The Labor Sector

The Labor Sector

Third Edition

Neil W. Chamberlain
Graduate School of Business
Columbia University

Donald E. Cullen
New York State School
of Industrial and Labor Relations
Cornell University

David Lewin
Graduate School of Business
Columbia University

McGraw-Hill Book Company

New York   St. Louis   San Francisco   Auckland   Bogotá   Hamburg
Johannesburg   London   Madrid   Mexico   Montreal   New Delhi
Panama   Paris   São Paulo   Singapore   Sydney   Tokyo   Toronto

THE LABOR SECTOR

1 2 3 4 5 6 7 8 9 0   DODO   7 8 3 2 1 0 9

This book was set in Times Roman by Progressive Typographers.
The editors were Bonnie E. Lieberman and Susan Gamer;
the cover was designed by Robin Hessel;
the production supervisor was Leroy A. Young.
The drawings were done by J & R Services, Inc.
R. R. Donnelley & Sons Company was printer and binder.

Library of Congress Cataloging in Publication Data

Chamberlain, Neil W
    The labor sector.

    Includes bibliographies and index.
    1. Labor and laboring classes—United States. 2. Trade-unions—United States. 3. Industrial relations—United States. I. Cullen, Donald E., joint author. II. Lewin, David, date   joint author. III. Title.
HD8072.C373 1980   331'.0973   79-14014
ISBN 0-07-010435-2

Contents

Preface   xi

CHAPTER 1 Population, the Labor Force, and the American
           Economy   1

Introduction   1
Population Changes and Distribution   2
Participation in the Labor Force   3
Unemployment, Underemployment, and Full Employment   10
    Unemployment Abroad
The Shift to Services   16
    Some Qualifications / Government Employment
The Shift to White-Collar Jobs   22
Processes of Occupational Choice   24
    The Nature of Occupational Mobility / Determinants of
    Occupational Achievement / Some Appraisals
Personal Income   37
    Poverty
Dual Labor Markets and Beyond   41
The Search for Security   43

Summary   46
Notes   46
Additional Readings   49
For Analysis and Discussion   50

CHAPTER 2   Job Mobility and Job Attitudes   52

Introduction   52
Job Mobility   53
      The Anatomy of Job Mobility / Types of Job Mobility /
      Determinants of Job Mobility / An Interim Appraisal
Attitudes toward Work   67
Job Design, Job Enrichment, and Workers' Participation
   in Management   74
Summary   84
Notes   85
Additional Readings   89
For Analysis and Discussion   90

CHAPTER 3   The Organized and the Unorganized   92
            Part One   Development and Legal Treatment of Unions   93
Workers' Objectives and the Agency Relationship   93
      Why Workers Join Unions / How Unions Represent
      Workers
Origins of the Labor Movement   95
Unions as Conspiracies   97
      Civil Conspiracy and the "Illegal Purpose" Doctrine
Idealism and Reform   98
      The Knights of Labor / The Rise of the AFL
The Development of Business Unionism   102
      Opposition to the AFL
Labor and the Sherman Antitrust Act   105
New Dimensions of Opposition to Unionism   106
      Depression and Governmental Intervention
Union Power and the Taft-Hartley Act   115
      The AFL-CIO Merger
Organizing the Public Sector   118
      Growing Pains and Legal Treatment
Other Developments and New Initiatives   120
      Summarizing the Development of Labor
*Part Two   Contemporary Patterns of Labor
   Organization*   123
The Extent of Unionism   123
      Organization by Industry / Organization by Occupation /
      Labor Organization among Women
Racial Discrimination and Labor Organizations   139
Managerial Unionism   144
Membership in Individual Labor Organizations   147
Explaining the Unorganized   150

Summary   153
Notes   153
Additional Readings   156
For Analysis and Discussion   157

CHAPTER 4   Union Government and Labor's Political Activity   159

The Structure of the Labor Movement   160
    The Principle of Autonomy / The Principle of Exclusive
    Jurisdiction / Functions of Union Organizations / Two
    Kinds of Government
Regulating Internal Union Affairs: Presumptions and
    Dynamics   172
    The Landrum-Griffin Act / Evaluating Internal Union
    Controls / Variations in Internal Union Government /
    Democracy in Unions and Union Administration
Political Activity of Labor   194
    The Effectiveness of Labor's Political Activity / Party
    Alignments / Political Activity and Public Employees /
    A Labor Party / Labor Leaders in Government
Summary   206
Notes   207
Additional Readings   210
For Analysis and Discussion   211

CHAPTER 5   Collective Bargaining in the Private Sector   213

Bargaining Power   214
The Behavioral Bases of Negotiations   215
Internal Bargains   216
The Bargaining Unit   218
The Scope of Bargaining   222
    The Bugaboo of Management's Prerogatives
Negotiating Tactics and Strategy   230
Administering the Labor Agreement   235
    The Grievance Procedure / Seniority / Work Rules
The Dynamics of Bargaining   248
    The Electrical Equipment Industry / The Steel Industry /
    The Automobile Industry
New Dimensions of Bargaining and Labor Relations   254
Multinational Bargaining   257
Summary   259
Notes   260
Additional Readings   264
For Analysis and Discussion   265

CHAPTER 6   Collective Bargaining in the Public Sector   267

How Different Is Public-Sector Bargaining?   268
    Multilateral Bargaining and Wage Determination

Legal Regulation of Public-Sector Bargaining   272
  Strikes / Supervisory and Managerial Personnel /
  Union Security
Currents of Change   282
  Two Examples: San Francisco and New York / Diversity in
  Public-Sector Bargaining
Selected Issues in Public-Sector Bargaining   293
  Productivity Bargaining / Personnel Administration /
  Management Policy / The Structure of Public-Sector
  Bargaining
Labor Relations in the Federal Sector   299
  Interpreting the Experience in the Federal Sector
Some Unresolved Issues   304
Experiences of Other Countries   306
Summary   309
Notes   309
Additional Readings   313
For Analysis and Discussion   314

CHAPTER 7   The Labor Market: Private and Public   316

Part One   Theories of a Competitive Labor Market and a
            Segmented Labor Market   317
Theory of a Competitive Labor Market   317
  The Individual Firm's Demand for Labor / The Aggregate
  Demand for Labor / The Aggregate Supply of Labor / The
  Supply of Labor to the Firm / Equilibrium in the Labor
  Market / Competitive Theory and Empirical Wage
  Patterns / The Human Capital Approach to Labor
  Supply
Segmented-Labor-Market Theories   336
  More on Segmented-Labor-Market Theories

Part Two   Wage Determination   341
Processes of Wage Determination   341
Political Influences on Wage Bargaining   344
Impact of Unions on Relative Wages   347
Impact of Unions on Wages in the Public Sector   349
  More on the Public Labor Market
Other Elements of Decisions on Wages   354
Summary   357
Notes   358
Additional Readings   362
For Analysis and Discussion   363

CHAPTER 8   Discrimination in the Labor Market   365

Introduction   365
Discrimination as a Social Issue   366
Experiences in the Labor Market   366
Contrasting Economic Perspectives on Discrimination   371

Measuring Discrimination   373
Sex-Role Stereotyping   375
Changes in Discrimination over Time   376
    More on Occupations and Education / The Question
    of Illegal Aliens
Regulating Discrimination in the Labor Market   388
    The Equal Employment Opportunity Commission / The
    Office of Federal Contract Compliance Programs / The
    Department of Health, Education, and Welfare / The Equal
    Pay Act / The Taft-Hartley Act / U.S. Office of Personnel
    Management / Apprenticeship Programs and the
    Construction Industry / Recent Cases and Court Decisions
    Involving Discrimination / Evaluating the Regulation
    of Discrimination in the Labor Market
Summary   409
Notes   410
Additional Readings   415
For Analysis and Discussion   415

CHAPTER 9   Equality and Income Distribution   417

Introduction   417
The Distribution of National Income   418
    The Impact of Unions on Labor's Share
The Distribution of Personal Income   424
    Taxes / Transfer Payments
The Distribution of Wealth   442
    Inheritance and Economic Success / Choice of a Mate /
    Other Evidence
Income Equality and Redistribution   451
    Equality as a Trade-off / Limiting Producers' and Consumers'
    Choice / Inequality and Meritocracy / Equality and
    Efficiency / The Labor Market, Once Again
Summary   462
Notes   462
Additional Readings   466
For Analysis and Discussion   466

CHAPTER 10   Income Supplements and Social Protection   469

The Philosophy of American Social Insurance   470
The Aged and Their Economic Circumstances   472
    Social Security Benefits / Private Pension and
    Benefit Programs
Workers' Compensation   490
    Protection of Workers and Federal Standards
Unemployment Insurance   496
    Coverage and Eligibility / Evaluating Unemployment
    Insurance / Adequacy of Benefits
Minimum Wage and Maximum Hours   505
    Union Views of Minimum Wage Laws / Economic

Consequences of Minimum Wage Legislation / Further
Aspects of FLSA and Related Laws
Social Welfare in the United States   515
Summary   519
Notes   520
Additional Readings   525
For Analysis and Discussion   525

CHAPTER 11   Human Resources Planning and Development   527

The Public Employment Service   528
The Human Resources Revolution of the 1960s   533
Public Service Employment   535
      The Comprehensive Employment and Training Act
Education and Human Resources Development   550
The Role of the Business Sector   556
      Human Resources Planning in the Firm
Human Resources Policy in Comparative Perspective   565
Some Unresolved Issues   569
Summary   575
Notes   575
Additional Readings   580
For Analysis and Discussion   580

CHAPTER 12   Full Employment and Inflation   583

Introduction   583
The Extent and Measurement of Unemployment   585
Unemployment as an Issue of Public Policy   591
      Patterns of Unemployment—And Employment / Inflation
      and Unemployment: Is There a Trade-off? / More on
      Inflation
Incomes Policies   614
      Wage and Price Controls in the Early 1970s / The Impact of
      Incomes Policies / Experiences of Other Countries
National Economic Planning   627
Notes   632
Additional Readings   638
For Analysis and Discussion   639

Appendix   Data Sources   641

Indexes   645
   Name Index
   Subject Index

Preface

In preparing this third edition of *The Labor Sector,* we have attempted to preserve the best features of the previous editions while incorporating material on the most significant developments of recent years. In addition, we have shortened this revision so that the entire text may be covered more easily in a one-semester course. These changes required several hard choices, not to mention some spirited negotiations among the authors, but we think the result is an improved text for both students and instructors.

On the one hand, we have retained the stress of the previous editions on the rich diversity of industrial relations as a field of study. A scholar can easily spend a lifetime exploring only the economic dimensions of the labor sector or only its historical, legal, or psychological dimensions. We believe it is most important, however, that the student new to the field see the labor sector in its fascinating entirety rather than as one corner of a particular discipline. We have therefore continued to draw on all the social sciences in an attempt to make the book useful and interesting to students in a wide variety of academic programs.

On the other hand, the book has been thoroughly rewritten to accommodate the considerable changes that have occurred in the labor sector since the publication of the previous editions. For example, the earlier editions dealt with the role of women and minorities in the labor market in a diffuse manner, describing different aspects of this issue in different chapters, but the present edition devotes an entire chapter (Chapter 8) to this critically important subject. Similarly, the second edition allotted only a few pages in a chapter on labor law to the complex problems of collective bargaining in the public sector, but bargaining has since grown so rapidly in that sector—as have the laws and academic research dealing with the subject—that it too now merits an entire chapter (Chapter 6).

The earlier editions also covered human resources planning and development in rather piecemeal fashion, under headings as diverse as "unemployment policy" and "personnel management," whereas this edition pulls together in Chapter 11 such related topics as the Comprehensive Employment and Training Act of 1973, the experimentation in recent years with public service jobs for the unemployed, the role of education in economic development, the pressing problem of teenage unemployment, and the growth of human resources planning and development within private firms. We have also introduced in this edition more extensive material on the experience of other countries with the labor problems that give us so much trouble. In Chapter 11, for example, we include a section on human resources policies in the Scandinavian countries and some other European countries, examining not only the ways in which their policies differ from ours but also the reasons for those differences.

Developments have also occurred on the theoretical front since the publication of the previous editions. In Chapter 7, for example, we now give more attention than before to the human capital approach to the analysis of labor markets, on which much research has now been done. We also analyze in that chapter the challenges to neoclassical theory recently posed by two groups of economists: the "dualists," who argue that relatively little competition occurs between certain primary and secondary segments of the labor market; and the "radicals," who argue that class divisions and class conflict are the major forces at work in the labor market. There have also been many tests by now of the Phillips-curve analysis of the possible trade-off between inflation and unemployment, and in Chapter 12 we review new evidence on this crucial issue (together with evidence on the effectiveness of the wage and price controls program adopted by the Nixon administration and the provisions of the Carter administration's wage and price standards program).

Finally, in shortening the text we have altered its emphasis in three respects. First, this edition places less stress on economic theory than the earlier editions did. We certainly have not jettisoned all or even most of our earlier reliance on such theory, for, after all, the labor sector consists of the relationship among workers, employers, and jobs—a relationship that is necessarily economic in large part. But the earlier editions probably carried the discussion of economic theory well beyond the level necessary to introduce the subject adequately to the general reader, and we have therefore attempted in this edition to confine such discussions to the absolutely essential concepts.

Second, we have considerably compressed our treatment of social welfare programs such as social security, unemployment insurance, workers' compensation and minimum wage laws. This edition retains, in Chapter 10, a description of the principal features of these programs and in fact adds new material on the Occupational Safety and Health Act of 1970 and the Employee Retirement Income Security Act of 1974. For the sake of brevity, however, we have deleted many of the institutional details of such programs that occupied several chapters in the earlier editions.

Third, we have incorporated into the text some of the behavioral research on workers and jobs which has come to prominence in recent years. This is most clearly evident in the discussion in Chapter 2 of the relationship between performance and satisfaction at the workplace, of job redesign, and of various other means of improving the quality of modern working life, including the freedom to move from one job to another. The behavioral science literature is also considered in Chapter 5, where we deal with recent new developments in collective bargaining and joint labor-management committees; and in Chapter 11, where the management of human resources in the firm is discussed.

We believe these changes have not only brought *The Labor Sector* up to date but also made it a better-balanced and more useful text. We hope that students and instructors alike will agree with this judgment, and will enjoy reading the book as much as we enjoyed writing it.

Finally, we wish to acknowledge the contributions of those who reviewed this book in manuscript form: Professor James E. Martin of Wayne State University, Professor Bernard Samoff of the University of Pennsylvania, and Professor Keith E. Voelker of the University of Wisconsin—Oshkosh. The thorough and perceptive criticisms, comments, and suggestions of these scholars were invaluable in preparing this revised edition of *The Labor Sector*.

Neil W. Chamberlain
Donald E. Cullen
David Lewin

The Labor
Sector

Population, the Labor Force, and the American Economy

INTRODUCTION

The labor sector is an extraordinarily diverse mix of more than 100 million persons who have in common the fact that they work for money, although at the time of this writing over 6 million of them were searching for, rather than actually holding down, jobs.[1] This group differs in terms of sex, age, race, occupation, income, and education, to name but a few characteristics. In this opening chapter we shall identify some of the most salient of these characteristics to provide the reader with an overview, a snapshot if you will, of the contemporary American work force. Where appropriate, historical material and data are used to trace the evolution of the labor sector to its present state.

We shall also introduce and explore briefly some important economic and social issues with which students of the labor sector should properly be concerned. These include unemployment and underemployment; the changing structure of employment, especially the shift to services; occupational mobility and achievement; family income and poverty; theories concerning segmented labor markets; and the search for security. Some of these issues are more fully examined in subsequent chapters. We begin with a review of some recent population trends in the United States.

POPULATION CHANGES AND DISTRIBUTION[2]

As of mid-1979, the population of the United States, including nonresidents and military personnel, was estimated to be 220,232,000. That figure represents an increase of some 97 million since 1930, 68 million since 1950, and 15 million since 1970. But while the population continues to expand in absolute terms, in recent years it has done so only at relatively low rates. As the data in Table 1-1 demonstrate, the post-World War II baby boom began to run its course in the early 1960s; thereafter, both the birthrate and the overall rate of population growth moved sharply downward. Since 1970, the population has grown by less than 1 percent per year, and during the period 1973–1978 it grew by only about 0.75 percent annually.

Clearly, the birthrate is the key variable affecting population growth. It dropped from a high of 26.5 births per 1000 population in 1947 to a low of 14.7 in 1975 and 1976, with an especially precipitous drop taking place in the early 1970s. The declining birthrate has been only very mildly offset by a reduced death rate and has been unaffected by the virtually stable rate of net civilian immigration since 1947.

The phenomenon of declining birthrates in the United States is attributable to a variety of factors, most notably increased job opportunities for women and improved methods of, and knowledge about, contraception—a combination of the birth-control pill and women's liberation. Responses to surveys in 1975 showed that women aged 18 to 24 expected to have an average 2.2 children each, in contrast to the average of 3.1 children per woman already born to females between 35 and 39 years of age. These articulated preferences for smaller families are, in part, a function of increasing schooling levels among, and expanded employment opportunities for, women. Census data provide strong evidence that the number of children per woman is inversely related to level of education and to participation in the labor force. This is true for both black and white women, though to a greater degree for the latter.

Also of relevance to declining birthrates are the postponement of marriage and the increasing divorce rate. Some 43 percent of American women in their early twenties were single in 1976, as compared with only 28 percent in 1960. The divorce rate per 1000 population doubled between 1966 and 1976, from 2.5 to 5.0, and the marriage rate per 1000 population dropped to 9.9 in 1976 from 11.0 in 1972. These patterns of marriage and divorce—reflecting changing conceptions of the style and importance of family life—clearly have contributed to the lowering of birthrates since the mid-1960s.

In terms of geographic dispersion, the south contains the largest proportion of the nation's population (32.1 percent), followed by the north central region (26.9 percent), the northeast (23.1 percent), and the west (17.9 percent). The continued westward migration of the American population throughout the twentieth century is, of course, well known, and for several decades that region's rate of population growth was several times greater than the rates of all regions. In recent years, however, the south has rivaled the west in population expansion. Thus between 1970, the date of the last decennial census, and 1978, the west and the south accounted for about 85 percent of the nation's population growth. Internal migration from the northeast and north central regions to the south and west, particularly to the so-called "sun-belt states," was especially noticeable during this period. Indeed, some migration of blacks to southern states was observed in the early 1970s, indicating a possible reversal of a historic trend.

Over the same period, another important pattern of population growth—the rate of expansion of major metropolitan areas—was modified, declining by 3 percent. These areas are made up essentially of counties with 50,000 or more inhabitants, together with neighboring counties that are closely associated with them by daily commuting ties, and they are more formally known as "Standard Metropolitan Statistical Areas" (SMSAs). They grew by 5.5 million persons, or 4.0 percent, between 1970 and 1976, compared with a rise of 5 million persons, or 8.2 percent, in nonmetropolitan populations. In previous decades, the rate of population growth in SMSAs outpaced that of nonmetropolitan areas, as the American populace became increasingly urbanized. Now some diminution of the earlier trend toward urbanization is occurring.

PARTICIPATION IN THE LABOR FORCE[3]

We have been talking about the growth and dispersion of the total population, but of course only a portion of that population offers its labor for sale. In 1978, more than 100 million persons, all but 2.1 million of them civilians, were in the labor force (Table 1-2). This translates into 63.7 percent of the noninstitutionalized population 16 years old and over, a figure known as the "rate of participation in the labor force." This is a figure of major importance, for it reveals much about people's attachment to work and changes in that attachment as economic conditions vary. The remainder of the group—some 58.5 million persons, or 36.3 percent of the noninstitutionalized population aged 16 and over—was classified as not in the labor force in 1978.

More interesting and informative than the measured participation rate at a given point in time are changes in the rate over time and among major subgroups of the work force. As Table 1-2 shows, the overall participation rate rose by about 5 percent during the post-World War II period. Not only did the noninstitutionalized population 16 years old and over increase by some 58 million persons, but also proportionately more persons were either employed or looking for work. Note, too, that the rate fell slightly at various times between 1947 and 1978. Though more will be said about this later, such declines generally follow aggregate economic contractions.

In terms of subgroups of the labor force, Table 1-3 shows that the participation rates of men have declined by 10 percentage points since 1948, while those of women have increased by more than 16 percentage points, and, in fact, reached a record high of 50 percent in 1978. Indeed, women now account for over

Table 1-1 Components of Population Change in the United States, 1930–1978
(Numbers in Thousands; Includes Alaska, Hawaii, and Armed Forces Overseas for 1940–1978 but Not for 1930 and 1935)

Year	Population at beginning of the year	Net change during the year		Components of change during the year					
		Number	Percent	Births	Birthrate	Deaths	Death rate	Net civilian immigration	Net civilian immigration rate
1978[1]	217,739	1,744	0.80	3,345	15.4	2,001	9.2	400	1.8
1977	216,022	1,717	0.79	3,313	15.3	1,901	8.8	305	1.4
1976	214,446	1,576	0.73	3,163	14.7	1,914	8.9	327	1.5
1975	212,748	1,698	0.80	3,149	14.7	1,911	8.9	450	2.1
1974	211,207	1,541	0.73	3,160	14.9	1,935	9.1	316	1.5
1973	209,711	1,496	0.71	3,137	14.9	1,974	9.4	331	1.6
1972	208,088	1,623	0.78	3,258	15.6	1,965	9.4	325	1.6
1971	206,076	2,012	0.98	3,556	17.2	1,930	9.3	387	1.9
1970	203,849	2,227	1.09	3,739	18.2	1,927	9.4	438	2.1
1969	201,760	2,089	1.04	3,605	17.8	1,934	9.5	453	2.2
1968	199,808	1,952	0.98	3,535	17.6	1,948	9.7	398	2.0
1967	197,736	2,072	1.05	3,555	17.9	1,961	9.4	414	2.1
1966	195,539	2,197	1.12	3,642	18.5	1,869	9.5	455	2.3
1965	193,223	2,315	1.20	3,801	19.6	1,830	9.4	373	1.9
1964	190,668	2,555	1.34	4,070	21.2	1,799	9.4	317	1.7
1963	188,013	2,655	1.41	4,142	21.9	1,815	9.6	361	1.9
1962	185,242	2,771	1.50	4,213	22.6	1,758	9.4	351	1.9
1961	182,287	2,955	1.62	4,317	23.5	1,703	9.3	373	2.0
1960	179,386	2,901	1.62	4,307	23.8	1,708	9.5	327	1.8
1959	176,447	2,939	1.67	4,313	24.3	1,663	9.4	292	1.6
1958	173,533	2,915	1.68	4,279	24.5	1,655	9.5	292	1.7
1957	170,571	2,961	1.74	4,332	25.2	1,641	9.5	272	1.6
1956	167,513	3,058	1.83	4,244	25.1	1,572	9.3	387	2.3
1955	164,588	2,925	1.78	4,128	24.9	1,537	9.3	337	2.0
1954	161,690	2,898	1.79	4,102	25.2	1,489	9.1	287	1.8
1953	158,973	2,717	1.71	3,989	24.9	1,531	9.6	261	1.6

Year									
1952	156,309	2,663	1.70	3,933	25.0	1,512	9.6	242	1.5
1951	153,622	2,688	1.75	3,845	24.8	1,501	9.7	336	2.2
1950	151,135	2,486	1.65	3,645	23.9	1,468	9.6	299	2.0
1949	148,580	2,556	1.72	3,667	24.5	1,452	9.7	323	2.2
1948	146,047	2,533	1.73	3,655	24.8	1,453	9.9	280	1.9
1947	143,394	2,653	1.85	3,834	26.5	1,455	10.1	238	1.6
1946	141,229	2,165	1.53	3,426	24.1	1,409	9.9	151	1.1
1945	139,767	1,462	1.05	2,873	20.5	1,549	11.0	162	1.2
1944	138,170	1,597	1.16	2,954	21.3	1,582	11.4	202	1.5
1943	136,371	1,799	1.32	3,118	22.7	1,503	10.9	148	1.1
1942	134,657	1,714	1.27	3,002	22.2	1,407	10.4	83	0.6
1941	133,275	1,382	1.04	2,716	20.3	1,415	10.6	60	0.4
1940	132,054	1,221	0.92	2,570	19.4	1,432	10.8	77	0.6
1935	126,874	853	0.67	2,377	18.7	1,421	11.2	−2	(Z)[2]
1930	122,487	1,128	0.92	2,618	21.3	1,419	11.5	113	0.9

[1] Estimates based on interpolation of 1977–1978 and 1978–1979 projections.

[2] (Z) rounds to zero.

Sources: Adapted from U.S. Bureau of the Census, *Current Population Reports: Population Profile of the United States, 1977,* ser. P-37, no. 324, 1978, pp. 6–7; and U.S. Bureau of the Census, *Current Population Reports: Projections of the Population of the United States: 1977 to 2050,* ser. P-25, no. 704, 1977, p. 23.

Table 1-2 Employment Status of the Noninstitutionalized Population 16 Years and Over, 1947–1978, Annual Averages
(Numbers in Thousands)

Year	Total noninsti- tutionalized population	Total labor force		Civilian labor force							Not in labor force
					Employed			Unemployed			
		Number	Percent of population	Total	Total	Agri- culture	Nonagri- cultural industries	Number	Percent of labor force		
1947	103,418	60,941	58.9	59,350	57,038	7,890	49,148	2,311	3.9		42,477
1948	104,527	62,080	59.4	60,621	58,343	7,629	50,714	2,276	3.8		42,447
1949	105,611	62,903	59.6	61,286	57,651	7,658	49,993	3,637	5.9		42,708
1950	106,645	63,858	59.9	62,208	58,918	7,160	51,758	3,288	5.3		42,787
1951	107,721	65,117	60.4	62,017	59,961	6,726	53,235	2,055	3.3		42,604
1952	108,823	65,730	60.4	62,138	60,250	6,500	53,749	1,883	3.0		43,093
1953	110,601	66,560	60.2	63,015	61,179	6,260	54,919	1,834	2.9		44,041
1954	111,671	66,993	60.0	63,643	60,109	6,205	53,904	3,532	5.5		44,678
1955	112,732	68,072	60.4	65,023	62,170	6,450	55,722	2,852	4.4		44,660
1956	113,811	69,409	61.0	66,552	63,799	6,283	57,514	2,750	4.1		44,402
1957	115,065	69,729	60.6	66,929	64,071	5,947	58,123	2,859	4.3		45,336
1958	116,363	70,275	60.4	67,639	63,036	5,586	57,450	4,602	6.8		46,088
1959	117,881	70,921	60.2	68,369	64,630	5,565	59,065	3,740	5.5		46,960
1960	119,759	72,142	60.2	69,628	65,778	5,458	60,318	3,852	5.5		47,617
1961	121,343	73,031	60.2	70,459	65,746	5,200	60,546	4,714	6.7		48,312
1962	122,981	73,442	59.7	70,614	66,702	4,944	61,759	3,911	5.5		49,539
1963	125,154	74,571	59.6	71,833	67,762	4,687	63,076	4,070	5.7		50,583
1964	127,224	75,830	59.6	73,091	69,305	4,523	64,782	3,786	5.2		51,394
1965	129,236	77,178	59.7	74,455	71,088	4,361	66,726	3,366	4.5		52,058
1966	131,180	78,893	60.1	75,770	72,895	3,979	68,915	2,875	3.8		52,288

6

Year										
1967	133,319	80,793	60.6	77,347	74,372	3,844	70,527	2,975	3.8	52,527
1968	135,562	82,272	60.7	78,737	75,920	3,817	72,103	2,817	3.6	53,291
1969	137,841	84,240	61.1	80,734	77,902	3,606	74,296	2,832	3.5	53,602
1970	140,182	85,903	61.3	82,715	78,627	3,462	75,165	4,088	4.9	54,280
1971	142,596	86,929	61.0	84,113	79,120	3,387	75,732	4,993	5.9	55,666
1972	145,775	88,991	61.0	86,542	81,702	3,472	78,230	4,840	5.6	56,785
1973	148,263	91,040	61.4	88,714	84,409	3,452	80,957	4,304	4.9	57,222
1974	150,827	93,240	61.8	91,011	85,935	3,492	82,443	5,076	5.6	57,587
1975	153,449	94,793	61.8	92,613	84,783	3,380	81,403	7,830	8.5	58,655
1976	156,048	96,917	62.1	94,773	87,485	3,297	84,188	7,288	7.7	59,130
1977	158,559	99,534	62.8	97,401	90,456	3,244	87,302	6,855	7.0	59,025
1978	161,058	102,537	63.7	100,420	94,373	3,342	91,031	6,047	6.0	58,521

Source: Adapted from U.S. Bureau of Labor Statistics, *Employment and Earnings, March, 1978,* p. 31; and Council of Economic Advisers, *Economic Indicators,* January 1979, pp. 11–12.

Table 1-3 Rates of Participation by Civilians in the Labor Force by Age, Race, and Sex, 1948–1978

	Male					
	Total		White		Nonwhite	
Age group	1948	1978	1948	1978	1948	1978
Total	87.0	77.9	86.5	78.6	87.3	72.1
16–17	53.4	51.9	51.2	55.3	59.8	33.2
18–19	79.9	73.0	76.2	75.3	77.8	59.5
20–24	85.7	86.0	84.4	87.2	85.6	78.0
25–34	96.1	95.4	96.0	96.0	95.3	90.9
35–44	98.0	95.7	98.0	96.3	97.2	91.0
45–54	95.9	91.3	95.9	92.1	94.7	84.5
55–64	89.5	73.5	89.6	73.9	88.6	69.1
65 and over	46.8	20.5	46.5	20.4	50.3	21.3

	Female					
	Total		White		Nonwhite	
Age group	1948	1978	1948	1978	1948	1978
Total	32.7	50.0	31.3	49.5	45.6	53.3
16–17	31.4	45.5	31.7	48.9	29.1	27.7
18–19	52.1	62.1	53.5	64.6	41.2	48.6
20–24	45.3	68.3	45.1	69.3	47.1	62.8
25–34	33.2	62.1	31.3	61.0	50.6	68.7
35–44	36.9	61.6	35.1	60.7	53.3	67.1
45–54	35.0	57.1	33.3	56.7	51.1	59.8
55–64	24.3	41.4	23.3	41.2	37.6	43.6
65 and over	8.1	8.4	8.6	8.1	17.5	10.7

Sources: Adapted from *Employment and Training Report of the President, 1978*, pp. 181–182, table A-2; and U.S. Bureau of Labor Statistics, *Employment and Earnings*, January, 1979, pp. 158–159, table 4.

40 percent of the total work force, up from 28 percent in the late 1940s and from 18 percent at the turn of the century.

Reductions in the participation rates of men in the post-World War II era have been especially great in the older age categories, largely as a result of the spread and liberalization of private retirement plans and social security benefits. The participation rates of both white and nonwhite males declined over this period in all major age categories.[4] In 1948, the overall participation rate for males was slightly higher for nonwhites (87.3 percent) than for whites (86.5 percent), and the rates for the two groups were quite similar among those between the ages of 20 and 44 years. By 1978, the overall participation rate of white males exceeded that of nonwhite males by about 6.5 percent, and notable racial differences in participation rates existed in the groups aged between 20 and 44 years. Indeed, participation rates of white males exceed those of nonwhite males in all age categories, with the differentials most pronounced in the younger groups.

Why is this so? If men enter the job market primarily because of economic pressures, sometimes taking on two or even three jobs to make ends meet, why are the participation rates of nonwhite males, principally blacks, generally lower than those of white males? Given the relatively low income of the average black family, shouldn't adult black males have, if anything, even higher participation rates than their white counterparts, as is the case with black females relative to white females aged 25 to 44?

In reality, there is no simple economic explanation for this. Many men just give up the search for work (and hence drop out of the labor force) after bitter experience teaches them the facts of discriminatory hiring practices. Even when black men stay in the job market (as most obviously do), their employment experience is often so unstable and low-paying that there is far more need for the black wife to work than for the white wife to do so.

But if there is a greater need for black women to work than there is for white women, the empirical fact is that by far most of the increases in the participation rates of women in all age groups since World War II have taken place among whites. In 1948, some 45 percent of the nonwhite women in the United States but fewer than one-third of the white women were in the work force. By 1978, about half the nonwhite *and* white women were in the labor force, the differential in participation rates being only about 4 percent. Interestingly, the participation rates of younger (16 to 24 years old) white women exceed those of younger nonwhite women, but the reverse is true among women aged 25 and over, especially those in the 25- to 44-year-old age group. It seems that the relatively inferior economic position of black families, which are more often headed by women than white families are, still compels higher participation rates among older black than among older white women.

The varying rates of participation in the labor force reviewed here have still other implications. To begin with, the trend among age groups, especially for whites, *partially* reflects what has been termed the "life cycle of the typical household." In the Unites States, people usually marry in their early twenties, and frequently both husband and wife work for the first few years in order to purchase household goods and perhaps save for a down payment on a house. With the arrival of a child, the wife usually quits her job, the earnings of the household drop, and there is an associated adjustment in family expenditures. Later, and particularly if other children are born, the young couple move into a home of their own, incurring a long-term debt (mortgage) to be paid off in installments out of current income. As has become increasingly common—in fact, commonplace—the wife may return to work sometime in her mid-thirties, when the children are in school. Eventually, younger members of the household may add to the family income by obtaining summer employment or part-time work during the school year, prior to leaving and starting households of their own. Finally, with the onset of retirement, the couple's income drops substantially, and expenditures are scaled down concomitantly.

In view of this familiar household life cycle, it is little wonder that four out of five males 16 years old and over are employed or are looking for work. Nor is it surprising that this proportion rises to 95 percent or even higher among those aged 25 to 54—the years between the completion of education and the appearance of the disabilities of old age. Our culture by and large expects the male head of the family to go to work, and the economic pressures for him to do so can appear nearly as unrelenting to the father in Scarsdale, New York, facing his children's Ivy League tuition rates and the monthly payments on a $200,000 home, as to the Alabama sharecropper struggling to pay food and clothing bills.

But if this "cultural" explanation suffices for the participation patterns of white male heads of households, it is less suitable for an understanding of women's rates of participation in the labor force. Clearly, over the last three decades, women of virtually all ages and differing marital status have increased their participation in the labor force. For some, notably married white women with school-age children, such participation represents a voluntary choice and a concern with using particular skills and abilities. The presence of economic hardship may play a part in this group's decision to work or to seek work, but less so than in the case of single women or especially married nonwhite women with children. (Black women, for example, are more likely than white women to be the only breadwinner in the household.) The increasing incidence of divorce, preferences for smaller families, growing awareness of employment opportunities, development of a career orientation among women, and, more generally, the growth of the women's liberation movement have combined to promote greater participation in the labor force among American women.[5] The fact that the economy has expanded rapidly enough to employ women in such large numbers, putting aside for the moment the question of their occupational and pay status relative to that of men, is one of the most significant developments of the post-World War II period. Further, through all these considerations of differential participation rates run questions about the role of social legislation as either a cause or an effect. For example, what would happen to the participation rates of both blacks and whites if welfare payments were slashed tomorrow—or if, on the other hand, we guaranteed every American family some minimum income, say $8000 a year? Clearly, Table 1-3 raises many issues that need to be explored in later chapters.

UNEMPLOYMENT, UNDEREMPLOYMENT, AND FULL EMPLOYMENT[6]

Recall that the labor force includes the unemployed as well as the employed. In 1978, the last year for which complete data are available, approximately 6 million persons, or 6.0 percent of the civilian work force, were unemployed (Table 1-2). This was the sixth highest annual rate recorded in the post-World War II period.

The unemployment rate frequently is used as a measure of the health of the economy, and, of course, it is the leading barometer of the state of the labor market. When the national economy expands, unemployment generally declines, and labor markets are characterized as "tight"—that is, there is an excess of the demand for labor over the supply of labor. Table 1-2 shows that labor markets were relatively tight in the United States during the immediate postwar years, the early 1950s, and the middle to late 1960s. When the national economy contracts, unemployment generally increases, and labor markets are characterized as "loose"—that is, there is an excess of the supply of labor over the demand for labor. Relatively loose labor markets existed in the United States at the mid-century mark, during the late 1950s and early 1960s, and in the mid-1970s. The particularly severe economic recession of 1974–1975 led to unemployment rates more than twice as large as those recorded in the last half of the 1960s. The aggregate unemployment rate began to decline in 1976 as recovery from the recession got under way and fell below 6 percent in late 1978.

Although for some purposes the aggregate unemployment rate is a useful economic indicator, it tends to mask as much as, or more than, it reveals. This becomes apparent when unemployment rates among subgroups of the labor force are examined. For example, Table 1-4 shows that the incidence of unemployment in 1978 varied considerably by sex, race, age, occupation, and work status. The unemployment rate for females was 2.0 percentage points higher than the rate for males, but that is a small difference compared with others shown in the table. At almost 12 percent, the unemployment rate for non-whites was more than double the rate for whites. This relationship has been relatively stable over time, indicating both the disproportionate burden of unemployment borne by nonwhites, principally blacks, and the apparent intracta-

Table 1-4 Selected Unemployment Rates, 1978, Percent

Total, 16 years and over	6.0
Male	5.2
Female	7.2
White	5.2
Nonwhite	11.9
Teenagers (16–19 years old)	16.3
White	13.9
Nonwhite	36.3
Males (20 years and over)	4.2
Females (20 years and over)	6.0
White-collar workers	3.5
Blue-collar workers	6.9
Service workers	7.4
Married males, wife present	2.8
Women who head families	8.5
Full-time workers	5.5
Part-time workers	9.0

Source: Adapted from U.S. Bureau of Labor Statistics, *Employment and Earnings, January, 1979,* pp. 154–155, 161, and 163–165; and *Economic Report of the President, 1979,* pp. 217–218.

bility of that burden, despite a variety of public policy measures intended to improve minorities' experiences in the labor market.

Even more startling are age differences in American unemployment rates. Almost one out of every six 16- to 19-year-olds in the labor force was unemployed in 1978, as compared with only about 5 percent of those 20 years of age and older. While unemployment rates of teenagers do not differ significantly between males and females, they vary enormously by race. In 1978, white teenage members of the work force had an unemployment rate of 14 percent, but the rate for black teenagers was 2½ times as large, 36.3 percent. Moreover, unemployment rates of between 40 and 60 percent have been reported for black teenagers living in some major urban areas.[7]

Observe also that blue-collar workers experienced almost twice as much unemployment as white-collar workers in 1978, 6.9 versus 3.5 percent. Among the former, operatives and nonfarm laborers had unemployment rates ranging between 8.1 and 10.7 percent, with a rate of 16 percent for construction laborers. Further, the unemployment rate for full-time workers was 3.5 percentage points below the rate for part-time workers. Finally, the unemployment rate for married men, considered by some to be the most critical of all unemployment indices, was 2.8 percent in 1978, or well below that for the remainder of the work force, but the rate for female-headed households was 8.5 percent.

The data in Table 1-4 indicate, in a way that no single aggregate index can, the marked variation in the incidence of unemployment among segments of the American work force. However, they do not provide much of a clue as to what may appropriately be considered full employment in the United States. Few would contend that full employment in a dynamic economy and a democratic society means zero unemployment. Nevertheless, there is a great deal of controversy about what level of unemployment is consistent with full employment.

In the 1960s, an unemployment rate of between 3.5 and 4.0 percent tended to be viewed as an indicator of full employment in the economy, although there was by no means unanimity on this point.[8] In the 1970s, some economists contend, the level of unemployment consistent with full employment rose to a range of between 5.0 and 6.0 percent. Proponents of this position point out that today's labor force contains larger proportions of teenagers, women, and part-time workers than the labor force of the 1960s. And because unemployment rates for these groups historically have been higher, and their attachment to the labor force lower, than is true of "prime aged" males, those aged 20 to 44, the level of unemployment consistent with full employment is higher today than in earlier years. Despite an element of circularity in this analysis, the argument cannot easily be dismissed, and we shall examine it more closely in Chapter 8.

The most widely used measure of unemployment is the percentage of the civilian noninstitutionalized population 16 years old and above who are not working but who are available and looking for full-time jobs. Some argue that this measure of unemployment is artificially inflated by requirements concerning work and the search for work contained in recently adopted welfare legislation. One study suggested that without such requirements, aggregate unemployment in mid-1977 would have been closer to 5 than to 7 percent; this further illustrates the problem of defining full employment in the American economy.[9]

Another important and related aspect of unemployment is its duration. In general, the longer the period of unemployment, the more severe the financial hardships associated with it. Of the average number of unemployed persons in 1978, 6.4 million, or roughly 23 percent, experienced 15 weeks or more of joblessness. For almost half of these, unemployment lasted for 27 weeks or more. These are especially important statistics because the American program of unemployment insurance generally provides a maximum of 26 weeks of benefit payments to the jobless person, provided he or she has actively searched for work.

The duration of unemployment differs by age, race, sex, and other factors. The average duration of unemployment during 1978 was 11.9 weeks. This was down noticeably from 14.3 weeks in 1977 and 15.8 weeks in 1976 but was well above the levels prevailing in 1973 and 1974. Note, too, that there is considerable flow through the ranks of the employed in any given year, as some find work and as others lose their jobs. Thus in 1977, when an average of 6.9 million persons were unemployed, almost 20 million people actually experienced at least one spell of unemployment.

Some of the complexities of defining and measuring unemployment should by now be apparent. Further illustration of this point is provided in Figure 1-1, which contains seven different measures of unemployment. For 1975, when the official unemployment rate was 8.5 percent, this series of measures yielded unemployment rates ranging between 2.7 and 10.7 percent. As noted by the Commissioner of Labor Statistics, these seven rates indicate the "range of value judgments on the part of many Americans about what kind of unemployment really matters."[10] Furthermore, they suggest "that there is no single 'true' rate of unemployment but rather many different rates reflecting different points of view about the economic and psychological hardship imposed by unemployment."[11]

*Under*employment provides still other problems of definition and measurement. Presumably, the underemployed include workers who have had to accept jobs below their educational or skill level, and the extent of this problem is simply not well known. One component of underemployment can be more readily measured, however: workers who would like a full-time job but who have to make do with shorter hours. In an average week during 1977, about 3.5 million persons were involuntarily employed on a part-time basis. Of these, all but 1 million were blue-collar and service workers, who represent well below half of all those in the total labor force.

In addition to the collection of data on part-time employment, there have been sporadic attempts to construct an index of underemployment. One of these efforts, based on the 1970 Census of Employment Survey, generated a subemployment index that included not only those who are conventionally classified as unemployed but also those who are involuntarily working part time, low-paid workers (those who earn hourly wages at full-time work which

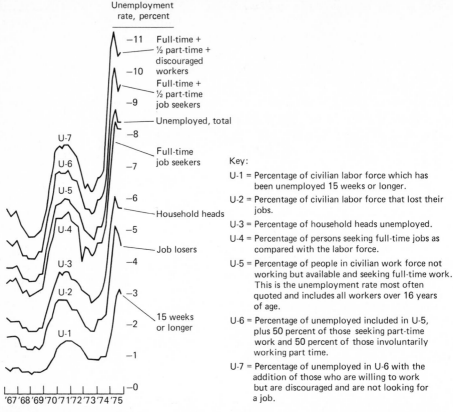

Figure 1-1 Seven different measures of unemployment. (*Source: Julius Shiskin, "Shiskin on the Unemployment Numbers,"* The New York Times, *Jan. 18, 1976, sec. 3, p. 14.*)

yield an annual income below the poverty line), and discouraged workers (those who give up looking for jobs but who want to work).[12] In 1970, the subemployment rate in the fifty-one urban areas that were surveyed was 61.2 percent, compared with an official unemployment rate of 4.4 percent for the nation as a whole.

There is little agreement concerning the usefulness of the concept of subemployment, and less still about the indices to which it leads. Nevertheless, the emerging efforts to identify and measure underemployment reflect a growing recognition of the limitations of conventional concepts and measures of unemployment. These limitations need to be kept fully in mind whenever the behavior of the economy and the work force is discussed.

Unemployment Abroad

Before moving on to consider the distribution of employment in the American economy, let us briefly examine the recent unemployment situation in other industralized nations compared with that in the United States. The relevant data are presented in Table 1-5.

Table 1-5 Unemployment in Nine Industrialized Countries, 1970–1978[1]

Measure and year	United States	Canada	Australia	Japan	France	Germany	Great Britain	Italy	Sweden
Unemployment rate			Data adjusted to U.S. concepts						
1970	4.9	5.7	1.4	1.2	2.8	0.8	3.1	3.5	1.5
1971	5.9	6.2	1.6	1.3	3.0	0.8	3.9	3.5	2.6
1972	5.6	6.2	2.2	1.4	3.0	0.8	4.1	3.6	2.7
1973	4.9	5.6	1.9	1.3	2.9	0.8	2.9	3.4	2.5
1974	5.6	5.4	2.3	1.4	3.1	1.7	2.9	2.8	2.0
1975	8.5	6.9	4.4	1.9	4.3	3.8[1]	4.1	3.2	1.6
1976	7.7	7.1	4.4	2.0	4.6	3.8[1]	5.5	3.6	1.6[1]
1977	7.0	8.1	NA	2.0	5.2	3.6	6.2	3.3	1.8
1978[2]	6.1	8.5	NA	2.2	5.4	3.4	6.3	3.5	2.3

[1] Data for the United States relate to the population 16 years of age and over. Published data for France, Germany, and Italy relate to the population 14 years of age and over; for Sweden, to the population aged 16 to 74; and for Canada, Australia, Japan, and Great Britain, to the population 15 years of age and over. Beginning in 1973, published data for Great Britain relate to the population 16 years of age and over. The adjusted statistics have been adapted, insofar as possible, to the age at which compulsory schooling ends in each country. Therefore, adjusted statistics for France relate to the population 16 years of age and over, and for Germany to the population 15 years of age and over. The age limits of adjusted statistics for Canada, Japan, Great Britain, and Italy coincide with the age limits of the published statistics. Statistics for Sweden remain at the lower age limit of 16, but have been adjusted to include persons 75 years of age and over.

[2] Data are averages for the first three-quarters of 1978.

Sources: Adapted from J. Moy and C. Sorrentino, "An Analysis of Unemployment in Nine Industrial Countries," *Monthly Labor Review,* **100:** 15 (1977), and U.S. Bureau of Labor Statistics, "BLS Study Reports on Unemployment in Major Industrial Nations," *News,* November 1, 1978, p. 4.

Historically, the United States has had one of the highest unemployment rates among all industrialized countries. Its rate of 6.1 percent for the first three-quarters of 1978 exceeded that of five of the other nations listed in Table 1-5. All these countries except Italy experienced increased unemployment between 1970 and 1978, especially during the mid-1970s. The unemployment rates for most of them would be considered low for the United States. However, most of them also have inflation rates that surpass those recently recorded in the United States. The apparent trade-off between unemployment and inflation, also known as the "Phillips relation," has been both a leading issue and a major problem in virtually all industrialized nations. It will be treated in depth in Chapter 12.

Before leaving this subject, though, three additional points concerning comparisons of unemployment in different countries are worth noting. First, such comparisons are only partial in nature, since unemployment is just one characteristic of a labor force, an economy, or a culture. For analytical and especially policy-making purposes, some of these other characteristics must be taken into account. Thus the United States' labor force dwarfs in size those of the other nations listed in Table 1-5, and these countries also differ in their rates of participation in the labor force, levels of employment, ratios of employed persons to the total population, social norms, forms of government, and cultural features. Only some of these characteristics can be quantified, and the unemployment rate is but one of those measures.

Second, different concepts of, and techniques for, measuring unemployment are used in the various countries, and even similar rates over time in any two of them may mask contrasting notions about joblessness. Table 1-5 presents unemployment rates for the countries shown adjusted to current concepts in the United States. These adjustments apparently make little or no difference for most of the countries, but they lead to significantly different rates from those originally derived in Great Britain (higher) and Germany (lower).

Third, a more complete comparative analysis of unemployment would include data from other nations, Russia and China in particular, but such information either is unavailable or is not made available to United States sources. One hears that "there is no unemployment in those countries," but that can be put down as either a matter of ideological wishful thinking or a matter of definition. In any event, the data in Table 1-5 present only a partial, if useful, picture of unemployment in the modern industrialized world.

THE SHIFT TO SERVICES[13]

Figure 1-2 portrays the dramatic transformation of the American labor force over the past century or so, from one in which four out of every five workers were engaged in goods-producing industries to one in which fewer than two in five are so engaged today. Using somewhat different data, Table 1-6 narrows the focus to the past 60 years or so and shows each sector's actual employment as well as its relative share of total employment.

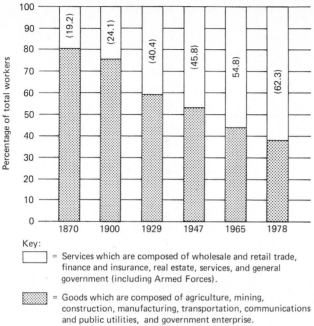

Key:

☐ = Services which are composed of wholesale and retail trade, finance and insurance, real estate, services, and general government (including Armed Forces).

▨ = Goods which are composed of agriculture, mining, construction, manufacturing, transportation, communications and public utilities, and government enterprise.

Figure 1-2 Distribution of employment by goods-producing and service-producing sectors, selected years, 1870–1978. Data on percentage of total workers for 1870 and 1900 include unpaid family workers and the unemployed. Data for later years are for self-employed persons plus wage and salary employees reduced to full-time equivalents; unpaid family workers and the unemployed are not included. (*Sources: Victor R. Fuchs*, The Service Economy, *National Bureau of Economic Research and Columbia University Press, New York, 1968, pp. 19, 24; U.S. Bureau of Labor Statistics*, Employment and Earnings, January 1979, *pp. 83–84, 154, 200.*)

Before discussing the implications of this "shift to services," we must first pin down that elusive term. In one sense, it is a contradiction in terms because *every* member of the labor force is selling his or her services in exchange for money. Even using it in a narrower sense, it is necessary to disentangle the service sector, the services industry, and the service-worker occupation.

The *service sector* consists of all the individual industries that produce something intangible like health care or education, in contrast to industries turning out physical goods such as food, clothing, and cars. When this definition is applied conventionally, as in Table 1-6, the data show that employment in the service sector broke ahead of employment in the goods sector in the middle 1940s. But Victor Fuchs, a leading authority on the service sector, excludes from that sector the group of industries called "transportation, communications, and public utilities" on the grounds that "in their use of physical capital and the nature of their production processes," those industries more nearly approximate manufacturing and other goods industries. By that classification, which is used in Figure 1-2, the data show that employment in the service sector did not surpass employment in the goods sector until the middle 1950s.

Table 1-6   Distribution of Employment by Goods-Producing and Service-Producing Industries, 1919 and 1978

	1919		1978	
Industry division	Employment (thousands)	Percen-tage of U.S. total	Employment (thousands)	Percen-tage of U.S. total
Total employment[1]	37,837	100.0	89,103	100.0
Goods-producing industries	23,562	62.3	28,723	32.2
Agriculture	10,749	28.4	3,342	3.8
Mining	1,133	3.0	837	0.9
Manufacturing	10,659	28.2	20,331	22.8
Construction	1,021	2.7	4,213	4.7
Service-producing industries	14,275	37.7	60,380	67.8
Transportation, communications, and public utilities	3,711	9.8	4,858	5.4
Wholesale and retail trade	4,514	11.9	19,392	21.8
Finance, insurance, and real estate	1,111	2.9	4,676	5.3
Services	2,263	6.0	15,976	17.9
Government	2,676	7.1	15,478	17.4

[1] Excludes military personnel and the unemployed. Data for agriculture include self-employed and unpaid family workers; data for all other industries exclude the self-employed and domestic servants.

Sources: Data on agriculture for 1919 from John P. Henderson, *Changes in the Industrial Distribution of Employment, 1919–59*, University of Illinois, Urbana, 1961, p. 12. Other data for 1919 from U.S. Bureau of Labor Statistics, *Employment and Earnings Statistics for the United States, 1909–67*, 1967. Data for 1978 from *Economic Report of the President, 1979*, p. 222, and Council of Economic Advisers, *Economic Indicators, January, 1979*, p. 11.

The issue is debatable, but we shall use the grouping in Table 1-6 unless noted otherwise.[14]

Table 1-6 also shows that within the service sector only a minority of workers are in the *services industry,* as it is labeled by the Census Bureau. There is no simple way of describing this industry, for it is a catchall group that includes the service activities which do not fit in any of the other industry categories.

More specifically, it includes the following:

Business and repair services—from advertising and modeling agencies to the repair of cars and television sets

Personal services—housework for pay; hotels and motels; laundries, dry-cleaning establishments, and barber and beauty shops; reducing salons; and many others (including brothels and funeral homes, both solemnly classified by the Census Bureau under "miscellaneous personal services")

Entertainment and recreational services—from professional wrestling and animated cartoons to bowling alleys and ballet companies

Professional and related services—nongovernmental medical, legal, educational, welfare, religious, engineering, accounting, and related services

The fuzziness and breadth of this industry's definition may well reflect our cultural lag in adjusting to the new shape of the American economy. Other industry titles also span a large variety of activities, of course, but everyone has a fairly workable notion of what is meant by "agriculture," "mining," and "construction," for example. Yet the services industry—which Table 1-6 shows to be larger than those three goods industries taken together and to have grown in payroll employment more rapidly than any other private industry over the past 60 years—has not achieved a clear identity outside the statistical tables. How many people have ever described themselves as working "in services," although about 16 million persons are now included in this industry category?

Finally, to compound the confusion, there is a *service-workers occupation*, and not all service workers are found in the services industry or even in the service sector. This too is a catchall category, but it includes jobs that do not neatly fit into any other occupational pigeonhole. For example, police officers are not exactly "craft workers" or "semiskilled operatives" or "laborers," and so they are termed "protective service workers" and may be found not only in government but also in manufacturing (plant guards), transportation (railroad detectives), and retailing (store detectives). Other occupations under the "service-worker" heading include firefighters, hospital attendants, barbers, bartenders, waiters, cooks, and domestic servants. Most of these are, in fact, part of the service sector, but this occupation as a whole has no more public identity than the services industry.

To recapitulate, it is more important to specify one's terms in discussing the shift to services. If "services" is taken in its literal sense, there has not been any shift at all, since labor has always sold its services. Also, we shall see shortly that the growth of the service *occupation* has been of only minor significance. It is the growth of the service *industry* and the service *sector* that is transforming the character of the American labor force.

Some Qualifications

Even the above statement must be interpreted carefully. For one thing, note in Table 1-6 that the growth in the service sector has been largely at the expense of agriculture and mining, rather than manufacturing and construction. Though we may talk about the coming of the "postindustrial society,"[15] any obituary notices for the factory worker or the building trades are decidely premature, and developments on the energy front seem already to be producing new, higher levels of demand for coal and for miners to extract it. Moreover, economic power does not necessarily flow to where the work force is largest. Much of the service sector is composed of small and medium-sized establishments. Galbraith, for example, argues that the economy is essentially bifurcated into "the world of the few hundred technically dynamic, massively capitalized and highly organized corporations on the one hand and of the thousands of small and traditional proprietors on the other" and that "the heartland of the modern economy" is still the world of the large corporation—"that part which is most subject to change and which, accordingly, is most changing our lives."[16] The large corporation to which Galbraith refers can no longer be identified only with the production of industrial goods—it encompasses many service activities as well—but the base of its operations is still frequently in manufacturing, transportation, and communications. Although it is true that factory jobs have dwindled as a share of nonfarm employment over the past 60 years, their share of *total* employment remains strong, at about 23 percent in 1978. And, among the major industry groupings, manufacturing stands as the single largest employer in the economy and a key to economic growth.

Even with these qualifications, the fact remains that a quiet revolution has occurred in the American labor force. In the underdeveloped countries, most of the world's population is still struggling with the massive problem of how to shift resources from agriculture to manufacturing within the goods sector. It is another index of our wealth that we now require less than one-third of our work force to produce not only the basic necessities of food, shelter, and clothing but also the cars and television sets and indoor plumbing and freeways and hair dryers and diet soft drinks that typify the American way of life to many friends and critics alike. That is not where the action is these days, though, at least in terms of employment growth; instead, it is in the still-expanding service sector. To illustrate the point quickly: from 1947 to 1978, nearly four out of every five new jobs added to the nonfarm economy were in the service sector; more people now work in hospitals than in the entire automobile and basic steel industries put together; more people work for the Postal Service than in all mining; and twice as many work in education as in construction.

Government Employment

Within the service sector, the mushrooming of government employment is particularly interesting for several reasons. Employment has grown more rapidly in government than in any of the major private industries (except services) over the past 60 years. In 1978 well over 17 of every 100 wage and salary workers were on a government payroll.[17] (Notice that the figures from Table 1-6 do not include members of the armed forces.) By way of comparison, the public sector in Sweden, which is often considered the epitome of the welfare state, employs one out of every four persons in that country's labor force. Although no one today expects the government to restrict itself to printing money and delivering the mail, these figures surely are surprising. Are there really 15 million or so bureaucrats somewhere in this country?

Table 1-7 should clarify matters considerably. Although employment of civilians by the federal government quintupled between 1929 and 1978, most of the increase took place during the three wars that occurred in that period, particularly World War II. The number of civilians employed by the federal government doubled during the New Deal era of the 1930s but did not pass the 1-million mark until August 1940 and increased by less than 1 million between 1947 and 1978. Employment by state and local governments, on the other hand, rose by a phenomenal 10 million jobs over the period 1947–1978—or by enough to have almost tripled government employment since 1947 even if the federal total had not changed at all.

Table 1-7 Government Employment, 1929, 1947, 1969, and 1978

Government level	All employees[1] (in thousands)			
	1929	1947	1969[2]	1978[3]
Government, total	3,065	5,474	12,195	15,478
Federal, total	533[4]	1,892	2,674	2,755
Executive		1,864	2,639	2,703
Department of Defense		689	1,050	908
Postal Service		467	769	653
Other agencies		708	820	1,142
Legislative		25	28	39
Judicial		3	7	13
State and local, total	2,532	3,582	9,521	12,723
Education	1,143	1,499	5,095	6,655
Other	1,389	2,083	4,426	6,068

[1] At the federal level, data exclude members of the armed forces and employees of the Central Intelligence and National Security Agencies. At the state and local levels, data exclude paid volunteer firefighters and elected officials of small local units.

[2] Data adjusted to yearly totals based on December 1969 distribution.

[3] Data adjusted to yearly totals based on November 1978 distribution.

[4] The distribution of federal employment is not available for 1929 in a form comparable to that for the other years.

Sources: Adapted from U.S. Bureau of Labor Statistics, *Employment and Earnings Statistics for the United States, 1909–67,* 1967, pp. 749–755; and U.S. Bureau of Labor Statistics, *Employment and Earnings,* February 1970, p. 115, and January 1979, pp. 83–84, 200.

If socialism is creeping in at the Washington level, these figures suggest that it is going at a mad gallop at the state and local levels. Obviously, such issues are a trifle more complicated than counting noses on the public payroll. Another reminder to the same effect is that more than half of all civilian workers in the government "industry" are engaged in defense, postal, or educational activities, areas seldom claimed by private industry.

But Table 1-7 presents only the narrowest measure of government-related employment. In 1977, when public employees numbered 15.5 million, all levels of government purchased about $189 billion worth of goods and services from private industry, a sum which generated another 8 million jobs outside government. There were also 2.1 million members of the armed forces who were part of the total labor force in that year. Adding all these up—direct civilian and military employment plus indirect employment—yields the staggering total of almost 26 million jobs, or about three out of every ten in the economy, that were underwritten by some unit of government in 1977.[18]

The effect of any industry on employment can be magnified by adding the employment it generates in other industries, of course, for every industry is always buying goods and services from others. Moreover, as Ginzberg, Hiestand, and Reubens emphasize in their study entitled *The Pluralistic Economy,* government employers compete in the labor market, just as private firms do (in hiring college graduates, for example); government employees often perform precisely the same tasks as their private counterparts (secretaries, teachers, doctors, and most others); and many government activities directly support or complement those of private industry (imagine what the demand for automobiles would be without the billions spent on public highways, or think of what farm output would be without the research done in state agricultural colleges).[19]

Thus it is misleading to think of the labor sector as neatly divided into private and public components. In short, the work force functions in complex patterns and systems which accurately reflect the pluralistic nature of the American economy as a whole.

THE SHIFT TO WHITE-COLLAR JOBS

The emergence of the white-collar worker as the dominant figure in the labor force is a familiar story by now, and yet the full significance of this occupational shift is not always recognized. In diagrams such as Figure 1-3, there is an appearance of historical inevitability about this trend, for employment among white-collar workers expanded almost without pause throughout this century, overtook that among blue-collar workers in the mid-1950s, and is still growing today. Until recently, however, few people saw anything inevitable about this trend, so firmly rooted was the belief that nonmanual occupations were reserved for a fortunate few. Even those who waxed most lyrical about the glories of the machine age usually stressed its advantages for blue-collar work-

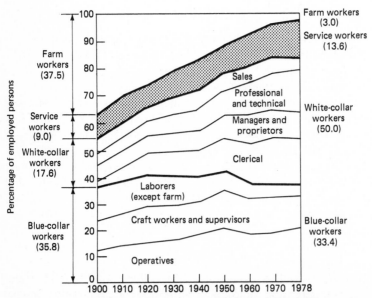

Figure 1-3 Occupational trends in the United States, 1900–1978. Data for 1900–1950 are for persons 14 years old and over; data for 1960–1978 are for persons 16 years old and over. (*Sources: U.S. Bureau of the Census,* Occupational Trends in the United States, 1900 to 1950, 1959, *table 1;* Manpower Report of the President, 1968, *table A-9; and U.S. Bureau of Labor Statistics,* Employment and Earnings, *January 1979, p. 171.*)

ers, in making their jobs easier and safer and better-paying, while critics were concerned that the independent farmer and artisan would be displaced by the robotlike assembler.

Certainly in the 1860s, when the industrial revolution took off in this country, no one could have predicted that it would take only a century to produce a work force nearly evenly split between white-collar and other workers. And only a generation ago, no one would have believed that more than *one out of every four workers* would soon be a professional or technical worker (15 percent of total payroll employment in 1978) or a "manager, official, or nonfarm proprietor" (11 percent of total payroll employment).

Again we must pause to straighten out our definitions. Just as the distinction between the service and goods sectors is partly arbitrary, so too is the boundary between white-collar and blue-collar occupations. If these terms had not taken on different connotations in the past, we would surely consider farm workers to be in the blue-collar category today, and probably also such manual service workers as cooks, porters, and janitors. On the other hand, should farm owners be grouped with farm supervisors and laborers (as in Figure 1-3) or with proprietors of drugstores and the like under the label "white collar"? And what do you call hospital attendants, police officers, waitresses, and hairdressers, if not something vague like "service workers," which does not clearly connote either a blue- or white-collar occupation? Clearly, these occupational groupings are as much in the province of the sociologist as of the economist or statistician.

Figure 1-3 also shows that several interesting shifts have occurred within each of the major occupational categories. In the blue-collar field, for example, the drop in the proportion of unskilled laborers must surely be chalked up as a major dividend of technology. It is tempting to romanticize those nineteenth-century stalwarts who carved a civilization out of a wilderness, but in fact much of the work in factories, mines, and construction of that period was incredibly dangerous and just plain brutish by today's standards. (Much the same argument could be made about a great number of the unskilled farm jobs that have vanished, but the nonwork values of farm life are so intertwined with this question that one generalizes at one's peril.)

The fact that skilled craft workers have apparently held their own since 1900, and have actually increased their numbers from 10 to 13 percent of the total of employed persons, has not settled the arguments over the net effect of technology on manual skills. For example, skeptics question whether a carpenter wielding a power saw and hammering together prefabricated forms today is the equivalent of yesterday's cabinetmaker, in terms of either skills or job satisfaction. On the other hand, electricians of today undoubtedly know more than their predecessors. And how does one appraise the net effects of something like numerical-control technology, a type of automation that reduces the skill required of machinists and increases that required of those who repair machines? In any event, by the only measures we have of manual skill, the proportion of craft workers has increased over the last 70 years.

PROCESSES OF OCCUPATIONAL CHOICE

These transformations in the structure of employment in the United States raise more general questions concerning occupational mobility, occupational choice, and the factors shaping the distribution of the populace among occupations. Concerning occupational mobility, John Kendrick, a leading researcher into productivity, contends that over the remainder of the twentieth century "a traumatic reversal of historical experience" will occur: "Children born to persons entering adulthood in the 1950s and the 1960s will, on average, experience relatively lower status than their parents. This will reflect both declining educational attainments, induced by the saturation of the highly educated labor market, and contracting career opportunities facing those who do in fact complete educational programs."[20]

The changes in the labor market that Kendrick forecasts, even if confined to more educated workers, serve as a harbinger of slower or reduced occupational mobility in American society generally. In order to evaluate Kendrick's projection and develop perspective on this issue, it is necessary to delve further into processes of occupational choice and recent patterns of occupational mobility in the American labor force.

The term "occupational choice" can be misleading indeed. It connotes a process of rational reflection which leads a person to a conscious decision to pursue a clearly identified career, usually of a skilled or professional nature. Such a process does occasionally occur, but it is the exception.

The word "occupation" has several operational meanings. Those who come from a middle- or upper-class background tend to identify it with a "calling" or a vocation, a readily identifiable activity which offers those who pursue it certain sources of satisfaction and which usually requires specialized training or skill or years of experience. In this sense, vocational choice is epitomized, perhaps, by the young acolyte who has been "called" to a lifetime of religious practice, but on a more mundane level it applies as well to the youngster who has "always liked to fool with machines" and who becomes a mechanic or an engineer; it covers all the professions and the licensed trades. From this perspective on occupations, there is always supposed to be some reason, some special attraction, which draws the individual to a particular line of work or holds the person there once in it.

But the term "occupation" is also often used as virtually synonymous with "job." It refers to a specific bundle of activities, to be sure—typing, filing, assembling, cleaning, clerking, digging, grinding—all of which may be necessary to the world's productive activity, most of which are perfectly respectable, and at least some of which carry with them their own minor satisfactions, but whose chief attribute is that they provide an income. If the individuals performing such tasks were to be offered different but higher-paying work with all other considerations—physical surroundings, social contacts, and commuting time, for example—remaining equal, they would make the switch with little hesitancy.

These two conceptions of occupation have been presented as antithetical, but they are actually polar positions on a spectrum along which all jobs can be spotted. Some people, though very few, are so dedicated to a profession that they will pursue it regardless of the income they earn from it. At the same time, even the person who is employed in a routine job calling for little skill can develop pride in the dexterity required for accomplishing the task well and will be reluctant to forfeit this claim to distinction by taking up some other equally unskilled job, even though it pays more. Nevertheless, although the distinction between a vocation and a livelihood is not one of black and white, the distinction does exist and is important to an understanding of the process which we label "occupational choice."

Note, too, that the second word in this label, "choice," is equally misleading. It does not adequately reflect the process of occupational selection, the diverse paths over which people may travel in their pursuit of occupations, or the dynamics of social conditions that result in some individuals' being chosen *by* occupations and livelihoods.

For some people, notably men and women of the middle class, the process of occupational choice involves the building of a mental picture, a self-concept, of the kind of person one wants to become. That self-concept, clearer for some than for others, develops out of a maturing process that brings with it a heightened ability to judge the realities of the world with which the person is confronted. Thus, the passage of time necessarily involves the person—the middle-class person—in a series of decisions, for example, whether to take an academic or a vocational high school curriculum, whether to work summers and at what jobs, and what major course of study to select in college if college itself is chosen. Indeed, a recent study by Freeman suggests that the process of deciding whether to enroll in college is a highly rational, systematic one that is closely responsive to changes in rates of return to investment in higher education.[21]

Each of the decisions described above closes certain lines of possible occupational activity and opens up others. In the process, adolescent fantasies give way to inescapable realities. Early ambitions, which generally prove excessive, are scaled down; new influences or experiences open up potentialities not previously recognized; and the pattern of "choice" becomes more and more determined. As Becker describes the process: "Somehow or other, the person becomes committed to a line of action . . . so many small steps are taken whose consequences are not foreseen. Each step tends to limit the alternatives available until suddenly . . . [there is] only one alternative to choose from."[22]

It would be foolhardy to pretend that these steps are always the product of conscious decisions or serious reflection, especially in terms of developing a career path. Various influences emanating from school, family, friends, chance exposure to new ideas, and repeated exposure to familiar ones mold a person without that individual's necessarily sensing the underlying forces at work. The particular set of personality characteristics in question may mean that the individual is more of a reactor than an initiator and that he or she makes little or no effort to control the forces that shape the future. This tendency, described by one writer as "default," is present in people to varying degrees, just as the capacity for decision making is.[23] It is reflected in more than a few cases by an absence of any conscious or sustained thought concerning occupational choice —something which appears to characterize a large proportion of high school students.

For one segment of the populace, then, occupational choice is something that occurs over a long period of time. Though it results from many decisions, many social pressures, and many defaults, the cumulative effect is that it marks out a path of *probable* occupational activity, a path which is at first shadowy but which, over time, becomes increasingly clear and determined. For others, however, this scenario hardly describes reality.

Consider the position of young people from minority groups, for example, who, if they live in urban centers, frequently have only tenuous connections to the conventional world of work. It is not merely that they are unsuccessful in finding work, as the data on unemployment presented earlier indicate. Rather, in such a setting, work itself, advancement on the job, and the designation of an occupation or career path are not highly valued. This view is richly documented by Liebow in his study of black streetcorner men:

> Putting aside, for the moment, what the men say and feel, and looking at what they actually do and the choices they make, getting a job, keeping a job, and doing well at it is clearly of low priority. . . . The man-job relationship is a tenuous one. At any given moment, a job may occupy a relatively low position on the streetcorner scale of real values.[24]

Rather than yielding to a simple explanation, however, this rejection of middle-class values concerning work and occupation is a complex phenomenon. It is related to the casual nature of much work offered to minority and disadvantaged groups; to the low pay that accompanies such work; to the lack of suitable transportation to search for work or the hardships imposed by the available transportation; to the relative instability of the family; to schools, which often must serve as custodial institutions instead of places of learning and from which large numbers of young people from minority groups drop out; and to the large (if short-term) rewards that "hustling" and illegal activity offer, relative to more conventional employment. As noted by Friedlander in his study of urban unemployment in thirty American cities:

> The illegal market of criminal activities is readily available and serves as an attractive alternative to the legitimate employment available to a slum dweller, offering high remuneration and status, flexible hours, glamorous activities, and excitement. Moreover, hustling and stealing and gambling and prostitution are alternatives to dying a slow death in the oppressive slums of the cities.[25]

This picture of the occupational and career "choices" facing individuals in the urban ghetto was heavily underscored by the comments of the Harlem,

New York, youth whom Friedlander and his staff interviewed and by the estimate that 20 percent of that community's population received income from illegal activities during the late 1960s.[26] One needn't have a precise accounting of the influence of illegal activities or the other forces mentioned here to recognize that, in combination, they promote a set of values antithetical to middle-class concepts of career paths and occupational choice.

Nor should it be thought that alternative conceptions of work and careers are confined to disadvantaged minorities residing in urban ghettos. Lower-class white families trapped in the rural poverty of Appalachia, the Tennessee backwoods, and parts of the southwestern plains also do not make the kinds of occupational choices or follow the career patterns that characterize middle-class families. For these poor whites, a son or daughter may represent another member of an extended (rather than nuclear) family who will help in the cultivation of crops, who may take on odd jobs, and who will sporadically attend school for a few years but whose horizons will not encompass steady employment, occupational mobility, or the planned choice of a career. Even when members of these families migrate to urban areas, they do not often find steady work, jobs with the potential for promotion, or educational and training opportunities that serve as avenues to occupational mobility for others. The culture and factual circumstances of this type of family militate against a strong concern for occupation, career, or the developmental process that characterizes middle-class families and individuals. In such a setting, conventional notions of individual choice and occupational mobility hardly seem applicable. Here the individual does not so much choose a livelihood as be chosen by it.

In sum, the social factors affecting occupational choice lead us to recognize that there is more than one selection process. For many, the process reflects values associated with career development and mobility, it is systematic, and it becomes increasingly clear over time, even if it involves haphazard elements and defaults. For others, the process contains contrasting characteristics that reflect very limited choices, with the individual more likely to be selected by the available livelihoods than to select an occupation from among a wide range of opportunities. If these contrasting processes are overdrawn, they nevertheless usefully depict the diversity that exists within the labor sector in terms of occupational decision making.

The Nature of Occupational Mobility

Though the above discussion provides insights into how individuals choose careers and how careers choose individuals, it is not very informative concerning the occupational mobility of individuals in the labor sector as a whole. In conceptual terms, the same process of decision making undoubtedly occurs in rich families as in poor ones and in recession periods as in prosperous years, but surely with very different results. It is necessary, therefore, to dig a bit more deeply to discover how individual decisions are translated into the sweeping changes in occupational structure that were described earlier.

Consider a point in time, specifically January 1973, when some 77.4 million persons 18 years old and over were employed in civilian jobs. Of that total, nearly 9 percent, or more than 6.7 million persons, were working in an occupation different from the one they had been in 1 year earlier. This would be astounding if the term "occupation," as used here, meant one of the eleven broad categories listed in Table 1-8. Instead, it refers to the several hundred detailed occupations into which the Bureau of Labor Statistics divides those eleven large groups. (Under "professional, technical, and kindred workers," for example, one finds such detailed occupations as accountant, mechanical engineer, dentist, and airline pilot, while such jobs as metal cutter, assembler, weaver, and driller are listed in the "operatives, except transport" group.) Still, a substantial proportion of occupational mobility occurred across the eleven major categories, involving about 3.5 million persons, or roughly half the total.[27]

A large volume of occupational shifts does not necessarily serve either economic or social ends, however, for the pattern of those shifts may or may not improve the lot of the individuals who make them. Table 1-8 presents a measure of the direction that those shifts took in 1972; the data are shown separately for men and women. The second row in the upper portion of the table shows that of the men who changed jobs during 1972 and wound up in the "professional, technical, and kindred workers" category, 32.7 percent came from the same group (that is, shifted from one detailed professional occupation to another, such as from professor to dean, mechanical engineer to sales engineer, or reporter to public relations man), 14.2 percent came from the managerial group, 7.3 percent came from the sales group, and so on. The data in the lower portion of the table show that 33 percent of the women who changed jobs and wound up in the professional group came from the clerical group, while 31.2 percent came from the professional category, 9.0 percent came from the managerial category, 6.8 percent came from sales, and so on. For each occupational group, the leading original occupation of those who changed jobs is underlined.

Note from the data presented in Table 1-8 the large amount of both upward and downward mobility that occurred during 1972. Surely "up" and "down" are subjective terms as used here, but most people would agree that an upward move was made by those men and women who were clerical workers one year and managers or administrators the next year (7.7 and 37.8 percent, respectively, of those who shifted into the managerial and administrative group), just as most would agree that the reverse was a downward move (8.5 and 3.8 percent, respectively, of those who shifted into clerical occupations had been in the managerial and administrative group the year before).

Perhaps the most interesting aspect of occupational mobility concerns the chances for blue-collar workers to move into expanding white-collar jobs. While the data in Table 1-8 offer only a partial view of this subject, they reveal that the chances are much greater that blue-collar workers, both men and women, will move to other blue-collar jobs than to white-collar ones. This does not mean that some blue-collar workers do not move to white-collar occupations, or vice versa, but only that, on balance, there is more movement within than between these two major occupational groupings.

Determinants of Occupational Achievement

A single year's data on occupational mobility do not reveal very much about this complex subject. In the broader perspective, we know from many studies that there is a good deal of "occupational inheritance" in American society. The occupation (or occupational group) of a father is an important "determinant" of the occupation (occupational group) eventually chosen by his son or daughter. Race is also a key factor related to occupational mobility. The nonwhite worker is less likely than the white worker to move—as quickly or as far—up the occupational ladder.

But these factors do not reveal the whole story. Everyone recognizes that educational achievement has enabled many persons to surpass their fathers in the occupational hierarchy. Additionally, a person's family background can be important not only because of the race and occupation of the father, and increasingly of the mother, but also for reasons such as place of residence (compare economic opportunities in the rural south with those in the urban north *or* the urban south) and the size of the family (compare per capita educational expenditures in large versus small families). And, adding to the complexity, education and family background may reinforce each other: the father in a well-paid profession and with a small family is often in the best position to provide the college education the offspring need to enter their own top-rated occupations.

Disentangling these several influences on occupational mobility is an enormous task which, fortunately, has been performed in part by Blau and Duncan, who utilized data from the same national sample of households that is the basis for reports on the labor force published by the federal government.[28]

Figure 1-4 presents Blau and Duncan's principal findings concerning the extent to which the distribution of men among more or less prestigious occupations can be explained by their education, their family background (broadly defined), or some combination of those two factors. These findings should give pause to both sides in that ancient debate over whether economic success is determined by "whom you know" or "what you know." The truth seems to be that education has an edge over family background, although both certainly are important to occupational achievement, and that there are other factors which are just as decisive but which no one has yet pinned down.

It is highly encouraging to note, as a measure of equality of opportunity, that the independent influence of education far outweighs the independent influence of family background in determining occupational achievement. After all, the American work force is now more educated than at any other point in its history, the median level of schooling having reached 12.6 years in 1978, with only a relatively small difference remaining between whites and nonwhites, and none between men and women.[29] This does not mean that life is an old movie in

Table 1-8 Major Occupational Groups in January 1973 of Men and Women Who Changed Their Occupations during 1972, by Major Occupational Group in January 1972, Percent Distribution

Men

Occupation in January 1973	Total who changed occupation	Occupation in January 1972											
		Professional, technical, and kindred workers	Managers and administrators, except farm	Sales workers	Clerical and kindred workers	Craft and kindred workers	Operatives, except transport	Transport equipment operatives	Laborers, except farm	Private household workers	Service workers, except private household	Farmers and farm managers	Farm laborers and supervisors
Total, 18 years old and over, not in school	100.0	9.3	9.1	8.6	7.0	16.4	18.0	7.6	11.4		9.5	0.9	2.1
Professional, technical, and kindred workers	100.0	32.7	14.2	7.3	11.5	12.7	6.1	4.5	3.9		6.1		0.9
Managers and administrators, except farm	100.0	19.6	14.0	18.3	7.7	16.6	8.3	6.2	2.8		6.0	0.5	0.6
Sales workers	100.0	7.9	22.0	24.2	9.7	11.9	7.9	5.7	5.3		3.1	1.6	0.4
Clerical and kindred workers	100.0	9.6	8.5	6.9	12.7	10.0	15.4	10.0	7.7		17.7	1.2	2.1
Craft and kindred workers	100.0	5.1	7.7	4.6	5.4	21.9	22.6	7.4	13.8		7.4	1.9	2.1
Operatives, except transport	100.0	2.4	5.4	5.0	5.7	16.9	28.2	9.0	14.0		9.6	0.2	3.6
Transport equipment operatives	100.0	2.5	3.8	2.5	4.2	20.8	18.2	9.7	18.2		14.8	1.3	3.8
Laborers, except farm	100.0	2.9	3.4	5.6	5.0	15.9	22.8	8.2	18.6		13.0	0.3	4.2
Private household workers													
Service workers, except private household	100.0	8.0	6.7	6.7	5.0	11.7	19.7	8.7	16.4		15.7	0.3	1.0
Farm workers													

Women

Occupation in January 1972

Occupation in January 1973	Total who changed occupation	Professional, technical, and kindred workers	Managers and administrators, except farm	Sales workers	Clerical and kindred workers	Craft and kindred workers	Operatives, except transport	Transport equipment operatives	Laborers, except farm	Private household workers	Service workers, except private household	Farmers and farm managers	Farm laborers and supervisors
Total, 18 years old and over, not in school	100.0	10.5	4.3	8.8	38.9	1.7	12.7	0.5	0.8	1.9	18.8	0.2	0.3
Professional, technical, and kindred workers	100.0	31.2	9.0	6.8	33.0		2.3		0.9	1.4	15.4		
Managers and administrators, except farm	100.0	14.3	12.2	6.1	37.8	3.1	6.1		1.0	1.0	18.4		
Sales workers	100.0	10.2	3.9	15.0	38.6	2.4	7.9			0.8	21.3		
Clerical and kindred workers	100.0	8.8	3.8	9.9	57.7	0.8	3.1	0.4	0.3	0.4	14.6	0.1	0.1
Craft and kindred workers	¹												
Operatives, except transport	100.0	4.0		9.0	12.3	4.0	42.9	1.0	2.0	2.0	19.3		3.7
Transport equipment operatives	¹												
Laborers, except farm	¹												
Private household workers	¹												
Service workers, except private household	100.0	5.4	4.7	6.5	26.1	1.4	17.4	0.4	1.1	5.1	29.3	1.1	1.4
Farm workers	¹												

¹ Percent not shown where base is less than 75,000.

Source: Adapted from James J. Byrne, "Occupational Mobility of Workers," *Monthly Labor Review*, **98**: 56 (1975).

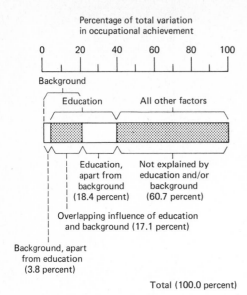

Percentage of total variation
in occupational achievement

Figure 1-4 Occupational mobility: sources of variation in occupational achievement for men 20 to 64 years old in the experienced labor force. Background factors included occupation and education of father, color, number of siblings, sibling position, parentage (native or foreign), birthplace, and region of residence. (*Source: P.M. Blau and O.D. Duncan,* The American Occupational Structure, *Wiley, New York, 1967, app. H., as presented in* Toward a Social Report, *U.S. Department of Health, Education, and Welfare, 1969, p. 23.*)

which the poor but honest lad always wins out over the rich young wastrel, but Figure 1-4 does suggest that, "all other things being equal," social background is decidedly less influential in the labor market than education is.

Unfortunately, as we shall note frequently in this book, all other things are seldom equal in the labor market. It is true that the laborer's son who becomes a doctor will usually do better than the doctor's son who drops out of high school, but it is also true that it is the doctor's son who is more likely to get a good education:

> This is true even after differences in academic ability have been taken into account, as can be shown by considering only those high school graduates who rank in the top one-fifth of [a national sample] in academic aptitude. If the parents of these relatively able youth are from the top socioeconomic quartile, 82 percent of them will go on to college in the first year after high school graduation. But, if their parents come from the bottom socioeconomic quartile, *only 37 percent* will go on to college in the first year. Even 5 years after high school graduation, by which time almost everyone who will ever enter college has done so, only 50 percent of these high ability but low status youths will have entered college, and by this time 95 percent of the comparable students from high status families will have entered college. . . .
>
> Differences in attendance at graduate or professional schools are even more striking. Five years after . . . graduation, those high school graduates in the top fifth by ability are *five times more likely to be in a graduate or professional school* if their parents were in the top socioeconomic quartile than if their parents were in the bottom quartile.[30]

It is facts such as these which underlie the tendency toward occupational inheritance mentioned earlier and the data provided in Figure 1-4, which shows that the overlapping influence of education and family background accounted for 17 percent of the variation in occupational achievement of American men in the 1960s. Observe as well that according to Figure 1-4, 60 percent of the variation in men's occupational achievement cannot be explained statistically by *either* education *or* family background (including color). This category presumably includes such intangibles as personality, motivation, mental health, "native intelligence," and a "natural aptitude" for composing music or fixing motors or leading other men and women—traits which everyone acknowledges to be important determinants of success in the labor market (and many of which are undoubtedly linked to family background) but which are not presently amenable to precise measurement.

Yet another insight into occupational mobility and the issue of "whom you know" versus "what you know" is offered by John Brittain. On the basis of the analysis of a sample of brothers for whom data on education, occupational status, and income earned during the mid-1960s were obtained and for whom hereditary influences could (in researchers' terminology) be "controlled," Brittain concluded the following:

> Some 34 to 67 percent of the inequality among the male younger generation in the sample studied here is explained statistically by their membership in a given family —that is, primarily by the characteristics of their parents. . . . Something on the order of one-half of inequality is caused by the fact that some people start life with substantial headstarts and others start from handicaped positions. This freezing effect is one measure of . . . inequality of opportunity as a determinant of overall inequality.[31]

That is as succinct a statement on this issue as we presently have available.

Some Appraisals

No matter how many statistics are amassed on this subject, we keep returning to the problem of how to judge them. On balance, are the volume and patterns of occupational mobility in the United States pretty good or pretty bad?

One test is to ask whether such mobility has met the changing needs of the economy. Unfortunately, this kind of question is difficult to answer with any precision or without becoming trapped in circular reasoning. At the most general level, our economy has been so successful over the long run that one can justify anything and everything in it—from monopoly to poverty—on the grounds that "it works." As for occupational mobility itself, clearly we have had enough to alter the entire structure of the labor force within a few decades, from the production of goods toward the production of services and from blue-collar toward white-collar jobs. But how do you measure what might have happened if, over the past 60 years, everyone had had an equal chance for adequate housing and medical attention, a good education, and employment opportunities based on merit instead of racial, religious, or other discriminatory grounds? Would the economy have performed about the same, except that the fruits of progress would have been distributed more fairly? Or would the economy actually have performed far better, with more for everyone, if the quality of the labor force and the chances for upward mobility had been even better than they were?

Because demand and supply interact in such a complex fashion in the labor sector (as they do elsewhere), it is difficult to disentangle the effects of one from those of the other. At the very least, however, one must be wary of assuming that whatever occupational mobility we have at the moment must be just right because the numbers of workers and jobs come out about even. They did in the Middle Ages, too.

Since economic criteria are difficult to come by, one might appraise the equity of our patterns of mobility against a statistical measure of "perfect mobility." That is, if occupational achievement were related solely to ability (and ability were randomly distributed throughout the population) and if there were complete equality of opportunity, then one would expect to find no relationship whatsoever between occupation and family background. By such a test, there is no question but that our patterns of mobility are inequitable and that racial barriers to mobility are the most egregious example of this inequity.

But how realistic is that test? There are many reasons other than inequality of opportunity why the sons of farmers might "disproportionately" prefer farming and why many sons of doctors choose medicine as a career. Unless one assumes a community like the one Plato envisioned, in which all children are removed from their parents at birth, it is obvious that a family must have *some* influence on its members' occupational choices, and this influence need not be socially pernicious. That fact certainly does not explain all (or perhaps even very much) of the occupational inheritance that exists in our society, but it does explain some unknown portion, and therefore it reduces the utility of "perfect mobility" as a test of equity.

Also, there has never been a major society that remotely approached a passing grade by the test of perfect mobility, and so perhaps it would be more realistic to mark on a curve—that is, to compare mobility in the United States today with mobility in the past or with mobility in other countries today.

Concerning historical trends within this country, two contradictory ideas prevail: first, that because of the increase in educational opportunities, Horatio Alger–type heroes could rise even further and faster today than in the past; and second, that the closing of the frontier and the growth of the modern corporation have choked off opportunities for the enterprising individual to rise from rags to riches. Neither idea is supported by the available evidence, which indicates instead that there has been little change in the influence of social background on occupational mobility since about 1910 (as far back as the data permit comparisons). More precisely, workers from farm backgrounds naturally tend to move out of farming today more frequently than in the past, and there may have been a slight increase in upward mobility during the years since World War II. But for most nonfarm workers and for most years since 1910, father-son measures do not show that occupational mobility has either increased or decreased to any significant extent.[32]

Finally, how does occupational mobility in the United States compare with that in other countries? Are we more of an "open society," as we have long claimed to be? There is a fascinating literature on this subject, and the most recent and comprehensive studies agree on two significant points: *The rate of mobility from blue-collar to white-collar occupations is about the same in most industrialized countries, including the United States, but the rate of movement of manual workers into "elite" occupations is higher in this country than in others.*

The startling conclusion that mobility from blue- to white-collar occupations is no greater in this than in other countries had been suggested by several scholars throughout the years, but the evidence to support it was first presented systematically by Lipset and Bendix in 1959 and was later confirmed by Miller and by the Blau and Duncan study.[33] The principal explanation for this observation is apparently that no country, regardless of its political ideology or class traditions, can transform its economy from an agricultural to an industrial base by keeping the lower classes "down on the farm" or in other manual occupations. Industrialization everywhere creates a growing need for professionals, managers, and sales and clerical personnel, and that need cannot be met simply by the favored few at the top when this revolutionary process is first touched off.

In the face of these similar experiences, why do many Europeans as well as Americans continue to believe that we have fewer barriers to occupational mobility? Lipset has suggested two reasons. First, because income in all classes has been higher in the United States than in most of Europe, the gap between the living standards of workers and those of managers is not so noticeable in this country, where the proportion of workers who own homes, cars, and so on, is higher than in Europe:

> But divergent value systems also play a role here, since the American and European upper classes differ sharply in their conceptions of egalitarianism. The rags-to-riches myth is proudly propagated by the successful American businessman. Actual differences in rank and authority are justified as rewards for demonstrated ability. In Europe, aristocratic values and patterns of inherited privilege and position are still upheld by many of the upper class, and therefore the European conservative wishes to minimize the extent of social mobility.[34]

Second, belief in our superior opportunities persists because they *are* superior when measured by access to the "elite" occupations instead of by access to all white-collar occupations. It can be argued that an upward move from a blue-collar position to a job as salesclerk is no longer regarded as a great achievement and that the prime test of opportunity is whether the upper classes have a monopoly on the professional and managerial occupations that rank highest in income, in prestige, and often in several varieties of power.

Table 1-9 shows that in this important respect the United States ranks at the top. The concept of an elite occupation is obviously a slippery one, but in all industrialized countries, professionals and managers usually form the bulk of what most people consider the elite. Although Table 1-9 uses only profes-

Table 1-9 Mobility into Elite Occupations: International Comparisons

Country	Percent of all men in elite[4] (1)	Working class[1] into elite		Manual class[2] into elite		Middle class[3] into elite	
		Percent (2)	Mobility ratio[5] (3)	Percent (4)	Mobility ratio[5] (5)	Percent (6)	Mobility ratio[5] (7)
Denmark	3.30			1.07	0.32	4.58	1.39
France I (Study I)	8.53	4.16	0.49	3.52	0.41	12.50	1.46
France II (Study II)	6.12	1.99	0.33	1.56	0.25	10.48	1.71
Great Britain	7.49			2.23	0.30	8.64	1.15
Italy	2.77	0.48	0.17	0.35	0.13	5.76	2.08
Japan	11.74			6.95	0.59	15.12	1.29
Netherlands	11.08			6.61	0.60	11.55	1.04
Puerto Rico	13.79	11.42	0.83	8.60	0.62	23.17	1.68
Sweden	6.66	4.43	0.67	3.50	0.53	18.09	2.72
U.S.A.	11.60	10.41	0.90	9.91	0.85	20.90	1.80
West Germany	4.58	1.55	0.34	1.46	0.32	8.28	1.81

[1] Blue-collar occupations.
[2] Blue-collar plus farm laborers.
[3] White-collar occupations excluding the elite.
[4] For the United States, elite is equivalent to professional, technical, and kindred workers. For other countries, see definition in source below.
[5] For column 3, ratio equals column 2 divided by column 1; for column 5, column 4 divided by column 1; and for column 7, column 6 divided by column 1.
Source: Adapted from Peter M. Blau and Otis Duncan, The American Occupational Structure, Wiley, New York, 1967, p. 434.

sionals to represent the American elite, Miller's study shows much the same results when American managers are included.[35] To illustrate the meaning of the mobility ratios in this table: column 2 shows the proportion of sons from blue-collar families who were employed in elite occupations in recent years (the dates vary), and column 3 corrects for differences in the size of these elite occupations (caused partly by differences in definition) by dividing the values in column 2 by those in column 1. The mobility ratios for both working-class people and manual laborers in this country are well above those in other countries. However, although the mobility ratio for American middle-class workers is high, it is partly depressed by the high ratio for manual workers and so is exceeded by the ratios of Sweden, Italy, and West Germany. Still, by the test of mobility into elite occupations, the United States is a more open society than most other economically advanced nations.

PERSONAL INCOME[36]

Because most individuals work in order to make a living, it is necessary to consider some income characteristics of the labor sector. For example, in 1977, per capita disposable personal income in the United States totaled $5494, which was double the 1967 figure and three times larger than the 1956 figure. When these data are adjusted for inflation, the per capita figure drops to $4141, but even that is about one-third larger than per capita disposable personal income in 1967 and more than half again as large as that in 1956. The total places the United States very near, but not at the top of, the per capita ranking of all nations.[37]

More interesting than per capita calculations, however, are data on occupations and family income. These will be considered in order. Table 1-10 provides information about occupational income and income differentials in 1977 for the American work force. Median income is reported by sex, first for all workers and then for year-round, full-time workers.[38]

Observe that in 1977 there were large differences in annual income among the occupational categories listed in Table 1-10. These incomes ranged from a median of $736 for all female private household workers to $16,850 for all male managers and administrators. The former figure is little more than 4 percent of the latter. As a group, male full-time blue-collar workers earned about $4000 less than male full-time white-collar workers in 1977, but they earned $7000 more than male full-time farm workers and roughly $3000 more than male full-time service workers. Four occupational groups—professionals, managers, sales personnel, and craft workers—had median incomes higher than the income of the full-time work force as a whole ($14,626), while the remaining groups earned below that level in 1977. The value of steady employment is clearly reflected in Table 1-10, which shows annual earnings levels for those who work full-time, year round to be about $3,600 and $3,900 for men and women, respectively, above those for the work force as a whole. Note particularly the

Table 1-10   Median Income by Sex, Occupation, and Work Experience, 1977

Occupational group	All male workers	Year-round full-time workers
Total labor force	$11,037	$14,626
White-collar workers	15,112	17,095
Professional, technical, and kindred workers	16,212	18,224
Managers and administrators	16,850	18,086
Sales workers	11,685	16,067
Clerical and kindred workers	10,822	13,966
Blue-collar workers	$10,202	$13,228
Craft and kindred workers	12,313	14,517
Operatives including transport	9,823	12,612
Laborers, except farm	4,566	10,824
Service workers	$ 4,961	$10,332
Private household workers	573	—
Service workers, except private household workers	5,077	10,338
Farm workers	$ 2,985	$ 6,412
Farmers and farm managers	4,317	5,601
Farm laborers and supervisors	1,988	7,278

Occupational group	All female workers	Year-round full-time workers
Total labor force	$ 4,674	$ 8,618
White-collar workers	6,218	9,467
Professional, technical, and kindred workers	9,161	11,995
Managers and administrators	$ 7,817	$ 9,799
Sales workers	2,425	6,825
Clerical and kindred workers	6,053	8,601
Blue-collar workers	$ 5,028	$ 7,524
Craft and kindred workers	5,600	8,902
Operatives including transport	5,109	7,350
Laborers, except farm	2,857	7,441
Service workers	$ 1,971	$ 6,108
Private household workers	736	2,714
Service workers, except private household workers	2,463	6,330
Farm workers		
Farmers and farm managers		
Farm laborers and supervisors		

Source: Adapted from U.S. Bureau of the Census, *Current Population Reports: Money Income and Poverty Status of Families and Persons in the United States: 1977 (Advance Report),* ser. P-60, no. 116, 1978, pp. 13–14, table 7.

effect of year-round, full-time employment on the earnings of sales personnel and private household workers.[39]

These data provide yet additional perspective on occupational mobility. With a 25-fold difference between the earnings of the lowest- and the highest-ranking (by income) occupational groups; with annual earnings differentials exceeding $6000 *among* white-collar occupations, and almost $8000 *among* blue-collar occupations; and with farm *employees* earning less than half as much as farm *owners* and *managers,* the access of an individual worker even to the next highest occupational category takes on special significance. It is one thing to compare alternative processes of occupational choice or mobility patterns among industrialized nations; it is quite another to examine income differences by occupation and to recognize from this examination the importance of even modest changes in occupational classifications. To state the point baldly, a machine operative who successfully pursues a craft job, a private household worker who obtains other *service* employment, or a professional employee who becomes a manager or administrator is likely to increase his or her annual earnings by some $2500 to $4500, according to the data in Table 1-10.

With respect to family income, the median figure in 1977 for about 56.7 million families was $16,009, a historic high. Again, because prices have increased sharply in recent years, the purchasing power of people at this income level was not as large as might be thought. More illuminating than the aggregate figure, though, is the distribution of family income. Tables 1-11 and 1-12 present the relevant data. Table 1-11 shows that about 46 percent of American families had incomes below $15,000 in 1977, about 32 percent were in the $15,000-to-$25,000 range, and roughly 22 percent received more than $25,000. Mean income deviates by almost $2000 from the median figure, reflecting the influence of a relatively few high-income families.

Table 1-12 shows that family income is unevenly divided among quintiles. The bottom 60 percent of families account for about 34 percent of total income, and the top 20 percent account for about 42 percent. Some 15.7 percent of total family income is received by the top 5 percent of families. While debate continues over the equity (or lack of it) of this distribution of family income, it is notable that the relative income shares received by each quintile have remained remarkably stable in the postwar period. This issue, and the more general one of equality in American society, will be more fully explored in Chapter 9.

Table 1-11 Total Money Income of Families, March 1977

Total money income	Number of families	Percent
Total	57,215,000	100.0
Under $5,000	5,343,000	9.5
$5,000–$9,999	10,424,000	18.1
$10,000–$14,999	10,552,000	18.4
$15,000–$19,999	10,166,000	17.9
$20,000–$24,999	7,962,000	13.9
$25,000–$49,999	11,326,000	19.8
$50,000 and over	1,482,000	2.6

Note: Median income was $16,009; mean income was $18,264.

Source: Adapted from U.S. Bureau of the Census, *Current Population Reports: Money Income and Poverty Status of Families and Persons in the United States: 1977 (Advance Report),* ser P-60, no. 116, 1978, p. 2, table 3.

Table 1-12 Percentage Share of Aggregate Income Received by Each Fifth of Families, 1947 and 1977

Income rank	Share of aggregate income received	
	1947	1977
Lowest fifth	5.0	5.2
Second fifth	11.9	11.6
Middle fifth	17.0	17.5
Fourth fifth	23.1	24.2
Highest fifth	43.0	41.5
Top 5 percent	17.5	15.7

Sources: Adapted from U.S. Bureau of the Census, *Current Population Reports: Household Money Income in 1976 and Selected Social and Economic Characteristics of Households,* ser. P-60, no. 109, 1978, p. 19, table 4; and U.S. Bureau of the Census, *Current Population Reports: Money Income and Poverty Status of Families and Persons in the U.S.: 1977* (*Advance Report*), ser. P-60, no. 116, 1978, p. 11, table 4.

Poverty[40]

Of special interest in the discussion of personal and family income is the issue of poverty, especially its changing incidence over time. The federally determined poverty index for the United States is constructed on the basis of assumptions about the consumption pattern and budget of a "typical" family and is adusted annually for changes in the Consumer Price Index.[41] In 1977, the last year for which complete data are available, just over 24 million persons, or 11.6 percent of the population, were below the poverty level. In 1959, the first year for which such data were collected, 39.5 million persons, or 22 percent of the population, occupied a poverty status. Among all poverty-stricken individuals in 1977, about 16.4 million were white, and 7.7 million were black. However, these figures translate into very different rates of poverty among the white and black populations: 8.9 and 31.3 percent, respectively. Among persons of Spanish origin, 22.4 percent (2.7 million persons) were below the poverty level in 1977.

In that year, the poverty-level income for a nonfarm family of four was $6191. By this standard, 10.2 percent of all families were below the poverty level, about the same as in 1976 but substantially less than the 18.5 percent recorded in 1959. Again, sharp racial differences exist in the distribution of poverty among families. Fewer than 8 percent (7.3 percent) of families headed by whites were below the poverty level in 1977, compared with over one-quarter (28.1 percent) of families headed by nonwhites. Both these figures have declined by half since 1959, however, when 15 percent of families headed by whites and 50 percent of families headed by nonwhites were below the poverty level.

It is especially important to recognize that possession of a full-time job does not necessarily provide a guarantee against poverty. Indeed, a worker who was employed at the legal minimum wage of $2.30 in 1977 and who was fortunate enough to work full time throughout the year earned about $4800, or about $1400 *less* than the amount that separated families below the poverty level from families above it. And, of course, that income level is more than $10,000 below the median family income recorded in the same year. In fact, in a majority of cases, the heads of families below the poverty level are at work on a full- or part-time basis or are available for work, although, not unexpectedly, they suffer more long-term unemployment than the heads of families above the poverty level. These data are all the more remarkable when we consider that almost half of all poverty-stricken families are headed by females who have no husband present. They also highlight once again the importance of occupational mobility and of access to channels of mobility.

In sum, the incidence of poverty in the United States has declined over time, but that was much more true of the expansionary 1960s than of the economically erratic 1970s. The problem of poverty remains an intractable one, and it is linked to the broader issue of inequality of income, the causes of which are not very well known. Why, for example, do private household workers and farm laborers earn an annual wage income below the official poverty line when the heads of some American corporations receive compensation exceeding $1 million per year? Or, if that comparison is too extreme, why were the average weekly earnings of workers in the construction sector about $314 in 1978, while those of wholesale and retail trade employees were about $152? Why should some public employees receive higher pay than their counterparts in the private sector, as was the case in the United States in the early 1970s—or, for that matter, why should college professors at Ivy League institutions receive about twice as much compensation as their counterparts in small southern colleges?[42] These questions are provocative, to be sure, but difficult to answer, and we shall be considering them at several points in this book, along with various proposals for the elimination of poverty.

DUAL LABOR MARKETS AND BEYOND

Recognition that the working poor are an important component of the population below the poverty level leads naturally to a consideration of the theories that have emerged in recent years about dual and segmented labor markets. These theories are usually offered as alternatives to the neoclassical labor-market theory (about which more will be said in Chapter 7), which assumes that workers have complete information about available employment opportunities; that they are able and willing to move to new jobs; that there are many employers, none of whom are very large or have a great deal of influence in the labor market; and that workers are paid the value of their (marginal) contribution to the final product.

One alternative theory divides the labor market into primary and secondary components.[43] Jobs in the primary market display such characteristics as high wages, good working conditions, employment stability, chances of advancement, and equity and due process in the administration of working rules. The last of these is frequently brought about by labor unions through collective bargaining. In contrast, jobs in the secondary market are characterized by low wages and few benefits, poor working conditions, high rates of turnover, little chance of advancement, and often arbitrary and capricious supervision.

Beyond specifying the characteristics of these two markets, the dual-market theory suggests that disadvantaged workers are more or less permanently confined to the secondary market by virtue of residence, inadequate skills, poor work histories, and, more generally, discrimination. The connections between the primary and secondary markets are, in this view, weak or nonexistent. However, through the mechanisms of subcontracting, temporary employment, and the like, employers may attempt to convert employment in the primary market into employment in the secondary market. Public policy is viewed as having the central goal of overcoming the barriers which confine the disadvantaged to the secondary market.

The dual-market theory has much to commend it. The discontinuities and rigidities of labor markets in the real world are central to this theory. For example, the concept of a port-of-entry job which is within the primary labor market and which provides the starting point for mobility up a well-structured occupational ladder—and the absence of such jobs and job ladders in the secondary labor market—has undeniable plausibility and adds to the credibility of the dual-market theory. So too do notions of steady employment and the protection of specific working rules negotiated between union and management or developed through formalized personnel procedures in the primary market.

Like any theory, that of the dual market also has its limitations. One of these is the confusion over the importance of the worker's characteristics as against that of job characteristics in determining the individual's fate in the labor market. In some formulations of the dual-market theory, workers are described as possessing behavioral traits—for example, unstable attachment to the work force, poor attendance at work, erratic behavior in the workplace, and negative attitudes toward work and supervision—that perforce confine them to the secondary labor market.[44] Another limitation of the theory is its lack of attention to the process by which some (perhaps many) workers make the transfer from jobs in the secondary market to jobs in the primary market. Additionally, the theory tends to treat alike all jobs within each market, distinguishing them not from one another but only from those in the other category.

Because of its provocativeness, however, the dual-market theory has led other labor economists to construct more sophisticated theories about segmentation of the labor market. One of these envisages the primary market as being composed of two parts, an upper tier and a lower tier.[45] The former consists of professional and managerial jobs, which are distinguishable from those in the lower tier by higher pay and status, greater promotional opportunities, the absence of elaborate working rules and administrative procedures, greater

educational requirements, and, most notably, more room for individual crea-
tivity and initiative, combined with superior economic security. This more
elaborate version of the dual-market theory has been supported by at least one
recent empirical investigation, though not without qualification.[46]

Other theories about segmentation distinguish labor markets by industrial
concentration, size of establishment, collective bargaining coverage, licensing,
and the proportion of full-time workers, to name but a few variables. A recent
empirical study utilizing 1970 data identified fourteen distinct segments of the
labor market, with variation in annual earnings among them ranging between
$2779 and $15,794.[47]

Clearly, the student of labor markets has available an abundance of
theories from which to choose—classical, neoclassical (human capital), dual,
segmented, radical, and others not easily categorized. No one of the theories
has so dominated the market (for theories, that is) that it has crowded out the
others, though a simple head count of labor economists probably would reveal
stronger support for neoclassical than for the other theories. Yet even neoclas-
sicists recognize that by calling "attention to class (or group) interests and behavior, and to the historical basis for these collective actions, which often extend into political markets,"[48] segmented-labor-market theorists have offered
important modifications of, and additions to, orthodox theory. These theories,
along with empirical evidence about them and some of the rich historical traditions from which they emerged, will be more fully examined in Chapters 7, 8, and
9. For now, it is worth remembering that the recent search for alternative
theories about the labor market was spurred largely by the underlying desire to
understand poverty in the United States and to develop remedies for it. In this,
the dual-market theory provides a most useful counterpoint to the view, sometimes derived from the types of data presented earlier in this chapter, that the
occupational structure and income profile of the American labor force fit into a
neat, continuous spectrum. The dual-market theory alerts us to the more disturbing ways of picturing both the contemporary labor sector and the job markets in which labor seeks its share of the nation's wealth.

THE SEARCH FOR SECURITY

The ethos of American capitalism has long stressed individual ability, initiative,
and enterprise. The importance of the individual is supposed to outweigh that
of the group and especially that of the political state. In the labor market, conventional theory proposes that workers are mobile, informed about alternative
work opportunities, and highly responsive to changes in the job market. And
certainly many American workers—and also business owners and managers—
exercise such free choice, taking advantage of various opportunities in the
market as they pursue the upward mobility which American society, perhaps
more than any other, seems to promise.

At the same time that changes in the economy, job opportunities, and technology apparently offer much to strive for and many potential rewards to the

work force, they also create numerous anxieties and wrenching dislocations. Furthermore, as the theory of the dual labor market suggests and as the data on poverty and unemployment underscore, not all workers are in a position to take advantage of these opportunities. In the cold logic of neoclassical economic analysis of the labor market, a black male who migrated from the rural south to the industrial north years ago, and who is now trapped in an urban ghetto, and a white male or female recipient of an M.B.A. from Harvard, Columbia, or Stanford are treated the same. The realities of the worlds they face are vastly different, however, and the opportunites available to them simply are not comparable. Or consider the difficulties encountered by a female clerical worker in a large municipal government who, though employed in presumably the most stable sector of the economy, found her job eliminated in the fiscal crisis that afflicted many of the nation's cities in the late 1970s. These burdens and dislocations may not be the same as those which accompanied the shift of the work force from the farms to the factories during the first half of the twentieth century or which were associated with the employment under treacherous conditions of women, children, and, yes, men in the sweatshops, factories, mills, and mines at the turn of the century, but they are nevertheless real and onerous to those who experience them.

Should it be any surprise, then, given the ceaseless turbulence of the job market, that the labor force searches for security even as it hopes to benefit from the rewards of a dynamic economic system oriented toward the individual? Invariably, those who are surprised by this occupy relatively secure positions of their own—for example, academic economists with lifetime tenure, senators with a guaranteed 6-year job and a long list of perquisities, and even displaced or retired top executives who receive handsome pensions and perhaps even long-term consulting contracts with their former employers.[49]

Even so, by historical standards, most workers and their families have greater economic security today than ever before, owing to developements on three fronts. First, and despite its being something of a cliché, there is much truth to the assertion that a healthy economy is the best guarantee of income security. By most standards, the American economy has done quite well, though clearly better in some periods than in others. This is especially important to ethnic, racial, and other minorities, for whom an expanding, vibrant economy seems a necessary condition for achieving income gains relative to those of whites. Second, the welfare state is an important part of the contemporary scene, though its scope and future direction are the subject of most serious debate. The term ''welfare state'' does not refer specifically to recipients of public assistance, but, rather, to the multitude of legislative measures adopted over the last four decades or so to protect and promote the welfare of the labor sector. Included here are not only unemployment insurance, regulations setting minimum wages and maximum hours, and laws covering occupational safety and pension reform, but also legislation pertaining to collective bargaining, employment training, and equal employment opportunity. The last is especially important, for it is aimed at preventing the hiring, placement, promotion, evaluation, or firing—the treatment in employment generally—of workers on the basis of race, color, religion, sex, and national origin. Students of the history of labor know full well the role that these factors have played in the American experience. Even though progress on this front has been slow, it seems unlikely that this country would retrogress to previous discriminatory practices.

Finally, and to be much more thoroughly explored in Chapters 3 to 6, there is the phenomenon of unionism and the gains achieved through collective bargaining. On the American scene, unionism has always been and remains today a minority movement, with less than one-fourth of the work force claiming membership in labor organizations. But to use this figure as a measure of organized labor's power and influence and of the labor movement's ability to provide workers with greater economic security than they could obtain from the market alone is misleading. In fact, bargaining gains are transmitted beyond the minority of the work force who are union members. For many reasons, all but the smallest nonunion organizations are likely to have adopted many, if not all, of the policies and benefits found in unionized firms. As examples, they typically place restrictions on the supervisor's authority to hire and fire, to set wages, and to impose discipline on the basis of personal whim; they provide lower- as well as higher-ranking workers with the paid vacations, holidays, sick leave, health insurance, and pensions that once were the exclusive prerogatives of top management or, at best, of white-collar workers; and, following formally bargained labor contracts, they have devised various ways of cushioning the impacts of technological change through such devices as seniority, retraining and relocation programs, and, in some instances, guaranteed wages for future periods.

Observe, however, that the bulk of the income supports reviewed in this section are designed and intended for those who have a permanent attachment to the labor force and who are more or less regularly employed, rather than for those outside the labor force. Claims to pensions, supplemental unemployment benefits, paid leaves, unemployment insurance assistance, training allowances, severance pay, and other financial resources generally require a prior pattern of steady employment on the part of the individual.

The Great Depression of the 1930s generated public concern for providing jobs to those who needed them, protecting workers from arbitrary treatment at work, compensating temporarily unemployed workers, and ensuring a modest pension to those retired from active employment. Nevertheless, after four decades of the welfare state, collective bargaining, and rapidly growing (if not always full) employment, many people are still left behind, economically speaking, because they are cut off from the labor force. Thus, in 1975 more than 40 percent of the heads of poverty-stricken families were not even in the job market because of illness, retirement, or the need to care for young children; another 15 percent suffered long-term (15 weeks or more) unemployment; and still another 5 percent were unable to find any work at all during the year, even though they looked for it.[50] For these individuals, public assistance provides at least a minimum of economic security, and most likely it will continue to do so even as the nation wrestles with policy proposals for more comprehensive income maintenance plans.[51]

SUMMARY

In this chapter, we traced some of the leading characteristics of the American labor sector, whose members' principal claim to a share of the national income is through their employment as wage and salary workers. This overview should have revealed the extraordinary diversity and pluralistic character of the labor sector. We cannot talk about the "unemployed worker," the "white-collar employee," or the "poor family" without some awareness of the great variety masked by these labels. As will be apparent later on, the same is true of the terms "union member," "employer," "training program enrollee," and others. Yet neither the citizen nor the policy maker can function in a world that is all complexity—without trends or tendencies. If we should be wary of easy generalizations, we should also avoid the reductionist assumption that no patterns whatever exist in the labor sector.

NOTES

1 Of this 100 million, some 8.5 percent were either self-employed or unpaid family workers in 1978. They should be distinguished from the remaining wage and salary workers, who made up the vast bulk of the labor sector.

2 Data in this section were obtained from U.S. Bureau of the Census, *Current Population Reports: Population of the United States: Trends and Prospects, 1950–1990,* ser. P-23, no. 49, 1974; U.S. Bureau of the Census, *Current Population Reports: Projections of the Population of the United States: 1977 to 2050,* ser P-25, no. 704, 1977; and *Economic Report of the President, 1979,* 1979, passim.

3 Unless otherwise noted, data reported here were obtained from U.S. Bureau of the Census, *Current Population Reports: Population Profile of the United States: 1976,* ser. P-20, no. 307, 1977; U.S. Bureau of Labor Statistics, *Employment and Earnings, January 1979,* 1979; and *Employment and Training Report of the President, 1978,* 1978.

4 The category "nonwhite" includes blacks (Negroes), American Indians, Eskimos, Asians, and others. At the time of the 1970 census, 89 percent of this population group was black. Thus, the reader should be aware that the term "black" is almost but not quite a synonym for the term "nonwhite." Further, at the time of the 1970 census, about 96 percent of the population of Spanish origin was classified as white. Hence, data on participation in the labor force for this group are not shown separately in Table 1-3.

5 For additional data on this issue, see U.S. Bureau of Labor Statistics, *U.S. Working Women: A Data Book,* Bulletin no. 1977, 1977; and Beverly L. Johnson, "Women Who Head Families, 1970–77; Their Numbers Rose, Income Lagged," *Monthly Labor Review,* **101**:32–37 (1978).

6 The data in this section were obtained from *Economic Report of the President, 1977, 1978 and 1979, passim;* selected issues of the *Monthly Labor Review* and of *Employment and Earnings,* both published by the U.S. Bureau of Labor Statistics; from

selected issues of *Economic Indicators,* published by the Council of Economic Advisers; and from the *Employment and Training Report of the President, 1977* and *1978.*

7 William Spring, Bennett Harrison, and Thomas Vietorisz, "Crisis of the Under-employed: In much of the Inner City 60 Percent Don't Earn Enough For a Decent Standard of Living," *The New York Times Magazine,* Nov. 5, 1972, pp. 43–44.

8 See, for example, the essays contained in Robert A. Gordon and Margaret S. Gordon (eds.), *Prosperity and Unemployment,* Wiley, New York, 1966; and Arthur M. Ross, (ed.), *Unemployment and the American Economy,* Wiley, New York, 1964.

9 See Kenneth W. Clarkson and Roger E. Meiners, Letter to the Editor, *The New York Times,* Aug. 10, 1977, Section A, p. 18.

10 Julius Shiskin, "Shiskin on the Unemployment Numbers," *The New York Times,* Jan. 18, 1976, Section 3, p. 14.

11 Shiskin. See also Julius Shiskin, *Employment and Unemployment: The Doughnut or the Hole?* paper delivered to the Metropolitan Economic Association, New York, Dec. 11, 1975.

12 Spring, Harrison, and Vietorisz, pp. 51 and 53. The reader should be careful in comparing data on underemployment and employment of the type reported here. The inclusion of so-called "low-paid workers" in the former group makes the sub-employment index much different conceptually from the unemployment index.

13 Unless otherwise indicated, the basic data for this section were obtained from U.S. Bureau of Labor Statistics, *Employment and Earnings, January 1979.*

14 In all his writings on this subject, Fuchs correctly insists that any definition of the boundary between the goods sector and the service sector must be partly arbitrary. For the quotation concerning his exclusion of the transportation and utilities group, See Victor F. Fuchs, *Productivity Trends in the Goods and Service Sectors, 1929–61,* Occasional Paper 89, National Bureau of Economic Research, New York, 1964, p. 2. The federal government has used both classifications, but generally includes transportation, communications, and public utilities in the service-producing category (see U.S. Bureau of Labor Statistics, *Employment and Earnings, January 1979,* p. 200).

15 See, for example, Daniel Bell, *The Coming of Post-Industrial Society: A Venture in Social Forecasting,* Basic Books, New York, 1973.

16 John Kenneth Galbraith, *The New Industrial State,* Houghton Mifflin, Boston, 1967, p. 9. A similar theme is sounded by Galbraith in his sequel to the earlier volume, *Economics and the Public Purpose,* Houghton Mifflin, Boston, 1973.

17 *Economic Report of the President, 1979,* p. 222.

18 Specifically, 29.4 percent of all civilian and military employment. On this point, see *Employment and Training Report of the President, 1978,* pp. 330–333.

19 Eli Ginzberg, Dale L. Hiestand, and Beatrice G. Reubens, *The Pluralistic Economy,* McGraw-Hill, New York, 1965, chap. 2–4, 9.

20 As quoted by Richard J. Levine, in "The Outlook," *The Wall Street Journal,* Aug. 10, 1977, p. 1.

21 Richad B. Freeman, "Overinvestment in College Training?" *Journal of Human Resources,* **10:**287–311 (1975).

22 Howard S. Becker, "The Implications of Research on Occupational Careers for Household Decision-Making," in Nelson N. Foote (ed.), *Household Decision-Making,* New York University Press, New York, 1961, p. 245.

23 Becker, p. 245.

24   Eliot Liebow, *Talley's Corner: A Study of Negro Streetcorner Men*, Little, Brown, Boston, 1967, pp. 34–35.

25   Stanley Friedlander, *Unemployment in the Urban Core: An Analysis of Thirty Cities with Policy Recommendations*, Praeger, New York, 1972, p. 113.

26   Friedlander, pp. 154–189.

27   James J. Byrne, "Occupational Mobility of Workers," *Monthly Labor Review*, **98**:53–59 (1975). This source provides the basis for much of the discussion in the present section. Also see Dixie Sommers and Allan Eck, "Occupational Mobility and The American Labor Force," *Monthly Labor Review*, **100**:3–19 (1977), which reports mobility changes between 1965 and 1970.

28   See Peter M. Blau and Otis Dudley Duncan, *The American Occupational Structure*, Wiley, New York, 1967. This study's major findings are condensed in U.S. Department of Health, Education, and Welfare, *Toward a Social Report*, 1969, chap. 2. For a recent examination of occupational mobility among women that addresses the question of whether the same methodology may be used to study both men and women in this regard, see Andrea Tyree and Judith Treas, "The Occupational and Marital Mobility of Women," *American Sociological Review*, **39**:293–302 (1974).

29   See Scott C. Brown, "Educational Attainment of Workers—Some Trends from 1975 to 1978," *Monthly Labor Reveiw*, **102**:54–59 (1979). In fact, this median educational level of the work force was achieved in 1976 and stabilized through 1978.

30   U.S. Department of Health, Education, and Welfare, p. 20.

31   John H. Brittain, *The Inheritance of Economic Status*, Brookings, Washington, 1977, pp. 35, 72.

32   Blau and Duncan, chap. 3 and pp. 424–425.

33   Seymour M. Lipset and Reinhard Bendix, *Social Mobility in Industrial Society*, University of California Press, Berkeley, 1959, chap. 2; Blau and Duncan, pp. 432–433.

34   Seymour M. Lipset, *Political Man*, Doubleday, Anchor Books, Garden City, N.Y., 1959, pp. 268–269.

35   S. M. Miller, "Comparative Social Mobility," *Current Sociology*, **9**:30–31, 58 (1960).

36   Unless otherwise noted, the data in this section are from U.S. Bureau of the Census, *Current Population Reports: Money Income and Poverty Status of Families and Persons in the United States: 1977* (*Advance Report*), ser. P-60, no. 116, 1978.

37   *United Nations Statistical Yearbook 1976*, United Nations, Department of Public Information, New York, 1977, p. 689, table 182.

38   The median splits the distribution of a sample into upper and lower halves. When significantly different from the mean figure, as is the case for the data shown in Table 1-10, it indicates that the distribution is not very even. In this case, some very high income individuals cause the mean figures to be well above the medians in almost all instances.

39   We are not at this point considering multiple jobholders, of whom there were about 4.5 million in 1977. *Employment and Training Report of the President, 1978*, p. 255.

40   Data in this section are from U.S. Bureau of the Census, *Current Population Reports: Money Income and Poverty Status of Families and Persons in the United States: 1977* (*Advance Report*), ser. P-60, no. 116, 1978.

41   For a detailed explanation of the concept of poverty, see U.S. Bureau of the Census, *Current Population Reports: Characteristics of the Population below the Poverty Level: 1975*, ser. P-60, no. 106, 1977, p. 195.

42 Data sources for this paragraph include U.S. Bureau of Labor Statistics, *Employment and Earnings, June, 1977*, pp. 73–87; Stephen H. Perloff, "Comparing Municipal, Industry and Federal Pay," *Monthly Labor Review*, **94:**46–50 (1971); and American Association of University Professors, *AAUP Bulletin*, **64:**193–266 (1978).

43 This exposition of the dual-market theory relies heavily on Peter B. Doeringer and Michael J. Piore, *Internal Labor Markets and Manpower Analysis*, Heath, Lexington, Mass., 1971, chap. 8.

44 Doeringer and Piore. The authors note (p. 166), for example, that "instability appears to be a characteristic of both jobs and workers."

45 Michael J. Piore, "Fragments of a 'Sociological' Theory of Wages," *American Economic Review: Papers and Proceedings*, **93:**377–384 (1973).

46 Paul Osterman, "An Empirical Study of Labor Market Segmentation," *Industrial and Labor Relations Review*, **28:**508–523 (1975).

47 Marcia Friedman (with the assistance of Gretchen Maclachlan), *Labor Markets: Segments and Shelters*, Allanheld, Osmund, Montclair, N.J., 1976.

48 Glen G. Cain, "The Challenge of Segmented Labor Market Theories to Orthodox Theory: A Survey," *Journal of Economic Literature*, **14:**1215–1257 (1976). Theories of human capital, about which little has been said so far, will be considered at length in Chapter 7.

49 On this last point, see "Few Duties Involved for Ex-Officers Named as Consultants," *The Wall Street Journal*, June 30, 1976, pp. 1, 20.

50 U.S. Bureau of the Census, *Current Population Reports: Characteristics of the Population below the Poverty Level: 1975*, p. 4.

51 See, for example, Daniel P. Moynihan, *The Politics of a Guaranteed Income: The Nixon Administration and the Family Assistance Plan*, Random House, New York, 1973; and, more recently, the Carter administration's proposals for welfare reform as reported in several issues of *The New York Times* during August 1977.

ADDITIONAL READINGS

Blau, Peter, and Otis Dudley Duncan: *The American Occupational Structure*, Wiley, New York, 1967.

Brittain, John: *The Inheritance of Economic Status*, Brookings, Washington, 1977.

Doeringer, Peter B., and Michael J. Piore: *Internal Labor Markets and Manpower Analysis*, Heath, Lexington, Mass., 1971.

Employment and Earnings, monthly publication of the U.S. Bureau of Labor Statistics.

Employment and Training Report of the President, annual report (formerly *Manpower Report of the President*).

Fuchs, Victor R.: *The Service Economy*, Columbia University and the National Bureau of Economic Research, New York, 1968.

Industrial and Labor Relations Review, published quarterly by Cornell University, New York State School of Industrial and Labor Relations, Ithaca.

Industrial Relations, published three times a year by the University of California, Institute of Industrial Relations, Berkeley.

The Journal of Human Resources, published quarterly by the University of Wisconsin, Institute for Research on Poverty.

Special Labor Force Reports, published by the U.S. Bureau of Labor Statistics as a series and also as occasional articles in *Monthly Labor Review*.

FOR ANALYSIS AND DISCUSSION

1 Briefly outline the ways in which you expect the composition of the labor force to change by the year 2000. Do these changes represent a continuation of, or a shift away from, the twentieth-century trends reviewed in this chapter?

2 Compare the decision to enter the labor market with the decision to enter college. In your own case, was the decision made principally by you or your parents? Was the decision based on economic considerations—the desire to earn more money, for example—or noneconomic ones—such as the desire to make new friends? Were differences in intellectual ability the only distinction between those in your high school graduating class who went to college and those who didn't? Estimate the "rate of participation in college" of your high school class and explain why it differs from the rates of some of your college classmates' high schools. On balance, is the decision to enter college basically similar to, or different from, the decision to enter the labor force?

3 To be counted as unemployed, an individual must provide some evidence of having searched for work, such as contacting a public or private employment agency, responding to a help-wanted advertisement, or being interviewed for a job. However, some persons become discouraged by the failure to find a job and stop searching for work, in which case they are considered to be not in the labor force rather than unemployed. Among those listed in Table 1-2 as not in the labor force in 1978, how many would you estimate might be "discouraged" workers? How would you go about finding out how many were discouraged? Would the unemployment rate be significantly affected by reclassifying discouraged workers as unemployed? Would the rate of participation in the labor force be affected?

4 Given the importance of education to occupational achievement, what do you consider the principal weaknesses of the present educational system, and what remedies should we consider adopting? In responding to this question, appraise the contribution of education *relative to that of other factors* in the process of occupational achievement.

5 Given that employment in state and local governments has grown very rapidly in recent years, what has been the growth of public employment in the area in which you live? What kinds of government jobs have provided the most employment opportunities? The fewest? What is the source of your information on this issue?

6 Why do you think that some of the countries listed in Table 1-5 have lower unemployment rates than the United States? Select one of these countries and compare some of the characteristics of its economy and labor force with characteristics of the American economy and labor force.

7 Suppose that you could redesign American society to fit your own specifications. How would you change the distribution of family income from that shown in Table 1-12? What are the main factors upon which you base your decision? Is there any reason to believe that shares of income should be divided equally among the five categories of families listed in Table 1-12? Explain.

8 "The broad categories of occupations used by the Bureau of Labor Statistics (such as those listed in Table 1-8) are not very suitable for assisting in the process of occupational choice. There is as much or more variation among jobs within each of these categories as between the categories." Appraise this statement. What are your sources of information about detailed occupational classifications? About occupations generally?

9 Making use of the appropriate statistical sources of the Bureau of Labor Statistics and the Bureau of the Census, estimate how many competitors you are likely to have in your chosen field upon graduation, as compared with your counterparts of 10 years ago *and* 10 years hence. Identify whom you include in your category of competitors.

10 In certain Eastern cultures, highly sophisticated individuals have cultivated asceticism in the belief that they are richer spiritually if they require few worldly goods. Thoreau came close to such a philosophy during his retreat at Walden Pond, and echoes of it appear today among those who wish to "drop out of the middle-class rat race." Discuss (*a*) the desirability of such a philosophy from the individual's perspective and (*b*) its desirability from the viewpoint of society as a whole.

Job Mobility and Job Attitudes

INTRODUCTION

In this chapter, we explore both the extent of job mobility within the labor sector and the attitudes of workers toward their jobs. Of particular interest are changes over time in both job mobility and work-related attitudes. Knowing simply that 15 percent of the work force changes jobs in a particular year or that 8 percent of workers surveyed report sharp dissatisfaction with their jobs is less interesting than knowing how such behavior and attitudes compare at various points in time.

A mobile work force contributes to an efficiently functioning economy and enables individual workers to improve their positions in the labor market. In the material to follow, we shall explore some of the determinants of job mobility, the sources and uses of information about jobs, the role of government in providing information on the labor market, and, briefly, some implications for competitive-labor-market theory of the empirical material on job mobility and job search.

Concerning the attitudes of workers toward their jobs, it would be difficult to identify another era in which the theme of alienation has been so widely propounded. Attitudinal data concerning alienation will be closely scrutinized in relation to the nature and structure of work, in relation to technology, and in relation to job design. Some remedies, actual and potential, for improving the quality of working life will be discussed, including job enrichment and participation by workers in managing the enterprise, areas in which the experiences of other nations are particularly relevant.

JOB MOBILITY

The most common employment shifts in the economy are the movements of workers from job to job, sometimes (but only sometimes) within the same occupation and industry. An individual obviously can pursue the occupation of truck driver, electrician, stenographer, nurse, engineer, or personnel director for any one of a number of companies or government agencies and in a variety of locations. Thus, the distinguishing characteristic of job mobility is usually a movement from one employer to another, whether or not the worker also changes occupation, industry, or geographic location. (Strictly speaking, job mobility also encompasses movement among jobs within the same firm, but this "internal mobility" has not been studied as extensively as the moves among employers.)

The practical implications of job mobility are far-reaching. For example, if American families want more and better medical care, highways, or petroleum products, workers must be attracted into these activities and away from areas of declining or lower-priority employment. And if workers within each industry move easily from marginal, high-cost firms to expanding, low-cost firms, this too serves the interests of consumers. In addition, such movement can serve the interests of the worker, for the efficient and expanding firm usually provides steadier employment and often higher wage rates, more fringe benefits, and better working conditions than the marginal firm.

Alternatively, "job mobility" can be a euphemism for disaster in the lives of many workers. It is one thing for a recent graduate of a high school located in an affluent suburb to shop around from job to job, but it is quite another matter for the 50-year-old coal miner with an eighth-grade education, a family rooted in a town in West Virginia or Pennsylvania, and seniority and pension rights concentrated in a fading job that provides fewer and fewer workdays each year to do so. Who would care to tell this worker that mobility is good for the economy and that he should welcome the opportunity to uproot his family and take a chance on finding a job in Chicago, Los Angeles, or Houston? Further, should society subsidize the worker's job search, as is the case in several nations, or will market forces match workers and jobs better than any arm of government?

Competitive-labor-market theory portrays job mobility in a very beneficial light.[1] For labor markets to function competitively, workers must be ready and able to move to new jobs that provide higher pay or offer some net advantage over their present employment. As some employers bid up the demand for labor, offering higher pay and more benefits (and perhaps better working conditions) than are available elsewhere, workers will move to them and away from other jobs. This dynamic process is the mechanism through which equilibrium in the labor market is approached if not fully attained. In equilibrium, resources are at the peak of allocative efficiency and all workers are paid the value of their (differing) contributions to the production of final products. Note that competitive-labor-market theory presumes that information about job opportunities is widely available and quickly acted upon.

However, several studies have revealed that most factory workers have only a limited, sketchy notion of the job alternatives available in the local labor market, let alone in other, more distant locations; that they value many other aspects of a job besides its wage rate (for example, the nature of supervision, steadiness of employment, and congeniality of the work group); that they are reluctant to change jobs and especially reluctant to change geographic areas; and that, when forced to move, they often take the first decent job they find rather than shopping around to "maximize the returns" to their investment in search activity. Reasoning from facts such as these, some economists argue that the orthodox model of competitive behavior in the job market is a poor guide to understanding how labor markets actually operate.

Defenders of the competitive-labor-market model respond that its critics have misread both the theory and the evidence. They point out that the theory calls for only some workers, not all, to be willing to move at any given time; that it is valid if workers tend to move as predicted, that is, as *if* they were indeed economic beings; and that the evidence shows that this is how workers do in fact move, from other countries to the United States, from farms to cities, from the south to the north earlier in the twentieth century, and, more recently, from the industrial northeast to southern and "sun-belt" states.

In short, we may inquire, "How competitive and predictable is the labor market?" To answer this question, at least on a preliminary level, let us consider how much job mobility takes place in the American economy and how purposeful or predictable that mobility seems to be.

The Anatomy of Job Mobility

Although several studies have been made of job mobility in local labor markets, particularly among factory workers, there have been very few surveys of all the job changes made within the entire labor force. Derived from the Current Population Survey, the most recent of these reports shows that, in 1976, the mobility rate was 16.4 percent.[2] This is the proportion of wage and salary workers in the labor force who worked for two or more employers during the year (excluding multiple jobholders), and it is larger than others previously reported—10.1 percent in 1961, 11.1 percent in 1955, and 15.1 percent rate in 1975.[3]

Like most such statistics, the figures themselves prove little. To those who believe that labor is basically immobile, the significant point is that five-sixths of all workers do not change jobs during the course of a year, in spite of the fact that a dynamic economy is constantly forcing some people to move involuntarily and is providing job openings for others who might want to move. As further support for this point of view, a study of job tenure showed that of all workers employed in January 1978, 40 percent had been with their current employer for 5 or more years, roughly one-quarter for 10 or more years, and almost 10 percent for 20 or more years.[4]

Conversely, those who stress the flexibility of the work force would be impressed by the fact that one out of every six workers changes jobs every year, in spite of the upheaval that such a move represents to most people, and by the fact that almost 60 percent of all workers have been on their current jobs for less than 5 years. Furthermore, and consistent with the increased mobility rate reported here, the proportion of male and female workers with 10 or more years of job tenure declined noticeably over the period 1963–1978, while the proportion with less than 5 years increased. With so much movement among workers, then, the competitive-labor-market model might seem to be applicable.[5]

Clearly, additional facts and judgmental criteria are required in order to evaluate these contrasting views of job mobility in American society. Table 2-1 presents data showing that the aggregate mobility rate is composed of quite different rates among subgroups of the labor force, each of which requires its own explanation.

The fact that men change jobs more frequently than women may partially reflect the greater concentration of women in white-collar occupations, in which mobility rates tend to be lower than those in blue-collar occupations. Perhaps more important, however, is the fact that when women lose or quit their jobs for any reason, they are more likely than men to drop out of the labor force for a time (as is suggested by the data in column 4 of Table 2-1). A survey of mobility in any one year would not count those dropping out of or reentering the labor force as job changers and in that sense would understate the mobility rate of women.

In view of the concentration of nonwhites in less desirable and less stable occupations, it is perhaps surprising that their mobility rate is not higher than that of whites; in fact, it is fully 5 percentage points below the rate for whites. This may indicate that nonwhites see fewer job opportunities than whites do, even if they are equally disposed to move. One must be wary of such an explanation, however, for it contains an element of self-fulfilling prophecy. Moreover, since nonwhites are more likely to be unemployed and to suffer longer spells of unemployment than whites, a single year's survey of the type reported in Table 2-1 could well understate mobility among nonwhites who are *between* jobs.[6]

In 1976, job mobility was greater among part-time than among full-time workers, 19 versus 14 percent. This is not surprising, since part-time work has fewer of the characteristics that promote attachment to a specific job—seniority rights, channels for promotion, deferred benefits, and the like. It is also easier for part-time than for full-time workers to locate a new job while working at the first one. Thus, fewer of them need to look for work *between* jobs.

Table 2-1 Wage and Salary Workers with Two Employers or More during the Year, by Age, Sex, Race, Hispanic Origin, and Occupation, 1976
(Numbers in Thousands)

Item	With two employers or more		Looked for work between jobs	
	Number (1)	Percent of all workers (2)	Number (3)	Percent of total with two employers or more (4)
Age				
Total, 16 years and over	15,578	16.4	7,338	47.1
16 to 19 years	2,916	28.9	1,354	46.4
20 to 24 years	4,631	30.2	2,416	52.2
25 to 34 years	4,216	17.6	1,946	46.2
35 to 44 years	1,842	11.3	777	42.2
45 to 59 years	1,592	7.2	717	45.0
60 years and over	379	5.1	129	34.0
Sex				
Men	9,174	17.2	4,589	50.0
Women	6,403	15.4	2,749	42.9
Race or Hispanic origin				
White	14,169	16.9	6,573	46.4
Black	1,138	11.8	630	55.4
Hispanic origin	759	17.8	414	54.5
Employment status (1975)				
Usually worked full time	10,388	14.1	5,300	51.0
Usually worked part time	3,604	18.9	1,603	44.5

Sources: Adapted from Anne McDougall Young, "Work Experience of the Population, 1976," *Monthly Labor Review,* **100**:47 (1977), table 6. Data for employment status, 1975, from U.S. Bureau of Labor Statistics, *Work Experience of the Population, 1975,* Special Labor Force Report 192, 1976, p. 8, table 5.

But of all characteristics of workers, *age is by far the most reliable predictor of job mobility.* Study after study has shown that as age increases, there is a steady decrease in the propensity to change employer, occupation, or geographic area. This is observable from Table 2-1, which shows mobility rates in 1976; as can be seen from the table, roughly 30 percent of workers below 25 years of age changed jobs in that year, while only about 7 percent of those 45 years of age and older did so. A study of job tenure by Hayghe found that in 1973, "the length of time on the job varied directly with age and . . . is longest for older workers and shortest for teenagers."[7] Table 2-1 also demonstrates that the incidence of looking for work between jobs declines with age, though irregularly.

These findings make sense, for young people just entering the labor force often have a difficult time adjusting to the discipline of working life; they may not know what to look for or what to expect when selecting the first job or two, and they sometimes move among temporary jobs while they are still in school. In addition, young workers are less encumbered than older ones with family responsibilities, such as mortgage payments and the desire to be near good schools, and they are less likely to have seniority and pension rights and specialized skills invested in a particular job. All this adds up to the fact that young workers have both the desire and the ability to shop around for jobs much more frequently than older workers do.

Types of Job Mobility

To this point, we have concentrated primarily on moves among employers, but a few words are in order about moves to other geographic areas and other industries. These types of mobility are, in general, less common than job mobility, with geographic mobility being the least common of all. In 1972, for example, among persons 18 years old and over, some 6 percent of the men and 7 percent of the women changed their employer but not their occupation. Less than 1 percent of both groups changed their occupation but not their employer.[8] As to industrial mobility, researchers have consistently found that workers are less firmly attached to an industry than to an occupation. Indeed, some analysts argue that "industrial mobility is not an important factor in itself; . . . industrial mobility rates may be more a function of varying occupational distributions across industries than of differences in the types of goods or services produced."[9]

There are at least two major deficiencies in the data on mobility. First, there are no national samples of movement *within* private firms and public agencies. Many employers are known to hire blue-collar workers primarily at the bottom of the skill ladder and then to promote from within, at least below the level of apprenticeable crafts. The same pattern is followed in some white-collar occupations. Yet we do not know the rate of such internal mobility, which can often be as important to the worker, the employer, and the economy as various types of external mobility.

Second, mobility rates are relatively meaningless without some standard of evaluation. Most economists would agree that a rate of 16 percent a year is perfectly adequate to meet the shifting needs of the economy and the expectations of competitive theory—but *only* if most of those changing jobs are the "right" workers moving at the "right" time and in the "right" direction. The rates shown in Table 2-1 demonstrate only that some workers are more likely than others to change employers, leaving unanswered the question to which we now turn: "How purposeful are all these job shifts?"

Determinants of Job Mobility

We shall concentrate on four measures of employees' attitudes and behavior: what workers say they look for in a job, why they leave one job for another, how they find and select another job, and whether their moves are predictably toward higher-paying jobs.

Workers' Opinions Orthodox economic analysis tends to stress the rate of remuneration as the major factor affecting choice of a job. If one job pays more than another, it is for that reason a better job and will be preferred. To this generalization is added the major qualification of *ceteris paribus:* "all other things being equal" about two jobs, workers will take the one paying the higher wage. Sometimes this basic proposition is broadened to state that workers will choose a job on the basis of total net advantages, meaning that they will compare jobs not only in terms of wage rates but also in terms of fringe benefits, stability, safety, cleanliness, opportunities for advancement, and so on, and that each worker will pick the job with features that he or she considers most important.

This approach has been challenged over the years by the so-called "institutional" economists, who have reasoned not so much from general principles as from empirical observations. As previously noted, almost every study of workers' attitudes concludes that workers value several aspects of a job in addition to its pay rate. First, there is a cluster of satisfactions related to the intrinsic nature of the work itself: some jobs are boring, and some are fascinating; some provide the worker with a great deal of independence, and some are closely controlled by a supervisor or a machine; some are dirty and hazardous, and some are clean and safe. Second, there is a cluster of factors which involve the social setting of the job: whether it permits frequent and pleasant interpersonal relations; whether it is characterized by congeniality and stability of the immediate work group; and whether supervisors are fair and value workers' opinions. These and other, similar nonwage matters are the things that neoclassical economists have impounded in the term *ceteris paribus,* but the institutionalists argue that they are too important to dismiss as mere qualifications in describing workers' values and behavior.

This argument cannot be settled by abstract logic alone. On the one hand, when the orthodox theory of workers' behavior is stated with its proper qualifications, it is correct but uninteresting. Who is surprised to learn that a worker will choose the higher-paying of two jobs that are identical in all other respects? The institutionalists argue that a worker seldom has that choice in the real world and that the actual choices are not illuminated by restating the theory to mean: "Depending upon circumstances, workers may maximize net advantage by moving to a new occupation which pays more, less, or the same rate (as their previous occupations), and any one of the three can be consistent with the classical doctrine."[10] By that test, anyone could explain any pattern of mobility after the fact, but would be hard pressed to predict a pattern before the fact.

On the other hand, the institutionalists' attitudinal surveys are not necessarily any better as predictors of human behavior. Workers who say that a fair supervisor is more important than wages on their scale of job satisfactions may be saying only that their current wages are closer than their current supervision to their expectations of what is normal and right; they might (or might not) move to a better-paying job with an unknown supervisor tomorrow. In other words, if the institutionalists' approach is pushed too far, it strains credulity by implying that there is no observable pattern whatever to mobility—that there are only individuals, each unique to some extent in terms of noneconomic preferences and each choosing unpredictably among jobs that have their own unique noneconomic characteristics.

In summary, if job changes are so unpredictable that they can be explained only by depth interviews with each individual after he or she has changed jobs, it matters little whether one says that mobility is determined primarily by "institutional" factors or by "total net advantages"—each theory is correct, but neither is useful as a basis for prediction or policy making. If there is a meaningful difference between these theories, it emerges only when their qualifications are largely ignored. Classicists really do expect mobility to be primarily from lower- to higher-income jobs, in spite of their bows to *ceteris paribus*. And institutionalists really do expect mobility to be only loosely related to differences in wages, even though they acknowledge that workers naturally prefer high to low wages. It is this difference in emphasis and expectation that has divided labor economists, and it cannot be resolved by more elegant models or better attitudinal surveys. The decisive test of theories about mobility is what workers *do,* not what they say or what theorists assume.

Why Workers Change Jobs Changing jobs can mean different things to different groups of workers. Generally speaking, white-collar workers change employers less frequently than blue-collar and service workers do, they are less likely to be unemployed between jobs, and *they are less likely to move because they have to* (that is, because of layoffs resulting from lack of work) *and more likely to move to improve their status* (that is, to quit to take a "better" job or to leave a job with which they are dissatisfied).[11]

All this suggests that mobility may be more purposeful among white-collar than among blue-collar workers. If workers can control their shifts in employment, in the sense of having a better job lined up before or shortly after quitting the old job, they might be expected to behave more like rational, calculating individuals than workers who are buffeted by forces beyond their control. The latter—those who are laid off with little advance notice, who are uncertain as to whether or when they will be recalled to their old jobs, and whose debts increase as they remain unemployed—are hardly in a position to hold out for a job that will bring an "improvement in status." By the same reasoning, one would expect the classical model of behavior in the labor market to give better predictions during periods of full employment, when job openings are plentiful, than during recessions or depressions. It is no accident, for example, that the quit rate closely follows the ups and downs of the business cycle.[12]

Yet all this is at best indirect evidence of the directions in which workers move. Those who change jobs voluntarily may quit to get more money, but they may also consider another job to be better because it is more interesting or steadier or because the boss is more to their liking, even if it does not pay more than the previous job. And those who change jobs involuntarily may end up in a higher-paying job almost in spite of things, as when a worker is forced to leave a dying firm or area and to look for work elsewhere for perhaps the first time in years. Finally, note that some shifts in employment occur for a hodgepodge of reasons—such as illness, school responsibilities, and the termination of a seasonal job known to be temporary when it was taken—from which it is difficult to infer anything useful about patterns of mobility.

Thus, we cannot settle the debate over theories about mobility; we can only indicate why the debate began and why it continues. In the real world, workers change jobs for many reasons—only one of which is the desire to make more money—and many workers, particularly in the blue-collar ranks, change jobs only because they have to, not because they want to.

How Workers Find Jobs   When workers do leave their jobs, voluntarily or otherwise, or when they reenter the labor force after having left it, how efficient is their search for the next job? The answer to this question is important not only from the worker's perspective but from society's as well, in that smoothly functioning labor markets add to the performance of the economy and ultimately satisfy consumers' interests.

Competitive-labor-market theorists and the institutionalists are alike in their concern for improving the functioning of labor markets, which means, in part, the quality and sources of information about the labor market. As Lansing and Mueller observed in their study of geographic mobility:

> It is only necessary that comparatively few workers move to areas where there is greater demand for their services, as indicated by more job openings and/or better pay. However, when moving decisions are made in a haphazard fashion without sufficient information . . . mobility is bound to be inefficient economically. Inefficiency means that many more moves occur than are needed to bring about the required reallocation of the labor force.[13]

Regarding blue-collar workers, the evidence is clear that they typically have only sketchy information about job alternatives, even within their local labor markets, and that they rely primarily on informal sources for information about jobs. More specifically, friends and relatives are the principal source of information that blue-collar workers use in finding out about possible job openings. It is "contacts" that count, and, for them, such contacts are most often found in the personal networks of informal informational sources. The direct application to a plant is also important, though primarily with respect to companies located in the worker's immediate neighborhood and to the large, well-known firms, whose very size guarantees enough turnover to give some expectation that they might always have some openings. Public and private employment agencies are not extensively used by blue-collar workers, although their purpose is to provide a maximum of choice to both employer and job seeker.[14]

In contrast, white-collar workers tend to rely more heavily on formal or impersonal sources of information about the labor market. This conclusion is evident from the data presented in Table 2-2, which reports sources of information about jobs during the late 1960s for a sample of workers in the Chicago area, and in Figure 2-1, which presents similar information drawn from a national sample of households during the late 1950s and early 1960s.

The Chicago study[15] shows that formal sources of information—newspaper advertisements and private employment agencies, in particular—were the

Table 2-2 Sources of Information about the Chicago Area Labor Market by Occupation, Percentage Distribution

Information source	Typist (557)	Keypunch operator (378)	Accountant (228)	Tab operator (216)
Informal sources				
Employee referral	23.0	26.2	17.5	22.2
Other informal referral[1]	2.0	3.7	6.6	1.9
Gate application	3.4	7.9	4.8	1.9
Total informal sources	28.4	37.8	28.9	26.0
Formal sources				
State employment service	0.9	1.1	2.6	0.5
Private agency	20.5	8.7	16.7	12.5
Newspaper ad	10.1	15.9	19.7	13.0
School or college[2]	1.1	10.3	6.6	6.0
Union	0.2			
Other formal sources[3]	0.5	0.3		0.5
Total formal sources	33.3	36.3	45.6	32.5
Rehires	5.0	10.3	5.7	4.2
Unknown	33.4	15.6	19.7	37.5

Information source	Material handler (650)	Janitor (473)	Janitress (173)	Forklift trucker (356)
Informal sources				
Employee referral	38.4	34.0	29.5	32.9
Other informal referral[1]	1.8	1.7	2.9	5.9
Gate application	3.6	6.8	3.5	3.9
Total informal sources	43.8	42.5	35.9	42.7
Formal sources				
State employment service	1.5	2.1	1.2	0.6
Private agency	2.7	1.7	1.2	1.7
Newspaper ad	2.0	2.5	5.2	3.7
School or college[2]				
Union	2.0	2.5	0.5	0.3
Other formal sources[3]		0.6	2.3	0.3
Total formal sources	8.2	9.4	10.5	6.6
Rehires	3.8	4.2	19.1	8.1
Unknown	44.2	43.8	34.7	42.7

(Continued on page 62)

Table 2-2 (Continued)

Information source	Punch press operator (303)	Truck driver (166)	Maintenance electrician (275)	Tool and die maker (278)
Informal sources				
Employee referral	28.7	22.9	26.9	24.5
Other informal referral¹	2.3	5.4	3.6	3.2
Gate application	2.6	6.0	8.0	8.3
Total informal sources	33.6	34.2	38.5	36.0
Formal sources				
State employment service	1.7	0.6	0.4	0.7
Private agency	1.7		1.1	
Newspaper ad	6.6	0.6	5.5	7.9
School or college²	0.3			0.4
Union		4.8	0.7	0.7
Other formal sources³			0.7	
Total formal sources	10.3	6.0	8.4	9.7
Rehires	11.2	8.4	5.5	11.9
Unknown	44.9	51.2	47.6	42.4

¹ Includes referrals by other employers and contacts initiated by present employer.

² Includes private trade schools, which account for all school placement of tab operators and thirty-three of thirty-nine for keypunch operators. Colleges account for fourteen of fifteen school placements of accountants.

³ Includes churches, welfare agencies, and professional associations.

Note: Sample size in parentheses.

Source: Adapted from Albert Rees and George P. Shultz, *Workers and Wages in an Urban Labor Market,* University of Chicago Press, Chicago, 1970, pp. 201–202.

dominant mechanisms through which white-collar workers obtained information about the labor market. Among the four white-collar occupations studied, only keypunch operators relied more heavily on informal than formal sources, but even here, more than one-third of them used private employment agencies, newspaper advertisements, school or college placement offices, and the like. By contrast, in only two of the eight blue-collar occupations studied did formal sources of information account for as much as 10 percent of all sources. And, as the authors of this study point out, because informal sources of information are not as likely to be recorded as formal ones, "the relative importance of informal sources for blue-collar workers is understated by the percentage distributions."[16]

The data shown in Figure 2-1 reinforce the findings of the Chicago study, though yielding a somewhat smaller set of differences between blue- and white-collar workers concerning the use of formal and informal sources of information about the labor market.[17] Additionally, the authors of this study investigated the deliberation with which workers make decisions to change jobs and job locations. They found that, among those in the sample who changed jobs, 44 percent of the professionals but only 22 percent of the blue-collar workers considered alternative places to which they might move and that 52 percent of the professionals but only 36 percent of the blue-collar workers used more than one source of information.[18] Though no one group utilizes all sources of informa-

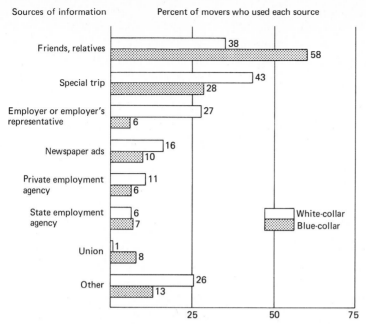

Sources of information   Percent of movers who used each source

Figure 2-1 Sources of information about jobs used in geographic moves, 1957–1963. "Movers" are heads of families who changed residence from one labor market to another between 1957 and 1962 or between 1958 and 1963 (depending on date of interview), excluding those transferred by their employers or not in the labor force. Percentages total more than 100 because some movers used more than one source of information. (*Source: John B. Lansing and Eva Mueller,* The Geographic Mobility of Labor, *University of Michigan, Institute for Social Research, Ann Arbor, 1967, p. 225.*)

tion or weighs all job alternatives, white-collar workers conform more closely than blue-collar workers to our idea of "economic man."

What of the attempts by government to improve the process of finding jobs and acquiring information about the labor market? Beginning in the late 1960s (a period of tight labor markets), the federal government embarked on a formal job bank program in which automated data processing equipment would be used to improve the functioning of labor markets. Each known job opening in a particular area would be recorded and stored in a computer. Lists of these jobs would be updated daily and distributed to all counselors and placement interviewers in the United States Employment and Training Service (ETS) and cooperating agencies, who would then use the data in referring applicants to jobs.

Though only one component of federal efforts to improve the functioning of labor markets, the local job bank program has not met with much success to date. Part of this has to do with long-standing organizational characteristics of the ETS, particularly the tensions and conflicts arising from the requirement that the agency provide both job-finding services and unemployment compensation payments. Nevertheless, the lack of success is also due partially to the informal nature of much information about the labor market. As noted in a recent study of this federal program, "job bank data may be less intensive than the labor market information produced in the non-job bank system."[19] Such a conclusion reinforces the view that the job-search process is, at least in part, haphazard and unpredictable. But then the operations of the labor market are not perfectly analogous to those of capital, commodity, or stock markets.[20]

Note that informal contacts and channels of information about the labor market may well reinforce discriminatory hiring practices, intentionally or otherwise. A firm that hires clerical personnel strictly on the basis of referrals from present clerical employees may well exclude from consideration individuals of a particular age, race, or sex who could perform the job about as well as those chosen for employment. The young white male construction worker who obtained his job through a relative's position in a craft union has taken advantage of informal contacts in the labor market, but the result, even if largely unintended, is to reinforce the low representation or absence of minorities and women in such jobs. On a larger scale, when labor and business groups informally combine to restrict the entry of other employers into a market, they may also restrict the entry of all but the "right kind" of workers into their labor forces.[21] Thus, informal contacts and channels of information in labor markets may promote and solidify discriminatory employment practices even if they benefit the individual worker.

Mobility and Income Do workers move predictably from lower- to higher-income jobs? Or, because of the inefficiency of search methods, the importance of nonwage aspects of employment, and the involuntary nature of many job changes, is mobility largely independent of wage differences?

In a review of the literature on this subject, Parnes concluded: "There is abundant evidence that net geographic migration—international as well as domestic—is generally in the direction of greater economic opportunity as measured by differentials in income, in employment opportunities, or both."[22] But he goes on to say: "There is disagreement . . . with respect to the relative importance of the two (income and employment), and it is frequently difficult to disentangle their effects empirically." As an example, one investigator found that differences in employment opportunities rather than differences in potential income explained the migration of Puerto Ricans to the United States, while a second investigator reached the opposite conclusion.[23]

Most analysts probably would agree that the relationship between mobility and income is strongest in the case of moves to a different geographic area. Migration among countries has been predominantly from lower- to higher-income areas, and this has also been true of the massive shifts from rural to urban jobs within all industrialized nations. Concerning long-run mobility within the United States, Raimon has shown that net migration is primarily from lower- to higher-income states, while Lansing and Mueller found that some two-thirds of those who moved earned more after their move than before, about one-quarter earned less, and one-tenth earned the same.[24] Perhaps the strongest evidence that mobility is functionally (and positively) related to income comes from studies that find a strong negative correlation between voluntary job changes, as reflected in the quit rate, and annual earnings.[25] Because these studies also control for factors other than earnings that may affect mobility (for example, skill mix, size of firm, extent of unionism, proportions of female and black employees, and quality of the work force), their findings in support of a positive mobility-earnings relationship—and, more generally, in support of orthodox economic theory—are impressive. Nevertheless, these studies also are limited, if not deficient, partly because data on turnover in the American labor market are collected only for the manufacturing sector and partly because the methodologies employed in these researches permit contradictory hypotheses about job mobility to be equally well supported. And, in still another example of this type of study, one investigator finds that "employment opportunities explain a larger proportion of voluntary job movement than wage differentials."[26]

Finally, there may well be differences between blue- and white-collar workers concerning the importance of income to the decision to change jobs. The early studies of manual workers in local labor markets suggest that little more than half of all voluntary job shifts and far less than half of all involuntary shifts (those resulting from layoffs or discharges) resulted in an improvement in wages for these workers.[27] The few studies of white-collar workers present a mixed picture: among clerical workers in Boston in the mid-1950s, three-fourths of job shifts were to higher-paying jobs when those who changed jobs stayed in the labor market, and among college professors who changed jobs in 1963–1964, 69 percent moved up in income; however, among scientists and engineers in the San Francisco area during the early 1960s, a period of heavy layoffs, job shifts resembled those made by blue-collar workers, with about half the shifts before layoff but only one-fifth of those after layoff being to higher-paying jobs.[28]

Though they illuminate the issue of job mobility, these studies do not prove that higher-paying jobs cause workers to change positions. What they show is a series of positive correlations between mobility and pay (or earnings) that permit inferences to be drawn about the underlying relationships between the two variables. But correlational analysis does not yield—or should not be interpreted to yield—causality. It does not tap workers' basic motivations or the dimensions of the decision processes that lead some workers to take higher-paying jobs, others to take lower-paying ones, and still others to remain in their positions over long periods of time. The danger of imputing causality from correlation is a general one in the social sciences and is especially to be guarded against in studying the labor sector.

Given the importance of mobility, it is surprising that so few economists have investigated it systematically. On the basis of the scattered evidence now available, it can be predicted only that moves from lower- to higher-paying jobs will be more frequent when job shifts are voluntary than when they are involuntary; when they are broad geographic rather than narrow, local shifts; when labor markets are tight rather than when there is high unemployment; and when they occur among white-collar rather than among blue-collar workers. Among all job shifts occurring at any given time, however, there is only a weak trend of low-to-high movement.

An Interim Appraisal

What does this welter of studies on mobility add up to, beyond the obvious fact that we need more and better data, particularly about white-collar workers, than are now available?

On the theoretical front, the facts suggest that the labor force is much more flexible and mobile than the institutionalist approach implies, but this extensive mobility is far less efficient and predictable than the competitive-labor-market model indicates. More specifically, about one out of every six American workers will change jobs next year, about half of the them will move their families to a different labor market, and most will move to a job paying as much as, or more than, the job they left—all of which suggests a fairly competitive labor market. However, much of this movement will be made involuntarily, few of even those who change jobs voluntarily will be efficient in their job search, and the safest prediction concerning change in income is that the average person who changes jobs will end up neither gaining nor losing very much.

None of this means that the labor market is hopelessly irrational. Informal job-search methods work quite well for many workers and employers, and formal channels are available when wanted. Each year the ETS fills many thousands of jobs, often helping the workers and employers who are most in need, and the agency is attempting to improve its usefulness to both the disadvantaged and white-collar groups. On the policy front, the United States has been cautiously following the lead of other countries and experimenting with subsidies to help workers move out of depressed areas, to train those left behind, and to entice new industry into such areas.

On balance, however, the evidence strongly indicates that the impressive mobility of the American work force is often inefficient, needlessly painful, and unproductive for many workers. This fact is central to an understanding of most other issues in the labor sector. For millions of workers the right to quit and seek a better job has provided great opportunities for advancement, but for millions of others mobility has often meant the right to be fired or laid off from a much-needed job and to join the ranks of the unemployed for whom no better job may exist or, if it exists, may never be discovered. To these workers, advancement may appear to lie not in job mobility but in concerted action through unions so as to protect and improve the jobs they already have.

Moreover, the occurrence of layoffs and the evidence cited earlier concerning the relationship between voluntary separations (quits) and the business cycle underscore the importance of full employment. If the job choices of the labor sector are to be expanded and the opportunities for job mobility enlarged, the economy must operate closer to full employment than it recently has. This is especially so in the case of racial minorities and women, but it applies to the work force as a whole. Without a rate of employment expansion sufficient to absorb a growing labor force and to provide new job opportunities for existing workers, job mobility is more a value than a characteristic of the work force. Later chapters will examine some of the difficulties encountered in attempting to achieve full employment simultaneously with other societal goals.

However, whether they are attained in present jobs or different jobs and with or without the help of unions, such things as advancement, rewards, and satisfaction may seem to some workers to reside in a broader, fuller participation in their work or, in other words, in improvements in the quality of their working lives. We now turn to that issue, beginning with a brief examination of employees' changing attitudes toward work.

ATTITUDES TOWARD WORK

The notion that work is a major source of dissatisfaction (as well as rewards) for employees in an industrialized society has a long and rich intellectual tradition. In his early writings, for example, Karl Marx discussed the growth of alienation among the working class resulting from the "lost control of the products of their own activity" and from the process of work itself, which, far from permitting workers to exercise "their natural powers" freely constrains them "to perform uninteresting and degrading tasks."[29] This growing alienation, together with other characteristics of dynamic capitalism, leads in the Marxian analysis to the eventual overthrow of the capitalists (the bourgeoisie) by the working class (the proletariat).

Considerably before Marx's time, Adam Smith, who otherwise extolled the economic virtues of the division of labor in society, noted the following:

> In the progess of the division of labor . . . the man whose whole life is spent in performing a few simple operations, of which the effects too are, perhaps, always the same, or very nearly the same, has no occasion to exert his understanding, or to exercise his invention in finding out expedients for removing difficulties which never occur. He naturally loses, therefore, the habit of such exertion and generally becomes as stupid and ignorant as it is possible for a human creature to become. The torpor of his mind renders him, not only incapable of relishing or bearing a part in any rational conversation, but of conceiving any generous, noble or tender sentiment. . . . His dexterity at his own particular trade seems, in this manner, to be acquired at the expense of his intellectual, social and marital virtues.[30]

Unlike Marx, Smith considered the negative attributes of specialization to be more than offset by the increases in production and in economic returns to worker and capitalist which are generated by the division of labor together with other characteristics of capitalism. In this view, human resources are the wealth of a nation but there are costs to be incurred in increasing that wealth, of which disenchantment with work and onerous working conditions are two examples.

Writing in the 1940s, Karl Polanyi viewed capitalism—or, more specifically, the "self-regulating" market—as an aberration which would eventually be replaced by some form of collective social organization. He argued that the development of the factory system caused workers to feel like mere appendages to machines.[31] In this view, the factory system disrupts social relations, helps perpetuate the "myth" that labor is a commodity, and sows the seeds of an eventual subordination of the market system, an idea somewhat similar to the Marxian philosophy. Polanyi's observations about changing attitudes of workers resulting from changes in the organization of work are especially relevant to contemporary discussion of this issue.

Perhaps the most significant, and certainly the most far-reaching and best-publicized, recent statement in support of the thesis that there is widespread dissatisfaction among workers is *Work in America,* a study sponsored by the Department of Health, Education, and Welfare (HEW).[32] This document, the report of a federally designated task force which employed dozens of consultants and commissioned some forty separate papers on one or another dimension of the subject, contended that the American labor force was becoming increasingly dissatisfied with dull, repetitive, boring work that provided little or no chance for the exercise of initiative and responsibility and little or no opportunity for self-fulfillment. Not only was this dissatisfaction presumably felt by blue-collar workers, but, according to the report, it was also widespread among white-collar workers and even managers. The discontent of workers—their "dehumanization," in the parlance of the report—led to such consequences as low productivity, increasing absenteeism and tardiness, wildcat strikes, industrial sabotage, low-quality products, and deteriorating physical and mental health of workers. The remedies for these ills suggested by the *Work in America* task force included basic restructuring of jobs to allow workers greater autonomy, massive federally sponsored retraining efforts to promote job mobility and second careers, and a commitment on the part of the federal government to full employment.

The chief villain in all this, according to the HEW report, was "Taylorism," the notion of organizing work *and* work organizations according to the principles of scientific management as defined by Frederick W. Taylor shortly after the beginning of the twentieth century.[33] Taylor argued that the careful study of jobs—all jobs, including managerial ones—the specification of their individual components, the measurement of standard times required to complete them, and the reconstruction of jobs on the basis of these key components would vastly increase production, thereby leading to greater profits for business owners and higher wages for workers.

There is little doubt that Taylor's view of the industrial world naively assumed that managers and workers would willingly permit an outside authority (the deity of science, no less) to govern their behavior. Moreover, Taylor presumed a one-dimensional worker, the proverbial "economic man," who would respond favorably to simplifying the job and pursuing higher pay through increased output. Taylor ignored the collective activities of workers, who, though organized on only a small scale in the early part of the century, nevertheless had for many decades manifested various dissatisfactions with the industrial system. Taylor didn't overtly oppose or support trade unions; he simply ignored them—and perhaps not too differently from the way the authors of the HEW-sponsored report ignored modern labor organizations.[34]

But if Taylor presumed too much about workers, he nevertheless proposed a doctrine (and methods of implementing it) of fundamental importance: that the operations of industrial enterprises could be subjected to systematic analysis and, where necessary, redesigned in accordance with the dictates of that analysis. The result would be greater efficiency in production, which would in turn be in the best interests of consumers, producers, and workers. The authors of the HEW report never came to grips with the questions of whether job satisfaction is compatible with the efficiency required by a profit-oriented industrial system and of whether some "costs" are required in order to obtain the benefits that may accrue from specialization in organization and work design. To raise these questions is not the same thing as to endorse Taylorism.

The evidence of dissatisfaction among workers contained in *Work in America* consists primarily of data from attitudinal surveys conducted by others, most notably the Institute for Social Research at the University of Michigan. Several uses were made of these data. The first was to support the notion of generalized and increasing dissatisfaction. Yet an extensive review by Kahn of the literature on job dissatisfaction, including attitudinal surveys of varying scope, design, and occupational coverage, yields a different conclusion.[35] While relatively few respondents described themselves as extremely satisfied with their jobs, still fewer reported extreme dissatisfaction. The most frequently voiced description of attitudes toward jobs in these surveys was "pretty satisfied," with the proportion of self-described dissatisfied workers ranging between 10 and 21 percent.[36] Further, data derived from numerous studies of various groups of workers do not substantiate a conclusion of increasing dissatisfaction over time, even though they consistently reveal selected pockets of it.[37] Whether the magnitude of such dissatisfaction is somehow too high requires a specific valuation standard. In that sense, it is analogous to evaluating the data on job mobility presented earlier, except that the mobility data are behavioral evidence while the survey data are attitudinal evidence. Put differently, the former indicate what workers actually do, whereas the latter indicate what workers believe but not necessarily what they will do.

The second purpose for which the aforementioned survey data were used was to construct rankings of the most highly valued characteristics of work. For this, the authors of *Work in America* relied on the 1970 *Survey of Working Conditions*, conducted at the University of Michigan, and they described these rankings as follows:

This unique and monumental study is based on a representative sample of 1,553 American workers at all occupational levels. When these workers were asked how important they regarded some 25 aspects of work, they ranked in order of importance: (1) interesting work; (2) enough help and equipment to get the job done; (3) enough information to get the job done; (4) enough authority to get the job done; (5) good pay; (6) opportunity to develop special abilities; (7) job security; (8) seeing the results of one's work.[38]

On its face, this is a striking set of findings which unexpectedly reveal that pay and security, traditionally thought to be central to the interests of workers, are less highly valued than the nature and characteristics of work itself. Thus the data appear to support some modern theories of motivation and job design which assign greater importance to intrinsic aspects of work, such as responsibility and autonomy, than to extrinsic factors, such as pay and supervisory policy.

These findings, however, are called into question by other analyses of the original data on which they are based. First, Fein disaggregated the composite data to permit comparisons of ratings of work characteristics among different occupational groups.[39] He found that interesting work, which, as noted above, was the most highly rated job characteristic for the composite worker (that is, for the total Michigan sample), was rated only fifth and seventh, respectively, by two groups of blue-collar workers and only third and sixth, respectively, by "partial blue-collar workers" such as service employees and truck drivers. Good pay, which placed only fourth in the composite worker's ranking, rose in importance for all these blue-collar workers, with service and factory employees ranking it first. Only white-collar employees ranked pay far down the list and interesting work at the top of the list of important work characteristics.

Then, White extended the analysis of the disaggregated data to construct a measure of the difference between (1) the importance of a particular job characteristic and (2) the extent to which that characteristic was present in the worker's own job.[40] After calculating the differences between these two ratings for eleven major work characteristics, White ranked them in order of magnitude. The result was to reveal sources of dissatisfaction at work, ranging from highest to lowest. Table 2-3 presents the findings, showing separate rankings for the composite worker and for the various occupational groups studied.

We see that for the four groups of blue-collar workers, pay and fringe benefits are the sources of greatest dissatisfaction (in White's terminology, "satisfaction discrepancy"). Pay ranks first and benefits second in two of these cases (columns 5 and 6), with the order reversed in the other two (columns 3 and 4). Job security is ranked either third or fourth by the blue-collar groups, alternating with opportunities to develop special abilities. In contrast, interesting work drops to either a fifth- or a sixth-place ranking as a source of job dissatisfaction among these groups, with other previously top-ranked characteristics such as enough help and equipment and enough information to get the job done also declining substantially in importance. Note that for the composite

Table 2-3 Difference between Importance and Availability as a Measure of Satisfaction with Working Condition Factors: A Comparison of the Difference Rankings of Several Occupational Groups and the "Composite Worker"

Working condition factor	Composite worker (1)	White collar	Partial blue collar		Blue collar	
		Professional, technical and managerial (2)	Service (3)	Miscellaneous and truck drivers (4)	Factory (5)	Structural (6)
Work is interesting	5	4	5	5.5	6	5
Enough help and equipment to get job done	6	3	6	5.5	5	7
Enough information to get job done	7	5	10	9	8	8
Enough authority to do my job	9	6	8	9	10.5	11
Pay is good	1	2	2	2	1	1
Opportunity to develop my special abilities	2	1	3	4	3	4
Job security is good	4	10	4	3	4	3
Can see results of my work	10	8	9	11	10.5	10
Co-workers are friendly and helpful	3	7	7	6	9	6
Responsibilities are clearly defined	11	9	11	9	7	9
Fringe benefits are good	3	11	1	1	2	2

Note: The rankings were derived as follows: Each respondent was asked to rate the characteristics of work along two dimensions: importance of a factor in a job, scored from 1, "very important," to 4, "not at all important," and availability of each factor in the respondents' job, scored from 1, "very true," to 4, "not at all true." The average (mean) scores of the respondents on these two dimensions were compared, and the differences recorded. Then for the composite worker, i.e., the total sample, and for each of the occupational groups listed, the eleven major work characteristics were ranked according to the differences in rating scores. The characteristic with the largest difference received a 1, and that with the lowest received an 11. As an example, white-collar workers in the sample rated the importance of pay at 1.64 and its availability at 1.79, the difference being −.15. This difference was the second largest among this group's scores on all eleven dimensions, so that for white-collar workers pay received a ranking of 2, as shown in column 2 of the table.

Source: Adapted from Bernard J. White, "The Criteria for Job Satisfaction: Is Interesting Work Most Important?" *Monthly Labor Review,* **100**:34 (1977).

worker, pay, fringe benefits, and job security now account for three of the four most dissatisfying job characteristics, with interesting work ranked only fifth.

The results are different in the case of white-collar workers. They, too, now rank pay high (second) as a source of dissatisfaction at work, but such characteristics as opportunities to develop special abilities and enough help and equipment to get the job done are ranked highly, while fringe benefits and job security are at the bottom of the list. Still, white-collar workers rank interesting work only fourth among the eleven factors listed in Table 2-3 as sources of dissatisfaction.

The refined analysis thus indicates that rankings of workers' sources of job dissatisfaction are not the same as the workers' rankings of order of importance. Perhaps white-collar and factory workers are kidding themselves, but what the data show is that while pay is not highly ranked as important to the job, workers are highly dissatisfied with their pay. Similarly, while interesting work is ranked more important than pay, the lack of interesting work is not as great a source of job dissatisfaction as pay.

These findings are unsettling not only because they partially contradict earlier results but, even more important, because of the doubts they raise concerning the quality of the analysis and conclusions contained in *Work in America*. White notes that "even the most kindly interpretation of the results of the present analysis vis-à-vis . . . *Work in America* would suggest an unacceptable lack of completeness in data analysis, interpretation, or reporting by the study's authors."[41] This conclusion, together with prior critiques questioning the report's assertions about wildcat strikes, sabotage, productivity, absenteeism and tardiness, and low-quality products, reduces the usefulness of *Work in America*.[42] Yet, as White himself suggests, it would be unfortunate indeed if such reanalysis led to a downgrading of the importance of interesting work or to the conclusion that lack of interesting work is not a source of dissatisfaction on the job, for neither result is supported by the data.[43] What is important, however, is that data on job satisfaction be soberly assessed and closely analyzed so that the magnitude of the problem can be better understood and the remedies for it carefully framed. Later on, we shall review some remedies for job dissatisfaction that have been tried in various work settings.

The third use of data from attitudinal surveys in *Work in America* was to discover what line of work people would choose if they had the opportunity to make the choice over again. The results of these surveys, drawn from a variety of sources, are shown in Table 2-4. The responses are remarkable for the range they exhibit—93 percent of university professors and 16 percent of automobile workers said they would look for the same type of work again—and for the sharp differences reported between professional and manual workers. Note, also, the considerable differences in responses *among* major occupational groups. To be sure, it would be not only careless but also inaccurate to conclude that the scores reported in Table 2-4 translate directly into relative amounts of job satisfaction. Nevertheless, these data offer yet another perspective on the issue of dissatisfaction. They can be interpreted to mean that even a largely satisfied steelworker might not choose that occupation over again and might well choose to direct his children away from it. The university professor, the physicist, and the chemist presumably would behave quite differently, being very likely to select their respective occupations over again, perhaps even if somewhat dissatisfied in them, and also to direct their offspring toward them.

On balance, then, the survey data examined here tell us several things

Table 2-4   Proportions in Occupational Groups Who Would Choose Similar Work Again[1]

Professional and lower white-collar occupations	Percent	Working-class occupations	Percent
Urban university professors[2]	93	Skilled printers	52
Mathematicians	91	Paper workers	42
Physicists	89	Skilled automobile workers	41
Biologists	89	Skilled steelworkers	41
Chemists	86	Textile workers	31
Firm lawyers[2]	85	Blue-collar workers[2]	24
School superintendents[3]	85	Unskilled steelworkers	21
Lawyers	83	Unskilled automobile workers	16
Journalists (Washington correspondents)	82		
Church university professors[2]	77		
Solo lawyers[2]	75		
White-collar workers[2]	43		

[1] Data in this table are based on responses to the question: "What type of work would you try to get into if you could start all over again?" Entries are primarily from a study of 3000 workers in sixteen industries, conducted by the Roper organization.

[2] Probability samples or universes of six professional groups and a cross section of the "middle class" (lower middle class and upper working class) in the Detroit area, stratified for comparability with respect to age, income, occupational stratum, and other characteristics. From Harold Wilensky, "Varieties of Work Experience," in Henry Borow, *Man in a World of Work,* Houghton Mifflin, Boston, 1964.

[3] From a 1952–1953 Massachusetts sample taken from Neal Gross, Ward Mason, and W. A. McEachern, *Explorations in Role Analysis: Studies of the School Superintendency Role,* Wiley, New York, 1958.

Source: Adapted from Robert L. Kahn, "The Meaning of Work: Interpretation and Proposals for Measurement," in Angus Campbell and Philip Converse (eds.), *The Human Meaning of Social Change,* Russell Sage, New York, 1972, p. 182.

about job satisfaction in the American workplace, and some of these seem to contradict the findings and interpretations contained in *Work in America.* Contrary to much popular opinion, dissatisfaction with work does not appear to be on the increase. This does not mean that all people love their jobs or that some of them are not truly dissatisfied with their work, but it hardly presages the demise of the work ethic or a major, tortuous restructuring of work and work organizations. At the same time, workers are not all alike in their valuations of work characteristics. Those who hold factory and construction jobs and who perform manual labor seem most strongly oriented toward the surrounding, or extrinsic, characteristics of work, principally pay, fringe benefits, working conditions, and job security. This is also true of service employees, labeled "partial blue-collar workers" by White, for whom pay is an even stronger source of job dissatisfaction than it is for traditional blue-collar workers. Professional, managerial, and clerical personnel, however, apparently are most heavily oriented toward the content of work, that is, toward the job itself, as reflected in their articulated concern for, and high rankings of the importance of, interesting work, having the tools to get the job done, and accomplishment of tasks.

It is possible, of course, that these differences in work orientation reflect simply the more favorable position *generally* occupied by professional, technical, and managerial workers with respect to compensation and stability of employment. From this perspective, they are able to focus their interests on the task itself because they are relatively well satisfied with other conditions of work—the external conditions. Such an interpretation clearly is consistent with the well-known theory of the hierarchy of needs developed by the psychologist A. H. Maslow, which postulates that higher-order needs (for recognition, prestige, and self-actualization) become salient only after lower-order needs (for food, shelter, and safety) are met.[44]

Proceeding further from the hierarchy of needs, one might venture to say that an increasing incidence of job dissatisfaction is not a necessary condition for the development of greater interest in, or efforts to improve the quality of, working life. After all, we now observe higher levels of educational attainment, enhanced *recognition* of dissatisfaction with work, an increasingly professional managerial cadre (who have their own job dissatisfactions), and perhaps even the growth of work as a central life interest of individuals. These factors may well combine with others to spur a new emphasis on humanism at the workplace, leading to new remedies for job dissatisfaction and to improvements in the quality of working life. Some current efforts along these lines are discussed in the next section.[45]

JOB DESIGN, JOB ENRICHMENT, AND WORKERS' PARTICIPATION IN MANAGEMENT

A variety of experiments and programs have been introduced in recent years to improve the quality of working life. Some of the most far-reaching of these have occurred outside the United States, notably in Norway and Sweden. Much of this attention has focused on the tasks that workers are required to perform in their jobs and on how these tasks—or, more basically, the jobs themselves—can be restructured to make them more meaningful, inherently more interesting, and more satisfying. This has necessarily involved a reexamination of the way in which jobs are designed and some attempts to specify how jobs may be enriched rather than simply rotated or enlarged. *Job enrichment* is the process of reordering a task in such a way that it "provides the opportunity for the employee's psychological growth."[46] In contrast, *job enlargement* merely makes a job structurally bigger, while *job rotation* simply exposes workers to more than one element of a basically unaltered task.

A popular setting for efforts at job redesign and enrichment is the assembly line, particularly in the automobile industry. Perhaps this is not surprising, as research has demonstrated that, among the major industrial technologies, the assembly line leads to the strongest feelings of alienation from work. Yet alteration of the traditional assembly-line format of automobile production has occurred outside rather than within the United States.

In Sweden, for example, both the Saab-Scania and the Volvo companies began in the late 1960s to develop new work environments, largely through the restructuring of production technology.[47] At the former's Sodertalje plant, the assembly line was done away with in assembling truck engines and was replaced by autonomous work teams. While the preassembly operation is much the same as before, each team has its own work area located near a moving track which serves as the repository for preassembled engine blocks as well as completed engines. Hand-pushed trolleys are used in assembling the engines, and thus each team controls its own work. Moreover, each three-person team decides whether to construct entire engines as a unit or to divide up specific tasks among the members. Clearly, this form of job design provides an element of autonomy not possible in the assembly-line context.

At Volvo, management's initial response to dissatisfaction, high turnover, and absenteeism took the form of job rotation.[48] Each day, groups of workers exchanged jobs with one another in the hope of relieving the boredom that accompanies the performance of a small, relatively simple task. No changes of technology were involved; workers were simply given the opportunity to perform a wider variety of assembly-line jobs. Later, however, in the design of its automobile assembly plant at Kalmar and in the manufacture of its gasoline and diesel engines, Volvo did indeed alter its technology, and in rather comprehensive ways. After consulting with employees from different levels of the organization, Volvo's management installed a production system using teams of between fifteen and twenty-five workers who had responsibility for different installation components such as electrical systems, brakes, and wheels. Each team was given its own work area and was allowed to control the allocation and rhythm of its work.

Between each of the work areas in the Kalmar plant are buffer zones for storing and retrieving completed work. Rather than using an assembly line, cars are transported on electric self-propelled trolleys. Each team procures its own materials from factory stores, manages its own parts inventory, and can decide to work on cars either in a stationary position or as they move along the trolleys. The tilting arrangements built into the trolleys facilitate working on the underside of the cars. Each work area has its own resting place, toilet facilities, and changing rooms. These innovations, and others, were subsequently adopted at Volvo's Skovderverken plant for the production of gasoline and diesel engines.[49] From the standpoint of technological change and job enrichment, the principal result of these efforts is that workers now control their work rather than being controlled by it. In the altered production context, the exchange and adjustment of tools and the overseeing of various aspects of the process have replaced short-cycle work and the close dependency of the worker on the machine.

American efforts to remedy the job dissatisfactions of automobile workers have not involved changes in technology, job redesign, or even the more conventional practices of job rotation and enlargement. Rather, on the American scene, emphasis has been placed on high wages, fringe benefits, reduced working hours and a shorter workweek, liberalization of qualifications for pension benefits (such as was provided by the collective bargaining agreement negotiated in 1973 by the United Automobile Workers—the UAW—permitting a worker to qualify for full pension rights after 30 years of work irrespective of age[50]), and, most particularly, the structuring of multistep grievance procedures to deal with problems and disputes at the workplace. As will be discussed in Chapter 5, this last—the grievance procedure—tends to distinguish the United States and Canada from other industrialized countries.

Work redesign and job enrichment have, of course, been attempted in sectors other than automobile manufacturing. At Cummins Engine Company, for example, a variety of actions were taken in the 1970s to reduce employee dissatisfaction and improve performance.[51] These included (1) the redesign of engine testing jobs in such a way that workers could inspect their own work, maintain measurement instruments, set the number of engines per shift to be tested, solve technical problems, and exercise responsibility for ordering and budgeting supplies; (2) the enrichment of keypunch operators' jobs so as to allow them to plan their work according to the needs of internal customers, set goals and target dates for the completion of work, update and correct computer runs, elect (within a 1-hour period) when to start work, and assist in the orientation and training of new employees; and (3) a basic structural reorganization of the fabrication machine shop and automated engine-block line. In each of these instances, workers and supervisors were actively consulted and made part of the design and implementation of new work processes.

At about the same time, the Xerox Corporation embarked on a program of job enrichment for its technical field representatives.[52] Preceded by detailed job analyses and attitudinal surveys of the employees occupying these positions, the enrichment experiment was put into operation in one branch of the company, with three other branches used as control groups to evaluate the effort. Among other things, the field representatives' job was altered to include (1) the authority to use specialized technical personnel, to determine their own working hours and to place a "hold" on machine installations that failed to meet standard requirements; (2) the responsibility for determining their own field assignments and size of work load and for maintaining their own parts inventories and tool supplies, and the partial responsibility for training new technical representatives and making presentations at service meetings; and (3) their involvement in the selection of technical representatives and the provision of input for determining their own merit pay increases during performance appraisals. Also developed as part of the enrichment initiative was a detailed plan for its introduction and implementation into the branch in question. The subsequent evaluation of the efforts at job enrichment revealed improved attitudes toward jobs, that is, increased satisfaction, higher levels of performance, and greater willingness on the part of upper management to delegate authority to field service representatives. The results of this admittedly experimental undertaking formed the basis for a slow if steady expansion of efforts at job enrichment at Xerox.

Another form of task modification aimed at improving the quality of working life can occur on a larger scale; that is, an entire organizational structure can be altered. A recent effort along this line involved the introduction of a "business-team" concept into the refining operations of a major oil company.[53] The business-team concept requires the development of four components: (1) a mission defined in terms of critical quantity, cost, and engineering standards; (2) a team made up of members with cross-functional skills (for example, in marketing, finance, production, and industrial relations); (3) a clearly understood set of intergroup relationships; and (4) a formal authority structure which permits the cross-functional team to carry out its mission. At the particular refining department that served as the site of this modification in organizational structure, the business team was introduced in conjunction with a changeover from manual to automatic, computer-controlled operations. Essentially, implementation of this change involved the development over time of higher levels of trust among the unit supervisors and the leaders of several functional organizations serving those units so that both the new production process and the new organizational format would be well received. Attitudinal surveys administered after the change provided data showing that the responses of workers and supervisory personnel were favorable and that the productivity of the refinery operation had improved. This rather sophisticated example of organizational redesign, which has been only lightly sketched here, subsequently was applied to other operating departments of the oil company.

Many other efforts at job design, job enrichment, and organizational restructuring intended to improve the quality of working life could be described. Instead, we shall turn our attention to some of their limitations. One of these is the lack of attention paid to the evaluation of such efforts. "Analysis" often has taken the form of anecdotal comments made by those who participate in, or observe the altered and enriched tasks, or even the remarks of those responsible for the redesign, who have a considerable stake in seeing them labeled a "success." Other evaluations, utilizing systematic surveys of participants both before and after job redesign or enrichment, yield somewhat better information, to be sure, but often they fail to employ control groups of workers whose tasks have not been altered, and very often the survey data are collected at only a single point in time following the experimental change. Consequently, some projects for improving the quality of working life report greatly improved attitudes—that is, increased job satisfaction—shortly after the restructuring of jobs, but one is at a loss to know whether these responses have lasting value. Put differently, evaluations of experiments in "work humanization" frequently fail to apply scientific procedures. For this reason, their reported results—favorable, unfavorable, or something in between—must be cautiously received and carefully scrutinized.[54]

Even more basic to this criticism, perhaps, are the heavy reliance on attitudinal data and the sporadic collection or virtual shunning of performance data. The focus on workers' attitudes is understandable, of course, because the reduction of job dissatisfaction usually is the principal rationale for these efforts, and often they are mounted in response to an overt sign of discontent. Yet if the movement to humanize work and improve the quality of working life is to be more than a fad, more than a repository for the favorite scheme of one or another self-styled expert on human behavior, it must be tested against the evidence pertaining to performance—that is, the quantity and quality of goods and services produced—and to the actual behavior of the labor sector at work. That behavior—the effort expended by employees at work; their commitment to their jobs, as reflected partially in data on absenteeism and turnover and partially in their reports concerning deficiencies at the workplace and in their recommendations for improvement; and the willingness of employees to participate in the resolution of conflicts at the workplace—is distinguishable from workers' attitudes, which, as noted earlier, are not always a useful or reliable guide to behavior.[55]

Fortunately, there are grounds for optimism about improving the design and evaluation of efforts to enhance the quality of working life. Social scientists presently are developing more refined survey instruments not only to measure the attitudinal effects of job restructuring on employees but also to "diagnose existing jobs to determine if (and how) they might be redesigned to improve employee motivation and productivity."[56] It is extremely important that these instruments be derived from well-developed conceptual frameworks which specify critical linkages between the worker, the job, and behavior at the workplace. An example of one such framework is presented in Figure 2-2; it has recently been used to develop the Job Diagnostic Survey, which, as its title suggests, is employed to assess the necessity for job enrichment and to measure the consequent effects on employees.[57]

Additionally, after many years and a voluminous amount of writing on the

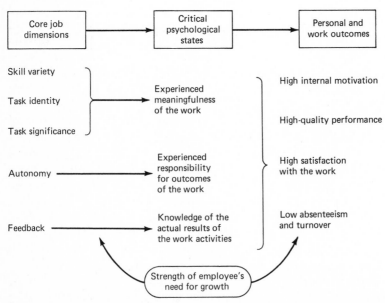

Figure 2-2 A theoretical model relating "core dimensions" of a job, critical psychological states, and on-the-job outcomes, as moderated by the strength of an employee's need for growth. (*Source: Adapted from J. Richard Hackman and Greg R. Oldham, "Development of the Job Diagnostic Survey,"* Journey of Applied Psychology, **60**:*161, April 1975.*)

subject, behavioral scientists have reached something of a consensus on the relationship between behavior on the job and attitudes toward work. Rather than being regarded as an independent variable that gives rise to different types of behavior at the workplace, workers' attitudes are now considered a function of—dependent upon—that behavior. Stated more succinctly, performance on the job determines the worker's satisfaction rather than being determined by it, as was presumed by so many of the early efforts at job enrichment (and is still presumed by a substantial number of the current ones).[58] A schematic model of the more recent performance-satisfaction relationship is shown in Figure 2-3.

Of course, as the reader might suspect, several factors moderate the relationship between performance and satisfaction on the job. These include the intrinsic and extrinsic rewards associated with performance or the accomplishment of tasks, the employee's expectations concerning the probability of receiving rewards for performance and the type of rewards that will be received, and the perceived equity of rewards for performance. These and other factors are shown as intervening variables in Figure 2-3, which also portrays the feedback effect of satisfaction on performance. The diagram suggests what should always be kept in mind concerning efforts at job enrichment, namely, that behavior at the workplace is complex, multidimensional, and rarely susceptible to a simple or single-minded manipulatory scheme.

Another important and unresolved issue related to improving the quality of working life concerns workers' participation in decisions which have traditionally been made solely by managers. In question form, the issue is, "What kind of participation by workers is required and at what levels should it occur?" Clearly, there is no single or ready-made answer to this question. Any type of

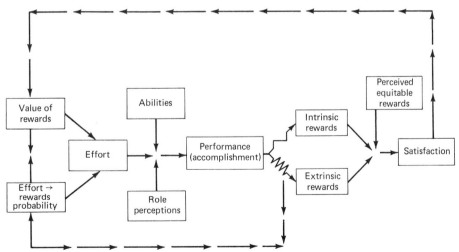

Figure 2-3 A model of performance and satisfaction at work. (*Source: Donald P. Schwab and Larry L. Cummings, "Theories of Performance and Satisfaction: A Review,"* Industrial Relations, *9:418, October 1970.*)

effort to redesign and enrich jobs requires some form of participation by workers, even it if involves only an initial questioning of workers about problems encountered at the workplace. The participation of various types and levels of workers was an integral part of all the efforts at job enrichment and restructuring described earlier. Yet the role of workers, especially organized workers, in the restructuring of jobs and work remains highly controversial. The "solutions" to this problem vary from country to country or, more accurately, from culture to culture, but at the center of the controversy is the question of authority.[59]

In the United States, it is instructive to note, the bulk of formal work restructuring has been carried out in nonunion settings and made operational in new plants, with new technologies, new designs, new patterns of work flow, new geographic locations, and often new personnel.[60] In these settings, the barriers posed by old technologies, the costs of conversion, poor or outmoded building designs, established work patterns, and formal collective bargaining relationships do not exist. Yet it is precisely in the settings where one or more of these barriers are present that work restructuring is most difficult to effectuate, even as it may be most needed. The key limitation of putting into operation a program of job enrichment in the older setting is, from a managerial perspective, the fact that something generally must be given up to buy out traditional work patterns. And though it may take the form of higher wages, bonus payments, greater protection against layoffs, increased shift differential, or membership in a worker-management transition committee, that "something" is at heart management authority.[61] This is a considerably less pressing issue in a new plant, office, or factory, where management largely controls the situation and largely reserves authority unto itself. With some oversimplification, it may be said that in the new plant or facility, participation by workers in job enrichment takes the form primarily of consultation and that management's authority faces few basic challenges.

Clearly, this is not the case in the unionized shop, plant, office, or factory. In fact, as assertions of job dissatisfaction grew more numerous in the 1970s, as various schemes for work redesign and enrichment were offered as a cure for this dissatisfaction, and as management (or part of management) adopted both the diagnosis and the remedy, American union leaders expressed suspicion of moves to improve the quality of working life. Thus, William Winpisinger, president of the International Association of Machinists and Aerospace Workers and an AFL-CIO vice president, wrote of job enrichment as "just another name for 'time and motion' study" and as the "introduction of gimmicks, like doing away with time clocks or developing 'work teams' or designing jobs to 'maximize personal involvement,' whatever that means."[62] He went on to say: "If you want to enrich the job, enrich the paycheck; . . . decrease the number of [work] hours; . . . do something about . . . nerve-shattering noise, heat and fumes."[63]

What Winpisinger and other American union leaders are opposed to is not job enrichment but, rather, the notion that management by itself (or with hired consultants) can diagnose and resolve ills in the workplace. Union leaders may well resent the failure of others to appreciate that the improvements in wages and working conditions they have negotiated over the years represent true advances in the quality of working life, and this inevitably colors their verbalized reactions to job enrichment and work redesign. But what they fear most is that the managers with whom they now share decision-making authority over a dearly valued (if, by European standards, narrow) set of issues concerning wages and working conditions may use the lever of job enrichment—improving the quality of working life—to reassert and broaden their so-called "prerogatives" and to narrow labor's influence. This, rather than any inherent negativism, explains organized labor's stated opposition to much of the movement to humanize work. And, it is instructive to note, where the concerns of unionized workers are truly recognized and considered legitimate to deal with, labor and management have evolved a variety of structures and cooperative arrangements to pursue joint efforts to improve the quality of working life.[64]

For example, under collective bargaining, most American workers have won the right to challenge management and, in a sense, to decide jointly the resolution of issues of major concern to them—discipline, job classification, overtime assignments, the order of layoffs, and many others. These challenges can be mounted formally through the grievance procedure, which may culminate in binding third-party arbitration, or informally through day-to-day negotiations with the supervisor, who often is anxious to settle such affairs "out of court."[65] This continued negotiation at the workplace over grievance settlement, though not widely recognized, reflects the influence that unionized American workers (and some nonunionized ones as well) are able to exercise at their places of work.[66] Surely these are examples of improvements in the quality of working life under collective bargaining.

The same may be said of productivity bargaining, instances of which are found in both the private and the public sectors. Here, unionized workers agree to relax or eliminate a working rule that limits productivity in exchange for a specific negotiated benefit such as a pay increase, a retraining allowance, or guaranteed job security. Such arrangements reflect the "buy-out" approach to productivity bargaining. Another, less common arrangement is "gain sharing," whereby labor and management agree to a particular plan for improving productivity, the fruits of which are to be distributed throughout the work force, including managers, according to a predetermined formula. These plans can also arise from formal suggestion schemes in union and nonunion situations. The Scanlon plan, which is perhaps the best known of the gain-sharing incentive schemes, provides for a departmental production committee through which workers participate in devising solutions to production problems. Again, the example has obvious implications for the quality of working life.

More generally, joint labor-management committees have emerged in a variety of industries, sometimes integrated with, and sometimes as adjuncts to, formal collective bargaining.[67] During World War II, when such committees proliferated, they were oriented almost exclusively toward improving the productivity of existing operations. More recently, they have focused on problems of industrial health and safety, plant location, automation, job satisfaction, and even economic development of the local community. Of course, all these issues involve productivity, but they also involve the quality of working life. We see that by widening the scope of union-management relations beyond traditional collective bargaining, some unionized workers and their leaders have indeed shown a willingness to join with management in efforts to improve the quality of their working lives. This is the reality which should not be overlooked in assessing the verbalized opposition of some union leaders to work restructuring.

In truth, such opposition is aimed at unilateral decisions by management to enrich or redesign jobs which threaten to decrease rather than increase participation by workers in the enterprise. Unionists tend strongly to equate participation with the quality of *their* working lives, which is why unilateral management decisions or the perceived threat of them is such a key issue. But whether through collective bargaining, through less formal consultative and committee arrangements, or through more formal approaches,[68] American union leaders have demonstrated a long-standing commitment to participation in decisions concerning the workplace, even if they, too, are sometimes slow to recognize the changing concerns of union members in this regard. Indeed, to do otherwise would virtually deny the very reason for the existence of labor organizations. What they ask is for others—notably managers and behavioral scientists—to recognize this commitment and the legitimate role of unionists in new efforts to improve the quality of workers' lives. We will have more to say about some of these efforts in Chapter 5.

In European countries, to which many proponents of work humanization look for examples of innovations in job restructuring, the issue of participation is not quite as newly volatile as it is in the United States. Perhaps this is due to the greater class consciousness in those countries. In western continental Europe, most nations have legislatively provided for some form of involvement by workers in management decisions. West Germany and Sweden have gone further in this direction; in both countries, joint decision making on a number of matters at the shop and plant level is sanctioned by law, as is representation by workers on boards of directors.

Representation by workers on boards of directors, which is still virtually unthinkable in the United States, reflects a view that workers should be involved in the very highest levels of managerial decision making. In West Germany, nationwide legislation authorizing codetermination recently was amended to permit fully half of the membership of boards of directors to be made up of workers' representatives, though one of these represents middle managers. (In the event of a tie vote, the chairman of the board, who is certain to be a representative of the shareholders, is entitled to a second vote, and so the interests of ownership still have the edge.[69])

In communist Yugoslavia, control by workers is complete. The workers' council makes or ratifies all major decisions and designates the management. The extent to which it actually exercises the powers allotted to it has been subjected to question, but there is no doubt of the intent. Workers are not assumed to "own" their enterprise, but they are entrusted with the discretionary authority to manage social assets and are charged with the obligations to maintain and improve them.[70]

In Japan, the workers' involvement in the enterprise, and the involvement of the enterprise with the workers, extends considerably beyond the workplace. There, the phenomenon of "permanent employment" is widely, if not exclusively, practiced. The university graduate, skilled craftworker, or semiskilled machine operative, especially when employed by a large firm, is considered to be a permanent asset of that organization. It is not at all unrealistic for such workers to expect a lifelong career with the firm, to be employed—and paid— even during recession periods, to be regularly promoted in rank, and to receive "fringe benefits" that include complete medical coverage for their families, educational payments for their children, special recreational allowances, and a host of other items. In turn, workers are expected to show unswerving allegiance and loyalty to the firm, identifying more strongly with it and assigning a far more important role to it than is common in the United States and elsewhere.

That workers are recompensed for this loyalty is reflected in the very heavy emphasis in Japan on length of employment service in the determination of wages. This practice has tended to confound those who view efficiency and competitive-labor-market theory as the rudiments of wage setting, but that only bespeaks the limitations of these analytical constructs, for seniority is a pervasive criterion in the Japanese wage system. True, the phenomenon of permanent employment has always been more characteristic of some types of workers than others (men rather than women, for example) and more common among large than among small firms.[71] Nor is this an immutable characteristic of the Japanese culture and labor market, for the system of permanent employment is breaking down somewhat under the pressures of advanced industrialization.[72] However, it reflects still another approach to the humanization of work, one that contrasts strongly with American (and most other) attempts to improve the quality of working life.

One need not accept these alternative philosophies of participation by workers in the enterprise or believe that these philosophies are fully implemented in practice to recognize how different the United States is from much of the rest of the world in this regard. Still, on the evidence, no society has to this point been able to escape or fully resolve the conflicts that inevitably emerge over the organization and performance of work. As long as there are tasks to be performed and as long as some must manage those tasks while some must be managed, conflicts ranging from mild to revolutionary will occur. Each society, each economy, and each culture attempts to work out its own resolution of such conflicts. In these efforts are reflected the power relationships and institutional forces that must inform any discussion of attempts to improve the quality of working life and, even more, any discussion of the labor sector.

SUMMARY

In this chapter, some key dimensions of the relationship between the worker and the workplace have been explored. We examined the incidence of job mobility in the American labor sector, the types of mobility that occur, and some of the factors influencing mobility. While, on balance, a pattern of mobility toward higher-paying jobs seems to exist, there are many individual variations. The available evidence is not so compelling as to yield a firm conclusion that actual movements among jobs are favorable to either workers or the economy.

We also explored some aspects of workers' behavior in searching for work; the job search was judged to be less efficient and predictable than economic theory presupposes, but less chaotic and patterned than the institutional approach would have us believe. The informal nature of much activity in a job search and the institutional intermediaries through which much information is obtained and filtered render the labor market qualitatively different from other kinds of markets. It is not so different, however, as to be unreceptive to rigorous analysis, whatever one's preferred blend of neoclassical and institutional perspectives.

Then we examined the attitudes of workers toward their jobs, attitudes which are popularly thought to have shifted in the direction of increased dissatisfaction with work. We found little evidence to support this view or the companion claim that the labor sector, *in general,* is more concerned with intrinsic dimensions of work, such as job content, opportunities to develop special talents, and recognition, than with its extrinsic characteristics, for example, pay, fringe benefits, and seniority. Nevertheless, recent analyses of data having to do with job satisfaction do support the view that segments of the labor sector differ in their valuation of, and concern about, key dimensions of work.

This led us to a brief review of recent attempts to improve the quality of working life, particularly through the redesign and enrichment of jobs. While interesting and in some cases notably innovative, most of these experiments and case studies do not provide sufficient scientific evidence to allow us to judge their consequences or label them "successes" or "failures." Moreover, the bulk of them have been put into operation in new settings, and thus the difficulties and problems of dealing with older structures and equipment, outdated work patterns, and, most important, long-standing labor organizations and labor-management relationships have been largely avoided. Despite all this, the issue of the quality of working life is not likely to disappear, especially in view of the changing occupational composition of the labor force. Further, the efforts of other nations to "humanize" work—whether so labeled or not—provide guidance to the United States in this regard, even if many of those experiences are not directly transferrable across differing cultures.

The linking of mobility with efforts to humanize work, as has been done in this chapter, has an intellectual logic in that the search for a new job or occupation and the attempt to enrich an existing job represent alternative yet complementary avenues for remedying dissatisfaction among members of the labor sector. The solution to the problem of a job that a worker judges to be especially unsatisfactory may well lie in movement to a new job rather than redesign of the present one. Or employment in a type of work (rather than a type of plant, employer, or area) judged by an individual to provide limited opportunities for promotion or advancement may presage a shift in occupations rather than a change of jobs or an attempt to restructure the work. Again alternatively, a group of employees whose work is particularly onerous or whose jobs have a "numbing effect" because they are especially repetitive or fractionalized can attempt, formally or otherwise, to alter the structure of such work. Or those same employees may work in an organization whose management is quick to detect the dissatisfactions of its labor force and is willing to restructure jobs, provide greater participation by workers in decision making, and pursue other attempts to humanize work.

All these scenarios represent expressions of the labor sector's freedom to alter and redefine relationships between the worker and the job. These multiple freedoms—or, more correctly stated, these multiple avenues for expressing such freedoms—represent a major strength of a pluralistic and, one should add, democratic system. The lesson inherent in this observation is that no single facet of society, of the economy, of work in general, or of a job in particular should be so dominant, so total, that the individual must virtually live and die by it. A dissatisfying job should perhaps be amenable to alteration and humanization, but that should not be the sole option. Selecting another task, another employer, or another occupation—having such alternatives available—represents not only a broad range of choice for the individual but also a pluralism that gives tangible meaning to the concept of freedom in society. And, as has been noted in this chapter, even if these freedoms and these choices exist in a society, there remains that age-old but always pressing question of their distribution among the populace. Such are the types of issues and questions that make the study of the labor sector so fascinating and whet the appetite for further examination. In Chapter 3, we shall explore yet another contentious issue of freedom in relation to the worker and the job, the freedom to organize into unions.

NOTES

1 A solid exposition of competitive-labor-market theory appears in Belton M. Fleisher, *Labor Economics: Theory and Evidence,* Prentice-Hall, Englewood Cliffs, N.J., 1970. Economists now recognize the vastly oversimplifying assumptions of competitive theory concerning information in the labor market, and much research into the role and uses of such information is now being carried out. Some of this research is discussed later in this chapter.

2 U.S. Bureau of Labor Statistics, *Work Experience of the Population in 1976,* Special Labor Force Report 201, 1977, p. 7, table 6.

3 See Gertrude Bancroft and Stuart Garfinkle, *Job Mobility in 1961,* U.S. Bureau of Labor Statistics, Special Labor Force Report 35, 1963; and U.S. Bureau of the Cen-

sus, *Current Population Reports: Job Mobility of Workers in 1955,* ser. P-50, no. 70, 1957.

4 U.S. Bureau of Labor Statistics, "Average Job Tenure Declines," *NEWS,* Apr. 23, 1979, p. 1.

5 U.S. Bureau of Labor Statistics, "Average Job Tenure Declines," p. 1.

6 See, for example, U.S. Bureau of Labor Statistics, *Employment and Unemployment in 1976,* Special Labor Force Report 199, 1977, passim.

7 Howard Hayghe, "Job Tenure of Workers, January, 1973," *Monthly Labor Review,* **97:**53 (1974).

8 James J. Byrne, "Occupational Mobility of Workers," *Monthly Labor Review,* **98:**56 (1975).

9 Byrne, p. 58.

10 Simon Rottenberg, "On Choice in Labor Markets," *Industrial and Labor Relations Review* **9:**198 (1956).

11 For survey evidence supporting these conclusions, see Bancroft and Garfinkle, pp. 7, A-12.

12 See, for example, George J. Stigler, "Information in the Labor Market," *Journal of Political Economy* **70:**94–105 (1962), supplement. Data on quit rates are published regularly by the U.S. Bureau of Labor Statistics in *Monthly Labor Review,* but these are for the manufacturing sector only.

13 John B. Lansing and Eva Mueller, *The Geographic Mobility of Labor,* University of Michigan, Institute for Social Research, Survey Research Center, Ann Arbor, 1967, p. 198.

14 For an early, but still useful, analysis of job-search patterns among blue-collar workers, see F. T. Malm, "Recruiting Patterns and the Functioning of Labor Markets," *Industrial and Labor Relations Review* **4:**507–525 (1954). See also Margaret S. Gordon and Margaret Thal-Larsen, *Employer Policies in a Changing Labor Market,* University of California, Institute of Industrial Relations, Berkeley, 1969.

15 Albert Rees and George P. Shultz, *Workers and Wages in an Urban Labor Market,* University of Chicago Press, Chicago, 1970.

16 Rees and Shultz, p. 200.

17 Lansing and Mueller. pp. 208–224.

18 Lansing and Mueller, pp. 212–213.

19 Joseph C. Ullman and George P. Huber, "Are Job Banks Improving the Labor Market Information System?" *Industrial and Labor Relations Review,* **27:**184 (1974).

20 For further elaboration of the special informational characteristics of labor markets, see Boris Yavitz and Dean W. Morse, *The Labor Market: An Information System,* Praeger, New York, 1973; and David Lewin et al., *The Urban Labor Market: Institutions, Information, Linkages,* Praeger, New York, 1974.

21 On this point see the discussion of the *Allen Bradley* case contained in Neil W. Chamberlain, *Business and the Cities.* Basic Books, New York, 1970, chap. 6.

22 Herbert S. Parnes, "Labor Force and Labor Markets," in *A Review of Industrial Relations Research,* vol. I, Industrial Relations Research Association, Madison, Wis., 1970, p. 59. This conclusion is further supported by a recent longitudinal study, U.S. Department of Labor, Employment and Training Administration, *Why Families Move,* Research and Development Monograph 48, 1977. This is one of the first analyses of geographic mobility to employ the National Longitudinal Surveys, conducted by Ohio State University and funded by the Department of Labor.

23 Cited in Parnes, p. 63.

24 Robert L. Raimon, "Interstate Migration and Wage Theory," *Review of Eco-*

nomics and Statistics, **44:**428–438 (1962); and Lansing and Mueller, pp. 247–249.

25 For example, John F. Burton, Jr., and John E. Parker, "Inter-industry Variations in Voluntary Labor Mobility," *Industrial and Labor Relations Review,* **22:**199–216 (1969); and Vladimir Stoikov and Robert L. Raimon, "Determinants of Differences in the Quit Rate among Industries," *American Economic Review,* **58:**1283–1298 (1968).

26 Alan K. Severn, "Upward Labor Mobility: Opportunity or Incentive?" *Quarterly Journal of Economics,* **82:**143–151 (1968).

27 Herbert S. Parnes, *Research on Labor Mobility,* Social Science Research Council, New York, 1954.

28 George P. Shultz, "A Nonunion Market for White Collar Labor," in National Bureau of Economic Research, *Aspects of Labor Economics,* Princeton, Princeton, N.J., 1962; David G. Brown, *The Mobile Professors,* American Council On Education, Washington, 1967; and R. P. Loomba, *A Study of the Re-employment and Unemployment Experiences of Scientists and Engineers Laid-off from 62 Aerospace and Electronics Firms in the San Francisco Bay Area during 1963–65,* San Jose State College, San Jose, Calif., 1967, pp. 85–86.

29 As described by T. B. Bottomore (ed.), *Karl Marx: Early Writings,* McGraw-Hill, New York, 1963, p. viii.

30 Adam Smith, *The Wealth of Nations,* Modern Library, New York, 1937, pp. 734–735.

31 Karl Polanyi, *The Great Transformation,* Beacon Press, Boston, 1944, especially chaps. 5, 6, 19, and 21.

32 Report of a special task force to the Secretary of Health, Education, and Welfare, M.I.T., Cambridge, Mass., 1972.

33 Report of a special task force to the Secretary of Health, Education, and Welfare, especially chap. 2.

34 On this point, see Reinhard Bendix, *Work and Authority in Industry,* University of California, Institute of Industrial Relations, Berkeley, 1956, especially chap. 5.

35 Robert L. Kahn, "The Meaning of Work: Interpretation and Proposals for Measurement," in Angus Campbell and Philip E. Converse (eds.), *The Human Meaning of Social Change,* Russell Sage, New York, 1972, pp. 159–204.

36 Kahn, pp. 169–175.

37 Kahn, pp. 169–175. For more recent evidence suggesting a decline in job satisfaction in the United States between 1973 and 1977, see Graham L. Staines and Robert P. Quinn, "American Workers Evaluate the Quality of Their Jobs," *Monthly Labor Review,* **102:**3–12 (1979).

38 Report of a Special Task Force to the Secretary of Health, Education, and Welfare, p. 48, referring to *Survey of Working Conditions,* University of Michigan, Institute for Social Research, Survey Research Center, November 1970.

39 See Mitchell Fein, "The Real Needs and Goals of Blue Collar Workers," *Conference Board Record,* **10:**26–33 (1973).

40 Bernard J. White, "The Criteria for Job Satisfaction: Is Interesting Work Most Important?" *Monthly Labor Review,* **100:**30–35 (1977).

41 White, p. 35.

42 See, for example, Harold Wool, "What's Wrong with Work in America?—A Review Essay," *Monthly Labor Review,* **96:**38–44 (1973).

43 White, p. 35.

44 Abraham H. Maslow, *Motivation and Personality,* Harper & Row, New York, 1954.

45 For a study reporting stronger support among blue- *and* white-collar workers for a humanistic approach to work over the traditional work ethic, see Rogene A. Buchholz, "The Work Ethic Reconsidered," *Industrial and Labor Relations Review,* **31:**450–459 (1978).

46 The quotation is from Frederick Herzberg, "One More Time: How You Motivate Employees," *Harvard Business Review,* **46:**57 (1968). Herzberg is perhaps the leading American exponent of job enrichment.

47 Accounts of the experiments presented here are based on Olle Hammarstrom, "Joint Worker-Management Consultation: The Case of LKÅB, Sweden," in Louis Davis and Albert G. Cherns (eds.), *The Quality of Working Life, vol. 2: Cases and Commentary,* Macmillan, New York, 1975, pp. 66–82; and Noel M. Tichy (with the assistance of Thore Sandstrom), "Organizational Innovations in Sweden," *The Columbia Journal of World Business,* **9:**18–28 (1974).

48 Additional data on the Volvo work experiments are provided in Noel M. Tichy, (with the assistance of Jay N. Nisberg), "When Does Restructuring Work? Organizational Innovations at Volvo and GM," *Organizational Dynamics,* **5:**63–80 (1976).

49 Tichy, "When Does Restructuring Work?"

50 As reported in Bureau of National Affairs, *Daily Labor Report,* no. **210:**AA1–2 (October 31, 1973).

51 These are more fully described in E. James Bryan, "Work Improvement and Job Enrichment," in Davis and Cherns, pp. 315–330.

52 These are more fully described in Carl D. Jacobs, "Job Enrichment of Field Technical Representatives—Xerox Corporation," in Davis and Cherns, pp. 285–299.

53 This organizational change is further described in George E. McCullough, "The Effects of Changes in Organizational Structure: Demonstration Projects in an Oil Refinery," in Davis and Cherns, pp. 232–252.

54 See, for example, the "evaluations" of work redesign experiments reported in Davis and Cherns, passim.

55 This criticism is comparable to that offered by John P. Campbell and Marvin D. Dunnette, "Effectiveness of T-Group Experiences in Managerial Training," *Psychological Bulletin,* **70:**73–104 (1968), with respect to the impact of laboratory education on managerial behavior.

56 J. Richard Hackman and Greg R. Oldham, "Development of the Job Diagnostic Survey," *Journal of Applied Psychology,* **60:**159 (1975).

57 Hackman and Oldham, pp. 159–170.

58 See Edward E. Lawler III and Lyman W. Porter, "Job Attitudes, Effort and Performance: A Theoretical Model," *Organizational Behavior and Human Performance,* **2:**122–142 (1967); and Edward E. Lawler III and Lyman W. Porter, "The Effect of Performance on Job Satisfaction," *Industrial Relations,* **7:**20–28 (1967).

59 On these points, see George Strauss, Raymond E. Miles, Charles C. Snow, and Arnold S. Tannenbaum (eds.), *Organizational Behavior: Research and Issues,* Industrial Relations Research Association, Madison, Wis., 1974, especially chaps. 2, 4, and 8.

60 This certainly is the case with respect to the efforts at work restructuring reported in *Work in America* and in Davis and Cherns.

61 The persistance of the issue of authority in American industrial relations is documented by Bendix, chap. 5.

62 William P. Winpisinger, "Job Enrichment—Another Part of the Forest," *Proceedings of the Twenty-Fifth Annual Meeting of the Industrial Relations Research Association, 1972,* Madison, Wis., 1973, pp. 157–159.

63 Winpisinger, p. 157.

64 See, for example, National Center for Productivity and Quality of Working Life, *Recent Initiatives in Labor-Management Cooperation,* GPO, Washington, February 1976.

65 As noted by Tannenbaum, "Systems of Formal Participation," in Strauss et al., p. 93.

66 See James W. Kuhn, *Bargaining in Grievance Settlement,* Columbia, New York, 1961.

67 See Charlotte Gold, *Employer-Employee Committees and Worker Participation,* Cornell University, New York State School of Industrial and Labor Relations, Ithaca, 1976; and Edgar Weinberg, "Labor-Management Cooperation: A Report on Recent Initiatives," *Monthly Labor Review,* **99:**13–22 (1976).

68 Tannenbaum distinguishes four systems of participation by workers: legal, collective bargaining, suggestive-consultative, and behavioral science. See his "Systems of Formal Organization," pp. 79–102, for examples of specific forms of participation under each of these categories.

69 See Robert J. Kühne, "Co-determination: A Statutory Re-structuring of the Organization," *Columbia Journal of World Business,* **11:**17–25 (1976).

70 See Veljko Rus, "Influence Structure in Yugoslav Enterprise," *Industrial Relations,* **9:**148–160 (1970); and Josip Obrodovic, "Participation and Work Attitudes in Yugoslavia," *Industrial Relations,* **9:**161–169 (1970). Both control by workers and codetermination are among the legal approaches to participation identified by Tannenbaum, pp. 84–90. Tannenbaum also discusses the kibbutz system of factory operation in Israel, whereby a democratic, participative community or group owns and operates each factory (pp. 81–84).

71 As reported by Robert E. Cole, "Permanent Employment in Japan: Facts and Fantasies," *Industrial and Labor Relations Review,* **26:**615–630 (1972).

72 Cole.

ADDITIONAL READINGS

Blauner, Robert: *Alienation and Freedom,* University of Chicago Press, Chicago, 1964.

Gold, Charlotte: *Employer-Employee Committees and Worker Participation,* Key Issues Series 20, Cornell University, New York State School of Industrial and Labor Relations, Ithaca, 1976.

Katzell, Raymond, and Daniel Yankleovich: *Work, Productivity and Job Satisfaction,* Harcourt, Brace, Jovanovich, New York, 1975.

Lansing, John B., and Eva Mueller: *The Geographic Mobility of Labor,* University of Michigan, Survey Research Center, Ann Arbor, 1967.

Monthly Labor Review, selected articles and tables published throughout the year.

Rees, Albert, and George P. Shultz: *Workers and Wages in an Urban Labor Market,* University of Chicago Press, Chicago, 1970.

Strauss, George, Raymond E. Miles, Charles C. Snow, and Arnold S. Tannenbaum (eds.): *Organizational Behavior: Research and Issues,* Industrial Relations Research Association, Madison, Wis., 1974, especially chaps. 2, 4, 8.

Survey of Working Conditions, 1970, University of Michigan, Ann Arbor, 1970.

U.S. Department of Labor, Employment and Training Administration: *Why Families Move,* Research and Development Monograph 48, 1977.

Weinberg, Edgar: "Labor-Management Cooperation: A Report of Recent Initiatives," *Monthly Labor Review,* **99:**13–22 (1976).

FOR ANALYSIS AND DISCUSSION

1 On balance, would you prefer to see more or less job mobility over the year than is reported in Table 2-1 for 1976? What is the basis of your response? Be sure to consider what a different overall rate might reflect or require in terms of the subgroups of workers listed in Table 2-1.

2 Compare different types of mobility, for example, job mobility, industrial mobility, occupational mobility, and geographic mobility. From your vantage point, which of these is most important? Why? Which is the best indicator of mobility in the labor sector? Why?

3 It is sometimes said that workers change jobs to maximize not income but, rather, "comparative net advantage." What do you believe are the main elements of work that constitute comparative net advantage? Could you devise a method to test this assertion? Ask your instructor whether he or she could devise such a test.

4 Does the dual-market theory presented in Chapter 1 provide insights into the process of job mobility? In what ways? How does it differ from competitive-labor-market theory in its applicability to job mobility?

5 Attempt to simulate the process of job search for two of the occupations listed in Table 2-2. That is, select two of these positions and then try to identify employment opportunities for each of them. What are the principal sources of information about these opportunities? How do they compare with the sources uncovered by a classmate who selected two other occupations?

6 A recent study of job satisfaction reported percentages of workers expressing negative attitudes toward work and life (see Table 2-5). What factors do you think "ex-

Table 2-5 Work and Life Attitudes

	Negative attitude toward work, Percent	Negative attitude toward life, Percent
Age		
Under 20	25	20
20–29	24	14
30–44	13	15
45–54	11	10
55 and over	6	10
Occupation		
Professional, technical, and managerial	9	10
Clerical and sales	18	14
Services	23	24
Machine trades	15	11
Structural work	10	7
Personal income		
Below $3,400	20	21
3,400–4,999	21	17
5,000–7,499	13	14
7,500–9,999	14	11
10,000 and over	8	6

Note: $n = 1524$.

Source: Neal Q. Herrick and Harold L. Sheppard, *Where Have All the Robots Gone?: Worker Dissatisfaction in the '70s*, Free Press, New York, 1972, p. 193.

plain'' these age, occupational, and income differences in job satisfaction? In satisfaction with life?

7 If you were charged with the responsibility for assessing the redesign of the jobs of semiskilled machine operatives, what evaluative criteria would you use? Briefly outline a research program for evaluating this redesign.

8 Are occupational mobility and job mobility substitutes for, or complementary to, job enrichment? In other words, are the types of jobs that seem to be most frequently redesigned or enriched the ones characterized by little or much mobility? Can you suggest ways in which the tasks making up the ''job'' of student should be redesigned?

9 Reconstruct the path by which your father or mother reached his or her present position. See whether you can identify the reasons for any job changes. To what extent would you say that economic or noneconomic considerations were an influence? Would your mother or father choose the same occupation if that choice could be made all over again?

10 Using the model presented in Figure 2-3, trace through the performance-satisfaction relationship in terms of your work as a student. How does this differ from the performance-satisfaction relationships you experienced in previous work or expect to experience in the future?

The Organized and the Unorganized

In Chapter 2, we noted that workers who are dissatisfied may attempt to change jobs or to bring about a restructuring of the kinds of work they perform. Another way for workers to deal with dissatisfaction is to form or join labor organizations and bargain collectively with employers over terms and conditions of employment. The phenomenon of unionism is the subject of this chapter. Collective bargaining in the private and public sectors will be treated in Chapters 5 and 6, respectively.

We begin with a brief review of the union's function and of the motivation of workers in forming and joining unions. This is followed by a historical sketch of the American labor movement which identifies some of the key themes that characterized its development during the nineteenth and twentieth centuries. Woven together with the historical overview is an exploration of the accompanying legal regulation of unionism and labor-management relations. We treat these topics together to show the interrelationships between the development of unions as institutions and the legal treatment of labor organization and labor relations in the United States. This completes Part One of the chapter. Part Two explores contemporary patterns of labor organization in the American work force. These include the recent growth record, in which the public sector has played a prominent role; membership differences by industry, occupation, sex, and race; and the emergence of employee associations. Where relevant, material on foreign experiences is incorporated into the discussion in order to highlight the distinctive as well as the shared features of American unionism and industrial relations.

PART ONE: Development and Legal Treatment of Unions

WORKERS' OBJECTIVES AND THE AGENCY RELATIONSHIP

For the individual worker, the union exists only to obtain some improvement in the elements of job satisfaction identified in Chapter 2. The union is the employee's advocate, the employee's agent, in dealing with the employer about job concerns and work satisfactions, especially rates of pay. In carrying out its function as agent, the union differs from the business firm, government, or non-profit institution with which it deals in that it derives its income not from those *with whom* it negotiates but only from those *for whom* it negotiates. The union does not bargain with the employer for income itself; it gets income only from its members, for whom it bargains, in the form of initiation fees, dues, or special assessments.

Individual job concerns can be translated into collective concerns and summarized as follows: steady employment providing an adequate income, the rationalization and receipt of justice in personnel policies, a voice by workers as a group in decisions affecting their welfare, and protection against economic hazards beyond their control.[1] Observe that none of these objectives can be described as revolutionary. If they sometimes lead unionists to make demands which managements vigorously oppose, they do not require modification of the social and economic system in ways that represent a sharp break with basic traditions.

Why Workers Join Unions

There is a difference between the functions which unions can perform on behalf of members, and which therefore constitute the *rationale* for membership, and the actual reason why at some moment or on some occasion individuals may decide to organize or join a union.

A specific grievance against management may cause a worker to "sign up." Many successful organizing drives have been based on some general employee reaction triggered by a management action. These are the dissatisfactions experienced by workers which, if unresolved, might push them to look for other jobs elsewhere or, at a minimum, leave them disgruntled and resentful. "An unpleasant personal experience becomes a powerful motivation that turns workers toward a union and may get them to become active and accept leadership positions in it."[2]

Other reasons also are influential. Some workers join unions because their parents were members and made the concept of labor organization seem appealing to their offspring. (Note, though, that many parents who worked in unionized settings might have encouraged their children to pursue other job specialties in white-collar or professional occupations, thereby failing to promote an intergenerational attachment to labor organizations.) Other members of local unions have been persuaded by the logic or the emotional appeals of union organizers. For still others, membership in a union results less from conviction than from pressure. A relatively mild form of coercion emanates from peers who, when they join a union, subtly induce conformity with this action on the part of those working closely with them. More coercive is a rationale such as, "I joined to get them to stop hounding me," and there are also cases of outright compulsion, as when the union and management negotiate a requirement (such as a union-shop clause) that workers must belong to, or remain in, the union in order to hold their jobs. However, even most workers who join a union not because of conviction but because of some sort of social or institutional duress come in time to accept the union as desirable, whether they actively participate in it or express enthusiasm for it or not.

One other factor can account for union membership, typically in "casual" employment situations where a person works not for the same company week in and week out but in a series of short-run jobs with different employers. Industries organized in this fashion are the construction industry, in which an electrician, for example, will work for one contractor and then for another and another, finishing a job for each before moving on to the next, and the maritime trades, in which seamen sign on for a long voyage and dockworkers unload the cargo of a particular vessel. In such industries, workers must be able to move easily from one employer to another if they are not to lose income, and the employer must be able to obtain a work force quickly while taking on one new piece of business after another. The arrangement that best satisfies these needs of employee and employer is a central employment office or hiring hall, where workers who have just finished with one job can be assigned to another and where employers who need a crew for a short-run contract can find a "pick-up" gang. In these industries, it typically is the union that performs this referral and employment function, and workers could hardly hope to compete for the available jobs without belonging to the appropriate labor organization. Many workers apply for membership in referral unions, but few are admitted and added to the pool of available craft labor.

How Unions Represent Workers

There are two principal arenas—public politics and private economics—in which organized workers seek achievement of their objectives. In most countries, political action has tended to assume greater importance than private economic bargaining. In the United States, in contrast, organized labor's effort has emphasized union-management negotiations over the terms of employment. In this regard, unions and their leaders attempt to reflect the diverse needs and desires of workers, reconcile that diversity into a manageable package, and represent the workers in collective bargaining.[3] The focus of American unions on "job-conscious" activity—on wages, hours, and working conditions at the individual workplace—sets them apart from labor unions in most other countries, which have been heavily absorbed in political activity.

Bargaining for themselves, individual workers are often at a disadvantage, selling perishable labor that cannot be stocked for sale at a later date and at a higher price (wage). Lacking capital and, in most instances, savings of more than a marginal amount, the individual may find it difficult to refuse work even at a wage below what he or she considers "fair." The recurrence of business cycles, with labor surpluses building up during slack periods, has contributed to the general view of a job as something to be prized, not cast aside lightly. Recession periods contribute to a feeling of insecurity, as employers can more easily find substitute workers. Selig Perlman, a leading labor theorist, long ago identified "scarcity consciousness"—that is, a conviction that workers always are more plentiful than jobs—as the basic factor explaining the development and character of the American labor movement.[4] Other economists have estimated that, to the contrary, labor has been a relatively scarce factor of production in the United States but that this has no bearing on workers' perceptions that a decent job is hard to come by. In this vein, then, employees understandably may come to believe that the imbalance between worker and employer might be redressed by the organization of a union that could reduce the competition for jobs. An employer could less easily replace an entire organized work force than individual unorganized members of it. Thus, unionization seemed to promise increased group bargaining power. Within limits and over time, that view received the approval of the public, which believed that an individual worker was little match for an employer in a contest of economic strength.

ORIGINS OF THE LABOR MOVEMENT

The modern labor union did not come into existence in the United States until shortly before 1800. The early unions were composed of skilled craft workers who typically served long apprenticeships and who anticipated eventually establishing themselves as their own masters. At that time, the distinction between employee and employer, so important to industrial relations at later stages, neither was very great nor was dependent on social class. Both were producers, and both were workers, with the employer—the master—standing simply as a journeyman who had made good.

Contrary to some popular opinions and to the experiences of other nations, the early American unions were not broadly concerned with proletarian causes. Instead, they were established by groups of skilled craft workers in response to changing economic conditions that threatened their social status and economic welfare. In the early part of the nineteenth century the principal threat

stemmed from production for a widening wholesale market which pitted producer against producer in a more intense kind of competition than had previously been experienced in local markets, thereby putting pressure on the
master to restrain wages or otherwise reduce costs. One cost-cutting measure
was increased specialization of the work process, but this violated craft workers' sense of professional integrity, since they saw themselves not merely as
workers who performed part of a job but as people whose status was based
foursquare on the ability to do the whole job. Shoemakers and weavers were
among the craft workers most subject to these pressures.

Some of the early efforts at unionization were directed less toward the
master employer than toward the public. All journeymen of a particular skill
(carpenters, for example) might join together and agree that none would work
for less than a specified rate. They all stood to benefit from such an arrangement, and a combination of them could be quite effective, provided that the
members were not in direct competition with workers of similar skill from
neighboring communities. This type of action often was precipitated in times of
rising prices, as workers faced with a declining standard of living sought remedy in association.

If the early unionists were not the most oppressed or least fortunate workers, even the very skilled among them operated under serious economic and
social disabilities, as compared with the more privileged propertied groups.
Ownership of property usually was made a requirement for voting, education
frequently was beyond the means of those who lived on what they earned, and
justice was unequally applied to the manual worker and the well-born. Thus,
workers could legitimately view themselves as members of an underprivileged
group in comparison with a propertied, nonworking group that reaped the rewards of workers' toil.

This set of circumstances gave rise to a dual orientation—some might describe it as an ambivalence—within the labor movement of the early period. On
the one hand, economic pressures spurred workers to attempt to improve their
lot "here and now." In this vein, they formed unions, sought higher wages, and
attempted to use the strategic skills embodied in their crafts to improve the conditions of their work. On the other hand, the broader disadvantages imposed on
them by a social system that seemingly favored the propertied class encouraged
workers to undertake various political actions in the pursuit of a more general
improvement in their condition. These twin themes of collective bargaining and
political action, sometimes focusing on different dimensions of the same issues,
are ever present in the history of American labor.

This is clearly evident from the ebb and flow of unionism throughout the
nineteenth century. In periods when the economy was weak and their bargaining power quite limited, urban craft workers participated in broad political reform movements, in which they were often joined by unskilled workers. In
prosperous periods, these same craft workers banded together in separate
unions to exercise their economic strength. Bargaining with the masters who
employed them tended to be sporadic and short-lived at first, but it became bet-

ter established as the century wore on. At the close of the nineteenth century, collective bargaining in some trades was almost as advanced as it is today.

UNIONS AS CONSPIRACIES

Throughout the legal regulation of labor unions in the United States, two themes, stated in question form, occurred repeatedly: (1) ''What is the appropriate relationship of the organized group to society at large and to the employer?'' and (2) ''What is the appropriate relationship of an organization of workers to the individual worker?''

The legal doctrine which sought to cope with these questions prior to the mid-nineteenth century was the common-law doctrine of criminal conspiracy. Common law is judge-made law rather than legislative statute—an interpretation of lawful conduct rendered by the courts in light of precedents and with regard for what Justice Holmes called, in an enduring phrase, the ''felt necessities of the times.'' In the early 1900s, judges tended to rule that the mere existence of labor unions was illegal, thus regarding them as criminal conspiracies. Though an individual worker might attempt to secure increased wages and improved working conditions from an employer, a group of workers who came together to accomplish the same thing was illegal—not because of what it sought, but merely because of the collective nature of such action. The courts, following English common-law precedents, viewed labor collectives as inherent monopolies that required prohibition. Otherwise, such organizations presumably would use their powers to benefit themselves at the expense of the community and to deprive other individuals (such as employers) of some of their liberties. As one court official noted in *Commonwealth v. Pullis* (popularly known as the *Philadelphia Cordwainers* case) in 1806, ''A combination of workmen to raise their wages may be considered in a twofold point of view: One is to benefit themselves; . . . the other is to injure those who do not join their society. The rule of law condemns both.'' The criminal conspiracy doctrine was invoked in well over a dozen cases in the early nineteenth century.

Civil Conspiracy and the ''Illegal Purpose'' Doctrine

In the celebrated *Commonwealth v. Hunt* case of 1842, the Massachusetts Supreme Court, headed by Chief Justice Lemuel Shaw, refused to apply the criminal conspiracy doctrine to the Boston shoemakers, who were enforcing a closed shop—an arrangement requiring a worker to be a union member in order to obtain employment in a particular trade or craft. Rather, Shaw reasoned that a labor organization might serve any one of a number of useful ends—promoting among its membership sobriety, adherence to high work standards, and the like—and that this case and others should be decided on the basis of the ends or purposes which the union sought to accomplish.

Although this ''illegal purpose'' doctrine was commonly interpreted by the courts in a way that condemned almost every concerted labor activity, nevertheless it represented an important shift in judicial doctrine. In essence, it rejected the position that labor organizations were per se illegal and instead looked to the purposes of such organizations. The fledgling unions whose actions were repeatedly curtailed by the courts following the *Commonwealth v. Hunt* case understandably might not have appreciated this shift in common-law doctrine, but it was later to become the basis of legislation that tolerated and protected various goals and activities of unions.

A most effective method of implementing and strengthening the doctrine of civil conspiracy as applied to organized workers was the labor injunction.[5] This device, which originated in cases of railway labor disputes, permitted an employer to petition a court to stop a union action such as a strike before it began rather than having to wait until the act was committed and then sue for the recovery of damages. In essence, the court was asked to enjoin or restrain the union from undertaking a threatened action which the employer argued would result in "irreparable" damage to the business. The labor injunction was used with impunity by the courts until 1932, when the Norris-La Guardia Act severely limited its use. Interestingly, however, in the latter part of the nineteenth century, the labor injunction often was issued to protect employers who identified themselves with the broader "community" or "public" interest against the concerted "monopoly power" of unions. If persuasive in making such arguments, as they often were, employers of this period could be presumed by the judiciary to be defending interests other than their own. Later on, as we shall see, the public became exceptionally concerned about employers' monopoly power, but, in attempting to combat it, inadvertently increased the legal sanctions applied to organized labor.

IDEALISM AND REFORM

Throughout most of the nineteenth century, the American labor movement was oriented less toward economic or political gain than toward protection of a way of life and a lessening of the divide between the rich and the poor. The labor unions of the period were by and large (though with notable exceptions) unstructured, faction-ridden, and impermanent. In the face of recurring recessions and unemployment, even skilled workers would abandon their unions and collective bargaining in favor of broader, politically oriented movements that sought amelioration of the workers' lot as a class by overthrowing the "wage system," which required that they sell themselves by the hour.

For these same skilled workers, the nineteenth century was one of gradual deterioration of their social status and economic conditions. Not only did competition and specialization press down their wage rates and parcel their tasks out to immigrants, women, apprentices, and others, but in the process, they were also converted from the dignified status of "producer" to the common one of "hired hand."

The resentment toward the wage system that emerged out of the shift from the sale of craft workers' products to the sale of their time took many forms, including unsuccessful attempts to preserve the status quo and retard the spread of competition and industrialization. Later in the century a cleavage developed within the labor movement between the reformist group, which sought to recapture a "golden age," and the realist group, which was ready to come to grips with the developing industrial system, provided that workers could obtain a rightful share of its benefits. The former emphasized political action to achieve its objectives and viewed labor as a class, while the latter relied on the economic strength of its special position in the industrial system and bargained for higher wages, more benefits, and improved working conditions.

Though the distinction between these contending schools of philosophy was never fully clear-cut, it sharpened over time. Out of the trial-and-error process of attempting to resolve the internal conflict within labor's ranks was to emerge the movement's dominant philosophy, bread-and-butter-oriented "business unionism." An early, dramatic example of the clash between the two approaches was evidenced in the founding—and eventual foundering—of the National Labor Union. Formed in 1866, the organization represented the culmination of efforts to bring together in a single entity all the country's diverse labor groups. Under the direction of William H. Sylvis, president of the Iron Molders International Union, the National Labor Union welcomed not only established labor groups but also various reform groups such as suffragettes, land reformers, antimonopoly types, and utopians of several other persuasions. The national trade unions, the first of which were formed in the 1850s to augment the bargaining power of local unions of a common craft, sensed that their strength would be dissipated in generalized reform programs at the expense of their own immediate objectives concerning wages and hours, and so they began to withdraw from the organization. The National Labor Union came to an end in just 6 years, with only a half dozen delegates attending its final meeting in 1872.[6]

The Knights of Labor

The contest between realists and reformers for control of the labor movement was even more sharply played out during the 25-year existence of the Knights of Labor. Founded in 1869 even while the National Labor Union was still alive, the Knights prospered from the Panic of 1873, which virtually destroyed the membership base of trade unions of cigar makers, machinists, typographers, and the like. Organized as a small society of reformers, secret to avoid retaliation by employers and led by an evangelist breed, the Knights held their first local assembly in 1872; added eighty new chapters the next year, which were made up largely of former members of national trade unions; and conducted their first national congress in 1878. One year later, Terence V. Powderly succeeded Uriah Stevens as Grand Master Workman of the Knights, a position he held for almost 15 years.

Like the National Labor Union, the Knights of Labor sought to reform industrial society by eliminating the wage system and establishing producers' cooperatives which would again make workers their own masters. Coupled with these objectives was an uncompromising attitude toward the economic program of the national trade unions, which, by 1880, had begun to recover from the preceding depression and were asserting their members' claims to better wages and shorter hours, backed by strikes when necessary. Powderly and his associates considered wage raises of a few cents per hour inadequate when the craft workers deserved the whole price of their labor. They eschewed the strike, denouncing it as a "relic of barbarism," and attempted to substitute for it reason, persuasion, and arbitration. They also devised an organizational structure for the Knights which, though composed of local, district, and national assemblies, was ill suited to collective bargaining and subordinated the narrower interests of individual members of trade unions to the broader ones of the reformist elements.

While these internal tensions continued within the Knights (and, indeed, the national trade unions formed their own federation to which individuals could belong while retaining their membership in the Knights), the situation was tolerable if uneasy. But the most compelling events were yet to come.

During the early 1880s, much to Powderly's embarrassment, numerous trade unions affiliated with the Knights became embroiled in strikes. Though overwhelmingly local in character, one of these attracted national attention: the 1885 strike over wage reductions and layoffs of Knights employed on Jay Gould's Wabash railroad. While the reasons for Gould's eventual capitulation to the Knights remain cloudy, the public image created was one of the business titan "surrendering" to an insurgent labor organization. Subsequently, in 1886, an especially historic year in the annals of American labor, membership in the Knights swelled to 700,000, rising from just 100,000 a year earlier.

The extreme irony of this situation rested in Powderly's heading an organization whose expanded membership was now overwhelmingly composed of unionists who sought gains in the areas of wages and hours and who advocated the strike to achieve them, precisely the objectives and tactics abhorrent to the Knights' leadership. As these contending interests jockeyed to and fro, the situation became more unstable. The mounting resentment toward Powderly's subordination of trade union interests within the Knights grew even stronger with the lack of progress on the 8-hour workday, to which the organization presumably was committed on paper.

The Rise of the AFL

If the Knights' lack of support of strikes and their attitude toward the 8-hour workday were the principal reasons for their eventual decline in the late 1880s, a contributing factor was the Haymarket Affair of 1886. In that year, a workers' protest meeting ended with the throwing of a bomb into a group of Chicago policemen. Though union members were not directly involved in this action (in fact, it is now generally conceded that the crime was falsely attributed to them), the preceding wave of strikes became connected with a state of anarchy of which the bombing incident was symptomatic. Consequently, public opinion turned against the Knights.[7]

But an even more important event in that year was the proposal by twenty national trade unions of a "treaty" to the Knights which required them not to interfere in bargaining efforts and which sanctioned exclusive jurisdiction of individual unions over their respective trades. The Knights were to abstain from organizing any trade for which a national union existed and were to withdraw the charter of any local trade assembly for which there was a national union. In return, the Knights would have exclusive control over reform functions and the mixed assemblies supporting them. The early optimism that the treaty issues could be resolved quickly faded, and the breach was irreparably widened, when, at a meeting of the general assembly later in the year, a resolution was introduced requiring workers who held memberships jointly in the Knights and the Cigar Makers International Union to resign from the latter. One month later in Columbus, Ohio, the trade unions, whose concern for their own survival was now paramount, established the American Federation of Labor (AFL).

Over the next several years the two organizations pursued a common understanding, but with little success. As the AFL prospered, the Knights' organization declined, its membership dropping to 500,000 in 1887, to half that number in 1888, and to less than 100,000 in 1890. By the end of the century, the Knights had virtually ceased to exist.

Because the AFL survived and succeeded and the Knights did not, it is easy and commonplace to regard the former as the eager challenger that displaced the champion and to seek understanding of that success. But the demise of the Knights is fully as important as the rise of the AFL. Not only did it constitute the end of an epoch, but it also brought about recognition that the economy had passed beyond the stage in which any person could eventually own a business or in which production could be organized along cooperative lines. The passing of the Knights reflected the emerging acceptance by workers of the wage relationship and the recognition that small workshops were rapidly being replaced by aggregations of capital and professionally managed enterprises. The AFL survived and grew because it came to terms with the capitalist, private enterprise system, adapting to it rather than seeking to destroy it.

At the same time, it should be recognized that the reformist element within the American labor movement did not wholly disappear with the passage of the Knights from the scene. Socialism continued the reform movement, which was less important in the United States than abroad, although even here it developed powerful advocates within the house of labor. Early in the twentieth century, the Industrial Workers of the World (IWW) arose out of the anarchic-syndicalist movement to challenge both the evils of capitalism and the conservatism of the AFL. Though it championed the cause of migrant and casual laborers who suffered truly miserable conditions and though it won several important industrial strikes, the IWW suffered from a bad reputation during World War I and the hysterical aftermath of that conflict. Branded a subversive organization, ruthlessly hounded by the authorities, and susceptible to considerable violence on the part of management in opposition to strikes, the "Wobblies" soon faded to insignificance. However, the pressure they exerted, together with the efforts of the Knights and other organizations before them, provides testimony to the persisting presence of a reformist tradition within the labor movement, despite the rise to dominance of the AFL. Indeed, the virtual absence of such a reformist element within the American labor movement today may, more than any other feature, distinguish it from that of the past.

THE DEVELOPMENT OF BUSINESS UNIONISM

The philosophy of labor that developed in the closing years of the nineteenth century under the direction of the AFL, headed by Samuel Gompers of the Cigar Makers International Union, cast unionism in the role of agent for labor within a contractual business system. Long-range, broad-scale reforms were eschewed in favor of immediate wage gains and improved working conditions. This philosophy became known as "business unionism" and was described in 1916 by Robert Hoxie, an eminent student of industrial relations, in the following way:

> The outlook and ideals of this dominant type of unionism are those very largely of a business organization. Its successful leaders are essentially business men and its unions are organizations primarily to do business with employers—to bargain for the sale of a product which it controls. . . . Its position and experience have been very much like that of a new and rising business concern attempting to force its way into a field already occupied by old established organizations in control of the market. Like the new business concern, it has to fight to maintain a foothold.[8]

The "trade agreement"—a contract negotiated between union and management setting forth the terms and conditions under which workers would be employed—was the clearest expression of the new realism in industrial relations. Though such contracts were negotiated from time to time and place to place throughout the nineteenth century, it was with the signing in 1891 of a national agreement in the stove foundry industry that the modern system of collective bargaining can be said to have begun. By the end of the century, national agreements no longer were novel, and local agreements proliferated in towns and cities. Of this development, Perlman commented: "Without the trade agreement, the labor movement could hardly come to eschew 'panaceas' and to reconstitute itself upon the basis of opportunism."[9]

If, by the turn of the century, American labor had come to accept private enterprise and the wage system, American business had no such feelings about unionism. Ironically, because the AFL rejected systemwide reform and producers' cooperatives in favor of mobilizing organized workers to wrest more favorable economic terms from employers, it posed a more substantial threat to business interests and sharpened labor-management conflict.

Opposition to the AFL

Reduced to its most basic form, the clash centered on differing conceptions of the role of private property in American society. Managers presumed that ownership of physical property—plants and capital equipment—carried with it the freedom, indeed the right, to organize production and to modify industrial processes as they saw fit.

But this concept of ownership was extended to include the workers who ran the machines or otherwise toiled in plants, shops, and factories. It seemed not to occur to owners and managers that a right of property does not automatically translate into a right of power and authority; that the freedom to use property as the owner wishes depends in reality on the acceptance by workers of rules, regulations, and instructions concerning the operations of machines and equipment; and that authority over human beings at work is not conferred by ownership of things.

In contrast, workers sought protection from management, represented at the workplace by the supervisor, and they joined with other workers in a concerted agreement to work only at a given place, at specified times, on particular pieces of equipment, and under conditions and on terms spelled out in a contract. In the workers' view, this was a claim to their "property" of labor power fully on a par with the claims of managers. That such claims to property in work might reduce the capital value of the owners' property didn't concern workers, for they viewed the issue as one of human rights rather than property rights. Thus was the collision of contending rights joined.

In defense of employers' property rights, opposition to the AFL took many forms in the first quarter of the twentieth century. Organizations such as the National Civic Federation, formed in 1900; the National Association of Manufacturers (NAM), organized 5 years earlier; the National Metal Trades Association (NMTA), founded in 1899; the American Anti-Boycott Association, organized secretly in 1902; and numerous local employers' associations, industry groups, and citizens' alliances fervently opposed unionism in any form. Their overriding philosophy was expressed in the NMTA's declaration of principles, which included the following propositions:

> (5) We will not permit employees to place any restriction on the management, methods or production of our shops, and will require a fair day's work for a fair day's pay. Employees will be paid by the hourly rate, by premium system, piece work or contract, as the employer may elect.
> (6) It is a privilege of the employee to leave our employ whenever he sees fit and it is the privilege of the employer to discharge any workman when he sees fit.[10]

With this philosophy as a guide, many employers felt justified in using every available weapon to prevent unions from gaining a foothold in their firms. These included firing workers even suspected of union sympathies, blacklisting union organizers and supporters, planting spies within labor organizations, obtaining sweeping court injunctions that prohibited most union activities, and, when milder methods failed, employing goons, thugs, private detectives, and the local police forces of "company towns" (who volunteered for duty in many cases) to beat up pickets, break up disturbances, and otherwise encourage "outside agitators" to get out of town.

Not all employers used such methods or took a strong antilabor stance, however. Some used subtler means of opposition, and in a few industries where bargaining was established early—for example, printing and construction at local levels and coal at the national level—unionism was at least tolerated. So it was that the labor movement grew steadily, if slowly, unionism reaching a level in 1904 of about 2 million workers, of whom four-fifths were in the AFL. But that was to represent a pre-World War I peak, as unions found it increasingly difficult to hold their own. One factor in this struggle was the scientific management movement, which was briefly described in Chapter 2 and which quickly became a new tool of opponents of unions in the first quarter of the twentieth century.

Recall that Frederick Taylor conceived of scientific management as a system to maximize efficiency through standardization of the elements of production. These included the planning of work by specialists, time-and-motion study of all mechanical movements to determine the most efficient mode of reconstructing tasks and organizations, and the payment of workers on the basis of their objectively measured contribution as revealed by systems of job evaluation or incentives. Because Taylor, an engineer, believed that all work could be reduced to a scientific basis of objective fact and law, it followed that "the laws of the workplace . . . are no more subject to bargaining than the tensile strength of steel."[11]

The reader can probably infer how management jumped on the scientific management bandwagon to oppose unionism further. The organization of industrial processes and production methods according to scientific laws constituted the rationale for portraying unions and collective bargaining as unnecessary. At the same time, the workers' well-being would be protected, according to managers, because they would be trained in the best and easiest methods, asked to perform only at "normal" rates of speed, and protected against arbitrary reductions in wages since they would be paid on the basis of their performance. Unionists rejoined that they didn't trust management to look after the workers' interests and, in any case, didn't regard their interests as being served by the continued fractionalization of work and reduction of skill. In their view, unions were required to protect them from just such actions by management. Moreover, the conversion of craft into industrial workers as a result of applications of scientific management to the production process boded ill for labor's success in organizing workers, since industrial workers were more easily replaced than skilled craft employees. To some extent, these differing perspectives are present today, although in more diluted fashion than before. Most significant for our purposes, though, unions fought scientific management not so much because it was part of the business system as because it denied them a place in that system.

LABOR AND THE SHERMAN ANTITRUST ACT

The law was another important factor retarding the growth of labor unions and preventing workers from reaching bargaining goals in the early twentieth century. In 1890, Congress enacted the Sherman Antitrust Act, a measure aimed at business organizations. The legislation emerged out of the heated agitation of the 1870s and 1880s over the growth of large-scale monopolies that restricted competition. But shortly after its passage, through the process of judicial interpretation, the act was applied principally to the activities of organized labor.[12]

These applications took two major forms. First, the law affected the labor union's use of the boycott. A ruling in the *Loewe v. Lawlor* case, first heard in 1908, declared the boycott to be an unlawful union weapon whenever it inhibited the flow of interstate commerce. In that case, the organized hatters of Danbury, Connecticut, conducted a strike and a nationwide boycott against the products of an employer who had refused to recognize their union. The AFL circulated a "we do not patronize" list that included the name of the struck employer. Sympathetic groups were urged not to patronize stores in which the hats of this manufacturer were sold. The Supreme Court ruled that, by its actions, the union had impeded the flow of the company's hats across state lines, thereby subjecting itself and its members to the terms of the Sherman Antitrust Act. The union was found guilty and was assessed a fine of $210,000 plus costs. For a time it looked as though the homes of members would have to be sold to satisfy the judgment, but the AFL appealed for contributions, and the fine was eventually paid without such a dire consequence. This decision and others like it limited the unions' use of the organized boycott and presumably dampened the organizing spirit of individual workers who did not want to risk their own assets to court judgments.

The second restrictive impact of the Sherman Antitrust Act on labor unions concerned the use of the strike. The key case, *Coronado Coal Company v. United Mine Workers,* was decided twice during the 1920s by the Supreme Court. The union had conducted an organizational strike against the company which prevented the movement of coal into normal channels of trade. The company sued the union on the grounds that it had restrained interstate commerce.

In the first case, the Court found for the union, concluding that the interruption of the flow of trade was an unintended by-product of a basic strike for recognition. In the second case, relying on new evidence offered by a disgruntled union official, the Court ruled against the union, finding that the primary purpose of the strike was to prevent coal from being shipped. Unions saw this as a distinction without a difference, since a strike, to be effective, necessarily has to restrain a company's trade relations and normal business. To them, one was a natural concomitant of the other.

The application of antitrust law to concerted activities of labor unions in the early part of the twentieth century also is illuminating for what it reveals about the ability and willingness of the judiciary to impose its own conceptions of right and wrong on labor-management relationships, apart from the more general public will expressed in legislative statute. In 1914, Congress passed the Clayton Act, the clear objective of which was to exclude labor disputes from the purview of the Sherman Antitrust Act. Yet, through its interpretations of law and fact in a series of cases, the courts essentially rendered the Clayton Act ineffective as they continued to find one union action after another illegal under the antitrust statute.[13]

NEW DIMENSIONS OF OPPOSITION TO UNIONISM

World War I brought to American unionists what they hadn't been able to achieve for themselves—acceptance and growth. Though these were to prove temporary, they resulted from two causes: the favorable economic conse- quences of a sudden increase in the demand for labor and the heavy emphasis placed by government on the resolution of conflicts within industry to ensure wartime production of vital goods and services. Less concerned with the rights of owners and workers than with the need for output, federal officials wrote into their procurement contracts with employers provisions for the 8-hour workday, overtime pay, recognition of unions, and grievance procedures. Labor representatives were appointed to various administrative agencies, most notably the War Labor Board, which later asserted the rights of workers to or- ganize and bargain collectively with their employers and which proposed the establishment of "works councils" to resolve disputes. Indeed, the works councils performed so well that their continuance after the war was recom- mended by the NAM in conjunction with the so-called "representation plans" (to be discussed below). Thus, between 1915 and 1920, membership in unions doubled, for the first time reaching the 5-million mark, with more than 4 million members in the AFL alone.

But the glory period was brief. With the end of the war and the failure of the National Industrial Conference, convened by President Wilson in 1919, to seek tripartite readjustment to a peacetime economy, employers resumed their opposition to unionism, aided by the aforementioned court decisions declaring illegal various power tactics of organized workers. Nevertheless, an important change in employers' attitudes had taken place. Managers in large corporations realized that the size of their firms rendered impractical any notion of dealing individually with thousands of employees. Personnel policy had to be made on a corporate basis, with the views of employees given collective consideration.

An NAM subcommittee in 1919 advised employer-members to establish representation plans to facilitate communications with employees. The basic element of these plans was a constitutional system, with employees in a com- pany plant, shop or department electing representatives to meet jointly with management. Workers' representatives were permitted to raise questions con- cerning wages and working conditions, but final decisions on these matters rested with management. They could advise, but their consent was not re- quired. In fact, these were company unions; ostensibly they were organizations that represented employees, but in fact they were instigated and dominated by management. The company union was a key device used by management to oppose legitimate, independent labor organizations in the 1920s.

A more pernicious form of opposition to unionism was the "American plan," which attempted to link labor organizations to subversive foreigners seeking to dominate native-born American workers and force them into unions against their will. The tone of this opposition is reflected in the words of Charles Schwab, chairman of the board of Bethlehem Steel Company, who, while allowing that workers should organize to protect their rights, believed that "they ought not to be controlled by somebody from Kamchatka who knows nothing about what their conditions are."[14] In a similar vein, the Associated Industries of Seattle warned against "ignorant, foreign-born workers" who had come to "seize property and control in the United States" assisted by "radicals in the ranks and particularly the leadership of labor."

Not all employers subscribed to this jingoism, but most were genuinely opposed to being told by "outsiders" what to do in their "own" plants. Some among them raised wages, reduced hours, and improved conditions in the hope of forestalling unrest among workers.[15] Many others continued to require workers to sign written pledges not to form or join a labor organization as a condition of continued employment. These were known as "yellow dog" contracts. As for unionists, they continued to pursue what they regarded as their rightful place in the industrial system. They opposed representation plans, company unions, and especially the American plan, offering instead joint union-management programs of cooperation to improve efficiency and increase productivity. Employers would have little or none of this, however, for the retention of decision-making authority seemed paramount to them, surpassing even the objective of profit maximization.

Depression and Governmental Intervention

Employers might have successfully continued to oppose unions and to obtain generally favorable judicial and legislative consideration of labor-management relations, if not for two factors. One of these, alluded to earlier, was the growing recognition that traditional concepts of individual employer-employee relationships were increasingly untenable in light of the massing together of large numbers of employees in large corporate entities. The powerlessness of the single worker in these circumstances, the virtual helplessness of the individual as a bargaining agent, spurred people to see more clearly than before the function of a labor union which did not deny liberty to the individual but, quite to the contrary, acted as his or her representative. Indeed, the acceptance by business itself of the company union during the 1920s and early 1930s underscores this more general shift in attitude toward employer-employee relationships.

The second major cause of a change in attitudes toward unions was the Great Depression of the 1930s. So profound were its impacts—more than one-quarter of the work force was unemployed, and one-third of the residents of some industrialized areas were on relief—that the citizenry willingly accepted President Franklin Roosevelt's view that something had to be done. In the area of labor, the first significant legislative initiative was the passage in 1932 (actually in the closing months of Herbert Hoover's administration) of the Norris-LaGuardia Act, later copied by many state legislatures. This curbed, though it did not actually forbid, the issuance of injunctions by federal courts. The circumstances under which labor injunctions might be granted were sweepingly restricted, their issuance being permitted only after the parties had exhausted all other channels for settlement of labor disputes. The effectiveness of this act subsequently was reflected in diminished use by the courts of the civil conspiracy doctrine in labor cases.

New Legal Doctrines   Moreover, the courts also were beginning to modify the structure of controls on labor union activity that resulted from their earlier decisions. Concerning picketing, which the judiciary had tightly restricted, a radically different legal doctrine emerged in the *Thornhill v. Alabama* case, decided in 1940. There, the Supreme Court, arguing that employers had many more means available than unions to publicize labor disputes, found picketing to be a form of free speech protected by the First Amendment to the Constitution. Though this protection of picketing was later to be diluted, at the time it represented a sharp departure from the past.

In the same year, 1940, the Supreme Court decided the first in a series of cases, *Apex v. Leader,* which had the cumulative effect of removing most union activity from the sanctions of the Sherman Antitrust Act. In the process of conducting a sit-down strike at the company's plant, organized hosiery workers had damaged equipment and prevented shipments of goods across state lines. The Court ruled that these effects were only incidental to the union's main objective of conducting a work stoppage. If strikes which interrupted a company's interstate business were to be ruled monopolistic exercises of economic power, then in effect every strike could be declared illegal under the Sherman Antitrust Act. This surely was not the intent of Congress, noted the Court in its opinion in the *Apex* case. Clearly, this decision reversed the ruling previously handed down in the second *Coronado* case.[16]

In 1944, in *Allen Bradley Co. v. Local 3, IBEW,* the Court further defined its view of what constituted legal union activities. Local 3 of the International Brotherhood of Electrical Workers (IBEW), in New York City, had effected an arrangement with the manufacturers' and contractors' associations that produced and installed electric fixtures in that city. Under this arrangement, Local 3 refused to supply electricians to any contractor who installed fixtures made outside New York City, in return for which the two employers' associations promised to use only union labor. The arrangement constituted an embargo on an otherwise competing product and allowed the wage increases for union labor to be fully passed along in the form of price increases to consumers, who had no other place to go in order to purchase fixtures or have them installed.

The Court found this arrangement to be a violation of the Sherman Antitrust Act, but only because the union had entered into a specific agreement with the employers' associations to enforce it. If it had undertaken to police the arrangement itself or had not had a formal agreement with employers, the union would have been untouched by the Sherman Antitrust Act. It was the employers' involvement which "tainted" the arrangement. Thus, the Court came to accept a doctrine which had previously been urged on it but which it had never before adopted, namely, that the Sherman Antitrust Act was designed to prevent only *business* practices from restricting competition.

Consider then that between 1932 and 1944, a panoply of controls on union activity had been struck down. The injunction and the illegal purpose doctrine were sharply limited; picketing was constitutionally immune from attack; and the Sherman Antitrust Act was largely inapplicable to organized labor. This is not to deny that, in many communities, employers' opposition to unions continued to receive judicial support. Nor were all unions suddenly placed in a strong offensive position. Nevertheless, the trend of events reflected a sharp lessening of legal controls over labor unions and their concerted activities. Organizing workers was still no picnic, but, where unions were able to organize, legal restraints on the exercise of their power had become notably weaker.

The Wagner Act   The most compelling labor legislation of the Depression era was the National Labor Relations (Wagner) Act, adopted in 1935, which for the first time committed the power of the federal government to support unionism and to promote collective bargaining as a national policy. It is true that government-encouraged labor-management accords were reached during World War I, that the Railway Labor Act of 1926 gave the politically effective railroad brotherhoods protections and advantages which were not extended to organized labor generally, and that unionism and bargaining were partially promoted in the National Industrial Recovery Act of 1933. But the Wagner Act was more sweeping than any of these, and its constitutionality was upheld by the Supreme Court in 1937.

The significance of this legislation can be judged only against its background. Prior to its passage, employers were completely free to fire or refuse to hire union members and to discriminate against them on the job. While the Norris-LaGuardia Act prevented employers from enforcing the aforementioned "yellow dog" contracts, it in no way promoted unionism or supported collective bargaining. Employers were not mandated to recognize unions, and they could hire *agents provocateurs* and industrial spies to disrupt and weaken labor organizations. If a union called a strike, the employer was free to use any device to break it, including the use of armed guards—"Pinkertons," as they were known, from the name of the company which supplied them—for "protection."

The Wagner Act deprived employers of all these rights and enunciated a new policy: that the federal government protected the organizing rights of workers and supported the practice of collective bargaining. To implement the new policy, the act created a three-member (later a five-member) National Labor Relations Board (NLRB). Its duties included protecting workers in their right to organize unions, administering an election procedure for determining which unions have the legal right to engage in collective bargaining, and ensuring that the parties make a genuine effort to arrive at a joint agreement governing their relations.

These purposes were provided for in a lengthy piece of legislation which we shall not attempt to review in detail here. As will be noted shortly, the Wagner Act was followed in 1947 by the Taft-Hartley Act, which modified a few of its provisions but primarily added new ones to it. The Taft-Hartley Act in turn was followed, in 1959, by the Labor-Management Reporting and Disclosure (Landrum-Griffin) Act, which modified the 1947 legislation, but only in minor particulars. The last of these acts, which will be discussed more fully in Chapter 4, was concerned principally with internal union affairs, as it attempted to promote democracy within labor organizations. These last two statutes are mentioned here only to emphasize that they did not substantially alter the legislative provisions of the Wagner Act, which provided then, as it does now, the framework for private-sector labor-management relations in the United States.

The National Labor Relations Board and Unfair Labor Practices In implementing the framework and central policies of federal labor law, the NLRB is empowered to rule on what are known as "unfair labor practice cases." The Wagner Act defined several practices of employers which, if engaged in, could be prosecuted by a union in a legal proceeding before the Board. The Taft-Hartley Act added a group of unfair labor practices by employees and unions which employers may bring before the Board. The law gives the NLRB the power to impose financial penalties and to issue cease and desist orders, where necessary, to effectuate its decisions involving unfair labor practices by employers and unions. These orders are enforceable through the courts if the parties do not comply with them.

Unfair labor practices chargeable to an employer are intended to protect employees in organizing, joining, or campaigning on behalf of a union. Thus the law categorizes as "unfair" an employer's attempted interference with, coercion or dominance of, and discrimination against, employees in the exercise of their rights to organize and bargain. It also labels "unfair" an employer's refusal to bargain in good faith with a union that legally represents employees.

The NLRB gives tangible meaning to the general and formal statutory phrases by its decisions on a case-by-case basis. In recent years, the Board has declared actions such as the following to be illegal: evicting strikers from company headquarters; discharging employees for filing grievances on their own behalf and that of their co-workers; threatening discharge, demotion, and loss of wages if employees persist in union activity; interrogating employees about union activities as part of a coercive pattern of conduct; and relocating and closing plants without prior discussion and negotiations with organized employees. Not infrequently, the Board faces the difficult task of ascertaining an employer's motivation for a particular action so that it can determine whether antiunionism was the principal factor. Keep in mind that the Board is also concerned with illegal—unfair—labor practices by unions and employees, but that is a matter which we will briefly defer.

Elections to determine representation of employees   A major function of the Board is to conduct elections to determine representation of employees. The Wagner Act permitted workers to organize and to be represented by an agent of their own choosing, but the process could have taken several different forms. As in a number of European countries, for example, a union might represent only its own members, and so several different unions would be involved in negotiating for the employees in just one shop or unit. To avoid the strife that such an arrangement might generate, the American law provides for "exclusive representation." Whenever a number of employees in a unit—a minimum of 30 percent is required—indicate their desire to be represented by some union, they may petition the Board to conduct an election. The name of the union is placed on a ballot, along with a possible choice of "no union." If another union (or unions) seeks representation rights within the same unit, its name is also placed on the ballot, provided it can show authorization cards signed by at least 10 percent of the unit. The NLRB then conducts an election in which all employees declared by the Board to be in the unit (known as the "election district") may vote. If a majority of those voting cast their votes for a particular union, that union is certified as the *exclusive* representative for all the employees in the unit. As such, it must represent and negotiate terms with the employer for all the employees in the unit, *whether they are members of the union or not.*[17]

The principle and practice of exclusive representation in the American system of industrial relations are distinctive and important. Exclusive representation provides a peaceful, democratic method of determining employees' preferences and gives to a certified union institutional security of a very high order. This same principle, however, by requiring labor organizations to represent members and nonmembers alike, impartially and fairly, also imposes on unions an obligation which a partisan and belligerent organization cannot easily measure up to.

The bargaining unit   Prior to conducting an election, the NLRB first has to determine the "appropriate bargaining unit." In general, the Board seeks to group together employees whose interests are sufficiently homogeneous to sustain a presumption that the labor relationship will be a reasonably stable one. Typically, the preferences of employees and management are given strong weight in this regard, but sometimes the Board must exercise its own discretion. For example, the Board may have to decide whether unskilled and semiskilled workers in the same plant constitute one bargaining unit or two separate ones; whether paraprofessional and nonprofessional employees merit separate units or a single one enrolling both groups; and whether similarly skilled workers employed by a multiplant firm constitute one comprehensive unit or a series of units, one for each plant.

Particularly nettlesome is the question, often raised in recent years, of whether skilled workers who belong to an industrial union such as the United

Automobile Workers (UAW) may break off and form their own organization, presumably because they seek more effective representation of their own interests than is provided by a union whose constituency consists largely of unskilled and semiskilled members. While the Board has tended to disallow such "craft severance," it applies to this issue on a case-by-case basis the criteria that it has evolved to make initial decisions on bargaining units: the history and type of employee organization; the history of collective bargaining in the plant, office, factory, or shop of the employer in question and in other firms in the same industry; the skill, wages, and working conditions of the employees; the desires and eligibility of the employees; and the relationship between proposed units and the employer's organization. Note that these criteria appear nowhere in the law; instead, they were formulated over time by the Board to provide a systematic basis for determining bargaining units. Thus they reflect both the Board's pragmatic response to industrial relations and its ability to shape those relations.

Jurisdiction of the law   The Board's discretion also extends to the scope of its jurisdiction. The law provides only a general guide on this score, authorizing the NLRB to assume jurisdiction over unfair labor practices and questions of representation "affecting commerce." Early on, the Board decided to eliminate from its purview businesses having little effect on interstate commerce. The need for limited coverage arises from several factors, most particularly the heavy case load which the Board historically has confronted and which remains a formidable one. A series of dollar-volume criteria were formulated for firms in different industries; if these are met or exceeded, this indicates that the Board has jurisdiction over these firms' labor-management relationships. The criteria include, among others, $500,000 annual gross volume of business for retail firms, $250,000 for public utilities and transit systems, and $100,000 for newspaper and communications employers, including radio, television, telegraph, and telephone companies. The implicit presumption of these dollar-volume tests is that employers who meet them must perforce be "significantly" engaged in interstate commerce.[18]

The Board sometimes feels called on to extend its jurisdiction to new sectors, typically situations in which unionism has gained new footholds or has enlarged its presence. Thus, in recent years the Board has extended its authority to private universities (provided they have at least $1 million of annual gross revenues) and to professional sports such as baseball, basketball, football, and hockey. The Board's jurisdiction may also be extended by Congress. As a result of 1974 legislation, for example, the Board now possesses jurisdiction over labor-management relations in nonprofit hospitals and other health care institutions.

The subject matter of bargaining   Over the years, the Board has evolved three categories of bargaining subjects: mandatory, permissible, and prohibited. The first includes subjects which must be discussed and on which agreement must be sought, if the union raises them or if management wishes to change existing conditions. Incidentally, the act does not *require* the parties to reach agreement on any issue or to conclude a contract; it requires only a good-faith bargaining effort. Mandatory items of bargaining include (in addition to wages and hours) health insurance, company housing, work loads and work standards, and subcontracting. The last of these was judged by the Board in 1966 to be a mandatory subject of bargaining in a case where a paper products company subcontracted part of its operations to another firm shortly after the expiration of its collective bargaining contract with unionized workers. The Board ruled that the company was obligated to discuss its decision with the union before putting it into effect. Note that the Board compelled discussion and negotiation, not agreement or a change in the company's decision to subcontract work.[19]

Permissible bargaining issues are those which labor and management may discuss and negotiate about at their own discretion, but a refusal to bargain about such subjects by one or the other party is not illegal. Permissible bargaining subjects include price and marketing policies, company finances (though this is a mandatory subject when the employer pleads inability to pay), and re-design of jobs. Prohibited subjects of bargaining typically involve illegal practices which one party tries to force on the other. The Taft-Hartley Act specifies the closed shop in the category of subjects on which agreement may not be sought.

Once labor and management have reached agreement on new terms and conditions of employment, they must reduce these to writing in a formal contract. This collective bargaining agreement is the output of the negotiations process, the underpinning of the union-management relationship. The rights and obligations of both parties are spelled out in the agreement so that neither side is left to rely on the oral statements or promises of the other. A refusal by either side to reduce the terms of an agreement to writing is grounds for alleging a violation of the duty to bargain in good faith—that is, charging the other side with an unfair labor practice.

The foregoing discussion provides only a summary version of the way in which the Wagner Act, somewhat modified by later legislation, changed the status of labor unions in the United States, affecting their relationships with society, with individual workers, and with employers. It offers only a sketch of the role of the NLRB and the way in which the Board's policies shape unionism and industrial relations. Nevertheless, it reflects the basic public policy position which emerged in the 1930s and which continues today, namely, that labor unions have a legitimate role to play in representing the interests of their members and that this role is sufficiently important to the preservation and pursuit of the democratic values of American society to warrant strong legal protection.

Craft versus Industrial Unionism   With the passage of legislation favorable to unionism and collective bargaining, the gauntlet was thrown squarely to the AFL, which, in effect, was challenged to show what it could do under government protection. What few had reckoned on, however, was the fundamental conflict that soon developed within the AFL over the issue of craft versus industrial unionism.

Controlled at the top by presidents of the powerful craft unions and building trades, the AFL leadership insisted that future efforts to organize be carried out on the traditional basis whereby workers possessing specific skills and training were enrolled in the same union, irrespective of the industry in which they worked. This *craft doctrine* required, for example, that machinists, whether employed in steel or rubber or electric appliances or the automobile industry, be organized into the machinists' union.

There was significant opposition to this policy within the AFL among a minority of leaders who advocated the formation of unions on an *industry basis* without regard to craft. With this approach there would be one union for the automobile industry, and all automobile workers, irrespective of craft, skill, or training, would be members of the union for that industry. Believing that modern technology made prior craft distinctions obsolete, advocates of industrial unionism sought to expand the union movement to embrace labor wherever it was employed. They believed that the all-encompassing industry approach was better suited to such a purpose than the more selective craft approach.

Finding no support for this view within the AFL, the proponents of industrial unions, with John L. Lewis of the United Mine Workers of America (UMWA) acting as their spokesman, formed an unofficial committee to promote their objectives. This was declared by the AFL executive committee to be a violation of AFL policy, and the fledgling committee was ordered to disband. The dissidents refused, were then expelled from the AFL, and proceeded to form the Congress of Industrial Organizations (CIO).

Though it never surpassed the AFL in membership, the CIO was an undeniable success. Moreover, its enormous mass appeal and its bold, dramatic actions gave it an electric quality that has yet to resurface within the labor movement. Under Lewis's leadership, expressing a new economic and political power, the CIO generated a virtual uprising of protest among workers across the nation that reached its peak in 1937 but continued into the 1940s. Sit-down strikes, mass picketing, and secondary boycotts were repeatedly conducted, and the key industrial sectors—automobiles, steel, rubber, electrical products —were organized one by one.[20] These successes led the AFL to begin organizing along industrial lines, with the machinists' union and the IBEW being especially prominent in this regard.

Other important changes occurred during this period, including the passage of much social legislation, all of which was supported by the new industrial union leaders, if not by the AFL.[21] What is most important to recognize, however, is that despite the novelty of their objectives, the militancy of their tactics, and their sharp departure from past traditions, the leaders of the CIO never abandoned their primary concern with building unions rather than reform movements. The CIO sought a larger measure of control over the economic system, to be sure, but with preservation of the system's essential characteristics modified only to suit the particular interests of its constituent unions. In

this, it followed the basic philosophy of the AFL, with which it otherwise so
sharply disagreed.

UNION POWER AND THE TAFT-HARTLEY ACT

Whether the American labor movement would have expanded as rapidly as it
did without the influence of World War II is a speculative question to which the
answer can never be fully known. Certainly the increased demand for labor
during the war period and the strong concern of the federal government for uninterrupted industrial production provided a climate favorable to union advances. What is undeniable is that, by the war's end, the labor movement,
which only recently had been struggling to survive, could count among its
members some 15 million workers. What is also undeniable is that the force of
this movement and its notable accomplishments raised in the public mind a
concern about the power of unions and the specter of domination by organized
labor.

An illuminating example of the intent of this new law was its treatment of
This concern was heightened by the large number of strikes that occurred
in the year immediately following the war's end, when a record, which still
stands, was set for the amount of working time lost in one year as a result of
labor-management disputes. The response of political leaders to this popular
concern was to enact, in 1947, the Taft-Hartley Act, which sought to swing the
pendulum of power in labor-management affairs back (but not too far back) in
the direction of employers. In this "rebalancing" process, several power tactics used by unions—the closed shop, secondary boycotts, and picketing to obtain the recognition of employers—were prohibited; a list of unfair labor practices by unions was added to the law; and supervisors were removed from the
legal protection of unions and bargaining, an amendment which subsequently
rendered ineffective all but a few of the supervisors' labor organizations that
had grown up in the early twentieth century.

An illuminating example of the intent of this new law was its treatment of
secondary boycotts. Declared an unfair (unlawful) labor practice, the secondary boycott is a device by which a union engaged in a dispute (e.g., a strike) with
one employer seeks more support for its cause by enlisting the aid of sympathetic
workers employed by a neutral employer. Such aid can take the form of refus-
ing to handle goods emanating from, or destined for, the struck employer, or,
more directly, a work stoppage by employees of the neutral employer. Faced
with either situation, the neutral, "secondary" employer presumably will be
motivated to apply pressure on the "primary" employer to resolve the labor
dispute. Such secondary boycotts had been conducted prior to the Wagner Act,
but they became especially pronounced following its passage. In the 1947
legislation, Congress sought to prohibit this "conscription of neutrals" by
outlawing secondary boycotts as well as the picketing activity undertaken
in conjunction with them. However, picketing designed truthfully to inform customers about a labor dispute with a primary employer was permitted to

continue as long as it did not occur at the business locations of secondary employers or induce employees to refrain from handling struck goods (sometimes referred to as "hot cargo"). Also legislatively prohibited in the Taft-Hartley Act were strikes resulting from disputes between two or more contending unions concerning jurisdiction over work.

The AFL-CIO Merger

The principal unanticipated consequence of the Taft-Hartley Act was a rekindling of interest in reunification of the two major wings of the labor movement for the purpose of combating what were regarded as the emerging forces of reaction.

The leading obstacle to reunification was the "jurisdictional dispute" between competing units within the main labor federations. Such disputes were not drawn strictly on a basis of craft versus industrial organization, for the old-line AFL unions in their rivalry with CIO-based organizations began to pull in larger and more comprehensive groups of employees, regardless of craft. Rather, the conflicts were between rival union organizations, each of which wanted to remain a going entity and continue to represent its constituents. To the credit of the two organizations, several member unions entered into "no-raiding" pacts, appointing an umpire to decide cases which could not be settled between the unions themselves. It was these agreements, together with new leaders at the top of each organization—George Meany at the AFL and Walter Reuther at the CIO—that facilitated the merger of the two federations in 1955.

Also of relevance to the merger were the changing internal policies of the two federations. The CIO, long regarded by AFL stalwarts as Communist-infiltrated (a charge justified in some measure), began to clean house, eventually expelling eleven member unions which in 1950 were found by a specially established committee to in fact be Communist-dominated. For its part, the AFL, viewed by some CIO partisans as racket-ridden and corrupt, expelled in 1953 the International Longshoremen's Association (ILA) for its failure to rid itself of gangster elements. The two organizations thus took steps which helped dispel the stereotypes that each had built of the other.[22]

Complacency, Corruption, and Discrimination The AFL-CIO merger led many within and outside the labor movement to expect a fresh impetus to organize the increasing numbers of unorganized workers. The most optimistic observers assumed that the conflicts between unions were resolved and that all labor organizations could unite in a push to even greater power and influence. This was not to be the case, however. In the 1950s the labor movement did not display the sense of urgency that characterized its earlier years. Indeed, by some accounts the movement had grown sluggish, complacent, and perhaps smug.

Even many who were sympathetic to labor recognized the emerging challenges to unionism.[23] Probably the most important was the changing structure of the economy: employment was expanding most rapidly in sectors which the labor movement historically had had difficulty organizing—white-collar and professional employees and government and service workers. Nor had much headway been made in organizing women, who were entering the labor force in record numbers; employees of small firms; or workers employed in the south.

In the late 1950s, moreover, some unsavory aspects of union behavior came under public examination. Senate subcommittees chaired by such well-know figures as Senators Ives, Kennedy, and Douglas uncovered notable malpractices in the management of union health, welfare, and pension trust funds. In 1957, the Senate Committee on Improper Activities in the Labor or Management Field, chaired by Senator McClellan, reported the first in a series of disclosures concerning corruption within the American labor movement. The committee's final report, issued in 1960, shocked even the top leadership of the AFL-CIO in its revelations of sordid union practices. These included the secret borrowing of funds by union officials, participation of the same officials in fraudulent real estate deals, payment of union officials' personal and family expenses out of members' dues payments, and the participation of a criminal element in the internal affairs of some labor organizations. This well-publicized investigation was a key event leading to the passage, in 1959, of the Landrum-Griffin Act.

Though corrupt practices were confined to relatively few unions, the AFL-CIO could hardly ignore them. It invoked its Ethical Practices Committee, formed at the time of the merger, to conduct hearings at which evidence of the offending unions' behavior was gathered. This formed the basis for the subsequent suspension and expulsion of several unions from the federation, notably the Teamsters and the Bakery and Confectionery Workers' International Union of America. These actions engendered much bitter feeling within the labor movement, and it is questionable whether they effected the reforms which many hoped they would. Nevertheless, they demonstrated the defensive posture which characterized the labor movement at the start of the 1960s.

Still another factor contributing to this posture was the widespread perception that blacks were discriminated against within the labor movement as regards access to well-paying craft jobs and to leadership positions. This was an especially virulent issue for organized labor, whose long-standing objective of taking wages out of competition could hardly sustain internal discrimination against any group of workers, whether based on race or some other factor.

Leaders of CIO unions, which were now included under the federation's umbrella, were particularly concerned with the issue of racial discrimination. Many of them were strongly committed to the goal of racial equality, and some of these organizations had large proportions of black members. Few could deny that some old-line AFL unions, especially the crafts and railroad unions, engaged in discriminatory practices. Thus, along with the other internal rifts and problems it suffered at the start of the 1960s, the labor movement experienced much strife over the issue of racial equality.

ORGANIZING THE PUBLIC SECTOR

At that point in history, then, an observer of the labor scene could hardly have been faulted for being pessimistic about the future of the labor movement.[24] But as had occurred before, the movement displayed at least some resiliency. After 1960, this took the form of attempts to organize public employees at the federal level and especially in state and local governments. The public sector had long been regarded as unorganizable, at least on a large scale, by traditional unionists and outside observers. Furthermore, since they were then, and remain today, totally excluded from the Wagner and Taft-Hartley Acts, public employees were not protected by law in their attempts to organize. Even if such attempts were successful, employers were not required to recognize them either by federal law or by individual state statute. Prior to 1960, only one state, Wisconsin, protected the organization and bargaining activities of public employees. Many states expressly forbade such activity, and most outlawed strikes by public employees. So it was not altogether surprising that fewer than one in ten public workers belonged to a labor organization while the ratio in the nonagricultural private sector was about one in three.

Beginning in the early 1960s, however, the environment of labor relations in the public sector began to change in a direction favorable to unionization. In 1962, relying on the recommendations of a specially appointed panel headed by Arthur Goldberg, former general counsel to the United Steelworkers of America (USA) and later an associate justice of the U.S. Supreme Court, President John F. Kennedy issued Executive Order No. 10988, which proclaimed the right of federal employees to organize and bargain and which directed each federal agency to establish procedures for resolving questions of representation.[25] These provisions were strengthened in Executive Order No. 11491, which was issued by President Nixon in 1969 and which, with slight modifications, remains in effect today. Under it, federal employees may not strike or negotiate a "union-shop" clause (a provision requiring new employees to become members of the union after 30, 60, or 90 days). However, it provides substitute procedures for resolving impasses in bargaining, and it bars federal agencies from engaging in the kinds of unfair practices prohibited in private industry by the Taft-Hartley Act.

Not only did Kennedy's Executive order spur unionization and bargaining in the federal sector, but it also spilled over to affect labor-management relations in state and local government, where employment was growing very rapidly, especially in the areas of education, welfare, health, and hospitalization. Employees in these levels of government began actively to agitate for organization and bargaining rights, pointing to the treatment of workers at the federal level and taking advantage of the rapidly increasing demand for labor in the public sector. They also pressed the argument that their employment position was not so different from that of their counterparts in the private sector as to warrant their complete exclusion from unionism and bargaining rights. Often public workers contended that such exclusion enabled government employers to compensate them at levels well below those prevailing in industry. This position received indirect support, again at the federal level, when Congress enacted the Federal Salary Reform Act of 1962, requiring the pay of federal employees to be based on rates prevailing in industry, for which periodic wage surveys would be required. This law was reaffirmed and extended in several respects in the Federal Pay Comparability Act of 1970.[26]

Growing Pains and Legal Treatment

The challenge of unionism among public employees has been felt not only by government employers and public policy makers but also by organizations of government workers that consider themselves professional rather than union-oriented. The National Education Association (NEA) is the leading example of such an organization, but there are others which seek to achieve their objectives through lobbying activity or close cooperation with civil service and management groups. Most of these organizations previously eschewed collective bargaining, were not affiliated with the AFL-CIO, and disavowed (if they were not silent about) the strike. But such a posture has become increasingly difficult to maintain in the face of changes in employees' attitudes and particularly the challenge of competing organizations—in education, specifically, the American Federation of Teachers (AFT). The professional organizations must either adapt to new circumstances or watch their memberships decline and their survival be threatened. The bulk of them have abandoned their opposition to bargaining and some forms of militant activity, even as they seek to preserve, if only philosophically, the distinction between professionalism and unionism.

As to public policy for government employees, during the 1960s and early 1970s individual states and localities enacted legislation, and executives issued directives, that permitted or actively supported unionism and collective bargaining. The so-called "Taylor law" (named after George W. Taylor, who headed a panel that recommended its adoption) was enacted by the New York State Legislature in 1967 and was among the earliest and most important examples of such legislation. It encouraged unionization, protected the bargaining rights of public workers, and established an administrative agency to oversee the act. Many other states followed suit, with the result that, by the mid-1970s, more than 80 percent of them regulated public-sector labor relations within their borders, and about half required government employers to recognize and bargain with their organized employees.[27]

Those states (e.g., California) which do not require full-blown collective bargaining in the public sector usually mandate some form of "meet-and-confer" procedure in which employers may consult with organized workers and may conclude collective agreements, but in which they retain final decision-making authority over terms and conditions of employment. Legislatures in a few states, located primarily in the south, continued to oppose unionization and bargaining rights for public employees, but the scene is changing rapidly there as well.

Consequently, in the absence of a comprehensive national policy for labor-management relations in the public sector, there has emerged a panoply of statutes, directives, frameworks, and practices among various levels of government. Even in the jurisdictions that protect public workers' organization and bargaining rights, diversity is the order of the day. On the question of the strike, for example, most of these jurisdictions continue to outlaw it, a few recently have sanctioned selective work stoppages by public employees, and many have experimented with various forms of mediation, factfinding, and arbitration to resolve impasses in negotiations.

Nevertheless, the trend is unmistakenly toward the institutionalization of unionism and bargaining in the American public sector. As early as 1970, the federal government was more than half organized. Two years later, the incidence of organization among full-time employees of state and local government exceeded 50 percent, with the bulk of them enrolled in employee associations. Such associations are composed of white-collar and professional employees who, while not necessarily regarding themselves as unionists, nevertheless pay dues to, and are represented by, their organizations in negotiations with employers. Thus, by about 1975, the composition of American unionism had changed dramatically to the point where the public sector, which only recently had been a weak sister as far as the labor movement was concerned, was approximately twice as heavily organized as the private sector. Underlying this pattern of labor organization was the very rapid growth of public employment during the years 1950–1975, compared with slower growth in the private sector, most notably in traditional areas of union strength. By 1976, almost one-quarter of all union and association members enrolled in American labor organizations worked for one or another level of government.[28] In Chapter 6, we shall treat in detail collective bargaining activity in the United States' heavily organized public sector.

OTHER DEVELOPMENTS AND NEW INITIATIVES

In the area of health care and hospitalization, labor organizations made significant inroads during the 1960s and 1970s. At first, these were mainly in public hospitals, principally at the levels of the federal government and local governments. Later, they extended to private, nonprofit hospitals which came under coverage of the Taft-Hartley Act as a result of a 1974 amendment. (As originally adopted in 1947, the Taft-Hartley Act applied only to employees of proprietary hospitals.) The upshot of all this activity was that substantial proportions of attendants, nurses, clerical workers, and other employees in the health field now bargain collectively with employers in proprietary, nonprofit and public hospitals.

Especially interesting in the health field have been labor disputes involving hospital interns and residents. Well organized in areas such as New York, Los Angeles, and Chicago, they achieved some early successes in negotiating with their employers, but usually only after conducting major work stoppages. The novelty of these disputes placed interns and residents as well as hospital bargaining generally in the forefront of public attention during the mid-1970s. In 1976, the NLRB ruled that interns and residents are students, not workers, and are not at hospitals "for the purpose of earning a living," but rather "to pursue the graduate medical education that is a requirement of the practice of medicine."[29] However, in early 1979, the United States appeals court for the District of Columbia overturned the NLRB's ruling, thus upholding the unionism and bargaining rights of interns and residents. Consequently, strikes by interns and residents are, at present, protected by the federal labor laws. It is problematic, however, whether even formal bans on strikes would be a formidable obstacle to the organization and bargaining goals of professionals who occupy a relatively strategic position within the system of technology by which hospital services are "produced."

In 1975, the state of California enacted the Agricultural Relations Act, which sought to bring some order to an industry with a history of chaotic labor relations. It is important to recognize that the entire agricultural sector is excluded from federal labor law, leaving individual states free to legislate in this area. Most of them have been unsympathetic to providing full unionism and bargaining rights to agricultural workers. The underlying reality, however, is that such workers, most of whom are employed on a seasonal, casual basis and who are predominently foreign-born and foreign-bred, have long been difficult to organize. The United Farm Workers of America (UFWA), led by Ceser Chavez, achieved a rare success in organizing California farm workers and in sponsoring nationwide consumer boycotts which led in the late 1960s and early 1970s to the negotiation of written labor agreements. Some of these contracts were not renewed, however, as the Teamsters subsequently challenged the UFWA for representation of workers in California agriculture, an event which brought about much consternation within the house of labor.[30] The key point for readers to keep in mind, however, is that the procedures contained in the Taft-Hartley Act for regulating labor relations in the private sector still do not apply to the American agricultural industry.

Nor does the Taft-Hartley Act cover the military, in which some rumblings of unionization have been heard. It may seem ludicrous, even unpatriotic, to some that military organizations, which rely on the discipline of command and unswerving allegiance to authority, should even entertain the notion of bargaining collectively with unionized soldiers. But this is in fact what occurs in some other nations—Norway, Denmark, and West Germany, for example—and proposals for organizing the American armed forces are being heard in several quarters. True, little actual headway has been made on this score; most labor leaders remain opposed to organizing the military, and, in 1978, Congress passed a law prohibiting unionism and bargaining in the United States armed forces. Still, the possibility of unionism in this sector should not be dismissed out of hand.[31] After all, it was only recently that most observers saw little prospect for the wide-scale organization of civilian government employees.

The Ninety-fifth Congress, convened in 1978, grappled with several proposals for the reform of labor law. Some of these were initiated by the Carter administration, while others were offered by employer and union lobbyists.

For its part, the administration proposed a series of measures—expansion of the NLRB from five to seven members, increases in penalties for employers who refuse to recognize and bargain with certified labor organizations, and reduction in the length of time required to conduct elections to determine union representation—whose purpose was to reduce the backlog of cases confronting the NLRB and to strengthen compliance with the Taft-Hartley Act. Congress failed to enact any of these proposals.

Organized labor continues to pursue repeal of Section 14(b) of the act, a provision which allows states to legislate in the area of union security. Some twenty states have forbidden various forms of union security—for example, the union shop, the agency shop, maintenance of membership agreements, and even the dues checkoff—which are otherwise allowable under federal law. On the other side of this issue, employers continue to push for amended legislation that supports the "right to work." What employers mean by this term is a ban on any form of compulsory unionism rather than any legal entitlement to a job. This issue, long a subject of contention between labor and management, remains one of several topics that are being debated by the parties and by government in their continuing efforts to shape American labor relations. The debate reflects the fact that the question central to the legal regulation of labor-management relations—"What is the appropriate relationship of the organized group to society at large and to the employer?"—has no final answer.

Summarizing the Development of Labor

The foregoing review of the American labor movement and of industrial relations has highlighted several themes. First, as it has evolved in the United States, the labor organization is an institution that acts as an agent on behalf of its members. The collective wishes of its constituents are what guide the organization's leaders in the formulation and pursuit of bargaining objectives in negotiations with employers. Second, the orientation of the labor movement is toward the bread-and-butter issues of wages and working conditions. The dominance of "business unionism" emerged only after the failure of repeated efforts to mount broadly based, reform-minded organizations. The philosophy of business unionism continues to characterize the labor movement even as the incidence of organization shifts toward white-collar, professional, and public employees and away from blue-collar, manual workers employed predominantly in manufacturing. Third, the legal regulation of labor-management relations reflects both the pragmatism and the political philosophy which are characteristic of American society. This is clearly evident in the principles of exclusive representation and elections to determine union representation.

With this overview as background, we turn in Part Two of this chapter to a more detailed examination of contemporary labor organizations in the United States. Of special interest are differences in the composition of union membership by occupation, industry, sex, and race. Also to be explored are data pertaining to unionization in developed and developing nations, which provide some perspective on the American experience.

PART TWO: Contemporary Patterns of Labor Organization

THE EXTENT OF UNIONISM[32]

In 1976, the last year for which complete data are available, 24.0 million persons belonged to American unions and employee associations. Of these, some 1.6 million were employed outside the United States, mostly in Canada. Seven times as many workers are members of labor unions as of employee associations, 21.0 versus 3.0 million, but the latter group has grown at a much higher rate than the former in recent years. Among all members in 1976, 16.6 million were in labor organizations affiliated with the AFL-CIO. This means that about 6 million organized workers, or more than one-quarter of the total, are enrolled in unaffiliated labor organizations.[33]

While, in absolute terms, membership in American labor organizations is near a record high level, a different picture emerges when trends in membership as a proportion of the labor force are considered. Figure 3-1 shows that whether expressed as a proportion of the total or the nonagricultural work force (agriculture often is excluded from such calculations on the ground that its high incidence of self-employment renders unionization inapplicable), union membership has declined steadily since the mid-1950s. Note that we refer here strictly to union membership, lines 2 and 4 of Figure 3-1, excluding for the moment employee associations. In 1976, just over 20 percent of the total work force was enrolled in labor unions, down from almost 26 percent two decades earlier; fewer than one-quarter of nonagricultural employees belonged to labor unions in 1976, which represented a drop of some 11 percentage points since the mid-1950s.

The organization of more than one-fifth of the nation's "organizable" employees into labor unions may be regarded as a remarkable development, since, as is evident from Figure 3-1, fewer than one in twelve was a unionist as recently as 1930. Alternatively, the result may be considered surprisingly modest in view of the substantial gains in membership achieved by organized labor by the mid-century mark and also in view of the important agency function which unions perform for their members.

Further supporting the second of these interpretations are the comparative data in Table 3-1 showing the incidence of labor organization in the nonagricultural work forces of twenty developed nations. Among the countries listed in Table 3-1, the United States is close to the bottom of the list in terms of the proportion of workers who are union members; its rate is far below the rates of Sweden (80 percent), Austria (67 percent), Denmark (65 percent), and Norway (60 percent). Many of these nations differ from the United States in several basic respects, notably size, economic organization, homogeneity of population, and political structure, but that does not obviate the conclusion that the rate of membership in labor unions in the United States is relatively low compared with rates in other industrialized countries.

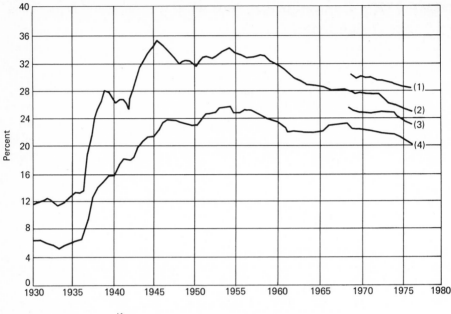

Key:
(1) = Employees who are members of unions or associations
      as a percentage of the nonagricultural labor force
(2) = Employees who are members of unions as a percentage
      of the nonagricultural labor force
(3) = Employees who are members of unions or associations
      as a percentage of the total labor force
(4) = Employees who are members of unions as a percentage
      of the total labor force

Figure 3-1 Union and association membership in the labor force, 1930–1976. (*Sources: U.S. Bureau of Labor Statistics,* Directory of National Unions and Employee Associations, 1975, *bull. no. 1937, U.S. Government Printing Office, Washington, D.C., 1977, p. 15; and U.S. Bureau of Labor Statistics, "Labor Union and Employee Association Membership—1976," NEWS, U.S. Department of Labor, Washington, D.C., September 1977, pp. 2, 5.*)

However, this conclusion requires some qualification. First, tabulations of union membership exclude those who belong to employee associations, which, as noted earlier, have grown rapidly in the United States in recent years. Data on membership in employee associations in the United States have been systematically collected only since 1968, but when added to union membership data, they show that the incidence of labor organization in this country exceeded 23 and 28 percent of the total and nonagricultural labor force, respectively, in 1976 (see lines 3 and 1 of Figure 3-1).

Second, the data which provide the basis for Figure 3-1 exclude members of single-firm and local unaffiliated unions, as well as members of organizations that negotiate agreements that either are not reduced to writing or are not reported to federal data-collection agencies. The magnitude of these exclusions is, of course, unknown, though the Bureau of Labor Statistics estimated, in

Table 3-1   Organized Labor as a Percent of the Nonagricultural Labor Force for Twenty Developed Nations, 1976
(Number in Thousands)

Country	Population	Labor force	Organized labor (percent of labor force)
Argentina	25,887	10,000	25
Australia	13,808	4,760	44
Austria	7,524	2,657	67[1]
Belgium	9,826	4,000	48
Brazil	111,666	30,000	50[2]
Canada	23,314	10,000	27
Chile	10,543	3,300	25
Denmark	5,079	2,500	65
Finland	4,738	2,200	60
France	53,096	22,100	17[3]
German Democratic Republic	16,778	8,200	88
Germany, Federal Republic of	61,590	26,700	31[4]
Italy	56,410	19,549	20
Netherlands	13,868	4,700	33
Norway	4,037	1,700	60
Spain	36,161	13,300	90[5]
Sweden	8,326	4,000	80
Switzerland	6,415	3,000[5]	20
United Kingdom	56,043	25,600	40
United States	215,966	92,000	23

[1] Rough estimate.
[2] Although 50 percent of the work force is organized, only 1.5 million members pay dues.
[3] This is an approximation; 23.4 percent of the salaried work force is organized.
[4] Thirty-one percent of the entire labor force is organized; 37.5 percent of the wage and salary workers are organized.
[5] Ninety percent of the labor force is in compulsory government-controlled syndicates.
Note: Population estimates are projections to January 1977.
Source: Adapted from U.S. Central Intelligence Agency, *National Basic Intelligence Factbook,* January 1977, pp. 10, 24, 67, 75, 189.

1974, that local unaffiliated and single-firms unions had about 475,000 members.[34] This means, for example, that a local clerical workers' union that concludes an agreement with a Los Angeles law firm, or a local police union that bargains a contract with a small New Jersey town, or an association of professional architects that "negotiates" an unwritten agreement with a suburban Chicago architectural firm is not included in the federal government's tabulations of membership in labor organizations.

Finally, the data do not fully reflect union representation under collective bargaining or, especially, the influence of unionism on terms and conditions of employment in the economy. Recall that the law and structure of American industrial relations are such that labor organizations are required to represent nonmembers who are in certified bargaining units and that nonmembers are bound by the terms of any collective agreement negotiated. Thus data on membership in unions and associations understate the true extent to which workers are represented by labor organization in the American work force. Moreover, the influence of unions on working conditions in the United States extends even further, since many nonunion employers grant to their workers terms and conditions of employment similar to those negotiated under collective bargaining agreements in the hope of meeting employees' expectations or forestalling unionization.

Nevertheless, it would be straining credulity to suggest that the American labor movement is prospering. Labor organization has not kept pace with the growth of the labor force, despite the recent surge of membership in the public and health sectors. There remain important areas of the economy, the country, and the labor sector—wholesale and retail trade, finance insurance and real estate, services, small firms, employers located in the south, female and professional workers—in which unions have made little or no headway. This may change quickly, in the way that the organization of government employees advanced so rapidly in recent years. But to penetrate and expand membership in these resistant sectors and groups would appear to require new approaches, new strategies, and tactics, and perhaps an altered image on the part of organized labor. And unionists can take little solace in the most recent data, which show that the number of union and association members declined, both absolutely and proportionately, between 1974 and 1976, following an apparent turnabout of the downward trends in 1973 and 1974.[35]

Organization by Industry

Table 3-2 shows that, roughly speaking, membership in unions and associations is distributed almost evenly between the manufacturing and nonmanufacturing sectors of private industry, but very unevenly within each of these categories. Fully 21 percent of all organized workers are in construction and transportation, while fewer than 5 percent are in the tobacco, textile, lumber, furniture, chemical, petroleum, and leather industries combined. The services and trade sectors, two of the most rapidly growing in the economy, are far more thinly organized than manufacturing or some other nonmanufacturing industries. More than 22 percent of members of unions and associations worked for government in 1974, with the majority of them employed in local government. By 1976 the proportion had risen to 24 percent. This is the highest proportion ever recorded for the public sector, where the incidence of labor organization rose by about two-thirds just between 1968 and 1976. Table 3-2 demonstrates the importance of the employee association as a form of labor organization for government employees—and its unimportance to the manufacturing and nonmanufacturing sectors. These associations enrolled almost half of all organized workers in the public sector in the mid-1970s (and one out of every eight organized workers in the economy), compared with only 1 percent of organized employees in the private sector (none in manufacturing). If membership in associations had been excluded from these data, as it was until the late 1960s, the proportion of organized workers employed in the public sector would have been 13.6 percent (instead of 24.3 percent) in 1976.

Table 3-2 can be misleading, however, for there may be fewer union members in a well-organized but small industry, such as mining, than in a weakly organized but large industry, such as retailing. Therefore, Table 3-3 presents a measure of the strength of labor organizations that attempts to correct for differences in size of industry. Observe that industries such as mining, petroleum, and tobacco now appear relatively well organized, though, as shown in Table 3-2, the incidence of organization is greatest in transportation and construction. Because these are only rough estimates and because they *exclude* membership in associations, some industries may be misclassified in Table 3-3. That is clearly the case with local government, which is about 50 percent organized. The service and trade sectors appear more weakly organized as a proportion of industry employment (Table 3-3) than as a proportion of total union membership (Table 3-2).

A similar problem arises in measuring the geographic pattern of membership in labor organizations. In 1974, over one-half of all members of unions and associations were concentrated in just six states—New York, California, Pennsylvania, Illinois, Ohio, and Michigan—but these are obviously the states which rank at or near the top in population and size of labor force. When union membership is considered as a percentage of nonagricultural employment, the most strongly organized states in 1974 were Michigan, Wisconsin, New York, Pennsylvania, Washington, and Hawaii. By the same measure, organization was weakest in North Carolina, South Carolina, South Dakota, Mississippi, Florida, and Texas. To be sure, unions are not uniformly weak in the south. In the automobile, rubber, and steel industries, for example, the southern plants of national corporations are usually organized, as is also true of longshoring in most of that region's ports, construction in some of its large cities, and public employment in a few locations. But in several industries of particular importance in the south—textiles, clothing, lumber, and furniture—unions are markedly weaker in that region than elsewhere in the country.

Another insight into industrial patterns of labor organization is provided by Table 3-4. It shows the dispersion (or lack of concentration) of membership in unions and associations in 1974. In order to expand membership, individual labor organizations have extended their organizing activities beyond traditional industrial and occupational boundaries. The data reveal that 58 percent of the labor organizations in the private sector had between 80 and 100 percent of their membership in a single industry. This compares with 60 percent in 1970, 67 percent in 1964, and 73 percent in 1958. Clearly, the membership of American labor organizations is, in general, becoming more dispersed across industries. The dispersion is greatest in the manufacturing sector, where labor organizations facing stable or declining industries have had to search elsewhere for members and where unionism has followed the corporate trend toward conglomeration.

Unions in the chemical industry provide a leading example of dispersion of

Table 3-2 Distribution of Membership of National Unions and Employee Associations by Industry Group and Affiliation, 1974

Industry group	Total unions and associations			Unions						Associations		
				AFL-CIO			Unaffiliated					
	Number[2]	Members[1] (thousands)	Per cent	Number[2]	Members[1] (thousands)	Per cent	Number[2]	Members[1] (thousands)	Per cent	Number[2]	Members[1] (thousands)	Per cent
Total[3]	212	24,194	100.0	111	16,879	100.0	64	4,705	100.0	37	2,610	100.0
Manufacturing	98	9,144	37.8	70	6,746	40.0	28	2,398	51.0			
Ordance and accessories	14	102	0.4	7	91	0.5	7	11	0.2			
Food and kindred products (including beverages)	26	908	3.8	17	570	3.4	9	338	7.2			
Tobacco manufactures	6	43	0.2	4	42	0.2	2	1	[4]			
Textile mill products	11	169	0.7	6	158	0.9	5	11	0.2			
Apparel and other finished products made from fabrics and similar materials	14	750	3.1	11	734	4.3	3	16	0.3			
Lumber and wood products, except furniture	18	261	1.1	10	254	1.5	8	7	0.1			
Furniture and fixtures	13	220	0.9	8	190	1.1	5	29	0.6			
Paper and allied products	21	366	1.5	16	324	1.9	5	41	0.9			
Printing, publishing, and allied industries	19	359	1.5	13	339	2.0	6	20	0.4			
Chemicals and allied products	22	268	1.1	17	232	1.4	5	36	0.8			
Petroleum refining and related industries	10	82	0.3	7	71	0.4	3	11	0.2			
Rubber and miscellaneous plastics products	24	275	1.1	17	248	1.5	7	27	0.6			
Leather and leather products	16	128	0.5	13	125	0.7	3	4	0.1			
Stone, clay, glass, and concrete products	17	325	1.3	14	281	1.7	3	43	0.9			
Primary metals industries	14	817	3.4	11	691	4.1	3	126	2.7			

Industry	No.	Members	%	No.	Members	%	No.	Members	%	No.	Members	%
Fabricated metal products, except ordnance, machinery, and transportation equipment	28	726	3.0	19	516	3.1	9	210	4.5			
Machinery, except electrical	16	726	3.0	11	425	2.5	5	302	6.4			
Electrical machinery, equipment, and supplies	14	1,074	4.4	10	820	4.9	4	254	5.4			
Transportation equipment	16	1,144	4.7	10	319	1.9	6	825	17.5			
Professional, scientific, and controlling instruments	12	65	0.3	7	37	0.2	5	28	0.6			
Miscellaneous manufacturing industries	40	338	1.4	30	282	1.7	10	56	1.2			
Nonmanufacturing	104	9,705	40.1	73	7,687	45.5	28	1,833	39.0	3	185	7.1
Mining and quarrying (including crude petroleum and natural gas production)	17	372	1.5	10	141	0.8	7	231	4.9			
Contract construction (building and special trade)	28	2,738	11.3	21	2,634	15.6	7	103	2.2			
Transportation	37	2,343	9.7	28	1,297	7.7	9	1,046	22.2			
Telephone and telegraph	11	672	2.8	9	606	3.6	2	55	1.4			
Electric, gas, and sanitary services (including water)	11	243	1.0	9	234	1.4	2	8	0.2			
Wholesale and retail trade	22	1,329	5.5	13	1,066	6.3	9	263	5.6			
Finance, insurance, and real estate	5	32	0.1	4	31	0.2	1	1	[4]			
Service industries	48	1,850	7.6	27	1,571	9.3	18	94	2.0	3	185	7.1
Agriculture and fishing	9	36	0.1	5	18	0.1	4	18	0.4			
Nonmanufacturing (classification not available)	7	91	0.4	6	88	0.5	1	3	0.1			
Government	101	5,345	22.1	39	2,447	14.5	25	474	10.1	37	2,425	93.0
Federal	53	1,433	5.9	26	955	5.7	23	437	9.3	4	42	1.6
State	52	1,035	4.3	13	438	2.6	3	6	0.1	36	592	22.7
Local	37	2,876	11.9	18	1,054	6.2	2	31	0.7	17	1,791	68.6

[1] Number of members computed by applying reported percentage figures to total membership, including membership outside the United States.

[2] These columns are nonadditive; many organizations have membership in more than one industry group.

[3] One hundred and forty-three unions reported an estimated distribution by industry; for thirty-two unions, the bureau estimated industrial composition. Estimates were also made for five of the thirty-seven employee associations. Three employee associations have members not in government. The Bureau believed those to be in service industries.

[4] Less than 0.05 percent.

Note: Because of rounding, sums of individual items may not equal totals.

Source: Adapted from U.S. Bureau of Labor Statistics, Directory of National Unions and Employee Associations, 1975, Bulletin 1937, 1977, p. 71.

**Table 3-3   Extent of Union Organization
by Major Industry Classification, 1974**
(In Percentage Categories)

75 percent and over
1   Ordnance
2   Transportation
3   Transportation equipment
4   Contract construction

50 percent to less than 75 percent

5   Electrical machinery
6   Food and kindred products
7   Primary metals
8   Mining
9   Telephone and telegraph
10   Paper
11   Petroleum
12   Tobacco manufactures
13   Apparel
14   Fabricated metals
15   Manufacturing
16   Stone, clay, and glass products
17   Federal government

25 percent to less than 50 percent

18   Printing and publishing
19   Leather
20   Rubber
21   Furniture
22   Machinery
23   Lumber
24   Chemicals
25   Electric and gas utilities

Less than 25 percent

26   Nonmanufacturing
27   Government
28   Instruments
29   Textile mill products
30   State government
31   Local government
32   Service
33   Trade
34   Agricultural and fishing
35   Finance

Source: Adapted from U.S. Bureau of Labor Statistics,
Directory of National Unions and Employee Associations, 1975
Bulletin 1937, 1977, pp. 70–71.

membership: in 1974, none among twenty-two labor organizations reported more than 80 percent of its members in that industry, while all but two had less than 20 percent of their membership in that field. Only one of ten petroleum unions had 80 percent of its membership in that particular industry. At the other end of the spectrum, twenty of thirty-seven unions had 80 percent or more of their members in the transportation industry, seventeen of forty-five labor organizations had 80 percent or more of their members in services, and twenty-two of forty-eight unions had 80 percent or more of their members in the federal government. This is but one indicator of the diversity that characterizes American labor organizations along several dimensions.

Organization by Occupation

The white-collar membership of national unions and employee associations reached 6.4 million employees, or 27 percent of the total, in 1976 (Table 3-5). The gain of almost 600,000 white-collar members between 1974 and 1976 was the second largest for a 2-year period, but it did not offset the overall decline in the incidence of American labor organization. White-collar membership in employee associations grew to 2.7 million in 1976, and these workers constituted more than 80 percent of all association members.

Care must be exercised in interpreting the type of data contained in Table 3-5. The category "white-collar" is not very precise, and the term itself is not defined uniformly by labor organizations that report data on membership. Additionally, because many such organizations do not maintain information on occupations, what they often provide is "estimated" data. In some cases, the Bureau of Labor Statistics will form its own estimates of the white-collar membership of labor organizations. In 1974, for example, it did so for thirty-seven unions and eleven employee associations. Further, the Bureau estimated the number of white-collar workers who were members of unaffiliated local and single-employer unions to be 154,800; this figure, added to the data in Table 3-5, yields a total membership in this category of more than 6 million in 1974. Thus, available data are best regarded as a close approximation of the number of white-collar workers who are members of labor organizations rather than as an exact count of them.

Table 3-6 provides information about the distribution of these white-collar members by occupation. More than 60 percent (3.5 million) are professional and technical workers, about one-quarter (1.4 million) are clerical employees, and the remainder (900,000) are salespersons. Just under four-fifths of the professionals and technicians belong to labor organizations whose membership is at least 90 percent white-collar. In other words, when they join a labor union or, more likely, an employee association, professional and technical workers are strongly inclined to select an organization that represents only their own kind. Relatively few of them prefer to enroll in labor organizations of "mixed" membership, occupationally speaking. This is consistent with the observation that professionals view themselves as being different from blue-collar, manual workers and as having little reason to join a "labor" union.

Table 3-4 Distribution of Membership of National Unions and Employee Associations by Membership in Industry Groups, 1974

Industry group	Total			Percent of membership in industry group									
	Number[1]	Members		Under 20 percent		20 and under 40 percent		40 and under 60 percent		60 and under 80 percent		80–100 percent	
		Number (thousands)	Percent	Number of organizations[1]	Number of members (thousands)	Number of organizations[1]	Number of members (thousands)	Number of organizations[1]	Number of members (thousands)	Number of organizations[1]	Number of members (thousands)	Number of organizations[1]	Number of members (thousands)
Unions:													
Manufacturing	98	9,144	42.4	16	182	6	917	6	610	3	444	67	6,991
Ordnance and accessories	14	102	0.5	10	98	1				2	3	1	
Food and kindred products (including beverages)	26	908	4.2	18	360	2	83	1	278			5	187
Tobacco manufactures	6	43	0.2	5	8							1	34
Textile mill products	11	169	0.8	6	12						107	4	50
Apparel and other finished products made from fabrics and similar materials	14	750	3.5	9	40	1	6			1	266	3	438
Lumber and wood products, except furniture	18	261	1.2	17	153							1	108
Furniture and fixtures	13	220	1.0	10	59							3	161
Paper and allied products	21	366	1.7	19	59							2	306
Printing, publishing, and allied industries	19	359	1.7	11	28					1	90	7	241
Chemicals and allied products	22	268	1.2	20	147	1	62			1	60		
Petroleum refining and related industries	10	82	0.4	8	22	1	57					1	3
Rubber and miscellaneous plastics products	24	275	1.3	21	77	2	11					1	188
Leather and leather products	16	128	0.6	11	24							5	104
Stone, clay, glass, and concrete products	17	325	1.5	9	126					3	69	5	130
Primary metals industries	14	817	3.8	10	62			2	597	2	158		
Fabricated metal products, except ordnance, machinery, and transportation equipment	28	726	3.4	16	376	5	157	4	43	1	6	2	145

Machinery, except electrical	16	726	3.4	11	483	4	235			1	8		
Electrical machinery, equipment and supplies	14	1074	5.0	9	265	1	19	2	455	2	335	1	25
Transportation equipment	16	1144	5.3	10	262	3	58	2	799	2			
Professional, scientific, and controlling instruments	12	65	0.3	11	65	1							
Miscellaneous manufacturing industries	40	338	1.6	31	257	4	44	2	24	1	7	2	7
Nonmanufacturing	101	9520	44.1	20	457	3	311	7	695	7	3044	64	5011
Mining and quarrying (including crude petroleum and natural gas production)	17	372	1.7	15	150							2	222
Contract construction (building and special trade)	28	2738	12.7	10	296	1	30	2	14	6	1524	9	874
Transportation	37	2343	10.9	11	78	3	31	2	998	1	22	20	1214
Telephone and telegraph	11	672	3.1	7	109							4	563
Electric, gas, and sanitary services (including water)	11	243	1.1	10	238			1				1	5
Wholesale and retail trade	22	1329	6.2	15	369	2	272	1	25	1		3	663
Finance, insurance, and real estate	5	32	0.1	4	10							1	22
Service industries	45	1665	7.7	24	223	2	35	1		1	358	17	1049
Agriculture and fishing	9	36	0.2	7	23	1	1					1	12
Nonmanufacturing (classification not available)	7	91	0.4	6	81	1	10						
Government	64	2920	13.5	34	313	2	190	2	23		65	26	2394
Federal	48	1392	6.4	25	257		389	1	13	1		22	1056
State	16	444	2.1	14	55	2	34				408		
Local	21	1085	5.0	15	32	2				1		2	610
Associations:													
Nonmanufacturing[2]	3	185	7.1	1	1		49	1	36	1	147		2340
Government	37	2425	92.9			1		1	36			35	
Federal	4	42	1.6	4	42		33						
State	36	592	22.7	3	31	1		3	156	2	24	27	347
Local	17	1791	68.6	8	1473	4	17	2	90	2	122	1	89

[1] These columns are nonadditive; many organizations have membership in more than one industry group.

[2] All members believed to be employed in service industries.

Source: Adapted from U.S. Bureau of Labor Statistics, *Directory of National Unions and Employee Associations, 1975,* Bulletin 1937, 1977, p. 72.

**Table 3-5   White-Collar Membership of National Unions
and Employee Associations, Selected Years, 1957–1976**

Year	Number of white-collar members (thousands)	Percent of total membership
Unions and associations		
1970	4917	21.8
1972	5202	22.6
1974	5881	24.3
1976	6460	26.9
Unions		
1956	2463	13.6
1958	2184	12.2
1960	2192	12.2
1962	2285	13.0
1964	2585	14.4
1966	2810	14.7
1968	3176	15.7
1970	3353	16.2
1972	3434	16.5
1974	3762	17.4
1976	3857	18.4

Sources: Adapted from U.S. Bureau of Labor Statistics, *Directory of National Unions and Employee Associations, 1975,* Bulletin 1937, 1977, p, 67; and U.S. Bureau of Labor Statistics, "Labor Union and Employee Association Membership—1976," *NEWS,* September 1977, p. 4.

Nevertheless, if membership of white-collar workers in unions and employee associations has grown rapidly in recent years, it still represents only a small proportion of all workers in that category. In 1976, the 6.4 million organized white-collar workers represented about 14 percent of all those actually employed in this broad occupational grouping. The "penetration rate" was roughly 28 percent for professionals and technicians, 9.5 percent for clerical workers, and 16 percent for salespersons. In contrast, blue-collar workers in the United States were about 60 percent organized in 1976, the proportion exceeding 90 percent in some occupational specialities within that broad category.

Labor Organization among Women[36]

The 6 million women enrolled in unions and employee associations in 1976 constituted one-quarter of the total membership of American labor organizations, or about the same proportion as in 1972 (Table 3-7). As a proportion of union membership (excluding associations), women increased their representation from one-sixth to one-fifth over the 22-year span between 1954 and 1976, but there was a proportionate decline in the 1970s. The 1.8 million female members

Table 3-6 Distribution of White-Collar Membership by Proportion in Occupational Groups, 1974[1]

Percent of membership in white-collar work	Professional and technical			Clerical			Sales		
	Number of organizations	Membership (thousands)	Percent of all professional and technical membership	Number of organizations	Membership (thousands)	Percent of all clerical membership	Number of organizations	Membership (thousands)	Percent of all sales membership
Unions and associations									
Total	129	3548	100.0	99	1462	100.0	33	872	100.0
Less than 10 percent	46	161	4.5	45	335	22.9	23	64	7.4
10 and under 30	22	350	9.9	25	411	28.1	5	122	14.0
30 and under 50	16	78	2.2	19	122	8.4			
60 and under 70	5	92	2.6	5	59	4.1			
70 and under 90	3	62	1.8	2	205	14.0	1	19	2.1
90 percent and over	37	2804	79.0	3	329	22.5	4	667	76.5
Unions									
Total	95	1600	100.0	67	1290	100.0	33	872	100.0
Less than 10 percent	43	154	9.6	44	335	26.0	23	64	7.4
10 and under 30	11	289	18.1	12	331	25.6	5	122	14.0
30 and under 50	2	25	1.5	5	58	4.5			
50 and under 70	3	30	1.9	2	39	3.0			
70 and under 90	3	62	3.9	1	199	15.4	1	19	2.1
90 percent and over	33	1039	65.0	3	329	25.5	4	667	76.5

[1] Based on reports of labor unions and employee associations and estimates of the Bureau of Labor Statistics when available. For professional and technical occupations, reports and estimates for fifty-four AFL-CIO unions yielded 1,416,585 members; for forty-one unaffiliated unions, 183,320; and for thirty-four associations, 1,947,969. For clerical occupations, reports and estimates for forty-six AFL-CIO unions yielded 948,386 members; for twenty-one unaffiliated unions, 342,106; and for thirty-two associations, 171,068. For sales occupations, reports and estimates for twenty-five AFL-CIO unions yielded 828,411 members; for eight unaffiliated unions, 43,267.

Note: Because of rounding, sums of individual items may not equal totals.
Source: Adapted from U.S. Bureau of Labor Statistics, Directory of National Unions and Employee Associations, 1975, Bulletin 1937, 1977, p. 68.

Table 3-7 Membership of Women in National Unions and Employee Associations, Selected Years, 1954–1976

Year	Number of women members (thousands)	Percent of total membership
Unions and associations		
1970	5398	23.9
1972	5736	24.9
1974	6038	25.0
1976	5991	24.9
Unions		
1954	2950	16.6
1956	3400	18.6
1958	3274	18.2
1960	3304	18.3
1962	3272	18.6
1964	3413	19.0
1966	3689	19.3
1968	3940	19.5
1970	4282	20.7
1972	4524	21.7
1974	4600	21.3
1976	4201	20.0

Sources: Adapted from U.S. Bureau of Labor Statistics, *Directory of National Unions and Employee Associations, 1975,* Bulletin 1937, 1977, p. 65; and U.S. Bureau of Labor Statistics, "Labor Union and Employee Association Membership—1976," *NEWS,* September 1977, p. 4.

of employee associations accounted for 60 percent of total membership in those labor organizations in 1976.

These limited gains in membership in the face of the greatly increased participation of women in the labor force during the post-World War II period meant that the proportion of all working women organized by labor unions fell to 11.9 percent in 1976, the lowest figure since 1952, when such data began to be collected. When membership in employee associations is added to the total, the proportion of working women in all labor organizations was 15.9 percent in 1976, down from 16 percent in the early 1970s. The decline contrasts with the relatively stable incidence of labor organization among men, which stood at about 30 percent in 1976.

Table 3-8 shows that women were dispersed over a large number of unions and associations in 1974. In that year, women constituted a majority of the membership of twenty-one national unions and fourteen employee associations. Together, these thirty-five organizations accounted for more than two-thirds of all female members of unions and associations, but even that figure represents a less concentrated pattern of membership than in prior years. Only twenty-eight unions and one employee association reported no female mem-

Table 3-8 Estimated Distribution of National Unions and Employee Associations by Proportion of Women Members, 1974

Women as a percent of membership	Total unions and associations				Unions				Associations			
	Number	Percent	Women members Number (thousands)	Percent	Number	Percent	Women members Number (thousands)	Percent	Number	Percent	Women members Number (thousands)	Percent
All unions and associations[1]	212	100.0	6038	100.0	175	100.0	4600	100.0	37	100.0	1438	100.0
No women members	28	13.2			28	16.0						
Under 10 percent	61	28.8	114	1.9	60	34.3	113	2.5	1	2.7	1	.1
10 and under 20 percent	22	10.4	888	14.7	20	11.4	886	19.3	2	5.4	2	.1
20 and under 30 percent	18	8.5	334	5.5	16	9.1	315	6.9	2	5.4	19	1.3
30 and under 40 percent	24	11.3	1272	21.1	18	10.3	1229	26.7	6	16.2	44	3.0
40 and under 50 percent	24	11.3	838	13.9	12	6.9	683	14.8	12	32.4	155	10.8
50 and under 60 percent	16	7.5	643	10.6	7	4.0	560	12.2	9	24.3	83	5.8
60 and under 70 percent	8	3.8	1024	17.0	6	3.4	108	2.3	2	5.4	916	63.6
70 and under 80 percent	6	2.8	341	5.6	5	2.9	341	7.4	1	2.7	[2]	[3]
80 and under 90 percent	1	.5	324	5.4	1	.6	324	7.0				
90 percent and over	4	1.9	261	4.3	2	1.1	41	.9	2	5.4	219	15.2

[1] One hundred and thirty-nine unions reported 3,729,519 women members; thirty-six unions did not report the number of women or failed to furnish membership data to which reported percentages could be applied. It was estimated that these unions had 870,056 members. Twenty-nine associations reported 1,173,401 women members. Estimates for eight associations totaled 264,997. In terms of union affiliation, it was estimated that women members were distributed as follows: AFL–CIO, 83.8 percent; unaffiliated, 16.2 percent. Women members of local unions directly affiliated with the AFL–CIO are not included in these estimates.

[2] Less than 500.

[3] Less than 0.05 percent.

Note: Because of rounding, sums of individual items may not equal totals.

Source: Adapted from U.S. Bureau of Labor Statistics, Directory of National Unions and Employee Associations, 1975, Bulletin 1937, 1977, p. 66.

bers in 1974, a decline of eleven organizations in this category from 1972. The International Ladies' Garment Workers' Union (ILGWU) claimed that 80 percent of its members, or 324,000 workers, were women. The International Brotherhood of Electrical Workers (IBEW) ranked second in the number of female members (297,368) in 1974, followed closely by the Retail Clerks International Association (RCIA) (292,894).

In tandem, the data on the membership of white-collar workers and women in American labor organizations can hardly be encouraging to unionists and supporters of the labor movement.[37] They imply that the dominant thrust of the movement, characterized earlier as "business unionism," is so closely associated with male, blue-collar, manual workers as to lack strong appeal to the most rapidly growing sectors of the labor force and, additionally, that it is unalterable by union organizations and labor officials. Like most generalizations, this one contains some truth.

White-collar workers, many of whom are employed in offices rather than in plants, shops, and factories, often work closely with managers and tend to associate themselves more intimately with them than with production employees. White-collar workers also are more highly educated—"schooled" is a more accurate term—than manual workers, which not only creates a social barrier between white- and blue-collar employees but also provides the former with an indispensable prerequisite to advancement into management ranks, something to which a manual worker can hardly hope to aspire. Some white-collar employees, notably professionals, shrink from traditional union tactics such as strikes, boycotts, and picketing, while others consider bargaining and collective activity to be anathema.

Concerning women, the failure to organize them on a larger scale or even in proportion to their representation in the work force is less easily explained. It is true that many women are employed only on a part-time basis and do not feel an especially strong attachment to the labor force, factors which historically have been unfavorable to efforts at unionization. But it is also true that although record numbers and proportions of women now work full time and identify strongly with a career, even among these women unionists apparently have not met with much success. Furthermore, labor organizations, including those such as the ILGWU, which have an overwhelmingly female membership, generally have been run by men. This dominance of male leadership conveys the impression that women have second-class status. Finally, employment of women is disproportionately high in clerical and sales jobs, the types of white-collar occupations in which labor organizations have met with little success in enrolling members.

Nevertheless, such apparent roadblocks to expansion of union membership may prove only temporary. Who would have thought just a few years ago that the nation's public school teachers, welfare workers, nurses, and other (predominantly female) employees in the health field would unionize and bargain with their employers? Who could have foreseen that the decline in the proportion of organized workers in the private sector since the mid-1950s would have been partially offset by the increased unionization of public employees, large numbers of whom are female? Who might have predicted in the mid-1960s that significant numbers of college teachers and professional athletes, possessors of independence and fame, respectively (and occasionally simultaneously), would turn to unionism?

In short, it is all too easy to presume that the composition of the modern labor sector in terms of industry, occupation, and sex is such as to be impervious to further unionization. True, several sophisticated analysts have used just such a "structuralist" argument in forecasting a continued decline in the proportion of union members in the work force.[38] But it is this same type of analysis which only recently identified public employment as being among the most unorganizable sectors. By contrast, advocates of the "historical school" of analysis seem to believe that it is inevitable that the labor movement not only will survive but also will surge again, overcoming whatever obstacles stand in the way of organizing new and previously unreceptive workers.[39] Those who hold this view, however, appear unwilling to recognize the real and formidable barriers that face present-day labor organizations. For the student of this subject, there can be no final resolution of this issue except as it will be revealed empirically. We offer only the observation that the labor movement in the United States, though a minority movement throughout its history, has survived and expanded when circumstances might have suggested it would do otherwise. If history teaches us anything, then, it is that it would be a mistake to underestimate the adaptive capacity of the American labor movement even while recognizing the imposing obstacles presently facing it.

RACIAL DISCRIMINATION AND LABOR ORGANIZATIONS

Critics of the labor movement have sometimes condemned unions for engaging in racial discrimination. The railroad workers' unions and, more recently, the building trades unions have been particularly subject to this charge. Perspective on this issue is provided by the data in Figure 3-2 and in Tables 3-9 and

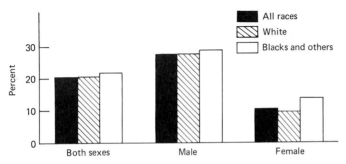

Figure 3-2 Percent of wage and salary workers in labor unions by race and sex, 1970. (*Source: U.S. Bureau of Labor Statistics,* Selected Earnings and Demographic Characteristics of Union Members, 1970, *U.S. Government Printing Office, Washington, D.C., 1972, p. 4.*)

Table 3-9   Wage and Salary Workers in Labor Unions, Membership Rates by Race, Occupation, and Industry, 1970

Occupation of longest job held in 1970	Percent in labor unions		
	All races	Whites	Blacks and others
All occupations[1]	20.4	20.2	21.8
White-collar workers	9.8	9.3	16.6
Professional, technical, and kindred workers	9.0	8.8	12.1
Managers, officials, and proprietors, except farm	7.5	7.3	14.2
Clerical and kindred workers	13.1	12.3	21.1
Sales workers	4.9	4.8	7.3
Blue-collar workers	39.3	39.8	35.5
Craft workers, supervisors, and kindred workers	42.7	42.9	39.8
Carpenters	45.4	46.4	[2]
Construction craft workers except carpenters	54.7	56.2	36.8
Mechanics and repairmen	32.9	33.0	31.5
Metal craft workers, except mechanics	63.3	63.2	[2]
Other	38.5	38.1	45.7
Operatives and kindred workers	40.4	40.8	38.2
Assemblers, checkers, examiners, and inspectors, manufacturing	48.8	47.7	56.6
Drivers and deliverymen	37.9	39.3	29.5
Other	39.6	39.9	37.5
Nonfarm laborers	28.9	29.2	27.7
Construction	29.9	30.2	29.0
Manufacturing	41.4	42.9	36.7
Other	22.1	22.3	21.0
Service workers, including private household	10.9	10.9	10.8

Industry of longest job held in 1970	Total		
	All races	White	Blacks and others
All industries	20.4	20.2	21.8
Agriculture	2.4	2.7	1.4
Mining	35.7	35.6	[2]
Construction	39.2	39.8	33.4
Manufacturing, total	23.8	33.1	39.4
Durable goods, total	37.4	36.4	46.5
Nondurable goods, total	28.7	28.4	30.8
Transportation and public utilities	44.8	45.0	42.9
Wholesale and retail trade	10.2	9.9	12.8
Services and finance	7.8	7.3	10.4
Public administration	22.2	21.2	28.9

[1] Includes farm workers not shown separately.
[2] Base less than 75,000
Note: Because of rounding, sums of individual items may not equal totals.
Source: Adapted from the U.S. Bureau of Labor Statistics, *Selected Earnings and Demographic Characteristics of Union Members, 1970,* Report 417, 1972, pp. 6–9.

3-10, which show differences in union membership by race in 1970.[40] Figure 3-2 reveals that among both men and women, proportionately more blacks (and other minorities) than whites were members of labor unions in 1970.[41] For black men, the membership rate was about 30 percent, or slightly higher than that for white men; among women, blacks had a markedly higher membership rate than whites, 14 versus 10 percent.

The tables provide more detailed data concerning the racial composition of union membership. Table 3-9 underscores the conclusion of Figure 3-2 that relatively higher proportions of black than of white men and women belong to labor unions, but it also shows the distribution of these differences by occupation and industry. For example, one-sixth of all blacks who were white-collar workers in 1970 belonged to labor unions, compared with fewer than 10 percent of whites in this occupational category. Among blue-collar workers, whites had a higher incidence of union membership than blacks, with the differential most pronounced in the case of construction craft workers. As to service workers, there was virtually no difference between the races in the proportion of union members.

Turning to industry breakdowns, the incidence of union membership was higher among whites than among blacks in agriculture, construction, transportation, and public utilities. In manufacturing, wholesale and retail trade, services, finance, and public administration, however, blacks were more heavily organized than whites, the difference being most pronounced in the last of these categories. That blacks seem to display a higher propensity to form or join labor unions than whites in the most rapidly growing nonmanufacturing sectors of the economy is a particularly intriguing implication of these data.

A somewhat different portrayal of the incidence of unionism among black workers is offered in Table 3-10. It compares the proportion of blacks who were unionized (and not unionized) in 1970 with their proportion of the total work force and of particular occupations and industries. In that year, blacks accounted for 11.6 percent of all workers, but for 12.4 percent of all union members. The incidence of union membership among blacks surpassed their representation in all major white-collar occupations, in some nonconstruction craft jobs, and in operative positions in manufacturing. On this basis, blacks were underrepresented in labor unions when they worked in construction and most other crafts, as drivers and deliveryman, and as laborers. Among blacks in the service occupations, union membership about matched their representation in the work force.

The data for industry both confirm and extend previous conclusions. Rates of membership of blacks in labor unions exceed rates of employment of blacks in industry in all cases except construction and transportation, precisely the areas in which it was suggested at the outset of this discussion that racial discrimination is most prevalent. Taken as a whole, the data imply that blacks are somewhat more likely to organize than whites and to do so in most if not all industries.

But of course the issue is more complicated than this, and the conclusions

Table 3-10 Blacks as a Percent of Total Wage and Salary Workers, by Occupation, Industry, and Membership in Labor Unions, 1970

Occupation of longest job held in 1970	Total wage and salary workers		In labor unions		Not in labor unions	
	Number (thousands)	Percent black[1]	Number (thousands)	Percent black[1]	Number (thousands)	Percent black[1]
All occupations[2]	84,256	11.6	17,192	12.4	67,063	11.4
White-collar workers	39,403	6.5	3,865	11.0	35,538	6.0
Professional, technical, and kindred workers	11,433	6.9	1,032	9.3	10,401	6.7
Managers, officials, and proprietors, except farm	6,850	3.2	514	6.0	6,336	3.0
Clerical and kindred workers	15,751	8.5	2,058	13.8	13,693	7.7
Sales workers	5,369	3.8	261	5.7	5,108	3.7
Blue-collar workers	30,293	13.0	11,893	11.7	18,400	13.8
Craft workers, supervisors, and kindred workers	10,131	6.3	4,328	5.8	5,803	6.6
Carpenters	861	5.6	391	3.6	470	7.2
Construction craft workers, except carpenters	2,040	8.3	1,115	5.7	925	11.6
Mechanics and repairmen	2,336	6.1	768	5.9	1,568	6.3
Metal craft workers, except mechanics	678	4.3	429	4.4	249	4.0
Other craft workers, supervisors, and kindred workers	4,217	5.9	1,625	7.0	2,592	5.2
Operatives and kindred workers	15,067	14.6	6,093	13.8	8,974	15.2
Assemblers, checkers, examiners, and inspectors, manufacturing	1,892	11.9	923	13.9	969	10.1
Drivers and deliverymen	2,699	13.7	1,024	10.6	1,675	15.5
Other operatives and kindred workers	10,476	15.3	4,146	14.5	6,330	15.8
Nonfarm laborers	5,094	21.4	1,471	20.5	3,623	21.8
Construction	1,139	23.9	341	23.2	798	24.2
Manufacturing	1,330	24.4	551	21.6	779	26.3
Other industries	2,625	18.9	579	18.0	2,046	19.2
Service workers, including private household	12,970	21.7	1,409	21.6	11,561	21.7

Industry of longest job held in 1970	Total wage and salary workers		In labor unions		Not in labor unions	
	Number (thousands)	Percent black[1]	Number (thousands)	Percent black[1]	Number (thousands)	Percent black[1]
All industries[2]	84,256	11.6	17,192	12.4	67,063	11.4
Mining	574	4.4	205	4.9	368	4.3
Construction	4,975	10.2	1,948	8.7	3,027	11.2
Manufacturing, total	22,503	10.7	7,600	12.4	14,903	9.8
Durable goods, total	13,094	10.0	4,900	12.4	8,194	8.5
Nondurable goods, total	9,409	11.7	2,700	12.5	6,709	11.3
Transportation, communication, and public utilities	5,642	10.7	2,527	10.3	3,115	11.1
Transportation	3,070	10.4	1,589	8.7	1,481	12.2
Communication and other public utilities	2,573	11.1	938	13.0	1,634	10.1
Wholesale trade	3,047	8.1	345	11.9	2,701	7.6
Retail trade	13,732	8.0	1,363	9.7	12,368	7.9
Services and finance	27,115	13.9	2,103	18.6	25,012	13.5
Public administration	4,761	12.8	1,055	16.5	3,706	11.8

[1] Columns nonadditive.

[2] Includes farm workers not shown separately.

Note: Because of rounding, sums of individual items may not equal totals.

Source: Adapted from U.S. Bureau of Labor Statistics, Selected Earnings and Demographic Characteristics of Union Members, 1970, Report 417, 1972, pp. 26–27.

derived from the kinds of data presented here must be cautiously regarded. Racial discrimination can take many forms, including, in the case of blacks, confining them to the lower-ranking occupational groups, relegating them to the lowest-paying jobs within broad occupations, and preventing their movement into leadership positions within labor organizations. These practices will be more fully discussed in Chapter 8, but even a brief perusal of the data in Table 3-10 shows that in terms of their overall participation in the work force (11.6 percent in 1970), blacks are underrepresented in goods-producing industries and in trade, while being overrepresented in services and public administration. Because wages tend to be higher in the industries in which blacks are underrepresented than in the industries in which they are overrepresented, their earnings are lower than those of whites. A similar pattern can occur within an industry: for example, in manufacturing blacks are overrepresented in the lower-paying nondurable-goods sector and underrepresented in the higher-paying durable-goods sector.

But even this characterization of its stance on racial discrimination is somewhat unfair to organized labor. More than any other institution, perhaps, the labor movement has offered to racial minorities protections against discrimination in employment and a form of representation in decision making at the workplace. It has done so in the past for a wide variety of minority groups—Jews, Italians, Irish, and Poles, to name but a few—and is doing so now for blacks within industry and government, as the data in Table 3-10 indicate. It is also attempting to do so on a larger scale for black workers in hospitals, Mexican-American farm workers, and other racial and ethnic minorities. These efforts emerge less out of altruism, surely, than out of the basic desire to redress grievances at the workplace, to secure for workers a larger portion of the economic pie, and to maintain and extend the labor movement as an important American institution. To recognize these efforts is not to deny the existence of racial (and other forms of) discrimination within the house of labor or to overlook the very real anger felt by some unionized minority workers, which has occasionally led them to form black and Chicano caucuses or rival union organizations. Rather, it is to suggest that in judging the labor movement along this dimension, one must assess—balance—the widespread organization and representation through collective bargaining of blacks and other minorities as against the discrimination that has been practiced against them or acquiesed in by some unions. An understanding of this ambivalent nature of the relationship between organized labor and minorities is necessary to making such a judgment.

MANAGERIAL UNIONISM

We noted earlier that supervisors and managerial employees are not covered by the Taft-Hartley Act. Even to suggest that this portion of the labor sector might pursue collective action and seek to bargain with employers may seem heretical

Table 3-11   Selected Survey Responses of Managerial Personnel

According to personnel executives		Key statements	According to middle managers	
Agree	Disagree		Agree	Disagree
335 (59%)	235 (41%)	Middle management is somewhat more receptive to the idea of collective bargaining today than it was, say, before the current economic recession.	340 (65%)	187 (35%)
160 (28%)	408 (72%)	Present laws should be changed to permit supervisory and middle-management personnel to organize for the purpose of collective bargaining, if they so desire	240 (47%)	272 (53%)
352 (62%)	214 (38%)	Middle managers should be allowed to organize informal groups to discuss conditions of employment with top management on a company-by-company basis	387 (75%)	132 (25%)

Source: Alfred T. Demaria, Dale Tarnowieski, and Richard Gurman, *Manager Unions?* American Management Association, New York, 1972, p. 5.

to some. Yet this is not at all uncommon in a variety of industrialized countries. Nor is it uncommon in the American *public* sector, where numerous supervisory and even some managerial personnel are represented by labor unions and employee associations. As the American economy becomes more complex, as those charged with decision making in organizations are buffeted by an increasingly broader array of external and internal forces (for example, regulatory legislation and a less pliant, younger work force), as some managers experience less upward mobility than they originally expected,[42] and as institutional protections develop for other interest groups, private and public managers may come to define more concretely than before their own rights within work organizations. In short, the emergence of managerial unions and associations in the United States is perhaps not as far off as might be suspected. Certainly it is a subject that cannot easily be dismissed.

Consider, for example, the responses, shown in Table 3-11, to a survey of some 1100 managerial personnel conducted in 1971 by the American Management Association (AMA).[43] A majority of personnel executives and middle managers felt that their colleagues in industry were more receptive than ever before to collective bargaining for themselves. While the respondents were more willing to support formation of informal management groups to discuss problems of employment than to support changes in the labor laws to permit formal organizations and bargaining among managers, well over one-third (400) of the entire sample (1080) expressed support for just such statutory changes. As to the factors underlying these sentiments, some of the conclusions offered by the authors of the report are instructive:

There is overwhelming agreement among surveyed middle managers and personnel executives alike that managerial frustration and discontent with corporate life are increasing. Bread and butter issues predominate [in] a list [of] conditions likely to alienate middle managers from their corporate superiors and drive them toward unionism, but most managers are also troubled by far more subtle conditions affecting their corporate lives.

In general, managers believe unionization would give them more job security, higher wages, and better health and fringe benefits. . . . More than one out of every three middle managers responding to the AMA survey would join, or consider joining, a manager's union.

The authors go on to point out that:

If these survey results are a valid representation of what's on management's mind, there is today widespread disenchantment among American middle managers with the prevailing state of corporate affairs. This disenchantment is largely the product of the dramatic changes in life styles throughout American society, of a painful and prolonged recession, and of increased external pressures for business and organizational reform.[44]

One could observe, further, that these findings and conclusions were reached prior to regulatory legislation enacted after 1971, the Arab oil boycott of 1973, the deep economic recession of 1974–1975, the Watergate revelations of the mid-1970s, and the discovery during the 1970s of widespread and often illegal corporate political contributions to domestic and foreign recipients, which brought to the fore questions about ethics and morality in management circles.

But just as this issue should not be ignored, so too the aforementioned responses should not be overemphasized. These are, after all, expressions of opinion which, however strongly worded, do not necessarily translate into action. Consider that most representatives of organized labor are somewhat cool to the idea of managerial unions. This apparently paradoxical view may be understood in light of the union leader's need, in continually seeking "more and more" for the membership, to be able to negotiate with a strong management from whom it can be claimed that every possible concession has been wrung but who has prevented even further gains from being made. The enrollment in unions of labor's opponents across the negotiating table might muddy the organizational and bargaining waters more than it would strengthen the labor movement.

In sum, we urge once again that it not simply be presumed that the present makeup of organized labor will be preserved immutably into the future. But even in the now unlikely event that managers should unionize, their organizational objectives and bargaining tactics would seem to be quite consistent with the philosophy of "business unionism."[45]

MEMBERSHIP IN INDIVIDUAL LABOR ORGANIZATIONS

As a diverse and changing institution, the American labor movement has within it organizations characterized by different size and growth patterns. Table 3-12 distributes national unions and employee associations by size of organization. Of the 212 reporting organizations, 139, or 56 percent, had fewer than 50,000 members in 1974. In total, they accounted for less than 8 percent of all members in that year. At the other end of the spectrum, the dozen labor organizations (5 percent of the total) with 500,000 or more members accounted for fully half of all membership in unions and associations. This distribution was almost the same as that recorded in 1972.

Over the period 1960–1974, labor unions were almost evenly divided between those which gained and those which lost members. About 30 percent of the unions increased their membership by at least one-fifth during these years (a few even doubled and tripled in size), while one-quarter of these organizations lost at least 20 percent of their members. Only 5 of the 126 labor unions providing data on changes in membership experienced less than a 1 percent gain or loss during this 14-year period.

Figure 3-3 provides data on trends in membership for the ten largest labor unions, circa 1976. In that year, the teamsters had 2 million members, two unions had over 1 million members each, and two others were not far below that mark. These five organizations accounted for more than 30 percent of all union members in 1976. Among them, the Teamsters recorded the most impressive growth since 1951, virtually doubling their membership. The United Automobile Workers, the United Steelworkers of America, and the International Association of Machinists and Aerospace Workers (IAMAW) had quite erratic membership patterns over the third quarter of the twentieth century, their size being closely related to changes in the economy generally and in the automobile industry in particular. The International Brotherhood of Electrical Workers experienced a steady if not spectacular pattern of growth between 1951 and 1976. Membership in the United Brotherhood of Carpenters and Joiners of America (UBCJA), the sixth largest labor organization, was not much different at the end of the period from what it had been at the beginning.

The labor unions ranked seventh through tenth have all recorded substantial gains in membership in recent years. Most impressive was the gain of the American Federation of State, County and Municipal Employees (AFSCME), which more than tripled its membership between 1960 and 1976 to approximately 750,000 workers. Indeed, AFSCME became the largest union affiliated with the AFL-CIO in early 1978, when it acquired the Civil Service Employees Association, Inc. (CSEA), of New York State, which has a membership exceeding 250,000. Its new total, estimated to be 1.1 million members, put it slightly above the United Steelworkers of America, which reported just under 1.1 million members for the same period.[46] The Retail Clerks International Association also achieved impressive gains during the period 1960–1976, its membership

Table 3-12 Distribution of National Unions and Employee Associations by Size of Organization, 1974

Size of organization	Total unions and associations		Unions — Total				Unions AFL-CIO	Unions Unaffiliated	Associations			
	Number	Percent	Number	Percent	Members Number (thousands)	Percent	Number	Number	Number	Percent	Members Number (thousands)	Percent
Total	212	100.0	175	100.0	21,585	100.0	111	64	37	100.0	2,610	100.0
Under 1,000 members	27	12.7	26	14.9	9	[1]	6	20	1	2.7	[2]	[1]
1,000 and under 5,000	37	17.5	26	14.9	71	.3	6	20	11	29.7	38	1.5
5,000 and under 10,000	14	6.6	9	5.1	61	.3	6	3	5	13.5	41	1.6
10,000 and under 25,000	29	13.7	21	12.0	337	1.6	16	5	8	21.6	103	3.9
25,000 and under 50,000	32	15.1	27	15.4	931	4.3	21	6	5	13.5	140	5.4
50,000 and under 100,000	20	9.4	18	10.3	1,281	5.9	14	4	2	5.4	161	6.2
100,000 and under 200,000	23	10.8	20	11.4	2,869	13.3	17	3	3	8.1	449	17.2
200,000 and under 300,000	10	4.7	9	5.1	2,233	10.3	8	1	1	2.7	207	7.9
300,000 and under 400,000	3	1.4	3	1.7	981	4.5	3					
400,000 and under 500,000	5	2.4	5	2.9	2,215	10.3	5					
500,000 and under 1,000,000	8	3.8	8	4.6	5,779	26.8	8					
1,000,000 and over	4	1.9	3	1.7	4,818	22.3	1	2	1	2.7	1,470	56.3

[1] Less than 0.05 percent.
[2] Less than 500 members.
Note: Because of rounding, sums of individual items may not equal totals.
Source: Adapted from U.S. Bureau of Labor Statistics, *Directory of National Unions and Employee Associations, 1975,* Bulletin 1937, 1977, p. 64.

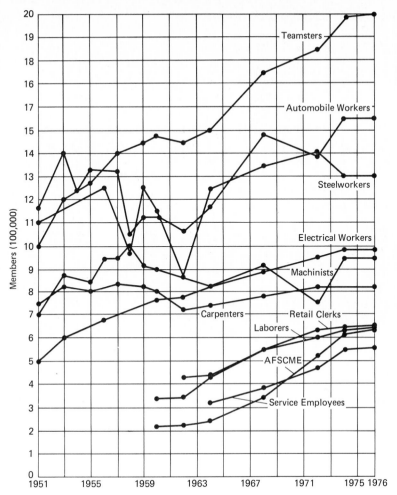

Figure 3-3 Membership in the ten largest labor unions, 1951–1976. (*Sources: U.S. Bureau of Labor Statistics,* Directory of National Unions and Employee Associations, 1975, *bull. no. 1937, U.S. Government Printing Office, Washington, D.C., 1977, pp. 64–66; suppl., February 1978; and previous bulletins.*)

about doubling to the same level as AFSCME's. The membership gains of these two labor organizations, together with those of the Laborers' International Union of North America (LIUNA) and the Service Employee's International Union (SEIU), occurred in the rapidly expanding sectors of the economy—government, services, and trade. The gains of the half dozen largest labor unions also were recorded partly in these expanding sectors, as those organizations pursued members outside their traditional industries and crafts. Thus, the Teamsters, for example, have organized various blue- and white-collar workers in several manufacturing and nonmanufacturing industries and in the public sector (though modestly), in addition to their traditional membership base of truck drivers.

Not shown in Figure 3-3, but listed in Table 3-13 together with other large national unions and employee associations, is the National Education Association, which enrolled almost 1.5 million members in 1974. This teachers' group is thus the nation's third largest labor organization, surpassed in membership only by the Teamsters and the UAW. The NEA has gained members steadily since 1960, its most recent increases having been obtained in competition with the more militant American Federation of Teachers. The AFT also prospered in the 1970s, however, its membership totaling 444,000 in 1974 and its ranking among all labor unions having risen from twenty-first to fourteenth place over the prior survey period (1970).

Indeed, perusal of the data in Table 3-13 reveals that one-sixth of the largest labor unions and four of the five largest employee associations represent government employees. Moreover, public workers constitute an important and growing segment of the membership of other large labor organizations such as the SEIU, the LIUNA, the Transport Workers Union of America (TWUA), and the American Nurses' Association (ANA). And, since Table 3-13 does not include the membership of unaffiliated, single-employer unions and associations, the high incidence organization among some other groups of public employees, such as the country's more than 200,000 police officers, may easily be overlooked. Despite their limitations, however, these data provide further illustration of recent gains in membership in the public sector and the importance of that sector to the modern labor movement.

Before leaving this subject, we should observe one other important aspect of the data contained in Table 3-13. The three largest labor organizations—the Teamsters, the UAW, and the NEA, which together enroll 5 million workers—are not affiliated with the AFL-CIO. It would be hard to imagine any other labor federation in the world which could be so widely accepted as the advocate for "labor" (all labor, not just organized labor) but which didn't enroll its country's largest workers' organizations. In Chapter 4, we will go more deeply into the structure of the labor movement. For now, we conclude by noting that this fact reveals the strand of individualism that persists in the American character even when collective actions occur and large institutions dot the landscape.

EXPLAINING THE UNORGANIZED

Before concluding this chapter, we would do well to say a few words about the unorganized among the labor sector, who, after all, substantially outnumber the one-quarter of the work force that belongs to unions and employee associations. Like organized workers, the unorganized represent a diverse mix of occupations, skills, interests, and motivations. Yet they apparently have in common the fact that they deal individually rather than collectively with their

Table 3-13. National Unions and Employee Associations Reporting 100,000 Members or More, 1974[1]

Organization	Number of members	Organization	Number of members
Unions		Painters	211,000
Teamsters (Ind.)	1,973,000	Rubber	191,000
Automobile workers (Ind.)	1,545,000	Iron workers	182,000
Steelworkers	1,300,000	Retail, wholesale	180,000
Electrical (IBEW)	991,000	Oil, chemical	177,000
Machinists	943,000	Firefighters	172,000
Carpenters	820,000	Textile workers	167,000
Retail clerks	651,000	Electrical (UE) (Ind.)	163,000
Laborers	650,000	Sheet metal	161,000
State, county	648,000	Transport workers	150,000
Service employees	550,000	Bricklayers	148,000
Meat cutters	525,000	Transit union	140,000
Communications workers	499,000	Boilermakers	138,000
Hotel	452,000	Bakery	134,000
Teachers	444,000	Printing and graphic	129,000
Operating engineers	415,000	Maintenance of way	119,000
Ladies garment	405,000	Typographical	111,000
Clothing workers	350,000	Woodworkers	108,000
Musicians	330,000	Government (NAGE) (Ind.)	[2]
Paperworkers	301,000	Graphic arts	100,000
Government (AFGE)	300,000	Federal employees (NFFE) (Ind.)	100,000
Electrical (IUE)	298,000	**Associations**	
Postal workers	249,000	Education association	1,470,000
Transportation union	238,000	Civil service (N.Y.S.)	207,000
Railway clerks	235,000	Nurses' association	196,000
Letter carriers	232,000	Police	147,000
Plumbers	228,000	California	106,000
Mine workers (Ind.)	220,000		

[1] Based on union and association reports to the Bureau with membership rounded to the nearest thousand. All unions not identified as (Ind.) are affiliated with the AFL–CIO.

[2] Membership estimated by the Bureau and not available for publication.

Source: Adapted from U.S. Bureau of Labor Statistics. *Directory of National Unions and Employee Associations, 1975,* Bulletin 1937, 1977, p. 65.

employers. We say "apparently" because, while for many of them this is no doubt true, others among them may be dealt with en masse—that is, collectively—*by* their employers.

Those who work in nonunion settings for large corporations, for example, often find their terms and conditions of employment established and maintained through the application of uniform personnel policies that have evolved over the years within those organizations. To be sure, these terms and conditions are not formally negotiated between employers and workers, but they are formally established, they are applied uniformly to groups of workers, and, most important, they often are administered by personnel departments staffed by professionals who regard their function in part as one of protecting the "rights" of employees. The institutionalization of such rights usually is most clearly expressed in formal systems for airing grievances and making appeals which, in nonunion organizations, provide a measure of due process to employees. One may legitimately doubt the extent to which such systems actually protect employees, just as one may be skeptical about the ability of personnel departments to serve effectively as buffers between employer and employees when such departments are themselves part of the management structure of organizations. Further, many nonunions firms develop personnel and labor relations policies to ward off unionization, and some are overtly antiunion. Nevertheless, these reservations should not obscure recognition of the many "collective" aspects of modern personnel policies, which reflect something less than a strict individual relationship between employee and employer. This observation is even more germane in the case of public employers who apply to virtually their entire work forces, managers included, the many policies contained in the typical civil service or merit system of personnel management.

Still, one must also recognize (as the data in Table 3-1 make clear) that individual rather than collective bargaining is the prevailing characteristic of employment relationships in the United States. To attempt to "explain" this phenomenon by saying that the majority of workers prefer individually over collectively determined terms and conditions of employment tells us very little, for we need to go beyond that observation to ask why it is so. We shall not undertake that task here. Keep in mind, however, that the dominant characteristics of American culture over the nation's history—individualism, self-sufficiency, a strong work ethic, aspirations to mobility, competition, and free enterprise—could hardly be without influence in labor-management relations.

Many workers do indeed value an individual employment relationship, viewing it as an expression of their self-sufficiency, enterprise, and initiative and perhaps also as an indicator of their potential for upward mobility. Other workers may not so much prefer individualistic employment relationships as they abhor or fear collective ones. And still others are not sufficiently powerful to form or adept at forming a labor organization or maintaining it as a viable entity. Workers in the less stable, lowest-paying jobs, for example, have never been heavily organized or prominently represented in the American labor movement.

In sum, the unorganized portion of the labor sector, not all members of which work in a strictly individual employment context, is as multifaceted and diverse as the organized sector. No one factor alone explains the preference for individual employment relationships and for individual bargaining with employers in this segment of the work force. It is for this very reason, then, that one should be cautious in presuming—or predicting—that the unorganized among the labor sector will remain so in the future.

SUMMARY

In this chapter we attempted to discuss some of the functions, trace out the history, and offer a contemporary picture of the American labor movement. Emphasis was placed both on the enduring characteristics of that movement— business unionism, for example—and on the dynamic changes which have marked its evolution and which may characterize its future. The most significant of these recent developments is the extent of organization in the public sector and the rise to prominence of the employee association.

Central to the legal framework of American labor-management relations is the principle of exclusive recognition, which is cemented in the Wagner and Taft-Hartley Acts and is more or less replicated in state laws governing public employment. That principle helps bring a measure of stability and democracy (along with some less favorable influences) to labor relations that is relatively unique within modern industrialized nations of the West. In Chapter 4 we examine the portion of the law that regulates internal union affairs. In so doing, we move inside labor organizations in order to gain a better understanding of their structure, dynamics, and internal politics, and of the forces that necessarily operate within any complex institution, however it is regulated by public policy.

NOTES

1 For an older but still relevant discussion of this issue, see Joel Seidman, Jack London, and Bernard Karsh, "Why Workers Join Unions," *Annals of the American Academy of Political and Social Science*, **274**:75–84 (1951).

2 Seidman, London, and Karsh.

3 Derek Bok and John Dunlop, *Labor and the American Community*, Simon and Schuster, New York, 1970, p. 207.

4 Selig Perlman, *A Theory of the Labor Movement*, Reprints of Economic Classics, A. M. Kelley, Publishers, New York, 1966, especially chap. 1. The work was originally published in 1928 by Macmillan.

5 For a detailed account of the origin and extension of labor injunctions, see Donald L. McMurray, "The Legal Ancestry of the Pullman Strike Injunctions," *Industrial and Labor Relations Review*, **14**:235–256 (1961). The classic treatment is by Felix Frankfurter and Nathan Greene, *The Labor Injunction*, Macmillan, New York, 1930.

6 The most exhaustive treatment of this subject appears in Lloyd Ulman, *The Rise of the National Trade Union,* Harvard, Cambridge, Mass., 1955.

7 This interesting event is thoroughly explored in Henry David, *The History of the Haymarket Affair,* Collier, New York, 1936.

8 Robert F. Hoxie, *Trade Unionism in the United States,* Appleton-Century-Crofts, New York, 1921, pp. 336–337. This book was published by Hoxie's students after his death. The remark quoted was actually written in 1916.

9 Selig Perlman, *A History of Trade Unionism in the United States,* New York, Macmillan, 1922, p. 145.

10 Perlman, *A History of Trade Unionism in the United States,* p. 189.

11 These claims were collected by Robert Hoxie in the course of his study for the 1915 congressional committee and are reported in his *Trade Unionism in the United States,* pp. 299–301.

12 An excellent discussion of the application of the Sherman Antitrust Act to organized labor is provided in Charles O. Gregory, *Labor and the Law,* 2d rev. ed., Norton, New York, 1961, chaps. 6, 8, 10.

13 On this interpretation of the Clayton Act, see Gregory, chap. 7.

14 Charles M. Schwab, "Capital and Labor," in *A Reconstruction Labor Policy,* Annals of the American Academy of Political and Social Science, January 1919, p. 158.

15 John A. Garraty describes some of the "benevolences" of the Morgan group that was in control of United States Steel (in contrast to the "steel men" themselves, as typified by Schwab) in "The United States Steel Corporation versus Labor: The Early Years," *Labor History,* **1:**3–38 (1960).

16 Note that the *Apex* decision did not declare the sit-down strike legal in every respect. For occupying the employer's plant and damaging his equipment, the Apex workers were still liable to discharge and to prosecution under the usual local laws prohibiting trespass and other damage to private property. The Supreme Court's decision said only that these activities were not a violation of the Sherman Antitrust Act.

17 In conducting such campaigns for elections to determine representation, the NLRB tends to regulate closely the behavior of employers and unionists, sometimes setting aside or requiring additional elections. For a sharply critical appraisal of the Board's assumptions in this area, see Julius G. Getman, Stephen B. Goldberg, and Jeanne B. Herman, *Union Representation Elections: Law and Reality,* Russell Sage, New York, 1976.

18 The complete list of jurisdictional standards is contained in National Labor Relations Board, *Summary of the National Labor Relations Act as Amended to 1959,* GPO, Washington, 1967, pp. 25–26.

19 This decision was reached in *Fibreboard Paper Products Corp. v. NLRB,* 130 NLRB 1958 (1961). The interested reader is referred to the NLRB's annual reports or to any of the standard labor law reporting services for a fuller discussion of all the cases and issues discussed in the remainder of the chapter.

20 For a thorough review of this subject, see Walter Galenson, *The CIO Challenge to the AFL,* Harvard, Cambridge, Mass., 1960.

21 For example, the AFL opposed the Social Security Act of 1935.

22 For more on these developments, see Philip Taft, *The AFL from the Death of Gompers to the Merger,* Harper & Row, New York, 1959.

23 For example, Solomon Barkin, *The Decline of the Labor Movement,* The Fund for the Republic, Santa Barbara, Calif., 1961.

24 Adding to the pessimism was the series of Supreme Court decisions during the 1960s which applied the Sherman Antitrust Act to labor unions that had joined—conspired —with employers to restrain the sale of products in the marketplace and to reduce competition in industry. The leading cases were *United Mine Workers v. Pennington* and *Local 189, Amalgamated Meat Cutters v. Jewel Tea Co.* An analysis of them is provided in Archibald Cox, "Labor and the Anti-Trust Laws: Pennington and Jewel Tea," *Boston University Law Review,* **46:**317–328 (1966).

25 For an analysis of the early response of federal managers to this order, see Wilson R. Hart, "The U.S. Civil Service Learns to Live with Executive Order 10988: An Interim Appraisal," *Industrial and Labor Relations Review,* **17:**203–220 (1964).

26 Like the Executive orders governing labor-management relations in the federal service, these laws have spilled over to affect the pay practices of state and local governments.

27 U.S. Department of Labor, Division of Public Employee Labor Relations, *Summary of State Policy Regulations for Public Sector Labor Relations: Statutes, Attorney General Opinions, and Selected Court Decisions,* 1975 and 1977.

28 As reported in U.S. Bureau of Labor Statistics, "Labor Union and Employee Association Membership—1976," *NEWS,* September 1977, p. 3.

29 As reported in U.S. Bureau of Labor Statistics, *Directory of National Unions and Employee Associations, 1975,* Bulletin 1937, 1977, p. 53.

30 For more on this subject, see the papers contained in "California Farm Labor Conflict," *Proceedings of the Twenty-Ninth Annual Winter Meeting of the Industrial Relations Research Association,* Madison, Wis., 1977, pp. 66–90.

31 For details of the congressional ban on military unionism, see Bureau of National Affairs, *Daily Labor Report,* no. 200, Oct. 16, 1978, A8–A9. For analyses of this issue, see Ezra Krendel and Bernard Samoff (eds.), *Unionizing the Armed Forces,* University of Pennsylvania Press, Philadelphia, 1977; Alan Sabrosky, *Blue-Collar Soldiers?,* Foreign Policy Research Institute, Philadelphia, 1977; and William Gomberg, "Unionization of the U.S. Armed Military Forces—Its Development, Status and Future," *Proceedings of the Thirtieth Annual Winter Meeting of the Industrial Relations Research Association,* Madison, Wis., 1978, pp. 47–55. This issue is taken up again in Chapter 5.

32 Unless otherwise stated, the bulk of the data in this and later sections are taken from U.S. Bureau of Labor Statistics, "Labor Union and Employee Association Membership—1976"; and U.S. Bureau of Labor Statistics, *Directory of National Unions and Employee Associations, 1975.* Note that we attempt to use the most recent data in the following sections. Sometimes these are available to 1976, at other times to 1974. Further, the term "unionism" is sometimes used to include membership in all types of labor organizations, that is, unions *and* employee associations. The latter are particularly important to public employees.

33 U.S. Bureau of Labor Statistics, "Labor Union and Employee Association Membership—1976," p. 6. This calculation is based on the number of members of unions and associations in the United States in 1976, that is, 22,463,000. If based on the total membership of 24,036,000, which includes workers employed outside the United States, the nonaffiliated group rises to better than 30 percent of the total. In 1977, the AFL-CIO itself reported 13.5 million dues-paying members of affiliated locals, leaving between 8.5 and 10 million (depending upon whether workers employed outside the United States are included) in nonaffiliated labor organizations. See AFL-CIO, *Proceedings and Executive Council Reports of the AFL-CIO,* The President's Report, Los Angeles, December 1977, p. 51. Obviously, these data are subject to many qualifications, exclusions, and interpretations. The important point is that a sizable segment of the unionized work force does not belong to organizations affiliated with the AFL-CIO.

34 U.S. Bureau of Labor Statistics, *Directory of National Unions and Employee Associations, 1975,* p. 67.

35 The data supporting this conclusion are shown in Table 3-14; see question 2 under "For Analysis and Discussion." They also underlie Figure 3-1. For evidence confirming the decline of unionization in the private sector during the past two decades, see Richard B. Freemaen and James L. Medoff, "New Estimates of Private Sector Unionism in the United States, *Industrial and Labor Relations Review,* **32:**143–174, (1979).

36 For additional data on this issue, see Linda H. LeGrande, "Women in Labor Organizations: Their Ranks Are Increasing," *Monthly Labor Review,* **101:**8–14 (1978).

37 See LeGrande, "Women in Labor Organizations: Their Ranks Are Increasing," for a somewhat different interpretation.

38 See, most recently, William J. Moore and Robert J. Newman, "On the Prospects for American Trade Union Growth: A Cross-Section Analysis," *The Review of Economics and Statistics,* **57:**435–445 (1975).

39 See Irving Bernstein, "The Growth of American Unions, 1945–1960," *Labor History,* **2:**131–157 (1961); and Irving Bernstein, "Discussion," *Labor History,* **2:**365–379 (1961).

40 Unless otherwise noted, the source of data for the discussion in the present section is U.S. Bureau of Labor Statistics, *Selected Earnings and Demographic Characteristics of Union Members, 1970,* 1972, passim. For additional information on employment of minorities and discrimination in unions, see the United States Commission on Civil Rights, *Equal Opportunity in Referral Unions,* 1976.

41 The discussion refers to blacks because they constitute about 90 percent of the grouping "Negroes and other minorities" used by the Bureau of the Census to tabulate data on labor force and union membership.

42 The term "managerial plateauing" has been coined to define this phenomenon. See, for example, Thomas P. Ference, J. A. F. Stoner, and E. Kirby Warren, "Managing the Career Plateau," *Academy of Management Reveiw,* **2:**602–612 (1977).

43 Alfred T. DeMaria, Dale Tarnowieski, and Richard Gurman, *Manager Unions?* American Management Association, New York, 1972.

44 DeMaria, Tarnowieski, and Gurman, pp. 1–2.

45 On this point, see DeMaria, Tarnowieski, and Gurman, pp. 1–2. For comparative perspective on this issue, see Howard Gospel, "European Managerial Unionism: An Early Assessment," *Industrial Relations,* **17:**360–371 (1978).

46 Bureau of National Affairs, *Daily Labor Report,* no. 78, Apr. 20, 1978, A–12.

ADDITIONAL READINGS

Barbash, Jack: *Labor's Grass Roots,* Harper & Row, New York, 1961.

Barkin, Solomon: *Worker Militancy and Its Consequences, 1965–75,* Praeger, New York, 1975.

Bernstein, Irving: *The Lean Years,* Houghton Mifflin, Boston, 1960.

Bok, Derek, and John T. Dunlop: *Labor and the American Community,* Simon and Schuster, New York, 1970.

Getman, Julius G., Stephen B. Goldberg, and Jeanne Herman: *Union Representation Elections: Law and Reality,* Russell Sage, New York, 1976.

Hill, Herbert: *Black Labor and the American Legal System,* vol. I: *Race, Work and the Law,* Bureau of National Affairs, Washington, 1977.

Marshall, F. Ray: *The Negro and Organized Labor,* Wiley, New York, 1965.

Perlman, Selig: *A Theory of the Labor Movement,* Reprints of Economic Classics, A. M. Kelley, Publishers, New York, 1966.

Ulman, Lloyd: *The Rise of the National Trade Union,* Harvard, Cambridge, Mass., 1955.

U.S. Department of Labor: *Directory of National Unions and Employee Associations, 1975,* Bulletin 1937, 1977.

Films   There are some fine films available on labor history, of which *The Inheritance,* available from the International Ladies' Garment Workers' Union (ILGWU), is a leading example.

FOR ANALYSIS AND DISCUSSION

1 Compare the unfair practices by employers and unions covered by the Taft-Hartley Act. Why are some the same and some different? Which of these would you recommend be stricken from the law or tightened up? Why?

2 Examine the data on union membership in Table 3-14 (on page 158). Explain the differences in trends in total membership and percent of the labor force organized. What would the data look like, in your judgment, if they were to be extended to 1980? 1985? 2000? Why?

3 Compare and contrast the National Labor Union, the Knights of Labor, and the AFL-CIO. Then prepare a short paper outlining the key characteristics of the AFL-CIO that "explain" its survival.

4 The Taft-Hartley Act does not cover public employees and farm workers. Should the law be extended to include either or both of these groups? Why or why not?

5 The principle of exclusive representation is almost unique to the American system of industrial relations. In what other ways could workers be represented for purposes of collective bargaining?

6 Under what circumstances are labor unions presently subject to the Sherman Antitrust Act? What is the source of your information in responding to this question? Outline the major changes in judicial treatment of labor unions under this act.

7 It is sometimes contended that professionalism is incompatible with unionism. Yet large numbers of professional workers, notably those employed by government, recently have formed or joined labor organizations. How can this apparent inconsistency be explained or resolved?

8 Assume that you are a staff assistant to a United States senator who will shortly be voting on changes in the Taft-Hartley Act and who has asked you to prepare an analysis of arguments for and against "right-to-work" laws. Prepare such an analysis, and also a recommendation as to whether Section 14(b) of the act, which permits individual states to legislate in the area of union security, should be retained or repealed.

9 The dismissal of labor organizations from the AFL-CIO on the basis of corrupt or unethical practices does not seem to have affected such practices significantly. What other ways of dealing with corruption in unions could you suggest? With racial discrimination?

Table 3-14 Membership in National Unions and Employee Associations as a Proportion of Labor Force and Nonagricultural Employment, 1958–1976[1]

Year	Membership excluding Canada	Total labor force		Employees in nonagricultural establishments	
		Number	Percent members	Number	Percent members
Unions and associations					
1968	20,721	82,272	25.2	67,951[2]	30.5[2]
1969	20,776	84,240	24.7	70,442[2]	29.5[2]
1970	21,248	85,903	24.7	70,920[2]	30.0[2]
1971	21,327	86,929	24.5	71,222[2]	29.9[2]
1972	21,657	88,991	24.3	73,714[2]	29.4
1973	22,276	91,040	24.5	76,896	29.0
1974	22,809	93,240	24.5	78,413	29.1
1975	22,298	94,743	23.5	77,051	28.9
1976	22,463	96,917	23.2	79,443	28.3
Unions					
1958	17,029	70,275	24.2	51,363	33.2
1959	17,117	70,921	24.1	53,313	32.1
1960	17,049	72,142	23.6	54,234	31.4
1961	16,303	73,031	22.3	54,042	30.2
1962	16,586	73,442	22.6	55,596	29.8
1963	16,524	74,571	22.2	56,702	29.1
1964	16,841	75,830	22.2	58,331	28.9
1965	17,299	77,178	22.4	60,815	28.4
1966	17,940	78,893	22.7	63,955	28.1
1967	18,367	80,793	22.7	65,857	27.9
1968	18,916	82,272	23.0	67,951[2]	27.8[2]
1969	19,036	84,240	22.6	70,442[2]	27.0[2]
1970	19,381	85,903	22.6	70,920[2]	27.3[2]
1971	19,211	86,929	22.1	71,222[2]	27.0[2]
1972	19,435	88,991	21.8	73,714[2]	26.4[2]
1973	19,851	91,040	21.8	76,895	25.8
1974	20,199	93,240	21.7	78,413	25.8
1975	19,473	94,793	20.5	77,051	25.3
1976	19,432	96,917	20.1	79,443	24.5

[1] Totals, include reported membership and directly affiliated local union members; Canadian membership and members of single-firm unions are excluded.

[2] Revised.

Sources: Adapted from U.S. Bureau of Labor Statistics, Directory of National Unions and Employee Associations, 1975, bull. 1937, 1977, p. 63; and U.S. Bureau of Labor Statistics "Labor Union and Employee Association Membership—1976," NEWS, September 1977, pp. 2 and 5.

10 Consider the following proposition: "To increase organization among women workers, the labor movement will have to alter its strategies, tactics, and approaches." Debate this proposition in front of your classmates, using teams of two students each to argue the opposing sides and with your instructor acting as moderator of the session.

Union Government and Labor's Political Activity

In Chapter 3, we raised but did not answer the question, "What is the relationship of the union to the individual worker?" We also noted that workers may engage in political activity to achieve their objectives, but we did not examine that aspect of unionism. It is these internal and external political dimensions of the labor movement upon which this chapter will focus.

We begin with the structure of the American labor movement, specifically relationships between local unions, national unions, and the AFL-CIO. Singled out for special attention are the twin cornerstones of the federation's operating philosophy, autonomy and exclusive jurisdiction. Next we examine the internal dynamics of labor organizations, contrasting the leaders' need for order and discipline with the members' claims for participation and perhaps even democracy. Some of the key issues addressed by the Labor-Management Reporting and Disclosure (Landrum-Griffin) Act, which regulates internal union affairs, are reviewed.

The remainder of the chapter is concerned with the role of organized labor in national and local politics. We examine the forms which this activity takes and the reasons why there is no unified labor vote but, rather, diverse positions and voting behavior among unionists. Selected aspects of the political activity of labor unions in other countries are also considered so as to highlight once again both the unique and the shared characteristics of the labor movement and of industrial relations in the United States.

THE STRUCTURE OF THE LABOR MOVEMENT

Far from having a simple structure, the American labor movement is characterized by an intricate web of interrelationships and a wide variety of organizations, ranging from local unions, of which there are about 70,000, to the AFL-CIO, under whose banner are some 17 million workers.[1] In between are municipal and state federations and regional and national bodies, as well as some specialized councils and coalitions. The apparent leading unit, the AFL-CIO, is not the most influential or most powerful of this complex. That distinction falls to the national unions (or international unions, in the case of organizations with members employed outside the United States); in 1976 there were 212 national unions and employee associations, each operating in some jurisdictional area vaguely bounded by occupational or industry lines.[2] They include such well-known organizations as the United Steelworkers of America (USA) and the American Federation of State, County and Municipal Employees (AFSCME) and such lesser-known bodies as the United Brick and Clay Workers of America (UBCW) and the International Die Sinker's Conference (DSC).

The local unions form the building blocks of which the nationals are constructed. The national trade unions emerged only when local unions in a particular trade felt the need for some sort of coordinating agency. The organizations which were thereby created were designed to systematize the conditions and relationships of workers in a particular skill or trade, who often traveled from one location to another or whose products competed with one another. Over time, the nationals came to dominate the local unions which had spawned them, especially as new locals were chartered or otherwise authorized by the larger body. Nevertheless, the local union remains the elemental unit upon which rest the national unions and, indeed, the entire labor movement. The local union corresponds roughly to local government in civil life.[3]

The structural interrelationships between the key components of the labor movement are displayed in Figure 4-1. At the apex is the federation, the AFL-CIO, with national headquarters in Washington, D.C. Its executive officers—President George Meany, whose tenure dates from the 1955 merger of the AFL and the CIO, and Secretary-Treasurer Lane Kirkland, who is regarded by some as the eventual successor to Meany as president—are joined on the executive council by thirty-three vice presidents, who themselves are presidents of one or another of the federation's affiliated national unions.

The executive council, which meets three times yearly and which concerns itself (1) externally with policies and legislation of interest to labor and (2) internally with matters affecting the relations between member organizations, is itself subordinate to the AFL-CIO convention. That body, which meets every other year, is composed of representatives of all the constituent national

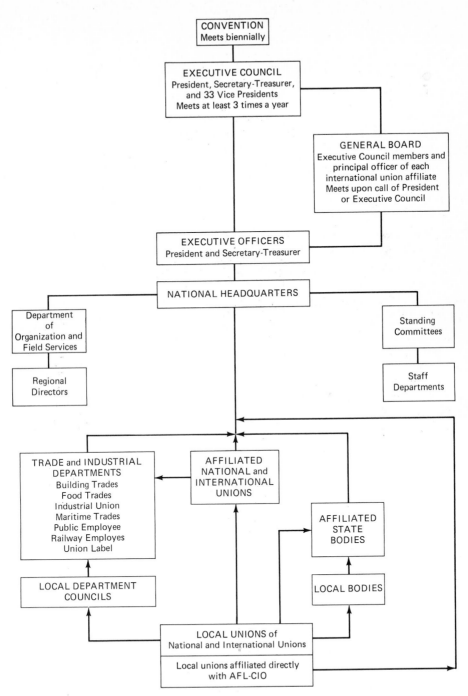

Figure 4-1 Structure of the AFL-CIO. (*Source: U.S. Bureau of Labor Statistics,* Directory of National Unions and Employee Associations, 1975, *bull. 1937, 1977, p. 2.*)

unions, with voting strength based upon the number of members on whom they pay a per capita tax to the federation treasury. The convention elects the president and secretary-treasurer, who, together with other members of the executive council, have final authority on all matters that arise during the periods between conventions. A general board composed of the principal officers (usually the presidents) of *all* the national unions meets upon call to act on any matter referred to it by the officers or the executive council. In voting, it follows the convention principle of casting ballots which are weighted by membership strength.

The Principle of Autonomy

The national (international) unions are *affiliated* with the AFL-CIO, as shown in Figure 4-1. Most local unions are in turn affiliated with their respective national union, though the affiliation of some local bodies is directly with the federation itself. The term "affiliation" signifies the voluntary nature of a labor organization's relationship with the AFL-CIO. A directly affiliated national or local union *voluntarily* chooses that status within the labor movement and is under no compulsion, no requirement, to join the AFL-CIO. Indeed, only about two-thirds of national unions in the United States and a handful of employee associations are affiliated with the federation. The rest have chosen to operate independently of the AFL-CIO, among them the powerful United Automobile Workers (UAW). By the same token, the federation may choose to reject a union's request for affiliation, or it may dismiss a member union for violation of one or another constitutional provision, as it did in 1959 with the International Brotherhood of Teamsters for failure to remedy corrupt practices.

The voluntary nature of a labor organization's affiliation with the AFL-CIO reflects one of the federation's basic operating principles, union autonomy. Despite their frequent appearance in the public eye, the officers of the AFL-CIO have very limited functions and powers, and the organization itself has nothing whatsoever to say or do about the collective bargaining policies of its constituent unions—what wages to seek, what pension benefits to pursue, what new items to negotiate over, or what tactics to adopt in applying pressure to employers. These decisions rest solely with the national unions themselves or their locals. Nor can the AFL-CIO control the political policies of its constituent unions. Even should its executive board decide to support the Democratic candidate in a presidential election, as it did in 1976, or to remain officially neutral, as it did in 1972, it could do nothing to prevent the International Typographical Union (ITU), for example, from actively campaigning for the Republican aspirant in the 1976 election or to stop AFSCME from supporting George McGovern over Richard Nixon in the earlier contest. The federation cannot take disciplinary action against its member unions for failing to conform to a recommended policy.

The principle of autonomy of the national unions has been absolutely central to the American labor movement ever since the birth of the AFL in 1886. To be sure, the constitution adopted at the time of the merger with the CIO in 1955 gave appreciably more authority to the central body to investigate, suspend, or expel member organizations on certain limited grounds. Further, the adoption of explicit codes of appropriate union conduct to which affiliated national organizations were expected to conform appears to have strengthened the control of the federation over its affiliates. Yet the national unions remain reluctant to cede any affirmative authority to the federation, and the power to expel member unions for racketeering or practicing racial discrimination does not seem to have been exercised very rigorously. The AFL-CIO may come to possess a greater measure of governmental power over its constituent members, but thus far the tradition of autonomy has helped it enroll a majority of national unions and associations that represent about 70 percent of all organized workers.

The Principle of Exclusive Jurisdiction

The AFL-CIO does exercise authority over its constituent unions—and by their consent—in the area of defining the jurisdiction within which each has the right to organize and represent workers. Much as the law and the NLRB promote exclusive representation for privately employed workers who choose unionization, a practice emulated in the public sector, the American labor movement follows the principle of one organizational spokesperson for one group of workers, whether the group is made up of workers in only one craft, such as bricklayers, or is composed of a broad assemblage of workers with different skills. If this objective is not fully carried out in practice—"rival unionism" is not always easily contained—the federation nevertheless attempts to enforce it within the practical constraints imposed by its voluntary membership and a labor movement characterized by diversity.

We noted in Chapter 3 that disputes between competing unions over jurisdiction had to be resolved—or a mechanism for resolving them had to be established—in order for the merger of the AFL and the CIO to become a reality. The "no-raiding" agreement developed at that time was a pragmatic convenience that pledged its signatories to recognize established bargaining relationships between organized workers and employers. Essentially this meant accepting the existence and respective membership bases of competing labor organizations in the same craft or industry—for example, the International Union of Electrical, Radio and Machine Workers (IUE) and the International Brotherhood of Electrical Workers (IBEW). It also meant accepting the judgment of the AFL-CIO concerning the jurisdiction of each of these competing unions in *future* organizational campaigns.

An amendment to the federation constitution adopted in 1961 further codified the procedures and criteria for resolving disputes over jurisdiction. It upheld the sanctity of established bargaining relationships recognized by the employer (public or private) or by the NLRB, defined valid defenses for a union's attempts to alter such relationships, and created a five-step internal appeals procedure, including at one stage an "impartial umpire from outside the labor movement" to assist in the resolution of future disputes over jurisdiction.

None of this, of course, guarantees the absence of rivalries among unions and over membership and representation. In fact, it is possible to argue that such rivalries are a healthy aspect of union behavior, reflecting a dynamic element within the labor movement and (ironically) the "production" of a better service for union members as a result of competition over their allegiance. Certainly the National Education Association (NEA) seems to have been largely unharmed and probably even helped by its rivalry with the American Federation of Teachers (AFT), and the same might be said of the American Association of University Professors (AAUP), which competes with the other two organizations to organize and represent college teachers. More broadly, most students of this subject conclude that the AFL was helped rather than harmed by the challenge in the 1930s and 1940s of the CIO.[4] Alternatively, such rivalries can be the basis for escalating wage demands, as one union tries to "outdeliver" another, thereby adding to an inflationary potential. The basic point, however, is that in attempting to deal with disputes over jurisdiction, the federation continues to demonstrate allegiance to another of the principles that have characterized its evolution over the better part of a century. Together with union autonomy, exclusive jurisdiction is a fundamental standard that guides the AFL-CIO in dealing with its constituent organizations specifically and in speaking for organized labor generally.

There is one important area, however, in which the principles of both autonomy and exclusive jurisdiction are diluted, and that is the role of public policy as interpreted by the NLRB. Through its determinations of bargaining units and its elections to determine representation, the Board shapes the structure and functioning of labor organizations and labor relations. These do not always follow a strict guideline concerning autonomy or exclusive jurisdiction, as when the Board prohibits a group of skilled craft workers from breaking off from an industrial union to form their own labor organization so as to escape being dominated by a majority consisting of semiskilled workers. In cases in which a dispute over jurisdiction has been resolved by letting both unions keep their territory (their existing memberships) and specifying ground rules for future organizing, the Board has generally tried to preserve the arrangement, believing that peaceful labor relations take precedence over adherence to the principle of exclusive jurisdiction. Indeed, one could go further and ask whether affording employees the right to pick a labor organization to represent them, as Section 7 of the Taft-Hartley Act provides, isn't inconsistent with the principle of exclusive jurisdiction. All this points out that even fundamental principles of union structure and function do not operate in a vacuum, but are subject to some qualification.

Functions of Union Organizations

The Local Union For the vast majority of organized workers, the local union is the principal institution of the labor movement with which they come in contact. They are members of a particular local, such as Local 12 of the UAW or Local 316 of the International Association of Fire Fighters (IAFF); their dues are paid to the local; their grievances are brought to, and processed by, the local; and they vote to elect officers of the local union. Such organizations may range in size from a handful of members to many thousands, and the members may be employed by a single plant or company or by a number of employers in one locality.

A local union is a multifunction organization. It attempts to expand its membership until all eligible employees are enrolled. It provides numerous services to its members, assisting them in applying for workers' compensation or unemployment benefits, securing medical or pension benefits, and sponsoring social activities. It negotiates or assists in the negotiation of a collective bargaining agreement for its plant, office, shop, craft, or occupation. It appoints or elects stewards who represent the members in defending their interests in the face of adverse actions by management. It processes the members' grievances, it conducts strikes when necessary, and it provides legal assistance to members who may be prosecuted for actions taken during a strike.

The governmental processes of local unions vary depending upon their makeup. For example, a small, local industrial or plant union of, say, steelworkers, automobile workers, or rubber workers will usually have officials who are not paid for their services or who receive only a token salary. These are regular jobholders who have sought union office; only in the larger locals, in which administration is a full-time job, are the officers paid a full salary, and this is likely to be about what they would earn in the plant or trade. The president of the local is, in fact, the chief executive and works closely with his or her associates, typically in committee activity. Relationships tend to be rather formal and prescribed, as is the administration of the collective bargaining agreement that has been negotiated with the employer. The common workplace of the local union's members facilitates informal contacts, both with one another and with union officers; sometimes these contacts may be no more than ''bull sessions,'' but at other times they are a vehicle for transmitting useful information about the union.

In contrast is the local dispersed union of the type commonly found in the building trades; this is much more informal than the local industrial union. Because the members are widely scattered—dispersed—throughout a number of jobs, many of short-term duration; because work crews are constantly being quickly formed and broken up; and because the gripes that may develop at a workplace require immediate attention rather than later consideration, there exists a clear need for a full-time agent to make the rounds of the jobsites where union members are employed to ensure that agreed-upon conditions are being observed. In local unions of this type, the full-time job of representing the members typically is performed by a "business agent," who is elected by the membership and who serves as the kingpin of the local organization, over and above its president. As in most industrial unions, the president of a local dispersed union usually is an unpaid officer. But the business agent is compensated on a full-time basis to police administration of the collective bargaining agreement with the employer or the employer's association. Thus it is easy to understand why the business agent is the union's most important officer. And, unlike the president of a local industrial union, in which the governing process tends to be quite formal, the business agent of a dispersed union personalizes and centralizes the function of administration and enforcement of the labor relationship. He or she must exercise initiative, judgment, and a capacity for quick decisions, for there seldom is time to hold a membership or committee meeting to resolve an issue. The difference is not so much one of philosophy as of structural necessity, reflecting the characteristics of employment in an industry such as construction. This also has the consequence, however, of deemphasizing participation by members in union affairs and of limiting opportunities for members to develop leadership capacities.

Despite these differences, the two leading types of local unions have some characteristics of government in common. Both have elected union officers, including a president, a secretary-treasurer, and an executive board; generally, both have trustees, a finance committee, and a negotiating committee; and both have shop or job stewards, who are the union's representatives in a division of a plant, in an office, or at a particular jobsite.

A local union is chartered by the national or international office of that union. To obtain such a charter, the local binds itself to conform to the international constitution of the union. The power of the international over the local union is quite considerable, usually including authority to approve or reject locally negotiated collective bargaining agreements; to sanction or refuse to sanction local strikes; to require a per capita dues payment from each of the local's members; to remove local officers for cause and, relatedly, to establish a trusteeship over a local union; to supervise, as required, the conduct of union elections; and to inspect the local union's financial books and records.

The National Union The ultimate source of authority in a national union is the convention, which is composed of delegates chosen by local unions. To avoid domination by a few large locals, the number of delegates allowed to a local is not strictly proportionate to its membership. The convention may amend the union's constitution, it has the final voice on all matters of union policy (for example, it can reverse prior decisions of its officers), and, in about two-thirds of the unions, it elects the national officers. The convention also serves as the highest tribunal in cases of disciplinary action which are appealed by the individual member or local union involved.

The interval between conventions is important, for that body constitutes the only effective check on the actions of national unions. The law (specifically the Landrum-Griffin Act, to be discussed below) requires national unions to elect officers at least every 5 years, and for most of them, this becomes the maximum amount of time permitted between conventions. Of the 212 national labor organizations reporting data in the mid-1970s, 30 percent said that they held conventions every year; 23 percent, every 2 years; 9 percent, every 3 years; 18 percent, every 4 years; and 12 percent, every 5 years. The data also reflect a trend toward shorter intervals between union conventions.[5]

During interconvention periods, the supreme authority of the union commonly resides in the general executive board, an elected body. In some labor organizations, however, the national president holds this power and, in general, tends to be the most influential person in union affairs. It is primarily where factionalism exists or where the president is new, weak, or inexperienced that an executive board takes on actual as well as intended power relative to that of the president. Thus, the union convention may be roughly compared with a corporate stockholders' meeting, and the union's executive board with a corporate board of directors.

The relations between a national union and its local unions are multifaceted. National staff personnel such as the editor of the union newspaper, the research director, and the education director provide assistance to the local in its bargaining activity and in servicing its members. In industrial unions particularly, the national representative, a full-time field officer appointed by the president, serves as the key link between national and local labor organizations. The national representative transmits the larger organization's policies to the local and also assists in, and is sometimes critical to, the negotiation of collective agreements. The national representative generally is treated with considerable respect by the local and the employer, for this is the person who will help define the national union's relationship to the local and the local union's relationship to the employer. After all, it is the national union which must sanction a locally negotiated collective agreement or a strike and which assists the local financially and otherwise when a labor dispute occurs.

The financing of union activity, local as well as national, stems from three sources: dues, initiation fees, and special assessments. Table 4-1 shows that, in 1974, most national unions and employee associations required monthly dues payments of $10 or less to their local affiliates.[6] Some unions have different arrangements; the UAW, for example, requires monthly dues from its members in the amount of 2 hours' straight-time pay. Initiation fees averaged less than $40 in 1974, though they exceeded $100 in several unions.[7]

Something more than one-half of the sums paid to a local union is retained for its own expenses of maintaining a hall or headquarters location and servicing the members. The remainder is paid to the national union in the form of a "per capita tax" that is set by the convention or, in a few cases, by a referendum of the membership. In 1974, the monthly per capita tax for national unions was $6 or less in about 85 percent of the organizations, with the smallest unions (by membership) having the highest rates of assessment.[8] More than half of the per capita tax revenues went to the general fund account of the national unions

Table 4-1   Monthly Dues of National Unions and Employee Associations, by Type and Amount, 1974
(Membership Figures in Thousands)

Dues	Total unions and associations Organizations	Membership	Total unions Organizations	Membership	AFL-CIO Organizations	Membership	Unaffiliated Organizations	Membership	Employee associations Organizations	Membership
Total	212	24,190	175	21,530	111	16,879	64	4,701	37	2,610
Fee set by national[1]	101	6,193	68	4,042	34	3,610	34	432	33	2,151
Single rate	80	4,255	50	2,292	22	1,934	28	359	30	1,963
Less than $6	47	2,603	18	653	6	644	12	9	29	1,950
$6–$10	10	202	9	189	4	77	5	112	1	13
$11–15	3	222	3	222	1	1	2	221		
$16 and over	7	7	7	7	1	1	6	6		
Percent or fixed rate	13	1,221	13	1,221	10	1,211	3	10		
Varying rate[2]	21	1,938	18	1,750	12	1,677	6	73	3	188
Less than $6	5	71	4	61	1	44	3	17	1	10
$6–$10	2	25	2	25	1	3	1	22		
$11–15	1	35	1	35	1	35				
$16 and over	3	6	3	6	2	6	1	[3]		
Percent or fixed rate	10	1,801	8	1,623	7	1,589	1	34	2	178
Fee set by local	111	17,997	107	17,538	77	13,269	30	4,269	4	458
Minimum rate only set by national	67	13,758	64	13,447	47	9,396	17	4,051	3	311
Less than $6	39	5,734	36	5,423	23	4,895	13	527	3	311
$6–$10	24	6,207	24	6,207	21	4,228	3	1,979		
$11–$15	2	235	2	235	2	235				
$16 and over										
Percent or fixed rate	2	1,582	2	1,582	1	38	1	1,545		
Maximum rate only set by national	1	14	1	14	1	14				
Less than $6										
$6–$10										
$11–$15	1	14	1	14	1	14				
$16 and over										
Percent or fixed rate										

Dues	Total unions and associations		Unions						Employee associations	
			Total unions		AFL-CIO		Unaffiliated			
	Organizations	Membership	Organizations	Membership	Organizations	Membership	Organizations	Membership	Organizations	Membership
Minimum and maximum rate set by national[4]	16	1,292	15	1,145	9	1,069	6	76	1	147
Less than $6	1	147							1	147
$6–$10	10	418	10	418	6	385	4	33		
$11–15	3	506	3	506	2	502	1	4		
$16 and over	1	182	1	182	1	182				
Amount not reported	1	39	1	39			1	39		
Percent or fixed rate										
No minimum or maximum rate set by national	27	2,933	27	2,933	20	2,791	7	143		

[1] Includes seventeen unions that charge dues but do not have locals.

[2] Amount listed is maximum charged by twenty labor organizations and minimum charged by one national union.

[3] Fewer than 500 members.

[4] Amount listed is maximum limit established by national.

Source: Adapted from Charles W. Hickman, "Labor Organizations' Fees and Dues," Monthly Labor Review, 100:21 (1977).

and employee associations. Of the remainder, the bulk was allocated to strike funds, with small percentages devoted to convention funds, publications, education funds, and funds for retired members. Interestingly, the AFT and the IAFF, whose members are almost universally prohibited by law from conducting work stoppages, nevertheless devoted part of their per capita tax receipts to strike funds. Labor organizations unaffiliated with the AFL-CIO were more likely than others to allocate their per capita tax revenues solely to their general funds. There are no aggregate data available concerning special assessments made by labor organizations, but these usually arise when a particularly difficult, widespread, or prolonged strike is expected.

Intermediate Bodies   Mention must also be made of the intermediate structures that sometimes characterize the system of union organization. One such body is the *joint board,* which enrolls and coordinates the activities of several local unions, usually located in close proximity, that belong to the same national union. A joint board might coordinate a wage demand to ensure that one local union does not undercut another in collective negotiations. An example of this structural form is the Joint Council of Teamsters, No. 13, centered in St. Louis, which is made up of locals of brewery drivers, taxicab operators, laundry drivers, and the like.

A second type of intermediate body is the *district organization,* which also consists of local unions or of several joint boards. Its director or president coordinates the bargaining activity of its member organizations. District Council 37 of AFSCME, located in New York, exemplifies this structure. It includes numerous local unions of blue-collar, white-collar, and professional employees of the city's municipal government.

A third intermediate form of labor organization, made up of locals of the same national union but representing several plants or locations of one employer, is the *council.* Like the district organization, it seeks to coordinate bargaining. Thus automobile workers who are members of several local unions have formed a council to deal with General Motors, and electrical workers' locals have formed a council at General Electric to coordinate bargaining with that employer.

Two Kinds of Government

We find, then, that even a relatively uncomplicated union is likely to be composed of a national office; a number of local unions; a parcel of joint boards or councils which coordinate bargaining in particular areas, districts, or regions and which serve as area coordinators for purposes of internal union administration; and special councils that perform or coordinate some specialized function. Note that these governing units perform two distinct activities: one involves the actual administration of the union as an organization, and the other affects the conduct of the collective bargaining relationship. Consequently, a labor organization can be said to possess two governments, one for internal affairs and one for external relations.[9] The duties of the occupants of positions within these twin governments may overlap considerably, as in most industrial unions, or they may be quite separate, as in most dispersed local unions. And the same division between internal and external affairs may well exist at the level of the national union.

The Teamsters provide an interesting example of this bifurcation. While some of their local unions still negotiate agreements with individual companies, by the end of World War II in major metropolitan areas joint councils generally had taken over the bargaining function and were concluding contracts with employee associations. The government of external relations thus was preempted by the joint council, leaving the internal governmental functions in the hands of the locals. Without deep national involvement in internal union affairs, some of the larger councils were able to accrue considerable power and establish veritable "baronies."

Later, the Teamsters established four "area conferences"—the western, central, eastern, and southern—each embracing all states in its territory. The conferences eventually took away the bargaining function of the joint councils, leaving them to find new activities to justify their existence. The justification took the form of an active involvement in internal governmental functions of the union, that is, nonbargaining activity. And, as a further consequence, the national president of the Teamsters has himself assumed a controlling role in the area conferences, thereby centralizing the power that previously had been dispersed among the baronies.

The area conference has its limitations, to be sure. Because it incorporates truck drivers from a variety of industries as well as other types of employees, the Teamsters found it necessary to establish "trade divisions" within the organization that, in effect, give a national dimension to what are otherwise *area* conferences. Most important for our purposes in this chapter, neither the area conference nor the national trade division has anything to do with the union's internal structure or administration. This illustrates how the members of American labor organizations have two kinds or lines of government: one (internal) which prescribes their duties and enlists their activity as members of their own union and one (external) which defines their rights as employees of a private company or public employer with which their union maintains a working relationship.[10]

Though it appears that those in charge of the bargaining apparatus in a union control the organization's power center, thorny questions have arisen concerning internal governmental procedures as they affect individual members—how much of a voice a member may have in the determination of union policy, the degree of disciplinary authority over the member that is appropriate for the union to exercise, the extent to which the member is required to support political causes that run counter to his or her own convictions, and related matters. Addressing these concerns necessarily brings us into contact with the Landrum-Griffin Act and, more basically, with the dual characteristics of a union's internal processes, which were aptly described many years ago by A. J. Muste as those of an "army" and those of a "town meeting."[11]

REGULATING INTERNAL UNION AFFAIRS: PRESUMPTIONS AND DYNAMICS

In 1959, Congress enacted the Landrum-Griffin Act, the principal objective of which was to promote democracy within unions. Before examining its specific provisions, however, let us consider the objective to which the statute is addressed and the extent to which it is possible for unions to be democratic.

The fact that, because of the way they are structured, labor organizations might be less than fully democratic may seem abhorrent to some and illogical to others. After all, don't unions act as agents of workers, countering the authority of those whom the union represents? But precisely because the union often has to approach the employer as an opponent, either on the offensive or on the defensive, it cannot afford internal disunity. This requires the centralization of authority and the maintenance of order within the ranks so as to build a strong organization. In that respect, the union does resemble a military unit such as an army, over which the leadership must exercise military control.

At the same time, determination within the union of its officers, its general policies and orientation, and its negotiating position with employers is presumed to be the product of participatory processes which reflect the resolution of conflicting internal interests. Out of discussion and debate, exchanges (often highly emotional) of contrasting positions, and a fair hearing of majority and minority views are supposed to emerge the labor organization's tone, its leaders, and its objectives, policies, and practices. In particular, individual workers should have the chance to dissent from a union policy, to oppose a specific practice, to run for an elective office against officials with whom they disagree, and generally to participate in the union. Such individual and group interchanges, debates, and disagreements contain elements of a town meeting, a basic democratic form which is sometimes said to characterize the labor organization as an institution.

It is the dual requirements of discipline and participation—of order and democracy and of behaving like an army *and* a town meeting—that make the union not only a complex institution but also one that is not readily understood. These dual requirements flow from the union's need to reconcile diverse interests, reflect them in its functioning, and represent them in collective bargaining with the employer. Critics of unions who focus on one of these dimensions— "It's just an oligarchy to perpetuate the leaders in office" or "They couldn't organize or effectively represent a Little League team"—invariably overlook the other and do not themselves have to decide when order should be imposed in the interest of representing the members or when a referendum should be conducted on a particular issue. Nor do they have to decide whether a union member should be fined for crossing a duly sanctioned picket line, how frequently contending election slates should be permitted to publish their views in the union newspaper, or whether a special assessment should be made to finance what promises to be a lengthy strike, and when.

To recognize the political "reality" of internal union affairs is not to support the oligarchies that some labor organizations have become, to deny that in others there is a lack of participation by members, or to condone the corrupt practices that still others engage in. The latter is a particularly disturbing aspect of modern unionism, even if confined to relatively few labor organizations; the legitimate labor movement and the vast majority of unionists oppose corruption within their ranks fully as much as they oppose domination by employers or interference with their right of self-determination in matters of labor organization. Rather, our comments are intended to spur readers to think critically about and to analyze for themselves the internal functions of labor unions, their self-government, and the extent to which public policy addresses the need for order as well as the rights of members to participate in such organizations. And in this respect, it is questionable whether Congress, in passing the Landrum-Griffin Act, truly sought to penetrate the real character of the labor organization in America, carefully judging the extent to which it is—and should be treated as—a membership or a service-type institution.

The Landrum-Griffin Act

For many years prior to the passage of the Landrum-Griffin Act, it was well known that in some labor unions the membership was prey to both gross and subtle forms of exploitation by entrenched officials, that democratic procedures for calling the exploiters to task were often deficient or lacking, and that civil judicial remedies for such malpractices were uncertain and not without their own dangers of retaliation when invoked. Periodically, some particularly onerous situation would be exposed and would evoke public interest. Even those favorably disposed toward labor unions—for example, the American Civil Liberties Union—have often remarked on the need for greater democracy within the internal governments of labor organizations. It was the McClellan Committee hearings of 1957–1959, however—at which were paraded across the congressional stage a collection of unsavory union officials, most of whom had been handpicked to make the committee's point—that generated sufficient steam to ensure passage of a bill designed to curb excesses within unions. If the public tended not to distinguish between unions and concluded that a general housecleaning was in order, despite the relatively small number of unions involved in the Senate hearings, even among the experts there was a widespread belief that some controls were called for. Indeed, that belief was shared, to a point, by officials of the AFL-CIO.

In part, the bill which eventually emerged as the Landrum-Griffin Act added to previous labor legislation. Its Title VII amended the Taft-Hartley Act to firm up prohibitions of secondary boycotts, clarify the boundary lines between federal and state jurisdiction over subjects of bargaining that came before the NLRB and, with some limitations, permit striking employees to vote in elections to determine representation. But the major thrust of the act, spelled out in Titles I to VI, was to provide a sweeping set of rules governing the relationship between union governments and their constituencies. The main sections of the law which remain fully in effect are (1) a "bill of rights" for union members, (2) provisions for the conduct of union elections, (3) limitations on "trusteeships" imposed by the national union over local unions, and (4) specification of the fiduciary responsibilities of union officials. The legislation is too lengthy and detailed to permit more than a brief discussion of its particulars. Therefore, we shall provide an overview of the law's main sections and the rationale for including them in the legislation.

The Bill of Rights   The bill of rights specifies that every member of a union shall have an equal right to participate in union meetings and elections. The member is entitled to freedom of speech and association with other members in discussions involving union affairs, both at union meetings and elsewhere. Dues and initiation fees can be increased, and special assessments levied, only by majority consent. Individuals may bring suit against their union, after having first exhausted any internal remedies available to them providing that the process does not require more than 4 months. Perhaps most important, "No member of any labor organization may be fined, suspended, expelled, or otherwise disciplined [by a union] except for nonpayment of dues . . . unless such member has been (A) served with written specific charges; (B) given a reasonable time to prepare his defense; and (C) afforded a full and fair hearing."[12]

These may sound like elementary privileges. However, it was necessary for federal legislation to provide for them mainly because, although many union constitutions contain provisions covering most of these liberties, they are frequently couched in general and ambiguous terms or are subject to additional provisions which weaken their effect. Particularly relevant is the customary constitutional injunction against any resort to the civil courts until all procedures for appeals within the union have been exhausted—without any limit as to time. Since the final appeals body is customarily the convention and since many conventions meet only every 4 years, disciplined members might have to wait that long before they would be—constitutionally—privileged to have their cases reviewed by an outside authority.

Moreover, the courts have frequently upheld such provisions in union constitutions. By and large, they have tended to look on labor unions as voluntary associations and to limit their own judicial function to interpreting the union constitution, which the member presumably accepted when he or she voluntarily joined:

One New York court stated that "the general policy of the courts is one of non-intervention with the internal affairs of labor organizations." As reasoned by the Oregon Supreme Court [in a suit brought by a member], there was no need for intervention, since "a union may, by its constitution, provide an exclusive and final method of resolving all internal disputes, including questions of constitutional interpretation." A Michigan court made the following unusually strong statement in declining jurisdiction over an election, complaining: "It is not the business of an equity court to assure union members that their union affairs shall be conducted in a thoroughly democratic manner."[13]

The reason for this attitude on the part of the courts was the fact that, once a court moved outside the framework of the union's own constitution, it lacked any specific standards, derivable from any relevant body of precedents, which it could apply. Nevertheless, in particularly flagrant cases of miscarriage of justice or abuse of power, the courts would sometimes intervene. Occasionally they would do so under the pretext of having found some procedural defect in the union's action. Occasionally they would look behind the surface facts to the reality of the situation, noting in some instances that further compliance with internal union remedies would be pointless since the result would be predictable.

That civil law did not provide satisfactory protection of the rights of individual members had already been recognized by the AFL-CIO in 1957, when it adopted its own Ethical Practice Code on Union Democratic Processes. While expressing pride in the record of the labor movement generally in this respect, it admitted that "a few unions do not adequately provide for these basic elements of democratic practice," and it went on to specify most of the provisions which the Landrum-Griffin Act was later to write into law. The most notable omission was any provision whereby aggrieved members could seek judicial relief before exhausting the often protracted internal procedures (recall that Landrum-Griffin provides a 4-month limit). The AFL-CIO code concludes: "When constitutional amendments or changes in internal administrative procedures are necessary to comply with the standards herein set forth, such amendments and changes should be undertaken at the earliest practicable time."

Despite the agreement in principle between the federation and the new law, AFL-CIO officials were unhappy with some aspects of its bill of rights. Their chief objection centered on the right of members to enter into civil suits against the union for alleged infringement of their freedoms. This, it was feared, constituted "an invitation to litigation" by dissident members, of whom there are some in every organization, which could result in harassment of officers even when engaged in entirely legitimate union activity. So far, these fears do not seem to have been borne out.

Consider that between 1959 and 1974, some 1560 private civil actions were brought against labor organizations or their leaders by union members, or a little more than 100 such actions annually.[14] The vast majority of these cases alleged violations of the law's bill of rights, though a large proportion were concerned with the officers' fiduciary relationship to the union and its members. Among the offenses over which unionists have sued their organizations and their leaders are denial of voting and contract ratification rights, barring from office those criticizing the incumbent leadership, "egregious" increases in dues over a period of several years, denial of fair disciplinary hearings, and lack of referenda on decisions to merge with other labor organizations. These issues illustrate why Congress believed it necessary to guarantee to union members freedom of speech and the rights of accused individuals. Note, however, that the decisions reached by the courts in cases involving abrogations of these rights have not uniformly found for the union members. They sometimes have supported the union or its officers and, in this way, have helped protect the labor organization *and* the membership from an overly strong emphasis on the individual's rights over the freedoms of the group or the majority. So, while no overall box score is available on the civil actions arising under the Landrum-Griffin Act, there is little reason to believe that the price of ensuring the rights of individual members has been to promote large-scale insecurity and instability among labor organizations.

Election Procedures A second major section of the Landrum-Griffin Act covering relations between a union's government and its constituencies deals with election procedures. Here the problem lay in the attempts of some union administrations to eliminate opposition to their reelection by means of such devices as prohibiting the circulation of campaign literature without the leaders' consent, threatening discipline for "causing dissension" or "creating disharmony," preventing members from participating in nominations by giving inadequate notice or by controlling procedures, expelling opposing candidates or their principal supporters, and manipulating or rigging the vote. In some unions, elections have been held so infrequently that members have been effectively disenfranchised. Moreover, the same attitude on the part of the judiciary which often rendered ineffective a member's protest to the civil courts concerning disciplinary actions operated with respect to complaints concerning irregular election practices.

The Landrum-Griffin Act sought to deal with abuses such as these in part through the protective provisions of the bill of rights and in part through measures having to do specifically with union elections. The law requires that national officers be elected by secret ballot or convention voting no less than every 5 years, that the officers of intermediate bodies such as joint councils be elected every 4 years, and that the officers of local unions be elected every 3 years. A reasonable opportunity must be given to nominate candidates, and the union must comply with reasonable requests to distribute campaign literature at the candidate's expense, with all candidates receiving equal treatment as to the cost of such distribution. Notice of an election must be mailed to each member no less than 15 days before it is scheduled to take place. Union funds may not be used to promote any individual's candidacy. Ballots and other election records must be preserved for at least 1 year.

Complaints alleging violations of any of these provisions must be directed to the Secretary of Labor, who is empowered to act through the federal courts to set aside an election held to be invalid. Table 4-2 provides an accounting of union elections challenged between 1965 and 1974, under procedures set forth

Table 4-2 Union Election Case Activity of the Labor-Management Services Administration, by Fiscal Year[1]

Item	Fiscal year										1965–1974
	1965	1966	1967	1968	1969	1970	1971	1972	1973	1974	
Cases active during year	119	174	116	144	148	154	159	170	162	220	
Based on complaints received											
This year	99	149	92	118	110	134	132	137	126	179	1296[2]
In prior years	20	25	24	26	38	20	27	33	36	41	1261
Cases closed during year	94	150	90	106	128	127	126	134	121	185	1261
Reasons for closing cases											
No violations found, complaint untimely, other reasons	41	24	27	42	58	48	49	47	48	60	444
Insufficient evidence that violations may have affected election outcome	25	56	27	24	20	24	22	35	30	60	323
Voluntary compliance achieved	16	35	21	17	21	21	20	29	27	32	239
New elections held											
Under LMSA supervision	10	26	14	11	19	10	13	18	19	24	164
Without LMSA supervision	4	9	4	3	2	7	6	7	8	6	56
Other corrective action taken	2	0	3	3	0	4	1	4	0	2	19
Civil actions filed under Sec. 402(b)	12	35	15	23	29	34	35	23	16	32	254[3]
Cases pending at end of year	25	24	26	38	20	27	33	36	41	35	35
Formal determinations issued	13	32	21	15	19	15	20	28	26	32	221
Elections supervised by the LMSA under federal court orders in civil actions based on Title IV of the Landrum-Griffin Act	8	10	16	7	11	17	35	27	24	10	165[4]
Civil actions pending in federal courts at end of year	35	52	35	46	59	71	71	54	41	54	

[1] The method of computing LMSA election activity was changed in 1963 from an alleged violation to a case basis; therefore, this table covers only the period from July 1, 1964 to date.

[2] Total includes all active cases since July 1, 1964, i.e., 1276 cases based on complaints received since then, plus the twenty cases based on complaints received before then which were active on July 1, 1964.

[3] Two cases were closed with the filing of a civil action against the United Steelworkers of America which challenged elections for the offices of district director of District 15 in McKeesport, Pa., and District 31 in Chicago.

[4] Figure does not include LMSA-supervised elections conducted in ten districts of the United Mine Workers (UMW) pursuant to orders entered in Title III trusteeship suits filed by the Secretary or by UMW members.

Source: Adapted from U.S. Department of Labor, *Compliance, Enforcement and Reporting in 1974 Under the Labor-Management Reporting and Disclosure Act,* U.S. Government Printing Office, Washington, D.C., 1975, p. 4.

in the Landrum-Griffin Act. In 35 percent of the 1261 cases closed during this time, no violation was uncovered, and in another 26 percent of the cases there was insufficient evidence of violations. In about one-fifth of the cases, the unions involved took voluntary action to meet requirements for compliance, while in the remaining 20 percent of the cases, civil suits brought by the Secretary of Labor were necessary to achieve compliance with election requirements. Some 165 union elections were supervised by the federal government between 1965 and 1974, and more than 300 formal determinations in cases of voluntary compliance by unions with election standards have been issued by the Secretary of Labor since this regulatory legislation was enacted.

Two interesting examples of issues having to do with union elections which attracted the attention of the Secretary of Labor involved the United Steelworkers of America (USA). In the first, the USA enacted a rule stating that no member of a local union would be eligible for office unless he or she had attended a minimum of half the local's meetings during the preceding 3-year period. The rule was first applied in the union's 1967 triennial election and subsequently was challenged in the courts in sixteen different suits brought by the Secretary of Labor on behalf of various local unions. Several district courts issued rulings on these cases, most holding the election rule to be reasonable. Responding to the Secretary's appeal of one of these rulings, the circuit court, in 1973, declared that the USA's rule concerning attendance at meetings "has a direct, substantial relationship to fitness to hold office in that participation in union meetings is one indication of interest in union affairs. Further it does not place any price tag on the right to be a candidate."[15] The court upheld the union's rule, and the Secretary did not appeal the decision further.

In the second case, a district court upheld as proper the Secretary of Labor's directive requiring an independent *district* labor organization to hold a referendum on its proposed merger with the USA before conducting an election of officers of the merged organization. The election itself had been ordered by the Secretary and was to be supervised by the Labor-Management Services Administration of the Department of Labor. Usually such elections are not delayed pending a direct or indirect appeal, but in this instance the court agreed with the Secretary that the district's membership should be afforded an opportunity to vote on the merger itself before voting for the organization's officers, even if the election campaign revolved centrally around the merger. The court commented that this course of action "in both method and objective reflected the ultimate principle of union democracy . . . [because] the merger referendum was the appropriate vehicle for resolving the then most crucial issues concerning the union's future."[16]

Other recent rulings by the Secretary and the courts have set aside union elections because the union failed to mail election notices to the members, barred the candidacies of discharged employees who were contesting their firing on grounds of unfair labor practices, or permitted incumbent candidates to use union funds to publicize their positions and criticize those of their opponents. As the data in Table 4-2 make clear, 1974 was the busiest year up to that time for federal regulation of union elections. More complaints were received and more cases closed in that year than in any one of the preceding 9 years. The number of formal determinations issued in 1974—thirty-two—equaled the previous annual high recorded in 1966.

Trusteeships A third major area in which the Landrum-Griffin legislation sought to reduce the power of union organizations vis-à-vis their members was that of trusteeships imposed on local unions. A trusteeship is an instrument for depriving the subordinate body of its autonomy and placing it under the control of agents usually appointed by the national office. It is a device which experience has shown to be necessary under certain circumstances, as when a national union must protect both its good name and its members' interests from local misgovernment or corruption or when a local union has shown itself unwilling to live up to its collective bargaining responsibilities. But there have also been occasions when trusteeships have been imposed to silence opposition to union officers or their policies or to make a raid on a local treasury. In some cases local unions have been deprived of the right to govern themselves for extended periods of time. The constitutions of a number of unions give the national office the power to determine when a trusteeship shall be instituted and when it shall be removed, sometimes with inadequate provision for a hearing or with no such provision.

> The hearings and findings of the Senate Select Committee on Improper Activities in the Labor-Management Field [the McClellan Committee] . . . focused primarily on trusteeships in three international unions, the Teamsters (Ind.), the Bakery Workers (Ind.) and the Operating Engineers. It also treated to a lesser extent trusteeships in the Allied Industrial Workers, the Meat Cutters, and the Jewelry Workers. It was found that in the Operating Engineers, 12 locals representing 20 percent of the membership were in trusteeship and that 7 of these had been in trusteeship for over 20 years and 2 for over 29 years. Roughly 13 percent of all Teamster (Ind.) locals were in trusteeship, some for more than 15 years. James R. Hoffa [then Teamster president was a favorite target of the Committee] was personally the trustee of 17 of these locals. Detailed investigations of a number of locals of the surveyed internationals revealed situations of impositions of trusteeship at gunpoint, looting of a local treasury by the trustees, and the placing of a dissident local under trusteeship on the pretext that such control was necessary for the conduct of an organizing drive. In one case, two local officers under indictment for extortion were appointed as business agents of the local after imposition of a trusteeship.[17]

The Landrum-Griffin Act recognizes four legitimate purposes for establishing trusteeships: correcting corruption or financial malpractice, assuring the performance of collective bargaining agreements, restoring democratic procedures, and "otherwise carrying out the legitimate objectives" of labor unions. (Included in the latter catchall category are caretaker trusteeships, the most common type, which may be installed when a local union has become inactive as a result of the closing of a plant or a sudden loss of leadership, as through illness or death, or because it is a new local and is still inexperienced in the conduct of its own affairs.)

The law provides that whenever a trusteeship is instituted for one of these reasons, the union must report to the Secretary of Labor the circumstances and the degree of participation which has been left to local members in the election of delegates to conventions and other policy-making bodies. Unless delegates to the union's convention from trusteed locals are elected by a secret ballot of the membership, their votes are not valid. No more than the normal per capita tax and legitimate assessments may be paid out of the local treasury to the national union, except upon bona fide dissolution. A trusteeship established in conformity with these provisions and the procedural requirements of the union's constitution (including authorization or ratification of the trusteeship after a fair hearing before the union's executive board) will be presumed effective for 18 months. During that period it is not subject to challenge except upon clear proof of bad faith. After the expiration of the 18-month period, the trusteeship will be presumed invalid unless it can be shown by convincing proof that continuation is necessary for one of the purposes specified in the act.

The provisions have acted to reduce drastically the number and duration of union trusteeships. Approximately 500 of them were in effect when the Landrum-Griffin Act was passed. None of these was still active in 1974, though several newer ones were in existence. Since 1959, the Secretary of Labor has sued four parent unions to enforce the law's trusteeship provisions, and all were settled in the Secretary's favor.[18]

The best known of these involved the United Mine Workers of America (UMW) in a case that was before the courts for more than 9 years. The original suit, filed in 1964, challenged the validity of trusteeships over a half dozen semiautonomous district unions. Rulings by district and circuit courts in 1972 and 1973, respectively, did indeed find these trusteeships to be in violation of the law and ordered the Secretary of Labor not only to conduct new elections but also to review the union's constitution to determine whether it protected the election rights of the membership.[19] This was done, and new elections subsequently were held for district officers, convention delegates, and members of the international executive board. Some of the more notorious recent aspects of internal machinations within the UMW will be discussed further below.

Fiscal Responsibility   The fourth major section of the act regulating the relationship between the governed and the governing in labor unions deals with the fiduciary responsibilities of officers. This was an area in which four ethical-practice codes of the AFL-CIO had earlier set out desirable standards to which their affiliates were expected to conform. The act first reminds union officers of their financial stewardship on behalf of the members and enjoins them to avoid any financial dealings in which there is a conflict of interest. If any officer is alleged to have violated this trust and the responsible union authorities fail to act to recover funds which have been misappropriated or misused, any member may institute a suit to that effect in either a federal or a state court. The expenses which a member incurs in so doing may be provided for, at the court's discretion, out of funds recovered.

Except in small unions whose annual receipts are less than $5000, all union officials must be bonded in an amount not less than 10 percent of the funds they or their predecessors handled in the preceding year, ranging from no less than $1000 for a local officer up to a limit of $500,000 for a national officer. A union cannot make loans to an officer totaling more than $2000, nor can it undertake to pay on an officer's behalf any fine to which he or she may be subject as a result of violation of the act.

Since 1959, more than 1000 persons have been indicted for violating the various criminal provisions of the Landrum-Griffin Act. Of these, some 75 percent were convicted; the remainder were acquitted, or their indictments were dismissed. The bulk of the charges and prosecutions have involved the embezzlement of union funds and the use of such funds for prohibited political purposes. In 1974, local officials of the Teamsters, the International Union of Operating Engineers (IUOE), and the IBEW, and national officials of the UMW, were among those convicted of criminal violations involving the illicit use of union funds.[20]

The public sector   Before we evaluate the Landrum-Griffin Act, it should be mentioned that Executive Order 11491 requires reporting, fiduciary, election, and trusteeship procedures of labor organizations in the federal sector very similar to those mandated in the law for unions and associations in the private sector. Table 4-3 shows that over the period 1970–1974, some 4500 federal labor organizations filed registration reports, more than 5000 filed annual financial reports (usually in abbreviated form), and information was received concerning thirty-one trusteeships established by these organizations. At the close of 1974, more than 3200 active federal labor organizations were in existence. Some of these were extremely small, while others were high on the list of all American unions and employee associations when ranked by size. These include the American Postal Workers Union (APWU) and the American Federation of Government Employees (AFGE).

There are no known statutory provisions regulating the internal affairs of state and local labor organizations. That is a rather remarkable, if not widely recognized, state of affairs in view of the size of some of these organizations—such as the American Federation of State, County and Municipal Employees (AFSCME), which has 1.1 million members—and the rapid growth of these unions and associations in recent years. Indeed, the extent to which democratic procedures characterize the internal affairs of labor organizations in state and local government is simply not known. One likely consequence of extending the Taft-Hartley Act to the nonfederal public sector would be to simultaneously extend the boundaries of the Landrum-Griffin Act. That particular point seems so far to have escaped the attention of those involved in the debate about federal standards for labor-management relations in the public sector.

Table 4-3 Federal Labor Organization Reports Received, by Fiscal Year and Type

Type of federal labor organization report	Form number	Fiscal year 1971[1]	Fiscal year 1972[2]	Fiscal year 1973	1970–1973 (adjusted)[3]	Fiscal year 1974	1970–1974 (adjusted)
Registration report	G-1	14,255	437	186	4,274	249	4,523
Financial reports							
Annual report	G-2	175	151	186	382	176	558
Simplified annual report	G-3	1,115	1,260	1,555	3,101	1,359	4,460
Abbreviated annual report	G-4	4,967	2,220	1,070	4,542	905	5,447
Trusteeship reports							
Initial trusteeship report	G-15	0	11	10	21	10	31
Semiannual report	G-15	0	4	10	14	14	28
Terminal trusteeship information report	G-16	0	8	12	20	7	27

Recapitulation of active federal labor organizations

	Form number	Fiscal year 1971[1]	Fiscal year 1972[2]	Fiscal year 1973	1970–1973 (adjusted)[3]	Fiscal year 1974	1970–1974 (adjusted)
Active organizations, start of fiscal year		14,255	14,255	3,256	3,205	3,205	
Add: Organizations reporting during year		14,255	437	186		249	
Adjustments, reinstatements, etc.			10,604	129		0	
Less: Organizations terminated during year[4]			0	0		0	
Organizations canceled during year[5]			832	108		200	
Net organizations, end of fiscal year		14,255	3,256	3,205		3,254	

[1] Includes reports submitted by postal unions.

[2] Excludes postal unions which were transferred under the Landrum-Griffin Act.

[3] Cumulative totals adjusted to exclude postal union filers.

[4] Includes organizations which lost their identity as a reporting federal labor organization through merger, consolidation, or otherwise.

[5] Includes organizations which submitted more than one G-1 and those which filed G-1s but were not federal labor organizations as defined by Executive Order 11491.

Source: Adapted from U.S. Department of Labor, Compliance, Enforcement and Reporting in 1974 Under the Labor-Management Reporting and Disclosure Act, U.S. Government Printing Office, Washington, D.C., 1975, p. 4.

Evaluating Internal Union Controls

These are the major provisions of the first piece of national legislation to deal explicitly with union government, and several evaluative observations may be made about them. First, while it is true that "democracy cannot be legislated," as some opponents of the act have argued, it is also true that legislation can facilitate the application and practice of democracy in labor organizations. In an analogous way, few would contend that good-faith collective bargaining can be legislated, but that does not deny the importance of the Wagner and Taft-Hartley Acts to the general acceptance by employers of an institution which they long had opposed.

Second, the act can assist in checking some of the worst abuses of union power, but the more effective remedy or preventive lies within the unions themselves. To the extent that they recognize society's legitimate interest in their exercise of power over their membership, union leaders can work to bring the internal procedures of their organizations into closer alignment with the values central to the society that fostered and protects their existence.

Third, the law has had negative consequences which were no doubt unintended by its framers. These include some centralization of power within labor organizations; greater difficulty in getting individuals to serve as unpaid union officials; increased union expenditures (and membership fees) for reporting, bonding, and litigation; and an increased incidence of strikes.[21] Further, the bulk of alleged union violations of the Landrum-Griffin Act are unproved.

Fourth, American labor law generally follows the doctrine of "trusteeship" in maintaining that a union's responsibility is to those whom it represents in its role as agent. An alternative view, that any person represented by a labor organization has a right to participate equally with others in the conduct of its affairs, appears not in any labor legislation but, instead, in the Civil Rights Act of 1964, to be reviewed in Chapter 8. The latter doctrine dispenses with the concept of labor unions as voluntary associations and, instead, regards their role as exclusive representatives as imposing on them the corollary duty of accepting any and all members as active participants in the administration of the organization.

Finally, even if the Landrum-Griffin Act were fully implemented and totally effective—the information required of unions by this legislation is slow to be processed and has been largely untapped by researchers, and so the law's impact remains to be determined—it provides only limited insight into the internal dynamics and government of labor unions.[22] In its emphasis on rules and regulations, on compliance and procedure, and on reporting requirements, the law provides only a partial picture of the characteristics, the vicissitudes, and the contending interests within the labor organization that make it inherently a political entity.[23] Put differently, the law attempts to treat in singular fashion the diverse institutions that make up the labor movement as a whole. While this is understandable—a similar comment can be made about the Taft-Hartley Act —we need to explore these dynamics and this diversity in somewhat greater detail.

Turnover of Union Officers It is widely presumed that labor leaders, once elected, are in office for life, occupying permanent positions and in some cases operating oligarchies rather than governments. Clearly this has occurred in some labor organizations, and it may appear to be a general characteristic of the American labor movement because of George Meany's nearly quarter-century reign as head of the AFL-CIO. Note, too, that the task of building and maintaining a well-functioning labor organization, and of developing collective bargaining relationships based on mutual respect and trust, may be best carried out by a stable, secure leadership. Unions must serve their members' interests by continuously representing them to management, and that objective might be frustrated rather than furthered by a high frequency of turnover among the leadership.

Nevertheless, recent data show that there has been a good deal of turnover in the leadership positions of national unions. For example, between 1971 and 1975, there were eighty-six changes of national union presidents, affecting some fifty different labor organizations, or about 30 percent of all those which reported to the Bureau of Labor Statistics.[24] Among the group were twenty-nine presidents who resigned or failed to seek reelection, twenty-three who retired, eleven who died in office, nine who were defeated in elections, seven whose terms were limited by constitutional provisions, and three who lost their jobs as a result of mergers with other labor organizations.

While the turnover of presidents during this period was proportionately greater in small than in large unions, it was certainly not confined to the former. Among the national union presidencies that changed hands in the first half of the 1970s were those of such well-known organizations as the Communications Workers of America (CWA); the United Brotherhood of Carpenters and Joiners of America (CJA); the Amalgamated Clothing and Textile Workers Union (ACTWU); the Hotel and Restaurant Employees and Bartenders International Union (HREU); The UMW; the United Textile Workers of America (UTWA); the Laborers' International Union of North America (LIUNA); the IUOE; the International Ladies' Garment Workers' Union (ILGWU); the International Typographical Union (ITU); the International Woodworkers of America (IWA); the Retail, Wholesale and Department Store Union (RWDSU); the AFT; and the AFGE. All these organizations have at least 10,000 members; some have many more (see Table 3-14). In 1977, Douglas Fraser succeeded Leonard Woodcock as president of the UAW, the nation's third largest labor organization.

Concerning turnover of officers in local unions, only fragmentary data (and few studies) are available. It has been widely assumed that the rate of turnover is considerably higher in local than in national labor organizations. That view received partial empirical support in a study of ninety-seven local unions located in and around Milwaukee, Wisconsin, which found 40 percent of those organizations experiencing at least one change of president during the early 1960s.[25] Interestingly, the same study revealed that there was a pattern of relatively low salaries for union officers of the Milwaukee locals (an average of $1230 in 1962) and that the salaries varied directly with the size of the membership. In a later investigation of more than 5000 local unions in Ohio and Wisconsin, the researchers found that turnover of officers during the mid-1960s was *negatively* related to their compensation.[26] The rate of turnover was 35 percent for officers who were paid less than $5000 but only 23 percent for those receiving $15,000 or more. Such findings suggest that, like other employers, the more labor unions pay their managers, the more likely they are to retain them. Just like high rates of turnover, "high" salaries for union officers are not necessarily a bad thing.[27] In any case, the available evidence indicates that turnover of labor union leaders is by no means an uncommon occurrence. If this does not prove that labor organizations are alive and well, it does indicate that they are not uniformly governed by self-perpetuating oligarchies.

Apathy among Members   That union officials are fairly often replaced by others also may seem at odds with the view that union members generally are apathetic about their organizations. By some measures, unionists do indeed appear uninterested in the internal affairs and the government of the institutions to which they belong. Attendance at local union meetings, for example, typically hovers at about 2 percent and rarely exceeds 10 percent of the membership. At some national conventions, furthermore, large numbers of local unions may be entirely unrepresented. Such apparent lack of participation in union affairs may imply that the members are dominated by labor "bosses" who will proceed unto themselves, pursuing their own special interests over and above those of the broader constituency that they are supposed to serve.

Other aspects of unionism, however, suggest that this conclusion is questionable. Low attendance at union meetings is somewhat comparable to the low turnout at the idealized town meeting or in American presidential elections. The latter are hardly undemocratic because not everyone, maybe even the majority, fails to participate actively in them. What concerns those who do not vote in elections, or, more narrowly, who do not attend monthly meetings, is that they be represented in the respective decision-making processes. To the extent that union members feel adequately represented in and by their labor organizations—by the leaders, by the shop stewards, and by those who do attend meetings—they may not actively participate in them. And, according to a study of a union of professional engineers, the level of satisfaction or dissatisfaction with the union has no significant relationship to a member's willingness to attend union meetings (or to represent the union).[28] Thus, if democracy is defined as full and continuous participation by members, then, by that standard, labor unions are not democratic—but perhaps neither is any institution.

More to the point, there are avenues other than meetings and periodic elections of officers through which unionists may make their wishes known to, or apply pressure on, their leaders. Central among these is the process of ratifying collective agreements negotiated with employers by the union's bargaining representatives. The vast majority of union constitutions require the membership, or in some cases delegates representing the membership, to ratify newly formed contracts through a vote. The union's leaders cannot simply presume to speak on behalf of the members in contracting for terms and conditions of employment. Rather, they must solicit the members' formal approval of their own negotiating efforts, and sometimes they must work quite hard to convince those whom they represent that all that can be gotten from the employer has in fact been obtained. For unionists, the ratification process is a clear way in which they may express approval or dissatisfaction with the leadership, whether or not they have voted in prior elections or attended monthly meetings and whether or not their vote is based on the terms of the contract or on some other issue—perhaps one of internal governance—of special importance to them.[29]

The ratification process again underscores the point that unions are not so much organizational democracies as interest groups that seek a larger share of resources for their membership.[30] In pursuing external bargaining objectives, unions and their leaders may indeed have to follow less than fully democratic, participative processes. They may have to operate more (but not totally) like armies than like town meetings. Further, the tensions that sometimes emerge within labor organizations between internal democracy and external bargaining objectives carry over to the public policies that regulate unions and labor-management relationships. The Taft-Hartley Act is intended to promote peace and stability in industrial relations, while the Landrum-Griffin Act seeks to preserve and promote democracy in labor organizations. But what if these two objectives occasionally conflict? What if union members in an industry that is critical to the nation's or to a locality's health and welfare—oil refining, steel manufacturing, or police protection, for example—exercise their democratic right to reject rather than ratify a contract, thereby causing a protracted strike? In such cases, democracy has prevailed over peace, but at what price and in whose interest? Should the government somehow enjoin the strike, and, if so, has not peace then been purchased at the cost of internal democracy? This is far from being an improbable scenario. It was precisely refusals by membership to ratify contracts that lay behind a 1971 proposal of the Nixon administration to permit privately negotiated labor agreements in the transportation sector to be put into effect without being voted on by union members. That proposal, subsequently rejected by the Congress, reflected a real concern for maintaining, in an uninterrupted fashion, key modes of transportation—trucking, rails, airways—through which are distributed much of the country's industrial, consumer, and farm products. But it also illustrated the many pressures and the differing values and objectives which are at work in a democratic, capitalist society and which make full-blown union democracy impractical.

Variations in Internal Union Government

If, because of their nature and functions, labor organizations cannot be totally democratic and if the law treats only some of the surface dimensions of the internal government of these institutions, it is nevertheless true that unions— and employee associations—differ widely in their responsiveness to members and in the extent to which members actively participate in them. Without pretending to be exhaustive in this regard, we shall briefly review and contrast the leading features of the internal union governments of five labor organizations—the Teamsters, the UMW, the UAW, the ITU, and the United Steelworkers of America (USA)—so as to illustrate the range of practices that exist along this dimension of the American labor movement. The analysis once again highlights the diversity that characterizes an institution which is too often presumed to be monolithic and unvarying.

The Teamsters   The Teamsters—the country's largest union, with about 2 million members—have long been regarded as among the more undemocratic and corrupt of American labor organizations. Revelations of sordid practices within this union were instrumental to the passage of the Landrum-Griffin Act and to the AFL-CIO's earlier effort to police more closely the internal governments of its affiliated organizations. The refusal of the Teamsters to adhere to the ethical practices set down by the federation led to the expulsion of that organization from the AFL-CIO in 1957; it continues its status as an independent, unaffiliated union.

The major manifestation of corruption within the Teamsters has been in the use—misuse—and management of their financial resources. Former president James Hoffa, whose predecessor, Dave Beck, was himself convicted and jailed for tax fraud in the 1950s, centralized collective bargaining within the union and proved to be a shrewd negotiator who secured the allegiance of the members by delivering substantial increases in wages and benefits and by eliminating certain pay differentials that were particularly irritating to his constituents. But Hoffa also permitted, indeed backed, the policy of using the members' dues and especially their pension funds (which he helped administer as the principal trustee of a joint labor-management group organized to oversee such matters) to finance a variety of construction and development projects, the materials for which were delivered to the building sites by Teamster drivers.[31] The considerable pressure that this brought to bear on trucking and other transportation companies, as well as on construction firms and their subcontractors, was augmented by direct loans to employers in a variety of industries and by bribes, kickbacks, and payoffs. The fact that many employers willingly accepted and in fact sought out these funds does not detract from the clear evidence that union members' financial resources were used in ways inimical to their interests and certainly to the public interest.

Following Hoffa's imprisonment in 1967 for tax fraud, he continued to run the Teamsters from his jail "office," but gradually his successor, Frank Fitzsimmons, assumed a real rather than a shadow leadership position. The overt misuses of funds and abuses of members' rights appear to have diminished somewhat in recent years, but some of them are still very real. For example, a group of dissident Teamsters, formed in 1972 and known as PROD (for Professional Drivers Council on Safety and Health), published a lengthy report documenting financial irregularities and violations of members' rights by the national organization and some of its local affiliates.[32] These included the payment to some union officials and organizers of multiple salaries and expenses by several different local or intermediate labor organizations (the total approaching $200,000 in some individual cases), members' lack of access to election processes and machinery, failure to process employees' grievances adequately, and patterns of cozy and close relationships between union leaders and company executives that seemed to defy rather than serve the members' interests. The PROD organization and another group, Teamsters for a Democratic Union, were indirectly referred to by President Fitzsimmons at the Teamsters' 1976 national convention, which he opened with the remark: "I will never allow any infiltration into this organization by those who would destroy it, unless by your majority you allow them to do so."[33]

The corrupt practices of a few can tarnish the many, and there are undoubtedly numerous local unions, local officers, and local officials within the Teamsters who do seek democratically to serve and protect the rights of the union's members. Further, the businesses in which members of the Teamsters are employed or with which they come into direct contact are usually highly competitive and relatively small. Such characteristics have been found by students of this subject to provide especially fertile ground for corrupt and unethical practices generally, and for corruption in unions in particular.[34] Thus the nature of a union's internal government does not stem solely from the composition of its membership, the character of its leaders, or its organizational dynamics.

The UMW Few labor organizations have had as stormy or as violent a history as the UMW. Again, that record and the union's internal government have been importantly shaped by the industry in which miners are employed and by the type of work they perform. The industry has generally been a fiercely competitive one containing many small firms, though a relatively few large companies have long played a prominent role in it. The work of miners is, of course, arduous, dangerous, and carried out in an isolated environment. To bargain effectively with the mine owners, John L. Lewis, the UMW's long-term president and founder of the CIO, centralized control over external and internal union affairs to a degree perhaps unmatched in the history of the American labor movement. That pattern of union governance was appropriate for its time and certainly for Lewis, and few doubted that he had a primary devotion to anything other than the interests of the union's members.

It is debatable whether the same could be said for Lewis's successors, however, and in the late 1960s and early 1970s the internal disputes in the UMW were constantly in the public eye. The attention stemmed from the notorious events and aftermath of the 1969 union presidential election, won by the incumbent, W. A. "Tony" Boyle, over the challenger, Joseph Yablonski. Three weeks after the election, Yablonski and his family were murdered in their home,and the subsequent federal investigation, which cost $500,000, into the union election resulted in its being set aside under provisions of the Landrum-Griffin Act. In a new election supervised by the Department of Labor, a slate of officers headed by Arnold Miller was elected, their campaign having been based primarily on democratic reform of the union. Yablonski's murderers subsequently were convicted, and their ties to the Boyle-led union and eventually to Boyle himself were established. Boyle was arrested, tried, convicted, and imprisoned in 1974 for ordering Yablonski's death, but he was released on bond in 1977 following a court ruling that he be retried because of irregularities in the handling of his case.[35]

Miller was reelected president of the UMW in 1975, but not without considerable opposition from those within the union who charged him with ineptitude and failure to serve the members' interests adequately in negotiations with employers. Later in that year, he was charged by the union's executive board with mismanagement and improper use of union funds, but an investigation by the Department of Labor found little evidence to support those claims. That opposition to Miller is in part led by former supporters of Boyle should not obscure the substantive concerns that are at issue here or the real dissatisfaction that some miners feel with the union's leadership. Wages, fringe benefits, job security, safety and health, and local grievance procedures head the list of items that miners are most concerned about. At least some of these unionists do not believe that under Miller's leadership the organization has made sufficient headway in bargaining with the mine owners over such items or in preventing the growth of nonunion mines. Miller's inability to control his union's members was widely commented on during, and fully evident in, the UMW strike against the coal operators in late 1977 and early 1978. And, while it is an oversimplification to suggest that the price of participatory union democracy is a weakened negotiating capability, this view is partly accurate and aptly characterizes the current internal tensions within the UMW. If a labor organization can only rarely and not for too long be operated *strictly* like an army, so too it cannot indefinitely be run like a town meeting.

The UAW At the other end of the spectrum—the spectrum of democracy within unions—from the UMW and the Teamsters is the UAW. Like the Teamsters, it is unaffiliated with the AFL-CIO, and like the UMW, it has experienced recent changes in leadership. But there the similarities end, for the UAW has long been regarded as among the most democratic of American labor organizations.

Formed during the mid-1930s as an affiliate of the CIO, the UAW was headed for almost 25 years, until his death in an airplane crash in 1970, by Walter Reuther, one of the most influential and charismatic figures ever produced by the American labor movement. Earning his spurs in the famous "battle of the overpass" and in the sit-down strikes conducted in American automobile plants during the late 1930s, Reuther became a powerful labor leader in part by promoting democracy within his union rather than by suppressing it. One dramatic example of that commitment to democratic government was the creation in 1957 of a UAW Public Review Board, composed of nonmember, nonofficer neutrals to hear and issue binding decisions in cases of appeal or complaint brought by individual members against the union. Hundreds of cases have been decided by the board during its tenure, and the parties have willingly lived by the rulings so rendered. The failure of all but a handful of other labor organizations to institute similar channels for appeals or review underscores the uniquely democratic features of the UAW.[36]

The withdrawal in 1968 of the UAW from the AFL-CIO was precipitated in an important sense by differing conceptions of democracy. Reuther felt that the federation should have been more receptive to contesting views within its own house concerning the economic, social, and political policies of the nation. He portrayed the labor movement's dominant institution as less than fully responsive to new and developing constituencies, blacks and women in particular, and as singularly intolerant of dissent over issues such as the Vietnamese war, "police brutality," and public assistance. His personal differences with George Meany over the leadership of the labor movement were considerable and the failure to transmit the union's per capita tax to the federation was the occasion for withdrawal from it. But the genuine commitment of Reuther's union to internal democracy and the real differences that it had with much of the rest of American labor over this issue should not be overlooked.

Reuther's successor, Leonard Woodcock, preserved the union's democratic traditions even as he proceeded in a relatively low-key fashion. Among Woodcock's innovations were conferences of production workers held in advance of the 1973 and 1976 bargaining rounds with the automobile firms, during which union members and their delegates informed the leaders about their negotiating preferences. In 1977, Woodcock, who left his post to become envoy to China in the Carter administration, was replaced by Douglas Fraser, a man clearly in the Reuther tradition. Despite the unstable economic position of the automobile industry in recent years and the long-standing conflicts between skilled craft employees and semiskilled automobile assemblers within the union, the UAW continues to steer a course that reflects a strong commitment to internal democracy and participative governance. And the organization's continued preference for remaining unaffiliated with the AFL-CIO persists in part because of differing views about participation by members and dissent over internal union affairs as well as external union politics.[37]

The ITU   The ITU is the only American labor organization to have maintained an internal two-party political system akin to that characteristic of the national political scene.[38] In this labor organization, the Progressive and Independent parties have vied for power for many years, but their conflicts over the internal governance of the union have become institutionalized within it. Dissent and opposition, debate between contesting election slates, campaigns soliciting members' votes, and other trappings of a party system of politics are present in the ITU. Most remarkable, perhaps, in comparison with other labor organizations (and institutions in which political campaigns are conducted), defeated officers willingly return to their positions as workers in the printshops.

There is no simple or single explanation for this continuing two-party internal political system. The history of the national union's development, arising as it did out of the federation of various and diffuse local printers' organizations of long standing, militated against the emergence of a dominant one-party, bureaucratic hierarchy. The printers' strong identification with their craft—an "occupational community," as it has been labeled—helped foster the notion of local autonomy even within a large labor organization. The borderline status of printing as between the middle class and the working class early on split the printers into "moderate" and "radical" groups, and this formed part of the enduring basis of the ITU's internal two-party political system. And the successful, if protracted, struggle of the printers against secret societies within their ranks early in their history inadvertently contributed to the maintenance of democracy, first by dividing those opposed to such societies from those supporting them, and second by providing a rationale for electing union officers on the basis of popular elections rather than conventions, for deciding many issues by means of popular referenda, and for enabling easy initiation of referenda by the rank and file.

One can hardly pretend that these factors, unusual but not unknown in other labor organizations, inextricably led to internal democracy or, least of all, to a functioning two-party system. Moreover, a variety of circumstances peculiar to this union are also relevant to its form of internal government. Nevertheless, the fact that the ITU has been able to sustain its unique internal political system, which offers the members considerable opportunities for participation in governing their union, indicates that a bureaucratic hierarchy led by a single faction is not the only way in which a viable labor organization can be structured. Note, too, that the printers have been employed not in a concentrated or monopolistic industry but in a highly competitive one which has experienced many sudden changes, periods of recession, and, particularly in major urban centers, decline of business and loss of jobs. Yet this has not caused the ITU to centralize its internal operations under one relatively permanent set of leaders —the union has been severely criticized by some of the members for not doing so—or engendered unwillingness among former officials to return to the shop floor. If the ITU's internal political system is not replicated elsewhere within the labor movement, its existence is noteworthy in and of itself, and in conjunction with the systems of the other unions reviewed above it indicates the diverse forms of governance within American labor. At the same time, a labor union or employee association need not maintain a two-party political system to be an internally democratic organization. If that were the standard of democracy, then only the ITU could pass muster.

The USA The fact that most labor organizations do not have formal political parties which vie for union offices and the fact that their leaders sometimes have long tenure in office should not mask the considerable challenges which officers sometimes face and which provide yet another sign of internal participation and at least partial democratic governance. The recent history of the United Steelworkers of America (USA) illustrates this point nicely.

The nation's fifth largest labor organization and the second largest within the AFL-CIO, the USA was headed for many years by Philip Murray, who also served as president of the CIO until his death in 1952. David McDonald succeeded Murray as the USA's president, and, while he was widely regarded by outside observers as an effective union leader, he became increasingly perceived by union members less as a spokesman for their interests than as a remote, aloof figure who was perhaps most comfortable with employers and company managers. The opposition to McDonald grew within the union to the point where, in 1965, he was defeated in a close election by I. W. Abel, who ran on a platform of returning collective bargaining to the members and of opposing the brand of "tuxedo unionism" which allegedly was practiced by McDonald.

Thereafter, Abel solidified his support within the union, continuing some but by no means all of the policies of his predecessor. In the process, he became perceived as a labor leader in firm control of his organization rather than as a reformer. In control he was, but some union members viewed Abel's leadership as increasingly autocratic and questioned some of his internal policies as well as his bargaining strategy with employers. The Experimental Negotiating Agreement (ENA), for example, which was concluded in 1973 and which permitted a form of compulsory arbitration to be substituted for the strike (and lockout), was strongly opposed by some unionists even as it was hailed by outside observers as a statesmanlike act intended to promote peaceful industrial relations.[39] In 1974, running on a platform of more militant bargaining and opposition to the national leaders of the USA, 35-year-old Edward Sadlowski was elected the head of District 31, the union's largest, with over 70,000 members.

Less than 3 years later, Sadlowski resigned as head of the Chicago district to run for the presidency of the USA against Lloyd McBride, who was strongly backed by retiring President Abel. The campaign was an aggressive and in some ways quite a bitter one. Sadlowski charged the leadership with "selling out," autocracy, and unresponsiveness to the members; McBride emphasized his experience and his key role as a shaper as well as an implementer of key union policies; and Abel threatened to resign before his scheduled retirement if Sadlowski was elected. In these respects, the contest for the presidency also reflected the ability of a challenger to mount an effective campaign against a strong incumbent and to generate internal as well as external debate over issues of critical importance to steelworkers. McBride defeated Sadlowski—326,000 to 249,000 votes— in the 1977 election, and the validity of the result was upheld by the Department of Labor in a response to an appeal brought by the loser.[40] Sadlowski remains on the staff of District 31, and he uses that position to voice his opposition to various union policies and bargaining positions, such as the 1977 decision to extend the ENA for 3 more years.

Democracy in Unions and Union Administration

If we ask, then, "How fares democracy in organized labor?" one answer is that it is certainly doing better than is popularly supposed, even if it falls considerably short of an ideal type of participatory governance. But if the internal politics of American labor organizations runs the gamut from the Teamsters to the ITU, it is nevertheless the corruption and violence and the occasional scandal that draw the attention of the media and tend heavily to influence public opinion about labor unions. Similarly, if there is considerable turnover among national union presidents and local union officers, it is nonetheless the continuance in office of 84-year-old George Meany as president of the AFL-CIO that helps to create the widespread impression that union leaders occupy their offices for life. Thus, even to union sympathizers the internal governance of American labor organizations remains a troublesome issue indeed, despite the fact that unions are probably more democratic than is generally presumed and, more fundamentally, that they are not established principally to promote internal democracy.

It would be most useful in evaluating democracy in labor oganizations to include in the analysis unions and employee associations in the public sector. As noted earlier, however, almost nothing has been written about the internal governments of these organizations, which now represent almost one-quarter of all organized workers and whose importance to the labor movement was reflected in the creation in 1974 of a public employees' department within the AFL-CIO (see Figure 4-1), which is one of only seven departmental entities in the federation's structure.[41] If anything, unions and associations in the public sector might be expected to exhibit greater internal democracy than their counterparts in the private sector, owing to the employment of their members in presumably democratic governments of the American political system. Without evidence contradicting or supporting it, however, this statement remains a speculative hypothesis.

Ironically, the extremely strong tendency of American unions to recruit their leaders from the ranks—in itself a practice that bespeaks democracy—contributes to an internal problem that is not well or widely appreciated: ineffective management and administration of labor organizations. In some ways, though certainly not all, democracy and efficiency conflict within an organizational context. To the extent that members benefit from efficient management and administration of internal union affairs, less in a direct sense perhaps than in relation to the benefits secured under collective bargaining, democratic governance may be overemphasized rather than underemphasized.

The many weaknesses in the management and administration of unions have been described by Bok and Dunlop:

> [The] principles of administration are little more than common sense, and labor leaders are instinctively aware of most of them. With few exceptions, however, union officials have not devoted much conscious effort to implementing these precepts. . . . The quality of administration in most unions is still at a primitive level, lagging behind the standards achieved not only in large business, but in many of the better-run foundations, hospitals and government departments.[42]

Among the key problems identified by these authors are excessive decentralization in some unions and excessive centralization in others; the maintenance of overly small local organizations, when aggregating them into larger units would yield real economies of scale; the failure of some craft and single-occupation or single-industry unions to diversify their membership base or mount an analytical capacity within the organization to investigate this potential; an unwillingness to adapt the structure of union organizations to their strategies, particularly as the latter are related to organizing women and white-collar and professional workers; and, most important of all, the lack of attention to long-rang planning of union objectives, goals, and strategies. To these could be added the limited short-run planning and budgeting carried out in most union organizations; the lack of incentives and rewards for administrative acumen; the low level of formal education and training among union officials, especially local officials; and, finally, the paucity of management development programs for high-ranking union leaders.

Where labor organizations have sought to improve their internal management and administration, they have generally done so in relation to, or as an offshoot of, their collective bargaining activity. For example, the growth of complex pension funds and fringe benefits programs, in which unions play a partial or major trusteeship-administrative role, has brought about the use of computers, the employment of computer specialists, and the glimmerings of systems analysis within labor organizations. More generally, the need to forecast the consequences—or respond to management's forecasted consequences —of alternative bargaining packages in terms of wage-benefit tradeoffs and service obligations imposed on the union also has underscored the need for internal analytical capability and similarly has spurred increased use of computers by labor organizations. There is likely to be even more emphasis on the management and administration of unions in view of the increased complexities of collective bargaining, the more intricate managerial structures such as conglomerates and multinational corporations with which unions must deal, the continued growth of fringe benefits relative to wage compensation, and the imperative of more closely identifying members' needs and views.

So, while the issue of internal union governance indeed merits debate and discussion and while truly democratic governance remains an elusive goal (where it is a goal) of many labor organizations and of public policy, in the last analysis efficient management and administration of union affairs may be even more important to the viability and effectiveness of these organizations. The point is further emphasized when the agency and representation functions of labor organizations are borne in mind.

POLITICAL ACTIVITY OF LABOR

Throughout much of its early history, organized labor in the United States eschewed external political activity. Under Samuel Gompers's leadership, the AFL adhered strongly to the collective bargaining approach, its member unions preferring to rely on their own strength rather than seek favors from government or those in elected political office. That posture was difficult to maintain when government continued to concern itself with the activities of labor unions, using the Sherman Antitrust Act to prosecute the concerted actions of workers. Gompers was pushed to dilute his preferred policy of noninvolvement, advocating that labor reward its political friends and punish its political enemies. In 1924, the AFL departed from its tradition of nonpartisanship to join with the railroad workers' unions in endorsing the third-term candidacy of Wisconsin Senator Robert LaFollette. The failure of that effort bespoke the desirability of not linking labor's political activity to a particular political party and of retaining the flexibility to choose labor-oriented candidates from any party. This remains the official policy of the AFL-CIO.

Early in this century, the political activities of the AFL were devoted largely to seeking removal of some of the legal disabilities from which unions suffered. Its greatest triumph of the pre-New Deal era was the inclusion in the Clayton Act (1914) of sections designed to limit the application of the Sherman Antitrust Act to unions. The subsequent judicial decisions that rendered these provisions meaningless could hardly have done other than increase the unions' distrust of government.

Somewhat more successful in their political bargaining during this period were the railroad workers' unions, which, in 1916, secured under the threat of a nationwide strike an 8-hour day on the railroads. Ten years later, the Railway Labor Act was passed, granting to the unions in this industry rights concerning organization and bargaining which were not extended to other unions until the adoption of the Wagner Act in 1935. The rest of the labor movement did not quickly follow the lead of the railroad workers' unions, however, and the AFL was noticeably lukewarm about the Wagner Act and actually opposed the Social Security Act, both of which were passed in the same year. It was the CIO that invigorated labor's political activity. Breaking away from the AFL, it contributed $770,000 to the Democratic National Committee in 1936; this was labor's first substantial contribution to a national political campaign.

In large part, the AFL's reluctance stemmed from a fear that government "paternalism" would sap the reliance of workers on their own organized strength, which was regarded as the only sure weapon in time of trouble. (Also, some union leaders feared that their own institutional roles would be diminished—do actors like to have their lines cut?) Thus the emerging doctrine that government is responsible for the welfare of people who cannot provide for their own well-being was one to which the leaders of the AFL (and of other institutions) were slow to adapt.

But adapt they did, and public policy soon reflected a concern with the actual or potential domination of the political process by labor and other major interest groups. The Hatch Act of 1940, which was applicable to managements as well as unions, established a ceiling of $5000 on individual cash contributions to campaign funds and also limited the total expenditures by any single campaign committee. The latter provision spawned diversified campaign committees, each of which could spend up to the legal limit. The Smith-Connolly Act of 1943 prohibited altogether contributions by labor unions to candidates in national elections, but it did not outlaw contributions to candidates seeking nomination. This led to the practice on the part of unions' political action committees of collecting funds from the unions to be contributed to friendly candidates and later to the legally allowable tactic of collecting smaller contributions directly from union members to be used in election campaigns. Nor did the law prohibit indirect political expenditures by the unions themselves, for example, purchasing space in a newspaper to endorse a candidate instead of giving the funds directly to the candidate.

In 1947 the Taft-Hartley Act prohibited unions from making expenditures on, or contributions to, elections, primaries, and conventions involving federal office; this matched a similar prohibition on corporate contributions and expenditures. Some states followed suit with legislation applying to state elections and primaries. However, as is still the case today, none of the laws affected the right of an organization to collect voluntary contributions directly from union members and the public, usually in very small sums. In the CIO, the Political Action Committee (PAC) performed this function, and in the AFL, it was carried out by Labor's League for Political Education; when the two federations merged to form the AFL-CIO, the Committee on Political Education (COPE) replaced the other political arms. Note, however, that the Supreme Court has permitted, as a form of free speech guaranteed by the Constitution, direct expenditures in the form of political advocacy in regular union publications and that the law touches neither unions' expenditures on state and local campaigns nor their lobbying activities on behalf of specific pieces of legislation.

The problem of labor's political spending is the age-old one of balancing the rights of the majority and the interests of the minority. From one perspective, unions are primarily instruments for bargaining with employers, and it is contrary to democratic ideals to allow union officials to spend members' dues, especially those required by union security clauses, in support of political causes and candidates that some members oppose. The contrasting view is that the activities of federal, state, and local governments have at least as much impact as collective bargaining on the welfare of workers; as long as a majority of a union's members want their leaders to support a particular cause or candidate, the minority should go along, as in any organization.

There is, of course, no easy resolution of these conflicting positions. The British have followed the practice of "contracting out," according to which each union specifies the proportion of its dues to be used for political purposes rather than for negotiating and administering the contract; the individual member who wishes to do so is permitted to pay only the "bargaining fee" and to be exempted (i.e., to contract out) from paying the political assessment by formally notifying the union of this desire. In 1961 the Supreme Court came close to permitting this system in the United States in a case involving six workers covered by the Railway Labor Act, in which it ruled that union members who are compelled to pay dues by a union-shop clause and who object to the nature of the union's political spending may file a formal protest which entitles them to a refund of the "political" portion of the dues. Since then, labor organizations such as AFSCME; the Brotherhood of Railway, Airline and Steamship Clerks, Freight Handlers, Express and Station Employees (BRASC); the International Association of Machinists and Aerospace Workers (IAM); and the UAW have adopted dues-rebate plans. To this point, however, most labor unions and employee associations have not developed comparable plans.

The importance of this issue naturally grew with labor's increased involvement in federal, state, and local politics. In the post-World War II period, organized labor began to involve itself more deeply than ever before in external politics. Its reported contributions totaled many millions of dollars by the late 1960s, and these notably unreliable (understated) figures exclude the large amount of union functionaries' indirect expenditures on, and direct participation in, numerous political campaigns. COPE, which has a paid director and staff, and some of the larger national unions offer extensive programs of political seminars and conferences for leaders and members and have substantial numbers of members who are ready to work in political campaigns. A legislative department was created within COPE to engage in lobbying activity and to coordinate that type of activity among member unions. On the state level, an AFL-CIO officer typically directs lobbying activities with the assistance of a professional staff, while an affiliated COPE plans and monitors labor's campaign efforts for statewide office. Similar functions are carried out at the local level by the leaders of county and municipal federations and their COPE organizations. The state and local levels are also a hotbed of political activity on the part of organized public employees, whether or not they are affiliated with the AFL-CIO.

In all this, the provisions of the Taft-Hartley Act limiting campaign contributions by labor (and business) organizations and permitting the individual union member to avoid paying for political activities inconsistent with his or her wishes make good sense. The thornier question involves their enforcement. And, as recently noted by Epstein, during the 25 years between the passage of the Taft-Hartley Act and April 7, 1972, when the Federal Election Campaign Act (FECA) became operational, the legislative restrictions on campaign activities by labor unions were seldom enforced.[43] Apparently, this lack of enforcement stemmed from judicial questioning of the constitutionality of the provisions prohibiting various campaign activities by labor unions.

In any event, the FECA, together with subsequent Supreme Court decisions and amending legislation in 1974 and again in 1976 arising out of the Watergate scandal, seems to firmly establish that labor unions' political action committees can contribute monies to political candidates and make expenditures on their behalf but that they must adhere to the legal restrictions concerning the size of contributions ($5000 per candidate, as before), the costs of internal communications to the members, and the solicitation of voluntary contributions from members and their families. This entire process is monitored by the Federal Elections Commission, created by the 1972 legislation. And, because the law permitted, both in form and in substance, unions to engage in political activities that previously were carried out in a clandestine fashion, it seems likely that such formerly undercover activity "has lost much of its previous utility except for those organizations determined to favor candidates or committees with extraordinarily—and illegally—generous contributions, or those particularly disposed toward secretiveness."[44] The same is expected of business corporations, whose covert as well as legal political contributions, especially to the 1972 Nixon campaign, dwarfed those of organized labor.[45]

The Effectiveness of Labor's Political Activity

The extent to which organized labor's political activity is translated into effective results—labor's "clout"—is the subject of considerable controversy. The fact that the AFL-CIO, its affiliated labor organizations, and those unaffiliated with it endorse candidates for political office or lobby for (or against) particular pieces of legislation does not mean that those candidates are elected or that those laws are passed.

On the second of these issues—labor's legislative record—both the CIO and the AFL, for example, strongly opposed the Taft-Hartley Act, which they characterized as a "slave labor law," but that hardly prevented Congress from enacting it. In the late 1950s, a heavily Democratic Congress, presumably favorably inclined toward organized labor, entertained a series of bills designed to restrict even further the concerted activities of labor unions and to regulate their internal affairs. The resulting legislation, the Landrum-Griffin Act of 1959, was not favorably viewed by the labor movement, but, according to a major study, it was more restrictive than it might have been if unionists and their representatives had better understood congressional decision-making processes.[46]

On other, more recent legislative issues, organized labor has fared somewhat better. There is no denying its pivotal role in supporting and lobbying for the passage of legislation concerning civil rights, poverty, and other social issues during the 1960s and also its role in the passage of the Occupational Safety and Health Act (OSHA) and the Employee Retirement and Income Security Act (ERISA)—the so-called "Pension Reform Law"—of the 1970s. Indeed, the AFL-CIO's prolonged support of the Vietnamese war and its "sitting out" of the 1972 presidential election, in the sense that it endorsed neither major candidate, tend to obscure labor's key role in legislation concerning social protection and economic security during the last two decades. But—and this is an important point—these legislative initiatives were supported by other groups in addition to organized labor: civil rights groups in the case of the 1964 Civil Rights Act; these same groups as well as spokespersons for the poor in the case of the Johnson administration's "War on Poverty"; environmentalists and consumer groups in the case of OSHA; and elderly persons representing "gray power" in the case of ERISA. Consequently, it is extremely difficult to separate out labor's distinctive impact on the underlying politics and the enactment of these laws.

When, in recent years, organized labor has lobbied or otherwise supported legislation concerned with its own particular activities, it has not fared very well. Thus, repeated attempts by labor to secure repeal of Section 14(b) of the Taft-Hartley Act, which allows individual states to legislate against union security provisions such as the union shop, have consistently been rebuffed. In the early 1970s, labor was unsuccessful in its campaign to convince legislators to support expanded picketing rights—"common situs" picketing—for workers such as those in construction who move from job to job and who typically are employed by one subcontractor among the several who normally operate at a building site.[47]

In terms of minimum wage legislation, which organized labor has strongly supported, increases in the base rates (the most recent congressional action provided for \$2.65 per hour in 1978 increasing to \$3.35 per hour by 1981) seem to have been authorized in response to larger social and political forces rather than in response to the pressures that unionists alone have brought to bear on legislators. In addition, the union movement has failed to ward off wage and price controls, such as the program imposed by the Nixon and Ford administrations between 1973 and 1975 and the Carter administration's program of wage-price standards adopted in 1978, or to achieve more than occasional import quotas or increased tariffs on imports as part of its attempt (from which some unions dissent) to restrict trade so as to "save American jobs."

This is not to say that the record of labor-supported political initiatives is entirely negative as concerns labor relations and collective bargaining. The extension in 1974 of the Taft-Hartley Act to nonproprietary hospitals, for example, represented a political success for organized labor, as did the administrative extension by the NLRB of that same law to labor relations in private universities and professional sports. But, again, efforts by organized public workers during the mid-1970s to have the federal labor laws extended to government workers were turned back by Congress.

In sum, two central points emerge from this discussion of the effectiveness of organized labor's political activity as it relates to legislative action: first, labor's specific impact is hard to measure precisely and to separate from that of other interest groups which have been especially active in the political process in recent years; second, organized labor has not demonstrated a consistent ability to translate its lobbying and other political efforts into legislative clout. Its successes are sporadic, uneven, and, in recent years, the exception rather than the rule. This is recognized by some unionists themselves who, in a critical self-examination, have called for new strategies to guide their political efforts and new tactics to achieve their political goals.[48]

Party Alignments

What of labor's effectiveness in backing political candidates for office? It is no secret that since the days of the New Deal, organized labor has backed Democrats far more than Republicans and that the Democratic party has appeared much more congenial than the Republican party to the interests of working people. But to infer from this that organized labor is monolithic in its political leanings, that the AFL-CIO directs a political machine that unswervingly supports and works for Democratic candidates, and that the labor movement is always able to sway elections in the direction it prefers is to misread the factual record.

Consider, first, that unionism per se does not form (though it may influence) workers' attitudes toward politics and economics or toward religious or social issues. It is the background characteristics of workers—their families, their income, their education, the environments in which they were raised—together with the nature of the society of which they are a part which shape the attitudes that they bring to the workplace and eventually to the union, if they happen to work in an organized setting. Thus, Centers and others have shown that the aforementioned factors combine to produce a strong orientation to the Democratic party among manual workers, a bit more than two to one on a proportional basis; a less strong but still majority orientation to the Democratic party among white-collar workers, about five out of eight on a proportional basis; and an overwhelmingly strong orientation to the Republican party among businesspeople and managers, eight out of ten, proportionately.[49]

But the fact that union members are oriented toward one political party more than another does not mean that they vote only for that party's candidates or for the politicians—of either party—whom their leaders endorse. Consider that between 1948 and 1968, the labor federations (the AFL and the CIO until 1955 and the AFL-CIO thereafter) consistently endorsed the Democratic candidate in presidential elections. Yet as the data in Table 4-4 demonstrate, the actual percentage of persons living in households headed by union members who voted for the Democratic presidential candidate varied from a high of 83 percent in 1964 to a low of 48 percent in 1968. In the last of those years, 13 percent of union members voted for a third-party candidate, George Wallace—votes which otherwise would presumably have gone largely to the Republican, Richard Nixon. More to the point, if labor had voted as a bloc in each of these elections, it could have reversed the results of all of them, including the Eisenhower landslides of 1952 and 1956. A similar voting pattern is evident in federal congressional elections (Table 4-4), the proportion of unionists voting for Democratic candidates having ranged from 80 percent in 1964 to 58 percent in 1968. In 1972, when the AFL-CIO adopted an official policy of neutrality, endorsing neither incumbent Richard Nixon nor the Democrat, George McGovern, a record low of 46 percent of families headed by union members voted for the Democratic presidential candidate. In 1976, organized labor endorsed Jimmy Carter for President, and 61 percent of families headed by unionists voted for him over Gerald Ford.[50]

This discussion is not, of course, intended to suggest that unionism makes no difference in voting behavior or that it has no influence on the outcome of elections.[51] The data in Table 4-4 show that unionists have a higher propensity to vote for Democratic candidates than nonunionists (again, though, not necessarily because of unionism). Further, the endorsement of a candidate for political

Table 4-4 Percentage of Members of Union and Nonunion Households Voting for Democratic Presidential and Congressional Candidates, 1948–1976

Year of survey	Presidential vote			Congressional vote		
	Union (1)	Nonunion (2)	Difference (3)	Union (4)	Nonunion (5)	Difference (6)
1948	80	44	36			
1952	56	36	20	61	44	17
1954[1,2]	52	31	21	65	49	16
1956	53	36	17	62	49	13
1958[2]	57	36	21	78	54	24
1960	63	44	19	69	51	18
1964	83	62	21	80	59	21
1966[2]	77	63	14	68	53	15
1968[3]	48(13)	39(10)	9(3)	58	50	8
1972	46	38[4]	8	NA	NA	NA
1976	61	53	8	69	54	15

[1] Congressional vote refers to voting intention prior to the election.

[2] Presidential vote refers to reported vote in the previous presidential election. These figures are likely to be less accurate than those reported immediately after the election.

[3] The Wallace vote is given in parentheses.

[4] Nonunion families not separated out; 38 percent is the national figure.

Sources: Arthur C. Wolfe, "Trends in Labor Union Voting Behavior, 1948–68," *Industrial Relations,* **9**:2 (1969); *Gallup Poll Reports,* **90**:12 (1972); and *Gallup Poll Reports,* **134**:8, 10 (1976).

office by labor organizations may have less influence on the outcome of an election than the services—office space, publicity, campaign volunteers, voter registration, and transportation for voters—which such organizations provide and which are directed toward the general public rather than union members in particular. Nevertheless, the labor movement is far from being and never has been uniformly made up of Democratic voters. The Republican-inclined unions of the old AFL by and large continue in that orientation today, notably the building trades unions and the railroad workers' unions. The Teamsters, with 2 million members, are also strongly oriented to the Republican party, as are a variety of other labor organizations and their members.

Moreover, as union members have prospered over the years and have moved more toward the middle class, they have also moved closer to non-unionists in their voting behavior; that is, they do not vote proportionately for Democratic candidates so much more than nonunionists. Columns 3 and 6 of Table 4-4 make this clear for the period 1948–1976. In displaying such behavior over time, unionists may be affirming the results of prior studies, such as Kornhauser's, which show that union members do not differ much from nonmembers on religious, social, and political issues and that their "liberalness" on economic issues, which seems to be the primary basis of their identification with the Democratic party, stems from their position as workers rather than businesspeople, managers, or property owners in the nation's economic system.[52]

The tendency of the populace to become more "conservative" as it becomes more prosperous is well known, and unionists are no exception to the rule. Ironically, the sustained economic expansion in the United States during the 1960s, engineered by (or under) Democratic administrations, may well have contributed to the election of a Republican President in 1968 and 1972. Similarly, the economic instability that occurred during the Republican administrations of those years apparently contributed to Carter's victory in the 1976 presidential election; it clearly spurred the labor movement to deemphasize its flirtation with the Republican party and to endorse the Democratic nominee— whoever that turned out to be—for the Presidency. In any event, it is clear that American labor leaders cannot manipulate union members in their political voting behavior, nor can they command delivery of the vote to candidates whom they endorse for political office. The individual union member remains relatively independent as a voter, reflecting the individualism that is characteristic of the American culture and demonstrating that the "political labor monolith" is a caricature of reality.

The political crosscurrents within labor are further demonstrated by the defections of some unions from the AFL-CIO's official position of neutrality in the 1972 presidential election and by the support in 1976 of the Carter campaign for the Presidency by a minority of unions in advance of the federation. The unions that endorsed or otherwise supported George McGovern over Richard Nixon in 1972—unions that tended to represent younger or more highly educated persons or whose memberships tended to be more heavily made up of minority-group workers than other labor organizations—took such action in defiance of the AFL-CIO. But apart from an occasional wrist slapping, demotion, or withdrawal of funds, there was little that the federation could do about it. In 1976, when the AFL-CIO preferred Hubert Humphrey and others over Jimmy Carter, its leaders found that they had little influence at the Democratic National Convention and were forced to scramble later to support the Carter candidacy in order to save themselves the embarrassment of playing second fiddle to the coalition of member and independent unions that organized itself early in that year to back the Carter nomination. Today, the labor movement continues to be criticized by persons both within and outside its ranks who fault its leaders for conservatism on a variety of social, political, and economic issues. It is no accident that the critics within the ranks of labor invariably represent younger, more militant, and often minority-group workers and that the leaders of such unions are dissatisfied with the AFL-CIO for political and other reasons. One expression of this dissent is offered by Victor Gotbaum, head of AFSCME's 100,000-member District Council 37, in New York City:

> All through the years of the Vietnam War, right up to the closing weeks, only Jerry Wurf, president of the American Federation of State, County and Municipal Employees, would cast a vote against Mr. Meany's support of the war. While the peace movement grew in the nation and in the unions represented in the Executive Council, there was never more than one vote in 33 cast against Mr. Meany's resolution

for support of the war. Nor did the union heads whose unions were committed to George McGovern's Presidential candidacy vote or press for national AFL-CIO support for Mr. McGovern when Mr. Meany insisted on a neutral posture. The labor movement is highly personal. Successful leadership accrues power that becomes personified in an individual. Opposition becomes inhibited, a gradual co-option of views and ideas takes place until one philosophy prevails. Debate and discussion are confined behind closed doors, rarely heard in the open, on-the-record meetings. . . . George Meany's contributions to American workers and their unions are historic . . . but the trade-union movement is larger than any one man. . . . The fitting cap to his career would be for George Meany to step down now for the good of the American labor movement.[53]

Needless to say, Gotbaum's position is a hotly debated one, but it serves to illustrate the diversity of political viewpoints that exists within the American labor movement. On political issues even more than others, unionists are a factious, independent breed, not susceptible to monolithic rule.

Political Activity and Public Employees

The political activity of organized workers takes on added dimensions—and is perhaps more influential—when these workers are public employees. After all, when government workers organize and bargain collectively, they are negotiating terms and conditions of employment not with a business firm that is dependent upon the market for its survival but with an employer whose principal function is to serve the electorate that has placed that employer in office. If economic pressure is the principal vehicle by which private employers may be induced to negotiate or conclude an agreement, political channels for many years were the only ones available to public employees to pursue their job interests. Direct and indirect lobbying of public officials took up the energies of public workers in the era before they could bargain collectively, and such lobbying is still common among organized and unorganized government employees. In the federal sector, wages are not negotiated in collective bargaining; instead, they are set by Congress. That is the decision-making body, the political forum, with which labor organizations in the federal sector must concern themselves if they are to have a say in the establishment of their pay. Consequently, organizations such as the American Federation of Government Employees (AFGE) devote much of their resources to lobbying Congress, informing their members of the votes of representatives and senators on issues about which they are especially concerned, and criticizing the political process by which their members' wages are set.

At the levels of state and local government, the situation is varied, but even formal collective bargaining operates in a fundamentally political climate which organized workers attempt to manipulate in ways favorable to them. In the mid-1960s, the strike, though illegal in most public jurisdictions, was more frequently used, but even that tactic was intended principally to bring public pressure to bear on elected officials. Beyond this, the tactics used include the kinds of activities, discussed earlier, that are common among labor organizations in the private sector. These include the endorsement of candidates for political office, financial contributions to their campaigns, and the use of union facilities by, and the provision of union services to, such candidates. The problem with these activities is that when directed toward the public official who also serves as the organized workers' employer, they might compromise the integrity of a government and place the interests of a special-interest group, public employees, ahead of those of the larger constituency, the general public.

There is no easy resolution of this problem or of others concerning labor relations in the public sector, except to attempt to regulate the political activity of government employees as they continue to exercise unionism and bargaining rights. In the federal sector, as noted earlier, the Hatch Act closely regulates some types of political activity by public workers and forbids others.[54] In state and local governments, the restrictions do not in general approach those found in the federal sector, according to a survey conducted in the late 1960s.[55] As to the prohibitions or controls that might suitably be placed on the political activities of organized public workers, Gerhart suggests the following:

> Activity on behalf of an elected official by employees working directly for the official (or the board to which the official is seeking election) should be prohibited in nonpartisan as well as partisan elections. Endorsements or identification with groups supporting the official need not be restricted. . . . Full time union officials should be permitted to contribute time to a political campaign if their membership directs them to do so. . . . Indirect means of reducing the threat of public employee political activity are likely to be even more effective. . . .[56]

The indirect means that Gerhart refers to involve improving the collective bargaining process so as to reduce the desire of public employees to rely on political channels in pursuing their objectives. More basic, perhaps, is the author's accompanying conclusion that "close alliances between union officials and candidates have more often than not had undesirable results for the union."[57] When placed alongside the views expressed by Bok and Dunlop, who, speaking of the private sector, say that "some union members may react to a [union] endorsement by voting for the opposing candidate," that "labor's endorsement can be the kiss of death in a deeply conservative area," and that "a portion of the electorate . . . uses the labor stand as a guide to how it ought *not* to vote,"[58] Gerhart's conclusions suggest again that we not overemphasize the impact of labor's political activity in any sector and that public policy be shaped in recognition of such limited impacts.

A Labor Party

As we conclude this chapter, the reader should be aware that in its relegation of political activity to a secondary role, the American labor movement is unusual among its counterparts around the world. In Great Britain, for example, workers long ago formed the Labor Party, which works in tandem with the Trades

Union Congress (TUC), the equivalent of our AFL-CIO. In other industrialized nations where a labor party as such does not exist, union federations are generally closely aligned with a social democrat, socialist, or communist party. Whether one looks to Italy, France, the Netherlands, Sweden, Norway, or Germany, labor's political role is more pronounced than in the United States, where organized workers remain largely committed to business unionism.

But is this difference, this uniqueness of the American labor movement, permanent? What in particular are the prospects for, say, a labor party in the United States? After all, we have in the past followed the British lead in treating several other dimensions of unionism and labor relations, and so this question is not totally inappropriate. It may be that at some future time a labor party will come into existence. Some workers harbor such a hope in the same way that some people continue to dream that eventually they will go into business for themselves. But among most union leaders in recent years, the sentiment has been against independent political activity by labor. Even as militant a unionist as the late Walter Reuther, who once identified himself with the labor-party adherents, later set his sights in the other direction and maintained that such a course would be folly.

The leaders of organized labor in the United States are aware of the difficulties that independent political action would bring. First, they realize that they cannot deliver the vote in the sense of controlling it. Hence, in times of prosperity, when the union membership most strongly exercises its prerogative of voting for a Democrat or a Republican, the infant labor party would suffer a loss of prestige that might be fatal. Even in times of adversity, there might be greater confidence among union members in an old and experienced political party, like the Democratic party, which, even if it did not support their interests as vigorously as labor leaders would like, would give greater promise of winning the election and hence of doing something about labor's demands.

Second, the leadership is aware of the common fate of third parties in the United States. The older parties (or one of them) adopt the new party's platform, and the reason for its existence withers away. Again, there would be a loss of prestige from which organized labor would suffer in future political bargaining. Third, any party must have a broad base in order to be successful in the United States. It must appeal to the independent vote if it is to win. But this would weaken the partisanship that would be a labor party's principal reason for existence.

Fourth, there is a danger that union leaders would be diverted from their job at the collective bargaining table, where they have made their greatest gains. Their energies would be drawn off into political activities, to the possible detriment of their economic program in negotiations with employers. Fifth, there is the persistent question of whether they could not gain almost as much and perhaps more, while escaping all the aforementioned difficulties, by acting as an effective pressure group within one of the established political parties.

The net effect of all this has been to create a situation in which American labor unions are quite unlikely to instigate an independent labor party unless they are so rebuffed in their political bargaining by both major parties that they have no other alternative. At the moment, this appears unlikely.

Labor Leaders in Government

Even if one views the emergence of a labor party in the United States as a hopelessly romantic notion or feels that business unionism is the appropriate orientation for organized workers, it is still possible to be concerned about labor's representation or lack of it in key decision-making positions of the federal government. One of the putative strengths of a democratic, pluralistic political system is the diversity of interests that it can encompass, which can be reflected in the composition of the governing administration that comes to power at a particular point in time and in the informal counsel that one or another leader of an interest group may provide to a President or high Cabinet official. In recent years, organized labor seems to have been very lightly represented in the high councils of government.

Consider, for example, that the only labor leader to occupy Cabinet status since the mid-1960s was Peter Brennan, Secretary of Labor in the first Nixon administration.[59] Brennan, formerly president of the New York Building and Construction Trades Council, proved so unpopular to, and unrepresentative of, organized labor that George Meany simply wouldn't talk to him, and he left office after less than 2 years in the post, having made no noticeable impact. President Nixon's unofficial confidant in the area of labor in the late 1960s and early 1970s was Frank Fitzsimmons, president of the Teamsters. The one prominent labor leader represented in the Carter administration is Leonard Woodcock, currently ambassador to China and formerly head of the UAW. The characteristic shared by Fitzsimmons and Woodcock, who, like their unions, otherwise have little in common, is that they are or come from outside the AFL-CIO. The federation has been largely unrepresented, on an official basis at least, in the leadership of the last several administrations. The fact that George Meany has been consulted from time to time by elected Presidents and their representatives does not obviate the lack of organized labor's voice in the executive branch of American government. Nor has a labor leader ever been appointed to the NLRB, although lawyers representing management have repeatedly sat on the Board. One needn't favor a labor party or unions in particular to recognize the problem for political democracy that is raised by the virtual absence of a representative of a major societal interest group in the ruling councils of government. This is an issue toward which unionists might wish to direct their attention and some of their resources.

SUMMARY

In this chapter, we set out some of the major structural interrelationships within the American labor movement; explored the dynamics of internal union government, including legal regulation; and reviewed selected aspects of organized labor's external political activity. We observed that, on all these dimensions, the labor movement is not monolithic. Indeed, although labor organizations do have certain structural, governmental, and political dimensions in common, it is their diversity in all these respects that is particularly notable. In Chapter 5, we examine that diversity within the domain of organized labor's major thrust: collective bargaining with employers.

NOTES

1 U.S. Bureau of Labor Statistics, "Labor Union and Employee Association Membership—1976," *NEWS*, September 1977, p. 6.
2 U.S. Bureau of Labor Statistics, p. 2.
3 This analysis must be qualified as far as the CIO is concerned: the CIO directly chartered national unions, which then authorized the formation of constitutents locals.
4 See, for example, Walter Galenson, *The CIO Challenge to the AFL*, Harvard, Cambridge, Mass., 1960.
5 U.S. Bureau of Labor Statistics, *Directory of National Unions and Employee Associations, 1975*, Bulletin 1937, 1977, p. 79. See previous directories for evidence of the trend noted here. Additionally, the directories provide useful information on a subject which we do not have space to review here, namely, the increase in union mergers. For an analysis of such mergers, see John Freeman and Jack Brittain, "Union Merger Process and Industrial Environment," *Industrial Relations*, **16:** 173–185 (1977). Also see Charles J. Janus, "Union Mergers in the 1970s: A Look At the Reasons and Results," *Monthly Labor Review*, **101:**13–23 (1978).
6 Charles W. Hickman, "Labor Organizations' Fees and Dues," *Monthly Labor Review*, **100:**21 (1977).
7 Hickman, pp. 19–20.
8 Hickman, p. 22.
9 This theme is developed in Alice H. Cook, "Dual Government in Unions: A Tool for Analysis," *Industrial and Labor Relations Review*, **15:**323–349 (1962).
10 The best treatment of the Teamsters can be found in Ralph C. James and Estelle D. James, *Hoffa and the Teamsters*, Van Nostrand, Princeton, N.J., 1975. On structural developments in this union, see Sam Rohner, "The Area Conferences of the Teamsters Union," *Monthly Labor Review*, **85:**1105–1109 (1962).
11 To be found in his essay entitled "Factional Fights in Trade Unions," in J. B. S. Hardman (ed.), *American Labor Dynamics*, Harcourt, Brace, New York, 1928, pp. 332–337.
12 From Title I of the act, Section 101.
13 Julius Rezler, "Union Elections: The Background of Title IV of LMRDA," in Ralph Slovenko (ed.), *Symposium on the Labor-Management Reporting and Disclosure Act of 1959*, Claitors Bookstore, Baton Rouge, La., 1961, p. 479 and citations therein.
14 U.S. Department of Labor, *Compliance, Enforcement and Reporting in 1974, Under the Labor-Management Reporting and Disclosure Act*, 1975, p. 43.
15 U.S. Department of Labor, p. 5.
16 U.S. Department of Labor, p. 6.
17 *Union Trusteeships*, A Report to the Congress by the Secretary of Labor, GPO, Washington, 1962, p. 171.

18 U.S. Department of Labor, pp. 10–13.

19 U.S. Department of Labor, pp. 10–12.

20 U.S. Department of Labor, pp. 16–18.

21 For evidence on this score, see Orley Ashenfelter and George E. Johnson, "Bargaining Theory, Trade Unions and Industrial Strike Activity," *American Economic Review*, **56**:35–49 (1969).

22 For recent confirmation of this view, see Joseph J. Klock, Jr. and Doris Palzer, "Democracy in the UMW?" *Labor Law Journal*, **25**:625–631 (1974).

23 This is not to say that unions behave only politically, for, as will be evident in later chapters, they are strongly subject to economic forces in carrying out their collective bargaining function.

24 U.S. Bureau of Labor Statistics, *Directory of National Unions and Employee Associations, 1975*, Bulletin 1937, 1977, p. 55; and U.S. Bureau of Labor Statistics, *Directory of National Unions and Employee Associations, 1973*, 1975, p. 62.

25 Leon Applebaum, "Officer Turnover and Salary Structures in Local Unions," *Industrial and Labor Relations Review*, **19**:224–230 (1966).

26 Leon Applebaum and Harry R. Blaine, "Compensation and Turnover of Union Officers," *Industrial Relations*, **14**:156–157 (1975).

27 For a different perspective on this issue, see "Sweet Salaries for Union Chiefs," *Business Week*, Aug. 18, 1973, pp. 62–63; and the source cited in footnote 32 below.

28 See Richard Walton, *The Impact of the Professional Engineering Union*, Harvard, Cambridge, Mass., 1961. For a more recent study of this issue, see John C. Anderson, "A Comparative Analysis of Local Union Democracy," *Industrial Relations*, **17**:278–295 (1978); and Anderson, "Local Union Participation: A Reexamination," *Industrial Relations*, **18**:18–31 (1979). More generally, see George Strauss and Malcolm Warner, "Research on Union Government: Introduction," *Industrial Relations*, **16**:115–125 (1977).

29 Note, too, that attendance at union meetings increases greatly when votes on strikes or contract ratification are taken.

30 The strategic use of the rejection of contracts for bargaining purposes is discussed in Donald R. Burke and Lester Rubin, "Is Contract Rejection a Major Collective Bargaining Problem?" *Industrial and Labor Relations Review*, **26**:820–833 (1973). See also William Simkin, "Refusals to Ratify Contracts," *Industrial and Labor Relations Review*, **21**:518–540 (1968).

31 For more on this, see James and James, chaps. 5–8. Recent evidence of corruption and dubious practices within the Teamsters can be found in a series of articles in *The Wall Street Journal* beginning in March 1977.

32 Professional Drivers Council on Safety and Health, *Teamster Democracy and Financial Responsibility?* Washington, 1976.

33 Frances E. Kauterman, "Dissidents Criticized, Leadership Strengthened at Teamster Convention," *Monthly Labor Review*, **19**:41 (1976). For further evidence of, and hearings on, corrupt practices in the Teamsters, see Jonathan Kwitny, "Big Firms Are Linked to an Apparent Racket Involving Teamsters," *The Wall Street Journal*, Oct. 20, 1977, p. 1.

34 For example, see John E. Hutchinson, *The Imperfect Union: A History of Corruption in American Trade Unions*, Dutton, New York, 1970. It is important to recognize that insofar as the Teamsters are concerned, abuses of the rights of union members tend to be concentrated in certain locals and in certain geographic areas. As an example, local unions of over-the-road drivers and intracity locals in metropolitan areas are more prone to commit violations of the Landrum-Griffin Act than other divisions of the Teamsters and truck drivers working in the south, the southwest, and rural areas.

35 See Ben A. Franklin, "Retrial of Boyle in Murder Case Starts Wednesday Amid Secrecy," *The New York Times,* Sept. 11, 1977, p. 26.

36 See Jack Stieber, Walter E. Oberer, and Michael Harrington, *Democracy and Public Review,* Center for the Study of Democratic Institutions, Santa Barbara, Calif., 1960.

37 The UAW's democratic traditions are once again reflected in the issue of affiliation. In 1977, the UAW's president and executive board favored reaffiliation with the AFL-CIO, but did not push for it because the membership was presumed to be against it.

38 The classic work on this subject is Seymour M. Lipset, Martin A. Trow, and James S. Coleman, *Union Democracy: The Internal Politics of the International Typographical Union,* Free Press, New York, 1956. It would be helpful to have a more recent analysis of the ITU, but none is available.

39 I. W. Abel, "Steel: Experiment in Bargaining," *The American Federationist,* **80:**1–6 (1973). The 1973 agreement provided for voluntary arbitration of a bargaining impasse at the expiration of the 1974 steel contract, should that have been necessary. The ENA will be more fully discussed in Chapter 5.

40 Leon Bornstein et al., "Developments in Industrial Relations," *Monthly Labor Review,* **100:**84–85 (1977).

41 But see Jack Stieber, *Public Employee Unionism: Structure, Growth, Policy,* Brookings, Washington, 1973.

42 Derek C. Bok and John T. Dunlop, *Labor and the American Community,* Simon and Schuster, New York, 1970, pp. 139–140.

43 Edwin M. Epstein, "Labor and Federal Elections: The New Legal Framework," *Industrial Relations,* **15:**259 (1976).

44 Epstein, p. 271.

45 It is estimated that some $30 million was legally and illegally contributed by business to the 1972 Nixon reelection effort. Epstein (p. 263) describes this as a response to "solicitation on a scale unprecedented in modern times."

46 See Alan K. McAdams, *Power and Politics in Labor Legislation,* Columbia, New York, 1964.

47 In 1977, the House of Representatives passed the AFL-CIO-backed Labor Law Reform Act, sending it on to the Senate for subsequent action, which never came about. The bill was reintroduced in the Ninety-fifth Congress in 1978, but again it was stalled in committee.

48 See, for example, Solomon Barkin, *The Decline of the Labor Movement,* Center for the Study of Democratic Institutions, Santa Barbara, Calif., 1961, p. 72.

49 Richard Centers, *Psychology of Social Classes,* Princeton, Princeton, N.J., 1949; and Arthur Kornhauser, Alber J. Mayer, and Harold L. Sheppard, *When Labor Votes,* University Books, New Hyde Park, N.Y., 1967.

50 Voting data for 1972 and 1976 are from *Gallup Poll Reports,* **90:**12 (1972); and *Gallup Poll Reports,* **134:**8,10 (1976). For additional analysis of union voting behavior in political elections, see Jong Oh Ra, *Labor at the Polls: Union Voting In Presidential Elections, 1952–76.* Univ. of Massachusetts Press, Amherst, 1978.

51 Specifically, the more closely unionists identify with their labor organizations, the longer they have been members, the more clearly the political norms of the union are communicated to them, and the more they regard labor's involvement in politics

as legitimate, the more they tend to vote in the way recommended by their leaders. See Angus Campbell, Phillip E. Converse, Warren E. Miller, and Donald E. Stokes, *The American Voter,* Wiley, New York, 1960, as summarized in Bok and Dunlop, pp. 419–420.

52 See Ruth Kornhauser, "Some Social Determinants and Consequences of Union Membership," *Labor History,* **2:**30–61 (1961).

53 Victor Gotbaum, "Wherein George Meany Is Urged to Step down Now," *The New York Times,* Oct. 5, 1977, p. 28.

54 Although the House passed a revised version of the Hatch Act on June 17, 1977, the bill was stalled in the Senate.

55 *The Commission on Political Activity of Government Personnel,* vol. 2, GPO, Washington, 1967.

56 Paul F. Gerhart, *Political Activity by Public Employee Organizations at the Local Level: Threat or Promise?,* International Personnel Management Association, Chicago, 1974, p. 72.

57 Gerhart, p. 72.

58 Bok and Dunlop, pp. 413–414. The passage was itself quoted by these authors from Donald E. Stokes, "Voting Research and the Labor Vote," in Charles M. Rehmus and Doris B. McLaughlin (eds.), *Labor and American Politics: A Book of Readings,* University of Michigan Press, Ann Arbor, 1967, p. 389.

59 Note, however, that in February 1976, President Ford appointed as Secretary of Labor Mr. William J. Usery, a Democrat who previously had served as director of the Federal Mediation and Conciliation Service. He was also once an official of the International Association of Machinists and Aerospace Workers (IAM).

ADDITIONAL READINGS

Edelstein, J. David, and Malcolm Warner: *Comparative Union Democracy: Organisation and Opposition in British and American Unions,* Wiley, New York, 1976.

Estey, Martin S.: *The Unions: Structure, Development and Management,* 2d ed., Harcourt Brace Jovanovich, New York, 1976.

Gerhart, Paul F: *Political Activity by Public Employee Organizations at the Local Level: Threat or Promise?,* International Personnel Management Association, Chicago, 1974.

Greenstone, David J.: *Labor in American Politics,* Knopf, New York, 1969.

Hutchinson, John E.: *The Imperfect Union: A History of Corruption in American Trade Unions,* Dutton, New York, 1970.

James, Ralph C., and Estelle D. James: *Hoffa and the Teamsters,* Van Nostrand, New York, 1965.

Lipset, Seymour M., Martin A. Trow, and James S. Coleman: *Union Democracy: The Internal Politics of the International Typographical Union,* Free Press, New York, 1956.

McAdams, Alan K.: *Power and Politics in Labor Legislation,* Columbia, New York, 1964.

Rehmus, Charles M., Doris B. McLaughlin and Frederick H. Nesbitt (eds.): *Labor and American Politics: A Book of Readings,* rev. ed., University of Michigan Press, Ann Arbor, 1978.

Taft, Philip: *Labor Politics, American Style: The California State Federation of Labor,* Harvard, Cambridge, Mass., 1968.

FOR ANALYSIS AND DISCUSSION

1 A local union which is directly affiliated with the AFL-CIO is known as a "federal union." Most locals are chartered by national (or international) unions, some two-thirds of which are affiliated with the federation. Using the latest *Directory of National Unions and Employee Associations,* contact a federal union and a local of an affiliated national union. Compare the two locals, especially in terms of their relationships to the federation. Do the same for two national unions, only one of which is affiliated with the AFL-CIO.

2 Select a national union, contact its officers, and inquire into the extent of control that it exercises over its constituent locals. From which locals did the current national officers come to their positions with the national? What are the differences in job duties among the national's principal officers? What secondary sources of information are available to help answer these questions?

3 Using the *Directory* referred to above, contact the research directors of any two national unions, one of which has a traditional craft orientation, and the other an industrial orientation. Ask for copies of their constitutions and compare them. How are they similar? How are they different? Why do you imagine that some of these differences exist?

4 Outline a set of criteria for evaluating the impact of the Landrum-Griffin Act on internal union affairs. What would be the principal sources of data in this regard? How do these sources compare with those available for gauging the Taft-Hartley Act's impact on labor relations?

5 Outline a set of arguments to support the following proposition: "Resolved: Because of their employment in government, organized public workers should operate unions and associations that surpass labor organizations in the private sector in the democracy of their internal procedures." (The instructor should moderate the debate.)

6 Consider the data in Table 4-5, pertaining to the financial resources of American unions. If organized labor was treated as a company—for example, Labor, Incorporated—where would its total assets (in 1969) place it on the "Fortune 500" list of the largest industrial corporations?

7 One criticism made of labor leaders concerns their "conservative" investment policies with respect to the assets shown in Table 4-5. For example, Troy reports that more than $850 million of labor's total assets (in 1969) was maintained in the form of cash and that only 8 percent was invested in common stock. Why do you think this pattern has developed? How would you suggest it be altered?

Table 4-5   Consolidated Total and Per Capita Assets, Liabilities, and Net Assets, American Labor Unions, 1962–1969 (End of Year)

	Consolidated assets		Consolidated liabilities		Consolidated net assets	
	Total (millions)	Per capita	Total (millions)	Per capita	Total (millions)	Per capita
1962	$1771	$111	$212	$13	$1559	$ 98
1966	2206	126	257	15	1949	111
1969	2647	143	361	19	2286	124

Source: Leo Troy, "American Unions and their Wealth," *Industrial Relations,* **14**:135 (1975).

8 Two conflicting points of view as to the political-economic role of unions have been
    expressed:
    a Unions, as powerful social agents, must engage in broader economic planning
        and assume greater responsibility for developing a social blueprint. As workers'
        organizations acquire power, they assume commensurate responsibilities. It is
        not enough for them simply to accommodate themselves to other forces in society;
        they themselves should be a force in the achievement of more clearly defined
        social goals. Labor groups cannot marshal their power for wage gains, fringe
        benefits, better housing, and so forth, without assuming the responsibility for
        determining where such programs fit into the larger framework. To ask unions to
        take responsibility for inflationary controls, for example, is really to say that
        unions should restrain their bargaining strength in the light of certain more
        broadly conceived social objectives. It is to a more explicit identification of such
        objectives that unions should pay more attention.
    b Any approach such as that suggested in item **a** will more sharply define class
        interests and draw ideological lines. The strength of American society lies in its
        freedom from rigid social groupings, which is carried over into political life. If
        unions act simply as one pressure group among other pressure groups, in a way
        that does not conflict sharply with public interests, then they can achieve most
        of their objectives without assuming larger responsibilities. Pragmatic and piece-
        meal change is more characteristic of the American scene than more comprehen-
        sive social planning; the unions will do well to continue an approach which is
        congenial to American political philosophy. It may be less dramatic, but in
        arousing less opposition it is almost certain to be more rewarding to those who
        follow it.
    Which of these two approaches would you prefer the American labor movement
    to follow? Which do you think would be better for unionists?
9 Select a western European and an Asian country and compare the external po-
    litical activity of their labor movements with that of the American labor movement.
    How do these activities differ? How are they similar? How do you account for the
    differences and the similarities?
10 While the Landrum-Griffin Act regulates the internal activities of labor unions, no
    comparable legislation exists for corporations. Should the internal activities of cor-
    porations be so regulated? Why or why not? If corporations as business entities dif-
    fer significantly from labor organizations, is that a rationale for not regulating their
    internal affairs? Should corporations be as internally democratic as labor unions?
    Why or why not?

Chapter 5

Collective Bargaining in the Private Sector

In this chapter and Chapter 6 we examine the process of collective bargaining in the private and public sectors. A major objective is to explore the essential differences and similarities between the two sectors in this respect.

The opening section of this chapter provides a review of some key models and concepts of the bargaining process. This is followed by a discussion of whether collective bargaining is necessarily subordinate to certain inherent prior rights of management and a discussion of the power tactics that are available to unions and employers in negotiating labor agreements. We explore how these contracts are administered at the workplace, and we examine the role which arbitration plays in this process. Some new dimensions and directions of collective bargaining are considered, which in turn serve to highlight the dynamic forces—economic, technological, social, political—that affect labor-management relationships. Finally, some comparative aspects of collective bargaining are taken up, including attempts by unions to coordinate negotiations with multinational corporations.

BARGAINING POWER

Underlying the process of collective negotiations between organized workers and employers is the concept of bargaining power, which may be defined as "the ability to secure another's agreement on one's own terms."[1] So stated, a union's bargaining power at any point in time is management's willingness to agree to the union's terms. Management's willingness in turn depends upon the cost of not agreeing to the union's terms, relative to the cost of agreeing to them.

Clearly, the cost to any one party of agreeing or disagreeing with its opponent's position is central to this concept of bargaining power. For example, if the cost to management of disagreeing with the union is high relative to the cost of agreeing, the *union's* bargaining power is enhanced. Thus if management judges a strike to be potentially very costly and the union's stated terms and conditions of employment to be relatively inexpensive, the union stands a good chance of gaining its negotiating demands—it has strong bargaining power. Conversely, if a company's sales are declining and production is down, the cost of a strike may be perceived by management as relatively low compared with the cost of meeting the union's demands. In this instance, the union has relatively weak bargaining power.

Note that these statements by themselves tell us nothing about the strength or weakness of the union relative to the strength or weakness of management; management might possess strong or weak bargaining power to press its own terms. Only if the cost to management of not agreeing to the union's terms exceeds the cost of agreeing to them, *and* if the cost to the union of not agreeing to management's terms is less than the cost of agreeing to them, does the union's bargaining power surpass that of management. Stated more generally, labor's bargaining power exceeds management's when the difference to management between the cost of not agreeing to labor's terms and the cost of agreeing to them is proportionately greater than the difference to labor between the cost of not agreeing to management's terms and the cost of agreeing to them.

From this perspective, bargaining power is not an attribute of the parties which is measurable in absolute terms. Rather, bargaining power may change over time in response to different tactics employed by the parties, shifting public opinion and government policy, and, especially, new economic conditions. The nature of demands made also influences bargaining power, generally in the following way: the greater the demand (made, for example, by the union), the greater the resistance to it (by management), and therefore the less the (union's) bargaining power.

The term "cost" is used here in the broad sense to include pecuniary and nonpecuniary types. Though it is common to focus on bargaining over wages and other monetary aspects of labor negotiations, it must be remembered that many nonmonetary issues and decisions—for example, seniority in layoffs and job assignments, the structure of the grievance procedure, and the type of union security clause to be adopted—face labor and management when they engage in bargaining. While it is not possible to reduce all costs to a common denominator, some balance must be struck, even if only judgmentally, among the pecuniary and nonpecuniary issues for an agreement to be reached.

As one authority on this subject has written, "The very incommensurability of certain issues makes possible the changing of minds that might be unpersuaded if all significant issues could be reduced by an economic calculus to a numerical balance or imbalance."[2] What the costs of agreeing and not agreeing may be to the bargainers involved, therefore, cannot be identified in a vacuum; rather, they are revealed only through the negotiation process.

THE BEHAVIORAL BASES OF NEGOTIATIONS

As the parties to negotiations attempt to exercise their own and influence their opponents' bargaining power by manipulating the costs of agreeing and not agreeing, the bargaining process in which they are engaged often takes on seemingly irrational characteristics, such as table thumping and threats, absurd or outlandish demands, all-night meetings as the strike deadline or contract expiration date approaches, and, on some occasions, the use of a third party (a mediator) to transmit proposals from union to management and back again. Why, many ask, don't the bargainers rely more on facts and rational approaches and less on propaganda and power? In particular, why should brute force, as reflected in the strike, be used and permitted by society to settle disputes?

In considering these questions, two analysts, Walton and McKersie, have suggested that labor negotiations actually consist of four systems of activity, which they identify as distributive bargaining, integrative bargaining, attitudinal structuring, and intraorganizational bargaining. Each of these processes makes different demands upon negotiators.[3]

Distributive bargaining is the familiar type of negotiation that involves straight-out haggling over how to split up a pie, with one party's gain being the other party's loss. Nearly everyone has engaged in this type of bargaining, as when buying a car or selling a house. In labor negotiations, wages are the leading example of a distributive issue. Within the broad parameters set by the competitive market, when labor and management bargain over wages, one's gain is the other's loss. But the parties may also be engaged in *integrative bargaining,* seeking to resolve a problem in such a way that both benefit (or at least neither loses).

Suppose, for example, that the parties have decided in principle on a job evaluation system, on retraining for technologically displaced (in British parlance, "redundant") workers, on an extension of the health insurance plan to cover dental expenses, or on a plan for job redesign and enrichment. Once the contentious issues of principle and money are out of the way, both parties may well gain from a cooperative search for the best job evaluation system, retraining program, dental insurance policy, or plan for job enrichment, one that will fit their particular needs and yield maximum results for each dollar they've agreed to spend.[4] Integrative bargaining requires a high level of trust between the parties, which is a relatively rare commodity in labor-management relations.[5]

The strategy and tactics of integrative bargaining contrast sharply with those of distributive bargaining, and this very contrast suggests the third element in Walton and McKersie's framework, *attitudinal structuring*. This refers to the shaping of such attitudes as trust or distrust and friendliness or hostility between the parties. Unlike many businesspeople and diplomats who occasionally negotiate agreements, union and management representatives must live with each other and their contracts the year round. Threats and bluffs are one thing when used on a one-time basis, but they can have quite different effects if used on someone with whom you must deal on a regular and continuing basis, as, for example, an industrial relations director deals with a union president. This factor can promote restraint, even collusion, between the negotiators, but it can also promote frictions which, if backlogged and tinged with bitterness, can erupt to make a shambles of contract negotiations. This potentially explosive situation may be further exacerbated by the fact that union officials employed by the company enjoy equal status with management during negotiations, even though, as employees, they are subordinate to management during the working year. One needn't be a psychologist to appreciate the stresses that can accompany this change of roles, particularly when local union officials lead a "successful" strike or, earlier on, when employees first organize a plant, an experience that many employers find deeply humiliating.[6]

INTERNAL BARGAINS

Finally, the most underrated aspect of labor negotiations is the process of *intraorganizational bargaining*. Most people view collective bargaining as a clash between two monolithic protagonists, for each party strives to present a solid front to the other and to the public. In fact, though, there are almost always divergent points of view within each party which must first be reconciled before an agreement can be reached. The depth and extent of these internal divisions have a pronounced effect upon bargaining between the parties. This is true in the private sector and even more so in the public sector, as will be demonstrated in Chapter 6.

In representing labor or management in collective bargaining, negotiators actually occupy a boundary role. On the one hand they negotiate with an opponent, and on the other hand they negotiate with their own organization's contending internal interests. This is more easily visualized in the case of the union than of the management organization.

Typically, the union's membership varies in age, skill, ambitions, and other characteristics. Invariably, some groups within the union feel that their interests are not being adequately served. Skilled workers may believe that the union unduly favors the less skilled members; women or members of minority groups may feel that their special problems are being ignored, to the advantage of white male members; workers in one local union of a multiplant company may believe that their interests are subordinated to those of other locals; and younger members may be convinced that the interests of older workers dominate their own in the setting of objectives for negotiation. Similarly, where bargaining occurs at the level of the national union, local organizations may dissent from the targeted wage increase, feeling that it should be higher or, perhaps, lower because they believe that employers may react to higher labor costs by cutting employment. All the competing interests within a union, whether it is a local, intermediate, or national organization, must be resolved (or at least papered over), and this resolution comes about through a bargaining process, informal rather than formal in nature. Indeed, bargaining with the employer cannot proceed to completion until this internal bargaining has taken place, although interorganizational bargaining may also affect intraorganizational negotiations. Moreover, the union negotiator must maintain vigilance over existing and developing internal pressures even after bargaining with the employer commences.

In all but the smallest employer organizations, a roughly similar process of internal bargaining occurs. For example, the sales manager and company treasurer may disagree strongly over the firm's negotiating posture. The former may urge that a settlement with the union be reached quickly and a strike avoided at all costs so that relationships with important customers can be maintained. The treasurer may insist that any wage increase beyond a given amount would seriously harm the company's financial situation. Similarly, there may be conflicts between those who believe that the best way to deal with the union is to be tough with it and those who think it wisest to try to work out more amicable relations.

Further, just as in the union, the company must harmonize the objectives of its local plants with those of the organization as a whole. Plant management may be directed by corporate headquarters to take a stand on some issue which is either contrary to its own best judgment or not suited to its own needs. This typically occurs when the company fears that the union will extract a condition of employment in one plant and then attempt to extend it to other plants. Where a firm bargains through an employers' association, as is common in the steel, shipping, and construction industries, the problem of reconciling differences among the companies that compose the association is directly comparable to that confronting the union in dealing with special-interest blocs among its membership. For management negotiators, all this means that they (like their union counterparts) must please the "constituents" on whom their jobs depend. Because no one can win everything that constituents would like, negotiators occasionally may have to make a show of militancy to prove that a sellout to the other party is not taking place.[7]

In summary, Walton and McKersie's analysis demonstrates that the negotiation process is far more complex than it appears to the casual observer. It is not just a poker game for high stakes or another buyer-seller relationship, although it contains elements of those and other types of economic and political (and theatrical) activities. Nor does it impugn the integrity of labor and management negotiators to point out the ritualistic nature of much of the bargaining process; the players usually know the rules of the game and understand that serious issues are at stake. But because there is no single "right" answer to the economic issues in dispute and because the union-management relationship also involves a clash of political, psychological, and organizational interests, the negotiation process inevitably bears little resemblance to a dispassionate search for truth. Each of the four subprocesses described above places severe and conflicting pressures upon a negotiator, some calling for candor and cooperation, and others for bluffs and threats to browbeat the opponents. Different negotiators respond to these conflicting pressures in different ways, and no one has discovered a foolproof formula for success at the bargaining table.

THE BARGAINING UNIT

Before collective bargaining actually begins, two questions must be addressed: "For whom are we bargaining?" and "Over what are we bargaining?" The first question involves the definition of the bargaining units, the specific employees or groups of employees covered by a collective bargaining agreement. When a firm signs an agreement with a union, as United States Steel does with the United Steelworkers of America (USA), this tells us little about who is covered by its provisions. It is unlikely to cover railroad employees on the rail facilities owned and operated by a steel company in conjunction with its plants. They will be provided for in separate agreements with the railroad workers' unions. It is similarly unlikely to cover the company's construction workers, carpenters, bricklayers, painters, and plumbers, who will be represented by other unions, or the company's truck drivers and warehouse workers, for whom the International Brotherhood of Teamsters acts as bargaining agent. It is unlikely to cover clerical employees and sales personnel, who may not be represented by any union at all. The workers who are covered by the agreement, in this case production employees in the steel plants, will be identified by the agreement itself; together with the employer, they constitute the *bargaining unit*.

In the United States, the National Labor Relations Board (NLRB) is legally empowered to determine the bargaining unit prior to an election held to determine representation. In carrying out this function, the Board may allow the parties to determine the composition of the unit in conformance with its own standards before holding the election. Such an election by "consent agreement" is what occurs in the large majority of cases. The Board has elaborated a number of rules as to what constitutes an "appropriate" unit for bargaining purposes—rules which specify what kinds of employees may appropriately be grouped together and what parts or divisions of a company (or what companies, when more than one is involved) constitute a fitting unit for collective bargaining.[8] For example, the more employees share a community of interest at work, receive similar wages and work under similar conditions, perform similar jobs or can be interchanged with one another, and desire to be in the unit, the more likely they are to be grouped into a single bargaining unit. Also taken into consideration by the Board are the history and pattern of collective bargaining in the industry or firm in question. There is often a difference, however, between the initial unit which is the basis for an election and the actual unit which evolves over time, after the election has taken place. Thus the NLRB may rule that all the production employees in a newly organized plant constitute an appropriate bargaining unit, but if those employees select as their agent the same union which is already representing the workers in the company's other plants, the chances are that a single agreement will cover all the plants of the company, including the new one. The *legal* determination of the bargaining unit in this instance would have been significant only for purposes of the election and not for the bargaining process itself.

Surprisingly, there are few statistics available on the incidence of collective bargaining in this country, for no complete census of bargaining units has ever been made. The Bureau of Labor Statistics (BLS) estimates that about 175,000 collective bargaining agreements were in effect in the United States during 1975.[9] The bulk of these apparently cover workers employed in the same plant or in several plants owned by a single company. Agreements covering more than one employer are still in the minority, but it is a growing minority as labor and management apparently continue the trend toward multiemployer negotiations.[10]

Note, too, that because unions certified by the NLRB must represent all the workers in a defined unit, whether they are members or not, data on membership do not reveal the total number of workers represented by unions. In 1974, approximately 25 million workers were covered by collective bargaining agreements, or about 2.5 million more than the number of members of American labor organizations in that year (excluding members employed outside the United States).

A bit more light is shed on the characteristics of bargaining units by the data presented in Table 5-1. These were obtained by the BLS in a study of roughly 1500 labor agreements which covered 1000 or more workers in 1975—the so-called "major units."[11] About 57 percent of the 7.1 million workers were covered by single-employer agreements; the remainder were covered by multiemployer agreements. The multiemployer agreement was the dominant type in the nonmanufacturing sector, particularly in construction, transportation, and services, and also in the apparel manufacturing industry. Of single-employer agreements in these units, about half were for firms having more than one plant, and they covered almost 75 percent of the 3.8 million workers (see columns 3–4 and 7–8 in Table 5-1). Six unions—the United Automobile Workers (UAW), the Teamsters, the USA, the United Brotherhood of Carpenters and Joiners of America (CJA), the Communications Workers of America (CWA), and the International Brotherhood of Electrical Workers (IBEW)—represented 3.3 million workers, or almost half of those covered by these "major unit" agree-

Table 5-1 Bargaining Structure by Industry
(In Agreements Covering 1000 Workers or More, July 1, 1975)

Industry	All agreements		Total		Single employer				Multiemployer	
					Single plant		Multiplant			
	Agreements (1)	Workers (2)	Agreements (3)	Workers (4)	Agreements (5)	Workers (6)	Agreements (7)	Workers (8)	Agreements (9)	Workers (10)
All industries	1,514	7,069,750	861	3,829,100	440	1,040,050	421	2,789,050	653	3,240,650
Manufacturing	815	3,750,950	661	3,002,750	390	930,850	271	2,071,900	154	748,200
Ordnance and accessories	12	32,250	12	32,250	8	16,550	4	15,700		
Food and kindred products	105	293,550	61	132,800	37	65,850	24	66,950	44	160,750
Tobacco manufacturing	8	26,350	8	26,350	4	11,000	4	15,350		
Textile mill products	13	38,850	10	23,350	8	19,650	2	3,700	3	15,500
Apparel	50	435,400	11	26,600	1	1,300	10	25,300	39	408,800
Lumber and wood products	6	11,000	3	5,100	2	2,600	1	2,500	3	5,900
Furniture and fixtures	21	33,450	12	19,150	7	9,300	5	9,850	9	14,300
Paper and allied products	53	101,600	47	87,950	33	50,800	14	37,150	6	13,650
Printing and publishing	23	47,200	5	5,950	4	4,950	1	1,000	18	41,250
Chemicals	47	108,750	47	108,750	40	88,850	7	19,900		
Petroleum refining	13	25,000	12	23,000	3	5,650	9	17,350	1	2,000
Rubber and plastics	19	94,950	19	94,950	11	17,600	8	77,350		
Leather products	14	39,800	7	24,500	4	12,500	3	12,000	7	15,300
Stone, clay, and glass	29	70,750	25	60,650	8	10,900	17	49,750	4	10,100
Primary metals	84	492,000	83	490,950	46	86,300	37	404,650	1	1,050
Fabricated metals	32	85,500	25	68,400	14	27,050	11	41,350	7	17,100
Machinery	90	278,950	88	275,750	59	111,000	29	164,750	2	3,200
Electrical machinery	95	437,550	93	433,650	60	257,550	33	176,100	2	3,900
Transportation equipment	84	1,058,300	79	1,034,800	37	123,800	42	911,000	5	23,500
Instruments	9	20,050	9	20,050	1	3,150	8	16,900		
Miscellaneous manufacturing	8	19,700	5	7,800	3	4,500	2	3,300	3	11,900

Nonmanufacturing	699	3,318,800	200	826,350	50	109,200	150	717,150	499	2,492,450
Mining, crude petroleum, and natural gas	13	150,750	11	21,950	8	13,550	3	8,400	2	128,800
Transportation[1]	65	572,750	14	37,850	4	4,750	10	33,100	51	534,900
Communications	65	495,750	63	440,750	4	7,350	59	433,400	2	55,000
Utilities, electric and gas	47	134,100	46	132,850	13	40,250	33	92,600	1	1,250
Wholesale trade	12	22,250	2	2,550	1	1,200	1	1,350	10	19,700
Retail trade	92	298,750	41	120,100	5	9,700	36	110,400	51	178,650
Hotels and restaurants	42	187,900	4	6,000	4	6,000			38	181,900
Services	70	369,350	13	50,700	7	18,800	6	31,900	57	318,650
Construction	291	1,084,650	5	12,100	3	6,100	2	6,000	286	1,072,550
Miscellaneous nonmanufacturing	2	2,550	1	1,500	1	1,500			1	1,050

[1] Excludes railroads and airlines.

Source: Adapted from U.S. Bureau of Labor Statistics, *Characteristics of Major Collective Bargaining Agreements, July 1, 1975*, Bulletin 1957, 1977, p. 12.

ments, and more than 13 percent of all American workers under collective bargaining contracts in 1975.

Still, the majority of bargaining units are small. Only 299 of those included in Table 5-1 covered 5000 or more workers; that is less than 20 percent of all major agreements. The contracts not included in Table 5-1 by definition cover fewer than 1000 workers, and most of them are negotiated in bargaining units of fewer than 100 persons. Thus, despite the public attention surrounding major negotiations, small bargaining units that conclude single-plant and single-employer contracts remain a central feature of the American system of industrial relations. To recognize this is not to deny the intricate system of "pattern setting" and "pattern following" which characterizes wage bargaining in particular and which will be discussed more fully in Chapter 7.

The fact that bargaining in the United States customarily proceeds on a single-employer basis is especially noteworthy in view of the experiences of other countries. Abroad, the characteristic pattern is negotiation on an industry or a regional basis. These industry agreements are often supplemented by local agreements, but the basic terms are negotiated in a multiemployer unit usually encompassing most of an industry. In some countries there is the further practice of "extending" by governmental authority the terms of an agreement negotiated by "representative" industry and union officials to all other establishments in that industry, whether they are organized by the same union, by another union, or by no union at all. Collective bargaining around the world is thus customarily collective on the side of employers as well as employees. The United States is the major exception to this rule. Here, collective bargaining is primarily collective only with respect to employees, and on the employer's side it is conducted largely on an individual-firm basis. A labor agreement typically is concluded with a relatively small, self-contained bargaining unit.

THE SCOPE OF BARGAINING

Several responses can be given to the question "Bargaining over what?": "wages and working conditions," "mandatory items specified by the NLRB," "anything but management policy," "whatever the parties decide," and others. None of these responses is inherently right or wrong, for specific examples can be found to support each of them. In some local negotiations, in some firms, and in some industries, the scope of bargaining is very narrow, while elsewhere it is quite broad. Furthermore, the scope of bargainable issues can narrow or broaden over time as circumstances change and affect the relative bargaining power of labor and management.

In Chapter 3 we discussed the distinction between mandatory, permissible, and prohibited subjects of bargaining, as defined by the NLRB. But those categories are not very helpful for understanding why the scope of bargaining develops in a particular way in a particular unit. Consider, for example, that product pricing policy is, in the Board's parlance, a nonmandatory subject of bargaining, and yet the International Ladies' Garment Workers' Union

(ILGWU) plays a central role in formulating just such policy in the apparel manufacturing industry. Grievance procedures certainly are a major (and mandatory) subject of bargaining, and yet they are much more a part of negotiations and labor relations in the steel, retail trade, and oil industries than in construction or the maritime trades. These examples, and many others which could be added, indicate that there is no single, stock answer to the question of "bargaining over what."

Nevertheless, it is possible, by systematically examining labor agreements, to learn what issues most commonly concern the parties to collective bargaining. In doing so, one should not be misled by the length of a contract, which can run to several hundred printed pages plus supplemental agreements. Much of this language and many of the contractual provisions are "boilerplate" in nature, describing in considerable detail the structure and process of the grievance procedure, the coverage and regulations of the pension or supplemental unemployment benefit plan, and the eligibility for, and scheduling of, vacations and overtime assignments. The fact that these provisions add up to many pages does not necessarily mean that the parties to the agreement negotiate over a broader scope of issues than their counterparts who have much shorter contracts, nor does it mean that the union in question has made a more substantial inroad than others into management's prerogatives. Further, it should be recognized that the scope of bargaining is not strictly discernible from a formal contract. Informal customs, practices, and relationships abound at the workplace, and these reflect a meeting of minds, a coming to terms, and a set of bargains over issues which are treated lightly or perhaps not at all in the written labor agreement. Such informal arrangements would have to be included in any complete assessment of the scope of bargaining between labor and management.

These caveats issued, some major contractual provisions of American labor agreements are shown in Table 5-2. Again, the information is based on a survey of just over 1500 agreements covering 1000 or more workers in 1975, which admittedly is hardly a random sample of the 175,000 collective bargaining contracts that exist in the United States.[12] Not all these provisions are present in every labor agreement, of course, and some are more common than others. For example, grievance procedures are included in all but 1 percent of the agreements, and arbitration procedures in all but 4 percent of them. Some 94 percent of the agreements contain antidiscrimination provisions; about 90 percent include clauses covering overtime pay, weekly work schedules, and paid holidays and provisions for strikes and lockouts; and 80 percent contain union security clauses, principally the union shop. At the other end of the spectrum, fewer than 5 percent of the agreements include provisions referring specifically to older workers or clauses that provide for joint labor-management committees to deal with issues of industrial relations. Roughly 10 percent of the contracts contain provisions for environmental protection and the protection of workers; these are concentrated in the construction, primary metals, and transportation industries. One-sixth of the agreements specify job evaluation systems, one-fifth include provisions for testing, and two-fifths contain clauses covering apprenticeship and training. Well over half of the agreements contain selected provisions concerning safety, such as the right to refuse to do unsafe work, the right of inspection by a union or a union-management safety committee, and the regulation of crew sizes.

Contractual provisions have varied considerably over time. At mid-cen-

Table 5-2   Illustrative Provisions of Collective Bargaining Agreements

Wages and related issues

Wage administration	Time and money differentials by shift
Methods of compensation	Pay differentials for hazardous work and
Basic rate structure for nonincentive jobs	abnormal working conditions
Progression plans	Wage adjustments
Travel	Issues and timing of contract reopeners
Provisions for tools, work clothing, and	Wage garnishment, equal pay for equal
safety equipment	work, and red-circle rates
Nonproduction bonuses	
Profit sharing, thrift, and stock purchase	
plans	

Hours, overtime, and premium pay

Overtime	Premium pay rates for Saturday work as
Scheduled weekly hours	part of regular workweek
Overtime rates for work outside regularly	Premium pay rates for Sunday work not
scheduled hours by industry	part of regular workweek
Provisions for graduated overtime	Premium pay rates for Sunday work as
Premium pay for weekends	part of regular workweek
Premium pay rates for Saturday work not	Premium pay for sixth and seventh days
part of regular workweek	of work

Paid and unpaid leave

Leaves of absence	Number of hours of reporting pay or work
Vacation plans	Number of hours of call-in or call-back pay
Maximum vacation weeks allowed	Total daily time allowances for paid rest
Number of paid holidays and pay for time	periods
worked	Applicability of provisions for paid meal
Selected payments for time not worked	periods and for pay for time on union
Pay for time spent on union business	business

Job security

Measures applicable in slack work periods	Supplemental unemployment benefit plans
Apprenticeship and training	and severance pay
Selected work rules	Wage and employment guarantees
Advance notice	

Dispute settlement

Provisions for grievance and arbitration	No strikes, no lockouts
Exclusions from grievance and arbitration	
procedures	

Table 5-2 *(Continued)*

Union security, management's rights, and other noneconomic issues	
Union security	Restrictions on posting or distribution of
Checkoff	union literature and moonlighting
Management's rights and "favored	Protection of the environment and of
nations" clauses	workers
Antidiscrimination clauses	Absenteeism and tardiness
Older workers	
Safety	
Labor-management committees on issues	
of industrial relations, safety, and	
productivity	

Seniority and related issues	
Seniority	Testing
Retention of seniority rights during layoff	Applicability of testing
and recall	

Source: Adapted from U.S. Bureau of Labor Statistics, *Characteristics of Major Collective Bargaining Agreements, July 1, 1975,* Bulletin 1957, 1977, passim.

tury, collective agreements consisted largely of provisions concerning wages and limited work rules. After 1950 they were expanded to include guarantees of job and income security, paid and unpaid leaves, specific treatment of special groups, and employee-benefit plans pertaining to health and welfare, life insurance, and pensions. Indeed, fringe benefits now constitute almost 40 percent of total compensation in the private, nonfarm sector, and a modern labor agreement may well include maternity leave, dental and eye care, disability pay, educational allowance, legal services, and retraining provisions, among many others.[13] Some more conventional subjects of negotiation also have changed in terms of treatment, complexity, and scope. Thus, well over half of the agreements covering 1000 or more workers contain limitations on the employer's subcontracting of work, a like proportion provide for jointly conducted time studies of industrial jobs, and well over one-third contain cost-of-living, or "escalator," provisions. These developments clearly indicate that the scope of bargaining has expanded in the American private sector in terms of both the number of items covered and the depth to which they are covered.

The Bugaboo of Management's Prerogatives

To say this is to recognize that, despite their continued adherence to "business unionism," American labor organizations have made major inroads on what were once thought to be exclusively "management's prerogatives." If this is the case in the private sector, as a review of contract provisions and an examination of decisions made by the NLRB suggest, it is even more the case in the public sector, where the presumed sovereignty of legislative bodies has been substantially eroded by organized employees. It is small wonder, then, that the reaction of many employers (private and public) is summed up in the despairing question, "Where will it all end?" In the words of one company official, "The legitimate areas of collective bargaining must be defined. Until that time, management is in the position of an army retreating and regrouping. At some point it will have its back to the wall and there will be no further retreat—without a new economic system, possibly along socialist lines."

Dispassionate analysis of this issue, perhaps the most hotly contested one in labor relations, is more readily undertaken when we recognize that it is as old as the master-servant and employer-employee relationships. Whenever one individual has authority over another, the exercise of that authority is bound to be called into question, precipitating an argument over the basis of the authority. Under what circumstances must the subordinate accept the rule of the superior as final? In the event of conflicts of interests, can resolution come through an appeal to rights which the other does not recognize? By whom is the scope of authority to be defined—by those who assert it or by those over whom it is exercised?

In the United States, charges that unions invade the realms of authority properly belonging to management go back to the earliest records and have persisted in one form or another over the years. Thus, the comment of George Baer, president of the Reading Railroad, on the occasion of a strike by coal miners in 1902, that "the rights of the labouring man will be protected and cared for, not by labor agitators, but by the Christian men to whom God in his infinite wisdom, has given the control of the property interests of the country," and the campaign during recent years by the National Right to Work Committee to repeal legally sanctioned union security arrangements, both reflect a basic concern for protecting management's authority and, even more, the view that unions are a threat to the private enterprise system.[14]

But what is the basic concept of the function of management that underlies this position and these views? What is the nature of this function upon which unions presume to trespass? From where derives the authority which managers seek to preserve? One approach has it that the function of management consists in the art and science of decision making. Since the business firm is the locus of decisions about what line of products or services to produce, on what scale, at what prices, and by what methods, the function of management is to make those decisions. But this conception fails to square with the fact that, through collective bargaining, organized workers participate with management in the making of many major business decisions. When, for example, unions negotiate clauses which determine the content of jobs, the assignment of personnel to those jobs, and how operations are to be performed, they are making basic production decisions. If the function of management is no more than decision making, then others besides those who have traditionally viewed themselves as managers can lay claim to a share of that function.

Further, it may not be possible to cordon off a set of issues to be decided exclusively by management from those to be decided in conjunction with the union. Who is to say that it is proper for unionists to bargain over wages but not job assignments, over fringe benefits but not plant location, or over seniority but not subcontracting? If the workers' livelihood depends upon strategic decisions involving major aspects of the business, aren't they legitimately interested in having a say in such decisions? These are disturbing questions for managers to face.

If there are problems in defining the function of management as decision making, it might be better to regard management as consisting of those who have been accorded a legal basis for exercising their authority. In fact, the grounding of decision-making authority in law is the basis for management's strongest stand on this issue. Management has argued that the right to make its own business decisions free from union intervention stems from property rights. As the actual owner or as the agent for shareholders, the argument goes, management is free to decide how privately held property shall be used. To accede to union demands for greater participation in corporate affairs would require management to abdicate an authority, which it derives from a position of trust, to another group exercising it on behalf of competing interests.

The major limitation of this formulation, however, is its failure to recognize that *property rights confer a control over things, not over people*. The owners and managers of a plant, office, shop, or factory can, it is true, decide how to employ physical capital, but they have no power to compel people to implement those decisions. Owners and managers can make all the decisions with respect to what and how many products or services to provide and the technological processes to be employed in providing them, but they cannot, on the strength of ownership or control of physical assets, force workers to conform to their decisions. Instead, workers must be induced to conform to those decisions, and the inducement generally takes the form of money—wages and salaries paid to employees in return for compliance with management's decisions.

But note that the workers who are being induced by management to accept its judgments may have differing views about the size of the inducement—the amount of pay—or about its composition. They may, as part of their "price" of putting physical assets to use, prefer to have a voice in matters of production, sales, and location, or even selection of supervisory personnel. Whether they can attain such demands depends upon their bargaining power, but it is equally true that management's ability to avoid such demands, if made, depends not on its legal status as owner or agent of private property but on *its* bargaining power. It is evident, then, that the function of management, when viewed as decision making, is based not on property law but on broader economic and political considerations.

From the workers' perspective, the labor organization that represents them justifies its claim to participation in business decisions on the democratic principle that all who are affected by such decisions should have a voice in making them. Interestingly, this rationale of "industrial democracy" has its counterpart in the human relations school of thought, fathered in the 1920s by Elton Mayo of the Harvard Business School. That philosophy of pragmatic management viewed decision making not as the cerebration of top executives sitting behind walnut desks but as practices that are translated into actions. And since a completed action generally requires the participation of a number of individuals, decision making is, in reality, a group process. It is not just the engineers, production supervisors, or general manager who decide on the amount of goods to be turned out and on the speed of the line or the frequency of a service, but the workers as well. From this perspective, it may indeed make good sense for management to try to obtain agreement on the part of all involved about the organization's overriding objectives. If concessions are required to be made in reaching such agreement, if some "prerogatives" must be shared, that is the price for achieving an overall better result than would have materialized if preservation of management's decision-making authority had been deemed the leading organizational objective.[15]

Nature of the Management Function   But however pragmatic this approach may be, it still fails to resolve what constitutes the function of management. By converting discretion into management, it makes the custodian's decision to clean out the stockroom equivalent to the directors' decision to go into the money market for new capital. If these two roles are to be distinguished, the function of management must be conceived of as something more or other than simply decision making.

Consider that each individual has a bundle of aspirations, some of which require an income for their realization. That is the reason most people work. Once in a job, however, other values become salient, and a variety of pecuniary and nonpecuniary objectives take hold which affect a person's behavior and aspirations. Each individual seeks to satisfy those aspirations through the medium of the business, and each may prefer a different set of company policies and practices or may assign different priorities to these policies and practices. A production worker has a primary interest in personnel policies that promote job satisfaction and good pay; the accountant emphasizes the need for systematic information on company finances and a sensible policy concerning depreciation; the chief executive officer stresses the requirements for conducting effective long-range planning; and a general sales manager may prefer as a first priority to have the firm develop an aggressive policy for advertising its products. When decisions are made on any one of these issues, moreover, they must be consistent and compatible with all the other decisions being made in the company.

How is this to be accomplished—how are decisions to be made in the face of conflicting demands of the organization's members? Part of the answer is this: *A decision is made on the basis of the relative bargaining power of those whose views and interests clash.* Remember that your bargaining power is my cost of not agreeing to your terms relative to my cost of agreeing to them. Similarly, my bargaining power is your cost of not agreeing to my terms relative to your cost of agreeing to them. But such bargaining cannot usually proceed directly between the parties concerned, particularly when the issue is only one of many which are continuously the subject of negotiation—bargains between functional groups within the management hierarchy, between workers and material and capital suppliers, between stockholders and customers, and typically numerous subcategories operating within each of these groups.[16] Each seeks to fulfill the aspirations of its members through the medium of the business organization, and each prefers the business to take certain actions or make certain decisions rather than others, with the result that each tries to influence the conduct of the organization to the extent of its bargaining power.

To address all these issues and to make bargains that are internally consistent and compatible requires that there be a coordinator of bargaining. *This task—coordination of the bargains among all those who compose the business —is the unique function of management.* It is an inescapable function and an isolatable one, performable only by managers of a firm and not by those who make demands on the firm. The coordination of the bargains that are struck with multiple interest groups is here defined as the function of management.

In carrying out this task, managers must bear the responsibility for securing a complex of bargains (decisions) which will maintain adherence to the organization of all those on whom it depends. Management must also bear the responsibility for doing so within a framework of money flows whereby total outflows are covered by total inflows. It is through the performance of these functions and the coordination of them that management reserves to itself all residual discretion and control of resources within the framework of the enterprise. Especially on the American scene, as long as managers meet the demands of the organization's members and constituents without bargaining away the whole of its discretion or the total of the firm's money inflow, the remainder of both is at its own disposal.

Implications of the Analysis   What does this conceptual approach imply for the union's alleged invasion of management's prerogatives? *It suggests that there is no barrier except relative bargaining power to the scope of the subject matter in which the union may interest itself.* For some unions that subject scope is broad and for others it is narrow, but in any case the union will be confronted by employers who are sometimes strong and sometimes weak relative to itself. In the aggregate, labor's bargaining power has ebbed and flowed, affected as it is by changing economic, technological, political, legal, and social forces.

Also, the fact that society may declare through law that certain subjects are not bargainable—such as discriminatory hiring practices—is perfectly consistent with the approach offered here. Such restrictions are based on a reasonable belief that the interplay of private power might thwart the public interest in some *specific* respect, such as encouraging racial discrimination. That is very different, however, from declaring a subject nonbargainable because it is an ''inherent prerogative of management.''

A second implication of the analysis is that unions, in seeking to extend the range of their decision making within the enterprise, are not trespassing on the function of management. As the locus of all bargains struck, management attempts to coordinate them in a never-ending process so that they are internally consistent and create for those on whom the organization must depend a cost of agreeing that is lower than the cost of not agreeing and so that inflows to the firm cover all outflows. No matter how extensive the range of the union's interests, that function of management must by its nature always remain unimpaired.

That unions may make life more difficult for managers of organizations by attempting to expand the scope of bargainable issues is undeniable. But managers are also capable of exercising their creative abilities to deal with these complex situations, for that is what they do and are paid for doing. Managers of nonunion enterprises are constantly bargaining with interest groups—banks, suppliers, stockholders, customers—and pursuing the coordination of those bargains. Managers retain that function irrespective of the extent to which their organization is unionized. For its part, the union remains to serve its members by negotiating over issues of central concern to them. If these issues change from time to time, if they sometimes seem to challenge entrenched conceptions of management's prerogatives, keep in mind that the resolution of these issues —the union's ability to make inroads on them—fundamentally rests on the relative bargaining power of the parties. Few unions and few managements have discovered sure ways of preserving undiluted bargaining power for very long. That, more than anything else, may be the best guarantee against dominance by management or tyranny by unions.

NEGOTIATING TACTICS AND STRATEGY

If relative bargaining power determines the scope of negotiable issues and the outcome of a particular negotiation, the parties are always trying to affect such power by manipulating the costs of agreeing and not agreeing. At the outset of a negotiation, the union and increasingly the management confront each other with a list of "demands" that may cover many pages and hundreds of issues. Even at this preliminary stage, each party's bargaining power is relative to what it is asking for. For example, if the United Automobile Workers (UAW), in its negotiations with Chrysler, makes an initial demand for a wage increase of $1 per hour, its bargaining power will be stronger than if it were seeking $2 per hour. Chrysler's cost of agreeing to the lower figure is less than its cost of agreeing to the higher one. Put in a different and more general context, if your bargaining power is based on my costs of agreeing and of not agreeing to your terms, then high demands by you make it more costly for me to agree and increase my resistance, whereas modest demands are likely to have the opposite effect. In the case of the UAW and Chrysler, each side will generally modify its opening position on a range of issues, being in general willing to settle for something other than what it originally wanted. The union may reduce its wage demand gradually to a level or a "bargaining zone" where management's cost of agreeing to the union's terms will actually be lower than the cost of a strike in the event of a lack of agreement.[17] Similarly, the company may reduce its demand concerning an increase in the penalty for repeated absence from work, attempting to reduce the union's cost of agreeing relative to the cost of striking in the case of a lack of agreement. Such maneuvering goes on with respect to virtually all negotiable items, and it includes the outright dropping of some issues, the merger of others, and the aggregation of remaining ones to form overall assessments of costs of agreeing and of not agreeing.

Observe that this discussion raises to the forefront the importance of bluffing in the bargaining relationship. Your bargaining power is based on my estimates of the costs of agreeing and of not agreeing to your terms, and my bargaining power similarly is based on your estimates of these costs. *But neither of us can know what the other's estimates truly are.* Consequently, each party is left to guess the other party's reactions to its proposals. In the example concerning wages given above, the union must guess at what point management's cost of not agreeing to the union's terms is sufficiently high that it would rather concede to the union's demands. At that point the union holds firm. If it guesses too high, it will find itself in a strike that it does not want (since it would prefer to settle at, say, an increase of 50 cents per hour rather than strike). But if it guesses too low, it will deprive its members of a wage gain that they otherwise might have had. Simultaneously, management is engaged in the same process of guessing, probing, and bluffing.

Even on distributive issues such as wages, the parties seldom come to the bargaining table with their own final offer absolutely fixed. It is part of each party's job to convince the other party that the cost of agreeing is actually lower than that party may have estimated, thereby changing the other party's final position. There have been numerous instances in which a union has become convinced, in the course of negotiations, that management could not give what the union genuinely expected to obtain as its "last-ditch" demand, and others in which management was persuaded of the reasonableness of the demands which it considered grossly unreasonable on first entering into negotiations. The bargaining process itself provides the opportunity for negotiatiors on each side to seek clues, from no more perhaps than facial expressions and tone of voice, that will reveal the other party's position and provide firmer ground for estimating the costs of agreeing and of not agreeing. Realizing that their counterparts engage in such behavior, negotiators will attempt to shape and influence the attitudes and opinions of the other side concerning their own party's position. This process of attitudinal structuring characterizes all labor negotiations, even when the parties are well known to each other and their bargaining representatives have developed a firm basis of mutual understanding. The mediation process similarly may be viewed as a device for attitudinal structuring that helps the parties overcome barriers to communication and enables each party to find out what the other really wants.

By themselves, tactics of the negotiating process are not always sufficient to obtain a collective bargaining agreement. Indeed, if there is no "right" answer to be discovered and if each negotiator has an incentive to conceal his or her real position for as long as possible, how do the parties settle anything? The answer is that nearly every union contract in the United States has a fixed expiration date; the union usually agrees not to strike during the life of the contract, but when the contract expires, the union is free to pursue a policy of "no contract, no work." Negotiations for a new contract thus begin some months before the current one expires,[18] frequently drag on in a desultory fashion for a few weeks, and then quicken in pace as the expiration date approaches—for that is the deadline at which all bluffs are called, all speeches end, and either the parties agree on a new contract or both will incur the costs of a strike.

It is important to understand the crucial role of the strike in the bargaining process. When labor and management disagree over wages or any other issue, how might their disagreement be resolved? One way, of course, is for the employees to quit and look for work elsewhere, but that is hardly what Congress meant when it said that workers could have an equal voice in determining wages and working conditions. Indeed, if this free market alternative worked satisfactorily, we would have no reason to permit unions to exist at all. Second, the workers could marshal all the facts at their disposal and plead their case before management. But even the most fair-minded employers are bound to disagree often with workers' views of the facts of industrial life, and in effect they win every dispute as long as workers can only talk, leaving employers free to determine wages and working conditions as they see fit. Third, society could require all parties to submit their disputes to a government agency or to a court for a binding decision. But most management and union officials and both major political parties oppose such compulsory arbitration as a method for settling disputes in the private sector (although we shall see that it is often supported in the public sector). There are several reasons for this opposition, but to illustrate: if the government is to fix wages, why should it not also fix prices and profits and make all the other economic decisions now left in private hands?

That appears to leave only the alternative of permitting workers to cut off their employer's income by means of a strike. No one can claim that the strike is an elegant or a precise weapon or that it has never been abused. But neither has anyone yet discovered an alternative generally acceptable to the parties which permits workers an *effective* voice in establishing their terms of employment. It is true that the strike can nearly obliterate some employers, but its effectiveness varies greatly from one situation to the next. Often overlooked, for example, is the fact that the strike cuts off the workers' income as well as the employer's, and so a union leader must think twice before recommending that the members walk out rather than accept the employer's last offer.[19]

This also suggests why, contrary to popular belief, the lockout is not usually the employer's equivalent of the strike. If a union strikes only the most vulnerable company in a multiemployer unit, the other companies may lock out their workers to preserve a united front. In the more typical bargaining relationships, however, employers would gain nothing by triggering a lockout upon the expiration of a contract; that would be tantamount to calling a strike against themselves. As long as the union continues to talk instead of strike, the employer is ahead of the game, with profits and production continuing as before, usually on the terms of the expired contract. The employer's real counter to the strike is, paradoxically, the ability to take a strike—or, stated differently, the ability to force the union, at the strike deadline, to choose between accepting the employer's last offer or calling a strike that will hurt its own members as well as the employer.[20]

For these reasons, the strike as a weapon has a pronounced impact upon negotiations *even when it is not used*. In the 1970s, only about 5300 strikes occurred per year, with 175,000 collective bargaining agreements in effect. Little more than 0.2 percent of all working time of the American labor force was lost each year during this period as a result of strikes.[21] But the mere availability of labor's right to strike for its demands and the countervailing "right" of the employer to take a strike rather than yield to those demands weigh heavily in the calculations of both parties as the strike deadline approaches. Therein lies the primary incentive for the parties to back off from their extreme positions and to inch toward a compromise agreement, most often without resort to an actual strike.

If the union uses the threat of a strike or the strike itself to increase the employer's cost of not agreeing to its terms, it may engage in picketing, conduct boycotts, and appeal for support from other unions. As the cost to the employer of not agreeing rises, the cost of agreeing seems relatively smaller than before, and the union's bargaining power is enhanced. The union also may use the contract ratification process to increase the employer's perceived cost of not agreeing. Whether the membership's rejection of a tentative contract settlement negotiated by its representatives is totally unexpected or, as is sometimes the case, results from a less than wholehearted recommendation for approval by the union leadership, making it in effect a bargaining ploy, it increases the threat of a strike and, hence, the cost to the employer of not agreeing.

For its part, a company may counter such actions and impose on the union a higher cost of not agreeing to its terms by shifting orders among plants, moving the equipment of a struck plant to a nonunion site, threatening to close the plant altogether, replacing labor with capital equipment, relocating operations in another country where labor costs are low, building up inventories of products so as to weather the strike, joining with other firms to conduct multiemployer negotiations, seeking legal restrictions on the union's picketing, mobilizing public opinion against the union, and, most directly, hiring nonunion labor to replace striking workers. A few of these practices have been limited by the law, but employers appear as ingenious as unionists in devising ways of raising the cost to the other party of not agreeing, thereby enhancing their own bargaining power. Some employers are perfectly capable of weathering a sustained labor dispute—the Wisconsin-based Kohler Company survived a 6½-year strike without noticeable impact,[22] and, more recently, the textile firms of J. P. Stevens and Farrah Manufacturing have been able to withstand prolonged labor-sponsored boycotts of their products. It is well to remember that, in some parts of the country and in several industries and occupations, unions are still struggling to gain a foothold and are hardly able to mount successful strikes.

There is yet another method of manipulating bargaining power to one's own advantage—by decreasing the other party's cost of agreeing to one's terms. Obviously, this can be done by improving one's offer—the union can shave its demands, and the company can increase its counterproposals. Because bargaining power is always relative to demands, such an action can be expected to improve one's capacity to settle on one's own terms. But because concessions also mean that one achieves less than one's goal, unions and managements offer them only as a last resort. Before that time, each party may seek to lower the other's cost of agreeing to its terms by such devices as:

On the union's part, giving assurances of stimulating greater cooperation of its members, thus potentially reducing the impact of the increased wage bill to management; promising to take a stronger hand in the curbing of wildcat strikes; or agreeing that an international representative of the union will work more closely with a local union leader who has been giving management trouble.

On management's part, promising to consult with the union before undertaking any major changes in production processes; agreeing to talk to an obstreperous supervisor who consistently ignores the collective bargaining agreement; promising to talk over the company's economic position with the union leadership at regular quarterly meetings; or establishing a labor-management committee to anticipate problems.

Such devices may be treated by the other party as "concessions," particularly for public relations purposes, but as long as they do not constitute any sacrifice of aspiration by the party who resorts to them, they are actually a mean of improving that party's bargaining power by lowering the other's cost of agreeing while *avoiding* concessions. In some instances, they may be only face-saving gestures, but using such an escape hatch is an important way in which a party that has perhaps trapped itself by a bluff that failed can reduce its cost of agreeing to the other's terms.

If all this sounds somewhat Machiavellian, bear in mind that manipulation of interpersonal relations, whether in business organizations, in educational or religious institutions, in political groups, or in the family, takes place in virtually all but the most primitive societies. From this perspective, the issue being debated is not manipulation or pressure itself, but rather the permissible extent of it and the forms that it is allowed to take. In union-management relations, as in product markets, we have been uncertain about how far the parties may be allowed to go. Some boycotts and some types of picketing are permitted, while others are not; an employer can say some things but not others to workers as an election to determine union representation approaches; and the parties must bargain over some issues but not others.[23] Clearly, it is not pressure itself that we object to, but only pressure past some point.

What we so frequently forget, however, is that pressures are applied by the parties in the pursuit of their aspirations, and these aspirations have to do not only with money (profits or wages) but also with people's conception of the kind of life they hope to carve out for themselves and of the kind of society in which they would like to live. The use of pressure thus involves social values and standards of morality, however inchoate these may be in the minds of most people. That can be seen not only in the context of collective bargaining but also in disputes over such issues as civil rights (minority groups, for example, have organized and brought pressure on employers to revise their personnel practices) and human rights (for example, the Carter administration has pushed various allies to pressure the Soviet Union to adopt practices more closely in keeping with western notions of personal freedom). In short, pressure tactics are used during negotiations over all important social as well as economic issues.

ADMINISTERING THE LABOR AGREEMENT

There is a tendency to believe that once the terms of a collective bargaining agreement have been established and reduced to writing, there is almost no activity in the area of labor relations until the preliminaries of the next round of negotiations get under way. That is an erroneous view, however, for once the contract comes into being, it is up to the parties—labor and management—to enforce it. The leaders and representatives of these two groups must see to it that their respective constituencies are informed not only about the terms of the agreement but also about their rights and obligations resulting from those terms. Though neither an obvious nor an especially glamorous activity, policing of the labor agreement helps set the tone of, and give definition to, a labor-management relationship. Three aspects of contract administration will be discussed in the following pages: the grievance procedure, seniority, and work rules. The first of these is the main form of contract administration, while the others are subjects in the typical labor agreement over which administrative issues frequently arise.

The Grievance Procedure

Among the most important areas of contract administration are discipline and due process. In one form or another, these operate in all organizations, but in the unionized setting they are made manifest through the grievance procedure. This mechanism has multiple purposes. First, it is an avenue through which workers (and less frequently employers) may appeal an action that runs counter to the provisions of the agreement. For example, the contract may contain a clause that requires a senior employee to be promoted to a higher position or to a more favorable shift than a junior employee when the two are of equal ability. In the event of such a promotion or assignment, union and management may be faced with a grievance filed by a junior worker which requires them to decide whether he or she has greater ability than a senior worker. As further examples, management may transfer one employee between departments when the union believes that the contract calls for the movement of another employee; it may temporarily assign an employee to a job which he or she believes calls for a higher rate of pay; it may deny full leave benefits to a pregnant employee who feels that she deserves such benefits; or it may deny paid holidays to craft workers who consider themselves eligible for such holidays under the provisions of the contract. The grievance procedure is the mechanism which has evolved in the private sector to handle and, it is hoped, resolve such controversies.

Second, the grievance procedure often is called into play to deal with issues about which the labor agreement says surprisingly little. The contract could well provide that discipline is to be invoked for "just cause," but the precise meaning of that phrase may be unclear.[24] The firm may have written or unwritten policies forbidding various types of behavior—pilferage and gambling, tardiness and alcoholism, physical violence and drug abuse—but few unions attempt to negotiate changes in such rules at the bargaining table. Instead, they usually prefer to let management initiate discipline for whatever reason and then, through the grievance procedure, challenge the decisions that they believe to be unfair. Consequently, most of the "bargaining" over discipline occurs *during the administration of the labor contract,* as the parties grapple with specific cases and eventually build up a set of rules concerning discipline that are relatively permanent and well understood in each relationship. In so doing, they are attempting to protect workers' rights under the contract and still satisfy the employer's need to respond quickly to the shifting pressures on the firm without endlessly debating the "legality" of every decision before an action is taken.

Third—and this is not often recognized—the grievance procedure permits an employer and a union to identify trouble spots and operating weaknesses within the work organization. When grievances are filed and work their way up the grievance procedure, they provide much valuable information about particularly troublesome issues. By maintaining and systematically analyzing such information, the employer is better able to determine what areas of personnel and labor relations management—for example, wages, seniority, overtime, work assignments, and sick leave—merit closer monitoring and perhaps changes in policy. The grievance procedure can thus be viewed as part of the organization's information system with respect to its utilization of human resources and the development of proposed contract demands in subsequent bargaining rounds. Tempering this interpretation, however, is the fact that employers often do not avail themselves of the grievance procedure (i.e., cannot file grievances) because "management access to the contractual grievance and arbitration procedure may be construed by management as a waiver by management of its right to act unilaterally instead of filing a grievance."[25]

How does the grievance procedure actually work in practice? Table 5-3 provides a listing of the steps in a typical grievance procedure and identifies the union and management representatives involved at each level. One of the most

Table 5-3 A Sample Grievance Procedure

Level	Employee's representative	Employer's representative
First	Employee, union steward, or both	Employee's supervisor
Second	Chief steward	General supervisor or department head
Third	Grievance committee	Plant manager or industrial relations manager
Fourth	Grievance committee plus representative of international union	Executive vice president for industrial relations
Fifth	Arbitration	

important characteristics of the grievance procedure is that relatively few disputes over the interpretation of existing contractual terms and conditions of employment find their way into a formal system, such as that shown in Table 5-3. On the American scene, most "grievances" are settled informally at the workplace following discussions between the employee and the union representative, the employee and his or her immediate supervisor, or the employee and both the union representative and the supervisor. No one knows what the scorecard of such informal settlements is—whether more disputes occurring at the workplace are settled in management's or the worker's favor. But the existence of the formal procedure, with its requirement that grievances be reduced to writing and its provision for group consideration of grievances at higher levels of the process and for the scheduling of hearings and the taking of testimony in cases of arbitration, serves to make the parties to a dispute more careful in following through on grievances and more cautious about making charges of unfair discipline or violations of the contract by workers.

To illustrate how the process works, suppose that a man is caught walking out of the plant at quitting time with tools in his jacket pocket and is fired outright for stealing by the supervisor, who does not accept the explanation that he simply forgot to remove the tools from his pocket. The grievance process has been triggered, as the worker, having been unsuccessful in convincing the supervisor of the absentminded nature of his act, explains the situation to his union steward. The latter is the worker's representative at the shop level; his jurisdiction roughly accords with that of the supervisor, whose counterpart he is. If the steward accepts the worker's explanation, he will urge the supervisor to reconsider his decision. If the supervisor persists in the decision, the steward will help the worker put the grievance in writing, will summarize his own position, and will help process the grievance to the second step of the procedure.

Which union and company officials are designated for the several additional stages of appeal varies from situation to situation. Typically, however, at the second stage the worker's complaint will be presented by a chief steward for the union (or by the chairperson of the local union's grievance committee) to the company's departmental supervisor. If the latter comes to the conclusion that the action of the worker's immediate supervisor was justified, the union might then proceed to a third step, in which the whole grievance committee (numbering perhaps nine people) or the local president might represent the employee, while the plant personnel manager or the general plant manager might appear for the company. If no settlement is reached here, an international representative of the union might take the worker's case up with someone from top management, perhaps a vice president in charge of labor relations.

If the company's reply is still to the effect that the discharge should stand and if the union is still persuaded that the employee is innocent, and with all the bilateral appeal stages now exhausted, the union might take the case to arbitration. More than 95 percent of all collective bargaining agreements specify arbitration as the terminal step of the grievance procedure.[26] The arbitrator, a neutral third party, is empowered by labor and management to make a decision which is final and binding upon them. This is referred to as "rights" or "grievance" arbitration—the resolution of disputes arising from different interpretations of the terms of an existing agreement—as distinct from "interest" or "contract" arbitration—the resolution of a dispute between the parties over a new contract, with the third-party arbitrator setting the terms and conditions of the agreement. Interest arbitration is hardly ever used in the private sector, but, as we shall see in Chapter 6, it has become quite common in the public sector.

In the present example, the arbitrator might find the worker completely innocent of the charge and could then reinstate him with back pay, restore his seniority privileges, and the like—that is, "make him whole." Alternatively, the arbitrator might find the worker guilty of the charge and judge the company's penalty appropriate to the infraction. Or the arbitrator might find the worker in violation of the contract, but require the company to modify its penalty, deeming it too harsh for the infraction committed.

In all this, the arbitrator relies on standards of equity and common law, solicits the facts of the case, and takes testimony from each side in hearings that generally are conducted in a less formal atmosphere than a court procedure. But the arbitrator also relies on custom, past practice, and the "law of the shop" in reaching a conclusion about the violation of the contract in question. Frequently, the arbitrator must base the decision purely on circumstantial evidence and the character of witnesses whose testimony cannot be fully verified.[27]

Appraising the Grievance Procedure   It is hard to overstate the significance of the grievance procedure in American industrial relations. In a diverse, decentralized, "business-union-oriented" labor movement, with literally hundreds of thousands of collective agreements in effect, and in a competitive economy featuring rapid changes in technology and no legally guaranteed employment, one might expect much conflict, including wildcat strikes and violence, to arise in the context of disputes over existing terms and conditions of work. That such open conflicts, strikes, and violence are the exception rather than the rule testifies to the grievance procedure's standing as a social invention of great importance. While a similar procedure is used in other countries, it is safe to say that almost nowhere else has it reached the high stage of development that it has in the United States, in the sense of being so widely employed and so vital a force at the local level. The parties to it often regard the grievance procedure as the heart of collective bargaining; more than others, they recognize that the negotiation of an agreement takes place every 2 or 3 years but that the grievance procedure handles the gripes, disputes, and individual problems which are bound to arise, perhaps almost daily, at the workplace.

Despite its virtues, though, the grievance procedure is not without limitations, and these seem to have grown and been better recognized in recent years. Among these limitations are the costs of arbitration, which in the mid-1970s, according to the AFL-CIO, averaged about $2200 per case just for the union's share, as shown in detail in Table 5-4. The important cost elements of the process include lawyers' fees; the arbitrator's fee, which can be very much larger than that shown in the table; the lost production time of witnesses from union and management, the cost of which is also conservatively estimated in Table 5-4; and various clerical expenses, which can be very large in a major

Table 5-4   The Union's Cost of Traditional Arbitration for a 1-Day Hearing

	Prehearing expense	
Lost time	Grievant and witnesses @ $5 for 32 hours	$ 160
Lawyer	Library research @ $40 for 4 hours	160
	Interviewing witnesses @ $55 for 4 hours	220
Filing fee	AAA (shared equally) $100	50
Total cost of prehearing		$ 590
	Hearing expense	
Arbitrator	Fee (shared equally) 1 hearing day	$ 100
	Expenses for meals, transportation, etc. (shared equally)	50
	Travel time one-half day (shared equally)	50
Total cost of arbitrator		$ 200
Transcript	$2.75 per page with two copies and 10-day delivery of 200 pages (shared equally)	$ 325
Lawyer	Presentation of case @ $55 per hour	330
Lost time	Grievant and witnesses @ $5 per hour, 32 hours	160
Hearing room	Shared equally (free under AAA)	25
Total cost of hearing		$ 840
	Posthearing expense	
Arbitrator	1½ days of study time (shared equally)	$ 150
Lawyer	Preparation of posthearing @ $55 per hour	440
Total cost to union		$2,220

Source: Adapted from John Zalusky, "Arbitration: Updating a Vital Process," *The American Federationist,* **83**:3 (1976).

case involving many witnesses, a long hearing, and the reproduction of numerous copies of supporting documents.

Of equal significance in diminishing the effectiveness of the grievance procedure is the often lengthy delay in resolving a dispute. In 1975, the average time between the occurrence of a grievance and an arbitrator's award was 7⅓ months, and it is not uncommon for a key case that goes to arbitration to take as much as 1 year or even more to resolve.[28] In such circumstances, the cliché "justice delayed is justice denied" has considerable application—to management as well as to the worker and his or her union. If the arbitration of grievances once was an informal, rather swift process often performed free as a service by a local minister, a college professor, a lawyer, an economist, or a public figure, it has now become more professionalized, costly, and time-consuming and has grown into a veritable industry.

One way of overcoming some of these problems is for a union and a company or employers' association to retain during the life of the agreement a permanent umpire or referee to hear and rule on those grievances which are not resolved at lower stages of the process. This has been a long-standing arrangement in some labor-management relationships and in some industries, but it usually requires a very large business and unionized labor force to make it viable and to pay the umpire or referee's sizable retainer. Additionally, it requires the parties to agree on a single individual whom they judge to be knowledgeable about the myriad of grievances that may arise out of a complex production technology and to be capable of handling them. Still further, it calls for labor and management to give up their right to choose or to veto during the life of the contract an arbitrator who might hand down a decision or a series of them which are unfavorable to one side or the other. Most unionists and most managements jealously guard that prerogative.

Another alternative to conventional grievance arbitration is "expedited arbitration," a process which is on the rise in the private sector. As the name implies, expedited arbitration seeks to reduce the costs of, and delays in, resolving grievances. It does this by eliminating some of the intermediary steps of the grievance procedure, such as the second to the fourth levels in Table 5-3, thereby going directly from the initial step to arbitration. It may also dispense with full written records and formal hearings, though retaining informal ones, and it may take place at the workplace or closer to it than traditional grievance arbitration. A simple decision without lengthy justification may be all that is required. This process is reported to have worked relatively well in several industries such as steel, coal mining, aluminum, glass, and copper. The cost of expedited arbitration appears to be as little as 10 percent of the cost of standard grievance arbitration.[29]

Another and possibly more fundamental challenge to rights arbitration stems from the legal treatment it has recently received. In 1960 the Supreme Court decided a series of cases which gave extremely strong legal standing to the process of arbitration.[30] The Court upheld as almost inviolate the right of neutral third parties to make binding decisions where labor agreements empowered them to do so. It suggested that such decisions would only in the rarest of circumstances ever be reviewed by the courts. This doctrine of "deferral to arbitration" placed the arbitrator in the position of, if not a supreme figure, then one whose authority to render decisions in grievance cases was very strong indeed. Moreover, since third parties are sometimes called on to resolve issues which are not well spelled out and occasionally not dealt with at all in the contract, the doctrine of deferral to arbitration undergirded the authoritative position of arbitrators who, in the 1960s, came to rule on an increasingly broader scope of issues. By deciding that work shifts, job assignments, leave in the event of the death of a family member, interdepartmental transfer, subcontracting, and other items which the contract dealt with only in general terms, if at all, could be questioned through the grievance procedure, the arbitrator could, in effect, expand the scope of bargaining. This clearly did not sit well with employers, who presumed that they knew the limits of joint decision making with the union when they negotiated an agreement in formal collective bargaining. As a consequence, employers sought more carefully to structure and implement clauses concerning management's rights in collective bargaining agreements.

On the employee's side, arbitrators' rulings strongly supported the position that workers had to seek resolution of their complaints through the grievance procedure established in the contract. In seeking redress of their grievances, unionized employees could not attempt to deal directly with the employer or try to bring pressure to bear on the employer by, for example, conducting a slowdown or engaging in picketing. If they did so, they could be disciplined by the employer (often with the support of the union), and their appeals were not likely to be upheld by the arbitrator, if in fact they did appeal and if their complaints reached the final stage of the grievance procedure. The NLRB and the judiciary supported this position by the aforementioned doctrine of deferral to arbitration and also by rulings which required workers to pursue fully their grievances using procedures spelled out in the contract before going on to seek further redress from the courts.[31] This is not to say that the Board and the courts failed to distinguish cases involving discrimination by employers against workers on the basis of their union activity—under Section 8(a)(3) of the Taft-Hartley Act—from cases involving the failure to bargain in good faith—under Section 8(a)(5) of the act—in deciding the extent to which they would defer to the decisions of arbitrators. Nor did these institutions for regulating labor-management relations in the United States display an identical proclivity for deferral as between actual arbitration awards and prearbitration procedures. Nevertheless, on balance, they continued through the 1960s to follow and strengthen the policy of deferring to arbitration and abiding by the decisions of arbitrators in labor relations matters.

More recently, however, the NLRB and the judiciary have shown a greater willingness to examine and, in some instances, to overrule arbitration procedures and decisions relating to the scope of negotiable issues and employees' rights. In the *General American Transportation Corporation* case of

1977, for example—a case which involved the discharge of an employee ostensibly for engaging in union activities—the Board majority held that it would no longer defer to arbitration in cases of alleged discrimination by employers or interference with protected employees' rights or in situations involving coercion by a union.[32] The Board will continue to defer to arbitration only when the dispute is strictly between the contending parties and when no alleged interference with individual employees' rights under Section 7 of the Taft-Hartley Act has taken place. In another case decided in 1977—that of *Roy Robinson, Inc.*, which involved an employer's alleged plant shutdown without prior notice to the union and, therefore, a presumed violation of the duty to bargain in good faith—the Board decided that it would defer to arbitration only if violations of the law were subject to, and actually resolvable by, grievance procedures set forth in the contract.[33] Otherwise, it would hear and rule on the case in an unfair-labor-practice proceeding.

As to the honoring of arbitration awards once they are rendered—postarbitration deferral—the Board and the courts are tightening the requirements here as well. For the decisions of arbitrators to be accepted, the contractual issues treated by the law must actually be presented and considered in arbitration, they must receive a fair and regular proceeding, the decision must be final and binding on all parties to the dispute, and the award may not be repugnant to the purposes of the Taft-Hartley Act.[34]

Recognize, too, that Congress enacted the Civil Rights Act of 1964 (amended in 1972), the Age Discrimination Act of 1967 (amended in 1978), the Equal Pay Act of 1967, and the Occupational Safety and Health Act of 1970, all of which provide avenues other than the grievance procedure for individuals and groups of workers to redress certain types of complaints arising at the workplace. In providing additional forums for protecting employees' rights, these statutes and the decisions subsequently rendered in light of them inevitably reduced somewhat the dominance of the grievance procedure and especially of arbitration in resolving disputes. Especially notable on this score was the Supreme Court's 1974 decision in the *Alexander v. Gardner-Denver* case, which found that a decision reached through arbitration—in this instance, upholding for just cause the firing of a black worker who had alleged racial discrimination—does not deny a person the right to pursue his or her statutory rights through other avenues *in addition to* those provided under a collective bargaining agreement, even if those actions deal with the same factual occurrence.[35]

These various decisions have been interpreted by some as spelling an end to the "golden age of arbitration."[36] A more circumspect view is that issues of the right of the majority versus the interests of the minority in the realm of employment are not resolvable solely through the machinery of collective bargaining. Grievance procedures by and large have been shown to work well—appeals procedures, typically without arbitration, have been widely adopted in nonunion firms—and they continue to be central to the administration of the collective bargaining agreement and to labor relations on the American scene. It is safe to say that this will be the case for some time to come.

Seniority

It is quite common in the private sector, the nonunionized as well as the unionized portion, to base some terms and conditions of employment on *seniority*. This term refers to the length of time an employee has served in an employment unit, for example, a job, department, plant, or company. There are two general types of seniority: benefit seniority and competitive-status seniority. The first involves benefits that are allocated to all workers who meet a standard concerning length of service, while the second involves benefits which some workers gain at the expense of other workers. If all workers with 10 years of seniority can take 3 weeks of paid vacation but workers with 1 year of seniority can take only a week, that is an example of benefit seniority. As an example of competitive-status seniority, if three out of thirty employees in a department must be laid off, the three who go are those who have worked there the shortest length of time. Of these two types of seniority, the second is far more controversial than the first.

In addition to decisions on benefits and layoffs, seniority is also widely used in decisions on transfers and promotions. Rarely does a strict provision concerning seniority govern in these areas, however, for seniority usually operates in conjunction with a standard in regard to ability. In the case of two employees who wish to be promoted to the same higher position, for example, seniority generally will prevail only if the two are judged to be of equal ability. Note that what counts as "service" for purposes of determining seniority depends upon the seniority unit, just as what counts as "residence" for purposes of voting depends on the governmental unit—national, state, or local. Length of residence in the United States does not count when it comes to voting in local elections, and, similarly, service in a particular plant does not count toward occupational seniority. Further, seniority units may be based on craft or occupation—as in the case of welders in an automobile plant or nurses in a private hospital—on a department or division of a company, and, in a few instances, on an entire industry. A professional baseball player with 10 or more years of service in the major leagues can veto a trade to another team irrespective of the employer for whom he works or the area in which his team is located. In general, the seniority unit reflects the nature of a company's operation, being broad where skills are uniform and interchangeable, and narrow where specialization of skills exists.

As to the rationale for seniority, some workers undoubtedly support it out of the fear that management will "play favorites" in the designation of employees to be rewarded or penalized. But seniority also constitutes a system of rules by which workers decide among themselves who shall be given preference in certain conditions of employment. It is thus an allocative device designed to deal with situations of scarcity: a scarcity of jobs, of better jobs, of preferred assignments, and of preferred conditions. Therefore, rather than being viewed strictly as a defensive mechanism intended solely to protect the worker from bias, seniority may be regarded as a positive claim to job rights, or property in work, which helps to rationalize an otherwise overly competitive and indeterminate employment context.[37]

From another perspective, seniority eliminates the troublesome question of deciding that one person is better than another, in favor of a system based on equity in which the virtue of time on the job is rewarded. It is perhaps this aspect of seniority more than any other that leads many to use the term pejoratively. A common criticism of seniority is that it promotes inefficiency, if not mediocrity, and fails to recognize individual ability. But in many jobs—though not all, to be sure—performance improves with length of service, and thus a decision based on seniority may also be the "best" decision. In other cases, the range of abilities required to perform a particular task is not so great that decisions based on seniority and those based on merit will have very different outcomes in terms of performance. In still other instances, seniority may indeed lead to less desirable consequences than management would like, but then management would have to look for some other justification for its decisions concerning promotions, transfers, layoffs, and other personnel matters. And it is precisely the difficulty of identifying truly objective criteria to guide such decisions that has led managers to accept seniority on a broader basis than they would otherwise prefer.

If the principle of seniority is not likely to be attacked by management on a wide scale, it is nevertheless subject to other pressures. For example, studies have shown that preferences among employees for use of seniority in decisions about promotions, transfers, layoffs, and fringe benefits are negatively correlated with their skill, educational, occupational, and income levels. The less skilled and less well educated, in particular, prefer a broadly based application of seniority to issues arising at the workplace.[38] An important implication of these findings, and it is only an implication at this point, is that as the work force becomes more skilled, better educated, more highly paid, and more heavily composed of white-collar workers, it may prefer that greater weight be placed on merit or ability than on seniority in personnel decisions.

Another set of pressures on seniority emanates from accords that management may reach with other interest groups which conflict with provisions of the collective bargaining agreement. Such a conflict emerged on many fronts in the mid-1970s, when, in the face of layoffs necessitated by a recessionary economy, many employers had to decide whether seniority provisions of collective bargaining contracts took precedence over affirmative action agreements that sought to preserve the jobs of minority-group workers and women on more than just a token basis. The latter agreements, negotiated between private companies and one or another agency of the federal government, required that layoffs be carried out in such a way that the agreed-upon proportions of minority-group members and women in the work force would be preserved. Generally, this meant that the use of seniority as the basis of layoffs had to be modified or abandoned. When these conflicts reached the level of the courts, various and often contradictory decisions were reached, some holding that collective bargaining (seniority) provisions took precedence over affirmative action (minority employment) plans, and others taking the opposite view.[39] Incidentally, the same Congress that enacted legislation in the 1960s and 1970s to support equal employment opportunity itself operates most strictly on the principle of seniority with respect to committee assignments, and that system has few admirers among labor leaders or business managers. In any case, our purpose is to point out, again, how changing legal, economic, social, and political conditions affect a particular dimension of collective bargaining and labor relations—in this instance, the principle and practice of seniority. And those effects may occur in spite of the preferences of labor or management. This is particularly true in the legal sphere, where public policy (as, for example, in equal employment opportunity and seniority) seeks primarily to serve society's interests.

Work Rules

Discussions of work rules in relation to collective bargaining agreements and the administration of contracts seem inevitably to degenerate into allegations of featherbedding, goldbricking, restriction of output, make-work practices, and so on. The common perception is that organized workers oppose technological change at every turn and try diligently to stave off its effects by negotiating and maintaining restrictive work practices.

Like other assertions, this one contains some truth. In a free enterprise system, in which economic development and technological change result in the displacement of portions of the labor force even as they bring substantial benefits to society, one might well expect groups of workers to seek protection of their jobs, income, and the ways in which they are used to "doing business" at the workplace. This is especially true if, as is the case in the United States, workers are legally permitted to bargain with employers over their conditions of work. That some of these bargains result in work rules and practices which on their face are inefficient, costly, and outmoded should hardly be unexpected, for that is undeniably part of the price of preserving free collective bargaining.

But the issue is vastly more complicated than this. First of all, like other provisions of a collective bargaining agreement, work rules are established jointly by labor and management. They are not simply imposed by one party on the other, and, more important, they are a part of the larger range of issues involved in most labor negotiations. This means that the employer and the union may make trade-offs between work rules and other negotiable items—wages, fringe benefits, overtime provisions, grievance procedures, and even length of the contract. This is a key point, for it means that to abstract for analysis and criticism the work rules of a labor agreement is to overlook the trade-offs that have gone into the making of such rules and the corresponding benefits or freedoms that the employer may have gained in negotiations by agreeing to a particular set of work practices.

Second, and no doubt surprising to some, the most common union policy toward technological change is to leave the initiative to the employer and by and large acquiesce in acceptance of the changes.[40] This is somewhat akin to labor's position on discipline and due process; in these areas, the employer is left free to take actions, some of which may subsequently be challenged by the union. The difference is that organized workers mount few retrospective challenges to technological change, being more concerned with the consequences of a particular change than with preventing it. By and large, technological change has not harmed organized American workers, *as they see it;* where it is perceived that harm may result, unionists will attempt to negotiate provisions for job protections and economic security in their written agreements with employers. As an example, when the containerization of cargo moving through American ports became a reality in the 1960s, the shippers and the longshoremen's unions on both coasts negotiated such provisions for dockworkers affected by that technological change. This issue remains a sticky one, however, and the East Coast union (the International Longshoremen's Association, ILA) conducted a strike in 1977 over what it viewed as employers' attempts to erode previously negotiated provisions for job protections on the docks. The parties eventually reached a new 3-year agreement later that year.[41]

The fact that unions do not seem to have asserted control over or play a prominent role in technological change should remind us that to pursue bargaining objectives is not necessarily to achieve them. Only if a union has strong bargaining power relative to that of the employer *and* only if it chooses to focus that power on an issue of technological change does it have the capability of affecting, controlling, or warding off the effects of such change. The employer is generally more concerned than the union with technological change, capital investment, and the like, for these are the lifeblood of the business, importantly determining the firm's capacity to compete and survive. In undertaking technological change so as to meet organizational objectives, the employer will have to strike bargains with several interest groups—workers, suppliers, customers, stockholders, creditors—and will work to coordinate those bargains so as to integrate them and permit the business to remain a going concern. In terms of labor relations, employers generally have been able to retain this coordination function and to exercise their prerogatives concerning the form, scale, and timing of technological change. In some instances, they have had to bargain about the consequences of technological change for organized workers and to "buy out" work rules that developed under older technologies.

This leads to our third point about collectively bargained work rules and practices: they cannot be preserved indefinitely unless both parties agree to them and unless underlying economic circumstances and conditions in the industry allow labor and management to continue them in force. In the printing industry, for example, the practice of setting "bogus type," whereby compositors belonging to the International Typographical Union (ITU) reset the type for advertising copy even though it would never be used, existed for about 100 years. As competition in the industry became more severe; as employment in printshops declined, particularly in urban areas; and as capital was increasingly substituted for labor in the production process, the setting of bogus type became less and less viable, and it was eliminated from the industry altogether in 1973. In the allied instance of newspaper publishing, bogus type and related work practices began to be eliminated in the mid-1960s, though employers had to buy out such practices by providing income protections, employment guarantees, and retraining programs and by using attrition (voluntary quits and retirement) rather than layoffs to reduce the work force. These changes in work rules facilitated—and to a degree were brought on by—the mechanization of newspaper composing rooms, which began to develop in the early 1970s, especially among big-city dailies such as *The New York Times* and *The Washington Post*.

In 1970, the railroad employers and railroad workers' unions negotiated a contract in which they agreed to phase out, through a policy of attrition, the employment of firemen on diesel locomotives. A roughly comparable arrangement had been negotiated in the airlines in the 1960s, when flight engineers without pilot training, who had been important members of the cockpit crew in the propellor age, were phased out of most large jet planes. In 1976, in the apparel manufacturing industry, the combination of foreign competition, declining domestic employment, and new labor leadership spurred the International Ladies' Garment Workers' Union (ILGWU) and several employers' associations to negotiate sweeping changes in work rules, the first in 40 years, which totally revised systems of wage payment, production incentives, and work standards in that industry. In the same year, the United Automobile Workers (UAW) and the major automobile companies negotiated a form of premium pay for work done on Mondays and Fridays to reduce absenteeism and tardiness, which were particularly heavy on those days, while a variety of labor contracts concluded in 1974 and 1975 provided for work-sharing arrangements among members of bargaining units that allowed them to share more equitably the burden of unemployment induced by the recession of that period.[42]

In all these instances, changes in work rules were not put into effect without some cost to management. Employers typically had to buy them out, for the workers had come to regard them as part of their property in the job which could be sold or recompensed, but certainly not just given away. In the workers' view, they should be compensated when management attempts to change their jobs.[43] That the aforementioned work rules were changed and that others constantly are being revised, discarded, and adopted reflects this idea of property in the job as well as the necessity to adapt to changing economic, industrial, and employment conditions. In summary, most workers and unions accept changes in technology, production methods, and work rules because they are not fundamentally threatened by them. When they are so threatened, however, the most common bargaining solution is one that permits the employer to innovate, but at the price of cushioning the impact of the change on employees. The extent of such cushioning depends upon the union's bargaining power, which, keep in mind, is always relative to that of management.

THE DYNAMICS OF BARGAINING

In order that the reader may more fully appreciate the ways in which labor and management respond to, and are affected by, shifting economic circumstances and relative bargaining power, we will briefly review recent developments in collective bargaining in the electrical equipment industry, focusing specifically on the General Electric Company, where coalition bargaining first developed; on the steel industry, which features multiemployer negotiations and, in recent years, continuous bargaining; and on the highly concentrated automobile industry, in which contracts are negotiated with individual firms and which has been the scene of several important innovations in bargaining.

The Electrical Equipment Industry

Throughout its history, the General Electric Company, which is one of the three dominant firms in the electrical equipment industry (the other two being Westinghouse and RCA), prided itself on its progressive personnel and labor relations policies. Following a bitter and unexpected 2-month strike in 1946, however, the company resolved to develop a new approach to collective bargaining. What emerged was "Boulwarism," named after a GE vice president of marketing, Lemuel Boulware, who was placed in charge of industrial relations. His distinctive contribution was a philosophy which condemned the haggling and bluffing of collective bargaining and sought to substitute a concept of managerial justice. Boulware advocated this approach partly in response to the aggressive personal style of the key union leader at that time, James Carey, president of the International Union of Electrical, Radio and Machine Workers (IUE). Before negotiation of the contract, the company undertook an extensive study of its own position and of wages, benefits, and working conditions prevailing elsewhere in the industry. It then made an offer to the union, leaving no doubt that this was also its final offer unless the union could clearly demonstrate some error in its analysis. GE sought to demonstrate that it would "do right voluntarily" by its employees, and it attempted to sell its offer directly to employees by means of an extensive communications program. In particular, the company felt that its approach substituted reason for force and realism for gamesmanship.[44]

For a number of years the company successfully pursued this policy, although the unions objected to it from the very beginning. Several charges of unfair labor practices alleging violation of the duty-to-bargain provision of the Taft-Hartley Act were filed against the company; the case became one of the most celebrated and prolonged in the history of American industrial relations, taking nearly a decade to resolve in the NLRB and the courts. But the rhetoric of Boulwarism and the legal argumentation that evolved over it should not mask the realities of a power relationship between labor and management in which the company held the upper hand.[45]

It is true that GE came to the bargaining table with a well-researched, clearly articulated, and internally cohesive negotiating position. Undergirding its stance, though, was a production process in which no single element or group of employees was particularly crucial. The maintenance of various production locations for each major component of the process meant that, for example, if workers at one facility went on strike, the work would simply be switched to another facility. In bargaining parlance, no single union was in a position to increase the cost to the company of not agreeing to its terms.

Moreover, the unions at General Electric were a factious lot, especially those composed of electrical workers—the IUE and the United Electrical, Radio, and Machine Workers of America (UE), the former having split off from the latter over the issue of Communist penetration in the union. This factionalism, together with the fact that no one among the thirteen unions representing segments of GE's work force of more than 150,000 members could mount a successful strike or otherwise bring strong pressure to bear on the company, reflected the relatively weak bargaining power of organized employees at the giant electrical manufacturer.

The frustrations of tackling a unified, powerful opponent across the bargaining table led the unions at GE to attempt a bargaining coalition to confront the company and simultaneously negotiate terms and conditions of employment. These efforts were hesitant at first but picked up steam, and in 1969 the thirteen unions formed a solid bargaining coalition that began to push the company away from its "final-offer-first, employer-knows-best" approach. Ironically, during the 1960s, the NLRB and the courts found that the company's bargaining did indeed constitute a violation of the legal requirement to bargain in good faith.[46] But it was the growing ability of the union coalition, manifested in a major strike in 1969 and 1970, to impose on the company a larger cost of not agreeing to its terms that led to further backing away from Boulwarism in the bargaining rounds of 1970 and 1973. By the time of the next contract renewal— June 1976—that approach to bargaining had been abandoned altogether, with GE participating in the give-and-take of negotiations with the unions.

This experience provides a good illustration of intraorganizational bargaining within a management and several unions; of attitudinal structuring, as each party attempted to reshape its opponent's views about its own negotiating position; and of a distributive-bargaining approach to labor relations. Most of all, it demonstrates how the conduct and outcomes of negotiations are dependent upon the relative bargaining power of labor and management.

The Steel Industry

Collective bargaining in the steel industry proceeds in large part on a multiemployer rather than an individual-employer basis.[47] The Coordinating Committee Steel Companies serves as the negotiating arm of the industry's ten largest firms, which bargain with the United Steelworkers of America (USA). The union's negotiating policy is formulated through a series of coordinating committees, the Wage Policy Committee, the Basic Steel Industry Conference, and a Negotiating Advisory Committee. These structures have evolved out of the need to give different local unions a say in the formation of bargaining goals while, at the same time, integrating these diverse needs into an overall negotiating position. Additionally, in recent years the union has attempted to coordinate its contract negotiations among several industries, such as aluminium, metal containers, and nonferrous metals, in which some of its members are employed or which are otherwise strategically important to the steel industry. Once the USA and the Coordinating Committee Steel Companies reach agreement on the major terms and conditions of employment, a separate pact is signed with each of the firms. As the largest firm in the industry, United States Steel plays an especially important role in this bargaining structure, which sets the pattern of wage and nonwage provisions that generally is followed by each of the major producers as well as other, smaller employers. ("Pattern setting" and "pattern following" occur in a number of other American industries as well.)

The recent bargaining history of this industry is fascinating. In 1959, a 116-day strike occurred, primarily over wages, cost-of-living provisions, and work rules. A board of inquiry appointed by the President of the United States investigated the dispute, the emergency strike procedures of the Taft-Hartley Act were invoked, and the Vice President of the United States and the Secretary of Labor became active mediators with the parties for several weeks. A new 3-year agreement was reached at the beginning of 1960 and was made retroactive to the previous year. Among other things that emerged out of the negotiations, a Human Relations Research Committee was formed to study and recommend solutions to a variety of difficult issues concerning wages and working conditions. That committee was itself to become an issue in the union's internal politics (reviewed briefly in Chapter 4), with the opposition, led by I. W. Abel, citing it as an example of incumbent president David J. McDonald's overly close association with key employers in the steel industry.

In any case, the steel companies responded to this major conflict by maneuvering production so as to stockpile large inventories of goods, which they believed would help them weather another prolonged conflict. The purchasers of the steel companies' products (automobile manufacturers and machine tool firms, for example), who also wanted to protect themselves in case of another prolonged strike of their major suppliers, did the same. Though these actions were taken in order to raise the cost to the USA of not agreeing to management's terms, one result was that much costly overtime work was done prior to contract expiration dates, but with considerable layoffs occurring thereafter owing to a slump in demand. The uncertainty about strikes at contract renewal time consequently harmed both labor and management. These developments, together with the intrusion of foreign competition—at first on a small scale and then on a larger one—made the union hesitant to conduct another work stoppage. Further, the earlier strike had severely depleted the union's treasury, thereby contributing to its weakened capacity to engage in militant activity.

Over the next several bargaining rounds, the parties sought to consolidate their respective positions, to resolve particularly pressing issues concerning working conditions and production, and even to engage in joint lobbying in

Washington in an effort to obtain import quotas and tariffs on foreign-made steel and steel products. Put differently, the parties began a process of "continuous bargaining" to deal with key issues during the 3-year periods between the renegotiation of labor contracts. Possibly more than any other American labor organization, the USA gave support to the increasingly fashionable view within labor that the strike in industry needs to be resorted to only in the rarest of circumstances. As noted in Chapter 4, this position culminated in 1973 in the signing of the Experimental Negotiating Agreement (ENA), covering some 350,000 workers, which guaranteed uninterrupted production through mid-1977, established voluntary interest arbitration of any unresolved issues in the 1974 negotiations, and pledged the parties to refrain from conducting a strike or lockout in support of their respective bargaining positions. The arrangement was a signal to customers of the steel industry that production would be ensured when an old contract expired. The ENA was reaffirmed in the 1977 negotiations, and its provisions were extended through 1980, including one that does permit strikes over local issues on a plantwide basis. This was not accomplished, though, without opposition from a substantial minority of union members, many of whom supported Ed Sadlowski over Lloyd McBride in the USA's 1977 presidential election (won by McBride). Thus it is that a union's bargaining strategy is influenced by internal political pressures and that candidates for union offices exploit bargaining issues for political ends.

The fact that labor and management in the steel industry have been led to the aforementioned actions—especially to continuous bargaining, which remains relatively rare within contemporary industrial relations—is due in large part to the external threats facing that industry. Domestic markets for steel products have shrunk, especially in automobile manufacturing, where lighter-weight and cheaper plastic, aluminum, and glass are being substituted liberally for heavier and costlier steel components; the industry's technology and production facilities are relatively old and inefficient and therefore do not provide a strong basis for competing effectively with foreign manufacturers; and political decision makers in Congress and the executive branch of government have been reluctant to enact the protectionist legislation so eagerly sought by the industry's employers *and* unionists. In 1977, several major producers reported record operating losses and closed some of their least efficient plants, leading to large-scale layoffs.[48]

These economic, legal, and political dimensions of the environment impinge upon collective bargaining in the steel industry, shaping the parties' negotiating strategy and behavior. That labor and management have chosen for the moment the route of industrial peace is a concrete manifestation of their desire to survive in circumstances in which they operate under numerous disadvantages.

The Automobile Industry

Collective bargaining in the automobile industry centers on contract negotiations between the UAW and the "big three" producers: General Motors, Ford, and Chrysler.[49] Unlike the steel producers, however, the automobile producers are not represented in a joint bargaining committee; each one deals separately with the UAW and negotiates a separate agreement with it. Despite the different structural form, however, pattern setting and pattern following are common to the industry, as the "big three," American Motors (the number four firm), and the several manufacturers of specialized vehicles and trucks generally adhere to a pattern of wages and other terms and conditions of employment set in an agreement between the UAW and one of the large companies.

Prior to the expiration of its major labor contracts, the UAW selects one of the "big three" companies as a "target" with which it will attempt to conclude an agreement, and it then spreads the major negotiated provisions to other firms. The fact that negotiations take place at the beginning of a new model year is important to bargaining and to the selection of a target firm in this industry. If that firm suffers a strike and a subsequent loss of production at the start of a new model year, it can well lose sales and market share to a competitor. Clearly, this acts to strengthen the union's bargaining power. Once individual contracts are reached, they will differ in some of their particulars, and a collective bargaining agreement in a multiplant firm will not cover all issues but, instead, will leave many of them to local negotiations within the framework of the master agreement. For more than two decades, 3-year contracts have been the rule in this industry.

Automobile manufacturing has been the scene of many unusual and innovative developments in bargaining. Escalator clauses, tying wage increases to changes in the Consumer Price Index over the life of the contract, first appeared in labor agreements in the automobile industry negotiated in the late 1940s. Later, the parties pioneered the concept of supplemental unemployment benefits, a set of payments to laid-off workers which, together with unemployment insurance funds, permits them to weather economic recessions and industry downswings at income levels that approach their earned wages. By the early 1970s, the combination of these two forms of payments enabled a laid-off automobile worker to receive up to 95 percent of his or her take-home pay.

Relatively few new bargaining initiatives took place in the industry during the 1960s, though at various times the UAW proposed that the companies negotiate over automobile prices, the duration of unemployment compensation, excise taxes, and other items. Thwarted in these efforts, the UAW nevertheless made substantial headway in increasing wages and the fringe benefits it had previously won, such as supplemental unemployment benefits, and in acquiring such benefits as severance pay and pay while serving on a jury, a prescription drug plan, and protection against layoffs due to subcontracting. An expansionary economy and a relatively prosperous industry provided the backdrop to bargaining in the 1960s, even though automobile imports rose steadily and foreign-made cars accounted for a considerably larger share of total sales in the United States at the end of the decade than at the beginning.

Nevertheless, several strikes were threatened during these years, and a 49-day strike at the Ford Motor Company took place in 1967. An internal dispute between skilled trades workers and production employees over differences in their wages, which had narrowed over time, and various local disputes over work rules were key issues in that strike. In 1970, there was a 2-month strike of General Motors employees. Once the strike was concluded, the terms of the settlement were extended in a virtually unchanged form to Chrysler and Ford, where employees had been working past the contract expiration date, that is, without a contract, awaiting the results of bargaining at GM.

Bargaining in the automobile industry in the 1970s provides another example of the fact that labor relations do not occur in a vacuum but, rather, are affected by major economic factors. Before the 1973 bargaining round, the UAW called a conference of production workers to "hear the members' views" concerning the leading issues and objectives of bargaining. Against the background of a generally strong economic recovery from the mild recession of 1969–1970 and very strong consumer demand for automobiles, which resulted in some employees' working 40 and 50 weeks of overtime annually, union officials subsequently identified "voluntary overtime" and "30 years and out" as major issues for negotiations. The first meant that within certain limits a worker could refuse management's request to work overtime, while the second permitted an employee to retire with full pension benefits after 30 years of service, irrespective of age. In late 1973, both provisions were incorporated into new labor agreements, along with other clauses more closely limiting the rights of supervisors at local plants to impose disciplinary measures on workers.

Shortly thereafter, the Arab oil embargo raised gasoline prices, thereby both reducing and changing the composition of demand for automobiles. This, combined with the severe recession of 1974–1975, dramatically reduced production in the industry. No longer was overtime an issue. The mass layoffs that occurred led the next conference of production workers to call for the union to negotiate job protection, work-sharing arrangements, and increased supplemental unemployment benefits in the 1976 contracts. This the union's leadership proceeded to do, though it obtained neither guarantees against layoffs nor complete job protection. Thus the UAW offers another example of the intraorganizational bargaining that occurs prior to distributive or integrative bargaining with the other side.[50]

Internal tensions between skilled trades and production workers remain an important issue within the union, while its leadership joins with employers in a mutual concern for the consequences to workers of increasing foreign competition and domestic regulatory policies, notably those dealing with environmental protection and consumers' and workers' safety. These are just some of the issues which can be expected to frame the next few rounds of negotiations in the American automobile industry, the outcome of which will again be shaped by the relative bargaining power of labor and management within an economic context over which they have only limited control.

NEW DIMENSIONS OF BARGAINING
AND LABOR RELATIONS

If the bulk of collective bargaining and labor relations deals with distributive issues or treats issues in a distributive way, there is nevertheless a variety of integrative, cooperative approaches presently in use to deal with specific labor problems. Such initiatives are not totally new. The B and O Railroad plan of the 1920s; the Scanlon plan, which emerged in the steel industry after World War II and which was copied elsewhere; the Union-Management Cooperative Committee at the Tennessee Valley Authority, which has functioned since the 1940s; and the committees on human relations and automation that were operative in several industries during the 1950s and 1960s all were concerned with improving productivity through labor-management cooperation in ways that typically went beyond the formal collective bargaining process and the labor agreement. These plans, committees, and joint ventures were mechanisms through which workers (in some cases running the gamut from unskilled laborers to executive personnel) could offer recommendations to increase efficiency, eliminate waste, improve methods and conditions of work, stabilize employment, facilitate technological change, and evaluate new working arrangements. One or another type of incentive scheme generally was necessary to secure the cooperation of workers. Some of these were oriented toward the individual, and others were group-oriented; some provided regular monthly bonuses, and others provided lump-sum annual payments; and still others carried with them income guarantees and job protections. But the notion underlying all of them was to distribute the fruits of productivity improvements to those responsible for recommending and effectuating them.

The 1970s have witnessed several new efforts to develop cooperation and joint consultation between labor and management.[51] In basic steel, the bargaining agreements of 1971, 1974, and 1977 provided for committees on employment security and plant productivity; so far these committees have explored such subjects as the avoidance of defects in quality, improved identification of warehoused steel, more efficient handling of scrap, energy conservation, more efficient phasing out of old equipment, and better care of new equipment. Workers' acceptance of, and participation in, these activities are encouraged by supplementary unemployment benefits, provisions for early retirement, a 13-week vacation every 5 years based on seniority, and other measures. The committees' activities are limited so as not to affect "the existing rights of either party under any other provision of the collective bargaining agreement."[52] Unfortunately, little detailed information is available about the experiences of the committees on plant productivity, numbering about 230, that have recently been established in the steel industry.

In automobile manufacturing, a joint union-management committee was formed in 1973 in each of the large companies to deal on a year-round, continuing basis with issues of the quality of working life. Interestingly, the committee structure emerged only after protests by the UAW that it was being excluded from company-initiated experiments beginning in 1970 to improve the quality of working life of automobile assemblers. Typical of the new structures is the National GM-UAW Committee to Improve the Quality of Work Life, which has to date sponsored several experimental projects that feature joint labor-management committees to supervise the progress of experiments and to hire consultants when necessary. This type of joint involvement has not been present in most projects for restructuring work and improving the quality of working life, such as those discussed in Chapter 2.

The UAW is also a party to joint experiments at Rockwell International and the Harmon International Company. The first of these features several innovative concepts, including training of employees for widened responsibility and job interchangeability; work teams within specific areas and departments; participation by employees in the setting of production standards and in the determination of policies for overtime, layoffs, break periods, and leaves; and the resolution of work-related problems at the lowest possible level of the employee-employer relationship. At Harmon's facility in Bolivar, Tennessee, union and management, assisted by grants from foundations and a consulting social scientist, conducted a survey of employees' attitudes to identify sources of discontent and then proceeded to organize experiments in work improvement featuring small groups of employees and supervisors who jointly decided on new methods of production. One project permitted workers who exceeded production standards to choose between higher pay and time off from work. Productivity was reported to increase in these circumstances, as did the volume of requests for in-plant training classes.[53]

In the railroad industry, a joint labor-management committee was formed in 1968 to study the difficult issues of manning that have perpetually confronted this sector of the labor force, but only relatively slow progress was achieved (though, as noted earlier, the employment of firemen on the diesels will be eliminated by attrition as a result of the 1973 collective bargaining agreement). Five years later, a fourteen-member Task Force on Terminals was established to develop and test innovative experiments in terminal operations. Early activities have focused on improved reliability of service, reduced time of car detention, creation of new business, better management planning and evaluation techniques, and greater job security and safety.

In the retail food industry, a joint committee composed of representatives of eight leading supermarket chains and three major unions—the Teamsters, the Retail Clerks International Association (RCIA), and the Amalgamated Meat Cutters and Butcher Workmen of North America (AMCB)—was organized in 1974 to discuss and seek cooperative action on such issues as work practices, technological change, productivity, and the structure of bargaining. Working closely with the Federal Mediation and Conciliation Service (FMCS), the committee focused on developing a national forum that might be used to improve local negotiations in an industry in which bargaining is highly fragmented; it was hoped that this would reduce the incidence of local strikes and promote long-run stability. The identification of the structure of bargaining as a

major issue of joint concern in the retail food industry is particularly noteworthy, as it accords with the policies of recent Secretaries of Labor to promote
tripartite labor-management-government committees in major sectors to study
industrial relations and collective bargaining problems.[54]

The food industry committee has also played a key role in gathering information about the impact of electronic check-out systems in supermarkets and
the elimination of conventional price markings on foodstuffs in favor of those
which can be detected by electronic scanners. Its subcommittee that dealt with
these issues recognized that management's attempts to use new technology and
improve productivity must be balanced with labor's "concern about the impact
on the size of the work force and the nature of changed job assignments."[55] In
addition, the joint committee commissioned a study by the Harvard University
School of Public Health to investigate the use of polyvinyl chloride film in retail
meat markets, with the longer-range objective of establishing safer work practices. The retail food industry is only one among many that have established
joint labor-management committees to deal with health and safety at the workplace. Such efforts were spurred in 1970 by the enactment of the Occupational
Safety and Health Act and generally have proceeded outside the framework of
collective bargaining.[56]

In addition to these cooperative initiatives in specific industries, the FMCS
has assisted with the formation of joint committees in a variety of plants and
localities to reduce the number of disputes and contribute to improved productivity. Important to these efforts is an FMCS mediation procedure that stresses
applications of behavioral science and management-by-objectives techniques
to enhance mutual trust between the parties and improve their problem-solv-
ing capabilities. In a sense, this is a tripartite form of attitudinal structuring,
which was identified earlier as a key component of bilateral negotiations between labor and management. Cooperative efforts sponsored by the FMCS have
been particularly notable in the pulp and paper industry.

In an unusual community self-renewal effort in Jamestown, New York, the
town's leading corporate employers and labor unions joined in 1972 to form an
Area Labor-Management Committee, which defined four principal goals: gains
in productivity in existing industries, improved labor relations, human resources development, and assistance to programs for industrial development.
This enterprise served as a vehicle for the creation of plant-level labor-management committees in a variety of Jamestown businesses that sought in particular
to secure the active participation of rank-and-file workers in meeting these four
major objectives. Early reports indicate something of a turnaround in Jamestown's business climate: the number of strikes and grievances has been reduced; several marginal plants have been improved; employment has increased; workers have been trained, and their skills upgraded; and at least one
company, an engine manufacturer, decided to locate a new plant in the city,
thereby creating 1500 new jobs in what had been for many years a depressed
area. The pattern of the joint committee subsequently was followed in nearby
Buffalo, a city of more than 400,000 population.[57]

From the perspective of our discussion in Chapter 2, the examples presented here of cooperative efforts by labor and management to improve productivity and the quality of working life, to confront issues of safety and health at the workplace, and to reinvigorate production processes and even the economic climate of some locales require the active involvement of organized workers who must come to regard such endeavors as serving their own interests as well as those of others. Some tangible benefits must accrue to employees, whether within formal collective bargaining processes and agreements or as an adjunct to them, if they are to be active participants in integrative negotiations over problems that arise within the general context of the labor-management relationship. For employers and managers, this requires that they be less concerned about preserving their "prerogatives," which in any case depends upon their bargaining power relative to that of organized workers, and more concerned with structuring the types of cooperative relationships from which they and their employees may derive mutual benefits. After all, because management has the final power of decision over business matters, organized workers are wary lest their role be undercut by cooperative undertakings with their adversaries at the bargaining table. To this point, it appears that as much art as science enters into the achievement of cooperative relationships between labor and management and that efforts to achieve these relationships often emerge where management faces especially pressing—or especially favorable—financial and market conditions.

MULTINATIONAL BARGAINING

Finally, the large amount of popular attention currently paid to the multinational corporation, as well as the attempts of some unions to deal with that type of institution on various labor matters, requires us to consider briefly the coordination of bargaining across national boundaries and in differing cultures. At present, few detailed studies have been made of multinational collective bargaining.[58] The incidence of such bargaining appears quite small, and those who have investigated the issue see few prospects for its emergence on a wide scale. However, it is undeniable that the decision of an American firm to undertake or expand business on a multinational scale can have important effects on domestic collective bargaining.

Consider, for example, the case of Litton Industries, a large conglomerate corporation which has followed the strategy of substantially diversifying its several business activities. As reported by Craypo,[59] in 1965 Litton acquired Royal Typewriter, the industry's second largest American firm, and in the following year it added German and British typewriter companies. In 1969, organized production workers struck Royal's Springfield, Missouri, plant over a dispute involving a challenge by a dissident group to the union's status as bargaining agent and over alleged unfair labor practices by management. The company made its first bargaining offer some 2 months after expiration of the contract, and on the very next day it announced a plant shutdown, with the transfer of some operations to Royal's plant in Hartford, Connecticut, and of others to a Portuguese firm.

The next year, some typewriter manufacturing operations were moved from Hartford to Litton's British subsidiary, Imperial Typewriter, and to its German firm, Triumph-Adler. In 1972, Litton announced plans to transfer production of its remaining manual office and electric portable typewriters from Hartford to the British facility, a move completed in early 1973. As noted by Craypo, "In this way, Royal Typewriter became a worldwide distributor of typewriters manufactured in Litton's foreign subsidiaries and sold under the Royal and [German] Adler brand name."[60]

The International Union of Allied Industrial Workers of America (AIW), which represented Royal's workers, had no prior knowledge of the transfer of production and jobs to foreign plants; indeed, it often was led to believe that no such transfer would take place. By moving to lower-cost operations in other countries, a conglomerate multinational firm such as Litton can severely curtail the bargaining power of some American labor organizations with which it has had to deal and can reduce that of others with which it continues to deal. If replicated on a large scale, this might well create "pockets of bargaining imbalance reminiscent of the 1920s" and "open-shop conditions under which real labor costs are minimized."[61] To offset such actions by employers, unions would have to consolidate their fractionalized domestic bargaining activity and bargaining units within particular firms and, on the international scene, would have to pursue coordinated bargaining in the various nation-states where the multinational firms with which they presently negotiate individually are located. However, "there is no record of effective global bargaining among the unrelated operations of a conglomerate, multinational firm."[62] Also, the legislative efforts of American labor to restrict the export of capital and jobs as well as the flow of imports into the United States have so far been largely unsuccessful.

In western Europe, multinational bargaining has made some inroads, but these have in general also been quite limited, despite claims to the contrary by some international union secretariats. In the highly concentrated western European flat glass industry, for example, the International Federation of Chemical and General Workers' Unions (ICF) seems to have had little success in coordinating bargaining across national boundaries with such major firms as Saint-Gobain-Pont-à-Mousson and Pilkington Brothers, Ltd. As reported by Northrup and Rowan,[63] labor settlements in the late 1960s and early 1970s at Italian, French, German, and American plants of Saint-Gobain differed substantially among the locations, indicating that the ICF's coordinated bargaining efforts had virtually no impact on the course of negotiations. The agreements at American plants seemed patterned after those set in the leading domestic firms, Libbey-Owens-Ford and PPG Industries, rather than after those arrived at in Saint-Gobain's western European facilities.

In late 1972, at the ICF Glass Industry Conference in Geneva, Switzerland, a Pilkington World Council was established, but it has never been officially recognized by the company, even though occasional meetings have been held between council representatives and company officials. In contrast, in 1975 the ICF, in coalition with other labor organizations, was able to negotiate a multinational agreement with BSN-Gervais Danone, a company based in France, to deal with employment problems at its locations in five countries. The agreement, which followed a series of shutdowns of the firm's Belgian plants, was narrowly confined to employment matters and did not intrude on prevailing labor agreements, but it nevertheless may be interpreted to represent a "long stride toward multinational collective bargaining and joint labor-management decision making."[64]

In generalizing from this experience and from the experiences of the metals and electrical equipment industries, Northrup and Rowan conclude that national unions are likely to be better equipped than international secretariats such as the ICF to handle the coordination of collective bargaining across national boundaries.[65] The secretariats most probably will continue to carry out the function of gathering and disseminating information. As to the more general prospects for multinational bargaining, most businesspeople continue to oppose it, while union officials seem unsure of the benefits to be derived from it. Union constituencies are national rather than international, and that fact is underscored in times of economic adversity. Moreover, the internationalization of collective bargaining would require some diminution of the power of national union officials, a factor likely to give them considerable pause before pursuing multinational negotiations.

Finally, political, economic, technological, and cultural differences between nations, as well as differences in the area of wages and working conditions, suggest real limits to the international coordination of collective bargaining, even if some union coalitions across national boundaries do emerge. The decentralized character of American industrial relations presents an especially formidable obstacle to multinational bargaining. Yet actions of the type engaged in by Litton Industries may spur further attempts by unions to coordinate negotiations with multinational companies. In this arena, as in others, the parties to collective bargaining will continue their efforts to alter their relative costs of agreeing and disagreeing, or, in other words, their relative bargaining power.

SUMMARY

This chapter focused on collective bargaining between labor and management in the private sector. Emphasis was placed on the concept of bargaining power and on processes of intraorganizational negotiations and attitudinal structuring which characterize both distributive and integrative bargaining. Each of the parties to negotiations has available various strategies and tactics which it uses in attempting to influence its relative bargaining power. The scope of negotiable issues varies from situation to situation and over time. Many items once regarded as involving strictly management's rights—prerogatives—are now seen as also involving the interests of unions and therefore have become subjects of negotiations. Once a collective bargaining agreement is reached, it requires active administration by both labor and management, which gives definition and tone to the working relationship between the parties. Some of the dynamic changes affecting such relationships were explored, as were several emerging cooperative ventures between labor and management and the prospects for multinational bargaining. In Chapter 6, we move on to examine developments in collective bargaining in the American public sector, where the labor movement has scored its most recent gains.

NOTES

1 For elaboration of this concept, see Neil W. Chamberlain and James W. Kuhn, *Collective Bargaining,* 2d ed., McGraw-Hill, New York, 1965, especially chap. 7.

2 Chamberlain and Kuhn, p. 171. Recognize that nonpecuniary items of the type mentioned here can have important cost implications. However, these are often hard to quantify, and so they must be qualitatively factored into bargaining decisions.

3 Richard E. Walton and Robert B. McKersie, *A Behavioral Theory of Labor Negotiations,* McGraw-Hill, New York, 1965, especially chaps. 1 and 10. The following discussion relies heavily on this source.

4 The integrative-bargaining approach can be thought of as a variable-sum game, in contrast to the zero-sum nature of distributive bargaining.

5 For more on this concept, as well as the nature of trust in society, see Alan Fox, *Beyond Contract: Work, Power and Trust Relations,* Faber, London, 1974.

6 For further development of this concept using different terminology, see Ross Stagner and Hjalmar Rosen, *Psychology of Union-Management Relations,* Wadsworth, Belmont, Calif., 1965.

7 On this point, see Walton and McKersie, chap. 9.

8 National Labor Relations Board, *Summary of the National Labor Relations Act,* 1970, pp. 20–22.

9 U.S. Bureau of Labor Statistics, *Directory of National Unions and Employee Associations, 1975,* Bulletin 1937, 1977, pp. 77–81.

10 This conclusion emerges from a comparison of multiemployer bargaining in major labor agreements in 1975 with that in prior years, as reported in U.S. Bureau of Labor Statistics, *Characteristics of Major Collective Bargaining Agreements, July 1, 1975.* Bulletin 1957, 1977, p. 12, and in previous editions of that series.

11 U.S. Bureau of Labor Statistics, *Characteristics of Major Collective Bargaining Agreements, July 1, 1975.* This source provides basic data for the discussion in the remainder of this section.

12 U.S. Bureau of Labor Statistics, *Characteristics of Major Collective Bargaining Agreements, July 1, 1975.*

13 U.S. Bureau of Labor Statistics, *Characteristics of Major Collective Bargaining Agreements, July 1, 1975.* See also Edward H. Friend, *Third National Survey of Employee Benefits for Full-Time Personnel of U.S. Municipalities,* Labor-Management Relations Service, Washington, 1977, pp. 1–2.

14 The quote by Baer is cited in James W. Kuhn, "Business Unionism in a Laboristic Society," in Ivar E. Berg (ed.), *The Business of America,* Harcourt, Brace & World, New York, 1968, p. 302. See also various publications of the National Right to Work Committee, headquartered in Fairfax, Va.

15 This line of reasoning is consistent with the integrative-bargaining approach as described earlier. There may be mutual benefits to management and the union as a result of shared authority—or there might be gains to neither side. To the extent that management seeks to preserve its prerogatives and authority in decision making, it engages in distributive bargaining with labor. Note that Elton Mayo and later advocates of the human relations philosophy of management overlooked unions as agents of the workers and thus tended to denigrate the role of power and authority in organizations.

16 Philosophical statements about corporate social responsibility often overlook the claims of interest groups to a role in organizational decision making, even when such statements emanate from businesses that negotiate agreements with labor unions. See, for example, *Social Responsibilities of Business Corporations,* Committee for Economic Development, New York, 1971. Concerning the effect that unions actually have had on management, see David Lewin, "The Impact of Unionism on American Business: Evidence for an Assessment," *Columbia Journal of World Business,* **13**:89–103 (1978).

17 For more on the concept of a bargaining zone, see Stagner and Rosen, chap. 7. The starting point for most modern theories of bargaining is John Hicks, *A Theory of Wages,* Macmillan, New York, 1932. This and other theories are summarized in John G. Cross, *The Economics of Bargaining,* Basic Books, New York, 1969.

18 The Taft-Hartley Act requires the parties to give each other 60 days' notice prior to contract expiration if either one wishes to change wages or conditions of employment. Additionally, organized workers may continue to work past the contract expiration date, hoping or expecting that their negotiators will reach a new agreement with management. This is far more common in the public than in the private sector, however.

19 Note that the strike may reduce rather than eliminate the workers' and the employer's income. Some unionists have access to union strike funds, public assistance payments, and food stamps. Also, in New York and Rhode Island strikers may collect unemployment insurance benefits following an 8-week waiting period. On the other hand, some employers are able to stockpile inventories, thereby continuing to sell goods during production workers' strikes, and others have mutual-aid pacts or strike insurance funds.

20 The employer lockout is legal only under certain conditions. It cannot be motivated by antiunion considerations, which the NLRB attempts to judge on a case-by-case basis. This can be difficult to determine, however, since even legal lockouts naturally seek to curb union power.

21 Derived from data in *Monthly Labor Review,* **102**:111(1979), table 37.

22 For an account of this dispute, see Walter H. Uphoff, *Kohler on Strike,* Beacon Press, Boston, 1966.

23 Prohibited bargaining tactics and strategies are generally defined by the rulings of the NLRB and to a lesser extent by the courts.

24 This point is emphasized in Paul Prasow and Edward Peters, *Labor Arbitration and Collective Bargaining,* McGraw-Hill, New York, 1970.

25 Benjamin Aaron, "The Impact of Public Employment Grievance Settlement on the Labor Arbitration Process," in Joy Correge et al. (eds.), *The Future of Labor Arbitration in America,* American Arbitration Association, New York, 1976, p. 15.

26 U.S. Bureau of Labor Statistics, *Characteristics of Major Collective Bargaining Agreements, July 1, 1975,* p. 94.

27 The grievance procedure is more fully analyzed in Chamberlain and Kuhn, chap. 6. The informal negotiations over grievances that occur between workers and managers are analyzed in James W. Kuhn, *Bargaining in Grievance Settlement,* Columbia, New York, 1961.

28 John Zalusky, "Arbitration: Updating a Vital Process," *The American Federationist,* **83:**2 (1976).

29 Zalusky, pp. 5–6. See also Ben Fischer, "The Steel Industry's Expedited Arbitration: The Judgement after Two Years," *Arbitration Journal,* **28:**185–191 (1973).

30 See *United Steelworkers v. Enterprise Wheel and Car Corporation,* 363 U.S. 593 (1960); *United Steelworkers v. Warrior and Gulf Navigation Co.,* 363 U.S. 574 (1960); and *United Steelworkers v. American Mfg. Co.,* 363 U.S. 564 (1960). These cases are commonly referred to as the "Steelworkers' trilogy."

31 See, for example, decisions in the following cases: *Collyer Insulated Wire,* 192 NLRB 150 (1971); and *Emporium Capwell Co. v. Western Addition Community Organization,* 95 U.S. 977 (1975).

32 228 NLRB 102, 94 LRRM 1483 (1977), as reported in American Bar Association, Section of Labor Relations Law, *The Developing Labor Law: The Board, the Courts, and the National Labor Relations Act, 1976 Supplement,* Bureau of National Affairs, Washington, 1977, p. 135.

33 228 NLRB 103, 94 LRRM 1474 (1977); and American Bar Association, p. 136.

34 See American Bar Association, pp. 138–141.

35 *Alexander v. Gardner-Denver,* U.S. (1974) 7 EPD P914S. Specifically, the Court held that an arbitrator's decision is not final and binding where Title VII of the Civil Rights Act of 1964 is involved. The complainant, Alexander, pursued his case through four tribunals, none of which upheld his claim of discrimination.

36 See David E. Feller, "The Coming End of Arbitration's Golden Age," in Barbara D. Dennis and Gerold G. Somers (eds.), *Proceedings of the Twenty-Ninth Annual Meeting of the National Academy of Arbitrators,* Bureau of National Affairs, Washington, 1976, pp. 97–126. For more on the issue, see J. A. Raffaele, "Labor Arbitration and the Law," *Labor Law Journal,* **29:**26–36 (1978).

37 On this concept of seniority, see Frederic Meyers, "The Analytic Meaning of Seniority," *Proceedings of the Eighteenth Annual Winter Meeting of the Industrial Relations Research Association, 1965,* Madison, Wis., 1966, pp. 1–9.

38 Phillip Selznick, *Law, Society and Industrial Justice,* Russell Sage, New York, 1969, chap. 5.

39 See, for example, *Jersey Central Power and Light Co. v. IBEW, EEOC, OFCC, USGA, et al.,* Third Circuit Court of Appeals, 74-2016 (1974), where the decision (reversing that of the lower court) upheld an affirmative action agreement, reached under provisions of the Civil Rights Act, concerning the seniority clause of a collective bargaining contract in determining layoffs. In other such cases, different courts have upheld seniority over provisions for affirmative action.

40 On this point, see Sumner H. Slichter, James J. Healy, and E. Robert Livernash, *The Impact of Collective Bargaining on Management,* Brookings, Washington,

especially pp. 348–349. This volume remains the single most comprehensive source on the nonwage impacts of unionism, but the subject could well stand reanalysis.

41 For an account of the 1977 agreement, see Bureau of National Affairs, *Daily Labor Report,* Apr. 19, 1977, p. A-10.

42 This discussion of changes in work rules is based on popular accounts. It remains for scholars to systematically investigate changes in work rules under recent collective bargaining in the way that was done in the 1950s by Slichter, Healy, and Livernash. For an example of a more recent study confined to one major sector, see Harold M. Levinson, Charles M. Rehmus, Joseph P. Goldberg, and Mark L Kahn, *Collective Bargaining and Technological Change in American Transportation,* Northwestern University, Evanston, Ill., 1971. Also, Charles Brown and James Medoff have concluded in a recent study that unions have had a positive impact on productivity in the manufacturing sector. "Trade Unions In the Production Process," *Journal of Political Economy,* **86:**355–378 (1978).

43 For more on this point, see William Gomberg, "Featherbedding: An Assertion of Property Rights," *The Annals of the American Academy of Political and Social Science,* **333:**119–129 (1961). Note that management may also seek to change the terms of the labor agreement that pertain to work rules and productivity. See, for example, Audrey Freeman, *Security Bargains Reconsidered: SUB, Severance Pay and Guaranteed Work,* The Conference Board, New York, 1978.

44 A sympathetic account of GE's labor policy is provided by Herbert R. Northrup, *Boulwarism,* University of Michigan, Bureau of Industrial Relations, Ann Arbor, 1964.

45 This dimension of bargaining at GE is explored in James W. Kuhn, "A View of Boulwarism: The Significance of the GE Strike," *Labor Law Journal,* **21:**582–590 (1970). For an updated account of labor relations in this industry, see James W. Kuhn. "Collective Bargaining in the Electrical Products Industry," Columbia University, New York, 1977, processed.

46 See *General Electric Company,* 150 NLRB 192 (1964); *NLRB v. General Electric Co.,* CA 2d (1969), 72 LRRM 2530, cert. denied U.S. Sup. Ct. (1970), 73 LRRM 2660. For a critical analysis of the NLRB's 1964 decision, see James A. Gross, Donald E. Cullen, and Kurt L. Hanslowe, "Good Faith in Labor Negotiations: Tests and Remedies," *Cornell Law Review,* **53:**1023–1035 (1968). On coalition bargaining generally, see William Chernish, *Coalition Bargaining* University of Pennsylvania Press, Philadelphia, 1969.

47 A useful account of bargaining in this industry is provided in U.S. Bureau of Labor Statistics, *Wage Chronology, United States Steel Corporation and United Steelworkers of America, March, 1937–April, 1974,* Bulletin 1814, 1975; and U.S. Bureau of Labor Statistics, *Wage Chronology, United States Steel Corporation and United Steelworkers of America, May, 1974–June, 1977,* Supplement to Bulletin 1814, 1977. The narrative presented here relies heavily on these sources.

48 Some accounts of Bethlehem Steel's declining economic situation are provided in *The Wall Street Journal,* Apr. 27, 1977; June 7, 1977; July 19, 1977; Aug. 19, 1977; Sept. 9, 1977; and Oct. 27, 1977, passim.

49 This account draws liberally from U.S. Bureau of Labor Statistics, *Wage Chronology, Ford Motor Company, June, 1941–September, 1973,* Bulletin 1787, 1974; and U.S. Bureau of Labor Statistics, *Wage Chronology, Ford Motor Company, October, 1973–September, 1976,* Supplement to Bulletin 1787, 1977.

50 Changes in foreign competition and domestic regulatory policies in the 1970s, to cite but two factors, also brought pressures to bear on company managements, which had to bargain over them as they approached labor negotiations with the UAW.

51 Several such efforts are reported in National Center for Productivity and Quality of Working Life, *Recent Initiatives in Labor-Management Cooperation*, GPO, Washington, 1976. A summary of that report is provided in Edgar Weinberg, "Labor-Management Cooperation: A Report on Recent Initiatives," *Monthly Labor Review*, **99**:13–27 (1976). Unless otherwise indicated, this summary is the source of information for the discussion presented in this section.

52 Weinberg, p. 16.

53 Weinberg, pp. 17–18.

54 See, for example, "Remarks Prepared for Delivery by Secretary of Labor Ray Marshall," United States Department of Labor, *NEWS*, Oct. 20, 1977, in which such a tripartite arrangement in the airline industry is discussed.

55 Weinberg, p. 19.

56 For a preliminary analysis of such committee efforts, see Thomas A. Kochan, Lee Dyer, and David B. Lipsky, *The Effectiveness of Union-Management Safety and Health Committees*, W. E. Upjohn Institute, Kalamazoo, Mich., 1977.

57 Weinberg, pp. 19–20.

58 See, however, Robert J. Flanagan and Arnold R. Weber, *Bargaining without Boundaries: The Multinational Corporation and International Labor Relations*, University of Chicago Press, Chicago, 1974; Herbert R. Northrup and Richard L. Rowan, *Multinational Collective Bargaining Attempts: The Record, the Cases and the Prospects*, University of Pennsylvania, The Wharton School, Philadelphia, 1978; and "Some Perspectives on Multinational Bargaining," *Proceedings of the Thirtieth Annual Winter Meeting of the Industrial Relations Research Association, 1978*, Madison, Wis., 1979, pp. 81–112.

59 Charles Craypo, "Collective Bargaining in the Conglomerate, Multinational Firm: Litton's Shutdown of Royal Typewriter," *Industrial and Labor Relations Review*, **29**:3–25 (1975).

60 Craypo, p. 17.

61 Craypo, p. 21.

62 Craypo, p. 23.

63 Herbert R. Northrup and Richard L. Rowan, "Multinational Bargaining Approaches in the Western European Flat Glass Industry," *Industrial and Labor Relations Review*, **30**:32–46 (1976).

64 Northrup and Rowan, "Multinational Bargaining Approaches," p. 44.

65 Northrup and Rowan, "Multinational Bargaining Approaches," pp. 45–46.

ADDITIONAL READINGS

American Bar Association, Section on Labor Relations Law: *The Developing Labor Law: The Board, the Courts, and the National Labor Relations Act*, Bureau of National Affairs, Washington, 1978.

Corrège, Joy, et al. (eds.), *The Future of Labor Arbitration in America*, American Arbitration Association, New York, 1976.

Kuhn, James W.: *Bargaining in Grievance Settlement*, Columbia, New York, 1961.

Levinson, Harold M., Charles M. Rehmus, Joseph P. Goldberg, and Mark L. Kahn: *Collective Bargaining and Technological Change in American Transportation*, Northwestern University, The Transportation Center, Evanston, Ill., 1971.

Mills, Daniel Q.: *Industrial Relations and Manpower in Construction*, M.I.T., Cambridge, Mass., 1972.

Morley, Ian, and Geoffrey M. Stephenson: *The Social Psychology of Bargaining*, G. Allen, London, 1977.

Northrup, Herbert R., and Richard L. Rowan: *Multinational Collective Bargaining Attempts: The Record, the Cases and the Prospects*, University of Pennsylvania, The Wharton School, Philadelphia, 1978.

Rehmus, Charles, et al.: *The Railway Labor Act at Fifty: Collective Bargaining in the Railroad and Airline Industries*, National Mediation Board, Washington, 1977.

Reynolds, Lloyd G.: *Labor Economics and Labor Relations*, 7th ed., Prentice-Hall, Englewood Cliffs, N.J., 1978.

Walton, Richard E., and Robert B. McKersie: *A Behavioral Theory of Labor Negotiations*, McGraw-Hill, New York, 1965.

FOR ANALYSIS AND DISCUSSION

1 Select a major American union and go on to examine the types of intraorganizational bargaining issues with which its leaders must deal before negotiating with an employer. Attempt to do the same for a major company that negotiates an agreement with the union you selected for analysis.

2 Figure 5-1 depicts a bargaining zone in labor-management relations. What power tactics and strategies would you expect the parties to use in order to influence each other's "tolerance limits" of this bargaining zone?

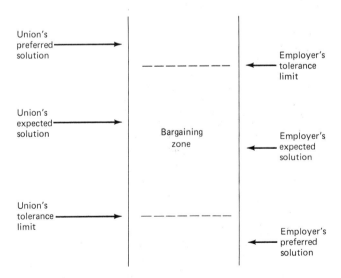

Figure 5-1 (*Source: Ross Stagner and Hjalmar Rosen,* Psychology of Union-Management Relations, *Wadsworth, Belmont, Calif., p. 96.*)

3   Why do some industries feature multiemployer bargaining while in others negotia-
    tions occur on a single-employer basis? Select an industry in which multiemployer
    bargaining takes place and trace out the factors which seem to have led to that form
    of labor-management relations. Have a classmate conduct an independent analysis
    of labor relations in the same industry and then compare your conclusions. Did the
    two of you identify similar "explanatory factors"? Different ones? Explain.

4   Two teams of two students each should debate the following proposition: "Re-
    solved: The Taft-Hartley Act should be amended to protect management's rights
    and restrict the scope of bargainable issues." The instructor should moderate the
    debate, and the rest of the class should critically examine the arguments offered by
    each side, questioning the participants about their respective positions at the con-
    clusion of the debate.

5   How does the definition of management given on page 229 compare with other defi-
    nitions that you've encountered, perhaps in textbooks on management? What are
    some of the kinds of "bargains" that management negotiates other than with labor
    unions?

6   How does the incidence of strikes in the United States during the 1970s compare
    with that during the 1960s? The 1950s? What are your sources of information on this
    issue? How does the incidence of strikes in this country compare with that in other
    nations? What are your sources of information on this issue? Besides the actual
    number of strikes in a given time period, what other measures of the incidence of
    strikes are available?

7   The Bureau of National Affairs (BNA) regularly reports the outcomes of grievance
    arbitration cases in *Labor Arbitration Reports*. Peruse recent editions of this pub-
    lication and then prepare your own report summarizing the principal issues that
    arbitrators are being called on to resolve. Discuss with your classmates and instruc-
    tor the viability of a grievance procedure for college students. What form might such
    a procedure take? How might it differ from the procedure outlined in Table 5-3?

8   Outline a set of criteria by which conflicts between seniority and requirements for
    affirmative action (equal employment opportunity) might be resolved in cases of lay-
    offs. How would your criteria differ if younger minority-group and female work-
    ers challenged older minority-group and female (rather than white male) workers
    for rights of job retention?

9   Prepare a position paper examining the prospects for multinational bargaining in the
    1980s. Why do you believe that such bargaining will or will not increase? What key
    factors will affect the future course of multinational bargaining? What aspects of
    your analysis might help a member of the Senate or the House of Representatives in
    deciding whether to support the legal strengthening of multinational bargaining?

10 How can cooperative labor-management efforts to improve productivity be inte-
    grated with collective bargaining? Are there limits to such integration? What are
    they? Consider the same questions in relation to safety and health at the workplace
    and to job satisfaction and the quality of working life. What types of incentive plans
    might be used to encourage labor-management cooperation on these issues?

Chapter 6

Collective Bargaining in the Public Sector

The rapid rise of unionism and collective bargaining in the public sector since the mid-1960s has been the most dramatic recent development in American labor-management relations. In this chapter, we focus on collective negotiations between organized public employees and their government employers, first at the state and local levels and then more briefly in the federal sector.

We begin by examining some of the unique characteristics, alleged and observed, of collective bargaining in the public sector. Next, the legal regulation of bargaining and of labor-management relations in government is reviewed, with policies concerning strikes and procedures for resolving impasses singled out for special attention. This is followed by an analysis of the changing economic, political, and legal climates of bargaining in the public sector, with San Francisco and New York used as illustrative cases. Next, some important contemporary issues in governmental labor relations are explored, especially as they relate to the scope of bargainable issues and the impact of public employees' unions on management. The chapter concludes with an overview of labor relations in the federal sector, a discussion of several unresolved issues of bargaining in the public sector, and some selected experiences of other countries with unionism and labor-management relations in the public sector.

HOW DIFFERENT IS PUBLIC-SECTOR BARGAINING?

Most treatments of labor relations in the public sector point to the unique aspects of the government as employer or, in other words, to the great difference between the public sector and private industry. Representative of this position are Wellington and Winter, who assert that "the public sector is *not* the private, and its labor problems *are* different, very different indeed."[1]

Chief among these presumed differences is the legal position of government. Elected officials possess rights and powers as representatives of the citizenry which voted them into office. They constitute the government of a political unit and exercise its sovereign—ultimate—power, which cannot be delegated to, or shared by, nongovernmental authorities. This lofty conception of governmental sovereignty was used for many years by elected officials to oppose unionism and collective bargaining in the public sector, but it became increasingly difficult to maintain as the growth of service obligations, revenues, employment, and the size of governmental units inevitably required the delegation of authority not only to staff personnel and specialized departments, bureaus, and agencies but also to private contractors. As collective bargaining in government emerged on a large scale during the 1960s and 1970s, the doctrine simply became untenable.

Another commonly cited difference between the public and the private sectors is the monopolistic aspect of government services. The underlying premise is that consumers have few or no alternatives available to them in the marketplace when they need police, fire, sanitation, welfare, and other such services. But not all state and local governments occupy a monopolistic position with respect to the services they provide. Private and sometimes nonprofit enterprises offering sanitation, transportation, and hospitalization and health services, to cite but a few examples, often operate alongside their public counterparts. This is not to say that governments do not indeed have a monopoly over some services, but that is quite different from saying that governments everywhere have strict monopolies over the whole range of their services.

What particularly concerns those who propound the thesis of government as monopolist is the greater bargaining power which this confers on organized public workers. If the government is a monopoly and there are no other sources from which citizens may obtain their services, some of which are highly essential, the union is in a bargaining position to extract excessively advantageous terms and conditions of employment, the costs of which will be passed on to the consumer-taxpayers, who have little or no choice in the matter. As described by Wellington and Winter:

> Market imposed unemployment is an important restraint on unions in the private sector . . . but no such restraint limits the demands of public employee unions. Because much government activity is, and must be, a monopoly, product competition, nonunion or otherwise, does not exert a downward pressure on prices and wages. Nor will the existence of a pool of labor ready to work for a wage below

union scale attract new capital and create a new, and competitively less expensive, governmental enterprise.[2]

Aside from the fact, noted above, that government is not necessarily the pervasive monopolist that popular characterizations suppose, public employees' unions do not uniformly occupy positions of power that far surpass those of their counterparts in the private sector. For example, public anger may be focused on them in ways which jeopardize their employment security. Moreover, a government does not go out of business as a result of a strike, however prolonged, and it continues to receive tax revenues throughout the strike's duration. Thus, while the bargaining power of public employees' unions—and of government employers—is a worthy subject for analysis, it should be dealt with empirically rather than taken for granted as a consequence of the thesis of government as monopolist.

Another alleged difference between employment in the public sector and that in the private sector concerns personnel administration. In the twentieth century, and especially after 1940, the civil service, or merit, system of personnel administration became widespread in state and local governments. Promoted by reformers who sought to do away with the spoils system, political patronage, and corrupt practices in the selection, promotion, and classification—indeed, the general treatment—of public employees, the civil service system promised merit as the basis of all personnel decisions. To ensure the implementation of merit principles in public personnel administration, many governments formed civil service commissions and sought to ensure their independence by separating them from the executive and legislative branches—for example, from a mayor and city council. To the extent that organized public workers pursue collective bargaining over issues of classification, promotion, selection, discipline, discharge, and related matters, they challenge fundamentally the authority of civil service commissions to make personnel decisions. Certainly most civil service officials have opposed collective bargaining in government, even if their functions have been only narrowed rather than totally supplanted by formal labor-management negotiations over terms and conditions of employment.[3]

But far from being unique to government, a clearly defined, comprehensive personnel function operated on the basis of merit evolved (partly or wholly) in many large American businesses during the twentieth century. If not as broad or as common as governmental civil service systems, personnel departments of business organizations nevertheless formulated policies, developed practices, and provided record-keeping services and expertise in human resources management to other line units and staff functions of the firm. Moreover, these personnel departments often were viewed by those who ran them as repositories for the protection and defense of employees' rights, a vision still operative in numerous nonunion organizations.[4] But this did not prevent their authority from being substantially eroded or shared as unionism and collective bargaining advanced in the private sector. Thus, the personnel management systems of government and their interactions with collective bargaining are in many ways comparable to the systems and interactions of private industry. What is perhaps unique about "civil service" is the term itself rather than the substantive function which it is intended to describe.

Multilateral Bargaining and Wage Determination

If governments are in fact not unique in terms of decision-making authority, provision of services, or personnel management, is it fair to say that they are not unique in any respects and that labor relations and labor practices may proceed there as elsewhere? The answer is "no," for there are some characteristics of government that indeed are peculiar to public institutions.

With respect to the conduct of labor relations, the most important of these is that formal union-management negotiations over terms and conditions of public employment reflect a "multilateral" bargaining process rather than the bilateral type found in the private sector. Multilateral bargaining takes place in a situation in which "a clear dichotomy between the employee and the management organization does not exist."[5] To elaborate, a state or local government typically distributes its decision-making authority and responsibility among a number of public representatives. This stems from the American emphasis on the separation of powers in a political system of checks and balances. In a local municipal government, for example, these public agents might include a mayor, a city council, a chief administrative officer or controller, a civil service commission, and independent or quasi-independent "authorities" or boards. This type of management structure, which is based upon representation rather than efficiency and which is thus more fractionalized than that generally present in private business firms, means that the public employer finds it very difficult to speak with a single voice at the negotiating table or away from it. Consider that some organized public employees who negotiate an agreement with a major department head subsequently approach the mayor or city council to bargain for better terms and conditions of employment, a process known as the "end run." Or the public employees' group might first negotiate with the mayor or the mayor's representative and then seek to improve on that agreement by conducting an end run to the city council. Or, in still another instance, state approval may be required before some provision can be negotiated by a municipality (which is the state's creation).[6] And, by virtue of the principle of separation of powers in a political democracy, each of these management actors legitimately has a voice in labor relations as well as in other areas of decision making.

Recognizing their fractionalized management structure and lack of expertise in labor relations, many public employers have responded to the unionization of their workers by establishing a separate collective bargaining office and bringing in a professional negotiator to bargain labor agreements. As Burton has pointed out, this has had the effect of increasing the centralization of governmental management, with the executive branch generally gaining authority at the expense of the legislative body.[7] But, contrary to expectations, the professional negotiator and collective bargaining office do not eradicate the influence of legislators, department heads, civil service commissions, and chief executive or administrative officers on the process or the outcomes of collective bargaining. Each of these actors retains the view that it occupies a legitimate role in setting terms and conditions of employment with organized workers, even if that role is an indirect one and even if the governmental entity of which it is a part operates a collective bargaining office and employs a professional negotiator. In other words, the attempt to centralize and professionalize labor relations in government does not act to convert the bargaining process from a multilateral to a bilateral one. As noted by Kochan with respect to municipal government:

> The nature of the collective bargaining process in city governments is a natural outgrowth of the political context in which it operates. . . . The type of bargaining often found in city governments is [not] an abnormal deviation from "normal collective bargaining" that will be eliminated as the parties and the laws under which they operate become more sophisticated. Such an argument simply ignores the underlying forces that influence the bargaining process in the public sector. . . . The process responds to the nature of the relationships that exist among the diverse interests that share power over bargaining issues.[8]

Kochan's conclusions derive from a study of collective bargaining in municipal fire departments, but investigations of public education, police departments, and other government services support the view that multilateral bargaining is a basic characteristic of American labor relations in the public sector.[9] In terms of intraorganizational bargaining, negotiators in the public sector, even more than those in private industry, must attempt to resolve conflicting internal interests.

The fractionalized, multiparty structure of management in the public sector influences various dimensions of human resources utilization and labor relations in addition to collective bargaining. Consider just one of these, compensation. Several recent studies have found that, contrary to the widely espoused principle of prevailing wages, which holds that pay in the public sector must be based upon rates existing in private industry, government employers systematically overpay (relative to industry) low-skilled, blue-collar, and lower-ranking white-collar employees, while at the same time undercompensating (again relative to industry) high-level professional, managerial, and executive personnel.[10] Put differently, wage structures in the public sector are more egalitarian and more compressed than those in private industry, and this despite the stated adherence of government to the principle of prevailing wages.

In attempting to understand this phenomenon, which began to be observed in the late 1960s and early 1970s, several authorities have pointed to the politics of governmental wage-setting processes within the framework of a fractionalized, multiparty management structure as a key explanatory factor.[11] For example, low-paid workers constitute an effective lobby for a wage above subsistence levels, irrespective of what rates prevail in the private market for the same work. Citizens' groups argue against high salaries for executives, managers, and professional employees of government, which have to be financed by less affluent taxpayers, even if similar jobs command higher payment in private industry. Or in exercising the discretion they possess within a general standard of prevailing wage rates, public officials—to gain political support—enact generous minimum wage statutes; pay "craft" workers hourly rates based on those which are paid in the construction industry, even though these employees do not suffer from seasonal unemployment in government; and survey the wage rates of semiskilled, blue-collar, and lower-level white-collar workers only in the larger, higher-paying firms in the private sector. The multiple points of access to public decision makers allow one or another interest group, notably the relatively large aggregations of workers at the lower levels of the occupational structure (whether or not unionized), to press first one and then another management actor to grant its particular wage objective.

This fractionalized, multiparty nature of political decision making, which arises out of the separation of powers in governmental entities, has its impact upon wage determination, collective bargaining, and other elements of labor relations and human resources management in the public sector. Here indeed is an element of uniqueness about the public sector which, if not widely appreciated, nevertheless is germane to an understanding of labor practices and labor-management relations in American government.

LEGAL REGULATION OF PUBLIC-SECTOR BARGAINING

While scholars may study and debate the differences between bargaining in the public sector and that in the private sector, policy makers have tended to regard many private-sector bargaining practices as applicable to labor-management relations in government. Since the late 1960s, all but a handful of states have enacted some type of statutory framework to permit unionism among public employees and to guide labor relations in the public sector in their respective local governments. Some twenty-five of these state laws authorize collective bargaining for public employees, several others permit "meet and confer" arrangements between public workers and public employers, while still others allow unionism but say little more. This is quite a change from the situation in 1959, when Wisconsin enacted the first state law supporting a policy of collective bargaining for local government employees and when most public jurisdictions were opposed to unionism and bargaining rights for public workers.

The most developed state laws typically (1) grant rights of unionization to public employees that closely match those of privately employed workers, (2) define unfair labor practices by employers and unions, and (3) establish administrative agencies along the lines of the NLRB to decide unfair-labor-practice cases and conduct elections to determine representation. They differ from the Taft-Hartley Act, which regulates labor relations in the private sector, primarily in their treatment of strikes and bargaining impasses, supervisory and managerial personnel, and union security.

Strikes

The strike has been the leading issue in labor relations in the public sector. That this was true long before the advent of bargaining laws in the public sector is reflected in this statement made by President Franklin D. Roosevelt in 1937:

> A strike of public employees manifests nothing less than an intent on their part to prevent or obstruct the operations of government until their demands are satisfied. Such action looking toward the paralysis of government by those who have sworn to support it is unthinkable and intolerable.

Ten years later, in enacting the Taft-Hartley Act, which otherwise covers only privately employed workers, Congress wrote the following policy into the law:

> It shall be unlawful for any individual employed by the United States or any agency thereof including wholly-owned government corporations to participate in any strike. Any individual employed by the United States or by any such agency, who strikes, shall be discharged immediately from his employment, and shall forfeit his civil service status, if any, and shall not be eligible for reemployment for three years by the United States or any such agency.

Several states also have adopted antistrike legislation, in some cases imposing substantial penalties for public employees who engage in work stoppages. Even those state statutes giving public employees the right to organize and bargain have tended to contain outright bans on strikes and to prescribe penalties such as fines, jail sentences, and loss of seniority rights for striking public workers.

Interestingly, these antistrike statutes were almost all enacted as a consequence of actual strikes by public employees, which, while occurring more frequently in recent years than ever before, have hardly been unknown in the American past. For example, a study by Ziskind documents more than 1000 strikes by public employees that occurred in the United States between the 1830s and the 1930s, a period in which few laws dealt explicitly with labor disputes in government or, indeed, with labor disputes of any kind.[12] A rash of strikes by municipal employees in 1946, when private workers also struck in record numbers, was largely responsible for the adoption of the Taft-Hartley antistrike provision for federal employees. The number of strikes by public employees then declined until the mid-1960s, but rose precipitously thereafter, as shown in Table 6-1. From forty-two strikes involving 11,900 workers and totaling 146,000 days of idleness in 1965, the number of stoppages by public employees rose to more than 400 in 1969 and 1970 and to almost 500 in 1975, and these involved hundreds of thousands of workers and millions of days of idleness. Most of these labor disputes took place in local government, the bulk of

Table 6-1 Work Stoppages by Level of Government, 1942–1978
(Workers Involved and Days Idle in Thousands)

Year	Total[1] Number of stoppages	Workers involved	Days idle during year	Federal government Number of stoppages	Workers involved	Days idle during year	State government Number of stoppages	Workers involved	Days idle during year	Local government[2] Number of stoppages	Workers involved	Days idle during year
1942										39	6.0	23.7
1943										51	10.2	48.5
1944							2	0.4	8.0	34	5.3	57.7
1945										32	3.4	20.0
1946							1	[3]	[3]	61	9.6	51.0
1947										14	1.1	7.3
1948										25	1.4	8.8
1949										7	2.9	10.3
1950										28	4.0	32.7
1951										36	4.9	28.8
1952										49	8.1	33.4
1953										30	6.3	53.4
1954							1	[3]	0.8	9	1.8	9.6
1955							1	0.2	0.5	16	1.3	6.7
1956										27	3.5	11.1
1957										12	0.8	4.4
1958	15	1.7	7.5	—	—	—	1	[3]	[3]	14	1.7	7.4
1959	25	2.0	10.5	—	—	—	4	0.4	1.6	21	1.6	8.9
1960	36	28.6	58.4	—	—	—	3	1.0	1.2	33	27.6	57.2
1961	28	6.6	15.3	—	—	—		—	—	28	6.6	15.3
1962	28	31.1	79.1	5	4.2	33.8	2	1.7	2.3	21	25.3	43.1
1963	29	4.8	15.4	—	—	—	2	0.3	2.2	27	4.6	13.2
1964	41	22.7	70.8	—	—	—	4	0.3	3.2	37	22.5	67.7
1965	42	11.9	146.0		—	—		—	1.3[4]	42	11.9	145.0
1966	142	105.0	455.0		—	—	9	3.1	6.0	133	102.0	449.0
1967	181	132.0	1250.0		—	—	12	4.7	16.3	169	127.0	1230.0

Year												
1968	254	201.8	2545.2	3	1.7	9.6	16	9.3	42.8	235	190.9	2492.8
1969	411	160.0	745.7	2	0.6	1.1	37	20.5	152.4	372	139.0	592.2
1970	412	333.5	2023.2	3	155.8	648.3	23	8.8	44.6	386	168.9	1330.5
1971	329	152.6	901.4	2	1.0	8.1	23	14.5	81.8	304	137.1	811.6
1972	375	142.1	1257.3	—	—	—	40	27.4	273.7	335	114.7	983.5
1973	387	196.4	2303.9	1	0.5	4.6	29	12.3	133.0	357	183.7	2166.3
1974	384	160.7	1404.2	2	0.5	1.4	34	24.7	86.4	348	135.4	1316.3
1975	478	318.5	2204.4	—	—	—	32	66.6	300.5	446	252.0	1903.9
1976	378	180.7	1690.7	1	(3)	(3)	25	33.8	148.2	352	146.8	1542.6
1977[5]	385	183.6	2149.3					NA				
1978[6]	344	224.0	1950.0					NA				

[1] The Bureau of Labor Statistics has published data on strikes in government in its annual reports since 1942. Before that year, they had been included in a miscellaneous category—other nonmanufacturing industries. From 1942 through 1957, data refer only to strikes in administrative, protective, and sanitary services of government. Stoppages in establishments owned by governments were classified in their appropriate industry; for example, public schools and libraries were included in education services, not in government. Beginning in 1958, stoppages in such establishments were included under the government classification. Stoppages in publicly owned utilities, transportation, and schools were reclassified back to 1947, but a complete reclassification was not attempted. After 1947, dashes denote zeros.

[2] Includes all stoppages at the county, city, and special district levels.

[3] Fewer than 100.

[4] Idleness in 1965 resulted from two stoppages that began in 1964.

[5] Estimates based on percentage of work stoppages in the economy accounted for by government, entire year.

[6] Estimates based on percentage of work stoppages in the economy accounted for by government during the first ten months of 1978.

Note: Because of rounding, sums of individual items may not equal totals.

Sources: Adapted from U.S. Bureau of Labor Statistics. Work Stoppages in Government, 1976, Report 532, 1978, p. 4; Monthly Labor Review 102:111, table 37 (1979); and U.S. Bureau of Labor Statistics, "Work Stoppages: October 1978 and a 9-Month Summary of Selected Characteristics," NEWS, U.S. Department of Labor, November 30, 1978, table 3, n.p.

them in public education, which accounts for about half of all employment at this level of government. Such strikes provide ample testimony to the new militancy that has developed among American public employees in recent years. They also explain the response of legislators who have outlawed strikes in the public sector and, in many jurisdictions, have substituted other methods for resolving impasses, such as mediation, factfinding, and eventually arbitration.[13]

Even with such laws on the books, work stoppages still occur in the public sector, as Table 6-1 shows. On the other hand, Table 6-2 shows that, at least by some measures, there is less strike activity in the public than in the private sector. The most comprehensive measure of strike activity is the total days of "idleness" (that is, the total number of work days in a year that strikers were not on their jobs) as a percent of estimated total working time (average number of employed workers multiplied by the average number of days worked in a year). By that measure, strike activity was much lower in the public than the private sector both in 1975, when the actual number of strikes hit a record level (see Table 6-1), and in 1976. Also, the average days of idleness per striker— roughly, the length of the average strike—were fewer in the public than the private sector in both years. Interestingly, however, the number of workers involved in the average strike was larger in the public sector, and strikers as a percent of total employment showed no clear pattern in these two years.

Of the strikes by public employees that occurred in 1976, almost half involved professional and technical personnel (including teachers and nurses). Wages were the dominant issue in disputes, followed by plant administration, union organization and security, and job security. More than 60 percent of these strikes involved governments located in five states—Pennsylvania, Ohio, Illinois, New Jersey, and Michigan. Another three states—California, New York, and Wisconsin—accounted for an additional 13 percent of such strikes. These data should be kept in mind when we discuss the regulation of labor relations in the public sector, especially at the point of an impasse in bargaining.[14]

Resolving Impasses   If the strike was to be almost universally disallowed in the public sector, then substitutes had to be found for it or collective bargaining would be little more than a charade. As already noted, mediation, factfinding, and arbitration of the terms of a contract became increasingly common in the late 1960s. In this respect, regulatory policy for labor relations in the public sector differs from that for private industry, in which mediation is provided only on a request or voluntary basis by the Federal Mediation and Conciliation Service (FMCS), in which factfinding occurs only in those (relatively few) labor disputes which are declared by the President to be national emergencies, and in which arbitration of the terms of a contract is rare indeed.

Mediation, sometimes termed "conciliation," involves the use of a neutral third party who attempts to get labor and management to resume negotiations which have broken off or been stalled and to bargain toward a settlement. The mediator facilitates such bargaining by offering suggestions about negotiable items, by carrying proposals from one side to the other and back again, and by

Table 6-2 Selected Work Stoppage Measures, All Industries and Government, 1975–1976

Item	1975				1976			
	All industries	Government			All industries	Government		
		Total	State	Local		Total[1]	State	Local
Days of idleness as a percent of estimated total working time	0.16	0.06	0.04	0.09	0.19	0.04	0.02	0.07
Average days of idleness per worker involved in stoppages	17.9	6.9	4.5	7.6	15.6	9.4	4.4	10.5
Average number of workers involved per stoppage	347	666	2081	565	428	478	1352	417
Workers involved as a percent of total employment	2.2	2.2	2.1	2.9	3.1	1.2	1.0	1.6

[1] Includes data for two work stoppages in the federal government.
Source: Adapted from U.S. Bureau of Labor Statistics, *Work Stoppages in Government, 1976,* Report 532, 1978, p.5.

serving as a general resource person on whom each side can try out possible proposals and tactical considerations. Mediators have no power to decide a contract or impose a settlement on the parties. They must rely on persuasion, argument, and force of personality to make the mediation process effective. Most laws concerning bargaining in the public sector *require* the parties to accept mediation of a deadlocked labor negotiation, and this typically is the first in a series of mandated procedures for resolving an impasse.

Another of these procedures is *factfinding,* in which an outside individual or neutral panel takes testimony from each side and then makes a report to the parties and to the agency administering the relevant law. Such factfinding reports, which contain a digest of the issues in dispute and recommendations for resolving them, normally are made public a short time after they are submitted. Though the recommendations usually are not binding on the parties, their general release is presumed to put public pressure on labor and management to accept them. In some instances, moreover, if the parties are recalcitrant, the factfinder's recommendations may become the basis for a legislated settlement or for a contract imposed on the parties as a result of *compulsory arbitration.*

This last method of settling disputes, which has grown rapidly in government, is probably the key feature distinguishing labor relations in the public sector from those in the private sector on the contemporary American scene. Where operative, a state or local government statute requires that where other means of settlement have proved ineffective, the parties must accept the terms and conditions of employment handed down by an arbitrator or arbitration panel. They do not have the discretion to reject either the procedure or the award. To repeat, compulsory arbitration of the terms and conditions of public employment exists in many state and local governments (the extent of its use is not fully known), but it is employed on only a very small scale in private industry, reflecting a major difference in the regulatory treatment of labor relations in the public and private sectors.[15]

In requiring procedures to resolve impasses in labor disputes in the public sector, governments do not necessarily apply them uniformly across all the services they provide. Those services which most directly affect public health, welfare, and safety, and which are therefore labeled "essential," are singled out for special treatment. It is no coincidence, then, that compulsory arbitration is more common in police and fire departments than in other government services.

Final-Offer Arbitration   Among the more intriguing aspects of compulsory arbitration in labor relations in the public sector is the search for procedures that will encourage the parties to negotiate a contract settlement on their own. After all, if collective bargaining is supported by law as a preferred means for determining terms and conditions of employment in the public sector, then public policy should seek to encourage labor and management to conclude their own written agreements rather than relying on third parties to do that for them.

Labor and management should view compulsory arbitration as a threat which, if utilized, will impose higher costs on *both* sides than would have resulted from a bargained settlement.[16]

Proceeding from this perspective, several state and local governments have adopted the approach of "final-offer arbitration" to bargaining impasses in the public sector. There are two main types of final-offer arbitration. The first allows the arbitrator to select *either* the union's *or* management's final (last) offer as the basis for a new agreement. The total package so selected, its provisions for wages, fringe benefits, work rules, grievances, and other matters, will constitute the new collective bargaining contract. The second type of final-offer procedure permits the arbitrator to select labor's or management's last position on each major bargaining *issue*. Thus, the arbitrator might select management's final offer on wages and work rules and the union's last position on fringe benefits and grievance procedures. Whether structured on the basis of a total package or issue by issue, final-offer arbitration is intended to provide greater incentives than conventional arbitration for labor and management to settle agreements by themselves and on their own terms. The incentive is contained in the threat or risk that the arbitrator will select the other party's (say, management's) last offer, in which case the first party (say, the union) will have incurred a very heavy cost of disagreeing with its opponent in negotiations. That possibility should make each party more cautious, more realistic, and less extreme in formulating its final bargaining offer. Thus, a common ground of agreement may emerge as the result of each party's not wanting to risk a worse outcome—under final-offer arbitration—than it could achieve by "voluntarily" negotiating a contract with the opponent.

Has this objective of final-offer arbitration been borne out in practice? To answer that question requires a comparison between final-offer and conventional arbitration, focusing on the extent to which each procedure encourages or fails to encourage labor and management to bargain in good faith. Such a comparison was recently made by Feuille, who summarized studies of experiences with conventional arbitration in American and Canadian governments over the period 1960–1974 as well as experiences with final-offer arbitration in other American governments (and in major league baseball) between 1972 and 1975. His conclusion is instructive:

> Final offer arbitration procedures appear to have less of a chilling effect on bargaining than do conventional arbitration procedures. This finding is consistent with the increased "strikelike" foundation of the final offer process: the sudden death possibility of "losing the ball game" in final offer arbitration apparently induces the parties to negotiate their own agreements proportionately more often than occurs under the less costly conventional arbitration procedures. This finding suggests that the final offer process increases the compatibility of arbitration and bargaining to a greater extent than the conventional process. . . . The purpose of the final offer concept is to make it costly for the parties to disagree, and the discretionless arbitrator is the mechanism for imposing these costs. . . .[17]

Supervisory and Managerial Personnel

A second important area of difference between regulatory policies concerning labor relations in the public sector and those concerning labor relations in the private sector involves the treatment of supervisory and managerial personnel. Recall that such employees in the private sector were given the right to organize and bargain when Congress passed the Wagner Act in 1935, but these rights were withdrawn from them by the Taft-Hartley Act in 1947. In contrast, supervisory and even some managerial employees in the public sector tend to be included under laws and policies concerning collective bargaining in state and local governments. Typically, these statutes deny the right to organize and bargain only to top executives and their immediate subordinates and to "confidential" employees who play a role in high-level governmental policy making. All other employees enjoy whatever rights are provided for in legislation.

One consequence of this rather expansive collective bargaining coverage is that some supervisors and managers in the public sector not only are unionized and negotiate written agreements but, in some cases, also are represented by the same unions that enroll the subordinate workers whom they supervise and manage. In New York and Los Angeles, for example, the American Federation of State, County and Municipal Employees (AFSCME) and the Service Employees' International Union (SEIU) represent clerks, stenographers, and many other entry-level white-collar employees in municipal government and also many of the supervisors of these employees. The only restriction on this practice is that supervisory personnel are required to be in separate bargaining units from nonsupervisory workers.

In these same cities and in many others, public school teachers are highly organized, as are public school administrators, principals, assistant principals, deputy principals, and the like. In numerous school districts, only the superintendent and members of the board of education are considered fully "management" and are not represented by a union in collective bargaining. Much the same is true in the protective services, where, in addition to a patrolmen's benevolent association, which represents police officers, and a local union of the International Association of Fire Fighters (IAFF), which represents basic fire department personnel, one typically finds separate labor organizations representing and bargaining for police sergeants, police lieutenants, and comparable officers in the fire department. Such government personnel as registered nurses, assistant district attorneys, engineers and architects, social caseworkers, and even interns and residents, many of whom have supervisory and some of whom have policy-making authority, are organized and negotiate collective agreements with their employers.

A second consequence of this expansive bargaining coverage, and of signal importance, is that it blurs considerably the division between managerial and nonmanagerial employees in government. For whatever benefits that may bring in terms of a broader egalitarianism in public employment, it adds to the difficulty of defining a managerial presence in government, whether on the job, in a department, or at the bargaining table. Thus, in addition to providing procedures for resolving strikes and impasses, regulatory policies for labor relations in the public sector differ considerably from those for labor relations in private industry in permitting supervisory and managerial personnel to organize and bargain with their employers over terms and conditions of employment.

Union Security

We noted previously that the dominant policy toward union security in private-sector labor relations is to permit the dues checkoff, the union and agency shop, and other forms of protective arrangements (but only rarely the closed shop) for labor organizations, provided that they can negotiate these with employers. Section 14(b) of the Taft-Hartley Act allows individual states to legislate in this particular area, and twenty states maintain legal prohibitions on such union security arrangements in private industry.

In the public sector, the dues checkoff is a common (though by no means fully accepted) practice, but only a few state statutes authorize any form of union security arrangement. This is a carry-over of the doctrine of sovereignty in that public officials have been almost totally unwilling to cede or delegate authority to managers or to labor organizations to make retention of a job in the public sector dependent upon membership in any organization, including one that represents workers in collective bargaining. Yet the bargaining laws in virtually every state and local government follow the private-sector practice of exclusive representation, in which a single labor organization that is certified as a bargaining agent must fairly represent all the members of the bargaining unit.

As a result of these policy directives, some labor organizations in the public sector represent many more employees than they enroll as dues-paying members. Such multioccupational organizations as AFSCME and the SEIU are cases in point, as only about half of the workers represented in bargaining by some of their big-city locals are dues-paying members. Not unexpectedly, leaders of these labor organizations complain loud and long about having to represent and service some employees upon whom they are not able correspondingly to impose "taxes." By virtue of custom, practice, and relative homogeneity of membership, labor organizations of police officers, firefighters, sanitation personnel, craft employees, and engineers and architects generally have high proportions of dues-paying members and therefore are less inclined than the multioccupational unions and associations to press for union security in the public sector. Nevertheless, even they and some public officials see merit in the "representation without taxation" argument. They may also believe that stable, effectively functioning labor organizations in the public sector require as a condition of their existence some sort of security arrangement, probably the most suitable being the agency shop, under which all workers in a bargaining unit pay the equivalent of union dues even if they are not union members. With a few exceptions, however, the prevailing practice in the public sector is to deny labor organizations the type of security arrangement, including the union shop, that is common among unions in the private sector.[18] Here, then, is another respect in which the policies governing public-sector labor relations in the United States are far from a mirror image of those which govern the private sector.

CURRENTS OF CHANGE

If the public sector has been treated differently from the private sector in terms of the regulation of labor relations, it nevertheless is similar to private industry in that it is subject to the pressures of shifting economic, political, and legal forces. It is the particular responses of public managers and public workers to these pressures, however, which merit our attention. In this regard, keep in mind that state and local governments were the leading growth sector of the American economy during the third quarter of the twentieth century. Unionism and bargaining in the public sector, especially during the 1960s and early 1970s, developed against a backdrop of rapidly expanding government services and employment, massive infusions of revenues from the federal government to state and local governments and from state to local jurisdictions, swiftly rising levels of wages and benefits for public employees whether unionized or not, and a political climate that strongly supported the participation of organized workers in determining pay and conditions of employment. Such supportive economic and political trends were most pronounced in the period 1965–1970, but they also continued into the early 1970s. For at least a major portion of the public sector, this period might suitably be labeled the "first generation" of collective bargaining.[19]

The economic recession of 1974–1975, however, marked the beginning of a new era of bargaining in the public sector. Many state and local governments were faced with shortfalls in revenue, even as expenditures continued to rise. The fiscal plight took on the dimension of a "crisis" in several locations, most notably New York City, where the full-time municipal work force was reduced from roughly 300,000 to 235,000 over the period 1975–1977. In fiscal 1975, governments located in agricultural and energy-poor states accounted for the bulk of 140,000 layoffs that occurred at the state and local levels. Capital construction projects in the public sector that would have cost some $8 billion were postponed or eliminated in that year, and the federal government and state governments cut back sharply on their revenue-sharing contributions to other levels of government. Public officials often were confronted with rejection by voters of increased expenditures for public services and with various signs of the citizenry's opposition to—some say revolt against—higher income, property, and sales taxes. Perhaps the ultimate sign of this increased resistance to the cost of government was the approval in June 1978 by California voters of Proposition 13, a measure which reduced property taxes in that state by an estimated $7 billion.[20] Further, the fiscal crisis of the mid-1970s was most pronounced among governments located in the northeastern states, where unionism in the public sector gained its earliest and strongest foothold and where bargaining is most firmly established.

These developments brought with them a climate less conducive to unionism and bargaining in the public sector than had previously existed. They reflect the emergence of a "second generation" of public-sector bargaining, in which public officials, policy makers, and the citizenry more carefully assess the bargaining demands of organized government employees, act to limit the access of unionized public workers to political decision makers, and more closely scrutinize regulatory policy toward collective bargaining in government. Most fundamentally, the constrained rather than expansive economic climate of second-generation union-management relations in the public sector leads to a reappraisal of the costs of peace in relation to the costs of other bargaining outcomes.

Such a reappraisal questions, for example, the wisdom of blanket prohibitions on the strike, which imply that the cost of a stoppage always exceeds the cost of a peaceful settlement. But that is an assumption, no more and no less, which is more easily acted on during an economic expansion than during periods of slow growth or contraction. Indeed, a reconsideration of that assumption was under way in some areas even before the recession of 1974–1975, and by 1978 approximately a dozen states had authorized strikes by government employees *under certain conditions*. Some of these states and their policies concerning strikes are listed in Table 6-3. Observe that some permissions to strike cover all public employees, while others cover only selected groups. Several of the laws link strike authorizations to the public's health, safety, and welfare; a few assign a key decision-making role to the judiciary; and all but one apply to employees of both state and local governments. Importantly, none of these policies allow a strike by public employees to occur unless one or another procedure—advance notice, mediation, factfinding, nonbinding arbitration, injunctive relief—intervenes between an impasse in bargaining and a work stoppage. Consequently, the statutes support a limited rather than an unqualified right of public employees to strike.

Observe further that the legislation also attempts to distinguish more sharply than before degrees of essentiality among public services. Policies concerning strikes are in general less permissive for protective service workers and sometimes for public health workers than for other government employees. Alaska's statute is notable for its threefold categorization of essential, semiessential, and nonessential employees. These laws represent a sharp departure from the tendency in the first generation of public-sector bargaining to view all government services and employees as equally essential.

For those who might be nervous about the specter of increased strikes by public employees as a result of liberalized regulatory policies, consider what is known about the effectiveness of bans against strikes in the government sector. On the basis of an examination of strikes by public employees (other than educational workers) that occurred in the United States between 1968 and 1971, Burton and Krider conclude the following:

Those elements that can be controlled by public policy seem to have little impact on strikes. For example, the statutory prohibition on strikes has little apparent impact on the incidence of strikes, nor does the enactment of a law either prohibiting or encouraging collective bargaining by public employees appear to affect materially the number of local government strikes.[21]

While these findings seem to support the popular view that bans on strikes by public employees are ineffective, they may also be interpreted to mean that governments which accept collective bargaining for their employees do not thereby encourage strikes to any significant degree. As Burton and Krider put it, "Our findings may encourage the enactment of statutes supporting bargaining rights for public employees."[22]

The treatment of governmental supervisory and managerial personnel and of union security may also proceed differently in the second than in the first generation of collective bargaining in the public sector. The voting public's reaction to the financial plight of many state and local governments in the mid-1970s was not focused solely on unionism and bargaining; rather, it reflected a larger concern about the performance of government in the provision and delivery of public services.

Criticism of the efficiency and effectiveness of public services caused elected officials to pay greater attention to the management—or lack of it—of these services. The possible productivity-inhibiting consequences of having public supervisory and managerial personnel represented in collective bargaining by the same union that represents their subordinates—or by any union—began to be recognized, as did the need for a better-defined, more cohesive management cadre which would be held more closely accountable than before for the peformance of government agencies and functions.

While it is problematic whether the performance of management in the public sector will be improved as a result of these developments, it is very likely that a more clearly defined management presence will emerge at the bargaining table. Regulatory policies are likely to be modified to withdraw the rights of union representation and bargaining from supervisors and managers in the public sector, a reform which has been advocated by several students of this subject.[23] Such a development might well breed greater independence among managers and diminish the boundary role presently occupied by supervisors and managers in the public sector, though it would likely have to be accompanied by revised government policies concerning pay, job classification, and performance evaluation.

The "compensation" to public employees' labor organizations for a reduced membership base may well be a legislatively sanctioned union security provision. That such a condition of employment—specifically, the agency shop —is not unconstitutional and may be a proper subject of negotiations in bargaining in the public sector has recently been affirmed by the Supreme Court.[24] More fundamentally, those labor organizations in the public sector which typically bargain for supervisors and some managers—organizations such as

Table 6-3   Summary of State Bargaining Laws That Permit Strikes by Public Employee

State	Strike policy
Alaska	Strike prohibited for essential employees; permitted for semiessential employees (utilities, schools, snow removal, sanitation) but may be enjoined if there is threat to public health, safety, or welfare; strike permitted for nonessential employees if approved by majority of unit in secret ballot election; no direct provision governing teachers.
Hawaii	Pertains to state and local government employees, police, firefighters, and teachers; strike prohibited for 60 days after factfinding report; 10 days' notice required; strike not permitted where public health or safety is endangered; can be enjoined by circuit court.
Minnesota	Pertains to state and local government employees, transit workers, police, firefighters, and teachers; strike prohibited except where employer refuses to comply with arbitration award or refuses request for binding arbitration.
Montana	Pertains to state and local government employees, transit workers, police, and firefighters; strike permitted; also pertains to nurses, but stoppage prohibited if simultaneous strike occurs within 150 miles; labor organization must give written notice and specify strike date.
Oregon	Pertains to state and local government employees, police, firefighters, and teachers; limited right to strike for employees in bargaining units for which final and binding arbitration is not provided; mediation and factfinding and other statutory procedures must have been exhausted; injunctive relief can be granted if the strike is a threat to public health, safety, and welfare; strike is prohibited for police and firefighters, but the dispute must be submitted to binding arbitration if unresolved after mediation and factfinding.
Pennsylvania	Pertains to state and local government employees and teachers (court employees excluded); limited right to strike after exhaustion of impasse procedures unless strike creates clear and present danger to public health, safety, and welfare; injunction may not be issued prior to strike.
Rhode Island	Strike prohibited with qualification that courts may not enjoin the stoppage unless it causes irreparable injury.
Vermont	Pertains to local government employees, police, firefighters, and teachers; limited right to strike; stoppage is prohibited and enjoinable if it occurs 30 days after a factfinder's report, after parties have submitted dispute to arbitration, or if it is shown that the strike will endanger public health and safety; for teachers, a strike may be disallowed if it is ruled a clear and present danger to a sound program of education by a court of competent jurisdiction.

Sources: Adapted from Bureau of National Affairs, *Government Employee Relations Report* 501, December 1974, p. 51; Deborah T. Bond, "State Labor Legislation Enacted in 1975," *Monthly Labor Review,* **99** 17–29 (1976); and Richard R. Nelson and David A. Levy, "State Labor Legislation Enacted in 1977," *Monthly Labor Review,* **100**:3–24 (1977).

AFSCME and the SEIU rather than single-occupation unions of police, fire-fighters, sanitation workers, and teachers—are, as noted earlier, the ones for whom the issue of union security, or the "free rider" problem, is paramount. They might be quite content to accept a somewhat smaller membership base in exchange for enhanced security arrangements.

To the extent that these developments occur in the public sector—that prohibitions against strikes are liberalized, compulsory arbitration is less heavily relied upon, the right to organize and bargain is withdrawn from supervisors and managers, and union security arrangements are permitted—they will bring government closer to the private sector in terms of the structure, process, and functioning of labor relations and collective bargaining. They signify, therefore, that the differences between the public and private sectors are less important than the similarities between them insofar as union-management relations are concerned. And the fundamental reason for this is that, far from operating independently as monopolists in a continuously expanding economy, most governmental entities face some competition in the delivery of services that vary in essentiality, and they are also subject to changes in their economic climate.

On the upside, economic expansion has produced political forces that promoted laws favorable to unions and supported collective bargaining in government, but in a policy framework significantly different from that in the private sector. On the downside, a less expansive and, in some instances, contracting economic environment has energized a political attitude less favorable to unionism and bargaining, and it has fostered policy initiatives that (perhaps ironically) move the regulatory framework of labor relations in the public sector closer to that of private industry. The first set of events seems to have characterized the period 1960–1975, which we labeled the "first generation" of bargaining in the public sector, while the second appears to depict the years since 1975, or the "second generation."

Two Examples: San Francisco and New York

The structure, process, and function of bargaining are dependent upon the characteristics of the parties to negotiations, on their organizational structures, and on the environmental contexts in which they operate. To appreciate how quickly these external forces can change and influence labor relations in the public sector, consider recent developments in the local governments of two major American cities, San Francisco and New York.

San Francisco This city operates under a consolidated city and county government, while New York has a more conventional municipal government. Formal bargaining between organized employees and the municipal government has existed for many years in New York, which has a local labor relations ordinance patterned closely after New York State's Taylor Law (1967), which specifies the right of public employees to organize and bargain. In contrast, formal collective bargaining has not traditionally characterized San Francisco's public sector, even though government workers in that city are well organized and have been quite militant, as indicated by the four major strikes by public employees that occurred there between 1970 and 1976. Unlike that of New York State, California's law covering labor relations in local government, the Meyers-Milias-Brown Act of 1968, calls for public employers and organized workers to "meet and confer" over terms and conditions of employment, but they are not required to reach agreement about these matters. If they do, a memorandum of understanding rather than a labor contract expresses the terms of agreement.

San Francisco is known as a "labor town"; its private sector is very well organized, with wages and other matters in many major industries set through collective bargaining.[25] The city's public workers, also well organized, historically have engaged in lobbying and other forms of political activity in pursuit of their objectives (wages and other issues) and have been quite skillful in pressuring the various management actors in the fragmented municipal government structure to agree to their objectives. In particular, organized employees made their influence felt during the 1950s and 1960s in the implementation of the city's regulations concerning prevailing wage rates, and this resulted in some of the nation's highest pay rates for blue-collar and some white-collar municipal government employees.

In spite of these achievements, San Francisco's public workers pressed in the late 1960s for at least quasi-collective bargaining or a "meet and confer" system along the lines of the provisions of the Meyers-Milias-Brown Act. Some of the city's key elected officials, notably Mayor Joseph Alioto, supported that objective, and thus, between 1968 and 1975, a local employee relations ordinance was developed. Representation units were officially certified, management formed a negotiating team, and wages and other terms of employment began to be bargained rather than administratively determined. None of these developments occurred quickly, though, and the growing militancy of the city's public employees seemed to reach its peak in the summer of 1975, when police and firefighters struck in dissatisfaction with the wage offer of the Board of Supervisors (BOS), management's representative in negotiations.

The strike was marked by several unsuccessful legal efforts to order the police and firefighters back to work and by a continued hard line on the part of the BOS, which steadfastly opposed the union's proposal for pay increases about double what the board was willing to offer. Even as this work stoppage was in progress, Mayor Alioto recommended to a gathering at the National Conference of Mayors that any public employee who struck should be summarily dismissed. After 4 days with only minimal police and fire service, however, Alioto, who in San Francisco's weak-mayor form of government appeared to lack the decision-making power to set wages and negotiate memorandums of understanding, declared a state of emergency and imposed a wage increase of 13.05 percent that he had "negotiated" with the police and firefighters.

Alioto's action, which was not illegal under the city's charter and which did not result in a settlement very different from what had been proposed by the BOS, nevertheless created a storm of protest and bitter public backlash against police and firefighters. First, the BOS rescinded memorandums of understanding previously reached with these groups, citing their violation of the no-strike pledge contained in those agreements. Then, in early November, voters passed several propositions revising the city's formulas for prevailing wage rates in ways that led to substantially lower pay rates than previously permitted under the charter. For example, some city employees later incurred annual pay cuts of up to $4500, or more than 18 percent. Another of the approved propositions required a majority of the BOS to agree in advance to a mayoral declaration of a state of emergency. And still another required the firing of police and firefighters who engaged in strikes (the state law is silent on the issue of strikes).

That these new political and legal postures toward unionism and labor relations in the public sector were not just temporary reactions rooted in momentary anger was demonstrated by the response of elected officials and the San Francisco citizenry to a strike during the spring of 1976 of municipally employed craft workers, whose wages were to be slashed under the city's new pay-setting procedures. When these unions refused to accept the city's wage "offer," the BOS simply incorporated it into a new salary ordinance.

The craft workers' bargaining power seemed to be augmented by a sympathy strike conducted by municipal transit workers and by the decision of several SEIU locals to honor craft workers' picket lines. But other city employees ignored or looked with disfavor on the strike, and the municipal craft workers had trouble gaining any support from craft workers in the private sector. City officials took the work stoppage in stride, but continued to negotiate with the craft workers even as the strike progressed. The city solidified its bargaining position behind its chief negotiator and proceeded to put on the ballot two propositions which extended wage cuts for 2 additional years and which permitted multiyear salary ordinances.

Most notably, the public reacted with equanimity, if not indifference, to the work stoppage, adjusting commuting schedules and making other arrangements to ward off the effects of the transit workers' strike, which had a more direct impact than the loss of services of city construction and maintenance workers. On the last day on which the two punitive propositions could be removed from the ballot, the city and the craft unions announced an agreement that provided for a factfinding committee to be chaired by George Moscone, Joseph Alioto's successor as mayor. The BOS removed the aforementioned propositions from the ballot and granted amnesty to the strikers, but the factfinding committee unexpectedly recommended that the wage cuts of 1976 be maintained, with the union members of the panel dissenting, but doing no more than that.

The aftermath of these events included further changes in work assignments and methods of pay, which had the effect of reducing some municipal workers' wages still more; the trial and conviction of the leader of a plumbers' union for violating his duties as an airport commissioner; and additional litigation over actions taken by both the union and management during the strike. The main point of this account, though, is that the economic, political, and legal climate within which labor relations in San Francisco's public sector take place has changed from one that was very supportive of unionism and bargaining to one that is far less supportive. The imposition of wage cuts, the hardening and consolidation of management's negotiating position, and the public's demonstrated support for such actions, along with its relatively easy adjustment to the absence of transit services, illustrate the reappraisal that has recently taken place of the cost of "buying" peace relative to the cost of other outcomes of bargaining in the public sector.

New York[26]   Undoubtedly, more has been written about public-sector labor relations in New York City than about those in any other American municipality. That should not be unexpected of the nation's largest city, which also possesses the country's largest municipal work force (about 200,000 at the beginning of 1979) and was among the first cities to adopt a formal collective bargaining system for public employees. The foundations of that system were established between 1954 and 1965 under the administration of Mayor Robert Wagner, who was a strong supporter of the labor movement in general and who was particularly keen on permitting public employees in the city to organize and bargain collectively. In each of his three terms as mayor, he issued executive orders which enhanced the rights of municipal workers to organize and bargain, and it was Wagner himself who negotiated agreements with leaders of the major public employees' unions.

This did not mean that the city was always able to avoid labor troubles. In 1965, a strike by public welfare workers stimulated Mayor Wagner to appoint a commission to study the municipality's labor relations and make recommendations for improving them. In brief, the panel recommended that the bargaining system be further formalized to include procedures for determining bargaining units and for hearing unfair-labor-practice charges and that the authority for these functions be vested in an independent Office of Collective Bargaining, structured along the lines of the NLRB. The commission also recommended that the city's labor relations function not rest with the mayor himself but, rather, reside in a separate office headed by a director, who, together with a professional staff, would negotiate contracts with labor unions and employee associations.

These recommendations were put into practice not by Mayor Wagner but by his successor, John Lindsay, late in 1966. On his first day in office, Mayor Lindsay was confronted with a transit workers' strike, which by all accounts the union "won" and the city "lost." Burned by that event, Lindsay strongly supported creation of an Office of Labor Relations (OLR) to negotiate contracts and administer the city's labor relations and an Office of Collective Bargaining (OCB) to certify units, to hear unfair-labor-practice charges, and—very important—to provide third-party neutrals in cases of impasse in negotiations. This system was a precursor of New York's state law governing bargaining in the public sector, and it remained largely intact after passage of that law the following year. Compared with Wagner, Lindsay was thereafter in a secondary, behind-the-scenes role in municipal labor relations.

Lindsay's two-term administration (1966 to 1973) was marked by a major expansion of public services, increased revenues and employment, and rapidly rising expenditures, notably for public employees' wages and fringe benefits. Whether the last of these was due primarily to unionism and bargaining or to other factors (for example, the demand for public services) is a matter of considerable debate, but there is no question that organized city employees became a powerful force and, even more, that the citizenry perceived them as such. When, not long after taking office in 1973, Mayor Abraham D. Beame proclaimed the existence of a major budget deficit, and later, when reports of a fiscal crisis and possible bankruptcy surfaced with increasing regularity, popular opinion held public employees' unions to be a major culprit in creating that state of affairs. It is true that wage rates in the city were not appreciably higher (and in some cases were lower) than those in other large urban governments, that federal and state financial contributions to New York had fallen considerably since 1970, that the recession of 1974–1975 acted to create financial crises in many state and local governments, and that this municipal government was asked to provide types and levels of services unknown elsewhere. Most of New York's citizens nevertheless appeared to hold public employees' unions largely responsible for the city's financial plight.

In any event, to avoid bankruptcy, the state legislature created two bodies in 1975, the Municipal Assistance Corporation (MAC) and the Emergency Financial Control Board (EFCB). The first was concerned mainly with financial and accounting practices, but the second possessed substantial authority to intervene in the management of city government and was to oversee the creation of a 3-year financial plan designed to produce a balanced budget by 1978. The EFCB was instrumental in pushing the city to reduce employment by means of a combination of layoffs and attrition, to lower pension benefits for a variety of employees, and, through its power to affirm or reject *all* labor contracts, to negotiate deferrals of previously bargained wage increases. In November 1975, the EFCB imposed a 1-year wage freeze on all city employees, which subsequently was extended for 2 additional years. Cost-of-living adjustments were permitted to occur under these arrangements, but only if they could be offset by improvements in the production of services, the particulars of which would be monitored by the EFCB.

Perhaps most dramatic of all, when the specter of bankruptcy emerged for a second time in November 1975, a complicated financing arrangement was worked out which included the purchase of $2.5 billion worth of city and MAC bonds by the trustees of the municipal employees' pension funds. Thus, the city's public employee unions became direct financiers of the city, especially AFSCME and the American Federation of Teachers (AFT). These organizations were forced by circumstances not only to forgo most increases in wages and benefits for a 3-year period but also to render their members' future income flows dependent upon the financial solvency of New York itself. These developments of the 1970s were startlingly different from those which characterized public-sector labor relations in America's largest city during the expansionary 1960s and the relatively stable 1950s. If a second generation of bargaining has occurred anywhere in the public sector, it has taken place in New York in the 1970s.

In terms of the future course of labor relations and collective bargaining in the public sector of New York, it is safe to say that they will not remain unchanged. Even as Mayor Beame's successor, Edward I. Koch, assumed office in 1978, he faced a group of leaders of municipal labor unions who were determined to negotiate new gains for their members as the 3-year moratorium on wage increases came to an end. And, indeed, that was the result of the 1978 negotiations, although pay increases were tied to improvements in productivity. More interesting, perhaps, was the city government's encouragement of a bargaining coalition among the municipal unions and the setting of a common expiration date for all but a few of the city's labor agreements.[27] If the city's economic status improves in the future, these new structural arrangements may well enhance the bargaining power of organized public workers relative to that of management. Nevertheless, neither the city's organized workers nor its managers will soon be able to ignore the continuing fragile economic structure of the municipal government and of the city's economy more generally.

Diversity in Public-Sector Bargaining

Bargaining relationships in the public sector are not everywhere alike, even if they share some similar characteristics. This was evident just from a review of the situations in San Francisco and New York, and it is underscored by the experiences of other state and local governments. Further, diverse types of labor-management relationships may exist within a single government. For example, in Los Angeles, where formal labor negotiations emerged in the early 1970s, Lewin has identified four types of labor organizations: unions composed of the traditional craft or skilled workers, organizations of workers in the "neocrafts" such as the police and firefighters, multioccupational associations (such as the SEIU and AFSCME), and professional associations (of which the Engineers and Architects Association is a leading example in Los Angeles).[28]

The importance of this organizational diversity is that it spills over to affect the scope and substance of collective bargaining. According to Lewin:

> The traditional craft has the narrowest objectives among these groups, largely confined to wages and fringe benefits, while the multioccupational type probably has the widest interests, extending to case loads and management policy. The neo-craft group pursues rather narrow interests at the bargaining table, but a larger—or at least different—range of issues than the traditional craft in its relations with department personnel, given the strong tradition of . . . [settling all disputes within

the family] in the police and fire services. The professional association pursues a relatively broad range of issues, as much through political and management channels as through bargaining, but retains a marked identification with management and a disdain for if not an abhorrence of unions. Unlike the multioccupational union, the professional association has no interest in the agency shop or other security arrangements, and alone among public employee organizations in Los Angeles, utilizes the Civil Service Commission rather than an independent third party as the final arbiter of grievances.[29]

Diversity in labor relations and bargaining in the public sector emerges not only from the characteristics of employee organizations but also from variation in mechanisms for governmental control, organizational structures, and composition of work groups. Some local governments have a mayor-council form of administration, and others have a city-manager form. Within the mayor-council type, some cities (such as San Francisco) follow a weak-mayor, strong-council form, while others (such as New York) have a strong-mayor, weak-council type of administration. In some cities, certain departments or agencies —for example, water and power, education, and hospitalization—operate autonomously or even independently of the municipal government, whereas elsewhere they come under the control of the city administration. Often, selected local service agencies are funded by the state government, but equally as often they are funded by local sources of revenue. States vary widely in their financial contributions to local governments for public education; in some communities, but not in others, the property tax (rather than the income tax) is almost the sole source of revenues to pay for teachers' salaries. In some areas, the responsibility for public services is partitioned between a city and a county government, in others this responsibility overlaps or is shared, and in still others only the municipal government provides services. And, of course, the political orientation of voters may vary widely among communities and may also change over time, spilling over to affect the operations of government, including labor relations policies and practices.

With so many forces at work on labor relations in the public sector, one might conclude that diversity renders each situation unique and therefore subject to explanation only on an ad hoc basis. But such a view is as inappropriate as the one which maintains that labor relations in the public sector are everywhere the same. What informed students of this subject propose is that *patterns* of similarity and difference in public-sector labor relations be empirically identified across a wide base of data.[30]

This thesis of diversity is especially useful in analyzing the subject of management's prerogatives in the public sector. As is true of the private sector, no absolute or permanent line can be drawn separating the interests of public employers from the rights of public workers. Not only do these change over time, as we have observed in both the public and the private sectors, but they also vary across major types of employee groups and major types of government management.

SELECTED ISSUES IN PUBLIC-SECTOR BARGAINING

What are some of the specific issues and items that form the substance of collective bargaining in the public sector? For teachers, social workers, nurses, and probation officers, one of the most important is student, patient, or case load. Teachers have been shown systematically to accept lower wages or rates of wage increase in return for smaller classes.[31] Social workers and probation officers bargain with public employers over the size of their case loads, and nurses in many big-city hospitals do the same with respect to patient loads. Also, in a few instances, assistant district attorneys and public defenders have organized and have negotiated limits on their client loads.

Organized public workers contend that by negotiating more suitable limits on their work loads, they benefit the public in that more productive government services are provided. From this perspective, when a public employee bears a client, student, or patient load that is too large, he or she can provide only cursory service, which may be inadequate to give the care required or to resolve the problem at hand.

Clearly, there is some merit to this position, and few would argue that additional time spent instructing a student, caring for a patient, or consulting with a client does not qualitatively improve the service rendered. The difficulty with this position, though, is in knowing how far to pursue it. Extension of the principle to its outermost limit would result in one worker per case, client, patient, or student, which would clearly be untenable. Both the quantity and the quality of the service provided have to be considered in any decision on work load or the utilization of labor. In fact, there may be a real danger that only small proportions of the student, patient, or client population will be served when work load is a subject of bargaining in the public sector, since managers sometimes view lowering work loads as a way of holding down the increases in wages and benefits which they might otherwise have to grant. At other times, though, especially in strained economic circumstances, public employers seek to increase work loads and to base wage hikes on measurable gains in "productivity." Workers, too, may pursue these objectives, arguing that their increased work load merits higher pay and more benefits. As is true of labor relations everywhere, there is no single practice or posture concerning the issue of work load in the public sector; there are only patterns. This discussion should indicate, though, why questions of work load are important to some groups of public employees and why decisions concerning them rarely remain solely a prerogative of management.

Productivity Bargaining

The issue of work load is a useful one for raising the more general problem of productivity in the public sector and of the role that productivity bargaining may play in governmental labor relations. Pressures for improved productivity on the job began to emerge in the public sector during the early 1970s, as the financial base of government became less stable and as wages and benefits rose to levels that often surpassed those in private industry. A variety of schemes to improve productivity emerged at the state and local levels, offering further wage increases only in return for a higher level of performance, that is, increased productivity; hence the term "productivity bargaining." Some of these schemes involved reassigning police, fire, and sanitation personnel on the basis of the changing hourly, daily, or seasonal demand for their services. In one southern California city, police were given incentive pay increases that were based upon reduction in the town's measured crime rate—a policy that may unfortunately serve to reduce only the reporting of crime rather than its actual incidence. Elsewhere, some labor agreements provided for joint labor-management committees to study (1) ways of reducing absenteeism, tardiness, and abuse of provisions for sick leave; (2) rearrangement and redesign of work methods and work assignments; (3) methods of monitoring employees' performance; (4) modifications of pay structures to allow greater use of incentive pay; and (5) ways of revising narrow job classifications to permit more flexible use of public personnel.

The early efforts at productivity bargaining in the public sector tended to be relatively unsuccessful. For example, in examining what went wrong in productivity bargaining between the New York State government and the Civil Service Employees Association, Inc. (CSEA), during the early 1970s, Osterman cites a lack of commitment on the part of both management and the union, a lack of technical expertise, overly rigid adherence to a gain-sharing formula that raised employees' expectations beyond the ability to deliver, and the inclusion of job security within the overall effort.[32] The last is especially interesting, for real savings from a scheme for improving productivity in the public sector may be realizable in large part only through reductions in the size of the work force. After all, public services are heavily labor-intensive, with payroll costs accounting for 90 percent or more of total cost in some cases. Even though reductions in personnel might be accomplished through voluntary attrition rather than layoffs, unionists in the public sector should not be expected generally to support policies that result in fewer union members.

When improvements in productivity are sought through the vehicle of collective bargaining, different approaches may be used. For example, the buy-out approach requires management to develop objectives and methods of implementing improvements in productivity and then to proceed to the bargaining table in order to secure the cooperation of the union in the adoption of a specific plan. Alternatively, the gain-sharing approach is more open-ended, requiring cooperation between labor and management and a sharing of rewards after the plan for improving productivity has been implemented, and its consequences measured. In commenting on the first of these approaches, which he commends over the second, McKersie warns that it must be used sparingly because "the exchanging of money for productivity improvements is a high risk process."[33] If the union demands that every change made by management be reimbursed as part of a program to improve productivity, counterproductive results will ensue. To be sure, if the buy-out approach is followed, financial rewards generally must be provided "up front" to induce workers to accept the planned changes. But it is then management's function to measure results so as to determine whether savings have been achieved and whether the bargain with the union has worked to the government's advantage.

In sum, productivity-bargaining initiatives are likely to be more carefully framed and evaluated as the parties develop further experience with them and if the financial climate of the public sector continues to be threatening. It is well to remember, though, that government services are heavily labor-intensive, that they are not readily subject to capital innovation and new technologies, and that they are not likely to yield increases in productivity that approach those recorded in other parts of the economy. This is a problem which labor and management as well as the public will continue to face, no matter how imaginative the schemes for productivity bargaining and for improving productivity may be.

Personnel Administration

Like organizations of privately employed workers, labor organizations of government employees have significantly affected the personnel management function. One of the major areas of impact has been discipline and due process; here, collectively bargained grievance procedures that culminate in binding arbitration have supplanted internal appeals systems, in which a civil service commission typically rendered an authoritative decision. As public employees organized and bargained on a wider scale in state and local governments, they no longer accepted the civil service commission as an independent, neutral adjudicatory body in cases in which employees appealed employers' actions. Rather, they regarded such commissions as an arm of management. To remedy this situation and to achieve a counterpart to "industrial justice" in the private sector, public employees negotiated grievance procedures into their labor agreements, and they did so in the face of strong opposition from civil service officials, who (rightly) perceived a challenge to their authority.

Despite this development, grievance procedures in state and local governments are not as comprehensive as those in private industry. Labor agreements in the public sector tend to exclude proportionately more issues from the grievance process, to provide a narrower interpretation of violations of contracts, and to contain more general definitions of issues that are properly dealt with through the grievance procedure than labor agreements in the private sector.[34] The scope of arbitrable issues is considerably narrower in state and local governments than in the private sector, with the former often excluding wages, classification of positions, employment status, plant administration, and sometimes even discipline from neutral third-party rulings.

If unions have made inroads into some personnel management functions in the public sector—discipline, work rules, job assignments, and job classifications—they have had little impact on others. One researcher studied fifteen city and four county governments in the late 1960s and early 1970s and concluded that labor organizations in the public sector had little effect on employment standards, methods of personnel selection, promotions, and employee training and development.[35] Other investigators have found evidence of a partial impact on one or more of these functions, as in the case of nurses who negotiate over promotions to higher classifications, police officers who bargain over staffing levels, and multioccupational organizations such as AFSCME which negotiate with management over training programs for their members. Here, as in other areas of labor relations, diverse patterns of union influence emerge. On balance, civil service commissions survive rather than fade from the scene as a result of collective bargaining, but with less authority and a narrower set of responsibilities than they had previously.[36]

Management Policy

Unions of government employees sometimes have an impact on management policy. In some police departments, for example, organized officers have eliminated residency requirements (that police officers live in the cities for which they work), have minimized restrictions on their own use of firearms, have prevented the functioning of civilian review boards, and have engaged "in electoral politics on behalf of local candidates whom they perceived as ideologically compatible with rank-and-file law enforcement interests."[37] In public education, where the overall impact of organized teachers on management policy seems slight, some teachers' unions have successfully opposed changes in the areas of methods of financing schools, curricula, procedures for merit review, and the employment of paraprofessional teachers' aides. Other labor organizations have attempted to include such items in the scope of negotiations, official or otherwise, arguing that they are critical to the professional interests of teachers. Indeed, professionals are more likely than nonprofessionals to pursue bargaining over issues of so-called "management policy,"[38] and they may be more successful in making progress on these issues during the second generation of bargaining in the public sector than they were during the first generation.

In some cities which lack sufficient supervisory personnel or well-trained managers, union leaders and members sometimes themselves fill the void. This may put them in the position not only of making decisions on work assignments, work methods, overtime scheduling, staffing levels, and so forth, but also, in effect, of deciding which services get performed, which geographic areas receive services, and how often services are provided. This may result indirectly but nevertheless importantly in the shaping, by union leaders and unionized personnel rather than by elected officials and career managers, of basic policy concerning human resources management and the delivery of services.[39] The consequences of this may not be bad, but they come by default rather than by design.

Note that to the extent that productivity bargaining widens and proves successful, this is likely to increase the union's involvement in the formulation of management policy, whether in the area of personnel and human resources or, more generally, in the area of delivery of services. Such an outcome is most likely to occur when bargaining involves professional workers and when the parties to negotiations have engaged in attitudinal structuring (which, it should be remembered, is one aspect of bargaining) to the point where a high level of trust has developed. Alternatively, the multiplicity of management actors in the multilateral bargaining process of the public sector, the growing public concern about the power of public employees' unions, the rising pressures for stricter accountability of both elected officials and the parties to bargaining, and a stringent economic climate may limit or reduce the role of organized government workers in making basic policy decisions. As we have seen before, this issue cannot be effectively decided by labeling one group of subjects "management's prerogatives" and another "the union's interests." The scope of bargaining in the public sector will change over time as conceptions of rights and interests are modified; it will vary in diverse patterns across relationships between labor and management in government; and, in a particular context, it will be determined by the relative bargaining power of the parties to negotiations. Such power is, in turn, fundamentally shaped by the economic, political, and legal climates in which collective bargaining in the public sector takes place.

The Structure of Public-Sector Bargaining

As we conclude this section, the structure of collective bargaining in the public sector merits brief comment. Unlike bargaining in the private sector, bargaining in government almost universally takes place between an individual employer and an individual union. A particular government may be very large, a single union may have many locals and many members, and a specific agreement may set the pattern for others within the same government or neighboring jurisdictions. But, with the exception of negotiations between the Minnesota Twin City Metropolitan Area Managers Association and Local 49 of the International Union of Operating Engineers (IUOE) and some sporadic efforts in other locales, multiemployer bargaining is unknown in American state and local governments.

Why is this so? Why would public employers not join forces in an attempt to offset the bargaining power of organized workers? That option would seem especially appealing to boards of education in small communities, to police and fire departments, to town councils, and to city managers. Some answers were provided in a study conducted in 1975 by Feuille and his associates of public-sector interemployer relationships in four diverse metropolitan areas. Finding no formal alliances among the 114 municipalities and 112 school districts which they examined, the researchers concluded:

> Employer respondents anticipated considerable procedural difficulties in coordinating bargaining across several bargaining units with different employment condi-

tions, different abilities to pay and different union leaders . . . compounded by different management structures and decision processes. . . . The respondents spoke of employer decision autonomy in strongly positive terms as a behavioral dimension worth preserving. . . . Union and management representatives had little or no desire to reduce . . . duplication [of negotiations] because to do so would reduce their organizational stature or even eliminate their current livelihood.[40]

Perhaps the most interesting among these reasons for not pursuing multiemployer bargaining in the public sector is the desire of management and union officials to preserve their autonomy, that is, their decision-making prerogatives. In joint bargaining by employer-governments, shared interests would have to dominate those of individual jurisdictions, and the decisional powers of some would have to be subordinated to those of others. The respondents in the aforementioned study clearly felt uncomfortable about such a bargaining relationship. Claims that multiemployer bargaining would avoid "whipsawing" (using one unit's concession to pry a similar concession from another unit) and duplication and that it would assure greater expertise at the bargaining table seemed of less importance to the respondents than the consequent loss of autonomy.

Again we urge the reader to consider that the conclusions of a study like this may be affected by changing economic, political, and legal circumstances. If the resources available to the public sector become scarcer, if the pressures on governments to improve efficiency and hold down costs continue to mount, and if elected officials are motivated by a critical electorate to counteract the power of unions, then there may be broader efforts to structure multiemployer bargaining relationships. Similarly, labor organizations of public employees might respond to those developments by pursuing coordinated and coalition bargaining to preserve or augment their negotiating power. The dynamics of bargaining are such as to constantly challenge the present status of any aspect of labor-management relations.

Note, further, that the determination of the appropriate bargaining unit in the public sector presents some especially difficult problems. There are some who contend that broad occupational bargaining units are most appropriate for state and local government employees because they facilitate the maintenance of uniform benefits and working conditions; simplify the bargaining process; reduce the number of separate negotiations, thus permitting more centralized bargaining and more sophisticated approaches to bargaining; and, of major importance for management, dampen the tendency toward whipsawing. On the other side of this issue are those who favor smaller facility or departmental units, on the grounds that they best allow the needs of specialized groups of employees to be addressed, are more effective than broad units in dealing with purely local issues, avoid the inflated demands that leaders of conglomerate public employee unions may feel required to make, and reduce the number of intramanagement conflicts over job assignments, work rules, vacation scheduling, and the like.[41]

Lacking conclusive evidence about the suitability of broad versus narrow bargaining units in the public sector, we can nevertheless observe that those charged with determining such units (for example, public employment relations boards) usually follow the criteria adopted by the NLRB for determination of bargaining units in the private sector, which were reviewed in Chapter 5. Of those, the "community of interest" among employees is of major importance, though weight is also given to the similarity of skills and working conditions, common supervision, and the functional distinctiveness of work. Again, the diversity of labor relations in the public sector is reflected in bargaining units, which run the gamut from those consisting of workers in a narrow occupational specialty—police officers, operating engineers, or nurses, for example—to those encompassing all the office workers or professional personnel employed by a state or local government. However, even a large multioccupational labor organization—such as AFSCME in New York or the SEIU in Los Angeles—typically has several bargaining units, even if there is some coordination of negotiations among them. And the number and composition of these bargaining units change over time in response to the economic, political, and legal factors that also affect management's collective bargaining structure. In general, public employers tend, for reasons of efficiency, to prefer fewer, larger bargaining units, while, for reasons of effective representation, organized public employees favor smaller, narrower units.

LABOR RELATIONS IN THE FEDERAL SECTOR

The framework for labor relations in the federal government of the United States, which employs 2.7 million civilian workers, originally was set forth in Executive Order 10988, issued by President Kennedy in 1962. That order was revamped in 1969 by Executive Order 11491, issued by President Nixon, which was itself amended in 1971 and 1975. Briefly, Executive Order 11491 did the following:

1 Protected the rights of federal employees to join labor organizations

2 Established (a) the Federal Labor Relations Council, composed of the chairman of the Civil Service Commission, the Secretary of Labor, and the director of the Office of Management and Budget, to administer and interpret the order; (b) the Federal Service Impasses Panel to resolve impasses in negotiations by taking "any action it deems necessary" (usually mediation, followed by factfinding and, if necessary, a form of arbitration); and (c) the Office of the Assistant Secretary of Labor for Labor Management Relations to handle union elections, determinations of bargaining units, unfair-labor-practice complaints, and questions about the grievance procedure

3 Provided procedures for exclusive jurisdiction and national rights of consultation for employee organizations (concerning agencywide personnel policies)

4 Specified the scope of bargaining and enumerated management's rights

5 Required the negotiation of grievance procedures

6 Required the approval of all labor agreements by the top agency administrator

7 Enumerated several unfair labor practices prohibited to employers and organizations of employees

In part, this framework for labor relations conformed to that governing the private sector and large parts of state and local governments. However, federal employees were prohibited from striking, and the scope of bargaining at this level of government was narrower than elsewhere. For all but postal workers, it excluded wages, fringe benefits, civil service provisions, and many other agency policies. This narrow scope of bargaining has been a particularly controversial issue in the federal sector, and the history of labor relations there can be read as a continuing struggle between organized workers and agency managers over the range of negotiable items.

The latest chapter in that struggle occurred in 1978, when Congress debated the bill that became the Civil Service Reform Act when signed by President Carter in October of that year. This act superseded Executive Order 11491 and for the first time gave the federal labor relations program a statutory basis. During Congressional debate over the bill, union representatives sought to widen the scope of bargainable issues that had been provided by the executive order, while some agency managers attempted to maintain or even narrow that scope. It appears, however, that under the new law "the basic scope of collective bargaining will remain generally the same as . . . under the Executive order."[42]

Also noteworthy about the new law, which took effect on January 1, 1979, was its establishment of three new agencies: the Federal Labor Relations Authority (FLRA), an NLRB-type agency to administer the law's provisions—similar in most respects to those of the executive order—dealing with organization, representation, and bargaining rights; the Office of Personnel Management (OPM) to handle the personnel management function for the federal government; and a Merit Systems Protection Board (MSPB) to hear appeals in adverse action and grievance cases involving employees not represented by a union. The last two agencies supplant the long-standing U.S. Civil Service Commission.

As in other levels of government and in private industry, issues of union representation are of key importance in labor relations in the federal sector. Executive Order 11491 and subsequent amendments provided for exclusive representation and for the types of determinations of bargaining units found elsewhere. Before they came on the scene, an unwieldy system of formal, informal, and consultative recognition and negotiating statuses characterized the federal sector. Now, when a union or association wins an election to determine representation, it is accorded exclusive recognition—formerly by the Assistant Secretary of Labor for Labor Management Relations and now by the FLRA—and the union can begin to bargain with federal managers for the workers it represents. Spirited competition has developed in parts of the federal sector for the right to represent employees in collective bargaining. It is these elections which establish the structure of bargaining in the federal government.

The federal sector is highly organized, although the extent of membership in unions and employee associations varies across the three major classifications of workers in this level of government.[43] Among the roughly 500,000 *wage board* employees—that is, blue-collar workers in the trades, crafts, and manual occupations—more than 80 percent are enrolled in bargaining units that have exclusive recognition status. The compensation of wage board employees is set by the department or agency management and was coordinated by the Civil Service Commission (now replaced by the OPM and MSPB), but members of unions and associations are represented on the eleven-member National Wage Policy Committee and on comparable bodies at local levels. This gives labor an official voice in wage board deliberations, and, although this is not the same as a bargaining role, unions of federal employees have been able to affect their pay rates through this wage-setting process.[44]

Approximately half of all federal workers, or 1.35 million persons, are *classified employees*—white-collar workers in clerical, technical, and professional occupations—who are slotted into eighteen job grades, the pay for which is set by the Congress with the participation of the President, who may adjust salaries to make them comparable to rates for similar jobs in the private sector. A Federal Pay Council advises the President in this respect, with several of its members chosen from labor organizations that represent large numbers of federal workers.

Classified employees are the least organized category of federal personnel, but their membership rate of 50 percent far exceeds that for privately employed white-collar workers (about 17 percent). Approximately one-seventh of organized federal classified employees are professionals—accountants, engineers, nurses, statisticians, lawyers—who, while distributed across numerous departments, are concentrated in the Departments of Treasury, the Army, and Labor and in the Veterans Administration.

The Postal Service employs over 700,000 workers, who are extremely well organized and who, since 1970, have negotiated wages and other conditions of employment with the management of the quasi-public corporation that operates this service. The 1970 Postal Reorganization Act established the corporation and, in effect, extended provisions of the Taft-Hartley Act and jurisdiction by the NLRB to this portion of the federal sector. The legislation followed closely on the heels of a 1-week strike conducted by 200,000 postal workers. That action and a strike by air traffic controllers later in 1970 were the last major work stoppages to have occurred in the federal government as of this writing.

Postal employees are the most heavily unionized of all federal workers. About 87 percent of them are enrolled in unions with exclusive recognition. Almost all of these are affiliated with the AFL-CIO, the two largest and most important being the American Postal Workers Union (APWU) and the National Association of Letter Carriers of the United States of America (NALC). National bargaining agreements have been negotiated regularly in the Postal Service since 1970 without strikes, which are still banned by law, but binding arbitration was used to settle the negotiations in 1978. Various local agreements supplemental to national pacts also are negotiated on a regular basis in the Postal Service. Thus workers in the Postal Service are covered by more or less conventional collective bargaining agreements, while other workers in the federal sector—especially classified employees—have a more restricted role in decision making in labor relations matters.

For the most part, union security provisions are banned in the federal sector, which means that a relatively small proportion of employees actually covered by collective bargaining agreements are dues-paying members of labor organizations. For example, the American Federation of Government Employees (AFGE), the largest single labor organization in the federal sector, represented almost 650,000 employees for bargaining purposes in 1973, but it had fewer than 300,000 dues-paying members. Some other federal labor organizations, particularly unions of blue-collar workers, have considerably higher proportions of active, dues-paying members. Nevertheless, in the federal sector, as elsewhere in the public sector, the issue of union security remains a particularly contentious one, and debate over the issue of "representation without taxation" can be expected to continue in this level of government.

Earlier we observed that the scope of negotiable issues has been the most troublesome aspect of labor-management relations and collective bargaining in the federal sector, even though the regulatory framework established in presidential executive orders broadened that scope. Not only are wages not a negotiable matter for any federal employees except postal workers, but many personnel administration and management policies also are excluded from joint labor-management determination in the federal sector. This is so in part because the U.S. Office of Personnel Management (formerly the U.S. Civil Service Commission), which operates the merit system for the entire federal sector, retains considerable decision-making responsibility under federal regulations. In both the 1960s and the 1970s, the Commission warded off major attempts by unions to curb its authority. The narrow scope of bargaining in the federal sector is also due partly to the fact that agency and department heads still have the discretion to define some terms and conditions of employment as nonnegotiable, despite 1975 amendments to Executive Order 11491 which sought to broaden the scope of negotiations by requiring agency managers to demonstrate a "compelling need" not to bargain about certain items. The FLRA, established by the Civil Service Reform Act of 1978, is now the final arbiter about what is and what is not a negotiable subject, and the precedents established in its future decisions should help define and structure the scope of collective bargaining in the federal sector.

The 1978 law removed many of the restrictions that previously existed on the scope of grievance procedures in the federal sector. Subjects over which the Civil Service Commission exercised authority—such as discharge, demotion, and job classification—were not permitted to be handled under grievance procedures negotiated under the executive order, but the new law permits most of those subjects to be covered by negotiated procedures. Also, whereas grievants previously could choose to use either a negotiated procedure or the civil service procedure to handle other subjects, the new law states that grievants must use the negotiated procedure if one exists. Finally, binding arbitration of grievances had been accepted only reluctantly by many federal managers under the executive order, but the 1978 law makes clear that such arbitration—rather than "advisory arbitration"—is perfectly legal.

With respect to procedures for resolving impasses in the federal sector, only in the Postal Service are the parties permitted to utilize binding arbitration (it is not compulsory for them to do so), but this must be preceded by mediation and factfinding. These last two processes were used in the 1978 postal negotiations, but, as noted above, binding arbitration eventually was required to conclude a new contract.[45] For the remainder of the federal sector, impasses in bargaining are handled by the FLRA, which in effect can authorize any action necessary to resolve a federal labor dispute, such as mediation or factfinding. Also, although the parties themselves may not agree to binding arbitration of negotiation disputes, the FLRA can order such arbitration.

To reiterate, the strike remains a legally prohibited action in the federal sector, which is why organized workers are anxious to have suitable procedures for resolving impasses developed there. However, managers in the federal sector are not especially keen about this idea or others which would reduce their decision-making power.

Interpreting the Experience in the Federal Sector

The federal experience in labor-management relations is an especially provocative one for analysis. One might well have expected collective bargaining in the federal sector to have grown more rapidly and developed more fully than anywhere else in the public sector. After all, the Executive order of 1962 not only established a bargaining framework for the federal sector but also, by all accounts, spilled over to affect substantially the development of collective bargaining in state and local governments. Yet it is in the latter governments, especially those of large urban municipalities, that bargaining grew most quickly and developed furthest.

To supporters of collective bargaining, the federal experience has so far been disappointing. In 1976, one group of authors wrote:

> It is the general resistance of agency bureaucrats and the general inertia of the federal bureaucracy that has impeded the development of collective bargaining. A federal manager whose discretion already is circumscribed by reason of agency and civil service regulations is not too enthusiastic about negotiating contracts that will further delimit the scope of authority. . . . Restrictions on the scope of negotiations have impeded the development of meaningful bargaining and true bilateral decision making about major conditions of employment in the federal service.[46]

A similar viewpoint was expressed 10 years earlier by another student of labor relations in the federal sector.[47] On the other hand, at the local agency

levels of the federal sector, collective bargaining and labor relations sometimes operate much as they do in private industry. One study of six federal government installations located in the midwest concluded that differences in the
patterns of union-management relations between the federal sector and private
industry were "more of degree than of kind" and that they "should not be
allowed to obscure the similarities that exist."[48] It remains to be seen whether
these conclusions will be altered by developments under the Civil Service Reform
Act of 1978.

Beyond this, federal employees have available to them routes of access to
elected and appointed officials who set their salaries and who determine some
other conditions of employment. Several federal labor organizations have mas-
tered lobbying and political techniques and were influential in the writing of laws
such as the Federal Salary Reform Act of 1962 and the Federal Pay Comparability Act of 1970 and in gaining representation on the councils that set pay for
wage board and classified employees. At least some of them—notably the
AFGE—have indicated that they prefer this political method of influencing
terms and conditions of employment. As one group of writers put it, "With a
limited scope of bargaining, there is little incentive for unions and associations
to prefer the practice of bargaining over the time-honored political route of congressional lobbying."[49] To this we might add that lacking the right to strike,
workers in the federal sector have little alternative but to rely on political
channels and methods to influence their terms and conditions of employment,
even if that reliance is somewhat diminished by the growth of collective
bargaining.

SOME UNRESOLVED ISSUES

To round out our discussion of labor relations and collective bargaining in the
public sector, three contemporary issues that have received considerable attention will be briefly discussed. The first of these is unionization of the military,
which, while as yet unknown in the United States, has occurred in other countries, for example, Denmark, Sweden, and Germany. We noted in Chapter 3
that the concept of sharing decision making with organized workers in an institution which requires strict discipline and which maintains a notably hierarchical
chain of command is anomalous and even repugnant to some. That was clearly
the majority view in Congress in 1978, when a law was adopted that forbids
military personnel to unionize and imposes stiff penalties on those who attempt
to do so.[50] The proponents of such laws raise the specter of the casualties that
might be suffered in a "democratically" reached deployment of troops in a
military engagement and question what would happen if rank-and-file members
consulted their union representatives about filing grievances over certain orders
of senior officers or if they simply refused to obey them.

Yet some of these same objections were raised in the debate over the
unionization of American police departments, which are now so thoroughly organized that many of even the smallest police forces have a patrolmen's benev-

olent association or its equivalent representing its members in collective bargaining. Also, many recent developments—such as the Vietnamese war and its attendant anxieties, elimination of the military draft, changing attitudes of military and nonmilitary personnel toward the armed forces, the extension of unionism to previously unorganized sectors, the enrollment of women in the major service academies, and the growing sentiment toward unionization among the enlisted ranks and among some officers as well—have altered the climate of discussion in such a way that proposals concerning organization of the military are receiving serious thought and comment.[51] In particular, attempts to make noncompulsory military service competitive with other employment are likely to modify traditional military procedures relevant to labor-management relations, in spite of the 1978 law prohibiting unionism in the military forces.

The second issue for discussion concerns the potential for federal collective bargaining standards for the entire public sector.[52] Some unionists in and out of government have advocated the extension of the Taft-Hartley Act to the public sector as a whole. As might be expected, labor unions affiliated with the AFL-CIO—for example, the Service Employees' International Union (SEIU) and the American Federation of Teachers (AFT)—have been the strongest advocates in the public sector of this policy initiative. Other labor organizations favor creation of a separate bargaining law for the public sector, one patterned after the Taft-Hartley Act, that would establish an administrative agency along the lines of the NLRB to regulate labor-management relations in this sector alone. The National Education Association (NEA) and the American Federation of State, County and Municipal Employees (AFSCME) are the leading supporters of this approach to labor relations and bargaining in the public sector. A third view, prominent among neutrals and some expert observers and practitioners of labor relations in the public sector, is that the federal government should establish minimum standards ensuring government workers the right to organize and bargain, wherever they are employed, but individual jurisdictions should be free to expand on these. Those who support this position often cite the desirability of preserving the laboratory or experimental nature of labor relations policies and practices in the public sector.

In the early 1970s, several bills were introduced in Congress supporting one or another of these three policy alternatives. Some of the bills were extensively debated, and though none was enacted, it seemed only a matter of time until Congress took some initiative in this regard. Following the recession of 1974–1975, however, and the attendant fiscal crisis in parts of the public sector, the intensity of debate over, and support for, a federal bargaining law covering the entire public sector diminished considerably. Right or wrong, Congress (like many state legislatures) is at present more concerned with checking the power of organized public workers and with maintaining the financial soundness of government than with extending the bargaining rights of government workers. Further, the propriety of federal standards for all labor relations in the public sector was cast in doubt by a Supreme Court decision declaring unconstitutional the 1974 extension of the Fair Labor Standards Act to state and local government.[53] Nevertheless, serious debate over this aspect of labor relations in the public sector is almost certain to resurface.

The last issue to be dealt with here concerning collective bargaining in the public sector is a proposal to permit the public in some sense to "ratify" agreements negotiated between governments and their employees.[54] One version of this recommendation is for a representative of the public to be present at the negotiating sessions. Another is for the bargaining sessions to be open to the public. Still another would result in referenda's being put to the voters on the affirmation or rejection of negotiated labor agreements. The extent to which any of these proposals for strengthening the public's interest in public-sector labor negotiations might actually accomplish its objective is problematic; however, here is another example of a policy issue that has emerged as a serious subject of discussion largely as a result of the financial plight of many state and local governments in the United States in the 1970s.

What is perhaps more likely to occur than public representation in, or formal public approval of, collective agreements is a closer integration between the bargaining and budget-making processes of government.[55] In the first generation of bargaining in the public sector, it was common for labor and management to agree on terms and conditions of employment without elected officials, managerial personnel, or the citizenry knowing what their financial implications might be. Property, sales, and income taxes or combinations thereof sometimes had to be raised after the fact to finance the terms of labor agreements in the public sector, and some governments, notably that of New York City, financed these obligations by long-term debt or expenditures out of capital funds. In the second generation of bargaining in the public sector, which is now upon us, substantial pressures have been brought to bear on the parties to calculate in advance the budgetary implications of their negotiated agreements and on elected officials to integrate bargaining and budget-making processes so that everyone will know before the fact what the fiscal consequences of the projected agreements will be. The impetus for such integration seems likely to grow rather than diminish in the near future.

EXPERIENCE OF OTHER COUNTRIES

What of public-sector labor relations elsewhere? Are other countries undergoing experiences similar to, or different from, those of the United States? At a high level of generalization, the similarities apparently outweigh the differences.[56]

In neighboring Canada, public workers have enjoyed bargaining rights longer, and they have been far more militant. The differences in bargaining between the federal and state (provincial) levels in Canada are quite similar to those observed in the United States. Professional workers employed by Canadian governments are more heavily organized than their American counterparts, and contract arbitration, particularly the compulsory type, is considerably more common in Canada than in the United States. Canadian public employers often are pattern setters for the private sector.

In Great Britain, the largely nonstatutory basis of labor relations in private industry is also evidenced in the public sector. The important period of union growth in that country's public sector occurred during the immediate post-war years, 1945 to 1951. Today, organized employees bargain agreements with the national government, the civil service, local governments, and the public corporations of nationalized industries. Management is highly centralized in the civil service, but is much less so at other levels of government, where only "large, urban local authorities have developed any managerial professionalism and been exempted from widespread public criticism of their inefficiency in recent years."[57] Labor organization is far more extensive in the public than in the private sector of Britain, and collective bargaining occurs at more centralized —that is, national or "industrywide"—levels in government than in industry. The scope of negotiations is relatively broad in the British public sector, but comparability of wages with those in the private sector remains the leading issue in contention. Public workers are treated similarly to private workers in terms of the right to strike (no such rights are constitutionally guaranteed), and in terms of the procedures, including voluntary arbitration, that are used to settle bargaining disputes.

In France, unionism and collective bargaining recently have developed on a wide scale in the public sector, where once they were almost unknown. Unionism is legally permitted for French public workers, and the incidence of organization is particularly high among employees of nationalized and partly state-owned industries, so-called "public undertakings." Organized public employees are represented on the boards of management of state-owned credit, insurance, rail and air transportation, and utility enterprises. However, French unions, including those of public employees, are not centrally involved in day-to-day management operations, since they focus their energies less on problems of the immediate workplace than workers in the United States do. Unionists in the public sector have struck with increasing frequency in recent years— these strikes are not legally banned—largely over the failure of their wage rates to keep pace with those offered by private employers for the same work. Collective bargaining in the sense that it is known in the United States now exists in the French civil service, but the government employer has "insisted on exercising its sovereign authority."[58] Such insistence seems to be weakening over time, however, as bargaining over wages and continuous consultation with employees are becoming increasingly characteristic of labor relations in the French public sector.

In the Federal Republic of Germany, public employees are granted legal rights to organize and to be represented in the determination of "working and economic conditions." Well over one-third of West Germany's public employees are organized, but the incidence of organization is higher among the 1.4 million professional civil service personnel, known as *Beamte*, than among other white- and blue-collar workers, known as *Arbeitnehmer*. An important issue in West Germany is whether the prohibition of strikes by *Beamte* should be continued; this prohibition seems to be in the process of erosion, as is the rather special status that this group historically enjoyed in the German tradition of civil service. Bargaining in the public sector in West Germany occurs at the federal, state, and local levels, and multiemployer negotiations are quite common among nonfederal employers.

In the Scandinavian countries—Denmark, Finland, Norway, and Sweden—public employment has grown enormously in recent years, and government workers, like others in the economies of those countries, are heavily organized. Collective bargaining in the public sector has a relatively long history in the Scandinavian countries, especially Denmark. An important distinction is made in these nations between disputes over rights and disputes over interests (that is, between disputes arising under a contract and those arising over the terms of a contract), and a system of labor courts is used to settle the former. This contrasts with the reliance in the American public sector on negotiated grievance procedures, including arbitration, to resolve disputes over existing terms and provisions of labor agreements. Public employees in the Scandinavian countries by and large possess rights to strike, but these are more pervasive in Sweden and Finland than in Denmark and Norway, where heavy reliance is placed on mediation and compulsory arbitration of impasses in bargaining. However, in Sweden and Finland special procedures are available for resolving labor disputes in the public sector that constitute a national emergency.

In Japan, public employment is not growing; in fact, the number of public workers has declined as a proportion of the total work force from about 20 percent in the immediate postwar period to roughly 13 percent today. Wage settlements in the public sector are not as dominant as they once were in terms of establishing patterns for the rest of the economy. About two-thirds of Japan's public employees are organized, compared with about 30 percent of the privately employed workers. The Japanese public sector is a multifaceted system, ranging from the 1.5 million employees of nationalized industries, who may not strike but who are covered by provisions for compulsory arbitration, to the 14 million workers who bargain individual contracts with different levels of government. In between are wage board employees and administratively determined wage-setting processes not unlike those in the federal sector of the United States. Japanese public employees have been forbidden to strike since 1948, when the policy was instituted by General Douglas MacArthur, Supreme Commander of the Allied Powers, but they nevertheless have conducted frequent work stoppages in recent years. Present public policy attempts to distinguish degrees of essentiality among Japanese workers and to permit (by not enforcing prescribed penalties) work stoppages in nonessential services.

In conclusion, unionism and collective bargaining in the public sector are growing rapidly in a number of countries, not simply in the United States, and such issues as the scope of bargaining, management's prerogatives, the right to strike, procedures for resolving impasses, and the efficiency of government operations seem to be universal concerns. No one nation's record in structuring and attempting to resolve the thorny issues presented by collective bargaining in the public sector commends itself above all others. If the experience of the United States in this regard is experimental and characterized by diverse patterns of labor-management relations, the same may be said of bargaining in the public sector elsewhere in the world—or at least in the western-style democracies we selected for comparison. Perhaps the commonality of such democracy in these nations is the key to explaining why the similarities in their public-sector labor relations outweigh the differences.

SUMMARY

This chapter concludes our examination of collective bargaining within the American system of industrial relations. The discussion of public-sector labor relations in state and local governments covered such topics as the differences between collective bargaining in the public sector and that in the private sector; the regulation of collective bargaining in government, especially the legal treatment of strikes and procedures for resolving impasses; the changing economic, political, and legal climates of bargaining in the public sector; the scope of bargaining and selected key issues in contemporary negotiations in the public sector; the framework for labor relations in the federal sector; and some comparative aspects of labor relations in the public sector. Two key conclusions of this chapter are that labor relations and collective bargaining in the American public sector are characterized by a diverse rather than a uniform behavioral pattern and that bargaining relationships in the public sector are moving from a first generation, which stressed peace to preserve continuity of public services, to a second generation, which weighs more critically the cost of a peaceful settlement against the cost of a strike. In Chapter 7, we turn our attention to the labor market and processes of wage determination in both the private and the public sectors.

NOTES

1 Harry H. Wellington and Ralph K. Winter, Jr., *The Unions and the Cities*, Brookings, Washington, 1971, p. 8. For a critique of this view, see David Lewin, "Public Employment Relations: Confronting the Issues," *Industrial Relations*, **12**:309–321 (1973). The discussion in this section relies in part on Raymond D. Horton, David Lewin, and James W. Kuhn, "Some Impacts of Collective Bargaining on Local Government: A Diversity Thesis," *Administration and Society*, **7**:497–516 (1976).

2 Wellington and Winter, pp. 18–19.

3 The narrowing rather than the eradication of the authority and functions of civil service commissions as a result of collective bargaining is examined in David Lewin and Raymond D. Horton, "The Impact of Collective Bargaining on the Merit System in Government," *Arbitration Journal*, **30**:199–211 (1975); and David Lewin, "Collective Bargaining Impacts on Personnel Administration in the American Public Sector," *Labor Law Journal*, **27**:426–436 (1976).

4 See, for example, Howard M. Vollmer and Patrick J. McGillivray, "Personnel Offices and the Institutionalization of Employee Rights," *Pacific Sociological Review,* **3:**29–34 (1960).

5 Thomas A. Kochan, "A Theory of Multilateral Collective Bargaining in City Governments," *Industrial and Labor Relations Review,* **27:**526 (1974).

6 It could be argued that such higher approval is not very different from the bargaining process in the private sector, where top management must sanction the terms of a new labor agreement. However, it is more common in business for top management to delegate full authority to its chief negotiator before agreeing to a new contract.

7 John F. Burton, Jr., "Local Government Bargaining and Management Structure," *Industrial Relations,* **11:**123–140 (1972).

8 Kochan, p. 542.

9 See Kenneth McLennan and Michael H. Moskow, "Multilateral Bargaining in the Public Sector," *Proceedings of the Twenty-First Annual Winter Meeting of the Industrial Relations Research Association, 1968,* Madison, Wis., 1969, pp. 34–41; and Peter Feuille, "Police Labor Relations and Multilateralism," *Proceedings of the Twenty-Sixth Annual Winter Meeting of the Industrial Relations Research Association, 1973,* Madison, Wis., 1974, pp. 170–177.

10 See David Lewin, "Aspects of Wage Determination in Local Government Employment," *Public Administration Review,* **34:**149–155 (1974); Walter Fogel and David Lewin, "Wage Determination in the Public Sector," *Industrial and Labor Relations Review,* **27:**410–431 (1974); David Lewin, "The Prevailing Wage Principle and Public Wage Decisions," *Public Personnel Management,* **3:**473–485 (1974); and Sharon P. Smith, "Government Wage Differentials," *Journal of Urban Economics,* **4:**248–271 (1977).

11 Lewin, "Aspects of Wage Determination in Local Government Employment," pp. 149–155; Fogel and Lewin, pp. 410–431; Lewin, "The Prevailing Wage Principle and Public Wage Decisions," pp. 473–485; and Smith, pp. 248–271.

12 David Ziskind, *One Thousand Strikes of Government Employees.* Columbia, New York, 1940.

13 For further discussion of this issue, see David Lewin, "Public Sector Collective Bargaining and the Right to Strike," in A. Lawrence Chickering (ed.), *Public Employee Unions: A Study of the Crisis in Public Sector Labor Relations,* Institute for Contemporary Studies, San Francisco, 1976, pp. 145–163. Although the data in Table 6-1 cover the years through 1978, the more detailed data in Table 6-2 were available at the time of writing only through 1976.

14 In Ohio and Illinois, which have no laws governing bargaining in the public sector, some striking employees, notably teachers, have argued for statutes and impasse procedures as a means of reducing the number of strikes.

15 For an insightful analysis of the subject, see Carl Stevens, "Is Compulsory Arbitration Compatible with Bargaining?" *Industrial Relations,* **5:**38–52 (1966).

16 The literature on final-offer interest arbitration has grown very rapidly in recent years. See, in particular, "Symposium: Public Sector Arbitration," *Industrial Relations,* **14:**302–326 (1975); and Peter Feuille, *Final-Offer Arbitration: Concepts, Developments, Techniques,* International Personnel Management Association, Chicago, 1975.

17 Peter Feuille, "Final-Offer Arbitration and the Chilling Effect," *Industrial Relations,* **14:**302–310 (1975). For a critique of the methodology employed in this and related studies, see Henry S. Farber and Harry C. Katz, "Interest Arbitration,

Outcomes and the Incentive to Bargain: The Role of Risk Preference," *Industrial and Labor Relations Review* (forthcoming).

18   In the absence of union security provisions, the loser of an election to determine representation may continue to maintain its identity and challenge the established bargaining agent from within. On this point, see Eli Rock, "Bargaining Units in the Public Service: The Problem of Proliferation," *Michigan Law Review*, **67**:1001–1016 (1969).

19   For more on this theme, see Lewin, "Public Sector Collective Bargaining and the Right to Strike;" and David Lewin, Peter Feuille, and Thomas A. Kochan, *Public Sector Labor Relations: Analysis and Readings*, Thomas Horton and Daughters, Glen Ridge, N.J., 1977, pp. 1–10, 16–21.

20   See Bureau of National Affairs, "Proposition 13's Passage Estimated to Lay Off 75,000 California Employees," *Government Employee Relations Report 763*, June 12, 1978, pp. 16–18; and Public Employment Relations Service, *Information Bulletin 1*, June–July 1978, pp. 1–2.

21   John F. Burton, Jr., and Charles E. Krider, "The Incidence of Strikes in Public Employment," in Daniel Hammermesh (ed.), *Labor in the Public and Nonprofit Sectors*, Princeton, Princeton, N.J., 1975, p. 171.

22   Burton and Krider, p. 171. That liberalized rights concerning strikes by public employees may be coupled with restrictions on compulsory arbitration of labor disputes in government is proposed in Raymond D. Horton, "Arbitrators, Arbitration and the Public Interest," *Industrial and Labor Relations Review*, **28**:497–507 (1975).

23   See, for example, Stephen Hayford and Anthony Sinicropi, "Bargaining Rights Status of Public Sector Supervisors," *Industrial Relations*, **15**:60 (1976).

24   See *Abood* v. *Detroit Board of Education*, 45 U.S.L.W. 4473 (U.S. May 23, 1977). This decision is discussed in "Significant Decisions in Labor Cases," *Monthly Labor Review*, **100**:46–48 (1977). At least two states, Hawaii and New York, have authorized the agency shop for public employees.

25   This account relies in part on Harry C. Katz, "The Impact of Public Employee Unions on City Budgeting and Employee Remuneration—A Case Sudy of San Francisco," unpublished doctoral dissertation, University of California at Berkeley, 1977. See also Harry C. Katz, "Municipal Pay Determination: The Case of San Francisco," *Industrial Relations*, **18**:44–58 (1979).

26   The principal sources for this account are Raymond D. Horton, *Municipal Labor Relations in New York City: Lessons of the Lindsay-Wagner Years*, Praeger, New York, 1973; and Raymond D. Horton, "Economics, Politics and Collective Bargaining: The Case of New York City," in Chickering, pp. 183–202.

27   For an account of these developments, see various issues of *The New York Times*, March 1978 to July 1978.

28   David Lewin, "Public Sector Labor Relations in Transition: The Case of Los Angeles," *Labor History*, **17**:191–213 (1976).

29   Lewin, "Public Sector Labor Relations in Transition," pp. 211–212.

30   For more on this theme, see Horton, Lewin, and Kuhn, pp. 497–516.

31   See, for example, W. Clayton Hall and Norman E. Carroll, "The Effects of Teachers' Organizations on Salaries and Class Size," *Industrial and Labor Relations Review*, **26**:834–841 (1973).

32   Melvin Osterman, "Productivity Bargaining in New York—What Went Wrong?" in Lewin, Feuille, and Kochan, pp. 166–178.

33 Robert B. McKersie, "Afterword," in Lewin, Feuille, and Kochan, p. 180.

34 See Joseph C. Ullman and James P. Begin, "The Structure and Scope of Appeals Procedures for Public Employees," *Industrial and Labor Relations Review*, **23**:323 –334 (1970).

35 David T. Stanley (with the assistance of Carole L. Cooper), *Managing Local Government under Union Pressure*, Brookings, Washington, 1972.

36 Some writers have argued that collective bargaining will doom the civil service system. See John F. Burton, Jr., "Local Government Bargaining and Management Structure," *Industrial Relations*, **11**:123–140 (1972).

37 Hervey Juris and Peter Feuille, *Police Unionism*, Heath, Lexington, Mass., 1973, p. 161.

38 See Archie Kleingärtner, "Collective Bargaining between Salaried Professionals and Public Sector Management," *Public Administration Review*, **33**:165–172 (1973).

39 For an example of this behavior in New York City, see David Lewin, Raymond D. Horton, and James W. Kuhn, *Collective Bargaining and Manpower Utilization in Big City Governments*, Allanheld, Osmun, Montclair, N.J., 1979, chap. 5.

40 Peter Feuille, Hervey Juris, Ralph Jones, and Michael Jay Jedel, "Multiemployer Negotiations among Local Governments," *Proceedings of the Twenty-Ninth Annual Winter Meeting of the Industrial Relations Research Association, 1976*, Madison, Wis., 1977, p. 130.

41 This complex subject can be only briefly reviewed here. For further treatments of it, see James E. Martin, *Appropriate Bargaining Units for State Employees*, Sangamon State University, Springfield, Ill., June 1977, and the references contained therein; Rock, pp. 1001–1016; and James P. Begin, *Multilateral Bargaining in the Public Sector: Causes, Effects, Accommodations*, Rutgers University, Institute of Management and Labor Relations, New Brunswick, N.J., 1977.

42 This account is based on Bureau of National Affairs, "Civil Service Commission's Analysis of Provisions of the Civil Service Reform Act of 1978," *Government Employee Relations Report* 781, October 16, 1978, pp. 73–78; and "Analysis: Civil Service Reform Clearly Top Story of the Year," *Government Employee Relations Report* 791, January 1, 1979, pp. 5–7. It should be noted that this law dealt with aspects of the civil service program other than union-management relations.

43 For a more detailed treatment of this subject, see Robert F. Repas, *Collective Bargaining in Federal Employment*, University of Hawaii, Industrial Relations Center, Honolulu, 1970.

44 See, for example, William C. Valdes, "The Trend of Negotiations in the Federal Service," *The Bureaucrat*, special issue, *Labor-Management Relations in the Federal Government*, **2**:51–52 (1973); and American Federation of Government Employees, *The Government Standard*, January 1973, p. 7, where it is claimed that in local areas without a wage board for some reason, federal employees earned an average of 33 cents per hour less than their counterparts in areas with a wage board.

45 See "Binding Pact for Postal Workers," *The San Francisco Chronicle*, Sept. 16, 1978, pp. 1–12.

46 Edwin F. Beal, Edward D. Wickersham, and Philip K. Kienast, *The Practice of Collective Bargaining*, 5th ed., Dorsey-Irwin, Homewood, Ill., 1976, p. 487. See also Murray B. Nesbitt, *Labor Relations in the Federal Service*, Bureau of National Affairs, Washington, D.C., 1976.

47   See Wilson R. Hart, "The Impasse in Labor Relations in the Federal Service," *Industrial and Labor Relations Review,* **19:**175–189 (1966).

48   James E. Martin, "Application of a Model from the Private Sector to Federal Sector Labor Relations," *The Quarterly Review of Economics and Business,* **16:**75 (1976).

49   Beal, Wickersham, and Kienast, p. 485.

50   For an account of this Congressional action, see Bureau of National Affairs, "Number Seven: Military Union Ban," *Government Employee Relations Report* 791, January 1, 1979, pp. 10–11.

51   See, for example, Ezra Krendel and Bernard Samoff (eds.), *Unionizing the Armed Forces,* University of Pennsylvania Press, Philadelphia, 1977; Alan Sabrosky, *Blue-Collar Soldiers,* Foreign Policy Research Institute, Philadelphia, 1977; and William Gomberg, "Unionization of the U.S. Armed Military Forces—Its Development, Status and Future," *Proceedings of the Thirtieth Annual Winter Meeting of the Industrial Relations Research Association, 1977,* Madison, Wis., 1978, pp. 47–55.

52   See the discussion of this subject contained in Bureau of National Affairs, *Government Employee Relations Report* 577, October 21, 1974, pp. AA1–5; and Thomas R. Colosi and Stephen B. Rynecki (eds.), *Federal Legislation for Public Sector Collective Bargaining,* American Arbitration Association and International Personnel Management Association, New York and Chicago, 1975.

53   See Bureau of National Affairs, "Supreme Court Rejects Extension of Minimum Wage and Overtime Requirements to States," *Government Employee Relations Report* 663, June 28, 1976, pp. AA1–AA3. The decision in which this ruling was handed down, *National League of Cities and Others v. Usery,* is reprinted on pp. E1–E14 of this report.

54   See Economic Development Council, *Reforming Municipal Labor Relations in New York City,* New York, 1975.

55   For a study of this subject, see Milton Derber, Ken Jennings, Ian McAndrew, and Martin Wagner, "Bargaining and Budget Making in Illinois Public Institutions," *Industrial and Labor Relations Review,* **27:**49–62 (1973).

56   The discussion in this section draws heavily from Charles M. Rehmus (ed.), *Public Sector Labor Relations: An Overview of Eleven Nations,* University of Michigan, Institute of Labor and Industrial Relations, Ann Arbor, 1975.

57   David Winchester, "Labour Relations in the Public Sector in the United Kingdom," in Rehmus, p. 67.

58   Jean-Maurice Verdier, "Labour Relations in the Public Sector in France," in Rehmus, p. 93.

ADDITIONAL READINGS

Aaron, Benjamin, James L. Stern, and Joseph R. Grodin (eds.): *Public Sector Collective Bargaining,* Industrial Relations Research Association, Madison, Wis., 1979.

Chickering, A. Lawrence (ed.): *Public Employee Unions: A Study of the Crisis in Public Sector Labor Relations,* Institute for Contemporary Studies, San Francisco, 1976.

Gunderson, Morley (ed.): *Collective Bargaining in the Essential and Public Service Sectors,* University of Toronto Press, Toronto, 1975.

Hammermesh, Daniel (ed.): *Labor in the Public and Nonprofit Sectors,* Princeton, Princeton, N.J., 1975.

Horton, Raymond D.: *Municipal Labor Relations in New York City: Lessons of the Lindsay-Wagner Years,* Praeger, New York, 1973.

Juris, Hervey, and Peter Feuille: *Police Unionism,* Heath, Lexington, Mass., 1973.

Lewin, David, Peter Feuille, and Thomas A. Kochan: *Public Sector Labor Relations: Analysis and Readings,* Thomas Horton and Daughters, Glen Ridge, N.J., 1977.

Lewin, David, Raymond D. Horton, and James W. Kuhn: *Collective Bargaining and Manpower Utilization in Big City Governments,* Allanheld, Osmun, Montclair, N.J., 1979.

Rehmus, Charles M. (ed.): *Public Sector Labor Relations: An Overview of Eleven Nations,* University of Michigan, Institute of Labor and Industrial Relations, Ann Arbor, 1975.

Wellington, Harry H., and Ralph K. Winter, Jr.: *The Unions and the Cities,* Brookings, Washington, 1971.

FOR ANALYSIS AND DISCUSSION

1 Outline the major differences between collective bargaining in the public sector and that in the private sector. As part of this exercise, compare a recent agreement reached in the public sector with one negotiated in the private sector. How are they similar? How do they differ?

2 Examine the labor relations system in your city's municipal government. Are employees unionized? Do they negotiate contracts with the city government? Does your state have a law governing bargaining in the public sector? When was the law enacted? Analyze the key labor relations issues in your city government.

3 Examine the data contained in Table 6-1 on strikes by public employees in the United States. What factors might account for the sharp increase in such work stoppages between 1965 and 1966? Why did the incidence of such strikes decline in the early 1970s and rise thereafter? Is the number of work stoppages the best or most useful measure of strikes by public employees? Why or why not?

4 Compare and contrast the processes of mediation, factfinding, and interest arbitration in the public sector. How effective have these processes been to date? What are the sources of your information, and what criteria did you use to judge the effectiveness of these devices for resolving impasses?

5 Two teams of three students each should debate the following proposition: "Resolved: the Labor-Management Relations (Taft-Hartley) Act should be extended to public employment." The debate should be moderated by the instructor and followed by questions and comments from your audience of classmates.

6 Prepare a position paper outlining a legislative policy by means of which your state could regulate labor relations in the public sector. Be sure to cover such issues as union recognition, scope of bargaining, and procedures for resolving impasses. In carrying out this task, assume that you are a staff member advising an elected official who must choose from among several proposed bills dealing with the regulation of labor relations in the public sector.

7 A recent *New York Times* article described the growing opposition in many cities to raises for public workers such as police officers and firefighters. The article went on to observe: "Although the salaries of New York City policemen have been assailed as one major factor in that city's [fiscal] crisis, they lag considerably behind the sal-

aries of policemen in Los Angeles and in some other large cities.'' How might this apparent inconsistency between fact and opinion be explained?

8 Evaluate the current status of collective bargaining in the federal government of the United States. What are your criteria for evaluation? Upon what evidence do you base your evaluation? How have labor relations in the federal sector been altered by the Civil Service Reform Act of 1978? What recommendations would you propose for improving labor relations in the federal government?

9 Compare the major characteristics of labor relations in the public sector in the United States, Great Britain, and Japan. How do they differ? How are they similar? Trace out the common features of bargaining in the private and public sectors in Great Britain or in Japan. Compare your conclusions with those of a classmate who selected the other country for analysis.

10 Prepare an outline for a short presentation to your classmates on the subject ''Models of Collective Bargaining: Their Application to the Private and Public Sectors.'' Indicate whether different models are required for the two sectors or whether one or more such models may usefully be applied to both sectors.

Chapter 7

The Labor Market: Private and Public

This is the first of three chapters dealing with the labor market. Chapter 8 explores the roles of race and sex in the labor market as well as efforts to combat discrimination in employment by means of public policy. Chapter 9 examines the allocational consequences of labor markets in terms of income distribution and the issue of inequality.

Part One of this chapter lays the intellectual groundwork for the material to follow by setting forth the fundamentals of the theory of a competitive labor market (including the demand for, and supply of, labor) and the concept of equilibrium in the labor market. The application of this neoclassical theory to the contemporary scene is examined in a way that incorporates the newer human capital approach to labor market analysis. We then consider recent challenges to neoclassical labor economics as reflected in a variety of theories of a segmented labor market, most notably the theory of the dual labor market.

Part Two of this chapter is concerned with the determination of wages. Here we focus on various processes of wage determination within which institutional forces, such as labor unions, and market forces are conjointly at work, determining specific wage rates, pay differentials, and occupational wage structures. Evidence pertaining to the impact of unions on wages in the private and the public sectors is reviewed. The discussion of this impact and of other elements of structure and organization in labor markets highlights the role of political as well as economic forces in wage determination in both the private and the public sectors.

PART ONE: Theories of a Competitive Labor Market and a Segmented Labor Market

THEORY OF A COMPETITIVE LABOR MARKET

What is meant by the term "labor market"? Is it something real and tangible? Can it be observed in the real world, or is it instead an intellectual abstraction? In general, the labor market is not a single place where employers offering jobs and prospective employees searching for work meet to strike a bargain over wages, even though such places do exist, such as union hiring halls and private employment agencies. Except in rare instances, these locations do not attract all the jobs and prospective workers that flow through and make up the labor market. Rather, the labor market can be thought of as an area within which a set of exchanges takes place between buyers and sellers of labor. From the perspective of competitive-labor-market theory, these buyers and sellers are in close enough communication that the price of labor tends to be similar throughout the area. In geographic terms, some labor markets are very broad, while others are quite narrow. For example, high-level managers, administrators, and professionals typically "sell" their labor in markets that are national and even international in scope. Employers search for (that is, recruit) such workers throughout the country because local areas do not provide sufficient numbers of qualified personnel. Managers and professionals usually are able to obtain accurate information about job vacancies, salaries, and related matters in both nearby and distant locations through personal contacts and through trade and professional associations. For such employees, the costs of relocating typically are small when compared with the potential benefits to be derived from working in another area.

For manual, clerical, and nonprofessional workers, labor markets generally are narrower in scope. Employers search for these workers primarily in local markets, which generally can provide sufficient numbers of them to meet existing levels of demand. Individuals in these occupations will look for jobs within the boundaries of local markets and will not be especially interested in, or knowledgeable about, positions in distant locations. For them, the costs of relocating or of increased commuting time generally are large relative to the benefits to be derived from taking a job in a faraway location. Again, the presumption of competitive theory is that workers with similar skills will be paid roughly similiar wages within each local market; otherwise, some portion of the manual, clerical, and other nonprofessional groups would leave lower-paying jobs and move to higher-paying ones.

Within a specific locality, moreover, there is more than a single labor market. A medium-sized city such as San Antonio will contain a market for clerks, another for data processors, yet another for public school teachers, and so on for hundreds and even thousands of occupations. Each of these occupational specialties constitutes a separate local labor market, in which employers are trying to fill their jobs and prospective employees are searching for paid employment. When some among these many specialized markets are similar to others in terms of the skills required to perform the job, there exist additional possibilities of transfer of labor among them, as when a clerk becomes a clerk-typist or a technician becomes an engineer. Further, the possibility of migration can extend the boundaries of a labor market and help correct its imbalances, as when some job seekers moved from Appalachia to the midwest after World War II and others moved from the northeast to the sun-belt states in the 1970s. Thus, labor markets may be linked together even though they are separated by certain boundaries of both geography and levels of skill.

The notion that workers respond to differences in conditions in the labor market is central to competitive theory. It is the individual's desire to maximize "comparative net advantage" which leads to the prediction of this theory that workers will move away from markets paying lower wages to those paying higher wages.[1] The term "wage" is used here to include pay, fringe benefits, and working conditions (so-called "nonpecuniary benefits"), for competitive theory recognizes that it is not simply the hourly rate or monthly salary that dictates a worker's choice of jobs or movement between jobs. Critics of the theory sometimes overlook this point and mistakenly assert that neoclassical economists take the narrow view that workers are motivated solely by a desire for higher wage rates.

Nevertheless, because the wage rate or salary is the most easily available and understandable piece of information about a job, it tends to dominate discussions of behavior in the labor market and to be regarded as the principal "signaling" device affecting the job-search behavior of workers.[2] Furthermore, if competitive-labor-market theory is to consist of more than tautological statements to the effect that all movement and lack of movement by workers in the labor market is explained by comparative net advantage and if it is to generate testable hypotheses about behavior in the labor market, then one or more independent variables must be specified which affect workers' decisions about where and on what terms to sell their labor services. For this purpose, too, the wage rate or salary is the most useful job characteristic.

Beyond the requirement of workers' responsiveness to differences in wages, competitive theory specifies several other conditions. One of these is that information about jobs is readily available and easily communicated. Another is that workers are ready and able to move among alternative job opportunities; they are informed and mobile. Yet another is that employers view workers as being relatively interchangeable and equally efficient and that no single employer or group of them affects—dominates—wages by its individual decisions concerning pay. In fact, employers must pay the prevailing rate to attract workers, and they can fully satisfy their need for labor as a factor of production at the going rate. Finally, competitive theory assumes that all job vacancies are filled through the market rather than through internal systems for promotion and that there are as many workers in the market as there are jobs available. Unemployment is absent from this scenario; by definition, there is full employment.

Anyone who is familiar with labor markets in the real world knows that these perfectly competitive conditions hardly ever exist, singly or in combination. In actual labor markets, information is costly, some workers are not mobile, some employers have considerable power to affect the terms and conditions of work, and unemployment always exists, even though its incidence varies over time. Classical and neoclassical economists have made simplifying assumptions which seem to ignore these conditions, but not (as some would have it) because they are naive. Rather, they have sought to develop and rigorously test a model of labor markets that will accurately depict and, it is hoped, predict central behavioral tendencies. The danger comes about when those who employ the competitive model to analyze labor markets wittingly or otherwise accept it as a precise characterization of actual conditions. These caveats issued, let us now consider the derivation of the demand for, and supply of, labor in competitive theory.

The Individual Firm's Demand for Labor

In almost any line of business, the producer is faced with the problem of choosing the particular combination of factors—natural resources, labor, capital—to be employed in the production process. Within limits and over time, one factor of production may be substitutable for another, as when capital equipment displaces labor. The producer seeks to combine factors of production in such a way as to maximize profits. This requires weighing the marginal cost of a factor of input, such as a unit of labor, against the marginal revenue earned by that same unit, as well as against the marginal costs and revenues of other factors, for example, capital and raw materials.

Under competitive conditions, the marginal cost of a factor of production to the individual firm—that is, the cost of adding one more unit of that factor to production—is simply its price. This is so because, by definition, competitive-labor-market theory presumes the firm to be a "price taker," receiving information from the market about the going rate for a factor of production. The marginal revenue of a factor of production has two components: marginal physical product (MPP) and the market price of the good or service produced (P). Multiplying these two yields marginal value product (MVP), which is the net addition to revenue attributable to the marginal factor unit of production.

Having derived the marginal cost of a factor of input and marginal value product, we can relate these to the producer's problem of maximization, which involves the selection of combinations and quantities of factors of input. Whenever one factor makes a greater proportionate contribution to marginal revenue than another factor, a producer will prefer the former. The producer seeks to equate the relative contributions of factors of input to marginal revenue, measuring each factor's contribution in relation to its price. Using lowercase subscripts to denote particular factors, the producer's equilibrium position in combining factors of production requires that $\text{MVP}_a/P_a = \text{MVP}_b/P_b = \text{MVP}_c/P_c$, and so on.

As an example, assume unit labor costs to be \$8, marginal value product of labor to be \$20, unit capital costs to be \$15, and marginal value product of capital to be \$25. The ratios—20:8 and 25:15—reveal that the marginal dollar spent on labor adds \$2.50 to total revenue, while the marginal dollar spent on capital yields only \$1.60. The producer could—should—substitute more profitable labor for less profitable capital. *But the producer cannot continue to do so indefinitely* because the marginal physical product (and, with a constant price, marginal value product) of a factor must eventually decline if other factors are not increased in the same proportions. *This is the law of diminishing returns*, a fundamental tenet of economics. Past some point, the greater the number of factor units, the smaller the marginal value product, and vice versa. Thus the producer should add labor, whose marginal value product will fall, and subtract capital, whose marginal value product will rise, until the ratios are brought into balance.

Observe that attainment of this condition of equilibrium depends upon the time period assumed. In the short run, capital items such as buildings and machinery are fixed and, consequently, have no marginal product, just an average value product. Only variable factors such as labor and raw materials are substitutable for one another in the short run, and therefore they yield marginal value products. In the long run, all factors are variable and may be differentially combined so as to render equivalent contributions to profitability.

Note, too, that as the prices of factors change, so does the producer's preference for them. If the ratios of the previous example now appear as

$$\frac{\text{MVP}}{\text{P}} = \frac{\overset{\text{Labor}}{\overset{16}{8}}}{} \quad \frac{\overset{\text{Capital}}{\overset{30}{30}}}{}$$

the producer will find it advantageous to add labor and use less capital until the MVPs are equated, as in

$$\text{MVP} = \frac{\overset{\text{Labor}}{\overset{12}{8}}}{} = \frac{\overset{\text{Capital}}{\overset{45}{30}}}{}$$

But this result alone does not resolve the producer's problem of maximization, for there remains the question of the number of units of each factor to be employed. The rule for making a decision in this regard is that MVP = factor price.

In the individual firm, for which the price of factors is given, additional units of the factor will be used as long as their contribution to revenue (MVP) is greater than their addition to cost. If the marginal value product of each particular factor is just equal to its supply price, the condition of equiproportionate marginal contribution of *all* factors is met. With prices of $8 for labor and $30 for capital, as in the previous example, units of the two factors will be "hired" up to the point where

$$\frac{MVP}{P} = \frac{Labor}{\dfrac{8}{8}} = \frac{Capital}{\dfrac{30}{30}} = 1$$

Following this example, we can construct a factor demand schedule for the individual firm, as shown in Table 7-1. This example presumes homogeneous units, constant prices of all other factors, a constant product price, and a given state of technology. The only relevant range is one in which marginal product in both physical and value terms is diminishing. Before that, the producer will always add more of a factor input—for example, labor—since each additional unit of output creates more value than the previous one (as long as the factor price remains constant).

The data from Table 7-1 provide the basis for constructing Figure 7-1, which plots the MVP of labor at varying levels of employment. Since the firm will add units of factors, in this case labor, until their price (wage) is equal to MVP, "wage rate" can be substituted for MVP on the vertical axis. The result is the individual firm's demand schedule for labor, which shows the producer willing to hire three units of labor when the price and marginal value product of the third unit are $15, but unwilling to hire a fourth unit of labor until its price falls to $12, the value of its marginal product.

The Aggregate Demand for Labor

The demand schedule for labor (or any other factor of production) at the level of industry or the whole economy is the sum of the demand schedules of individual firms. However, at the level of industry or the economy, the simplifying

Table 7-1 Data for Derivation of a Firm's Demand Schedule for a Factor of Production

Number of factor units (1)	Marginal physical product (given) (2)	Price of the good (given) (3)	Marginal value product (column 2 × column 3) (4)
3	15	$1	$15
4	12	$1	$12
5	10	$1	$10
6	9	$1	$ 9
7	8	$1	$ 8
8	7	$1	$ 7

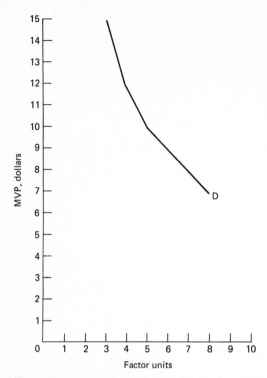

Figure 7-1 Demand schedule for labor of the individual firm.

assumption of a constant product price, which is appropriate for analyzing a single firm in a competitive market, becomes untenable. We have said that as more units of a factor are employed, its marginal physical productivity declines. If, then, the price of the factor declines, the individual producer will expand employment of the factor to the point where lowered marginal physical productivity times product price equals the new factor price. But, if all firms in an industry take the same action, total industry output will increase, creating downward pressure on the price of the product, the demand curve for which has not changed. As product price falls, so too does the marginal value product of the factor of production. With declining MVP, producers in the industry will be willing to hire fewer additional units of factors than before. Thus, the industry demand schedule for a productive factor must take into account whatever impact on product price results from variation in industry output as the use of factors increases or decreases. The result of all this is that the industry demand schedule for a productive factor such as labor, as portrayed in Figure 7-2, is steeper in slope than the demand schedules of individual firms.

The demand for factors of production cuts across industry lines, and so a change in the price of a factor affects many, if not all, industries. The MVP of an industry which is expanding to meet rising consumer demand for a new or long-standing product could be expected to be above the wage rate paid to

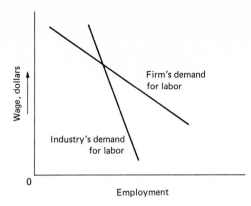

Figure 7-2 Demand schedules: industry versus firm.

labor. To recruit additional labor, firms in the industry might well have to increase wages, and they could afford to do so because of the high MVP. But as workers move to this industry away from lower-paying ones, the reduced outputs in the companies they leave will result in higher MVPs in those companies, which can then pay higher wage rates and stem the flow of workers to the expanding industry. In this competitive scenario, movement of workers ceases when MVPs, and hence wages, are equalized among the industries in question. In this way labor is distributed and redistributed among firms to produce products in amounts and at prices that satisfy the desires of consumer.

The Aggregate Supply of Labor

In competitive-labor-market theory, consumption is treated as a good, and work as a cost. The rational individual seeks to balance off the pleasure of consumption versus the pain of work. Where these are equal, the preferred position has been achieved, since any further work will create more pain than pleasure and any less work will decrease pleasure more than pain. Such reasoning leads to the familiar upward-sloping supply curve of Figure 7-3, which shows additional labor forthcoming at higher wages.

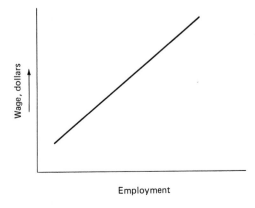

Figure 7-3 Aggregate labor-supply schedule.

Clearly, there is much validity to this view of why people work, but it also has shortcomings. For example, when a family determines how much time its members will work for pay, it must consider alternative uses of that time. Paid employment and the goods that it will buy must compete with unpaid uses of time for education, leisure, household maintenance, and other activities—all of which are substitutes for one another. Stated differently, the opportunity cost of leisure time is the goods that could have been obtained by selling that time to an employer, just as the opportunity cost of selling time to an employer is the leisure forfeited, the education forgone, the necessity of having someone else care for a young child, and the like. Decisions about whether a son or daughter should seek work, whether a husband should get a second job, and whether a wife should take a part- or full-time position, for example, all involve such trade-offs. A mixture of economic and cultural factors affects the values that individuals and families consider in deciding how to allocate their time between paid work and other activities. Such values are relatively fixed in the short run and more varied over longer periods.

The competitive model is less certain in predicting activity in the labor market when linkages between wage rates and individual behavior are more complex. For example, assume that all wage rates increase significantly tomorrow, while prices and other cultural variables remain constant. Will the number of married women seeking employment rise, fall, or remain about the same? In Chapter 1 we observed that women's rates of participation in the labor force (notably the rates of married women) have increased substantially in the twentieth century—over half of all married women are now in the work force—just as wage rates have been rising in the same period. But the inference that rising wages call forth larger numbers of female workers is complicated by the many other forces, such as the women's liberation movement, the shift from rural to urban areas, the decline in family size, and the proliferation of laborsaving devices in the home, which affect the participation rates of married women. One might conclude that these rates will continue to rise over the long run, but will not be very responsive to short-run increases in wages if the aforementioned cultural factors remain constant. Alternatively, however, in the face of sharply increased wage rates one could predict a decline in the number of working wives because the higher incomes earned by husbands alone would more adequately meet the family's needs. Depending on the value placed on alternative uses of a married woman's time, then, the competitive model's assumption concerning maximization seems to support any prediction one might care to make about the effect of a wage increase on this important source of labor supply.

Similar problems complicate the prediction of men's rates of participation in the labor force. Recognizing that leisure and paid employment each represent opportunity costs to the other, a male head of a household may indeed choose to supply more of his labor at higher wages—but only up to a point. Thereafter, he may choose *fewer* hours of work, since with higher wages he can consume as much as before, while leisure becomes more costly to forgo. In the

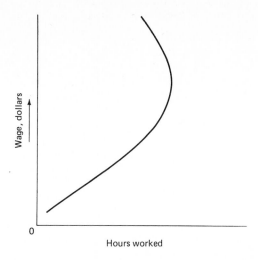

Figure 7-4 The backward-bending labor supply curve.

aggregate, such behavior is depicted by the "backward-bending" supply curve of Figure 7-4. Observe further that, in the short term, male heads of households might not adjust their work patterns at all in response to higher wages because of cultural expectation that they work full time. Again, the competitive model of labor markets seems consistent with any of these scenarios, and thus only empirical evidence can determine which of several plausible alternatives best describes the actual behavior of the labor supply.

The Supply of Labor to the Firm

How will a given labor force distribute itself among firms offering employment? The answer of the competitive model is an uncomplicated one. Workers' preferences for jobs depend on comparative wage rates when all other conditions of employment are similiar. Assuming this condition of *ceteris paribus,* higher wage rates at one firm will attract workers from another firm paying lower rates. The further assumptions of competitive theory that workers are perfectly mobile and that information about job vacancies and wage rates is fully available are central to the predicted reshuffling of workers among jobs so that they always move to the highest-paying positions for which they are suited.

To the individual firm in a competitive market, the supply curve of labor is horizontal, as shown in Figure 7-5. This perfectly elastic labor supply reflects the competitive firm's position as a "price taker" in the marketplace for factors of production. The firm pays the prevailing market rate for labor and can hire all that it chooses at this rate. It need not pay more than the market rate to attract a labor supply, but it cannot pay less, for then it would attract no workers. The firm's operations are presumed to be sufficiently small so that any expansion or contraction in the size of its work force has no effect on the aggregate labor supply or on the competitively determined market wage rate for labor.

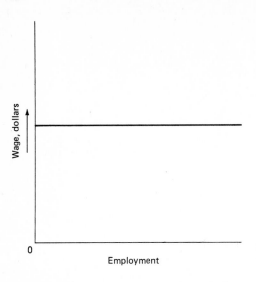

Figure 7-5 Supply curve of the firm under perfect competition

It is not difficult to criticize or identify the limitations of the competitive model in terms of labor supply to the individual firm. Except in rare instances, workers are not perfectly mobile, they usually do not possess full information about job vacancies and wage rates, and they are concerned with, and responsive to, nonwage aspects of employment. Also, if some firms operate in labor markets where they must take factor prices as given, other firms face labor markets in which they have considerable discretion in determining what wage rates they will pay for labor. Because the latter firms exercise varying degrees of power in the market, they face something other than a perfectly elastic supply curve of labor. Remember, though, that competitive-labor-market theory adopts simplifying assumptions in order to have testable hypotheses. Without such assumptions, prediction and validation would be impossible, and every decision to move or not move to a higher-paying job would have to be explained after the fact. For now, we simply note that a range of pay rates (for the same type or grade of labor) may exist in the market without necessarily affecting the supply of labor to a given firm.

Equilibrium in the Labor Market

Analysis based on competitive-labor-market theory assumes a market within which employees compete directly for jobs and in which employers bid against one another for labor services. The assumptions of maximizing behavior, ready substitutability of labor units, the ready mobility of factors, and the availability of information about jobs, factors, and wages lead to a single integrated supply schedule in which more labor will be forthcoming only at higher rates and to a single integrated demand schedule in which more labor will be purchased only at falling rates. In the short run, these two schedules intersect at a single point, which is the equilibrium rate, as shown by Q in Figure 7-6a. In each firm, production will take place to the point where MVP is equal to the market-deter-

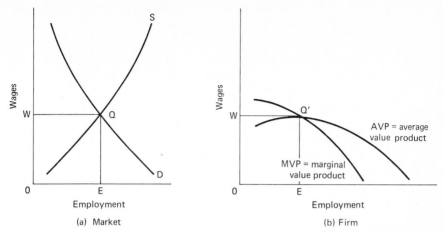

Figure 7-6 Equilibrium in the labor market: (*a*) the market, (*b*) the firm.

mined wage rate, indicated by Q' in Figure 7-6*b*. In these diagrams we observe competitive clearing of the labor market.

To establish long-run equilibrium in the labor market, additional assumptions about population, growth of the labor force, and both fixed and variable factor imputs to production would have to be made. Once that is done, the intersection of the demand and supply curves again determines the equilibrium price (wage) and quantity (employment) of labor. At the equilibrium price. firms will hire labor up to the point where its MVP in *all* uses equals its price. Further, for general equilibrium to exist in the long run, the marginal value products of the various factors of production must be equal in all industries where they are employed, and they must be equal to the common factor price. Wherever the factor price is less than MVP, producers will seek additional units of that factor, bidding for it until its price is equal to MVP. In competitive theory, this is as true in the market for labor as it is in the markets for capital and raw materials.

Competitive Theory and Empirical Wage Patterns

Because competitive theory presumes a perfectly mobile, completely interchangeable labor force undifferentiated by skill, economists often speak of one wage rate and of one level of employment and equilibrium conditions in the labor market. But, in reality, the labor force is spread among a variety of occupations, industries, and jobs, and it is compensated at widely different wage rates. Competitive theory is consistent with some of these empirical facts of life, but it is less so or even inconsistent with others.

For example, that workers in different occupations—electricians, machinists, nurses, lawyers, clerk-typists, salespersons—should be differentially compensated is consistent with competitive-labor-market theory when the classical model is applied to the particular labor markets for each of these occupations. Adam Smith suggested over 200 years ago that wage differentials between workers would arise out of differences in the "inconstancy" and "disagreeableness" of employment, the "trust to be reposed" in the worker, the "costs of learning" the occupation, and the "probability of success" in the occupation.[3] In the terminology of competitive-labor-market theory, the factors proposed by Smith to account for occupational wage differentials reflect the different marginal products of workers in these occupations. Thus, lawyers are expected to earn more than machinists, and professional workers are expected to earn more than laborers. Empirically, we find that, in 1975, professional, technical, and kindred workers in the United States had median earnings of about $14,300 and that nonfarm laborers had median earnings of about $4000, with the earnings of most other major occupational groups generally falling between these extremes of the distribution.[4]

Within specific occupations, however, there also are substantial wage differentials, and competitive theory is less satisfactory in explaining these phenomena. Consider the 1977 data on earnings in Table 7-2 for the nine occupations common to the six cities listed there. In the four white-collar jobs, weekly earnings varied widely across cities. There were differentials as large as $55 for payroll clerks, $61 for stenographers, $91 for computer systems analysts, and $95 for registered industrial nurses. In the blue-collar occupations, maximum differentials in hourly earnings across the cities totaled $1.63 for forklift operators, $1.83 for stationary engineers, $1.94 for janitors, $2.12 for truck drivers, and $2.21 for maintenance electricians. Assuming a standard 40-hour workweek, a truck driver earned well over $15,000 in 1977 if employed in Newark, New Jersey, but only $11,000 if working in Hartford, Connecticut. In the same year, a registered industrial nurse earned over $16,000 if employed in Detroit, Michigan, but less than $12,000 if working in York, Pennsylvania.

The existence of such intraoccupational wage differentials may seem inconsistent with competitive theory, which apparently postulates a single pay rate for workers of the same skill (in the same occupation). However, two additional points need to be considered. First, because labor markets are dynamic, with demand and supply constantly shifting, a condition of equilibrium is hardly ever reached. Thus, the key question becomes, "Are intraoccupational wage differentials diminishing over time?" A positive response to this question would be consistent with the predictions of competitive theory, while stable or widening differentials would be inconsistent with the theory. Second, we noted previously that labor markets have geographic properties and therefore may be at or near equilibrium for the occupations and cities listed in Table 7-2. More specifically, stenographers in Atlanta, Georgia, probably do not compete for jobs with stenographers in Newark, New Jersey; truck drivers in Hartford, Connecticut, probably do not compete with truck drivers in Milwaukee, Wisconsin; and janitors in Detroit, Michigan, probably do not compete with janitors in York, Pennsylvania. In light of this, the existence of intraoccupational wage differentials across cities by no means renders competitive theory inapplicable to labor market analysis.

Table 7-2 Earnings in Selected Occupations and Areas, 1977

Occupation	Atlanta, Ga.	Detroit, Mich.	Hartford, Conn.	Milwaukee, Wis.	Newark, N.J.	York, Pa.
			Straight-time weekly earnings			
Stenographers	$200.50	$213.50	$179.00	$169.50	$183.50	$152.50
Payroll clerks	$181.00	$204.50	$172.00	$187.00	$174.50	$149.50
Computer systems analysts	$354.50	$399.50	$308.50	$345.00	$375.00	$306.50
Registered industrial nurses	$264.50	$311.00	$230.50	$245.50	$246.50	$226.00
			Straight-time hourly earnings			
Maintenance electricians	$7.66	$8.60	$6.39	$8.27	$7.06	$6.67
Stationary engineers	$7.06	$8.24	$6.41	$7.23	$7.86	$7.20
Truck drivers	$6.11	$7.14	$5.29	$7.00	$7.41	$6.27
Forklift operators	$5.31	$6.84	$5.21	$6.46	$5.81	$5.24
Janitors	$3.01	$4.95	$3.28	$3.89	$3.61	$3.78

Source: Adapted from U.S. Bureau of Labor Statistics, Occupational Earnings and Wage Trends in Metropolitan Areas, 1977, Summary 77–11. 1978, passim.

More germane to this issue, then, are intraoccupational data on wages for a specific area of the labor market. Such data are presented in Table 7-3 for New York City, ranging across the nine occupations previously considered. In all instances, large intraoccupational wage differentials existed in 1977. For both blue- and white-collar jobs in New York City on this list, the top pay (in the full range of rates) was more than double the lowest pay. In the cases of truck drivers, forklift operators, and janitors, the top rates were almost three times as large as the bottom rates. And, while relatively few workers in any of these occupations were employed in jobs that paid the bottom or top rates of the ranges, those who received pay in the middle ranges nevertheless experienced considerable variation in wages. Again, it is necessary to analyze these intraoccupational wage differentials over time to see whether they move in the direction proposed by competitive theory, but their existence and magnitude well illustrate that labor markets do not yield a single, equilibrium rate even for "homogeneous" labor.

Finally, lest it be thought that the data on wage differentials presented above are peculiar to blue-collar and lower-level white-collar jobs, and thus that competitive-labor-market theory is most applicable to other occupations, consider the evidence presented in Table 7-4 for professional and administrative positions. Geographically, labor markets for professional and administrative personnel are relatively broad; the data shown here are for workers in such occupations who were employed anywhere in New York State in 1977. Additionally, Table 7-4 reports data for the entry-level job in each occupational category; because these jobs lead to higher-ranking positions within job ladders, they should be characterized by the smallest wage differentials among the positions making up those hierarchies. Once more, however, substantial differentials

Table 7-3 Distribution of Earnings in Selected Occupations in New York City, 1977

	Straight-time weekly earnings		
Occupation	**Median**	**Middle range**	**Full range**
Stenographers	$165	$148–$185	$110–$320
Payroll clerks	$189	$157–$231	$130–$360
Computer systems analysts	$430	$384–$480	$260–$640
Registered industrial nurses	$254	$224–$284	$170–$440

	Straight-time hourly earnings		
Occupation	**Median**	**Middle range**	**Full range**
Maintenance electricians	$7.00	$587–809	$4.40–$9.60
Stationary engineers	$7.77	$6.91–$8.48	$4.20–$9.60
Truck drivers	$7.11	$6.03–$7.78	$3.20–$8.60
Forklift operators	$6.42	$5.11–$6.51	$3.00–$7.80
Janitors	$5.56	$5.18–$5.56	$2.30–$7.80

Source: Adapted from U. S. Bureau of Labor Statistics, Middle Atlantic Regional Office, *Wages in New York City, May 1977,* Regional Report 56, March 1978, passim.

**Table 7-4   Earnings in Selected
Occupations in New York State, 1977**

Straight-time monthly salaries		
Occupation	Median	Middle range
Accountant I	$962	$869–$1000
Attorney I	$1333	$1291–$1546
Buyer II	$1250	$1125–$1463
Job analyst II	$1136	$992–$1377
Chemist I	$1086	$1000–$1269
Engineer I	$1225	$1136–$1374

Source: Adapted from U.S. Bureau of Labor Statistics,
*National Survey of Professional, Administrative, Technical and
Clerical Pay, March 1977,* Bulletin 1980, 1978, passim.

are observable, the middle range yielding variations of $131 per month for accountants, $385 for chemists, and more than $200 for five of the six occupations. This evidence further illustrates that labor markets do not behave in the pure form envisioned by competitive theory, whereby a single rate is paid for a single type of labor.

The Human Capital Approach to Labor Supply

Not only are labor markets in the real world diverse in terms of wage rates, occupations, and sectors of employment, but also the labor supply to those markets is made up of diverse groups: men and women, blacks and whites, and persons with different educational attainment and work experience. The relationships between individual workers' characteristics and their success in the labor market are of central interest to labor economists, many of whom believe that competitive theory, by assuming away diversity, is not well suited to understanding these relationships. However, one group of economists argues strongly that the conventional demand-supply framework can indeed be applied to labor market analysis, once allowance is made for the differences in skills possessed by members of the work force. Reasoning from this position, such economists have pursued research into the demand for, and the supply to workers of, labor skill itself, or, if you will, the acquisition of skills. This has become known as the "human capital approach" to labor supply, the term reflecting the underlying view that individuals invest in themselves by incurring costs to develop marketable skills, pursuing such investments to the point where marginal cost (MC) equals marginal revenue (MR).[5]

Because proponents of the human capital approach proceed on the assumption that employers do indeed view labor as a factor of production, as a commodity, the approach has been severely criticized by other economists, especially those who believe that labor markets are highly segmented and contain many discontinuities.[6] More will be said shortly about these alternative views, but note that some critics of the human capital approach focus primarily on its value judgments rather than on its empirical usefulness in explaining distributions of earnings and employment in the labor market. To be sure, some proponents of the human capital approach have brought such criticism on themselves by denying that the approach contains any normative dimensions.[7] Nevertheless, this theory, like others, should be judged on its ability to explain phenomena in the real world, even as its underlying value premises receive close scrutiny.

In brief, the human capital approach views expenditures on acquiring or improving skills as an investment—an investment in human beings. The term "investment" purposely conveys a long-term orientation because the costs of, and especially the benefits to be derived from, such investments typically are incurred and enjoyed, respectively, over a period of years. From this perspective, expenditures on education, training, relocating, and even health are regarded as investments, for they serve to enhance future benefits to individuals by making them more productive. Thus, rather than representing short-term outlays and unrelated events, the costs of more education, of on-the-job and institutional training, and of health care are systematically related to an individual's future earnings, which will be larger than they would have been had such expenditures not been made. This is the essence of the investment concept central to the human capital approach.

To some, this notion of individual decision making may seem farfetched. After all, aren't some expenditures on education, training, and health undertaken to maximize personal satisfaction, not monetary return? An advocate of the human capital approach might respond that indeed they are but that they also increase future earning power and therefore have an undeniable investment component. Do individuals and families sit down and rationally debate the money returns to investments in different educational curricula, different training programs, or different forms of health care? Do they systematically consider the comparative monetary values of a son's or daughter's going to college instead of entering the labor market after graduating from high school? Our hypothetical advocate of the human capital approach might respond negatively to these questions but then go on to point out that such individual and family decisions implicitly compare alternative choices and opportunities and that the pursuit of any of them has monetary consequences which can be examined through an analysis of return over cost. And what of the notion that so many (perhaps all) personal decisions are reduced solely to their monetary motives and outcomes? The advocate of the human capital approach most likely would have little to say about motives, but would remind us that a person's success in the labor market is widely (if not exclusively) judged by his or her earning power and that such judgments are therefore not the sole province of the human capital approach.

What are the costs and benefits that go into the formation of human capital? The costs consist of both direct and indirect expenditures. Direct costs are actual dollar outlays such as those for tuition, books, and supplies. The indirect costs consist of earnings forgone by an individual while he or she is investing in human capital. Because such investments typically occur over a long period and require full-time commitment, as in the case of a college education, an individual usually (though not always) is precluded from simultaneously engaging in other activity such as paid employment. The earnings that would have been received by an individual had he or she chosen not to undertake formal schooling are a measure of the indirect costs of investment in human capital. In the case of schooling, such forgone earnings have been estimated to account for roughly two-thirds of the indirect costs of investing in human capital.[8] Where on-the-job training is offered, the firm almost always provides it to employees without charge, but a worker nevertheless pays for it by accepting a lower rate of pay than could have been obtained elsewhere, with the intent of maximizing the future return to training.

These examples lead us to consider the benefits of investments in human capital, which also are of two types. The first redounds to the individual and consists of a higher rate of pay or salary than would have been received without the schooling, training, or other investment activity. The second type accrues to the firm which has invested in employees. In this case, the benefits are the difference between the worker's contribution (marginal value product) to the firm and the wage paid to the worker. If a firm does not pass on to workers in the form of higher wages the full value of increased productivity resulting from training programs, for example, the firm will benefit from conducting such programs.

If decisions to invest in human capital required only a comparative listing of the costs and benefits described above to see which is larger, our discussion might end here. But the value of money, of costs and benefits, varies over time. The money market establishes a price, the interest rate, which tells us the value of future dollars in relation to current dollars. At an interest rate of 5 percent, $1 placed in a bank is worth $1 today but $1.05 after a year. If a person borrows $1 today at this interest rate, he or she will owe $1.05 a year hence. The value today of such future costs and revenues is known as "present discounted value" or simply "present value." Because the value of each cost and revenue varies depending upon when it occurs in the future, a mechanism is required to compare them today; the calculation of present value serves that purpose.

For an investment to be undertaken, it must have a positive present value. No one wants to invest when the sum of future costs exceeds the sum of future benefits, for that is a losing proposition. The present value of costs and benefits depends upon the interest rate. The higher the interest rate, the lower the values of costs and benefits that will occur in the future, since their values can be matched by putting aside a small amount of money today. In the case of investments in human capital, costs usually are incurred early on, while benefits subsequently flow in a longer stream to the recipient. Thus, at higher interest rates, the value of returns on investments declines relative to costs, and so must present value. In the extreme case, the interest rate is very high, and the present value of future returns is or approaches zero. In fact, the interest rate which equates the costs and returns of an investment is known as the "internal rate of return," and it yields a simple rule to use in making such investment decisions: invest or continue to invest in human capital until the internal rate of return equals the market rate of interest. Through this formal analysis, then, we see that the market for human capital (workers' skills) can be examined using the neoclassical demand-supply framework, which generates an optimal combination of price and quantity for each individual investor.

Before considering some of the empirical evidence from studies of human capital, a brief discussion of the implications of this approach for on-the-job training is in order. Decisions to invest in schooling are those to which the human capital approach has been most frequently applied, especially in the expansionary period 1961–1969, when the idea of increasing the nation's stock of human capital was used to support increased public expenditures on higher education. But the merits of this approach to explaining on-the-job training in the labor market should not be overlooked.

Consider two types of training: general and specific.[9] General training raises the value of a worker to all employers, while specific training raises the value of a worker only to the employer who provides it. Workers who complete general training may be bid away by other employers, and so no single firm has an incentive to provide such training. If the firm could extract a promise from a worker to remain in its employ, it could obtain a return on its investment and would be willing to provide this type of training. Since that is not feasible, employers seldom provide general training *unless the employees themselves pay for it*. And that, following the human capital approach, is what occurs. Figure 7-7a illustrates this circumstance.

An untrained worker receives a wage W equivalent to his or her limited productivity throughout working life. The trained worker, however, initially receives a wage W_1, which is lower than his or her productivity prior to the completion of training, but he or she subsequently receives a wage W_2, which is equivalent to productivity after training. Thus the worker pays for training, ac-

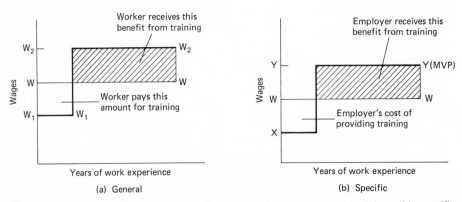

Figure 7-7 Costs and benefits of on-the-job training: (a) general training, (b) specific training.

cepting wage W_1 instead of W in return for future benefits, the difference between W_2 and W. A worker can decide whether to participate in a program of general training by determining the net present value of the investment in on-the-job training, exactly as is done in the case of decisions about schooling. Apprenticeship programs in the construction industry and management internships in medium-sized and large firms provide two good examples of general training which accord with the human capital approach.

Where specific training takes place, as shown in Figure 7-7b, the worker neither pays the costs nor receives the benefits of this investment. He or she is paid a wage W that is the same as that received by other untrained workers. But during training, this wage is above the worker's productivity, represented by X, because some working time is given over to participation in the program. This amount, the difference between W and X during the training period, is the cost to the employer of providing specific training. But the benefits to that same employer are represented by the difference between W, the wage which continues to be paid to the worker, and the increased marginal value product (MVP) of the employee, represented by Y, over the employee's remaining working life following the completion of training. The employer is "assured" this return because specific training does not raise the worker's value to other employers, who might then be disposed to bid the worker away from the firm which had already provided the training. An example of such training would be that designed to teach employees how to operate a machine patented and used only by one employer.

This human capital approach to on-the-job training seems consistent with a variety of experiences in the labor market in the real world. For example, quits should be lowest among specifically trained workers, who are more valuable to a present employer than to alternative employers. Empirical evidence tends to support this prediction.[10] So, too, do more educated and more experienced members of the labor sector exhibit more stable employment patterns—smaller fluctuations of unemployment—than less well educated and less experienced members. The former are more likely to have received specific training than the latter. Further, the participation of employees in various types of on-the-job training programs which carry temporary pay rates below initial productivity levels supports the hypothesis that it is they, not the employer, who pay the costs and receive the benefits of general training.

What of the more general explanatory power of the human capital approach? This depends upon what one wishes to explain. Numerous studies have found that workers' earnings can be reasonably well predicted on the basis of a combination of educational attainments (quantity of schooling) and experience in the labor market, the latter standing as a proxy for the effects of on-the-job training. But is not age an important determinant of earnings, irrespective of how much work experience—training—one has accumulated? Yes, but studies which hold age constant find earnings to be more closely related to experience (the human capital variable) than to age.[11]

Where education is concerned, its correlation with earnings is positive and often statistically signficant, but it is not very strong. Put differently, when workers' levels of schooling are held constant, substantial variation in earnings is still observed. Such a finding does not surprise supporters of the human capital approach, who contend that the correlation between education and earnings will increase if work experience (the training proxy) also is controlled. This contention tends to be borne out by empirical studies of workers' earnings profiles over the life cycle.[12]

In sum, the human capital framework of labor market analysis has considerable strengths. It is a well-developed, internally consistent, and logical conceptualization, and it follows closely upon the fundamental principles of neoclassical economics. It is supported—though not fully, to be sure—by empirical research and by casual observations, such as that earnings increase with work experience. Yet this approach has numerous limitations, not the least of which is its reliance on the simplifying assumptions of competitive theory, which tend to downplay the inequality of opportunities that often confronts individuals when they enter the labor market or seek to augment their "human capital." It is precisely such inequality that is the central focus of theories of a segmented labor market, which we explore next.

SEGMENTED-LABOR-MARKET THEORIES

Segmented-labor-market theories differ fundamentally from both classical theory and human capital theory in their focus on the fragmentations, rigidities, and discontinuities observed in labor markets in the real world. Such segmentation seems to run counter to notions of competitive-labor-market theory concerning mobility of workers, information about jobs, and continuous demand and supply schedules that generate optimum combinations of prices and quantities (wages and employment) of the labor factor of production. In viewing labor markets as highly structured and in many ways highly organized rather than as fluid and unorganized, this approach follows the rich historical tradition of institutional economists, who have always occupied a "counterculture" position relative to that of advocates of the dominant neoclassical school of thought.[13]

The leading theory of this type is that of the dual labor market, which distinguishes between primary and secondary labor markets.[14] Jobs in the former feature stable employment, relatively high wages, opportunities for training and advancement, due process in the handling of disputes arising at the workplace, and a high degree of unionization. A production job in a large automobile or steel company and an engineering job with an aerospace firm are examples of opportunities in a primary labor market. But if workers who enter a primary labor market obtain "good" positions, those who enter secondary labor markets find "bad" jobs, which feature intermittent employment, relatively low wages, few opportunities for training and promotion, little due process in settling disputes, and little or no union representation. Employment as a busboy in a restaurant and a job as a field hand on a farm are examples of positions in the secondary labor market.

An important implication of the dual-market theory is that primary and secondary labor markets impose different behavioral requirements on workers or attract different types of workers. Those who are employed in a primary labor market exhibit stable work patterns, are highly motivated and committed, show up for work regularly and on time, participate willingly in training programs, and make use of negotiated grievance procedures in attempting to settle disputes. In contrast, jobs in a secondary labor market make relatively few demands on workers, and the climate is such that tardiness and absenteeism are customary, turnover is high, petty thievery is more or less condoned as a concomitant of low pay, workers are not expected to develop commitment to a career or attachment to an occupation, and reactions to problems arising at the workplace take the form of insubordination, quits, and violence. Indeed, the secondary labor market can be extended to include the "underground" or "irregular" economy, featuring such illegal sources of income as gambling, prostitution, and sale of drugs.[15]

Perhaps the key aspect of the dual-market theory is that workers do not move between the primary and secondary labor markets. Those who initially are employed in jobs in a primary labor market continue to find such positions, and over the course of their employment they develop a strong orientation and commitment toward steady work as a central goal in life. This experience is totally at odds with that of workers who are employed—or, more accurately, trapped—in jobs in a secondary labor market; for them, the irregularity of employment, poor working conditions, and low wages combine to inculcate a value orientation in which steady work plays little or no role. Those who hold such jobs thus are a class apart from jobholders in the primary labor market, and so the two factions are noncompeting groups in the labor market. Clearly, this is a vastly different conceptualization of the labor market from the one offered in competitive theory.

The dual-market theory also distinguishes between external and internal labor markets.[16] The external market consists of the familiar process by which a firm hires a new employee who applies for a job. However, only some positions are filled in this way. In other instances, job vacancies are filled through internal sources by transferring or promoting employees already on the payroll. To meet staffing requirements by promoting from within the internal market, the employer often provides specific training to employees. But observe that for such upward internal job movement to occur, employment must be relatively steady, and workers must be committed to work as a central value in life. The characteristics of jobs in a primary labor market in fact suggest that only in this portion of the labor market are structured and specific training programs —investments in human capital—to be found. Employers who offer jobs in a secondary labor market have little incentive to invest in on-the-job training, and workers in these jobs have few expectations that such training will be provided. Consequently, many "transactions" in the labor market occur within internal markets, but such vertical structuring of markets is present solely in primary labor markets. Secondary labor markets feature only external transactions between buyers and sellers of labor, and the notion of a functioning internal market has little or no validity in this context.

The distinction between internal and external labor markets also contains implications for wage determination. Whereas competitive theory pictures all jobs and all workers arrayed in the labor market, with the interactions between them establishing wage rates and levels of employment, the dual-market theory envisions only some jobs available for bidding by workers outside the firm. Such jobs are ports of entry into employing organizations, providing points of access to other positions within the job ladders and occupational structures of the internal market. For non-entry-level positions, then, wages are set internally. Particular attention is paid to an equitable structure of pay rates among different jobs. Internally established pay rates for given jobs bear some relationship to market rates for the same jobs, but the relationship may be a loose one. In any case, the dynamics of internal labor markets are such that only for some jobs—the entry-level jobs, for the most part—are pay levels actually set by the external labor market.

More on Segmented-Labor-Market Theories

In positing the dichotomy of the primary labor market and the secondary labor market, the dual-market theory derives in part from Marxian analysis, which is based on class distinctions: mobility between these two segments of the labor market does not occur, and the income gap between them widens as workers in the primary labor market progress up career and pay ladders, while those in the secondary labor market move intermittently between entry-level jobs—when they can find them. To some, however, this dichotomy is an oversimplification, for significant differences exist among jobs *within* each of these segments of the labor market.

Responding to such criticisms, one dual-market theorist has identified upper and lower job tiers within the primary labor market, noting that this is "as important as the distinction between the primary and secondary sectors."[17] He goes on to say:

> The upper tier of the primary sector is composed of professional and managerial jobs. Such jobs tend to be distinguished from those in the lower tier by the higher pay and status, and the greater promotion opportunities which they afford. They also are distinguished by the mobility and turnover patterns, which tend to more closely resemble those of the secondary sector except, in contrast to the patterns of that sector, mobility and turnover tend to be associated with advancement. . . . Formal education in the upper tier seems to be an essential requisite for employment, and educational requirements . . . tend to be absolute barriers to entry. Finally, upper tier work seems to offer much greater variety and room for individual creativity and initiative, and greater economic security.[18]

The upper and lower tiers of the primary market, together with the secondary market, form a threefold segmentation of the labor market which seems an improvement over the simple dichotomy of the dual-market theory. Yet, one might inquire, would further segmentation eventually lead to an array of jobs in the labor market not very different from the continuous demand schedule of competitive theory? Perhaps, but as is true of human capital theory, the more important issue concerns the explanatory power of segmented-labor-market theories. On this point, a recent test of the refined (that is, three-segment) theory provided some instructive results.

Studying a sample of black and white male heads of households, Osterman found that differences in the annual earnings of workers in the secondary labor market depended almost solely on the amount of time worked.[19] In contrast, for workers in both the lower and the upper tiers of the primary labor market, earnings were significantly related to age and education as well as to hours worked. For workers in the lower tier, but not for those in the upper tier, race was strongly related to earnings, with whites receiving more than blacks when other important variables were controlled. Thus, "secondary employers do not distinguish among workers; they all appear equally unskilled and unstable."[20] It is the upper tier of the primary labor market which most closely conforms to the human capital model and where racial discrimination apparently loses its force. Such discrimination persists in the lower tier of the primary labor market, and the human capital model is a less useful predictor of earnings there than in the upper tier. This study therefore argues for the empirical validity of the refined dual-market theory, though that conclusion must be cautiously regarded since 90 percent of the sample was in the lower tier of the primary market and only 5 percent was in the upper tier and 5 percent in the secondary labor market.

Another "radical" group of theorists believe that it is "impossible to develop a simple, historically permanent, and universally determinant theory about economy and society."[21] They identify class and class conflict as the major forces at work in the labor market. Class is defined in terms of the relations of individuals to the process of production and to one another. People who work under similiar conditions, share a strong sense of identification, and receive roughly the same income form a class even if they do not profess a strong consciousness of this. Those who own or manage processes of production and are in roughly comparable income brackets form another class. Clearly, much more than the dual-market theorists, the radical theorists proceed from a Marxian base. In this view, capitalists accumulate wealth, exploit labor, and keep workers disunited so that they will not rebel against the economic system, all with the purpose of maintaining their privileged position over time. The time dimension means that capitalists must be able to transfer their wealth to later generations and to limit mobility into the ownership group; in other words, the class structure must be perpetuated.

Such a view of economic relationships in society leads to the judgment that formal education and on-the-job training are devices controlled by capitalists and used by them to maintain the working class in a subordinate position.[22] Public schools are seen by the radical theorists as institutions which socialize the young to accept authoritarian organizational structures, to be obedient and punctual, and to follow commands unquestioningly—precisely those elements of hierarchy and routinization which characterize the workplace. Also cultivated by the public schools is the notion of merit as the basis of advancement, but the radical theorists believe that the "mirage of merit" serves merely to legitimize the perpetuation of class differences, with the sons and daughters of the rich systematically exposed to better-endowed, more innovative, and less structured educational settings than the offspring of the poor and the middle class. Teaching systems reinforce the dichotomy of advantage, and so the educational establishment not only contributes to class divisions in the society but also "promotes the heritability of socioeconomic class."[23]

On-the-job training, too, is regarded by the radical theorists as a device to prevent workers from recognizing their common interests. More broadly, job ladders, salary structures, training programs, and formal job progression plans are seen as creating artificial distinctions between groups of workers, such as that between blue- and white-collar workers, which serve to prevent any discontent that might otherwise arise. According to the radical theorists, fractionalization of work and piece-rate systems of payment in industry also tend to smother workers' discontent and to reduce whatever power and control strategically placed production workers might be able to exercise. What the dual-market theorists identify as structural dimensions of internal markets and the primary labor market the radical theorists view as part of the machinery to prevent the working class from competing with the owner-capitalist class for power, wealth, and status in society. The radical theorists likewise consider the forms of technology to be dictated principally by the capitalists' desire to maintain their class in power. The demand for skills, then, evolves not from evolutionary forces in a decentralized market economy but, instead, from conscious control by the dominant producer class in society.

What is one to make of this argument? To begin with, it is virtually irrefutable, for it does not take the form of testable propositions. It is one thing to contend that technological change and patterns of industrial organization foster divisiveness in the working class and quite another to show that "keeping the masses in their place" was the principal objective of economic development rather than a by-product. Further, the imperatives of establishing hierarchies and routinization when organizing and completing large-scale productive tasks are hardly peculiar to capitalist societies; they also characterize the planned economies of socialist and communist societies. Indeed, such characteristics of work and the labor market emerge in the course of industrialization, whatever the particular "ism" that is used to label an economy and a society. Interestingly, the radical theorists also tend to overlook the decentralization of decision making which behavioral scientists have shown takes place in organizations that operate in service-producing and continuous-process industries.[24] Finally, the radical theorists tend to underestimate and homogenize the working class (and the "capitalist" class), judging them to be more malleable and gullible than their actual behavior and opinions suggest.

Yet the radical theorists have called attention to some fundamental problems of industrialized society. Chief among these is the persistence of inequality, which, if it has not generated in the United States two major classes that are violently antagonistic to each other, nevertheless has defied numerous public policies aimed at its eradication. Related to this inequality, of course, is the disparity in the educational, employment, and training opportunities available to various groups within our society.

The presence of racial discrimination in the labor market is another issue about which the radical theorists have helped spark contemporary debate, despite their own less than fully satisfactory explanations of this phenomenon. So too is the use by employers of such credentials as degrees, diplomas, and certificates to "screen" potential employees, irrespective of the actual relationships of formal qualifications to performance on the job, a subject which the radical theorists have pushed into the public eye.[25] Finally, in addressing the problem of alienation of workers from their jobs, the radical theorists have again raised public consciousness about an important issue, even if, like some behavioral scientists and popular writers, they have exaggerated the incidence of discontent with work or have failed to systematically confront evidence about it. The issues of discrimination based on race and sex in the labor market, income inequality, and meritocracy will be discussed in Chapters 8 and 9.

One result of the challenge of segmented-labor-market theorists to orthodox theory has been to spur champions of neoclassical analysis to consider more concretely the policy implications and other practical applications of their predictive models. This is particularly crucial for modern economic analysis, whether applied to labor markets or to other spheres, which runs the danger of becoming "terribly inbred and out-of-touch."[26] If the unorthodox theorists, like their institutional predecessors, serve to make neoclassical theory less sterile, they will have performed an important service in helping to improve our understanding of labor markets, an area in which no one theory or school of economics can claim a monopoly of explanatory power.

PART TWO: Wage Determination

PROCESSES OF WAGE DETERMINATION

We have seen that competitive-labor-market theory presumes an absence of structure in the labor market, whereas segmented-labor-market theories define structure not only as central to the labor market but also as an immutable characteristic of it. However, in examining processes of wage determination, it may be more useful to think about the degree of organization in labor markets and the extent to which decisions about wages are made "collectively" rather than individually. The most important collective force affecting such decisions is, of course, the labor union.

The economic approach to wage determination under unionism emphasizes the labor organization's desire to maximize its objective, which is analogous to the business firm's desire to maximize its profits. But what is the union's objective? What is its maximizing function? One possible answer is the wage rate.[27] A union might attempt to secure the highest possible wage rates for its members, not just in a single negotiation, but over several bargaining rounds, In that case, however, an employer would reduce his or her employment of increasingly costly labor, the amount of the reduction depending upon the shape of the demand curve, and union membership would decline. Clearly, the union cannot indefinitely pursue the single-minded goal of maximization of wages if it is to be a viable organization. The logical outcome of a strategy which says "maximize the wage rate" is one worker—one union member—employed at an astronomical rate of pay.

Alternatively, the labor organization might attempt to maximize the "total wage bill" of its constituents and, hence, its own revenues secured through dues payments. To achieve this end, the union could negotiate large wage increases with employers who have highly inelastic demand curves for labor, the increased revenue to the workers who remained employed more than offsetting the losses of revenues incurred by laid-off workers. But the labor organization would have to accept lower wages from firms facing relatively elastic demand curves if total revenues from members are to be increased. Apart from the knowledge of different demand elasticities which this strategy presumes on the part of union leaders, their agreement to wage cuts may be politically unacceptable. This strategy also is at odds with organized labor's fundamental goal of "taking labor out of competition." Thus, "maximizing the wage bill" seems as unlikely a characterization of a union's bargaining behavior as "maximizing the wage rate."

But the criticism applies only if these strategies for maximization are taken separately. If joined, they begin to suggest the multiple objectives and hint at the contending values and interests with which labor organizations must deal. Figure 7-8 depicts the trade-off between wage rates, scaled on the vertical axis, and employment (union membership), shown on the horizontal axis, which presents itself to unions in formulating and carrying out their bargaining goals. The wage rate is meant to encompass those aspects of compensation and of nonmonetary items which typically enter into any employment situation. Similarly, the employment-membership axis is meant to reflect the multiple interests, values, and points of view that operate within any labor organization.

In this model, which heavily emphasizes the economics of collective bargaining, each union selects for itself the particular combination of wages and employment that seems to best fit its own circumstances. The points of trade-off will differ among labor organizations, and so they should be arrayed all along the curve of Figure 7-8. But relatively few unions will be found at or very near the end points of the curve because few if any of them can pursue one or another narrow objective, in tunnel-vision fashion, to the exclusion of all others.

There is one instance, however, in which a labor union may negotiate higher wages and not endanger the employment of its members. This is the case of bargaining with a monopsonist, or single buyer of labor, as shown in Figure

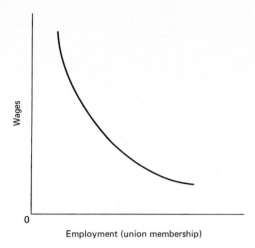

Wages

0

Employment (union membership)

Figure 7-8 A model of union wage policy in collective bargaining.

7-9. Unlike the competitive firm, the monopsonist faces a rising labor-supply curve, shown as AC, which requires that higher wages be paid in order to attract more workers. But the cost of additional employees is, besides the wages of new workers, the increase in pay for those already employed to bring them up to the new "hiring" rate or rates. Therefore, the marginal cost of labor increases by more than the average cost, as also shown in Figure 7-9. If, as is usually the case, the monopsonist is producing a unique or highly differentiated product, marginal revenue similarly will fall by more than average revenue as output increases. Following the rule to use in decisions on maximizing profits, which is to equate marginal cost with marginal revenue, the monopsonist will produce output Z and pay wage W. At this wage rate, labor is being paid less than the value of its marginal product (MR); these are the technical circumstances under which labor is, in fact, being "exploited."

If a labor union enters this situation, organizes the work force, and negotiates a new wage rate W_1, the employer will maintain a work force of the same size since the condition MC=MR still exists. Indeed, if the union-negotiated

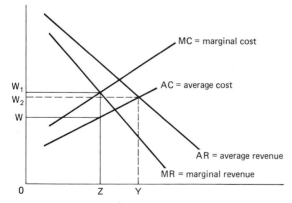

MC = marginal cost

AC = average cost

W_1
W_2
W

AR = average revenue

MR = marginal revenue

0   Z   Y

Figure 7-9 "Exploitation" of labor under conditions of monopsony.

wage rate is the lower W_2, the employer can still expand employment (to amount Y) over the level (Z) associated with the original wage W. In either circumstance, wages of W_1 or W_2, the union has succeeded in capturing some of the monopsonist's excess profits—profits over and above those required to maintain the firm in business.

Once this is done, however, the product market comes into play in determining wage rates for unionized workers, as it does in determining those for nonunionized workers. As a maximizer, the firm will hire and pay only as many workers as can produce a profit for it. Wage increases beyond this point will increase the cost of operations and reduce the firm's output; at a higher wage rate, and thus higher marginal cost, the firm simply cannot afford to produce as much as before. If it tries to recoup the costs of increased wages or other costs by raising the price of its products, the firm will lose customers, and output again will fall, reducing the employment of union members. As long as the demand curve remains about what it has been, the union's power to extract wage gains will be limited by the circumstance that such gains will create unemployment among its members. To be sure, this model allows that unions can sometimes help limit competition in the product market and aid the employer in increasing consumer demand. Examples in the real world include the efforts of the United Steelworkers of America (USA) to limit imports of steel products, the maritime unions' lobbying of Congress for increased subsidies to the shipping industry, the International Brotherhood of Teamsters' support of the trucking industry's attempt to escape restrictive state legislation, and attempts by organizations of workers in apparel manufacturing, printing, and agriculture to promote "buy union label" campaigns.

But just as these and other efforts by unions to manipulate conditions in the market to their advantage should not be overlooked, neither should they be exaggerated. In this and in other models that emphasize the economics of bargaining, it is the firm's state of profitability arising out of its competitive position in the product market which is the primary determinant of its cost of agreeing or not agreeing to the union's terms—the firm's bargaining power. And it is the trade-off of wages and employment, which is again closely related to the firm's position in the product market, that is the principal determinant of the union's cost of agreeing or not agreeing to the employer's terms—its bargaining power. The economic approach emphasizes that product markets, in association with their elasticities of demand, define and shape wage rates in the organized and unorganized sectors alike, thereby providing the underlying explanation of what labor unions are able to do for their members.

POLITICAL INFLUENCES ON WAGE BARGAINING

Another approach to wage bargaining, however, argues that there are important forces at work in union organizations which have an effect on wage determination independent of economic variables and that it would be as erroneous to ignore one set of forces as to ignore the other.[28] This approach—which we may call the "political" approach—is to some extent also sociological, for it begins with the premise that workers judge their pay rates and changes in pay not in isolation but with reference to the treatment accorded other workers with whom they compare themselves and who are similarly situated in terms of occupation, level of skills, industry, or employer. From this perspective, each group of organized workers will compare itself with an appropriate reference group for wage-setting purposes.[29]

Certain comparisons may be so important to a particular group of workers that if the comparisons are adverse, the workers feel compelled to take corrective action. These may be called "coercive comparisons."[30] For example, if the Mitchell Machine Tool Company of Weehawken, organized by the International Association of Machinists and Aerospace Workers (IAM), gives its employees a 50-cent-per-hour wage increase, the employees of the Horton Machine Tool Company, in the same town and organized by the same union, will be extremely restless until their employer grants them a similar pay increase. The same will be true of the employees of the Farley Lock Company, operating in a different product market but in the same town and organized by the same union, and of the employees of the Whitestone Machine Parts Company, located in a neighboring town and operating in a related product market but organized by the United Automobile Workers (UAW). That is, if employees' expectations of what constitutes an equitable pay relationship with another group are violated, they will seek remedial action through their union. Officers of the union will be judged by their success in winning wage gains comparable or superior to those won by other labor organizations. Here is the source of pressure on union negotiators to make good or to run the risk of being voted out of office. This seems to be a distinctly political rather than an economic force on wage determination in unionized labor markets.

But just how coercive can a wage gain won by one union be on another? What if economic circumstances differ between two firms, one of which negotiates a labor agreement that sets a pattern for employees of the other? What if the two firms operate in different industries or different labor markets? The "equitable" wage settlement based on a pattern reached elsewhere may be self-defeating for the union if it is inconsistent with the conditions of the firm's product market and thereby leads to reduced output and employment. Those who remain employed receive a higher income, to be sure, but others lose their jobs and their income and the union loses membership.

While this disemployment effect would appear to dilute the political approach to wage determination under trade unionism, some claim otherwise, saying that "the union is not automatically or mechanically concerned with the 'quantity of labor' sold" and that its leaders are not in a position to consider the disemployment effect of a bargained decision on wages inasmuch as "they do not have the means to predict it."[31] The problem of union leadership is to strike wage bargains which satisfy the various factions within the local union, are acceptable to national union officials, and increase the prestige of the union and its leaders. The same requirements are present in the case of nationally bargained settlements.

How well do these coercive comparisons and the underlying political process from which they derive explain wage determination under collective bargaining? Reasonably well in some instances, it seems, given the similarity between key bargains in the labor market which cannot be explained by economic factors alone. Wage settlements covering production workers in such diverse industries as automobiles, steel, aircraft, meat-packing, and shipbuilding have been shown to be systematically related, increasing over time by very similar amounts.[32] Likewise, key settlements in one portion of a community's construction industry set the pattern for others, and such "wage patterning" is also present in service-producing industries—hospitals, for example. Especially powerful labor leaders like John L. Lewis and James R. Hoffa were able to substantially reduce pay differentials in coal mining and trucking, respectively, despite significant differences among firms in each industry with respect to their cost structures and the markets in which they operated.

But other evidence confirms that, for economic reasons, negotiated wage settlements often deviate from key bargains. In the steel industry, for example, the wage agreement negotiated between the USA and United States Steel— or, more broadly, the multiemployer Steel Companies Coordinating Committee —sets the pattern only for the largest, fully integrated companies. The partially integrated firms follow the key pattern less closely, and the small, nonintegrated firms follow it sporadically, if at all. Moreover, such pattern following tends to be strongest in periods of economic expansion and weaker in stable or recessionary periods, when the costs to many employers of agreeing to the union's terms rise. On a more general note, unions very often use a national wage pattern as a goal, but permit myriad departures to cope with local differences in employers' ability to pay and in conditions in the product and labor markets.[33]

Consequently, it is *both* economic and political forces that shape the behavior of unions in regard to wages under collective bargaining, with the relative weights of the two depending upon time, place, and circumstances. Coercive comparisons of pay clearly make the wage structure different from what it would be if it were shaped by economic forces alone, but just as clearly economic forces set limits to every union's political tendencies. Changes in a firm's market position and processes of production bring about adjustments in wage rates whether workers are unionized or not, and these call for new patterns to be set (and new ones to be followed) when wages are bargained collectively. In every labor-management relationship, the parties refer to one or another wage pattern, but this hardly means that market forces are always overridden by—or dominate—political forces. What is certain is that both economic and political influences are present in a collective bargaining relationship. Devotees of competitive-labor-market theory often seem ignorant of the latter, while champions of segmented-labor-market theories often overlook the former. Students of the labor sector should recognize both as important to wage determination under collective bargaining.[34]

IMPACT OF UNIONS ON RELATIVE WAGES

Recognizing that there are both economic and political dimensions of wage setting in unionized labor markets, let us now consider how much unions have actually raised the wages of their members over the wages of other workers, thereby contributing to the differentials found in every labor market. For many years this issue has intrigued economists, who receive little help in resolving it from the participants in collective bargaining. Union leaders naturally claim that they are fully responsible for increasing their members' wages; employers sometimes support this claim (if decrying its outcome), but at other times they argue that unions can do little or nothing for workers.

The question of a union's impact on wages is a difficult one to resolve empirically. A few examples illustrate the point. That heavily organized automobile workers earn more than partially organized farm workers or unorganized domestic servants says little about the impact of unionism on wages, since there are important differences among these groups with respect to skills and product and labor markets. What is needed is a comparison of the wages of two groups of workers who are identical in every respect other than unionization. But, using the above example, there are few nonunionized automobile workers whose wages we can compare with those of members of the UAW. Alternatively, we might compare wages in a particular labor market for identical jobs across different industries, perhaps the pay of custodians working for companies located in New York City. But if custodians employed by firms in the highly profitable cosmetics industry received higher pay than custodians employed by firms in the less profitable apparel manufacturing industry, would the difference be due to profitability, size of firm, or some other unspecified factors, rather than degree of unionization? These problems might be avoided by comparing changes in the pay of unionized and nonunionized workers over time, but then the demand for (or supply of) labor may have risen over time in one instance and declined in the other, with markedly different consequences for changes in wages. Finally, even if the wages of nonunionized workers rise as rapidly as those of unionized workers over time, how is one to know whether the employers whose workers are not unionized are simply matching bargained wage rates to avoid the unionization of their employees?

These and other complicating factors for many years permitted no more than the safe generalization that the evidence concerning the impact of unions on wages was mixed. However, in 1963, H. G. Lewis provided a more comprehensive and precise set of estimates of the impact of unions on wages than had previously been available.[35] He reviewed all prior studies of the subject, adjusting them in the light of more recent findings and data; combined and added to the studies by means of newer, more sophisticated statistical techniques; and applied these findings to estimate the overall effect of unions on wage differentials at different points in time. The methods Lewis used to resolve the many problems of measurement noted above are too involved to discuss in detail here, but his principal findings are summarized in Table 7-5.

The data in Table 7-5 show the relative effects of unionism on wages to

**Table 7-5 Average Relative Effects of
Unions on Wages in Selected Periods**

Period	Average extent of unionism in the economy[1] (percent)	Average wage effect: union labor relative to nonunion labor[2] (percent)
1923–1929	7–8	15–20
1931–1933	7–8	Greater than 25
1939–1941	18–20	10–20
1945–1949	24–27	0–5
1957–1958	27	10–15

[1] Number of union members as a percent of number of persons employed in the civilian economy.

[2] The percentage difference between union and nonunion wages attributable to unionism alone.

Source: Adapted from H. Gregg Lewis, *Unionism and Relative Wages in the United States,* University of Chicago Press, Chicago, 1963, p. 193, table 50.

have been largest during the Great Depression, smallest in the immediate post-World War II period, and of intermediate size in times of mild expansion (1939-1941) and transition to recession (1957–1958). This seeming paradox of greatest success in unfavorable economic climates was explained by Lewis and later by others as a consequence of "wage rigidity" under collective bargaining. In times of economic contraction, employers cut the wages of unorganized workers, but they meet sharp resistance from unionists, who fear that they may never be able to win back higher rates later on. Hence, the wages of unionized workers are said to be "sticky" in terms of downward adjustments. In a sharp economic expansion, especially if accompanied by inflation, the wages of non-unionized workers are rapidly bid up, but employers of unionized workers, fearing the lasting consequences of a bad contract, strongly resist unusually large wage increases. Additionally, if labor agreements are negotiated before the start of a new expansionary period in which demand subsequently rises, the wages of unionized workers will remain stable, while those of nonunionized workers will increase. Thus it is that the relative effects of unionism on wages are more clearly manifested during periods of economic decline than during periods of economic expansion. This countercyclical effect of unionism on relative wages has been confirmed in subsequent studies.[36]

Several other aspects of Lewis's work merit brief discussion. First, the summary finding that, for the periods studied, American unions had an overall relative effect of increasing wages by between 10 and 15 percent has been confirmed by others, but somewhat larger estimates have been made for later years. Thus, Rees concludes that the average effect of all American unions on the wages of their members, relative to the wages of nonunion workers, has been between 15 and 20 percent; the larger effects reported in the 1960s and 1970s resulted less from an increase in the power of unions than from the availability of new data and the use of more refined methods of measurement.[37] Note, however, that several students who employ these methods warn that the chain of causality may run from wages to unionism rather than the reverse— that is, high wages lead to greater unionization.[38]

Second, Lewis found that the impact of unions on relative wages varies considerably among industries, ranging from increases of over 50 percent in bituminous coal to no increases in apparel manufacturing. Some investigators have sought to discover whether unionists do better in bargaining with employers in concentrated industries (such as automobiles and electronics) than in competitive industries (such as apparel manufacturing and retail food). One student found quite the reverse: unions have larger relative effects on wages in competitive than in concentrated sectors of the economy.[39] However, other researchers have questioned this conclusion, claiming that unionists do indeed enjoy an advantage in bargaining with firms in concentrated industries.[40]

Third, Lewis estimated that unions increased the dispersion of wages (the range from high to low) among industries, though not by much: "Unionism may have made the relative inequality of average wages among industries . . . about 6 to 10 percent higher than it otherwise would have been."[41] A later study, which found that the wage gains of unionized blue-collar workers do not spill over to inflate the salaries of nonproduction workers, supported this conclusion. In other words, contrary to popular belief, the salaries of white-collar workers are not systematically higher in industries where unions have raised the wages of blue-collar workers.[42]

What does all this say about the impact of American unions on wages? One answer is that it depends on where you look, since there are individual instances of very great impact, very small impact, and no impact. On a disaggregated basis, almost any response is possible. Another answer, an aggregate one, is that the impact is smaller than is commonly or popularly thought, a judgment with which most scholars would probably agree. A third answer is that while the impact was relatively modest up to the late 1950s, it may have increased since then, especially during the early 1970s.[43] Unfortunately, the evidence stops short at the very time when spreading recession was having an adverse effect on some of the most highly unionized sectors, such as construction. In addition, such a conclusion is based on evidence about the impact of unions on wages in the private sector alone, whereas the fastest-growing portion of the economy and the labor movement since the 1950s has been the public sector. This last observation suggests the desirability of examining the public sector before reaching an overall judgment about the impact of unions on wages in the American economy. We turn to that task next.

IMPACT OF UNIONS ON WAGES IN THE PUBLIC SECTOR

Many articles dealing with the impact of public employees' unions on wages in the United States have been published since 1970. Most have employed Lewis's approach to the study of this subject, and most have used cross-sectional methodology in which, for example, the wages of unionized firefighters are compared with those of unorganized firefighters, with the investigator attempting to hold constant other factors that affect wages such as location, city size, government structure, and alternative job opportunities in the labor market. While some of the most conclusive of these studies have analyzed the salaries of firefighters, the bulk of them have focused on teachers, others have dealt with the police, and still others have examined the wages of craftworkers, bus drivers, workers in health care, and even broader occupational groups commonly found in state and local governments.

The empirical results of these studies are most interesting. They reveal that the effects of unions on wages in the public sector are somewhat smaller than their effects on wages in the private sector. As one survey of this literature recently concluded:

> The "average" wage effect of unionism in government, according to these studies, is roughly on the order of five percent, a much smaller impact than is popularly supposed. . . . In education, which accounts for half of all nonfederal public workers, union wage impacts generally range between one and four percent, while in other functions, impacts range between −6 and +15 percent. Organized firefighters apparently have the largest relative wage impact among public employee unions, having achieved this outcome as much or more through reductions in working hours as through salary increases.[44]

The importance of these findings is that they run counter to the thesis of union power in the public sector, which, as we observed in Chapter 6, has so frequently been propounded. Specifically, the empirical studies suggest that unionized government workers have not been able to impose large relative wage costs on their employers, and that other basic factors are at work which, far more than the union status of public employees, determine pay levels in the public sector. In particular, wage rates in the private sector and levels of tax revenue in the local community are important determinants of the pay rates prevailing in local government.

This conclusion should, however, be qualified in some respects. Studies of the impact of unions on wages in the public sector have not dealt adequately with fringe benefits, which account for more than 40 percent of every payroll dollar in state and local governments.[45] Nor do some of the studies control for the spillover effects of the wages of unionized workers on those of nonunionized government employees.[46] But these limitations are also common to similar research on the private sector, and since the same designs and methodologies have been employed in studies analyzing the two sectors, there is no basis for placing any less confidence in the results obtained for the public sector than in those obtained for the private sector. Indeed, the evidence gathered for the public sector has the virtues of being more recent and more consistent in its estimates than that obtained for the private sector.

It is also worth noting that these impacts of unions on wages were by and large recorded during the first generation of collective bargaining in government. As labor relations in the public sector move into an era which features a more constrained economic climate, it might be expected that the impact of unions on wages will be even smaller than in the earlier, buoyant period. On the other hand, the experience in the private sector suggests the hypothesis that the impact of unions on wages in the public sector will be larger in a stable or contracting economy than in an expansionary one. Only by observing the impact of public employee unions on wages under different economic conditions will it be possible to develop a complete picture of this phenomenon and to determine which of these contrasting predictions stands up best.

What emerges from this necessarily brief review of the impact of unions on wages in the public sector is compatible with the conclusion reached earlier concerning the private sector. The organization of workers into unions, which are unquestionably political institutions, does not somehow transform the process of wage determination from a purely economic one into a purely political one. Both sets of forces are important to an understanding of wage setting in organized labor markets. In the private sector, the characteristics of the firm's product market and the relative costs of the factors of production set the parameters within which the political process of bargaining occurs. The most strategically placed, most powerful groups of workers can have a strong relative effect on wages, but the more common result is a relatively modest wage gain, roughly 10 to 20 percent rather than the much larger differential that popular discussion often suggests. In the public sector, where labor relations and collective bargaining are by definition more political than they are in private industry, the economic environment nevertheless delimits the parties' behavior. Unionized public employees have not been able to put great distance between their wages and those of their nonunionized counterparts. This doesn't mean that their pay has not risen rapidly, for it clearly did in the 1960s and 1970s, but so did the pay of public workers in general, as the rapid expansion of government services sharply bid up the demand for labor in the public sector. In this environment, public employees' unions apparently achieved relative wage gains of about 5 percent, on the average, though for some the increases were in the neighborhood of 15 percent.

If these wage gains are modest rather than extreme, they nevertheless reflect the conscious efforts of millions of workers and their union leaders to take wages out of competition. By collectively bargaining the terms and conditions of employment with private and public employers, the roughly 22.5 million unionists in the United States provide clear evidence that more than the competitive model is needed to explain the workings of labor markets. And, if the pattern-setting effect of negotiated agreements on the nonunion sector could ever be precisely gauged, the workings of an even larger proportion of labor markets would be less than satisfactorily depicted by competitive theory.

More on the Public Labor Market

One of the most recent studies of the impact of unions on wages (and one of the few which focus on *both* the public and the private sectors) found that organized hospital workers had more effect on private than on public institutions. However, the same study reported that "wages are higher in government hospitals than in private hospitals" and attributed this in part to "the growing politicization of the public wage-setting process."[47] Such a result suggests that we need to examine more broadly how wages are determined in the public sector, which is now such a large part of the American economy.

Because government services are, by definition, public or collective goods, there is no "market" for them in the traditional sense. A government has political jurisdiction over a particular geographic area, derives its revenue through taxes paid by the citizenry, and delivers services to all members of the community. There are no conventional demand and supply schedules of these services which relate the quantity provided by the government producer to the amount purchased by the consumer. But since government obviously must employ workers to provide services—and public services are especially labor-intensive compared with other types of economic activity—how does it go about deciding what pay rates are required to attract and retain a work force? What guides its decisions in this regard if the rule that MVP=W, available to firms in the private sector, does not exist in the public sector?

Most governments apparently follow either an explicit or an implicit policy of paying rates comparable to those paid in the private sector. Where explicit, this policy is known as the "prevailing-wage rule," an example of which is described below:

> In fixing the compensation to be paid to persons in the City's employ, the [City] Council and every other authority authorized to fix salaries and wages shall, in each instance, provide a salary or wage at least equal to the prevailing salary or wage for the same quality of service rendered to private persons, firms, or corporations under similar employment in case such prevailing salary or wage can be ascertained.[48]

Such policies became quite common in the public sector during the 1960s. The federal government made the prevailing-wage criterion the basis of its compensation policy in 1962, when Congress enacted the Federal Salary Reform Act, and in 1970, when it passed the Federal Pay Comparability Act. These actions by the federal government in the area of compensation spilled over to influence state and local governments' pay policies, which increasingly came to incorporate prevailing-wage provisions.

The prevailing-wage principle makes good sense on two grounds: equity and efficiency.[49] Paying public workers what their counterparts in the private sector receive seems an equitable policy, fair to everyone concerned, and responsive to the argument that government employees should not subsidize public services by accepting low pay. In terms of efficiency, payment of the prevailing wage permits public employers to attract and retain a work force equal in quality to that of the private sector. To pay less than the prevailing wage is to attract relatively low-quality employees—or perhaps none at all.

While the relative merits of basing wage determination in the public sector on equity or efficiency may be seriously debated, the most noteworthy aspect of the prevailing-wage policy is that its implementation has yielded a wage structure in the public sector quite different from what might have been expected. On the premise that pay in private industry is the appropriate guide for compensation in the public sector, one would predict parallel occupational wage structures to exist in the two sectors, except for a small differential owing to the lag time in collecting and processing data on pay in the private sector. This is shown in Figure 7-10a. What has actually resulted is something quite different. Occupational wage structures in the public sector are flatter and more egalitarian than those in private industry.[50] This is portrayed in Figure 7-10b.

Why has this occurred? Why are wage rates higher in the public than the private sector for blue-collar and lower-level white-collar jobs, the type examined in the aforementioned study of hospitals, but lower in government than in industry for high-level professional, managerial, and executive positions? Two students of this subject suggest the following:

> Public-private pay relationships in the United States can be explained, at least in part, by a combination of two factors: the discretion that public employers must exercise in implementing the prevailing-wage rule adopted by most cities and larger governmental units, and the nature of the political forces that affect governmental wage decisions.[51]

Public employers exercise such discretion in several ways: by choosing to pay the least skilled government workers rates which are above those prevailing in private markets so that they may enjoy more than subsistence or poverty-level earnings; by selecting as an appropriate reference group for wage-comparison and data-collection purposes large private firms that pay more for labor

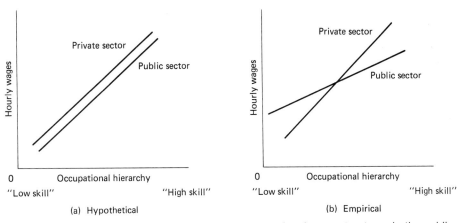

Figure 7-10 (a) Hypothetical and (b) empirical occupational wage structures in the public and private sectors.

than smaller employers; by accepting pay rates in private construction for public craft workers rather than the lower rates prevailing elsewhere in the private
economy; and by publicly proclaiming their resistance to higher salaries for
managerial personnel, irrespective of what the private sector pays to such personnel, on the grounds that this is wasteful of tax revenues and inappropriate to
the public sector. The political forces prevalent in the governmental wage-setting process reinforce these practices, as when low-skilled or craft workers
lobby a legislative body for higher pay, a group for "good government" or a
"budgetary watchdog" group opposes "high" salaries for managers, and entry-
level white-collar personnel contend that their large government employer
should compensate them on the basis of rates prevailing in large private organizations. Since the bulk of government personnel are employed in the lower and
middle ranks of the occupational structure, public officials in their political role
respond favorably to this group's wage goals, while opposing those of the much
smaller group of professional and managerial employees. These wage-setting
dynamics are present in governments irrespective of the degree of unionization
among employees.

   This is not to criticize the wage-setting process in the public sector or to
decry the occupational wage structure which it seems to generate. Rather, it is
to point out that, as in the private sector, so, too, in government do we observe
empirical realities which do not fully square with formal, conceptually sound
rules for making decisions, such as the prevailing-wage policy. The labor market
in the public sector contains important institutional elements, and in this respect
it is like key portions of the private economy.

OTHER ELEMENTS OF DECISIONS ON WAGES

Earlier we noted that equity and efficiency enter into decisions on wages in the
public sector, but that is also true of such decisions in the private sector. An important aspect of wage equity in both industry and government concerns the
pay relationship among jobs in the same firm or agency. A popular management
tool for establishing these pay relationships is job evaluation. Originally adopted
by several large private firms in the immediate post-World War II period as a
response to unionism and collective bargaining, job evaluation quickly spread
throughout the private sector. Its appeal was and remains the increased rationalization of the internal wage structure which it seems to provide. By studying
jobs, identifying their key behavioral requirements, and weighting these elements quantitatively according to their importance, organizations can attempt
systematically to establish the relationships of jobs and job groupings to one
another and to use these relationships for internal wage-setting purposes. A
typical job evaluation plan is shown in Table 7-6, and its related wage structure
is illustrated in Figure 7-11.

   The word "attempt" is used advisedly, for contrary to some popular opinion, job evaluation is not a fully scientific process since it requires the judgmen-

Table 7-6 Hypothetical Job Evaluation Plan

Factor	Definition	Point values
Education	Number of years of formal education required to adequately perform the job or its equivalent	55
Supervision received	Amount and type of supervision received	30
Physical demand	Measures and compares application, endurance, fatigue, and strength under normal or abnormal conditions; relates to expenditure of physical exertion inherent in a job to be performed at a normal pace	30
Working conditions	Involves general working conditions and extent of exposure to disagreeable factors	40
Experience and training	Time required to learn the job or experience necessary to perform the job competently	55
Complexity of duties	Amount of judgment, initiative, mental ability, knowledge, and independence from supervision necessary to perform the job	40
Contact with others	Frequency, importance, and diversity of contacts with others in the performance of the job	45
Responsibility for equipment	Degree of responsibility required to prevent loss of, or damage to, equipment and/or tools	55

Source: Adapted from Allen N. Nash and Stephen J. Carroll, Jr., *The Management of Compensation*, Brooks/Cole, Monterey, Calif., 1975, p. 118.

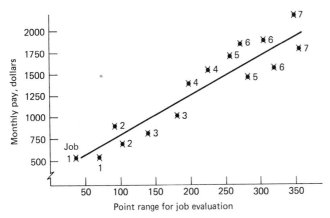

Figure 7-11 Hypothetical occupational pay structure based on job evaluation. The line shows "best fit" of pay to point values generated by the job evaluation system; points marked "X" represent actual point totals of jobs.

tal specification of key elements of performance and the application of a judgmental weighting system to them. Nevertheless, the existence of job evaluation plans on a wide scale indicates how pervasive is the criterion of internal equity in the making of wage decisions. Nothing in the competitive model would predict this close attention to the structuring of intraorganizational pay relationships. Yet such activity is clear evidence that the concept of structured internal labor markets has considerable validity.

Additional evidence confirming the importance of structure in labor markets emerges when occupational wage relationships and wage movements are considered.[52] Rather than being individually determined, the pay rates of most positions in an organization's occupational structure are set with reference to job groups or clusters. For example, an entry-level job such as that of clerk, stenographer, engineer, accountant, or assistant professor may be a "key" position, in that an employer surveys the labor market to determine the going (prevailing) rate for it. Once known, however, external information about pay for a key job is used to set compensation not only for that position but also for others which are related to it in a cluster or grouping that derives from the organization's processes of production, technology, or customs. The clerical group, for example, may contain several intermediate positions, two supervisory positions, and the position of a chief or head clerk, in addition to the basic entry-level job. The professorial group will include assistant, associate, and full professors. Pay rates for all jobs in one or another of these groups or clusters will be systematically related and will tend to change by similar amounts and at the same time.

When a job cluster is common to several organizations rather than peculiar to any one of them, pay rates for those groups of positions tend to be similar across organizations and to change by the same (or similar) magnitudes at the same time. Such interrelatedness among organizations in terms of wages for particular job clusters yields wage contours, as when changes in pay for jobs comprising the clerical group in several large manufacturing firms, or those for jobs in the nursing cluster in a group of proprietary hospitals, are closely similar in amount and timing. If job clusters are internal administrative devices for vertically structuring organizational decisions about wages, wage contours are the key mechanism for horizontal wage structuring in labor markets. Once more, the group or collective nature of these decisions and relationships underscores the incidence of organization and structure in labor markets.

Finally, consider the widespread use of seniority within organizations as a basis for determining wages, not to mention its many other applications to the employee-employer relationship. In both union and nonunion settings, seniority plays a prominent role in decisions about wages. Lacking the ability (or the willingness) to measure workers' productivity in particular jobs, employers often use length of service as a criterion for setting wage rates and making adjustments in wages. This is especially the case where a clearly defined personnel or human resources management function exists, since those who staff this function seek to establish rules and procedures which in part serve employees' needs for equity as they also facilitate achievement of organizational objectives.[53] Seniority in decisions about pay typically is one such rule, though it usually operates in conjunction with others.

As still another element of structure in internal labor markets, seniority is not necessarily at odds with competitive theory. Indeed, as a measure of work experience, which is itself a proxy for specific training in studies of human capital, seniority can be considered quite consistent with neoclassical theory. The limitation on this argument, however, is that it has selective application: seniority (experience) may be positively related to individual productivity in some kinds of work or occupations—professional and managerial positions, for example—but less so or not at all in others—blue-collar and semiskilled jobs. Yet seniority is used along with other criteria to set pay and determine changes in wages in a broad variety of jobs, occupations, and organizations. And the reason for its use in internal labor markets appears to be its appeal to equity rather than efficiency, despite the frequent compatibility of these two wage-setting principles. From this perspective, seniority, like job evaluation, job clusters, and wage contours, is another element of structure and organization in labor markets.

SUMMARY

To speak of "the labor market" is to aggregate under one phrase many sets of exchanges between buyers and sellers of labor. Some markets conform quite closely to the competitive model of classical and neoclassical theory, and some of the variation in earnings among individuals can be "explained" by variation in individuals' investment in human capital. However, other labor markets are highly structured and organized, featuring collectively bargained wage rates, job clusters, wage contours, and wage structures based on job evaluation and seniority. The labor market in the public sector, like that in the private sector, has many of these structural and organizational characteristics, and it also contains numerous interest groups that seek to influence legislated decisions about wages. Consequently, political forces seem to be pervasive in the labor market, and for that reason it would be erroneous to judge wage determination as a process in which economic factors alone dictate in an automatic fashion the wage rates paid for labor. Simply the presence of power in the market—the absence of purely competitive conditions—in some industries and sectors would indicate that not all employers necessarily pay wages equal to labor's marginal value product.

However, although the process of determining wages is in many ways political, it is nevertheless guided by economic forces which management and other parties to decisions about wages ignore only at their peril. Such is the nature of private- and public-sector labor markets in a capitalist economy, which are not so highly structured or segmented as to negate basic linkages between wages and employment and between pay and productivity.[54] There are both economic and political forces operating in labor markets. We have argued that the former set the basic conditions within which the latter operate, but we have also stressed that students of the labor sector should not focus so heavily on one set of forces as to overlook the other. Labor is undeniably a factor of production, and yet it is embodied in human beings, who inevitably seek to structure economic activity and who sometimes organize into unions and press for laws and employment practices to protect themselves from the more unfortunate consequences of competitive markets. Recognition of such tendencies leads quite naturally to a consideration of discrimination in the labor market against racial minorities and women, perhaps the most critical issue in contemporary labor market analysis. That is the subject of Chapter 8.

NOTES

1 See Simon Rottenberg "On Choice in Labor Markets," in Walter Galenson and Seymour M. Lipset, (eds.), *Labor and Trade Unionism*, Wiley, New York, pp. 40–55.

2 See Michael A. Spence, "Job Market Signaling," *Quarterly Journal of Economics*, **87:**355–374 (1973).

3 Adam Smith, *The Wealth of Nations*, Modern Library, New York, 1937, pp. 100–107.

4 U.S. Bureau of the Census, *Current Population Reports: Money Income in 1975 of Families and Persons in the United States*, ser. P-60, no. 105, 1977, p. 227, table 52.

5 The leading work on this approach is Gary S. Becker, *Human Capital: A Theoretical and Empirical Analysis*, 2d ed., National Bureau of Economic Research, New York, 1975.

6 See Neil W. Chamberlain, "Some Second Thoughts on the Concept of Human Capital," *Proceedings of the Twentieth Annual Winter Meeting of the Industrial Relations Research Association, 1967*, Madison, Wis., 1968, pp. 1–14; and Michael J. Piore, "The Importance of Human Capital Theory to Labor Economics—A Dissenting View," *Proceedings of the Twenty-sixth Annual Winter Meeting of the Industrial Relations Research Association, 1973*, Madison, Wis., 1974, pp. 251–258.

7 These supporters assert that the human capital approach is "essentially a positive theory of the labor market" that does not prescribe how things should be but, instead, attempts to explain how they are and predict what they will be. F. Ray Marshall, Allen M. Cartter, and Allan G. King, *Labor Economics: Wages, Employment and Trade Unionism*, 3d ed., Irwin, Homewood, Ill., 1976, p. 242.

8 For evidence on the returns to investment in schooling, see B. F. Kiker, *Investment in Human Capital*, University of South Carolina Press, Columbia, 1971, pp. 211–323.

9 This section relies heavily on Becker, especially chap. 2. See also Jacob Mincer, "On-the-Job-Training: Cost, Returns, and Some Implications," *Journal of Political Economy*, **70:**50–73 (1962), supplement.

10 See, for example, Walter Oi, "Labor as a Quasi-Fixed Factor," *Journal of Political Economy*, **70:**538–555 (1962); Donald O. Parsons, "Specific Human Capital: An Application to Quit Rates and Layoff Rates," *Journal of Political Economy*, **80:**1120–1143 (1972); and John H. Pencavel, "Wages, Specific Training, and Labor Turnover in U.S. Manufacturing Industries," *International Economic Review,* **13:**53–64 (1972).

11 For example, Jacob Mincer, *Schooling, Experience and Earnings,* Columbia, New York, 1974; and Sherwin Rosen, "Learning and Experience in the Labor Market," *Journal of Human Resources,* **7:**326–342 (1972).

12 Mincer, *Schooling, Experience and Earnings;* Barry R. Chiswick, *Income Inequality,* Columbia, New York, 1974; and Sherwin Rosen, "Human Capital: A Survey of Empirical Research," in Ronald G. Ehrenberg (ed.), *Research in Labor Economics,* vol. I, Jai Press, Greenwich, Conn., 1977, pp. 3–39.

13 See, for example, John R. Commons, *Institutional Economics,* vol. I–II, Macmillan, New York, 1934.

14 This concept of labor markets is developed in Peter B. Doeringer and Michael J. Piore, *Internal Labor Markets and Manpower Analysis,* Heath, Lexington, Mass., 1971, especially chap. 3. See also Piore, "On-the-Job-Training in a Dual Labor Market," in Arnold R. Weber et al. (eds.), *Public-Private Manpower Policies,* Industrial Relations Research Association, Madison, Wis., 1969, pp. 101–132.

15 For more on this, see Stanley M. Friedlander, *Unemployment in the Urban Core: An Analysis of 30 Cities with Policy Recommendations,* Praeger, New York, 1972, chap. 5; Bennett Harrison, "Employment, Unemployment and the Structure of Labor Markets," *The Wharton Quarterly,* **1:**4–7, 6–31 (1972); and Peter Passell, editorial, *The New York Times,* Apr. 15, 1978, p. 22.

16 Doeringer and Piore, chaps. 2–4.

17 Michael J. Piore, *Notes for a Theory of Labor Market Stratification,* Working Paper 95, M.I.T., Department of Economics, Cambridge, Mass., October 1972, p. 3; and Michael J. Piore, "Fragments of a Sociological Theory of Wages," *American Economic Review,* **63:**377–384 (1973), pt. 2.

18 Piore, *Notes for a Theory of Labor Market Stratification,* pp. 3–4.

19 Paul Osterman, "An Empirical Study of Labor Market Segmentation," *Industrial and Labor Relations Review,* **18:**508–523 (1975).

20 Osterman, p. 519.

21 David M. Gordon, *Theories of Poverty and Unemployment,* Heath, Lexington, Mass., 1972, p. 54.

22 See especially Samuel Bowles, "Unequal Education and the Reproduction of the Social Division of Labor," *Review of Radical Political Economy,* **3:**1–30 (1971); and Samuel Bowles, *Schooling in Capitalist America,* Basic Books, New York, 1975.

23 Samuel Bowles, "Unequal Education and the Reproduction of the Hierarchical Division of Labor," in Richard C. Edwards, Michael Reich, and Thomas E. Weisskopf (eds.), *The Capitalist System,* Prentice-Hall, Englewood Cliffs, N.J., 1972, pp. 218–219.

24 See, for example, Robert Blauner, *Alienation and Freedom,* University of Chicago Press, Chicago, 1964; Joan Woodward, *Industrial Organization: Theory and Practice,* Oxford University Press, London, 1975; and Gene W. Dalton, Paul R. Lawrence, and Jay W. Lorsch, *Organizational Structure and Design,* Irwin, Homewood, Ill., 1970.

25 This subject has also been broached by other, nonradical theorists. See, for example, Ivar Berg, *Education and Jobs: The Great Training Robbery,* Praeger, New York, 1970.

26 Glen G. Cain, "The Challenge of Segmented Labor Market Theories to Orthodox Theory: A Survey," *Journal of Economic Literature,* **14:**1248 (1976).

27   For more on union wage policy in collective bargaining, see Albert Rees, *The Economics of Trade Unions,* rev. ed., University of Chicago Press, Chicago, 1977, chap. 3; and John T. Dunlop, *Wage Determination under Trade Unions,* A. M. Kelly, Publishers, New York, 1950.

28   A leading work on this approach to wage bargaining is Arthur M. Ross, *Trade Union Wage Policy,* University of California Press, Berkeley, 1948.

29   See Seymour M. Lipset and Martin A. Trow, *Reference Group Theory and Trade Union Wage Policy,* Reprint 106, University of California, Institute of Industrial Relations, Berkeley, 1958.

30   This term was coined by Ross, chap. 3.

31   Arthur M. Ross, "The Tie between Wages and Employment," *Industrial and Labor Relations Review,* **4:**99–100 (1950).

32   For a summary of this evidence, see Rees, chap. 3, especially pp. 57–63; and David H. Greenberg, "Deviations from Wage-Fringe Standards," *Industrial and Labor Relations Review,* **21:**197–209. (1968).

33   Greenberg.

34   A study which attempts to reconcile the economic and political approaches to wage bargaining is Daniel J. B. Mitchell, "Union Wage Policies: The Ross-Dunlop Debate Reopened," *Industrial Relations,* **11:**46–61 (1972).

35   H. Gregg Lewis, *Unionism and Relative Wages in the United States,* University of Chicago Press, Chicago, 1963. The following discussion draws liberally from this source.

36   See Rees, pp. 53–57; Orley Ashenfelter, George E. Johnson, and John H. Pencavel, "Trade Unions and the Rate Change of Money Wages in the United States Manufacturing Industry," *Review of Economic Studies,* **39:**27–54 (1972); and Robert J. Flanagan, "Wage Interdependence in Unionized Labor Markets," *Brookings Papers on Economic Activity* 3, Brookings, Washington, 1976, pp. 635–673, plus discussion comments to p. 681.

37   Rees, p. 74. For an example of the type of study to which Rees refers, see Orley Ashenfelter, "Racial Discrimination and Trade Unionism," *Journal of Political Economy,* **80:**435–464 (1972), pt. 1.

38   See Orley Ashenfelter and George E. Johnson, "Unionism, Relative Wages and Labor Quality in U.S. Manufacturing Industries," *International Economic Review,* **13:**488–507 (1972); and Peter Schmidt and Robert Strauss, "The Effect of Unions on Earnings and Earnings on Unions: A Mixed Logit Approach," *International Economic Review,* **17:**204–212 (1976).

39   Leonard Weiss, "Concentration and Labor Earnings," *American Economic Review,* **56:**96–117 (1966).

40   James A. Dalton and E. J. Ford, Jr., "Concentration and Labor Earnings in Manufacturing and Utilities," *Industrial and Labor Relations Review,* **31:**45–60 (1977). These contradictory results can be explained only in part by differences in data sources and statistical methods.

41   Lewis, p. 297.

42   Robert L. Raimon and Vladimir V. Stoikov, "The Effect of Blue-Collar Unionism on White-Collar Earnings," *Industrial and Labor Relations Review,* **22:**358–374 (1969).

43   As previously noted, the larger impact suggested by recent studies may reflect newer and better measures rather than a real increase in the impact of unions.

44   David Lewin, "Public Sector Labor Relations: A Review Essay," *Labor History,*

18:138–139 (1977). For a somewhat different view, see Orley Ashenfelter, *Union Relative Wage Effects: New Evidence and a Survey of Their Implications for Wage Inflation,* Working Paper 89, Princeton University, Industrial Relations Section, Princeton, N.J., August 1976. Lewin's article summarizes the studies of the impact of unions on wages in the public sector reported in the literature to 1977. For a more recent version of that summary, see David Lewin, Raymond D. Horton, and James W. Kuhn, *Collective Bargaining and Manpower Utilization in Big City Governments,* Allanheld-Osmun, Montclair, N.J., 1979, appendix 1.

It should be noted that a recent study found police unions to have relative effects on wages of up to 19 percent and relative effects on fringe benefits of up to 40 percent. See Ann Bartel and David Lewin, "Wages and Unionism in the Public Sector: The Case of Police," Working Paper Series, Columbia University, Graduate School of Business, 1979.

45 As reported in Edward H. Friend, *Third National Survey of Employee Benefits of U.S. Municipalities,* Labor-management Relations Service, Washington 1977, p.2.

46 One that does is Ronald G. Ehrenberg and Gerald S. Goldstein, "A Model of Public Sector Wage Determination," *Journal of Urban Economics,* **2**:233–245 (1975).

47 Myron D. Fottler, "The Union Impact on Hospital Wages," *Industrial and Labor Relations Review,* **30**:352, 354 (1977). Fottler's results tend to confirm the hypothesis of politicization in wage determination in the public sector originally presented in David Lewin, "Public Employment Relations: Confronting the Issues," *Industrial Relations.* **12**:309–321 (1973). Two other studies which have examined the relative impact on wages of unions in both the public and the private sectors are Daniel Hamermesh, "The Effect of Government Ownership on Wages," in Daniel Hamermesh (ed.), *Labor in the Public and Nonprofit Sectors,* Princeton, Princeton, N.J., 1975, pp. 227–255; and David Shapiro, "Relative Wage Effects of Unions in the Public and Private Sectors," *Industrial and Labor Relations Review,* **31**:193–204 (1978).

48 Charter of the City of Los Angeles, Sec. 425. See also *Pay Policies for Public Personnel: A Report of the Municipal Government Section of Town Hall,* Robert Kingsley, Los Angeles, 1961, p. 35.

49 These points are further elaborated in Walter Fogel and David Lewin, "Wage Determination in the Public Sector," *Industrial and Labor Relations Review,* **27**:410–431 (1974).

50 See Fogel and Lewin; and David Lewin, "Aspects of Wage Determination in Local Government Employment," *Public Administration Review,* **34**:149–155 (1974).

51 Fogel and Lewin, p. 430. For further discussion of this phenomenon, see David Lewin, "The Prevailing Wage Principle and Public Wage Decisions," *Public Personnel Management,* **3**:473–485 (1974).

52 The following discussion draws on concepts developed by John T. Dunlop in "The Task of Contemporary Wage Theory," in George W. Taylor and Frank C. Pierson (eds.), *New Concepts in Wage Determination,* McGraw-Hill, New York, 1957, pp. 117–139. See also, Doeringer and Piore, chaps. 3 and 4, where the authors make use of the concepts described here.

53 See Howard M. Vollmer and Patrick J. McGillivray, "Personnel Offices and the Institutionalization of Employee Rights," *Pacific Sociological Review,* **3**:29–34 (1960).

54 This is a general conclusion which does not deny that, in some labor markets, political forces seem to far outweigh economic ones. See, for example, Boyce Rensenberger, "Health analysts ask if nation can afford more physicians," *The New York Times,* May 7, 1978. Rensenberger writes: "In the 1930's it was believed that supply-demand balances did operate, and the American Medical Association sought to hold down the supply of doctors in an attempt to maintain higher incomes for doctors. With the rapid expansion in the 1960's of private and public medical insurance plans, the way Americans paid the bulk of their medical costs changed dramatically, and classical market economics, to the extent they operated, went out the window.

"In yet another flouting of conventional economic theory, the increasing concentration of doctors in affluent areas has not resulted in price competition. Although data on office visit fees are not available, a study of surgeons' fees indicated that they were highest where the doctor supply was greatest, according to the Federal Council on Wage and Price Stability."

ADDITIONAL READINGS

Adams, J. F., Vernon M. Briggs, Brian Rungeling, and Lewis H. Smith: *Employment, Income and Welfare in the Rural South,* Praeger, New York, 1977.

Becker, Gary S.: *Human Capital: A Theoretical and Empirical Analysis,* 2d ed., National Bureau of Economic Research, New York, 1975.

Cain, Glen G.: "The Challenge of Segmented Labor Market Theories to Orthodox Theory: A Survey," *Journal of Economic Literature,* **14:**1215–1257 (1976).

Cross, John G.: *The Economics of Bargaining,* Basic Books, New York, 1969.

Doeringer, Peter B., and Michael J. Piore: *Internal Labor Markets and Manpower Analysis,* Heath, Lexington, Mass., 1971.

Ehrenberg, Ronald G. (ed.): *Research in Labor Economics,* vol. I, Jai Press, Greenwich, Conn., 1977.

Freeman, Richard B.: *The Market for College Trained Manpower,* Harvard, Cambridge, Mass., 1971.

Rees, Albert: *The Economics of Trade Unions,* rev. ed., University of Chicago Press, Chicago, 1977.

Smith, Sharon P.: *Equal Pay in the Public Sector: Fact or Fantasy?* Princeton University, Industrial Relations Section, Princeton, N.J., 1977.

Solomon, Lewis C., and Paul J. Taubman: *Does College Matter: Some Evidence on the Impact of Higher Education,* Academic, New York, 1973.

FOR ANALYSIS AND DISCUSSION

1 It has sometimes been argued that if the returns to factors of production are based on marginal productivity, this constitutes an ethical justification for whatever wages workers receive. Others contend, in rebuttal, that the value of the services rendered by a worker is based on effective consumer demand, the pattern of which is determined by the existing income distribution, which has no ethical justification. Critically examine these opposing views, indicating which of them (if either) you believe to be valid.

2 How might the elasticity of the supply of labor to a large firm in an isolated, heavily agricultural, rural area differ from that of a competitive firm in an urban, industrial-

ized location? Which supply curve would show greater responsiveness of workers to wages in the labor market? Why?

3 Examine the occupational wage structure of the community in which you live. How do pay rates differ by industry, employer, and occupation? How do they differ, if at all, between the public and the private sectors? If you observe large intraoccupational wage differentials, does this conform or run counter to competitive-labor-market theory? Explain your answer.

4 In a recent study ("Overinvestment in College Training?" *Journal of Human Resources,* **3:**287–311 (1975), Richard B. Freeman found: "(1) There was a significant decline in the college labor market in the 1969–74 period, with salaries and job opportunities [of new graduates] falling relative to those elsewhere in the economy; (2) the rate of return to investing in college was, as a consequence, reduced from 11–12 percent in the early 1960s to about 8 percent in the early seventies; (3) as salaries, rates of return, and job opportunities worsened, enrollments in college began to decline, apparently as a rational response to changed market incentives; and (4) the downturn resulted from shifts in relative demand due to changes in the industrial structure of employment and in relative supply, whose 'timing' produced the sudden change in conditions."

Evaluate these findings and write a short report indicating whether (and why) the downturn in the college labor market continued into the late 1970s. Select one educational specialty—for example, engineering, chemistry, or law—and determine whether it reflected the general pattern reported by Freeman for the period he studied and for the late 1970s.

5 Select two teams of students to debate the following proposition: "Resolved: The human capital approach to labor market analysis is superior to approaches based on segmented-labor-market theories." Be sure to identify the particular segmented-labor-market theories to be covered in the debate. The instructor should moderate the session and should poll the class on this proposition before and after the debate.

6 Briefly evaluate the dual-market theory and the radical theories of the labor market presented in this chapter. Indicate to what extent these theories contribute to your understanding of poverty, racial discrimination, wage determination, and the mobility of workers. Compare your conclusions with those of a classmate who also evaluated these theories and with those of another who explored neoclassical theory in these respects.

7 Sample the opinions of the members of your family concerning the impact of labor unions on wages. Are their judgments consistent with the estimates reported in the literature? If not, how would you go about explaining the different conclusions to your family? To union members? To employers? To your classmates?

8 Suppose that you were interested in studying the relative effects of labor unions on wages and that you were especially interested in the spillover of collectively bargained wage rates to the nonunion sector. Briefly describe a method for controlling such spillovers. Would the method be equally applicable to the private and the public sectors? Why or why not?

9 In Japan, seniority is a major determinant of wage rates. Indeed, a college student who takes a job with a company after graduation is generally considered to be employed for life. That person will continue to be paid during slack periods or periods of layoffs and will be provided with numerous benefits, including allowances for the education and health care of family members. Consequently, in Japan, rates of turnover in the labor market are low, job mobility is defined in terms of longevity,

and pay increases are based on seniority to a great extent. Appraise this type of labor market in terms of its applicability to the American scene and its susceptibility to the analytical framework of competitive theory.

10 Is the concept of an internal labor market equally applicable to blue- and white-collar jobs? Does your answer depend at all upon the extent of unionization in these broad occupational categories, given that unions seek "equal pay for equal work?" Select a firm or a government employer and identify the major elements of its internal labor market.

Chapter 8

Discrimination in the Labor Market

INTRODUCTION

We have seen the great diversity of prevailing views about the operation of labor markets. In this chapter we take up the subject that, more than any other, seems to shape individual perceptions about the labor market: discrimination in employment based on race and sex. The initial portion of the chapter presents evidence about the existence of such discrimination and the extent to which it has changed over time. Though the data are not conclusive, some progress unquestionably has been made in reducing discrimination in the labor market.

Then we review the major efforts that have been mounted in recent years to combat discrimination in the labor market and ensure equal employment opportunity by means of public policy. The federal system for enforcing equal employment opportunity legislation, which involves the executive and judicial branches of government and several key administrative agencies, is taken up next. Then we discuss several key issues that have emerged as part of the drive to eliminate discrimination in the labor market, including the validation of devices for selecting employees, clashes between affirmative action and collective bargaining agreements, and the use of racial quotas for admission to schools and in employment. The last part of the chapter focuses on the effectiveness of efforts to regulate discrimination in the labor market.

DISCRIMINATION AS A SOCIAL ISSUE

It would be difficult to overstate the importance of racial discrimination as a social issue on the American scene. The nation's only civil war, which lasted from 1861 to 1865, was fought over the issue of slavery, and some 100 years later urban riots and violence were commonplace, as blacks protested discrimination at the hands of whites. The National Advisory Commission on Civil Disorders, appointed in 1967 by President Johnson to investigate the particularly virulent unrest that occurred that year, concluded its report with the following statement:

> Our nation is moving toward two societies, one black, one white—separate and unequal. . . . Discrimination and segregation have long permeated much of American life; they now threaten the future of every American. . . . To pursue our present course will involve the continuing polarization of the American community and, ultimately, the destruction of basic democratic values.[1]

Racial violence in the United States during the 1960s led to various efforts aimed at overcoming racial discrimination. Later, discrimination based on sex became a major social issue, and its resolution also an object of public policy. For the purposes of this book, however, what is most important and interesting about discrimination based on race and sex is that both its existence and the proposed cures for it have been defined to a considerable extent in terms of the labor market. Specifically, such discrimination has been viewed, in part, as an economic phenomenon potentially susceptible to amelioration by legally mandated fair employment policies and practices. Later in this chapter we shall review some of these efforts by government to regulate discrimination, and we shall also attempt to judge their effectiveness. But first it is necessary to sketch some of the key dimensions of race and sex in the labor market and to examine changes in discrimination in the labor market over time.

EXPERIENCES IN THE LABOR MARKET

Chapter 1 pointed out some of the differences between the experiences of men and women and of blacks and whites in the labor market.[2] For example, in 1978, the rate of participation in the labor force of white men exceeded that of black men by a few percentage points, while the rate of white women was a few percentage points below that of black women.[3] Thirty years earlier, black men were slightly more likely to be in the work force than white men (their rates were 87.3 and 86.5 percent, respectively, in 1948), and nonwhite women were far more likely to be employed or looking for work than white women (rates of 45.6 and 31.3 percent, respectively, in 1948). In terms of unemployment, the rate for nonwhites is roughly double the rate for whites, a relationship that has prevailed over several decades, while the rate for women has generally been about 1.5 times the rate for men. But if rates of participation in the labor force and of unemployment differ by race and sex, most men and women, blacks and whites, who belong to the labor force are at work—are employed for pay. Thus, it behooves us to examine data on comparative earnings, work experience, and occupations if we are to gain a fuller appreciation of the roles of race and sex in the labor market.

In 1975, the median income of all persons 14 years old and over in the United States was $5564.[4] The median income of whites was $5889, and that of blacks was $4055; men had a median income of $8853, and women had a median income of $3385. These figures are not terribly surprising, nor are they very useful, for they mix different rates of participation in the labor force, different rates of unemployment, different occupations, and different work characteristics. Consider, for example, that year-round, full-time workers in the United States during 1975 had a median income of $11,078, with figures of $11,-384, $8593, $13,144, and $7719 recorded for whites, blacks, men, and women, respectively.[5] Thus, it is necessary to take into account—to hold constant—certain characteristics of individuals in order to speak meaningfully about the relationships between race, sex, and income. For this purpose, consider the data on earnings in 1975 presented in Table 8-1 for some 50 million year-round, full-time workers 16 years old and over.

Observe first that white men earned about two-thirds more income than white women, while for blacks and others, there was an earnings differential of about one-third between men and women. Consider next the very large differences in earnings by occupational category. Among white males, managers and administrators earned about three times as much as farm laborers and supervisors in 1975. *Within* the category of managers and administrators, however, men earned roughly 80 percent more than women, and white males earned 25 percent more than black and other nonwhite males. Among sales workers, men's earnings exceeded women's earnings by almost 150 percent—$13,710 versus $5682—and the differential between men's and women's earnings exceeded 50 percent in several other occupational categories. Even among professional and technical workers, where one might expect to find the smallest pay differentials by sex, median earnings were about one-third greater for men than for women.

In every occupational category, white men earned more than nonwhite men, the differentials ranging between 4 and 25 percent. Among women, whites earned more than blacks in most occupational groupings, but the differences were quite small, exceeding 5 percent only in the case of private household workers. In two categories, service workers and clerical workers, the median earnings of black women exceeded those of white women, in the latter case by about 10 percent.

The positive effect of education on earnings is clearly shown in Table 8-1. In every instance except that of white male farm laborers and supervisors, median earnings increase with education. But, for most of the occupational categories listed in Table 8-1, earnings differentials by sex and race are not narrowed as a result of greater educational attainment. Among professional and

Table 8-1 Median Earnings in 1975 of Year-Round, Full-Time Wage and Salary Workers 16 Years Old and Over, by Educational Attainment, Sex, and Race, March 1976

Occupation and race	Men					Women				
	Total	Less than 4 years of high school	High school, 4 years only	College, 1 to 3 years	College, 4 or more years	Total	Less than 4 years of high school	High school, 4 years only	College, 1 to 3 years	College, 4 or more years
All persons										
Total	$12,680	$10,205	$12,289	$13,599	$17,118	$7,598	$5,835	$7,150	$8,284	$10,502
Professional and technical workers	15,682	12,480	13,385	14,607	16,775	10,501	7,222	9,308	10,343	10,896
Engineers	19,224	—	17,631	18,216	19,910	—	—	—	—	—
Physicians	25,000	—	—	—	25,000	—	—	—	—	—
Health workers, except practioners	11,440	—	—	—	12,570	10,552	—	9,664	10,676	12,029
Teachers, except college	12,483	—	12,644	—	12,873	10,255	—	—	10,201	10,382
Engineering and science technicians	12,813	—	12,939	12,941	16,755	8,805	—	9,310	—	—
Other professional, salaried workers	15,832	—	14,377	14,963	16,470	10,890	—	8,724	9,791	11,953
Managers and administrators, except farm	16,734	13,270	12,745	14,148	20,592	9,425	5,938	—	—	13,112
Sales workers	13,710	10,320	11,936	12,231	16,470	5,682	5,009	5,266	6,546	—
Retail trade	10,051	9,302	9,988	10,763	9,893	4,829	4,907	4,606	5,499	—
Other	15,750	11,381	14,624	16,060	17,352	9,028	—	8,424	—	—
Clerical workers	12,019	11,145	11,798	12,261	13,110	7,594	6,784	7,463	7,934	—
Craft and kindred workers	12,732	11,645	13,127	13,514	14,797	7,416	6,134	7,483	—	8,295
Operatives, except transport	10,962	10,027	11,516	12,146	—	6,295	—	6,459	—	—
Transport equipment operatives	11,150	10,439	9,683	10,335	—	—	—	—	—	—
Laborers, except farm	9,140	8,260	—	—	—	6,977	—	7,192	—	—
Private household workers	—	—	—	—	—	2,481	2,204	—	—	—
Service workers, except private household	9,628	8,112	10,047	12,075	10,522	5,542	5,085	5,609	6,771	—
Farmers and farm managers	—	—	—	—	—	—	—	—	—	—
Farm laborers and supervisors	5,539	5,365	5,066	—	—	—	—	—	—	—
Whites										
Total	$12,961	$10,544	$12,473	$13,839	$17,351	$7,617	$5,932	$7,133	$8,236	$10,575
Professional and technical workers	15,787	12,607	13,531	14,736	16,867	10,521	—	9,265	10,333	10,922
Health workers, except practitioners	11,477	—	—	—	12,697	10,576	—	9,892	10,602	11,992
Teachers, except college	12,636	—	—	12,697	—	10,237	—	—	10,182	10,370
All other professional, salaried workers	16,587	12,852	13,708	15,095	18,070	10,974	—	9,077	9,570	12,326
Managers and administrators, except farm	16,856	13,248	14,402	16,403	20,845	9,433	5,969	8,771	—	13,428
Sales workers	13,900	10,345	12,827	14,318	16,866	5,647	5,017	5,209	6,506	—
Clerical workers	12,074	11,056	11,975	12,276	13,264	7,511	6,610	7,409	7,806	—
Craft and kindred workers	12,875	11,758	13,278	13,822	14,852	7,304	—	7,363	—	8,387
Operatives, except transport	11,099	10,186	11,638	12,148	—	6,363	6,214	6,550	—	—

Transport equipment operatives	11,661	11,168	12,080	12,497	[1]	[1]	[1]	[1]	[1]	
Laborers, except farm	9,553	8,578	10,000	10,480	[1]	7,102	[1]	[1]	[1]	[1]
Private household workers						2,806	[1]	[1]	[1]	[1]
Service workers, except private household	9,927	8,355	10,356	12,408	10,449	5,441	5,018	5,426	6,646	[1]
Farmers and farm managers	[1]	[1]	[1]		[1]	[1]			[1]	[1]
Farm laborers and supervisors	5,930	5,976	5,019	[1]	[1]	[1]	[1]	[1]	[1]	
Blacks and others										
Total	$10,000	$ 8,413	$10,325	$11,602	$13,801	$ 7,486	$5,384	$7,265	$ 8,547	$10,061
Professional and technical workers	14,009	[1]	[1]	[1]	15,722	10,386	[1]	[1]	[1]	10,748
Health workers, except practitioners	[1]	[1]	[1]	[1]	[1]	10,440	[1]	[1]	[1]	[1]
Teachers, except college	[1]	[1]	[1]	[1]	[1]	10,354	[1]	[1]	[1]	10,449
All other professional, salaried workers	15,479	[1]	[1]	[1]	16,771	10,444	[1]	[1]	[1]	11,000
Managers and administrators, except farm	13,779	[1]	[1]	[1]	[1]	[1]	[1]	[1]	[1]	[1]
Sales workers	[1]	[1]	[1]	[1]	[1]	[1]	[1]	[1]	[1]	
Clerical workers	11,622	[1]	11,424	[1]	[1]	8,212	[1]	7,949	8,797	8,007
Craft and kindred workers	10,969	10,319	11,101	11,352	[1]	[1]	[1]	[1]	[1]	
Operatives, except transport	10,007	9,115	10,620	[1]	[1]	5,802	5,569	5,790	[1]	
Transport equipment operatives	9,264	8,564	9,968	[1]	[1]	[1]	[1]		[1]	
Laborers, except farm	7,866	7,619	7,947	[1]		[1]	[1]	[1]	[1]	
Private household workers						2,202	[1]	[1]	[1]	
Service, except private household	8,379	7,346	8,368	[1]	[1]	5,798	5,214	6,181	[1]	[1]
Farmers and farm managers	[1]		[1]							
Farm laborers and supervisors	[1]	[1]	[1]		[1]	[1]	[1]			

[1] Median not shown where base is less than 75,000.

Source: Adapted from U.S. Bureau of Labor Statistics, *Year-Round Full-Time Earnings in 1975,* Special Labor Force Report 203, 1977, p. 37.

technical workers, completion of 4 or more years of college reduces the earnings differential between white and black males, but enlarges the differential between men and women. These data may give pause to those who propose that attainment of higher education on the part of blacks and women will reduce earnings differentials in the labor market based on race and sex, though more education clearly leads to higher absolute earnings levels for all types of workers.

Another perspective on the role of race and sex in the labor market is provided in Table 8-2, which shows some of the characteristics of year-round, full-time workers who earned less than $5000 in 1975. Only 4.5 percent of all men but 18 percent of all women fell below that earnings level; the rate for blacks (15.7 percent) not only was almost double that for whites but also was about 2.5 points higher than the rate for persons of Spanish origin. That young workers earn less than middle-aged and older workers is hardly surprising, but the proportion of young women workers earning below $5000 is twice that of young men, and the proportion of young blacks earning below that level is one-third larger than that of young whites. Observe that less than 3 percent of the men but more than 11 percent of the women in full-time white-collar jobs earned less than $5000 in 1975. Among blue-collar workers, almost 5 percent of the men but fully 25 percent of the women were in the low earnings category, and the proportion of blacks earning under $5000 was more than double that of whites. Once more, we see that educational attainment is positively related to earnings, but in each

Table 8-2 Proportion of Year-Round, Full-Time Wage and Salary Workers Who Earned Less than $5000 in 1975, by Selected Characteristics, March 1976

Age, occupation, and educational attainment	Both sexes	Men	Women	Whites	Blacks and others	Persons of Spanish origin
Total	9.0	4.5	17.9	8.2	15.7	13.3
Age						
16–24 years	19.8	13.7	27.5	18.9	27.1	19.9
25–44 years	6.3	2.7	14.3	5.6	11.2	11.6
45 years and over	8.8	4.2	18.0	7.7	19.0	13.4
Occupation						
White collar	6.4	2.5	11.3	6.4	5.4	7.4
Blue collar	7.3	4.5	24.8	6.2	14.9	11.4
Service, including private household	26.9	10.3	45.1	25.2	32.0	29.2
Farm workers	44.8	42.4	1	40.6	1	31.6
Educational attainment						
Less than 4 years of high school	16.4	8.6	36.2	14.5	25.4	19.5
High school, 4 years only	9.7	4.2	18.3	9.1	15.1	10.4
College, 1 year or more	4.0	2.3	7.7	3.8	5.2	4.3

1 Percent not shown where base is less than 75,000.
Source: Adapted from U.S. Bureau of Labor Statistics, *Year-Round Full-Time Eranings in 1975,* Special Labor Force Report 203, 1977, p. 38.

educational category women and blacks are overrepresented (compared with men and whites, respectively) among those with annual earnings of less than $5000.

Numerous other data could be presented to illustrate the substantial earnings differentials that exist by race and by sex in the labor sector. However, to observe such differentials is not to establish the existence of discrimination or to know its magnitude. Consider, for example, that between any two individuals or groups of workers with different amounts of work experience, one would expect to find pay differentials. The same could be said—and expected —of workers with different amounts of on-the-job training. Since women tend to be in the labor force less regularly than men and to be more heavily represented than men in part-time employment, it is not surprising and it is not necessarily evidence of discrimination that their pay is below that of men, even where the two groups are in the same occupational category and have the same educational attainment.

Clearly, this line of reasoning proceeds from the neoclassical human capital approach to labor market analysis, which, as we noted in Chapter 7, seeks to explain earnings differentials among individuals on the basis of variations in expenditures on education, on-the-job training, health, and the like. Following this line of reasoning, we would attempt to identify those portions of the earnings differentials between men and women and between blacks and whites which are due to variations in individual investments in human capital. Alternatively, an approach to discrimination in employment based on a theory of a segmented labor market would emphasize the magnitude of these differentials and would underscore the disadvantaged position of women and racial minorities relative to that of white males. Segmented-labor-market theorists, more than proponents of the human capital approach, regard differentials in pay based on race and sex to be evidence of discrimination in the labor market, and they would be more likely to call for political action and legislative remedies to combat such discrimination.

CONTRASTING ECONOMIC PERSPECTIVES ON DISCRIMINATION

To appreciate more fully the nature of the contemporary debate about discrimination in the labor market, let us briefly consider the contrasting views of two well-known theorists, Gary Becker and Lester Thurow.[6] In providing the first systematic treatment of this subject, Becker defines discrimination as a "taste" on the part of an individual—say, an employer—for avoiding "transactions" with certain other individuals—say, black workers.[7] In this model, the employer would be willing to pay for indulging that taste by offering a wage premium to white workers, by searching more widely for them, and by avoiding transactions with black workers. All these activities are costly, however, and in Becker's analysis they may be measured by a discrimination coefficient. This is the real cost to the employer of exercising a taste for discrimination, but the employer is willing to pay it—to pay the price—because to him or her the psychic cost of dealing with black workers is even higher.

In effect, the employer who exercises a taste for discrimination—in this example, against blacks—restricts the available labor supply and thereby has higher labor costs than would be incurred by selecting and paying workers drawn from the entire labor pool. With higher labor costs and an unchanged demand for the firm's product, the discriminating employer will reduce output, revenues, and profits. Logical extension of this analysis indicates that this hypothetical employer may be forced out of business by pursuing discriminatory practices to the ultimate, for other firms will capture a larger share of the market and continue to operate with lower labor costs since they draw employees from the total supply of labor to the market. Even if many of them discriminate, there always is an incentive for the individual employer to reduce, if not entirely eliminate, discrimination in order to make greater profits. In much the same way that theorists who espouse a competitive labor market argue against the stability of a business cartel, Becker leads us to the conclusion that market forces will correct for the discrimination practiced by some employers.

Thurow challenges Becker's formulation on the grounds that it "implies a desire for physical distance from members of some recognizable demographic group,"[8] but in the real world one observes whites and nonwhites, as well as men and women, together at the workplace. Consequently, he contends, discrimination has more to do with a desire for social than for physical distance. Thurow conceptualizes the white male community as an enormous cartel wielding economic power to hold blacks and women in their place.[9] This is quite different from Becker's model, which envisions losses to both the black and the white communities as a result of discriminatory practices and hence also envisions inherent incentives to reduce discrimination. For Thurow, social pressures, custom, and even some government policies force white employers to discriminate against blacks, even if some, acting individually, would choose not to do so. This serves to reduce the costs to—that is, share the burden of costs among—those who discriminate. In Thurow's scenario:

> Less schooling [for blacks] leads to fewer job skills, easing [for employers] the problem of occupational, employment, and monopoly power discrimination. Together all of these lead to low incomes, which make price and human capital discrimination easier. Together they reduce Negro political power and make schooling discrimination possible. When all are viewed together, no white perceives great economic losses from discrimination, and consequently there are only minor economic pressures to put an end to it.[10]

Clearly, Becker and Thurow have fundamentally different views of the nature of the economy. Becker envisions competitive capitalism at work, or at least assumes its presence in formulating his model of discrimination, while Thurow sees much concentrated power in the economy and the insulation of employers from competitive forces. It is this basic difference which gives rise to their contrasting portrayals of discrimination in the labor market and of its consequences. As with other dimensions of economic behavior in which opposing models vie for supremacy, however, empirical analysis helps shed light on the phenomenon of discrimination in the labor market.

MEASURING DISCRIMINATION

Table 8-3 presents a summary compiled by Oaxaca of studies which have attempted to measure discrimination in the labor market against blacks and women or, more precisely, "to estimate how much of the observed race and sex wage differential can be explained by differences in average characteristics

Table 8-3   Estimates of Wage Differentials, by Sex and Race

Source [Author(s)]	Sample	Gross differential[1]	Unexplained differential[2]	Unexplained differential ÷ gross differential
Male/Female				
Blinder	White workers over age 25, 1967	0.57	0.68[3]	1.02
Cohen	Nonprofessional workers aged 22–64 who worked more than 35 hours per week, 1969	0.74	0.54[4]	0.73
Fuchs	Nonfarm employed workers, 1959	0.67	0.57[5]	0.85
Malkiel and Malkiel	Professional workers in a single firm, 1971	0.52	0.24[6]	0.45
Oaxaca	White urban workers, 1967	0.54	0.40[7]	0.74
Oaxaca	White year-round, full-time urban workers, 1960	0.79	0.56[8]	0.71
	1970	0.85	0.63[8]	0.74
White/Black				
Blinder	Male workers over age 25, 1967	0.66	0.43[3]	0.65
Oaxaca	Male urban workers, 1967	0.36	0.22[7]	0.61
	Male year-round, full-time urban workers, 1960	0.66	0.37[8]	0.56
	1970	0.53	0.29[8]	0.55

[1] The gross differential is calculated as the male (white)/female (black) wage ratio minus 1.

[2] The unexplained differential is calculated as the estimated female (black) wage in the absence of discrimination/actual female (black) wage ratio minus 1.

[3] Control variables: age, geographic region, parental income, father's education, place of birth/place grew up, number of siblings, labor market conditions, geographic mobility, seasonal employment.

[4] Annual hours of work, fringe benefits, absenteeism, seniority, education, unionization.

[5] Race, schooling, age, city size, marital status, class of work, length of trip to work.

[6] Schooling, experience, degree held, publications, marital status, field of study, absenteeism.

[7] Schooling, potential experience, health, part-time employment, migration, marital status, number of children for females, size of urban area, geographic region.

[8] Same as in footnote 7 minus health.

Source: Adapted from Ronald Oaxaca, "Theory and Measurement in the Economics of Discrimination," in Leonard J. Hausman et al. (eds.), *Equal Rights and Industrial Relations,* Industrial Relations Research Association, Madison, Wis., 1977, p. 26. This source provides a complete citation of the studies listed in this table.

[of workers] and how much is unexplained. . . .''[11] All these studies thus utilize a human capital approach to investigate discrimination in the labor market. In the absence of discrimination, any differences between blacks and whites or between men and women in terms of wages or wage structure would be based on differences in productivity between groups of workers. By dividing wage differentials into those which can be statistically explained by differences in workers' characteristics and those which remain unexplained, a preliminary estimate of the extent of discrimination in the labor market is obtained. As to the results of these studies, Oaxaca summarizes them as follows:

> On average, males earn 67 percent in excess of female wages. On average, 50 percentage points of the average gross differential cannot be explained by the sex differences in the selected personal characteristics. . . . Accordingly, discrimination would account for 75 percent (50/67) of the original 67 percent gross wage differential. On average, whites earn wages 55 percent in excess of the wages of blacks. Of this 55 percent wage gap, 33 percentage points cannot be explained by race differences in personal characteristics. . . . [Therefore] direct labor market discrimination is estimated to account for 60 percent (33/55) of the original 55 percent white/black differential.[12]

As Oaxaca himself points out, caution must be exercised in accepting these conclusions. Differences in personal characteristics having to do with race or sex, such as level of education or training, health, and work experience, can have a feedback effect on blacks and women which reduces their incentive to invest in themselves, compared with the incentive of white males. The "residual" approach to discrimination in the labor market takes these differences as given and therefore may underestimate the true incidence of discrimination. Conversely, it may be argued that, in the complete absence of discrimination, common wage structures might not exist among men and women or among blacks and whites.[13] One or another group may have innate preferences different from those of white males. Though that may seem an unlikely proposition to most readers and may even be offensive to some, it must be raised as a potential analytical limitation to any approach that indirectly measures discrimination in the labor market.

The studies listed in Table 8-3 have two additional limitations which must be noted in attempting to develop a balanced picture of discrimination in the labor market. The first is their inability to examine discrimination which takes the form of disproportionate representation of groups of workers among occupations. To be sure, a comparison of the earnings of men and women or of the earnings of blacks and whites for the purposes of detecting discrimination in the labor market could not proceed very far if it were not made on a "within occupation" basis. But by holding occupation constant, as was done by several of the researchers whose findings are included in Table 8-3, one cannot address the issue of differential access among men and women, whites and blacks, to job opportunities, professional or otherwise.[14]

This is hardly a minor issue. Consider that, in 1978, about 35 percent of all female workers but only about 6 percent of all male workers were employed in relatively low-paying clerical jobs. Well under one-quarter of female workers but well over one-quarter of male workers were employed in the relatively high-paying occupational categories of professional and technical workers and managers and administrators. That women tend to be concentrated in the lower-paying occupations is further demonstrated by the data on full-time, year-round workers, which show that 55 percent of female workers were employed in the occupational groups with the lowest median earnings—clerical, service, and farm—compared with 16 percent of male workers. Many factors other than discrimination may account for these different occupational distributions, but the data clearly reveal that women are more heavily represented than men in low-paying occupations, in addition to earning considerably less than men when employed in the same occupation. In general, a similar conclusion holds for blacks and other racial minorities relative to whites, which illustrates the intractability of discrimination in the labor market.

SEX-ROLE STEREOTYPING

Such comparisons provide a basis for applying to the labor market the concept of sex-role stereotyping, which has been developed in the feminist literature. The concentration of women in lower-paying occupational categories creates an impression or stereotype (one not confined to men, incidentally) that some jobs are women's work. The positions of clerk, public school teacher, nurse, social worker, and secretary would rank high on this list, in the same way that employment as an engineer, scientist, doctor, lawyer, or business manager has invariably been considered the province of men. These stereotypes reinforce employers' behavior in that women are recruited almost exclusively to fill the first group of jobs, and men to fill the second. The stereotypes as well as the actual distribution of men and women across occupational categories are fed back to the family and influence child-rearing patterns in such a way that young girls are encouraged to seek out jobs that are considered appropriate for women. In this scenario, aspirations toward professional, managerial, and scientific work are something to be developed principally, if not exclusively, by men. In this way, the different occupational distribution of men and women is maintained over time.

Recall from Chapter 1, though, that only in recent decades have women sought to participate in the labor force on a wide scale. This participation itself has undermined the traditional view that "a woman's place is in the home." As women's participation in the labor force continues to expand; as some women enter the professions, some become managers, and some are employed in skilled blue-collar jobs; and as women continue to gain experience and record accomplishments in these occupations, they will provide new role models for aspiring younger women in the way that older men do for younger men.

These observations lead to consideration of another limitation of the studies presented in Table 8-3, namely, their cross-sectional nature. Each investigator listed in Table 8-3 used data from a specific point in time; also, none of these data were for years before 1959 or after 1971. Apart from gross comparisons of the studies, which employed different samples, different independent and dependent variables, and different data bases, it is not possible to learn much from them about changes in discrimination in the labor market over time. For this, one needs longitudinal studies that compare changes in earnings differentials, occupational distribution, and other characteristics of the labor market among samples of men and women and of blacks and whites.

CHANGES IN DISCRIMINATION OVER TIME

To begin this type of analysis, we present in Figure 8-1 changes in the ratio of black men's median earnings (from wage and salary employment) to those of white men and changes in the ratio of black women's median earnings to those of white women in the post-World War II era to the mid-1970s.[15] Observe that the ratio for males was roughly constant until the mid-1960s, when it began to accelerate. The ratio grew to 0.70 in 1974 and 0.72 in 1975, but it then declined to 0.69 in 1976, about what it was in the early 1970s. The ratio for females shows steady upward growth since the mid-1950s, with acceleration again occurring in the mid-1960s and fluctuations characterizing the 1970s to levels of 0.95 in 1975 and 0.96 in 1976.

Figure 8-1 also presents changes in relative real family income during the postwar period. In this case, the ratio of the real income of black families to that of white families is generally constant throughout the period, except for brief growth in the mid-1960s, after which it fluctuated around 0.60. A plausible explanation of this pattern of stability is the rapid rise in the number of black households headed by women since the mid-1960s.[16] While the ratio of black women's income to that of white women rose in recent years, the income of women remains well below that of men, and so the increased proportion of black families headed by women acts to retard the growth of the income of black *families* relative to that of white families.

Taken alone, these data clearly suggest that, since the mid-1960s, blacks and other nonwhites have achieved gains in the labor market relative to whites, although the rates of gain slowed in the 1970s. Further, the gains have been greater among black women than among black men. As one student of this subject recently observed: "In the early 1950s, black women were further behind white women than black men were behind white men; by 1972 their relative income exceeded . . . that of black men."[17] Note, however, that the improvement in the income ratio for black women compared with white women has resulted as much from the slow increase in the income of white females as from the rapid increase in the income of black females.

What all this seems to add up to is a reduction in discrimination in the labor market against blacks and other nonwhites in American society over the last 10 to 15 years. If that is so, it suggests, in turn, a movement away from the racially divided society to which the National Advisory Commission on Civil Disorders

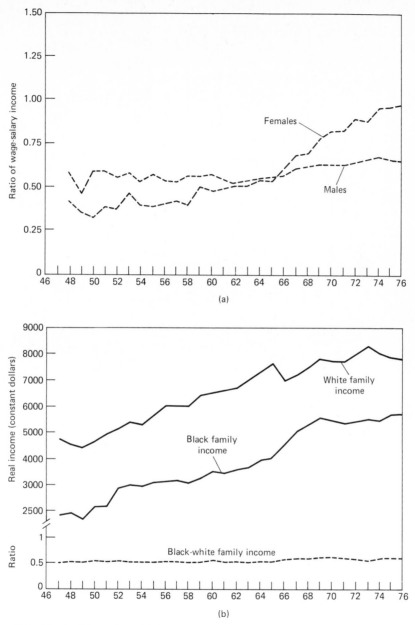

Figure 8-1 Black-white ratios of (*a*) earnings and (*b*) family income, 1947–1976. (*Sources: U.S. Bureau of Labor Statistics,* Current Population Reports: Money Income in 1976 of Families and Persons in the United States, *ser. P-60, no. 114, 1978, table 56, p. 246; U.S. Bureau of Labor Statistics,* Current Population Reports: Money Income in 1975 of Families and Persons in the United States, *ser. P-60, no. 105, 1977, table 56, p. 244; Richard Butler and James J. Heckman, "The Government's Impact on the Labor Market Status of Black Americans: A Critical Review,"* in Leonard Hausman et al., eds., Equal Rights and Industrial Relations, *Industrial Relations Research Association, Madison, Wis., 1977, pp. 237–243; James P. Smith and Finis Welch,* Race Differences in Earnings: A Survey and New Evidence, *Rand Corporation, Santa Monica, Calif., 1978; James P. Smith,* The Convergence to Racial Equality in Women's Wages, *Rand Corporation, Santa Monica, Calif., 1978.*)

referred in its 1968 report. The significance of such a development could hardly be overstated. But data on earnings and income tell only part of the story and may even lead to erroneous conclusions.

Recall that the rates of participation in the labor force of blacks—men and women—have fallen relative to the rates of whites. By 1978, the rate for black males was 6 points below that for white males whereas three decades earlier it had been 1 point above the rate for white males. In 1978, black women participated in the labor force at a rate less than 4 percentage points higher than that of white women, whereas the difference exceeded 18 points in 1948. These trends in rates of participation in the labor force are shown in Figure 8-2, where the rate for black men (women) is expressed as a ratio of the rate for white men (women). The decline in the rate for black women relative to that for white women reflects a slower growth of the rate for black women, but not a downturn in it. In fact, participation rates for black women remained steady in the 1970s, while rates for white women continued to grow, as they have done consistently in the post-World War II era. However, participation rates of black men have fallen, and more rapidly than those of white men; thus the black-white ratio of participation rates dropped to 0.93 by 1978. Moreover, the declines were not confined to older men, but occurred among black males of all ages.

The importance of the decline in the relative rates of black males' participation in the labor force is that it reduces the base of black members of the labor force who experience increased earnings relative to increased earnings of

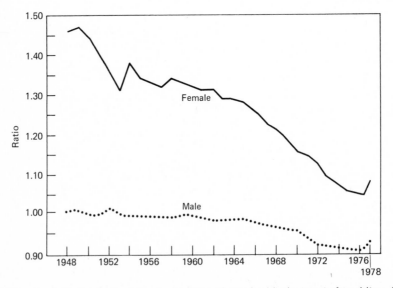

Figure 8-2 Participation in the labor force: ratio of rate for blacks to rate for whites, 1948–1978. (*Sources:* Employment and Training Report of the President, 1978, *U.S. Government Printing Office, Washington, D.C., 1978, table A-4, pp. 185–188; U.S. Bureau of Labor Statistics,* Employment and Earnings, January 1979, *1979, table 3, pp. 156–157; and Richard B. Freeman, "Changes in the Labor Market for Black Americans, 1948–72,"* Brookings Papers on Economic Activity I: 1973, *Brookings, Washington, D.C., 1973, p. 72.*)

white men. In other words, those black males who participate in the labor force may indeed have improved their position in the labor market (their earnings) relative to that of white males, but to have a more complete analysis of discrimination in employment, one has to take into account those black men who have been dropping out of the labor force in larger proportions than white men. Such withdrawal could result from discouragement about the prospects of finding a job, especially during periods of economic recession.[18] Alternatively, some black men apparently have been encouraged to drop out of the labor force by federal transfer payment programs, such as public assistance and unemployment insurance, particularly if their employment opportunities are limited to low-paying jobs. Thus, the apparent improvement in the relative earnings of black men in the labor force may be in part illusory. Indeed, two students of this subject forcefully conclude that "growth in relative black status (as measured by earnings) has nothing to do with a lessening of discrimination against blacks."[19] This interpretation is also supported by the evidence of stability in the family income of blacks relative to that of whites, except for brief improvement in the mid-1960s, even as the earnings of black men were rising relative to those of white men.

Data on unemployment provide additional insight into differences in experiences in the labor market due to race and sex. We know that for all workers unemployment varies with the economic cycle, rising during periods of contraction and falling during expansionary times. But the data on trends over several economic cycles in the post-World War II era show that unemployment rates for women have remained above those for men and that unemployment rates for blacks have remained well above those for whites, though the relative position of both "minority groups" was somewhat better in the 1970s than it had been in the 1960s. For blacks in particular, the continuation of unemployment rates about twice those of whites is a particularly troublesome characteristic of the labor market. Though these are gross statistics and probably mask as much as they reveal, the aggregate unemployment rate is perhaps the most widely accepted indicator of racial differences, if not discrimination, in the labor market. Thus, Figure 8-3 presents ratios of unemployment rates of blacks and whites separately for men and for women. Unlike ratios of relative earnings, the unemployment ratios for the two groups of black workers behave quite similarly over time. By this measure, in other words, the extent of relative discrimination in the labor market against blacks over time does not differ between men and women.

Two factors that are critical to the experiences in the labor market of the work force and its subgroups are age and education. This is startlingly revealed by the data from the decennial census shown in Table 8-4. These data yield several conclusions.[20] First, younger blacks do better than older blacks relative to whites, both in the aggregate and at different levels of education. For men, the income ratios decline fairly consistently by age, while for women, they drop for those 45 years old and over. Second, younger workers improve their position over time more than older workers. Black men 18 to 24 years of age improved their relative income position by 15 percentage points between 1959 and 1969;

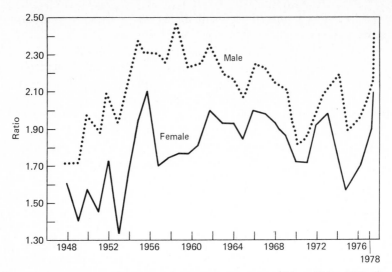

Figure 8-3 Unemployment: ratio of rate for blacks to rate for whites, 1948–1978. (*Sources:* Employment and Training Report of the President, 1978, *U.S. Government Printing Office, Washington, D.C., 1978, table A-20, pp. 213–214; U.S. Bureau of Labor Statistics,* Employment and Earnings, January 1979, *1979, table 3, pp. 156–157; and Richard B. Freeman, "Changes in the Labor Market for Black Americans, 1948–72,"* Brookings Papers on Economic Activity I: 1973, *Brookings, Washington, D.C., 1973, p. 72.*)

those aged 35 to 44 by 9 points; and those aged 55 to 64, by only 5 points. For women, the same patterns were evident, though the changes were considerably larger than those for men; the ratios increased by 37, 26, and 17 percentage points, respectively, for the three age groups over the period 1959–1969.

Third, the levels of, and changes in, income ratios vary by the educational attainment of black workers. Among young (18 to 34 years old) black men, the largest increases were recorded by college graduates, followed by high school graduates and grade school graduates. The pattern is different for black women, among whom the college-educated in 1959 were already earning as much as, or more than, white women. However, young female high school graduates increased their earnings ratios by larger magnitudes than young grade school graduates, and these two groups of women were far larger numerically than the group of black female college graduates. Finally, observe that among men a cohort of black workers experiences relative income stability over time. The 25 to 34-year-old group of black men, undifferentiated by education, had an income ratio of 59 in 1949. Ten years later, when this group constituted the 35 to 44-year-old age category, its relative income ratio was, again, 59 (using median data), and 10 years after that it was 58.

Not every group of workers who are similar in terms of age and educational attainment displays such relative income stability over time, and the experience of black women is considerably different from that of black men. Nevertheless, what these data indicate is that "the economic position of older men is less sensitive to market developments than that of other workers . . . pre-

Table 8-4   Average Income of Nonwhites as a Percentage of Average Income, by Age, Education, and Sex, 1949, 1959, and 1969

Education and age	Male				Female		
	1949, using median	1959		1969, using mean	1949, using median	1959, using median	1969, using mean
		Using median	Using mean[1]				
All levels of education							
18–24	70	70	67	85	46	55	92
25–34	59	61	61	70	56	70	95
35–44	55	59	57	64	55	65	91
45–54	54	55	52	58	49	46	76
55–64	49	52	51	54	49	52	69
Grade school graduates							
18–24	74	70	71	72	62	78	90
25–34	73	68	71	74	72	72	93
35–44	67	72	73	72	68	72	86
45–54	70	71	70	74	64	61	81
55–64	69	68	69	73	73	68	77
High school graduates							
18–24	74	68	73	87	52	57	95
25–34	72	70	69	76	67	78	103
35–44	67	72	71	71	70	84	102
45–54	63	68	62	70	62	68	92
55–64	63	67	57	66	66	61	80
College graduates, 4 years or more							
18–24	81	76	80	98	90	91	97
25–34	64	68	67	78	93	107	114
35–44	59	62	59	71	94	109	118
45–54	56	58	49	65	85	91	106
55–64	52	56	45	57	81	82	91

[1] Since median earnings in 1969 were not available, mean earnings are shown. This results in a small bias against nonwhites in 1969.

Source: Adapted from Richard B. Freeman, "Changes in the Labor Market for Black Americans, 1948–72," *Brookings Papers on Economic Acitivity 1, 1973,* Brookings, Washington, 1973, p. 83.

sumably because of the difficulty that older black men have in taking advantage of new market opportunities requiring occupational mobility and investment in skills."[21] For black women, among whom income ratios rise sharply as a cohort advances in age, investment in job skills and commitment (perhaps need) to work may be greater than for white women, and the types of clerical and factory-operative work which many of them perform do not require extensive training. Stated differently and using specific cases to illustrate the point, a black woman could enter into a clerical or an operative job with relative ease during the expansionary 1960s and thereby earn income equivalent to that of a white woman. But an older black male could not as easily switch into skilled construction work, for example, which may have also become available in the tight labor markets of the 1960s. Hence we observe the differential experiences in the labor market of black men and black women during the 1960s, when the nation experienced the most sustained economic expansion in its history. This illustrates why data on aggregate earnings by race tell only part of the story of discrimination in the labor market.

More on Occupations and Education

Additional perspective on the role of race and sex in the labor market is provided by the data in Tables 8-5 and 8-6. These show changes in the occupational distribution of blacks and whites—both men and women—over the period 1958-1978. Observe in Table 8-5 that the ratio of employment of blacks in white-collar jobs to that of whites increased from 0.30 to 0.70 during this 20-year span, with the largest relative increases recorded in the professional, technical, and sales categories. Blacks also increased their relative share of craft positions, while decreasing their shares of service, laboring, and farm jobs. The overall employment of blacks in blue-collar jobs relative to that of whites changed very little between 1958 and 1978. On balance, these data indicate considerable improvement over this two-decade period in the relative occupational position of blacks in the labor sector.

There is another side to this coin, however, for in the late 1970s blacks continued to be overrepresented (compared with whites) in relatively low-paying service and laboring jobs and to be underrepresented in relatively high-paying

Table 8-5 Occupational Distribution of Whites and Nonwhites, 1958 and 1978

Occupational category	Whites (percent)		Nonwhites (percent)		Ratio of nonwhites to whites	
	1958	1978	1958	1978	1958	1978
White collar	45.8	51.8	13.8	36.2	0.30	0.70
Professional and technical workers	11.8	15.5	4.1	11.7	0.35	0.75
Managers and administrators	11.6	11.4	2.4	4.8	0.21	0.42
Sales workers	6.9	6.7	1.2	2.8	0.17	0.42
Clerical workers	15.4	18.0	6.1	16.9	0.40	0.94
Blue collar	36.6	32.9	40.7	37.2	1.11	1.13
Craft and kindred workers	13.4	13.7	5.9	8.8	0.44	0.64
Operatives	14.3	14.6	20.1	20.5	1.41	1.40
Nonfarm laborers	4.5	4.6	14.7	7.9	3.27	1.72
Service	9.5	12.3	33.0	24.1	3.47	1.96
Private household workers	1.7	0.8	15.4	3.6	9.06	4.00
Others	7.7	11.4	17.7	20.5	2.30	1.80
Farm	8.0	3.0	12.5	2.4	1.56	0.80
Farmers and farm managers	5.0	1.7	3.7	0.4	0.74	0.24
Farm laborers and supervisors	3.0	1.3	8.5	2.0	2.93	1.54

Source: Adapted from *Employment and Training Report of the President, 1978,* 1978, p. 208, table A-16; and U.S. Bureau of Labor Statistics, *Employment and Earnings, January, 1979,* 1979, p. 171, table 22.

Table 8-6 Occupational Distribution of Men and Women, 1958 and 1978

Occupational category	Men, percent		Women, percent		Ratio of women to men	
	1958	1978	1958	1978	1958	1978
White collar	36.5	40.8	55.1	63.2	1.51	1.55
Professional and technical workers	10.4	14.7	12.3	15.6	1.18	1.06
Managers and administrators	13.6	14.0	5.0	6.1	0.37	0.44
Sales workers	5.7	5.9	7.6	6.9	1.33	1.17
Clerical workers	6.9	6.2	30.1	34.6	4.36	5.58
Blue collar	46.8	46.4	17.1	14.8	0.37	0.32
Craft and kindred workers	19.4	21.1	1.1	1.8	0.06	0.09
Operatives	19.4	17.7	15.5	11.8	0.80	0.67
Nonfarm laborers	8.0	7.6	0.5	1.2	0.06	0.16
Service	6.4	8.7	23.2	20.7	3.63	2.38
Private household workers	0.1	0.1	9.4	2.9	94.0	29.0
Others	6.3	8.6	13.8	17.8	2.19	2.07
Farm	10.4	4.1	4.7	1.3	0.45	0.32
Farmers and farm managers	7.0	2.4	0.6	0.3	0.09	0.13
Farm laborers and supervisors	3.4	1.7	4.1	1.0	1.21	0.59

Sources: Adapted from *Employment and Training Report of the President, 1978*, 1978, p. 206, table A-15; and U.S. Bureau of Labor Statistics, *Employment and Earnings, January, 1979*, 1979, p. 171, table 22.

craft, professional and technical, and managerial and administrative positions. Concerning sales jobs, which rank about in the middle of the occupational earnings hierarchy, blacks improved their position noticeably between 1958 and 1978, but they were still no better represented here than in managerial and administrative jobs. Keep in mind, too, that within occupational categories, blacks tend to be overrepresented in lower-paying jobs and underrepresented in higher-paying ones. Thus, blacks have made progress in the labor market in recent years, but they have by no means attained equality with whites.

Concerning women, the data in Table 8-6 show them to be disproportionately represented in service jobs, but less so in 1978 than in 1958. Over that span, however, the ratio of female to male workers in clerical positions increased by more than 1 point, and in 1978, about 35 percent of *all* working women were employed in such jobs, compared with about 6 percent of all working men. Between one-sixth and one-seventh of the women were in the professional and technical category, or approximately 1 percentage point more than men, with the differential having declined slightly (in favor of men) since the late 1950s. Similarly, little change was recorded over the period 1958–1978 in terms of proportions of men and women in craft employment. However, this occupational category accounts for 21 percent of all working men but for only about 2 percent of all working women. The ratio of females to males employed as operatives declined from 4 : 5 to 2 : 3 between 1958 and 1978. On balance, then, a snapshot of the occupational distribution of employment by sex taken in 1958 would show reasonably well the actual distribution some two decades later.

Turning to education, it is well known that the American work force has received—invested in—more formal schooling over time, but how has this differed by sex and by race? Table 8-7 provides the data necessary to answer this question. Between the early 1950s and the mid-1970s, the median number of years of schooling completed by men in the labor force climbed from 10.4 to 12.6. For women, the median number of years of schooling completed over this period also increased, but by a considerably smaller amount—from 12.0 to 12.6 years. Consequently, by 1977, men and women workers had completed the same number of years of schooling, but only because men had finally caught up to women.[22]

More impressive, however, were the relative educational gains of blacks in the labor force over the period 1952–1977. In 1952, black men trailed white men by more than 3 years in terms of median amounts of schooling, and black women trailed almost 4 years behind white women. By 1977, black men and black women workers had attained median levels of schooling slightly beyond high school graduation, and they trailed their white counterparts by only 0.5 and 0.3 years, respectively. As with earnings experiences, however, black women have done better than black men with respect to relative levels of schooling. In 1977, almost 11 percent of black women in the work force were college graduates, compared with about 15 percent of white women, while among men the corresponding percentages were 7.4 and 19.6. The percentages of women with 8 years of schooling or less in 1977 were 13.7 for blacks and 6.9 for whites; the percentages of men in this category were 21.3 for blacks and 10.8 for whites.

But if racial differences in schooling remain larger for men than for women, black men in the labor force nevertheless increased their median level of schooling by 5 full years between 1952 and 1977, significantly narrowing the advantage enjoyed by white men. Such relative increases in schooling account for some of the improved experience in the labor market of black men in the 1960s and to a lesser extent in the 1970s, even if they have not led to a fully equivalent narrowing of the earnings differentials between black males and white males. This conclusion is tempered, though, when we recognize the important differences in the quality of education that exist between blacks (and other minorities) and whites and their implications for success in the labor market.[23]

In sum, the welter of statistics presented here on the role of race and sex in the labor market are subject to varying interpretations, but we shall nevertheless risk some general conclusions. The most important of these is that discrimination in the labor market against racial minorities and women seems to be diminishing over time, but at a slower pace in the 1970s than in the 1960s. This is consistent with the more general view that tight labor markets are a necessary condition for combating discrimination in employment.

Concerning the *extent* to which discrimination has actually declined and the magnitude of the remaining discrimination, there are so many measures and interpretations of available data that a single conclusion is difficult to draw and

Table 8-7 Years of Schooling Completed by the Civilian Labor Force, by Sex and Race, 1952 and 1977

	Male			Female		
	All races	White	Black and other	All races	White	Black and other
1952						
Median years completed[1]	10.4	10.8	7.2	12.0	12.1	8.1
Percent distribution[2]						
Elementary school						
Less than 5 years	8.2	6.3	29.8	5.4	2.9	22.4
5–8 years	32.4	31.9	38.3	25.4	23.4	39.2
High school						
1–3 years	18.6	18.9	15.0	18.2	18.4	17.1
4 years	23.3	24.6	9.5	33.8	36.9	12.6
College						
1–3 years	8.0	8.4	3.4	8.8	9.6	4.0
More than 4 years	8.0	8.5	1.9	7.7	8.3	3.6
1977						
Median years completed[1]	12.6	12.6	12.1	12.6	12.6	12.3
Percent distribution[2]						
Elementary school						
Less than 5 years	1.9	1.5	5.5	0.9	0.7	1.8
5–8 years	9.9	9.3	15.8	6.9	6.2	11.9
High school						
1–3 years	17.2	16.5	24.8	17.0	16.1	23.9
4 years	36.0	36.4	33.1	44.6	45.6	38.2
College						
1–3 years	16.4	16.7	13.4	16.3	16.6	13.5
More than 4 years	18.7	19.6	7.4	14.4	14.7	10.6

[1] These figures are in years.
[2] These figures are percentages. Note that the percent distributions for each category may not add to 100, because of rounding.
Source: Adapted from Employment and Training Report of the President, 1978, 1978, pp. 248–249, table B-9.

would be too simple in any case. For example, women are as fully educated as men and have entered the labor force in record proportions in recent years, but they have less on-the-job training and work experience than men, that is, less human capital. But if this means that they would be expected to earn less than men, it does not explain why their occupational distribution has failed to improve very much relative to that of men or why greater educational attainment yields them smaller increases in earnings than it does for men.

By several measures, black women have approached, attained, or even exceeded parity with white women in the labor market, but they also have a demonstrably greater need to be in the labor market than white women. Black men have improved their position in the labor market relative to that of white men, but the pace has not been as rapid as for black women, and their relative earnings position has remained roughly constant in the 1970s. Finally, the cross-sectional research (see Table 8-3) provides important evidence of the continuing significance of this problem, even as the incidence of discrimination has moderated over time. Thus, if American society is less racially divided today than the National Advisory Commission on Civil Disorders concluded it was in 1967, there remain major divisions by race and by sex which are clearly reflected in the labor market.

The Question of Illegal Aliens

Before moving on to consider attempts to regulate discrimination in the American labor market, let us briefly turn our attention to a related topic of significance, illegal aliens.

Since 1964, the flow of illegal aliens, overwhelmingly Mexicans, into the United States has increased markedly. One measure of this increase is the number of illegal aliens apprehended, which rose from 85,000 annually in the early 1960s to 866,000 in fiscal 1976.[24] Of course, apprehended illegal aliens constitute only a small portion of all illegal aliens, about whom accurate information is, understandably, very difficult to come by. For the mid-1970s, estimates of the number of illegal aliens in the United States range from 1 million to 8 million. One appraisal of these estimates has recently concluded that "there are between three and six million illegal aliens in the U.S., with two to four million in the labor market."[25] The increase in the flow of illegal aliens into the United States was coincident with the ending in 1964 of the bracero program, originated during World War II, which permitted Mexican nationals to be employed in agricultural work on a contract-labor basis in California and Texas. The tremendous population growth in Mexican border cities between 1940 and 1970 also contributed to the increase in illegal entrants to the United States, but a more important factor was the great disparity between earnings opportunities in Mexico and those in the United States. Average *daily* earnings for landless rural workers in Mexico ranged from $2 to $2.80 in the mid-1970s, compared with the *hourly* legal minimum wage of $2.30 which then prevailed in the United States.[26] The recent devaluation of the Mexican peso has added to the incentives for migration to the United States. Additionally, the tight labor markets in this country in the late 1960s encouraged employers to hire illegal aliens, whom they often found to be reliable and productive, and "a cumulative effect then began to operate."[27] As to the immigration law, which seeks to control the flow of aliens, legal or otherwise, into the United States, it is easily broken and not vigorously enforced by American authorities.

The most controversial issue with respect to illegal aliens in the labor market is the extent to which they displace American workers and depress wage rates. The data do not permit very firm conclusions. Fogel tells us that "a complete removal of illegals tomorrow would . . . not result in their one-for-one replacement by resident workers; the amount of replacement would be governed by the wage elasticities of labor supply and demand."[28] Certainly some among the several million unemployed American workers would take jobs presently held by illegal aliens, but many would not. As to the effects of the employment of illegal aliens on wages, two studies have found wage rates increasing from the south to the north (away from border towns) in California and Texas, respectively, the implication being that an influx of illegal aliens across the Mexican-American border does act to lower wage rates compared with what they otherwise would be.[29] However, any increase in the labor supply relative to demand serves to lower wage rates, other things remaining constant, and the volume of illegal participants in the labor force is but one among several factors affecting geographical wage differentials. It is probably true, however, that the unavailability of illegal aliens would raise costs and, to some extent, the prices of goods and services in those industries where they are most heavily employed—agriculture, apparel manufacturing, hotels and restaurants, and others which we know little about.

The issue of illegal aliens raises questions of public policy which must take into account values and ethics as well as considerations concerning the labor market. Most of the present debate centers on the imposition of penalties on employers who hire illegal aliens. The AFL-CIO supports such penalties, believing that its efforts to organize the nonmanufacturing sector are undercut by illegal aliens, who willingly accept substandard working conditions (by American definitions). Employers and civil rights groups generally oppose penalties for the employment of illegal aliens.

Others advocate special treatment of Mexico in the formation of immigration policy, a position which flies in the face of recent congressional action, in 1976 and 1978, that amended the immigration law to treat all nations the same, to a considerable extent, in terms of immigration quotas (20,000 maximum from any one country) and rules establishing priorities among applicants. Also, while the United States might profit from a careful review of the policies of other nations concerning their "guest" (immigrant) workers, as some people have urged, most other nations have no unified policy and, in recent years, have experienced considerable disillusionment with their own efforts in this regard. Clearly, the question of illegal aliens will persist into the 1980s, and one would hope for better data about this issue in order to guide public policy.

REGULATING DISCRIMINATION IN THE LABOR MARKET

How has the incidence of discrimination in the labor market been affected by attempts to regulate it through public policy? This is an exceptionally important question, no matter what one believes about changes in, or the extent of, discrimination in the labor market. To answer it—more accurately, to approach an answer to it—we must review the legal treatment of discrimination in the labor market over the last 15 years or so.

The cornerstone of federal policy in this area is the Civil Rights Act of 1964, Title VII of which declares it illegal for an employer to discriminate against any individual on the basis of race, color, religion, sex, or national origin in any way that would deprive that person of employment opportunities or otherwise adversely affect his or her status. The act originally applied to private business, labor organizations, employment agencies, and apprenticeship programs; it was extended to state and local governments by legislative amendments enacted in 1972.[30] Those same amendments set a minimum of fifteen employees for a business or labor organization to be covered by the law. Title VII of the act is administered by the Equal Employment Opportunity Commission (EEOC), a five-member board appointed by the President of the United States, with headquarters in Washington, D.C., and branch offices in various locations throughout the country.

The circumstances surrounding passage of the Civil Rights Act are both interesting and instructive. The legislation came to fruition during the administration of Lyndon Johnson, who succeeded to the Presidency following the assassination in 1963 of John F. Kennedy. Earlier that year, civil rights advocates led the famous "march on Washington," which saw hundreds of thousands of people exercise their rights of peaceful assembly and free speech to petition the federal government for added protection of civil liberties in all aspects of social and economic relations. The highlight of that gathering, perhaps, was the fiery oration of Martin Luther King, Jr., delivered at the base of the Washington Monument, in which he articulated the desire of blacks to be truly "free at last." That speech and, more generally, the march itself exemplified the ferment in the early 1960s over the issues of greater rights and economic advancement for minorities.

These events, together with the assassination of President Kennedy and the leadership abilities of President Johnson, contributed to a legislative climate that supported liberal economic and social legislation in the mid-1960s. To be sure, none of these laws were automatically enacted at the behest of the executive branch of the government. Before passage, the Civil Rights Act in particular was subjected to extended debate and was adopted only after a major lobbying effort on its behalf, most notably by the AFL-CIO. Subsequent attempts to deal with racial discrimination practiced by some labor unions should not dim the memory of the labor movement's basic and critical support of the nation's key civil rights law.

Interestingly, the inclusion in Title VII of sex as a prohibited basis of discrimination emerged, according to informed observers, out of the efforts of southern Democrats and conservative Republicans, who added it as an amendment to the original bill in the belief that Congress would not vote into law so sweeping an antidiscrimination statute. Thus, women are today protected against discrimination in employment (in theory if not fully in practice) as a result of a fluke of the legislative process, rather than a careful, deliberate effort to address their particular problems in the labor market.

The Equal Employment Opportunity Commission

As the agency established to administer Title VII of the Civil Rights Act, the EEOC understandably has been at the center of efforts aimed at eliminating discrimination, and its activities have been widely scrutinized. It is important for the reader to understand the role and function of this agency. Unlike the NLRB, whose activities we reviewed in Chapters 3 and 5, the EEOC does not have the power to issue cease and desist orders which are enforceable in the courts, to reinstate workers who have suffered discrimination in employment, or to impose on employers financial penalties such as mandatory back-pay awards. Rather, the Commission's role is to seek on a case-by-case basis voluntary compliance by employers with the letter and the spirit of the law.

When such voluntary compliance is achieved, it takes the form of a conciliation or consent agreement between the employer and the Commission, in which the former pledges to refrain from discrimination, to provide equal employment opportunity, and to correct the underrepresentation of minority-group and women employees if and where that exists. This positive (or affirmative) action contrasts with the emphasis in earlier years on the elimination of racial bars to employment and the urging of employers to be "color-blind."[31] In pursuit of affirmative action, the employer specifies in the consent agreement numerical goals for the employment of minorities and women and a timetable for achieving them. The goals, which are established in consultation and negotiation with the Commission, depend in part on the nature of the labor market or markets from which the employer recruits workers. The agreement may also contain a methodology for analyzing the market to determine the firm's appropriate level of employment of minorities and women.

In its early years, the EEOC proceeded on a case-by-case basis to conciliate with employers and to conclude affirmative action agreements. These dealt almost solely with racial discrimination, the issue of women's representation in the work force being regarded at that time by both the Commission and employers as less pressing than that of employment of minorities. The Commission also encouraged some complainants to pursue legal action in the courts against employers who refused voluntarily to modify their allegedly discriminatory practices, and it referred to the Attorney General for prosecution selected cases involving a pattern of discrimination.

In 1972, however, when Congress amended the Civil Rights Act, the EEOC was given the power to pursue court actions on the behalf of complainants, and this added an important weapon to its meager stock of mechanisms for enforcement. But the Commission has yet to gain the authority to issue cease and desist orders, which many of its critics contend is essential to the enforcement of a meaningful antidiscrimination policy. Moreover, the 1972 amendments increased the EEOC's already large caseload, adding to a backlog which itself interferes with effective implementation of Title VII. Upon her appointment in 1977, the Commission's chairwoman, Eleanor Holmes Norton, identified the reduction of the backload as an item of top priority.

It should be recognized that the operations of the EEOC, which is to say its ability to implement equal employment opportunity, are linked to state and local commissions established to promote fair employment practices. In the two-thirds of the states in which such commissions exist, the EEOC must defer to them for at least 60 days any action on a complaint of discrimination. If the state commission cannot successfully resolve the complaint, the aggrieved individual can reapply to the EEOC for action, which is what in fact occurs in about eight out of ten cases. Apart from limiting the EEOC to indirect jurisdiction over discrimination in employment in a clear majority of the states, this arrangement for deferral has "prolonged the period during which the complainant waits for redress, constrained federal efforts to modify or amend the investigation, and . . . [failed to] alleviate the EEOC's enormous caseload."[32] Finally the EEOC has only limited power to investigate, hold public hearings, and subpoena witnesses, though it can hear voluntary witnesses and pay fees on the same basis as the federal courts.

The Office of Federal Contract Compliance Programs

The other major component of national policy in the area of equal employment opportunity is Executive Order 11246, originally issued in 1965, which is designed to prevent discriminatory practices among employers holding contracts with the federal government. This order, the sixth in a series dating back to the administration of Franklin D. Roosevelt, not only forbids federal contractors to discriminate on the basis of race, creed, color, sex, or national origin but also requires that they take affirmative action to guarantee potential employees equal access to jobs. Contractors must state in their help-wanted advertisements that they are equal opportunity employers; they must notify their subcontractors of this, thereby binding them to the provisions of Executive Order 11246; and they must comply with the federal government's requests for information.

To enforce this order, the Office of Federal Contract Compliance Programs (OFCCP) was established in the Department of Labor, and in 1968 it issued a requirement that contractors develop written affirmative action plans containing goals and timetables to correct deficiencies in equal employment opportunity. In early 1970, the OFCCP amended this requirement with Order 4, which was applicable to organizations with fifty or more employees and with contracts in excess of $50,000 and which called for federal contractors to do the following: analyze utilization of minorities in all job categories, establish goals and timetables to correct deficiencies, and develop data-collection systems and plans for reporting progress in achieving such goals. In late 1971 the order was revised to include women,[33] and in mid-1972 detailed, standardized procedures were established for complying with its provisions.

Executive Order 11246 is a potentially more powerful device than Title VII of the Civil Rights Act for promoting equal employment opportunity. Under the act, affirmative action can be ordered by a court only after a party has been found guilty of a legal violation, whereas no such legal determination is necessary for the OFCCP to require an affirmative action agreement from a government contractor. Sanctions for failure to comply with the Executive order include the cancellation of contracts, the suspension of a noncomplying employer from participation in future government contracts unless the employer shows a willingness to follow the intent of the order, publication and dissemination of the names of noncomplying contractors and unions, and recommendations by the OFCCP for legal actions to be taken by the EEOC and for court suits to be initiated by the Justice Department. Thus, Executive Order 11246 has considerably more teeth than Title VII of the Civil Rights Act, and the OFCCP's power of enforcement surpasses that of the EEOC. Note, however, that under the order, actual cancellations of contracts have been few and that individual complainants have only rarely been encouraged to file for redress. This is because the OFCCP places its major emphasis on compliance reviews and preaward programs that cover the entire scope of the employment activities of contractors and subcontractors.

The Department of Health, Education, and Welfare

Under the federal system for regulating discrimination in contracting organizations, the OFCCP delegated the enforcement of Executive Order 11246 and its accompanying revisions to other federal agencies that had contracts in particular industries. In the case of colleges and universities, delegation was to the Department of Health, Education, and Welfare (HEW), whose Office of Civil Rights (OCR) handled the actual negotiations over numerical goals and other aspects of affirmative action plans. Thus, HEW had the power to suspend or terminate all federal contracts with any institution of higher education that failed to comply with affirmative action in general or to meet specific goals and timetables set out in written agreements with the federal government. Beginning in late 1978, however, the OFCCP assumed all enforcement responsibility for the program for contract compliance, reversing the pattern of delegation that had prevailed up to that time. Also in 1978, the Department of Labor (in which the OFCCP is located), the Department of Justice, the EEOC, and the Civil Service Commission developed the first uniform guidelines for selection of employees, thereby further reflecting the federal government's intent to standardize the enforcement of antidiscrimination policy.[34]

In higher education, where HEW held sway, efforts to promote equal employment opportunities have focused more centrally on remedying discrimination against women than against blacks and other racial minorities. Indeed, as one student of this subject recently noted: "Women's organizations mounted an early and wide-ranging campaign charging that universities and their faculties, most of whom share in faculty personnel decisions, have been guilty of sex discrimination in violation of [federal] Executive Orders. . . ."[35] Women's groups have filed individual and class-action lawsuits against numerous colleges and universities, including the entire state systems of California, Florida, and New Jersey, alleging systematic underpayment, underrepresentation, and underpromotion of women on college faculties. They have also filed hundreds of similar charges with various federal enforcement agencies, leading federal officials to draw up guidelines for affirmative action plans in institutions of higher education which include the use of numerical goals and timetables for hiring women according to their estimated underutilization in particular job classifications.

Again, the clout of the federal government in this area is its ability to cut off funds to contracting colleges and universities; in some institutions, these funds amount to more than half of total revenues. Faced with the potential withdrawal of major funds, several of the nation's leading universities—the University of California, Columbia University, the University of Michigan, and Harvard University—signed formal agreements with HEW which committed them to specific goals concerning the employment of women and minorities in both the academic and the nonacademic ranks, together with timetables for achieving these goals. This process of enforcement and the related consent agreements have been highly controversial, especially because of what some critics contend are their unrealistic assumptions about the academic labor market and the time required to alter the racial and sexual composition of labor supplies to that market.[36] Nevertheless, these events illustrate how, under the procedure for contract compliance, the federal government has attempted to implement in the higher education sector a policy of nondiscrimination in employment.

The Equal Pay Act

It should be noted that the Civil Rights Act of 1964 and Executive Order 11246, issued in 1965, were not the first federal actions intended to combat discrimination in employment against women. They were preceded in 1963 by an amendment to the Fair Labor Standards Act of 1938 (to be reviewed in Chapter 10), which required "equal pay for equal work." Known as the "Equal Pay Act," this legislation is administered by the Wage-Hour and Public Contracts Division of the Department of Labor. The law is designed to eliminate wage differentials based on sex, and it prohibits employers from lowering wages in order to overcome existing pay differentials. Such differentials may, however, be based on merit, seniority, or incentive plans.

As the reader might guess, it is a rather tricky process to determine precisely the basis of pay differentials, that is, to know when they are based on the purportedly objective criteria of merit, seniority, and incentive plans, as opposed to the subjective, discriminatory standard of sex. Similarly, it is not always clear when equal work is being performed, but even when it is, pay rates can differ among individuals and yet be regarded as equal if they derive from differences in merit, seniority, and the like. Such difficulties confront officials of the Department of Labor who are charged with enforcing the Equal Pay Act, but these difficulties have not prevented them from investigating thousands of complaints and from helping bring hundreds of cases to the courts, resulting in back-pay awards that now total many millions of dollars. Incidentally, the Department's Wage-Hour and Public Contracts Division also bears the responsibility for enforcing the Age Discrimination in Employment Act of 1967, which was intended to protect workers 40 to 65 years of age from discriminatory treatment in matters of job classification, layoff, hiring, and compensation. Under both these laws, the Division seeks voluntary compliance from employers and assists complainants in bringing cases to court.

The Taft-Hartley Act

Another avenue for redress of discrimination in employment, this one confined to workers who are or who attempt to be represented by unions, is the Labor-Management Relations (Taft-Hartley) Act, administered by the NLRB. As originally set down in this law, "discrimination in employment" referred to an employer's differential treatment of a worker on the basis of that person's membership in, or support of, a labor organization. The Board could hear cases and, where warranted, find an employer guilty of discriminating against a unionized worker in matters such as pay, job assignments, discharges, and layoffs. After 1947, with the Taft-Hartley amendments to the Wagner Act, the Board could also remedy a union's discriminatory practices, but, again, only insofar as these pertained to an individual's exercise of his or her rights to join a union, to refrain from unionism, and to give testimony under the law. The act did not appear to cover discrimination in employment based on race or sex when such discrimination occurred in the context of union-management relations, and certainly for many years the Board did not interpret the law as applying to this kind of discrimination.

In the 1960s, however, the Board began to change its views and rulings, as it focused on discriminatory practices in unions. In the 1964 *Hughes Tool* case, for example, the Board refused to certify as the workers' bargaining representative a union that engaged in discriminatory practices.[37] The Board explained: "We . . . cannot validly render aid under Section 9 of the [Taft-Hartley] Act to a labor organization which discriminates racially when acting as a statutory bargaining agent."[38] In another case, the Board found an unfair labor practice to exist when a union had established separate all-white and all-black locals, dividing work unfairly between them.[39] The importance of these rulings and of others subsequently rendered is that they declared unions in violation of the duty of fair representation and hence guilty of an unfair labor practice when they engaged in racial discrimination. Rather than simply revoking a union's certification because it practices racial discrimination, a ruling that may have little practical effect on aggrieved minority-group workers, the Board can issue a cease and desist order, enforceable in the courts, which seeks to "make the worker whole." Recall that this is a stronger remedy than is available to the EEOC.

Moreover, in the 1969 *United Packinghouse, Food and Allied Workers v. NLRB* case[40] and in subsequent decisions, the Court of Appeals found in favor of the NLRB by ruling that where a union represents workers in collective bargaining or is sought as a bargaining agent, the practice of discrimination by an employer against employees on the basis of race or national origin constitutes a violation of Section 8(a)(1) of the Taft Hartley Act—the provision which bans interference with a worker's exercise of the right to protection by a union. The court indicated that an employer's action to deter minority-group employees from asserting their full rights under the labor law contributes to industrial unrest and apathy among employees, which the law was intended to remedy. Thus it is that the federal labor law, which is well over four decades old, is increasingly a vehicle by which some employees in the private sector can seek to eliminate racial discrimination practiced by employers and labor unions.[41]

U.S. Office of Personnel Management

For the federal government itself, affirmative action and equal employment opportunity are given formal expression in Executive Order 11478, issued in 1969, which was incorporated into the Equal Employment Opportunity Act of 1972. Guidelines were subsequently formulated by the Civil Service Commission and are now administered by the U.S. Office of Personnel Management, the Commission's successor agency. A variety of studies (including some of the Commission's own) undertaken in the late 1960s and early 1970s showed racial minorities and women to be concentrated at the lower occupational levels of the federal government and, therefore, to be heavily overrepresented in the lower portions of the General Pay Schedule.[42] The Commission's guidelines to federal managers specified the desired elements of an equal employment opportunity program, including specialized recruitment, selection, training, and development activities for minorities and women in the labor force and systematic monitoring and periodic evaluation of the progress of the program.[43]

Overall responsibility for this program in the federal sector rests with the Office of Personnel Management, which must review and approve the equal employment opportunity plans of diverse agencies and departments. This is in line with the Office's more general responsibility for promoting and ensuring employment and personnel practices based on merit in the federal civil service. Opinion is divided concerning the Office's ability to achieve (as distinct from its responsibility for) employment based on merit and equal employment opportunity in the federal sector. This important empirical issue aside, it is noteworthy that beyond its federal responsibility, the Office has jurisdiction over the equal employment programs in those state and local governments which contract with the federal sector, and it also helps set equal employment policy and guidelines for all state and local governments through its membership in the federal Equal Employment Opportunity Coordinating Council.

This council, which was created by the 1972 amendments to the Civil Rights Act and which enrolls—in addition to the U.S. Office of Personnel Management —the Departments of Justice and Labor, the EEOC, and the Commission on Civil Rights, attempts to resolve some of the differences and apparent inconsistencies in the approaches of various federal agencies to equal employment opportunity, especially in state and local governments. Its ability to perform this task has been questioned, but it recently published two documents to help guide state and local governments in achieving equal employment opportunity.[44]

Apprenticeship Programs and the Construction Industry

Finally, mention should be made of efforts by the federal government to combat discrimination in apprenticeship programs, which are pathways to relatively high-paying jobs in several industries, particularly construction. We noted earlier that the Civil Rights Act of 1964 is applicable to apprenticeship programs; even in 1963, however, Willard Wirtz, then Secretary of Labor, had approved new federal standards for apprenticeship programs designed "to provide full and fair opportunity for application."[45] The problem addressed by Wirtz was the very low representation of blacks and other minorities in the skilled construction trades and in the apprenticeship programs through which such skills were developed and jobs obtained.

Since craft unions largely control the supply of labor to the unionized sector of the construction industry through systems for job referral and apprenticeship, they, rather than employers, became the focus of attempts to racially integrate this industry's work force. Enforcement of the standards for apprenticeship programs rested with the Department of Labor's Bureau of Apprenticeship Training (BAT); however, the BAT possessed limited powers, and its principal sanction, the deregistration of a particular program, has been described as "more of an inconvenience than a serious deterrent to discrimination."[46] Beyond these federal regulations, apprenticeship programs are also subject to Title VII of the Civil Rights Act, the Taft-Hartley Act, governmental provisions for contract compliance, and various state regulations concerning apprenticeship programs and equal employment programs.

A key controversy over employment of minorities in the building trades and their enrollment in apprenticeship programs occurred in 1969, when Assistant Secretary of Labor Arthur Fletcher, acting under the authority of Executive Order 11246, issued an affirmative action plan for government contractors in the construction industry in Philadelphia. The order, similar to one previously drawn up but never introduced by Secretary Wirtz, required bidders on government contracts of over $500,000 to commit themselves to achieving goals for employing minorities in six different trades in which blacks constituted less than 2 percent of the work force and were rarely referred to jobs. Employers in the construction industry could not use the existence of a collective bargaining agreement as an excuse for failing to comply with the regulations. This action was strongly opposed by these employers and also by the trade unions and the AFL-CIO, who objected to the vague targets proposed by the OFCCP and asked for specific quotas, which were never supplied. But a legal challenge to the plan mounted by the employers in the construction industry in Philadelphia was rejected by the courts, which upheld the federal action as valid under Title VII of the Civil Rights Act and the Constitution.[47]

The experience in Philadelphia was repeated, with variations, in other locations. In some cities, employers in the construction industry, labor unions, and minority groups agreed voluntarily to achieve equal employment opportunity in this important sector of the economy. Such "hometown" solutions apparently were not very successful, though the data that would permit a complete assessment of these efforts are not available. The reader should be aware, however, that the proportion of minorities in the building trades and in apprenticeship programs has increased substantially over time, which may be due in part to efforts by the federal government to enforce civil rights legislation. For example, at the end of 1976, nonwhites constituted 18 percent of the roughly 250,000 registered apprentices in the United States.[48] That was about triple the representation that prevailed in the mid-1960s. In construction, which accounted for better than half of all apprentices in 1976, fully 20 percent of the total were nonwhites, of whom over half were blacks. Less than 2 percent of all apprentices were women in 1976; by industry, women were most heavily represented in services, petroleum, and printing and least well represented in construction.

It should be recognized further that the construction industry has been relatively depressed throughout much of the 1970s, that its workers have experienced very high unemployment rates, and that construction by non-unionized workers now accounts for a large portion of economic activity in an industry which was only recently considered a bulwark of unionism. Moreover, because construction workers do not enjoy seniority with any single firm, since they move from one completed job to another—that is, from one contractor or subcontractor to another—they must rely on control of the labor market to obtain and maintain employment. Many local construction workers' unions are organized along strict ethnic and geographic lines, and these practices are to some extent supported by Section 8(f) of the Taft-Hartley Act, which permits agreements with construction workers' unions that require contractors to refer employment opportunities first to such labor organizations. None of this is to deny that construction workers' unions have been more discriminatory than unions of industrial workers.[49] However, that discrimination stems fundamentally from the need of these unions to control the labor market, and thus it is not aimed at one or another minority group alone. In any case, the BAT continues to regulate apprenticeship programs in the skilled trades, unionized or not, and it shares responsibilities for enforcing equal employment opportunity legislation in this area with other federal agencies.

To sum up, the eradication of discrimination in the labor market has become a fundamental objective of public policy in the United States. The basic framework for achieving this goal, for ensuring equal employment opportunity, is laid out in the Civil Rights Act of 1964 and in Executive Order 11246. Numerous federal agencies, departments, and bureaus, as well as the courts, are in-

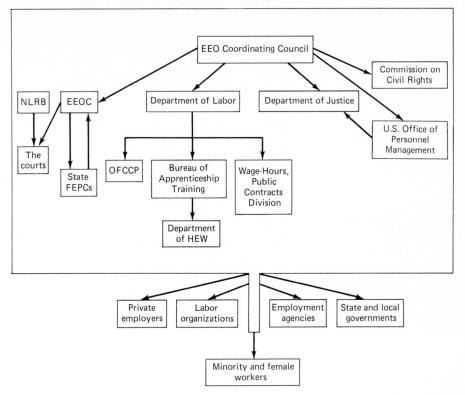

Figure 8-4 Federal system of enforcing equal employment opportunity policies. (*Source: Adapted from Phyllis A. Wallace, "Employment Discrimination: Some Policy Considerations," in Orley Ashenfelter and Albert Rees, eds., Discrimination in Labor Markets, Princeton University Press, Princeton, N.J., 1973, p. 156.*)

volved in the enforcement of these policy directives; Figure 8-4 depicts this complex federal system for delivering equal employment opportunity. However, while knowledge of these formal policies and enforcement agencies is important, to be sure, it provides only a partial understanding of the dynamics of equal employment opportunity in the United States. Consequently, below we shall review some of the key developments of the 1970s that pertain to the eradication of discrimination in the labor market.

Recent Cases and Court Decisions Involving Discrimination

Griggs v. Duke Power Company In 1971, the Supreme Court issued a decision in the *Griggs v. Duke Power Company* case which markedly affected discriminatory personnel policies.[50] The case involved a class-action suit, brought under the Civil Rights Act of 1964 by thirteen black employees of the North Carolina utility, alleging discrimination against them by the employer in matters of job assignments, transfers, and promotions. Blacks were employed solely in the company's labor department, where even the highest pay rates were below those in four other departments which employed only whites. While abandoning this formal policy in 1965 shortly after the Civil Rights Act became effective, Duke Power Company added a requirement of satisfactory scores on two professionally developed aptitude tests to its prior standard of high school graduation for individuals to qualify for employment in departments other than labor. Under these standards, no blacks qualified for transfer out of the company's labor department.

The importance of the Court's opinion in this case warrants the following lengthy quotation from it:

> The objective of Congress in the enactment of Title VII is plain from the language of the statute. It was to achieve equality of employment opportunities and remove barriers that have operated in the past to favor an identifiable group of white employees over other employees. Under the Act, practices, procedures or tests neutral on their face, and even neutral in terms of intent, cannot be maintained if they operate to "freeze" the status quo of prior discriminatory employment practices. . . . On the record before us, neither the high school completion requirement nor the general intelligence test is shown to bear a demonstrable relationship to successful performance of the jobs for which it is used. Both were adopted . . . without meaningful study of their relationship to job-performance ability. . . . Good intent or absence of discriminatory intent does not redeem employment procedures or testing mechanisms that operate as "built-in headwinds" for minority groups and are unrelated to measuring job capability. . . . Congress has placed on the employer the burden of showing that any given requirement must have a manifest relationship to the employment in question. . . . History is filled with examples of men and women who rendered highly effective performance without the conventional badges of accomplishment in terms of certificates, diplomas or degrees. . . . Nothing in the act precludes the use of testing or measuring procedures; obviously they are useful. What Congress had forbidden is giving these devices and mechanisms controlling force unless they are demonstrably a reasonable measure of job-performance.[51]

As this portion of the opinion indicates, the Supreme Court ruled in favor of Willie S. Griggs and his fellow employees, setting forth a decision which became the precedent for many others to follow in subsequent years. The central importance of the ruling is that it declared illegal indirect and unintended discrimination resulting from employment and personnel management practices. Thus, the Civil Rights Act, which was relied upon in this decision, is applicable to more than just explicit, overt forms of discrimination in the labor market.

But what does the *Griggs* decision actually mean for employers' selection, promotion, and transfer policies or, more broadly, for equal employment opportunity at the workplace? In declaring Duke Power's use of educational credentials and test scores illegal, the Court, as it was careful to point out, did not prohibit employers from using these and other devices for selecting employees. Rather, it prohibited their use only if management has not established them on the basis of demonstrated relationships to performance on the job or jobs in question. In a nutshell, employers must validate their tools for selection if the job qualifications that they set are to be in conformity with the law. This requirement, in turn, has several notable implications.

First, how is validation defined, and what type of validation procedure satisfies the doctrine that emerged from the *Griggs* case? To validate a test, educational credential, or other selection device is to systematically relate individual characteristics, known as "predictors," to the requirements of the job, known as "criteria," with the objective of empirically discovering those factors which differentiate levels of performance at work. Only in this way can the qualifications for entry into a job, transfer, or promotion be validly established.

As to the type of validation that an employer may use to set job qualifications, the Court was less specific. The voluminous literature on validation distinguishes two principal types—predictive and concurrent. The major difference between them is this: the former requires the gathering of data on individuals (say, through completed application blanks and test scores) after they have been randomly hired,[52] and the data are subsequently correlated with measures of job performance over several intervals; the latter involves the correlation of data on individuals with measures of performance among workers who have been nonrandomly selected for employment according to some preexisting standards.

Because concurrent validation begins with a sample of employees which excludes those previously weeded out—in research terminology, a "contaminated sample"—it is inferior to predictive validation for establishing valid and reliable job qualifications and standards for selection. But because predictive validation requires starting from scratch, in that workers are hired in the order in which they show up, it has major practical limitations and is used very sparingly in comparison with concurrent validation. To this point, concurrent validation seemingly satisfies the legal requirements for discriminating fairly in the selection of employees, in the sense of choosing among applicants on the basis of merit rather than whether they are men or women, blacks or whites, the young or the old, or the better-educated or the less well educated.

Second, despite the landmark nature of the *Griggs* decision, it did not remove management's decision-making power in terms of selecting employees, studying jobs, or establishing standards for entry, transfer, or promotion. Employers are required to validate their devices for selecting employees, but they retain their right to decide when and how to perform this task and by whom it should be performed. This aspect of the *Griggs* decision seems not to be widely recognized, even by those who claim that employers often set artificially high standards for selection in order to screen out minorities, women, and disadvantaged members of the labor force.[53] It is well known that job qualifications tend to rise when labor markets are loose and to fall when they are tight. Nevertheless, nothing in the *Griggs* decision removes from managers their control over the setting of standards for selection or the adjustment of job qualifications to changing conditions in the labor market.

Third, the onus of challenging as discriminatory an employer's selection standards and job qualifications is on aggrieved employees or prospective workers, though clearly they may be assisted in such efforts by the EEOC and other federal agencies. In the context of the American economic and legal system, no employee is guaranteed a job or a right to a particular job, and thus it is up to the individual to pursue redress of what he or she considers to be discriminatory employment practices. No one knows for sure what proportion of all discriminatory employment practices are actually challenged by employees or their representatives, but it seems to have increased in recent years. Individual (and class-action) challenges to allegedly discriminatory employment practices are not without risk. Apart from the fact that such challenges may fail, they frequently produce considerable personal stress and sometimes invite the retribution of employers and co-workers.

Further, for some who are subject to discriminatory employment practices, their freedom—their civil rights—may be better protected by seeking out alternative opportunities in the labor market than by working through the legal system, whether the latter produces favorable decisions for them or not. Of course, this is of little solace to those who have few or no alternative employment opportunities and whose recourse is thus limited largely to legal channels, nor is it a very satisfactory solution to the problem of persistent discriminatory employment practices in a nation which presumes to protect the civil rights of all workers. In sum, the decision in the *Griggs v. Duke Power Company* case, although certainly significant, may not be quite the landmark that it is often presumed to be.

The American Telephone and Telegraph Company Settlement In 1973, AT&T, which then employed more than 750,000 persons, signed a consent decree with the federal government in which it agreed to provide restitution in the form of back pay to several groups of female employees, as well as rights of transfer and promotion for women, members of racial minorities, *and* white males into jobs where these groups were underrepresented. In the first year of the agreement, the company "paid over $50 million for back pay and other charges," implying "at least institutional discrimination," although because a consent decree takes the place of a court proceeding, no formal admission of discrimination was required of the company.[54] Like the *Griggs* case, the AT&T action has several important ramifications.

First, the consent decree was worked out with the participation of the EEOC, the Department of Labor, and the Department of Justice, following protracted negotiations and a lawsuit filed against the company by the EEOC on behalf of female employees. While some critics of the settlement contend that it provided too little back pay, the coordination of federal agencies' efforts to enforce antidiscrimination legislation was one of the objectives of the 1972 Equal Employment Opportunity Act, inasmuch as competition among such agencies to "win" a settlement could frustrate the antidiscrimination goal of public policy.

Second, the focus of this effort to enforce antidiscrimination legislation on a very large employer reflected both a move toward replacement of the prior "shotgun" approach, in which targets were not very carefully selected, and an awareness of the demonstration, or spillover, effect of this action on other companies. That is, other employers were pushed by the circumstance of the AT&T settlement to "voluntarily" upgrade the pay and jobs of women and racial minorities. Such voluntary efforts are, in fact, a fundamental goal of the Civil Rights Act.[55]

Third, the consent decree tended to set affirmative action within the larger context of human resources management. It dealt with the underrepresentation of women and racial minorities in craft, telephone line, and telephone repair jobs, to be sure, but it also dealt with the underrepresentation of men in telephone operator and clerical jobs. In this regard, the decree provided a starting point for dealing with sex-role stereotyping on the job. It also assisted qualified women to move into "fast-track" management development programs, and it sanctioned the use of validated employment tests.

Finally, the decree provided mechanisms for systematically monitoring progress toward equal employment opportunity and for generating the type of information concerning the utilization of human resources within the firm's internal labor market that is useful for organizational decision making. This is one of the major, if not widely appreciated, by-products of federal regulatory activity in the areas of equal employment opportunity specifically and human resources management generally. It may also be one of the major reasons for the recent rise in importance of this management function in private firms and public organizations.

Affirmative Action versus Seniority The AT&T case was one of several that occurred in the mid-1970s in which the pursuit of equal employment opportunity was set against long-standing practices involving seniority. More specifically, a written affirmative action agreement arrived at voluntarily or by a consent decree typically contains criteria for upgrading, promotion, and transfer which differ from the criterion of seniority that usually governs such matters where workers are unionized—and often where they are not. In its starkest form, this clash emerged as one between racial minorities and women, on the one hand, and unionized white males, on the other. Also, the conflict was exacerbated by the recession of 1974–1975, which necessitated major layoffs. In deciding which employees to lay off, some firms had to choose between the seniority provisions of their collective bargaining contracts and the requirements concerning representation of women and racial minorities contained in their affirmative action agreements. A decision taken on either ground was certain to invoke opposition from one or another group of workers and might well have been declared illegal by the courts. A more painful dimension of efforts to remedy discrimination in employment by means of public policy could hardly be imagined.

When such conflicts reached the courts, they were decided on a case-by-case basis, and it was not uncommon for some decisions to uphold the primacy of seniority in layoffs and for others to favor affirmative action. Indeed, an employer with plants in several different states might have had to lay off workers according to seniority in some locations and according to race and sex in others, depending upon the legal doctrines prevailing at the time in the respective areas. Even if located in only one state, an employer may have had to alter the criteria for layoffs if different levels of courts rendered opposing decisions.

In the case of *Jersey Central Power and Light Company,*[56] for example, decided in 1975 by a court of appeals, seniority was given preference over affirmative action in determining layoffs at this utility. The case arose because of the conflicting criteria for layoffs contained in the company's conciliation agreement with the EEOC and its collective bargaining agreement with seven local unions of the International Brotherhood of Electrical Workers (IBEW). The IBEW and the company jointly challenged the ruling of a lower court that gave precedence to affirmative action requirements over seniority in layoffs conducted in 1974.

The court of appeals ruled that Congress had not intended so sweeping a remedy for discrimination in employment; indeed, bona fide seniority systems are expressly permitted in the Civil Rights Act of 1964 (although the term "bona fide" is not well defined), and the EEOC itself never developed systematic guidelines for affirmative action in layoffs, as it had for affirmative action in hiring, transfers, and promotions. Like others, the EEOC was caught unaware by the recession of 1974–1975 and only later began to formulate guidelines to layoffs under affirmative action. What the court of appeals concluded in the *Jersey Central Power and Light Company* case was that an agreement to maintain specific numerical proportions of women and racial minorities among a company's work force could not supplant the long-standing seniority rights of employees under a valid collective bargaining agreement. Subsequent court decisions have affirmed and extended this view, though they have also permitted awarding retroactive seniority to employees proved to have suffered discrimination in employment.[57]

These cases lead us to conclude that conflicts between affirmative action and collective bargaining—or, more narrowly, between women and minorities and unionized white males—should not be overdrawn. We saw in Chapter 3 that blacks are slightly more likely than whites to belong to labor organizations and that one-quarter of all union members are women, even though women are underrepresented in proportion to their participation in the labor force. Hence it is only in some circumstances, important ones to be sure, that blacks and women are pitted against white men in fighting for jobs and employment benefits. The question of affirmative action could become even stickier if, for example, younger blacks challenged older blacks or older women challenged younger women on issues of seniority rights, promotions, and the like. Note, too, that focusing on unionized workers and protections provided by seniority in attempting to achieve equal employment opportunity tends to deflect attention from upper-level professional and especially managerial jobs, where the underrepresentation of racial minorities and women is greatest. And, after all, in the

United States, employers rather than unions control the vast bulk of decisions on selecting and hiring workers. These observations testify to the complexity of the problem of discrimination in the labor market and its proposed solutions, a complexity that is sometimes overlooked in the debate over affirmative action versus seniority.

The *Bakke* Case　In mid-1978, the Supreme Court of the United States handed down its decision in the case of *The Regents of the University of California v. Bakke*.[58] No decision of the Court had been so eagerly awaited since the famous *Brown v. Board of Education* ruling in 1954, which outlawed so-called "separate but equal" public school facilities. One authority said that *Bakke* "poses issues of the utmost importance in constitutional law, educational policy, and race relations."[59] In brief, the facts of the case were these. Allen Bakke, a white male, was denied admission to the medical school of the University of California at Davis in 1973 and 1974, although sixteen blacks with lower scores on an admissions test were admitted. Bakke alleged "reverse discrimination" on the part of the university and took his case to court. In a 6 to 1 decision handed down in 1976, the Supreme Court of California held that in reserving a specific number of places for nonwhites, the university's admissions policy constituted unequal treatment of racial groups and was therefore illegal.[60] The university then appealed the decision to the Supreme Court of the United States and was permitted to maintain its admissions policy pending the outcome of the case.

What the Supreme Court rendered in *Bakke* was a two-pronged decision. First, it ruled by a 5 to 4 vote that the university's affirmative action program (specifically that of the medical school at Davis) was invalid because "it was inflexibly and unjustifiably biased against white applicants," thereby violating the Civil Rights Act of 1964. This was the first Supreme Court ruling on a case of reverse discrimination under the nation's civil rights legislation. Thus, Allen Bakke was ordered admitted to the Davis medical school, where he in fact commenced his studies in the fall of 1978.

But in another 5 to 4 opinion in *Bakke,* the Court upheld the constitutionality of college admissions programs that give special advantage to blacks and other minorities to help remedy past discrimination against them. Consequently, the University of California (and, by inference, others) can employ "a properly devised admissions program involving the competitive consideration of ethnic origin," but only where race is one among several factors considered. The admissions program of Harvard University was held up by the Court as a model in this regard, being described by one of the justices as an example of "diversity without fixed quotas." It was the quota aspect of the *Bakke* case which, perhaps more than any other, stimulated debate and intensified the feelings of those arrayed on both sides of the issue.

Consider that the establishment of numerical or percentage quotas for employment or admission to school is particularly offensive to those whose social, ethnic, or religious heritage contains historical examples of formal and explicit quotas which were used for the purpose of discrimination. Others who supported Bakke in his action against the University of California were deeply troubled by the specter of reverse discrimination, whereby efforts to achieve equal employment opportunity or choice of career for blacks—or, in other situations, women—might deny civil rights to whites who themselves do not discriminate on racial (or sexual) grounds and who have not been party to such discrimination in the past. In contrast, those who supported the university's position contended that rectifying past discrimination cannot be accomplished simply by permitting equal access to jobs or educational institutions and that any substantial remedy inevitably imposes hardships on others—for example, white males.

At first glance, the decision in the *Bakke* case may seem to have satisfied both sides. One part of the decision agreed that reverse discrimination is impermissible and that a person cannot be denied access to an educational institution simply because of his or her race. Remember that the principle underlying this ruling was absolutely central to the civil rights movement of the early 1960s, though at that time, denial of access—to jobs, educational institutions, and public facilities—was thought of in connection with the nation's black citizens. The other part of the *Bakke* decision, however, explicitly sanctioned affirmative action programs in educational institutions, which means permitting racially sensitive recruitment and admissions policies. The caveat is that such policies must appraise all applicants according to multiple criteria such as test scores, prior education, potential for community service, leadership ability, exceptional personal talents, maturity, a history of overcoming disadvantage, and unique work experience. Used flexibly, the Court noted, these and other criteria for admission can promote diversity in a student body without resorting to a fixed, racially based quota system. Here, the Court appeared to uphold the California tribunal, which found the Davis admissions plan illegal, while also approving a wide range of affirmative action programs prevailing at other educational institutions.

But a closer review of the *Bakke* decision may leave both sides uneasy, even perplexed. Very few of the nation's undergraduate colleges or professional schools seem to have maintained the type of rigid affirmative action plan found at Davis; most come closer to the flexible policy of Harvard, which met with the Court's favor. Hence, the *Bakke* decision permits these schools to do as they have done before and, like private employers in the aforementioned *Griggs* case, to decide what to do largely by themselves. This may please college admissions officers, who feared that the *Bakke* decision would hold them to a rigid legal standard, and more generally it may satisfy officials of educational institutions that their decision-making discretion is unimpaired. But it does not answer the question, "How much weight can or should be given to race as one among several criteria for admission?" The *Bakke* decision does not provide much guidance on this score, except to rule out race alone as a determining factor. In this light, Supreme Court Justice Blackman commented instructively that "the cynical, of course, may say that under a program such as Harvard's one may accomplish covertly what Davis says it does openly."[61]

Further, the Court did make clear in its *Bakke* ruling that a state institution which has not in the past been tainted with discrimination has no obligation to mount an affirmative action program. Conversely, it did not settle the issue of how full a remedy must be if an educational institution or a private firm is found to have excluded minorities. This awaits further Supreme Court rulings because, in *Bakke,* the Court was careful to limit itself to affirmative action plans for admission to state (public) institutions of higher education. Recognize, though, that many plans in the private and public sectors for affirmative action in employment incorporate the type of fixed quotas which the Court found unconstitutional in the *Bakke* case. Those plans have been approved in the past by various tribunals, and it is a matter of major import whether the judiciary will extend the doctrine of affirmative action that emerged from the *Bakke* case to cover employment in industry and government.[62] This is especially so because of two often unappreciated problems associated with the use of quotas for employment or admission to schools.

First, selection based on quotas may initially enlarge the representation of minorities or women in a company's work force, as in a school's student body. But it may also act as a ceiling or upper limit on such representation, bespeaking a mentality that "now that we've hit our target, we've solved the problem." Second, and related to the first point, setting numerical quotas for employment or admission to schools is in some respects an easy way out of dealing with a complex problem. Recall from our previous discussion of predictive validation that criteria for selection ideally should be established only after thorough study of the relationship between the characteristics of randomly selected workers or students and performance on the job or in school. That this ideal is not fully achieved in practice does not detract from the requirement that individual applicants—for employment or admission to a school—be appraised on the basis of their characteristics in relation to the performance required on the tasks for which they are being selected. If such relationships are not well known, then they should be investigated through the application of one or another strategy for validation. This is an essential component of competent management and administration, but it tends to be undermined by the contention that racial quotas are an appropriate basis of selection for jobs or for educational programs. The Supreme Court seems not to have addressed these issues in its *Bakke* ruling, but it may well have to do so in future cases that deal with affirmative action in employment.

What we do know from the *Bakke* case is that affirmative action programs in educational institutions are constitutional and that race may properly be taken into account in admissions policies, as long as it is not the sole criterion and is not used as the basis of a quota. This is a major decision, even if it does not resolve other important issues that have been raised in the contemporary debate over affirmative action.

**Evaluating the Regulation of Discrimination
in the Labor Market**

To evaluate fully the effectiveness of public policies that attempt to regulate
discrimination in the labor market is a herculean task, certainly not one that can
be accomplished in a few short pages. Further, despite the rapid growth since
the mid-1960s of civil rights legislation and Executive orders designed to provide equal employment opportunity, "it is remarkable that so little analysis of
these programs is available."[63] In this section, we summarize some of the limited evidence that is available about the effectiveness of governmental efforts
to regulate discrimination. The studies which provide this evidence have been
conducted mainly by economists; they focus heavily on the wages of blacks
relative to those of whites, and they do so largely for short-run periods. Hence,
they yield at best only a partial picture of the total impact of government on
discrimination in the labor market.

A key piece of research in this area was undertaken by Freeman, who conducted a time-series analysis of the position of blacks in the labor market in the
United States to the early 1970s.[64] He found that they had significantly improved their income and occupational position relative to that of whites, particularly in the 1960s. The gains in relative economic position were greater for
black women than for black men and were considerably larger for young than
for older black male workers. Most important, Freeman concluded: "Much of
the improvement in the black economic position that took place in the late sixties appears to be the result of governmental and related antidiscriminatory activity associated with the 1964 Civil Rights Act."[65]

These findings were challenged by other investigators. For example, Flanagan proposed that changes in expenditures by the EEOC during the 1960s,
which were Freeman's measure of the federal government's efforts to regulate
discrimination, were nothing more than a proxy for the sustained low unemployment rates in those years. Consequently, favorable economic circumstances rather than government policy may have improved the position of
blacks in the labor market in the United States.[66] Flanagan also argued that
Freeman's finding of an improved income and occupational position for black
males vanishes when relative education is taken into account.

Butler and Heckman examined these contentions by reworking and updating Freeman's analysis to the mid-1970s, when unemployment rates were high
compared with those in the previous decade.[67] They obtained results similar to
those of Freeman, indicating that Freeman's measure of activity by the federal government was not a proxy for conditions in the labor market. They also
examined differences in educational levels between black and white workers
and discovered that the impact of the EEOC reported by Freeman remained
in effect for both men and women. But when the researchers introduced participation in the labor force into the analysis, they concluded: *"There is no
impact of measured federal antidiscrimination policy on relative wage rates for
men or for women"* (emphasis in original).[68]

In his work, Freeman also found that the significant impact of antidiscrimination activities by the federal government on relative incomes had occurred only in the south, not in other regions. However, Butler and Heckman pointed out that the upward trend in the relative status of blacks in the labor market in the south began to occur in the late 1950s, or well before any federal regulatory statutes had been enacted. Moreover, when only data for the south since 1960 were analyzed, they showed no impact of antidiscrimination activities by the federal government on the relative income of blacks.

Several studies of other efforts to enforce equal employment opportunity legislation have also been reported. For example, Landes examined the impact of the provisions pertaining to wages and employment contained in state fair employment practice (FEP) laws.[69] Recall that the EEOC must cooperate with the regulatory bodies established to enforce such laws. Studying the forty-eight contiguous states, Landes found a statistically significant effect of the equal-pay provisions of FEP laws on the relative earnings of black males, though the size of the effect was small—roughly 3 to 4 percent. Even these results, however, were offset in part by the increased relative unemployment of blacks, which stemmed from the enforcement of the wage provisions of the laws. Thus Landes's work apparently shows that state FEP laws largely failed to achieve their intended effects. Note, though, that a reexamination of Landes's data, using new methods, doubled the estimated impact on the relative earnings of blacks to 7.5 percent, indicating that FEP legislation may be more powerful than was previously thought.[70]

No study of the EEOC compares the economic status of blacks or women employed in firms covered by the Civil Rights Act with that of blacks or women employed in firms not so covered. Instead, comparisons are made among private firms or states that are subject to different amounts of activity by the EEOC. For example, Adams examined conciliation efforts by the EEOC in the period 1966–1971, before the Commission acquired the power to initiate enforcement proceedings in the courts.[71] He compared changes in the relative employment and occupational positions of minority workers in twenty-six firms which had signed conciliation agreements with the EEOC with a comparable sample of firms in the same industry and Standard Metropolitan Statistical Area which had not signed such agreements. Finding no differences in the progress of minorities in these two sets of firms, Adams judged the EEOC's enforcement effort to have had little impact.

A similar judgment was reached by Wolkinson, who employed the case-study method to investigate seventy-five cases of alleged discrimination by unions against minority workers before 1972.[72] He found that the conciliation agreements negotiated by the EEOC provided little in the way of adequate relief and tended to be violated by the unions involved. Wolkinson attributed these outcomes to the EEOC's lack of any enforcement power. In a study of equal employment opportunity in the construction industry, Marshall and his associates found very limited implementation under Title VII, with long and costly legal suits frustrating the antidiscrimination objective of public policy.[73]

Focusing on employment of minorities during the early 1960s in the textile industry in the Carolinas, Kidder found a negative relationship between charges of discrimination brought by the EEOC against employers and subsequent increases in the employment of blacks.[74] She concluded that the presence of a government contract in a firm had no significant effect on employment of blacks and also that such employment rose sharply in the period immediately preceding the establishment of the EEOC.

More recently, Beller attempted to separate out the effects on wages from the effects on employment of enforcement of Title VII.[75] Using 1970 census data and reports by employers filed with the EEOC, she found that enforcement of the wage-equality provision of the law had a negative effect on employment of blacks, which outweighed the slight positive effect of enforcing the law's provision concerning employment. Hence, conflicting provisions of the Civil Rights Act itself may frustrate the objective of promoting equal employment opportunity.

Several studies of the OFCCP's impact on equal employment opportunity under Executive Order 11246 have been carried out. These seek to discover the impact of a government contract on the employment and occupational position of minority workers in private firms. For example, Ashenfelter and Heckman found that "in the short run, government contractors raised the employment of black males relative to white males 3.3 percent more than nongovernment contractors, while in the long run this effect was estimated to be 12.9 percent."[76] On the negative side, these researchers found that the OFCCP had had no significant impact on the relative wage and occupational position of black men and had produced no favorable results—in terms of employment, wages, or occupational position—for black women.

The sum and substance of this review of governmental efforts to regulate discrimination in the labor market may seem somewhat disappointing in the sense that most of the research evidence points to relatively modest or insignificant impacts. Yet such an overall conclusion must be qualified in several respects. First, evidence of the type presented earlier in Table 8-4 testifies to the recent improvement in the status of young black workers in the labor market. It is among this group that programs aimed at eliminating discrimination are likely to be most effective because employers prefer to train those with longer working lives and because young workers adjust more easily than older workers to new opportunities in the labor market.

Second, much of the evidence that is available to evaluate public policy in the area of discrimination in employment is crude, incomplete, or out of date. For example, most of the studies reviewed here rely on data from the late 1960s or from the 1970 census. Even if they were comprehensive for those times, they do not permit one to conclude anything about the federal government's efforts to enforce antidiscrimination legislation after 1972, when the EEOC was given expanded powers and when the Civil Rights Act was extended to additional sectors of the economy.

Third, the vast bulk of the research on efforts to regulate discrimination in the labor market focuses on racial minorities (and, within this group, almost exclusively on blacks). The issue of discrimination against women, to say nothing of religious groups and those with nontraditional sexual orientations, remains much less well explored. This no doubt reflects the evolution of the civil rights movement in the United States, in which the concern for racial equality in employment opportunity preceded the concern for other types of equality in employment; it also reflects the predilection of researchers to "go where the action is." A better balance must be struck in future studies if a complete picture is to be obtained of the effectiveness of public policies intended to remedy discrimination in employment.

Finally, research on discrimination which is conducted at the level of the economy, among firms or among states, seeks a relatively high order of generalization which can mask a wide range of outcomes, results, or actions. It is one thing to say that the average effect on a group of workers, a group of firms, or an entire industry of a particular law such as the Civil Rights Act of 1964 is small, nonexistent, or statistically insignificant. It is quite a different matter to move to a particular firm or to an individual worker for the purpose of inquiring into the effectiveness of the government's efforts to reduce discrimination. Few would doubt, for example, that black and female workers employed at AT&T in the early 1970s were aided by the consent decree awarding them back pay and giving them improved opportunities for promotion, or that black employees of the Duke Power Company were assisted by the Supreme Court's declaration that the company's procedures for selection, promotion, and transfer were illegal. The perceptions of individual black and female workers regarding the implementation of antidiscrimination laws may be critical to their subsequent behavior in the labor market, but this is another aspect of affirmative action that has not yet been studied.

Thus, in this area of human behavior and social relations, as in so many others, different levels and types of evaluation are possible. Is it any wonder, then, that no simple or single answer can be given to the question, "How effective is the regulation of discrimination in the labor market?"

SUMMARY

This chapter examined the role of race and sex in the labor market. We reviewed some of the changes in the position of racial minorities and women in the American economy and concluded from the data that the incidence of discrimination in the labor market, especially against blacks, seems to be diminishing over time. However, there remain substantial differences between blacks and whites and between men and women in terms of their status in the labor market, and only a minor portion of these can be "explained" by differences in human capital investments in education, training, and work experience.

Public policies to regulate discrimination in the labor market were discussed, especially the Civil Rights Act of 1964 and Executive Order 11246. The multifaceted governmental system for enforcing equal employment opportunity legislation was elaborated, and some key issues raised by the government's efforts to eliminate discrimination were presented. These included the validation of devices for selecting employees, the coordination of federal responsibility for enforcing antidiscrimination legislation, conflicts between affirmative action agreements and seniority provisions, and the use of racial quotas for employment and admission to schools.

Our review of the effectiveness of governmental programs to combat discrimination in the labor market indicated that they have had, at best, modest results to date, although young black workers seem to have been assisted by them more than others. However, limitations in terms of both available data and analytical capability prevent the drawing of final conclusions on this point. In Chapter 9, we turn our attention to the distribution of income in American society; this also requires a consideration of the issue of equality and of the role of government in transferring income among subgroups of the population.

NOTES

1 *Report of the National Commission on Civil Disorders,* Bantam, New York, 1968, p. 1.

2 In this chapter, the terms "black" and "nonwhite" are used interchangeably since blacks constitute about 90 percent of all nonwhites in the United States. Nonwhites also include American Indians, Eskimos, Asians, and others. Sometimes the government gathers separate data for persons of Spanish origin, also known as "Hispanics." These include persons who identify themselves as Mexican Americans, Chicanos, Mexicans (Mexicanos), Puerto Ricans, Cubans, or Central or South Americans or as being of other Spanish descent. The focus on blacks in our discussion of discrimination in the labor market is in no way intended to slight these other minority groups, who suffer many of the same disadvantages as blacks and also experience some unique forms of discrimination.

3 The data in this paragraph are from *Employment and Training Report of the President, 1978,* 1978, pp. 183–185, table A-4; and U.S. Bureau of Labor Statistics, *Employment and Earnings, January, 1979,* 1979, pp. 155–159, tables 2–4.

4 The data in this section are from U.S. Bureau of the Census, *Current Population Reports: Money Income in 1975 of Families and Persons in the United States,* ser. P-60, no. 105, 1977, passim. We use data for 1975 in this section because that is the most recent year for which complete data are available on the subjects covered.

5 U.S. Bureau of Labor Statistics, *Year-Round Full-Time Earnings in 1975,* Special Labor Force Report 203, 1977, pp. 36–37.

6 This discussion draws from the useful summary of this subject presented in Ronald L. Oaxaca, "Theory and Measurement in the Economics of Discrimination," in Leonard J. Hausman et al. (eds.), *Equal Rights and Industrial Relations,* Industrial Relations Research Association, Madison, Wis., 1977, pp. 1–30, especially pp. 3–11 and 18–19. Also see Gary D. Brown, "Discrimination and Pay Disparities Between White Men and Women," *Monthly Labor Review,* **102:**17–22 (1979).

7 See Gary S. Becker, *The Economics of Discrimination,* University of Chicago Press, Chicago, 1957.

8 Lester C. Thurow, *Poverty and Discrimination,* Brookings, Washington, 1969, as cited in Oaxaca, p. 18.

9 Thurow.

10 Thurow, p. 129, as quoted in Oaxaca, p. 19.

11 Oaxaca, p. 24.

12 Oaxaca, pp. 25–26.

13 See, for example, Nathan Glazer, *Affirmative Discrimination, Ethnic Inequality and Public Policy,* Basic Books, New York, 1975.

14 See, for example, Burton G. Malkeil and Judith A. Malkeil, "Male-Female Pay Differentials in Professional Employment," *American Economic Review,* **63:**693–705 (1973).

15 The data in this section are from U.S. Bureau of the Census, passim; U.S. Bureau of the Census, *Current Population Reports: Money Income in 1976 of Families and Persons in the United States,* ser. P-60, no. 114, 1978, passim; and Richard Butler and James J. Heckman, "The Government's Impact on the Labor Market Status of Black Americans: A Critical Review," in Hausman et al., pp. 235–281. Also see The National Commission for Manpower Policy, *The Economic Position of Black Americans: 1976,* Special Report no. 9, Washington, D.C., 1976.

16 This interpretation is offered by Butler and Heckman, pp. 235–281, especially pp. 237–243. Note that in 1977 the ratio of black family income to white family income was 0.57.

17 Richard B. Freeman, "Changes in the Labor Market for Black Americans, 1948–72," *Brookings Papers on Economic Activity 1, 1973,* Brookings, Washington, 1973, p. 76. For additional analysis of this issue, see James P. Smith and Finis Welch, *Race Differences in Earnings: A Survey and New Evidence,* Rand Corporation, Santa Monica, Calif., 1978; and James P. Smith, *The Convergence to Racial Equality in Women's Wages,* Rand Corporation, Santa Monica, Calif., 1978.

18 This hypothesis of the "discouraged worker" originated in the wake of the Great Depression and was offered by those who believed that unemployment rates during that period were understated. It has since been supported empirically. For a recent treatment, see Michael L. Wachter, "Intermediate Swings in Labor Force Participation," *Brookings Papers on Economic Activity 2, 1977,* Brookings, Washington, 1977, pp. 545–574.

19 Butler and Heckman, p. 265.

20 This discussion is based in large part on the analysis by Freeman, pp. 82–86.

21 Freeman, p. 85.

22 Actually, aggregate educational attainments of males and females equalized in 1970 at 12.4 median years of schooling. Since then, medians for both groups have risen to 12.6 years of schooling. See *Employment and Training Report of the President, 1978,* 1978, pp. 247–249, table B-9. On this issue, see also Scott C. Brown, "Educational Attainment of Workers—Some Trends from 1975 to 1978," *Monthly Labor Review,* **102:**54–59 (1979).

23 While there is reason to believe that such differentials in quality also have declined over time, there are no systematic data presently available to measure this phenomenon.

24 As reported in Walter Fogel, "Illegal Alien Workers in the United States," *Industrial Relations,* **16:**246 (1977). The present discussion draws liberally from this source.

25 Fogel, p. 253.

26 The minimum wage was raised to $2.65 in 1978 and to $2.90 in 1979, and it will rise to $3.35 by 1981 as a result of 1977 amendments to the Fair Labor Standards Act. These will be discussed in detail in Chapter 10.

27 Fogel, p. 248.

28 Fogel, p. 258.

29 See Walter Fogel, *Illegal Mexican Workers in the U.S.*, University of California, Institute of Industrial Relations, Los Angeles, 1977; and Barton Smith and Robert Newman, "Depressed Wages along the U.S.-Mexican Border: An Empirical Analysis," *Economic Inquiry*, **15**:51–66 (1977).

30 The amended statute is known as the "Equal Employment Opportunity Act of 1972." For a detailed analysis of the act, see Bureau of National Affairs, *The Equal Employment Opportunity Act of 1972*, Washington, 1973.

31 The affirmative support of nondiscrimination in employment as expressed in the Civil Rights Act can be compared with the affirmative support of collective bargaining contained in the Wagner Act of 1935. Just prior to that historic legislation, public policy as reflected in the Norris-LaGuardia Act (1932) limited the issuance of court injunctions in labor disputes—a neutral, hands-off stance—but supported neither unionism nor collective bargaining.

32 See Phyllis A. Wallace, "Employment Discrimination: Some Policy Considerations," in Orley Ashenfelter and Albert Rees (eds.), *Discrimination in Labor Markets*, Princeton, Princeton, N.J., 1973, p. 159.

33 This is known as "Revised Order No. 4," published in the *Federal Register*, Dec. 4, 1971, pp. 23152–23157.

34 See U.S. Employment Standards Administration, "OFCCP Adopts Standard Racial/Ethnic Definitions," *News*, Mar. 27, 1978; and Bureau of National Affairs, *Daily Labor Report*, Special Supplement, 166, Aug. 25, 1978.

35 Richard A. Lester, "Labor-Market Discrimination and Individualized Pay: The Complicated Case of University Faculty," in Hausman et al., p. 199.

36 See Lester for a review of these criticisms.

37 *Independent Metal Workers Union Local No. 1 v. Hughes Tool Company*, 147 NLRB 1573 (1964). Actually, this doctrine can be traced back to the *Lazrus and Bros. Company* case, 62 NLRB (1955), in which the Board ruled that a union which was unlikely to represent fairly all members of the bargaining unit would not be certified as the bargaining agent and that the certifications of unions which engaged in such unfair representation would be revoked. However, when based on race, instances of unfair representation were generally not disallowed by the Board until the 1960s.

38 *Independent Metal Workers Union Local No. 1 v. Hughes Tool Company*, p. 1595.

39 *International Longshoremen's Association, Local 1367*, 148 NLRB 44.

40 70 LRRM 2489 (1969).

41 For more on this issue, including a review of court decisions that deal with it, see Benjamin Aaron, *Employer and Union Responses to Anti-Discrimination Legislation*, Reprint 2706, University of California, Institute of Industrial Relations, Los Angeles, 1977.

42 U.S. Civil Service Commission, *Minority Group Employment in the Federal Government*, annual issues, 1965–1975.

43 These are reviewed in Robert E. Hampton, "The Response of Governments and the Civil Service to Antidiscrimination Efforts," in Hausman et al., pp. 141–165, especially pp. 147–149.

44 "Federal Policy on Remedies Concerning Equal Employment Opportunity in State and Local Government Personnel Systems," Mar. 23, 1973; and "Policy Statement of Affirmative Action Programs for State and Local Government Agencies," Aug. 26, 1976.

45 Sar A. Levitan, Garth L. Mangum, and F. Ray Marshall, *Human Resources and Labor Markets,* Harper & Row, New York, 1972, p. 182.

46 Levitan, Mangum, and Marshall, p. 182.

47 See *Contractors' Association of Eastern Pennsylvania v. Shultz,* 442 F. 2d 159 (3d Circuit), certiorari denied, 404 U.S. 854 (1971).

48 The data in this section are from *Employment and Training Report of the President, 1978,* 1978, p. 321, table F-15. See also pp. 56–57 of that volume for a brief discussion of apprenticeship.

49 Empirical support for this statement can be found in Orley Ashenfelter, "Discrimination and Trade Unions," in Ashenfelter and Rees, pp. 97–102. Ashenfelter's study showed that the overall effect of unionism in the building trades during the 1960s was to lower the ratio of the wages of black males to those of white males by roughly 5 percent; however, outside the construction industry, the effect was to raise it by 3.5 percent. Ashenfelter concluded more generally that unionism has little overall effect on wage differentials by race and sex in the American economy. It would be helpful to have a similar analysis for the 1970s, both generally and in the construction sector specifically.

50 *U.S. v. Duke Power Company,* 91 S. Ct. 849 (1971) 3 FEP.

51 *U.S. v. Duke Power Company.*

52 That is, the first 50 or 100 or 150 individuals who show up for available jobs would be hired without reference to their qualifications. The sample is random only in this sense, not in the sense of necessarily being representative of the larger population.

53 For a forceful statement of the hypothesis concerning "screening," see Ivar E. Berg, *Education and Jobs: The Great Training Robbery,* Praeger, New York, 1970, especially chaps. 3–5.

54 The quotations are from Theodore V. Purcell, "Management and Affirmative Action in the Late Seventies," in Hausman et al., p. 82.

55 Following the AT&T case, the federal government obtained consent decrees to remedy discrimination in employment from such companies as Uniroyal, El Paso Natural Gas, Pacific Gas and Electric, Standard Oil of California, Bank of America, United Air Lines, and Merrill, Lynch, among others. See Purcell, p. 84. A consent decree also was obtained from the major steel companies in 1974.

56 45 U.S.L.W. 4506 (U.S. May 31, 1977).

57 See, for example, *Teamsters v. United States* and *T.I.M.E.–D.C. v. United States,* 431 U.S. 324 (1977).

58 See Bureau of National Affairs, *Special Supplement: Decision of the Supreme Court in the Regents of the University of California v. Bakke, June 28, 1978,* Government Employee Relations Report, 766, July 3, 1978, pp. 1–42; Warren Weaver, Jr., "High Court Backs Some Affirmative Action by Colleges, but Orders Bakke Admitted," *The New York Times,* June 29, 1978, pp. A1, A22, and related stories on these pages and an editorial on p. A24; Anthony Lewis, "'Bakke' May Change a Lot while Changing No Law," *The New York Times,* July 2, 1978, Section 9, p. 1; William J. Bennett and Terry Eastland, "Why Bakke Won't End Reverse Discrimination," *Commentary,* September 1978, pp. 29–35, pt. 1; and Nathan Glazer,

"Why Bakke Won't End Reverse Discrimination," *Commentary*, September 1978, pp. 36–41, pt. 2. The present account relies heavily on these sources.

59 Louis B. Schwartz, as quoted in *MBA*, **12**:30 (1978).

60 Actually, Bakke first took his case to the trial court, which found that the program at Davis employed an impermissible quota but that Bakke hadn't proved that he would have been admitted to the medical school if no such program existed. Bakke subsequently appealed that ruling to the Supreme Court of California. For an analysis of some general implications of this case, see Charles G. Bakaly and Gorden E. Krischer, "*Bakke:* Its Impact on Public Employment Discrimination," *Employee Relations Law Journal*, **4**:471–484 (1979).

61 Weaver, p. A22.

62 In late 1978, the Supreme Court agreed to hear the case of *Weber v. Kaiser Aluminum and Chemical Corp.*, in which a white male employee (Weber) challenged his exclusion from a company-operated training program, alleging that blacks were favored over whites for entry into the program and that he had suffered lost income and promotional opportunities as a result of his exclusion. The Court's ruling in this case may decide the legality of most employers' affirmative action programs.

63 Butler and Heckman, p. 235.

64 Freeman, pp. 67–120.

65 Freeman p. 119.

66 Robert J. Flanagan, "Actual versus Potential Impact of Government Antidiscrimination Programs," *Industrial and Labor Relations Review*, **29**:486–507 (1976).

67 Butler and Heckman, pp. 255–256. See also Richard Butler and James J. Heckman, "The Impact of Social Transfer Programs on the Relative Status of Blacks," unpublished manuscript, University of Chicago, 1977.

68 Butler and Heckman, "The Government's Impact on the Labor Market Status of Black Americans," p. 256.

69 William M. Landes, "The Economics of Fair Employment Laws," *Journal of Political Economy*, **76**:507–552 (1968). This study and several others referred to below are summarized in Butler and Heckman, "The Government's Impact on the Labor Market Status of Black Americans," pp. 257–262.

70 James J. Heckman, "Simultaneous Equations Models With and Without Structural Shift in the Equations," in Stephen Goldfeld and Richard Quandt (eds.), *Studies in Nonlinear Estimation*, Ballinger, Cambridge, Mass., 1976.

71 Arvil V. Adams, *Toward Fair Employment and the EEOC: A Study of Compliance under Title VII of the Civil Rights Act of 1964*, Equal Employment Opportunity Commission, August 1972.

72 Benjamin W. Wolkinson, *Blacks, Unions and the EEOC*, Heath, Lexington, Mass., 1973.

73 Ray Marshall, Charles Knapp, Malcolm Ligget, and Robert Glover, "The Impact of Court Cases and Out-of-Court Settlements on Minority Employment," University of Texas, Center for the Study of Human Resources, Austin, February 1976.

74 Alice Kidder, "Federal Compliance Efforts in the Carolina Textile Industry: A Summary Report," *Proceedings of the Twenty-fifth Anniversary Meeting of the Industrial Relations Research Association*, Madison, Wis., 1973, pp. 353–361.

75 Andrea Beller, "The Effects of Title VII of the Civil Rights Act of 1964 on the Economic Position of Minorities," unpublished Ph.D. dissertation, Columbia University, New York, 1974.

76 Butler and Heckman, "The Government's Impact on the Labor Market Status of Black Americans," p. 264, citing Orley Ashenfelter and James J. Heckman, "Measuring the Effect of an Antidiscrimination Program,'' in Orley Ashenfelter and James Blum (eds.), *Evaluating the Labor Market Effects of Social Programs*, Princeton University, Industrial Relations Section, Princeton, N.J., 1976, pp. 46–84. In contrast to these results are those of Goldstein and Smith, who found a statistically insignificant decline in the economic status of blacks among firms holding government contracts. See Morris Goldstein and Robert S. Smith, ''The Estimated Impact of the Antidiscrimination Program Aimed at Government Contractors,'' *Industrial and Labor Relations Review*, **29**:523–543 (1976). This issue of the *Review* was devoted entirely to evaluating the impact of the federal government's program for compliance on affirmative action.

ADDITIONAL READINGS

Ashenfelter, Orley, and Albert Rees (eds.): *Discrimination in Labor Markets*, Princeton, Princeton, N.J., 1973.

Becker, Gary S.: *The Economics of Discrimination*, 2d ed., University of Chicago Press, Chicago, 1971.

Bureau of National Affairs: *The Equal Employment Opportunity Act of 1972*, Washington, D.C., 1973.

Hausman, Leonard J., Orley Ashenfelter, Bayard Rustin, Richard F. Schubert, and Donald Slaiman (eds.): *Equal Rights and Industrial Relations*, Industrial Relations Research Association, Madison, Wis., 1977.

Madden, Janice Fanning: *The Economics of Sex Discrimination*, Heath, Lexington, Mass., 1973.

Marshall, Ray: *The Negro and Organized Labor*, Wiley, New York, 1965.

Morgan, James N., et al. (eds.): *Five Thousand American Families—Patterns of Economic Progress*, vols. I–VI, University of Michigan, Institute for Social Research, Ann Arbor, 1972–1978.

Northrup, Herbert R., et al. (eds.): *Studies of Negro Employment in Basic Industries*, University of Pennsylvania, The Wharton School, Industrial Research Unit, Philadelphia, various dates to 1977.

Thurow, Lester C.: *Poverty and Discrimination*, Brookings, Washington, 1969.

U.S. Commission on Civil Rights: *The Federal Civil Rights Enforcement Effort*, 1978.

FOR ANALYSIS AND DISCUSSION

1 Compare the proportions of white and nonwhite workers who were in the labor force during each year since 1960. What factors account for changes in these rates of participation in the labor force over time, and how do the factors differ as between blacks and whites? Compare your answers with those of a classmate.

2 Table 8-2 shows that the proportion of blacks who had year-round, full-time jobs and earned less than $5000 in 1975 exceeded that of persons of Spanish origin. What explanation could you offer for this disparity in the incidence of poverty among these two minority groups? How does age enter into the analysis (see Table 8-2)? Would your explanation be equally applicable to the earnings differentials between white and nonwhite workers employed in year-round, full-time jobs?

3 Read one of the studies listed in Table 8-3, being careful to review its substance, data base, methodology, and conclusions. What factors are ''held constant'' by the author or authors to test for the incidence of discrimination? Why is it necessary to

use regression analysis to study discrimination in the labor market against racial minorities or women? Prepare a short review of the study you have selected for presentation to your classmates, incorporating responses to the questions posed here.

4 "Another very important factor operating to put a sex label on jobs, and more frequently to *keep* the sex label there, is tradition. . . . In other words, each time a job becomes vacant, the question of whether a man or a woman is to be hired is not up for debate. Rather, the job is usually considered a woman's or a man's job and, unless some difficulty is encountered, so it will remain" (Valerie K. Oppenheimer, *The Female Labor Force in the United States,* University of California, Institute of International Studies, Berkeley, 1970, p. 105). **a**   Select some jobs which you believe support or refute this statement and gather information about the representation of men and women in them. Briefly summarize your findings in a short position paper. **b**   Two teams of students should debate the above statement, viewing it as a proposition. The team supporting the proposition should be made up of men, and the team opposing it should consist of women. The teams should respond to questions posed by the remainder of the class after completion of the debate.

5 Suppose that you wanted to obtain reasonably accurate information about illegal aliens in the United States. How would you go about collecting such data? Would you contact employers, workers, or immigration authorities? Should the United States adopt a new policy toward employment of illegal aliens? Discuss your views with a *legal* alien, perhaps one of your classmates or a relative.

6 How effective do you believe the EEOC is in combating discrimination in the labor market? What is the basis of your judgment? Read the latest annual report of the Commission. Are the number of successful conciliations, the volume of legal actions pursued, and the backlog of unresolved cases sufficient for judging the EEOC's effectiveness? Consider your answer in light of the evaluative evidence presented in this chapter.

7 Contact the personnel officers of a large corporation, a large government agency, and a large university and interview them concerning their organizations' responses to the federal government's enforcement of equal employment opportunity legislation. Ask whether their organizations have affirmative action plans, what goals and timetables (if any) these contain, and what information they maintain about the composition of the work force in terms of race and sex. Summarize your findings in a report.

8 Select one of the broad occupational categories listed in Table 8-5 and compare the proportions of blacks and whites in the *detailed* occupations that make up this category. This information is obtainable from the Bureau of the Census. Why are blacks so underrepresented in some of these detailed occupations? Why are they overrepresented in others? Select one of these detailed occupations and examine changes over time in the racial composition of the work force.

9 Two teams of three students each should debate the decision handed down in the *Griggs v. Duke Power Company* case. Be sure to address the issue of validation raised by this case and consider how it has been affected, if at all, by the Supreme Court's decision in the *Bakke* case.

10 Analyze the issue of affirmative action versus seniority under layoffs. Summarize the arguments and evidence supporting each side of this controversy and then state your own position. Contact the highest court of your state to discover what its rulings have been in those cases, if any, which involved this issue. Also inquire of the EEOC whether it has prepared guidelines to resolve the conflict between affirmative action and seniority under layoffs.

Chapter 9

Equality and
Income Distribution

INTRODUCTION

In this chapter, we turn our attention away from the operation of labor markets per se and toward the distribution of national income among factors of production and among families. Of particular interest are the extent to which income distribution has changed over time and what this indicates about the incidence of poverty in the United States.

Data on income provide a point of departure for taking up one of the most widely debated issues of the day, economic inequality. The discussion of this issue will focus on the role of environmental factors and of inheritance in generating inequality, though the reader should bear in mind that in most cases such forces work through the labor market and employment to affect the distribution of income among the populace.

The other issue to be considered here is the redistribution of income through public policy. In the United States, governmental efforts to redistribute income intensified in the mid-1960s, and transfer payments have grown rapidly since then. We shall review some of the key components of these transfer payments, the policies from which they stem, and the evidence pertaining to their effectiveness in reducing poverty and economic inequality. Selected evidence on income distribution, inequality, and public policy in other nations will be provided throughout the chapter.

THE DISTRIBUTION OF NATIONAL INCOME

National income may be meaningfully disaggregated into three major components: compensation to employees, the income of unincorporated entrepreneurs, and income from property. The first includes wages, salaries, and fringe benefits (wage supplements); the second encompasses the income of farmers, independent professional people (like doctors and lawyers), and businesspeople (usually running small firms); and the third covers interest, rent, and corporate profits. Table 9-1 lists the proportion of national income accounted for by each of these categories for the period 1929 to 1978.

The clear message of Table 9-1 is that labor's share of national income has moved irregularly upward during this 50-year period. Note that in this instance, "labor" includes executives and managers and encompasses all employees, irrespective of the sectors in which they work. By the mid-1970s, labor's share was more than three-fourths of national income in the United States' trillion-dollar-plus economy. Correspondingly, the proportionate shares of national income going to other categories of recipients—that is, other factors of production—declined markedly from the late 1920s to the late 1970s. Why is it that the division of national income between labor and all other factors of production has shifted proportionately from less than 60:40 to more than 75:25 over the period in question?

First, just as a change in industry mix can change the wage level of a local area, so can a change in the industry mix of the economy affect the income share going to wages, salaries, and wage supplements. We saw earlier that the proportion of the labor force employed in agriculture has dropped sharply in the twentieth century, and thus millions of people who would have worked on a farm in earlier periods now work in offices, factories, shops, and plants. Among this group are some who owned or would have owned their own farms or other unincorporated enterprises (column 6 in Table 9-1); by shifting to employment in other sectors, they reduce the amount of national income credited to capital, and they increase that received by labor. And this shift occurs even if the farmer of yesteryear is a factory manager or top executive instead of a blue-collar or office worker because the salaries of all corporate executives and managers are counted in Table 9-1 as employee compensation instead of entrepreneurial income. Further, we know that the labor-intensive service sector—industries such as retail trade, health services, and especially government, in which wages and salaries often form a high proportion of total costs—has been expanding steadily. Consequently, labor's share of national income has increased mainly because of this shift in the industry mix of the economy, and not because the labor factor of production has augmented its earnings at the expense of profits and other shares. Stated differently, some increase in labor's share of national income would be expected to occur as the proportion of wage and salary workers among all those who expend labor at various tasks (owning a farm, renting a building, operating a business) rises over time.

A second difficulty in interpreting the apparent rise in labor's share lies in the puzzle of *entrepreneurial income*. Table 9-1 shows that the bulk of the increase in labor's share has been matched by a decline in the share going to unincorporated enterprises. That share (for farm and nonfarm enterprises combined) dropped from 17.4 to 6.6 between 1929 and 1978, or by 10.8 percentage points, compared with the increase of 17.5 points in labor's share. Everyone agrees that farmers, store owners, doctors, lawyers, and other owners of unincorporated enterprises receive two types of income simultaneously: a return on their hours of labor (the wage or salary that they could earn if they worked for someone else) and a return on their capital (the profit or interest that their capital might earn if invested in something other than their own business). Unfortunately, this distinction is much easier to make in theory than in fact, and no one really knows how this entrepreneurial income, amounting to $113 billion in 1978, should be divided between the shares of capital and labor—which is the reason why this type of income is always reported separately instead of being allocated (as the income of corporations is) among wages, profits, and other categories.

Related to this problem is that of the *government* or *public sector*, in which it is next to impossible to compute any returns to capital in the form of profits, interest, or rent. Indeed, the output of government operations is measured in the national income and product accounts of the United States solely by the input of labor, with the result that the large growth in the public sector since 1929 is portrayed in Table 9-1 exclusively as an addition to labor's share. This is a compromise that statisticians must make in the absence of any better concepts or measures, but obviously the public payroll does not reveal the total contribution to national output and income made by government operations in construction, education, health, law, and other fields.

Despite these imposing problems, we may conclude that labor's share of national income has increased rather dramatically over the years, especially since the late 1960s, and that corporate profits have declined noticeably. Observe from Table 9-1, though, that wage supplements—fringe benefits—account for virtually all this increase in labor's share. It may also be concluded that labor's share and profit's share tend to move in opposite directions with short-run swings in the business cycle. Table 9-1 shows this most clearly for the Depression years of the 1930s, when profits literally disappeared for a short period and the wage share rose simply by default, in spite of lower wages and massive unemployment. The pattern was also evident in the recession of 1974–1975. In an expansionary period, labor's share tends to drop, while the share of national income going to profits rises. This occurred between 1946 and 1948, in the mid-1960s, and in the post-1975 recovery period.

It is also generally agreed that government policy largely explains the decline in rental shares since 1929 and the changing pattern of returns to interest. The low levels of rental income in the Depression years of the mid-1930s were

Table 9-1 Distribution of National Income among the Factors of Production, 1929–1978

	Total national income (billions of dollars) (1)	Compensation of employees			Unincorporated enterprises		Rent (7)	Corporate profits (8)	Net interest (9)
		Total (2)	Wages and salaries (3)	Supplements to wages and salaries[2] (4)	Nonfarm (5)	Farm (6)			
Year									
1929	86.8	58.9	58.1	0.8	10.3	7.1	6.2	12.1	5.4
1930	75.4	62.1	61.3	0.9	10.1	5.7	6.3	9.3	6.5
1931	59.7	66.6	65.5	1.0	9.7	5.7	6.4	3.3	8.3
1932	42.8	72.7	71.3	1.4	8.4	4.9	6.3	(−)3.0	10.7
1933	40.3	73.2	72.0	1.2	8.2	6.4	5.0	(−)3.0	10.2
1934	49.5	69.3	68.1	1.2	9.5	6.1	3.4	3.4	8.3
1935	57.2	65.2	64.2	1.0	9.6	9.2	3.0	5.9	7.1
1936	65.0	66.0	64.5	1.5	10.3	6.6	2.7	8.6	5.8
1937	73.6	65.0	62.6	2.4	9.8	8.1	2.8	9.2	5.0
1938	67.4	66.8	63.8	3.0	10.2	6.5	3.9	7.3	5.3
1939	72.6	66.2	63.2	3.0	10.2	6.1	3.7	8.7	4.8
1940	81.1	64.2	61.4	2.8	10.6	5.5	3.6	12.1	4.0
1941	104.2	62.2	59.6	2.6	10.6	6.1	3.4	14.6	3.1
1942	137.1	62.2	59.9	2.3	10.5	7.1	3.3	14.8	2.2
1943	170.3	64.3	62.1	2.2	10.0	6.9	3.0	14.3	1.5
1944	182.6	66.4	63.9	2.5	10.0	6.4	3.0	13.0	1.2
1945	181.5	67.8	64.7	3.1	10.6	6.7	3.1	10.6	1.2
1946	181.9	64.8	61.6	3.2	11.9	8.2	3.6	10.6	0.8
1947	199.0	64.8	61.8	3.0	10.2	7.6	3.6	12.9	0.9
1948	224.2	63.0	60.4	2.6	10.1	7.8	3.6	14.7	0.8
1949	217.5	64.8	61.8	3.0	10.4	5.8	3.9	14.2	0.9
1950	241.1	64.1	60.9	3.2	10.0	5.6	3.9	15.6	0.8
1951	278.0	65.0	61.5	3.5	9.4	5.7	3.7	15.4	0.8
1952	291.4	67.0	63.5	3.5	9.3	5.1	3.9	13.7	0.9

Year	National income[1]								
1953	304.7	68.6	65.0	3.6	9.0	4.3	4.2	13.0	0.9
1954	303.1	68.6	64.8	3.8	9.1	4.1	4.5	12.5	1.2
1955	331.0	67.8	63.8	4.0	9.2	3.4	4.2	14.2	1.2
1956	350.8	69.3	64.9	4.3	8.9	3.2	4.1	13.1	1.3
1957	366.1	69.9	65.2	4.7	9.0	3.1	4.0	12.4	1.5
1958	367.8	70.1	65.2	4.9	9.0	3.6	4.2	11.2	1.8
1959	400.0	69.8	64.6	5.2	8.8	2.8	3.9	12.9	1.8
1960	414.5	71.0	65.3	5.7	8.3	2.9	3.8	12.0	2.0
1961	427.3	70.8	65.1	5.7	8.3	3.0	3.7	11.8	2.3
1962	457.7	70.7	64.7	6.0	8.1	2.8	3.6	12.2	2.5
1963	481.9	70.8	64.6	6.2	7.9	2.7	3.5	12.2	2.9
1964	518.1	70.6	64.4	6.2	7.8	2.3	3.5	12.8	3.0
1965	564.3	69.8	63.6	6.2	7.5	2.6	3.4	13.5	3.2
1966	620.8	70.2	63.6	6.6	7.2	2.6	3.2	13.5	3.3
1967	652.9	71.7	64.8	6.9	7.1	2.2	3.1	12.3	3.6
1968	712.8	72.0	65.0	7.0	6.7	2.1	2.9	12.5	3.7
1969	767.9	74.4	67.0	7.4	6.8	1.8	2.4	10.6	4.0
1970	798.4	76.3	68.4	7.9	6.4	1.7	2.3	8.5	4.7
1971	858.1	75.8	67.6	8.2	6.2	1.7	2.3	9.0	5.0
1972	951.9	75.1	66.6	8.6	6.1	1.9	2.3	9.7	4.9
1973	1064.6	75.1	65.7	9.2	5.7	3.0	2.0	9.3	4.9
1974	1136.0	77.1	67.3	9.8	5.4	2.2	1.9	7.4	6.1
1975	1215.0	76.6	66.3	10.3	5.2	1.9	1.8	7.9	6.5
1976	1359.2	76.2	65.5	10.7	5.1	1.4	1.7	7.3	6.2
1977	1515.3	76.1	64.9	11.2	5.2	1.3	1.5	9.5	6.3
1978	1703.6	76.4	64.6	11.8	5.1	1.5	1.4	9.4	6.2

[1] National income is the total net income earned in production. It differs from gross national product mainly in that it excludes depreciation charges and other allowances for business and institutional consumption of durable capital goods and indirect business taxes.

[2] Employers' contributions for social insurance and to private pension, health, and welfare funds; compensation for injuries; directors' fees; pay of the military reserve; and a few other minor items.

Source: Adapted from *Economic Report of the President, January, 1979*, 1979, pp. 204–205, table B-19.

continued by rent controls, imposed first by the federal government as a war-time measure and later by state and local governments. Such ceilings on rents have disappeared for the most part (although New York City is a major exception), but meanwhile other factors have been at work to keep the rental share of national income far below its 1929 level. In the case of interest, the federal government maintained an easy-money policy during the 1940s in order to accommodate the Treasury's problem of financing the national debt, which was swollen by wartime expenditures. Relatively tight money policies were adopted in the late 1960s and, in conjunction with the substantial deficits in the federal budget prevailing since that time, caused the share of national income going to interest to rise to more than 6 percent in the middle to late 1970s, its highest level since 1935.[1]

How does the distribution of national income among factors of production in the United States compare with that in other industrialized nations? It appears to occupy roughly a median position. In 1974, for example, when wages and salaries constituted about two-thirds of all national income in the United States, comparable proportions were 65 percent in Australia, 59 percent in Belgium, 62 percent in Canada, 59 percent in France, 62 percent in West Germany, 63 percent in Jamaica, 59 percent in Japan, 65 percent in the Netherlands, 67 percent in New Zealand, 66 percent in Norway, 69 percent in Sweden, and 71 percent in the United Kingdom. More important, every one of these nations, like the United States, experienced considerable growth in labor's share of national income from the mid-1930s to the mid-1970s, especially in the post-World War II period.[2] And even these data understate the proportion of national income going to labor, since they do not properly account for private and publicly provided wage supplements and fringe benefits, which tend to be proportionately larger outside than inside the United States. Thus, Atkinson writes: "The empirical evidence suggests that in most advanced countries, labor receives between two-thirds and three-quarters of national income and that its share has shown a long-run tendency to rise over time."[3]

The Impact of Unions on Labor's Share

Have labor unions been able to increase the share of national income flowing to wage and salary workers at the expense of other factors of production? The answer seems to be "very little, if at all," according to existing studies of this subject.[4] This is, of course, consistent with the view that labor's share of national income has remained relatively constant within homogeneous sectors of the economy, but let us consider further the lack of impact of collective bargaining on income distribution.

Recall from Chapter 7 that the influence of unions on wages in the United States is to increase them on the average from 10 to 20 percent and, from Chapter 3, that only about one in four American workers belongs to a labor organization. These two facts indicate that, as one observer puts it, "even if effective unions raise labor's share in their own industries, the effect would be highly diluted and thus difficult to observe when spread over the whole economy.''[5] Even more to the point, however, a union that achieves successes in bargaining —large relative impacts on wages—will not necessarily be able to raise its share even in the industry or industries in which it operates.

Labor's share of income may increase in the short run, but over the long haul employers will tend to substitute capital for labor, thereby rearranging the distribution of income so as to dilute the returns to labor. The exact adjustments of employers to negotiated wage increases will depend upon the elasticities of the demand for, and supply of, factors of production, but in the absence of a totally inelastic demand curve for labor, a union cannot augment its share of income simply by bargaining for a large wage increase. In fact, if the demand for labor is highly elastic, causing an employer to reduce the work force by a relatively large amount in response to a negotiated wage increase, it is ''entirely possible for a union simultaneously to raise the relative wages of its members and to reduce their aggregate share of income arising in their industry.''[6] According to some, it is only if unions seek to limit management's freedom to make such adjustments in the production process that they will be able to capture some portion of the income going to other groups. As yet, American unionists have shown little inclination to move along these lines.

But this argument should not be carried too far. Even within existing political and economic structures, unions can have some impact on income distribution through political channels or through a combination of bargaining and political pressure. Observe in Table 9-1, for example, the steep rise since 1929 in wage supplements, consisting primarily of employers' contributions to both public and private pension, health, and welfare funds. If labor's total share of national income adjusted for changes in industry mix has not risen over the last half century or so, as some contend, then this huge increase in wage supplements presumably means that bargaining by unions and the political pressure they have brought to bear have nevertheless served to redistribute employees' compensation away from immediate wages toward pensions and similar types of deferred income—a shift which many, if not all, workers would consider a distinct gain. Conversely, if labor's total share of income has actually increased beyond that accounted for by shifts in employment in industry—the ''unexplained'' portion of the shift was recently estimated to be about 2.5 points[7] —then a major source of that increase would seem to have been this rise in wage supplements. As with wage increases, employers can offset some enlarged fringe benefits by laying off workers, adding new equipment in place of labor, or raising prices. However, other costs of fringe benefits such as the cost of pension benefits paid to workers who have already retired cannot be offset in this fashion. Additionally, the data in Table 9-1 are for income shares before taxes, and the impact of unions on relative shares may be manifested in after-tax income, given organized labor's political support of the graduated income tax and public welfare measures. On balance, we can conclude by saying that labor unions have not significantly altered the shares of national income going to the major factors of production, while recognizing that the available evidence may not fully reveal this impact.

But if this is so, it leaves unanswered the question, "Is labor's share of national income too high or too low in relation to society's goals?" Is roughly 75 percent the "right" share for labor? Should it be larger or smaller? Should government policy be aimed at reducing or expanding that share? Obviously, answers to these questions depend on one's values, although the underlying forces at work which have generated the existing distribution of income between labor and capital would probably overmatch any explicit effort by government to impose a sharply different pattern of distribution. As to the social justice of the existing distribution of income among factors of production, consider that it might have been

> . . . delightful to have been born into an economy in which labor's share was only one percent while the capitalist owners of non-human goods got 99 percent. This could mean that people did almost no work and lived off a highly automated economy. Or it might mean that . . . most people were very poor with one person possibly owning the "capital." Obviously the situation [would] depend on the distribution of ownership of various forms of wealth and not basically on the human/non-human division of income.[8]

For this reason, most people are less concerned with the distribution of income between the two abstract factors called "labor" and "capital" than with the subject of the next section: how income is distributed among the millions of families and individuals in society, whether they are called "capitalists," "workers," or simply "human beings."

THE DISTRIBUTION OF PERSONAL INCOME

The United States is a rich and prosperous nation, and compared with people in most of the rest of the world, its citizens are indeed well-off. Perhaps the most commonly used indicator of well-being—of economic well-being, at any rate—is family income. In 1977, median family income rose to a record high of $16,009.[9] More important, however, is the distribution of income among families and changes in that distribution over time. Table 9-2 presents data relevant to these concerns.

In Table 9-2, the total number of American families is divided into fifths on the basis of their income level, and the proportion of total family income accounted for by each of the fifths is shown for the period 1929–1977. In 1977, the lowest fifth of families earned only 5.2 percent of total income, while the highest fifth earned more than 40 percent. In the same year, the top 5 percent of families earned almost one-sixth of total family income. Hence, family income is quite unevenly distributed in the United States. This has long been true, though, and observe that there was some reduction in the inequality of income

Table 9-2   Distribution of Family Income in the United States, 1929–1977[1]

Fifths of families	1929	1935	1941	1947	1952	1957	1962	1967	1972	1977
Lowest fifth	12.5	4.1	4.1	5.0	4.9	5.1	5.0	5.5	5.4	5.2
Second fifth		9.2	9.5	11.9	12.3	12.7	12.1	12.4	11.9	11.6
Middle fifth	13.8	14.1	15.3	17.0	17.4	18.1	17.6	17.9	17.5	17.5
Fourth fifth	19.3	20.9	22.3	23.1	23.4	23.8	24.0	23.9	23.9	24.2
Highest fifth	54.4	51.7	48.8	43.0	41.9	40.4	41.3	40.4	41.4	41.5
Top 5 percent	30.0	26.5	24.0	20.9	17.4	15.6	15.7	15.2	15.9	15.7

[1] Data are for consumer units, which include families and unrelated individuals.

Sources: U.S. Bureau of the Census, *Current Population Reports: Money Income and Poverty Status of Families and Persons in the United States: 1977* (Advance Report), ser. p-60, no. 116, 1978, p. 11, and Herman P. Miller, *Income Distribution in the United States.* U.S. Bureau of the Census Monograph, 1966, table 1-10.

distribution between 1929 and 1947. However, relatively little change in the distribution of family income has occurred in the post-World War II era.

How does the distribution of personal income in the United States compare with that in other countries? The data necessary to answer this question fully are not comprehensive or totally comparable, but we can nevertheless make some comparisons from the available information. Table 9-3 presents data which show that the United States had one of the more unequal distributions of personal income among industrialized countries in the late 1960s and early 1970s. On a before-tax basis, the income share of the lowest fifth of the population was smaller in the United States than in any of the other countries listed in Table 9-3, especially Japan and Australia. At the other end of the scale, the income share received by the top fifth of the population was greatest in

Table 9-3   Before-Tax and After-Tax Family Income Distribution in Selected Industrialized Countries, Selected Years[1]

Country	Year	Lowest fifth	Second fifth	Middle fifth	Fourth fifth	Highest fifth
Australia	1966–1967	6.7(6.6)	13.5(13.5)	17.8(17.8)	23.4(23.4)	38.9(38.8)
Canada	1969	4.3(5.0)	10.9(11.8)	17.3(17.9)	24.2(24.3)	43.3(41.0)
France	1970	4.3(4.3)	9.9(9.8)	15.8(16.3)	23.0(22.7)	47.0(46.9)
West Germany	1973	5.9(6.5)	10.1(10.3)	15.1(15.0)	22.1(21.9)	46.8(46.1)
Japan	1969	7.6(7.9)	12.6(13.1)	16.3(16.8)	21.0(21.2)	42.5(41.0)
Netherlands	1967	5.9(6.5)	10.9(11.6)	15.8(16.4)	21.6(22.7)	45.8(42.9)
Norway	1970	4.9(6.3)	11.6(12.9)	18.0(18.8)	24.6(24.7)	40.9(37.3)
Sweden	1972	6.0(6.6)	11.4(13.1)	17.4(18.5)	24.3(24.8)	40.5(37.0)
United Kingdom	1973	5.4(6.3)	12.0(12.6)	18.1(18.4)	24.2(23.9)	40.3(38.7)
United States	1972	3.8(4.5)	10.0(10.7)	16.8(17.3)	24.5(24.7)	44.8(42.9)
Italy	1969	(5.1)	(10.5)	(16.2)	(21.7)	(46.5)
Spain	1973–1974	(6.0)	(11.8)	(16.9)	(23.1)	(42.3)

[1] After-tax distributions are shown in parentheses.

Source: Adapted from Malcolm Sawyer, "Income Distribution in OECD Countries," *OECD Economic Outlook, Occasional Studies,* Organization for Economic Cooperation and Development, Paris, July 1976, p. 14, table 3.

France; West Germany followed closely in this respect, and then the Netherlands and the United States. The United Kingdom and the Scandinavian countries (Norway and Sweden) had the lowest percentage shares going to the top fifth of the population, but they nevertheless exceeded 40 percent in every instance. But while these and other important differences exist in the distribution of personal income before taxes in the first ten countries listed in Table 9-3, it is perhaps the similarities that are most striking. Thus, the percentage of income received by the middle 60 percent (the three middle fifths) of the populace in these ten nations ranged only from 47.3 in West Germany to 54.7 in Australia.

Table 9-3 also presents data on after-tax income distribution in these ten countries and in two additional ones. In this regard, the United States ranks above France but below all the other nations in terms of the proportion of income going to the bottom fifth of recipients, while ranking in the upper third in terms of the share of income going to the top fifth. The most unequal after-tax distributions of personal income occur in France, Italy, and Germany, and the most equal distributions in Sweden, Norway, Australia, Japan, and the United Kingdom. The United States is considerably closer to the first than to the second group of countries with respect to its after-tax distribution of personal income. The incidence of taxes as well as transfer payments in the United States will be discussed in considerable detail below.

It should be noted that the pattern of inequality in the distribution of personal income in developed nations pales considerably in comparison with that recorded in developing countries. This is evident from the data in Table 9-4, which lists the before-tax income shares for the bottom 40, top 20, and top 5 percent of the population in fifteen developing countries. (These data are slightly older than those presented in Table 9-3 for the developed nations.) Observe that the top 20 percent of income recipients in these countries generally earned 50 percent or more of total national income, with the proportion topping 60 percent in three nations and closely approaching that mark in three others. In fact, in two out of three instances, the top 5 percent of income recipients received a 25 percent income share or better. In contrast, the bottom 40 percent of the populace never received as much as 20 percent of total national income, they received more than 15 percent in only three countries, and they averaged about 14 percent.

Of course, it must be kept in mind that the level of per capita income in most of the developing nations is far below that prevailing in developed, industrialized countries, and the income gaps between these two categories of nations usually far outstrip the inequality of income distribution within either of them. Thus, India, with one-quarter of the world's population, accounts for only 4 percent of total world consumption. Finally, studies of eastern European countries (especially Czechoslovakia and Hungary) show them to have somewhat greater income equality than the developed nations listed in Table 9-3, though their distribution of income is hardly different from that of such largely capitalist countries as Australia, Japan, and New Zealand (not shown in the table).[10]

Table 9-4   Income Distribution in Selected Developed and Developing Countries

Country	Period	Percentage share of bottom 40 percent	Percentage share of top 20 percent	Percentage share of top 5 percent
United States	1966	15	44	19
Canada	1965	20	40	14
France	1962	10	54	25
Australia	1966	20	39	14
United Kingdom	1964	15	44	19
Japan	1962	15	46	20
Puerto Rico	1963	14	51	22
Argentina	1961	17	52	29
Uruguay	1967	14	47	21
Chile	1968	15	52	23
Mexico	1963	10	59	29
Lebanon	1955–1960	13	61	34
Brazil	1970	10	62	33
Zambia	1959	15	57	38
Phillipines	1965	12	55	30
Thailand	1962	13	58	34
Sudan	1969	15	48	17
Sri Lanka	1969–1970	17	46	19
India	1964–1970	17	49	25
Tanzania	1967	14	61	36
Pakistan and Bangladesh	1963–1964	18	45	20

Source: Adapted from A. B. Atkinson, *The Economics of Inequality,* Oxford Universiry Press, London, 1975, p. 248.

To return to the data for the United States, why did income differentials between families shrink between 1929 and 1947 and then level out? Most of the reasons are related to trends in the economy that were examined previously. We saw in Table 9-1, for example, that the share of national income going to wages and salaries increased between 1929 and 1947; the share going to rent dropped; and, while the profit share first dropped and then returned to its 1929 level, the high corporate income taxes imposed during and after World War II meant that a smaller proportion of profits was then available for distribution as stock dividends, the only portion of corporate profits that appears in the data on family income in Table 9-2. These shifts away from property income tend to narrow income differentials because, as one would expect, upper-income families receive a larger share of their income from property than lower-income families.

This trend has not halted completely since 1947, but it did slow down as corporate tax rates were eased, as the interest share rose, and as the rental share dropped more slowly than before. Also, we know that the labor force has continued shifting out of low-income farm and unskilled jobs toward jobs in higher-paying industries and occupations, but perhaps the postwar growth of employment in service-producing industries, where wages often are below those prevailing in goods-producing industries, has softened the equalizing impact of the shift from farm to factory. Finally, income differentials between occupations—between skilled and unskilled jobs, for example, or between professional and clerical positions—declined considerably between 1929 and 1947; since then, they have narrowed only slowly, have stabilized, or in some cases have actually widened. This also contributes to the postwar pattern of stability in the distribution of family income.

All this might suggest that the pattern of income distribution in the United States has achieved equilibrium, thereby solving the problem of what constitutes the "natural" or acceptable degree of income inequality in our society. That is most unlikely, however, since the constant changes that occur in the modern economy prevent competitive forces from working themselves out to that ultimate equilibrium envisioned in pure theory. To say this is not to deny the importance of market forces in shaping the present pattern of income distribution, but rather to warn against assuming that any economic pattern, even one persisting for three decades, is a long-run equilibrium position. More specifically, the fact that government policy has had a major impact on the trend of every component of family income—profit, interest, rent, transfer payments, and, more indirectly, wages and salaries—means that a shift in government policy can produce a change in income distribution at any time. We shall see this momentarily when we examine the effects of governmental income maintenance programs on the incidence of poverty in the United States. First, however, consider the data in Table 9-5, which show the distribution of families by income levels in the post-World War II era. Incidentally, the data are presented in terms of 1977 dollars, which adjusts for the effects of inflation on family income.

Observe that in 1947 almost two-thirds of all families received *less than* $10,000 of income, while by 1977 over 70 percent received *more than* $10,000 of income. During this 30-year span, the proportion of families with less than $5000 of income declined from 25 percent to under 10 percent. At the other end of the spectrum, 22 percent of all families received $15,000 or more of income in 1955, but 54 percent of all families were in this category in 1977. The proportion of families in the middle-income range, $5000 to $10,000, dropped from 39 percent to 18 percent between 1947 and 1977.

Table 9-5 also shows major differences by race in the distribution of family income, differences which have moderated but which have by no means been eliminated over time. Thus, we see that 22 percent of white families and 58 percent of nonwhite families received less than $5000 of income in 1947; by 1977, these proportions had declined to roughly 8 percent and 23 percent, respectively. In the mid-1950s, 24 percent of white families but only 5 percent of nonwhite families had incomes of $15,000 or more. Two decades or so later, 57 percent of white families and one-third of nonwhite families were in this category. By 1977, moreover, the median income of nonwhite families was 61 percent that of white families, up from 51 percent in 1947. However, in 1977, almost half of all nonwhite families received less than $10,000 of income, compared with

Table 9-5 Family Income by Level of Total Money Income and Race of Head of Family, Selected Years, 1947–1977

(In 1977 Dollars)

Total money income	1947	1955	1960	1967	1972	1977
All races						
Number (thousands)	37,237	42,889	45,539	50,111	54,373	57,215
Percent						
Under $3,000	12.7	11.2	8.6	4.8	3.7	3.6
$3,000–$4,999	12.2	8.9	8.5	6.5	5.6	5.7
$5,000–$6,999	19.4	10.1	8.8	6.8	6.6	7.2
$7,000–$9,999	19.8	20.0	15.0	11.7	10.5	10.9
$10,000–$11,999	⎫	15.3	14.8	9.0	7.7	7.2
$12,000–$14,999	35.9	12.5	13.2	14.3	11.9	11.3
$15,000–$24,999	⎬	17.8	23.6	32.3	33.5	31.7
$25,000 and over	⎭	4.3	7.4	14.6	20.5	22.4
Median income	$ 8,223	$ 9,999	$11,500	$14,398	$16,102	$16,009
Whites						
Number (thousands)	34,120	38,982	41,123	44,814	48,477	50,530
Percent						
Under $3,000	10.7	9.5	7.0	4.1	3.0	2.8
$3,000–$4,999	11.0	8.0	7.7	5.7	4.7	4.8
$5,000–$6,999	19.6	9.5	8.2	6.2	6.0	6.6
$7,000–$9,999	20.5	20.0	14.8	11.1	10.0	10.5
$10,000–$11,999	⎫	16.0	15.4	8.9	7.5	7.1
$12,000–$14,999	38.1	13.1	13.7	14.7	12.1	11.5
$15,000–$24,999	⎬	19.1	25.1	33.8	34.8	33.0
$25,000 and over	⎭	4.7	8.0	15.6	21.9	23.9
Median income	$ 8,566	$10,439	$11,940	$14,945	$16,729	$16,740
Blacks and other races						
Number (thousands)	3,117	3,907	4,333	5,020	5,896	6,685
Percent						
Under $3,000	33.6	27.4	23.1	11.2	9.7	9.6
$3,000–4,999	24.7	16.8	15.9	13.6	12.9	13.2
$5,000–$6,999	17.3	15.4	14.0	12.8	11.5	12.4
$7,000–$9,999	12.0	20.5	16.9	16.9	14.6	14.2
$10,000–$11,999	⎫	9.2	10.3	9.6	8.8	7.9
$12,000–$14,999	12.3	5.7	7.9	11.5	10.6	10.0
$15,000–$24,999	⎬	4.7	10.2	18.6	22.5	22.0
$25,000 and over	⎭	0.3	1.7	5.7	9.3	10.8
Median income	$ 4,378	$ 5,757	$ 6,610	$ 9,246	$10,293	$10,142

Source: Adapted from U.S. Bureau of the Census, *Current Population Reports: Money Income and Poverty Status of Families and Persons in the United States: 1977* (Advance Report), ser. P-60, no. 116, 1978, p. 10.

less than one-quarter of white families. Additionally, and as noted in Chapter 8, the ratio of the median income of black families to that of white families in the late 1970s was virtually unchanged from the late 1960s.

Turning more specifically to poverty, we see from Table 9-6 that its incidence has declined over time, although the poverty rate for 1977 (11.6 percent)

Table 9-6 Persons below the Poverty Level, by Family Status, 1959–1977
(Numbers in Thousands; Persons as of March of the Following Year)

Year	Number below the poverty level							Poverty rate						
	Total		By family status					Total		By family status				
	All persons	65 years and over	Total	Head	Related children under 18	Other family members	Unrelated individuals	All persons	65 years and over	Total	Head	Related children under 18	Other family members	Unrelated individuals
1977	24,720	3,177	19,504	5,311	10,028	4,165	5,216	11.6	14.1	10.2	9.3	16.0	5.9	22.6
1976	24,975	3,313	19,632	5,311	10,081	4,240	5,344	11.8	15.0	10.3	9.4	15.8	6.0	24.9
1975	25,877	3,317	20,789	5,450	10,882	4,457	5,068	12.3	15.3	10.9	9.7	16.8	6.4	25.1
1974ʳ	23,370	3,085	18,817	4,922	9,967	3,928	4,553	11.2	14.6	9.9	8.8	15.1	5.7	24.1
1974	24,260	3,308	19,440	5,109	10,196	4,135	4,820	11.6	15.7	10.2	9.2	15.5	6.0	25.5
1973	22,973	3,354	18,299	4,828	9,453	4,018	4,674	11.1	16.3	9.7	8.8	14.2	5.9	25.6
1972	24,460	3,738	19,577	5,075	10,082	4,420	4,883	11.9	18.6	10.3	9.3	14.9	6.6	29.0
1971	25,559	4,273	20,405	5,303	10,344	4,757	5,154	12.5	21.6	10.8	10.0	15.1	7.2	31.6
1970	25,420	4,709	20,330	5,260	10,235	4,835	5,090	12.6	24.5	10.9	10.1	14.9	7.4	32.9
1969	24,147	4,787	19,175	5,008	9,501	4,667	4,972	12.1	25.3	10.4	9.7	13.8	7.2	34.0
1968	25,389	4,632	20,695	5,047	10,739	4,909	4,694	12.8	25.0	11.3	10.0	15.3	7.8	34.0
1967	27,769	5,388	22,771	5,667	11,427	5,677	4,998	14.2	29.5	12.5	11.4	16.3	9.1	38.1
1966ʳ	28,510	5,114	23,809	5,784	12,146	5,879	4,701	14.7	28.5	13.1	11.8	17.4	9.5	38.3
1966	30,424	(NA)	25,614	6,200	12,876	6,538	4,810	15.7	(NA)	14.2	12.7	18.4	10.5	38.9
1965	33,185	(NA)	28,358	6,721	14,388	7,249	4,827	17.3	(NA)	15.8	13.9	20.7	11.8	39.8
1964	36,055	(NA)	30,912	7,160	15,735	8,016	5,143	19.0	(NA)	17.4	15.0	22.7	13.3	42.7
1963	36,436	(NA)	31,498	7,554	15,691	8,253	4,938	19.5	(NA)	17.9	15.9	22.8	13.8	44.2
1962	38,625	(NA)	33,623	8,077	16,630	8,916	5,002	21.0	(NA)	19.4	17.2	24.7	15.1	45.4
1961	39,628	(NA)	34,509	8,391	16,577	9,451	5,119	21.9	(NA)	20.3	18.1	25.2	16.5	45.9
1960	39,851	(NA)	34,925	8,243	17,288	9,394	4,926	22.2	(NA)	20.7	18.1	26.5	16.2	45.2
1959	39,490	5,481	34,562	8,320	17,208	9,034	4,928	22.4	35.2	20.8	18.5	26.9	15.9	46.1

Source: Adapted from U.S. Bureau of the Census, *Current Population Reports: Money Income and Poverty Status of Families and Persons in the United States: 1977* (Advance Report), ser. P-60, no. 116, 1978, p. 21.

was not much different from that prevailing in 1969 (12.1 percent). This poverty rate relates the proportion of persons below a specific threshold level of income in a particular year to the proportion of those above it. The threshold level, which is set by the federal government, is calculated by determining a "typical" family's expenditures on food and then tripling that amount (two-thirds of expenditures are presumed to be for nonfood items). The poverty threshold is updated annually to take into account changes in the Consumer Price Index. Stating the incidence of poverty as a rate allows one to control for changes in population over time, such as from about 179 million to 216 million between 1960 and 1977.[11] Still, some 25 million persons were below the poverty level in 1977, a figure which was down from almost 40 million in 1960 but which was unchanged from the late 1960s.

For a "typical" nonfarm family of four, the amount of income separating those below the poverty level from those above it rose from $3613 in 1959, the first year for which such data were collected, to $6191 in 1977. The change reflects adjustments in the threshold level of income to take account of inflation over that period.

Table 9-7 provides additional data profiling the poor. In 1977, almost half of the 5.3 million poor families were headed by women, and the poverty rate among families headed by women was about 32 percent, compared with the 5.5 percent rate prevailing among families headed by men. The incidence of poverty among black families, 28 percent, was four times greater than that among white families. And, whereas the poverty rate among families headed by black males was 13.5 percent, or almost three times as large as that among families headed by white males, this figure pales dramatically in comparison with the poverty rate of 51 percent among families headed by black women. Finally, note that among unrelated individuals the incidence of poverty in 1977 was almost one in four, though the female-male differential was much smaller than in the case of poverty-stricken *families*.

In sum, the data presented above suggest the continued presence of considerable inequality in the distribution of personal income in the United States, even if some of the sharpest disparities have lessened over time. But this picture may be misleading because the data we have reviewed so far fail to take into account the effects of taxes and of transfer payments—in other words, of government fiscal and income maintenance policies—on the distribution of personal income.

Taxes

Table 9-8 shows the federal income tax liability in 1978 of four-person families at different levels of adjusted gross income. The graduated, or progressive, structure of the United States federal income tax is such that a four-person family which claims the standard deduction begins to pay taxes only when its income rises above $7200 a year. Families at or slightly below that level pay no tax, while families substantially below the $7200 income level actually have their incomes

Table 9-7   Number, Poverty Rate, and Standard Errors: Persons, Families, and Unrelated Individuals below the Poverty Level, 1977

(Numbers in Thousands)

Selected characteristics	Below the poverty level		Poverty rate	
	Number	Standard error	Percent	Standard error
Persons				
All persons	24,720	366	11.6	0.2
Race and Spanish origin[1]				
White	16,416	305	8.9	0.2
Black	7,726	176	31.3	0.7
Other races	579	56	14.8	1.3
Spanish origin	2,700	154	22.4	1.1
Age				
Under 14 years	7,856	201	16.9	0.4
14–21 years	4,346	155	13.2	0.5
22–44 years	5,780	175	8.5	0.3
45–54 years	1,672	99	7.2	0.4
55–59 years	944	75	8.6	0.7
60–64 years	946	75	10.0	0.8
65 years and over	3,177	129	14.1	0.6
Total under 18 years	10,228	223	16.2	0.4
Related children under 18 years	10,028	221	16.0	0.4
Total 5 to 17 years	7,449	197	15.5	0.4
Related children 5 to 17 years	7,249	195	15.2	0.4
Metropolitan-nonmetropolitan residence				
Inside metropolitan areas	14,859	291	10.4	0.2
Inside central cities	9,203	232	15.4	0.4
In poverty areas	4,132	158	36.4	1.1
Outside central cities	5,657	184	6.8	0.2
In poverty areas	972	77	21.5	1.5
Outside metropolitan areas	9,861	240	13.9	0.3
In poverty areas	5,236	177	21.4	0.6
Families				
Race and sex of head				
All families: Total	5,311	74	9.3	0.1
Male head	2,701	53	5.5	0.1
Female head	2,610	52	31.7	0.5
White families: Total	3,540	61	7.0	0.1
Male head	2,140	47	4.8	0.1
Female head	1,400	38	24.0	0.6
Black families: Total	1,637	37	28.2	0.6
Male head	475	21	13.5	0.6
Female head	1,162	31	51.0	1.0
Unrelated individuals				
All unrelated individuals	5,216	73	22.6	0.3
Male	1,796	43	18.0	0.4
Female	3,419	60	26.1	0.4

[1] Persons of Spanish origin may be of any race, but the vast majority are white.

Source: Adapted from U.S. Bureau of the Census, *Current Population Reports: Money Income and Poverty Status of Families and Persons in the United States: 1977* (Advance Report), ser. p-60, no. 116, 1978, p. 20.

Table 9-8   Federal Income Tax Liability for One-Earner Four-Person Families, 1978

Adjusted gross income	Amount of tax	Tax rate (percent)
$ 5,000	$−300	−6.0
$10,000	$ 446	+4.5
$15,000	$1,330	+8.9
$20,000	$2,180	+10.9
$25,000	$3,150	+12.6
$30,000	$4,232	+14.1
$40,000	$6,848	+17.1

Source: Adapted from *Economic Report of the President, January, 1978*, 1978, p. 220.

increased by means of tax credits—a negative income tax. As shown in Table 9-8, a four-person family with an income of $5000 in 1978 thus was taxed at a rate of −6 percent, a family with $10,000 of income was taxed at a rate of +4.46 percent, and so on to the point where a family with $40,000 of income paid an effective tax rate of more than 17 percent. This progressive federal income tax structure thus seems to make the after-tax distribution of income more equal—less unequal—than the before-tax distributions shown in Tables 9-2 and 9-5 suggest.

But of course individuals and families must pay more than just federal income taxes. They are subject to a variety of state and local taxes, including property, payroll, sales, excise, and motor vehicle taxes, to name but a few. Further, those citizens who own or invest funds in corporations are subject to the indirect effects of corporate income taxes. Thus, to know how the after-tax distribution of income compares with the before-tax distribution requires taking all or as many as possible of these different taxes into account.

Such an analysis was recently undertaken by Pechman and Okner.[12] Using specially collected data from the mid-1960s, the authors calculated the total rates of taxation resulting from federal, state, and local sources for families in different income classes. The results are shown in Table 9-9 for two of the several different models of estimation employed in their study. The models differ primarily in their assumptions about the incidence of corporate income and personal property taxes—most importantly, about whether and to what extent these are borne by owner-producers of capital as opposed to user-consumers of goods and services. Here again, federal taxes (which now include corporate income, payroll, and personal income taxes) are progressive, though considerably more so in model 1 than in model 2. The difference between them results specifically from alternative assumptions made about the incidence of the corporate income tax.

State and local taxes are generally considered to be regressive, and they turn out to be so under model 2, which allocates property taxes on the more general basis of outlays for shelter and consumption. The effective state and

Table 9-9   Effective Rates of Federal, State, and Local Taxes, under Two Different Models

(Income Classes in Thousands of Dollars; Tax Rates in Percent)

Adjusted family income	Model 1			Model 2		
	Federal	State and local	Total	Federal	State and local	Total
0–3	8.8	9.8	18.7	14.1	14.0	28.1
3–5	11.9	8.5	20.4	14.6	10.6	25.3
5–10	15.4	7.2	22.6	17.0	8.9	25.9
10–15	16.3	6.5	22.8	17.5	8.0	25.5
15–20	16.7	6.5	23.2	17.7	7.6	25.3
20–25	17.1	6.9	24.0	17.8	7.4	25.1
25–30	17.4	7.7	25.1	17.2	7.1	24.3
30–50	18.2	8.2	26.4	17.7	6.7	24.4
50–100	21.8	9.7	31.5	20.1	6.3	26.4
100–500	30.0	11.9	41.8	24.4	6.0	30.3
500–1000	34.6	13.3	48.0	25.2	5.1	30.3
1000 and over	35.5	13.8	49.3	24.8	4.2	29.0
All classes	17.6	7.6	25.2	17.9	8.0	25.9

[1] Model 1 is the most progressive set of incidence assumptions examined in this study, and model 2 is the least progressive.

Source: Adapted from Joseph A. Pechman and Benjamin K. Okner, *Who Bears the Tax Burden?* Brookings, Washington, 1974, p. 62.

local tax rate declines from 14.0 percent to almost 4 percent as one moves from the lowest to the highest category of family income. Under model 1, however, which allocates property taxes on the narrower basis of property ownership, state and local taxes take on a U-shaped pattern, starting at 10 percent for the lowest income group, dropping to 6.5 percent for middle-income families, and rising to almost 14 percent for those earning $1 million and over.

Despite the differing assumptions concerning the incidence of corporate income and personal property taxes used in their study, Pechman and Okner conclude that "the tax system is virtually proportional for the vast majority of families in the United States."[13] This is the case because the true incidence of taxes lies well between the polar extremes of the two models discussed above. Even under the most progressive assumptions (model 1), taxes of all types and at all levels reduce income inequality, that is, the after-tax distribution of income, by less than 5 percent. Under the least progressive assumptions (model 2), the reduction is negligible, only about one quarter of one percent.

Table 9-3, which shows the redistributional effects of taxes in 1972, as compiled by the Organization for Economic Cooperation and Development (OECD), supplements and broadens Pechman and Okner's findings. Observe that in the United States, taxes reduced the income share of the top fifth of the population by about 2 percentage points. The bottom 40 percent of income recipients were the principal beneficiaries of this redistribution, their income share rising by 1.4 percentage points, compared with their before-tax levels. In most, but certainly not all, of the other developed nations listed in Table 9-3,

Table 9-10   Official Estimates of Distribution of Income, before and after Tax, United Kingdom, 1949–1974

	Percentage share of total income					
	Before tax			After tax		
	Top 10 percent	Next 60 percent	Bottom 30 percent	Top 10 percent	Next 60 percent	Bottom 30 percent
1949	33.2	54.1	12.7	27.1	58.3	14.6
1954	29.8	59.3	10.9	24.8	63.1	12.1
1959	29.4	60.9	9.7	25.2	63.5	11.2
1964	29.0	61.4	9.6	25.1	64.1	10.8
1967	28.0	61.6	10.4	24.3	63.7	12.0
1973–1974	26.8	62.3	10.9	23.6	63.6	12.8

Source: Adapted from A. B. Atkinson, *The Economics of Inequality*, Oxford University Press. London, 1975. p. 51 and Royal Commission on the Distribution of Income and Wealth, *Second Report on the Standing Reference*, Report 4, H. M. Stationery Office, London, October 1976, p. 12.

the redistributional effects of taxes on income shares were greater than in the United States.

An interesting pattern of income redistribution resulting from taxes has oc-curred in the United Kingdom. Note from the data in Table 9-10 that the share of before-tax income going to the top 10 percent of recipients dropped by 6.5 percentage points between 1949 and 1974 but that the share going to the bottom 30 percent also declined, in this case by roughly 2 points. In both 1949 and 1974, the bottom group's income share increased after taxes, but its after-tax share in the later year was just about the same as its before-tax share in the earlier period (12.8 versus 12.7 percent). It is the middle 60 percent of income recipients in the United Kingdom whose share of national income has steadily increased on a before-tax basis and who make up the bulk of the beneficiaries of the revenues generated by taxes imposed on the top 10 percent. Consequently, it appears that income redistribution in the United Kingdom has been "from the extreme ends to the middle ranges"[14] and that the burden of taxes is not, as it is in the United States, roughly proportional for the vast majority of income recipients.

Transfer Payments

Even more significant to an analysis of income distribution is the publicly fi-nanced income maintenance system in the United States. It is composed of two main elements: social insurance programs and public assistance or welfare programs. The first provide "partial replacement of earnings lost because of retirement, disability, or temporary unemployment," while the latter are directed toward "those unable to earn their own living—that is, the aged, the blind, the permanently disabled, and dependent children whose parents are un-able to support them."[15] The social insurance programs, notably social security and unemployment compensation, are financed through payroll taxes on a pay-as-you-go basis. These programs, which will be reviewed in detail in Chapter 10, do not subject the recipients to a test of income or earnings, and they are generally considered to provide benefits that have been "earned" by individuals who have been active in the labor market. In contrast, public assistance programs are financed out of general tax revenues, carry the label (perhaps stigma) of "public charity," and are generally available only to the low-income population. In this connection, recipients of public assistance are subject to tests of income. These social insurance and public assistance programs are listed in Table 9-11 together with the aggregate benefits paid and the number of recipients of benefits in 1977.

How effective have income maintenance programs been in altering the distribution of income in the United States? A precise answer to this question is unavailable because the Census Bureau, which gathers data on income distribution in the Current Population Survey, and the other federal agencies which dispense and monitor income maintenance funds provide information on very different samples of families and individuals. Nevertheless, an indirect answer may be inferred from the impact of income maintenance programs on the incidence of poverty in the United States. Table 9-12 provides the relevant data.

In the absence of cash transfer programs, some 21.4 million families would have been below the poverty level in 1975, according to estimates of the Congressional Budget Office. However, cash transfers, which are reported in column 2 of Table 9-12, reduced the number of poverty-stricken families in 1975 to 10.7 million, *thus cutting in half the amount of poverty in the United States*. But this would not alter the distribution of family income as shown earlier in Tables 9-2 and 9-5 because the Current Population Survey, the source of the data in those tables, takes account of cash transfers in tabulating family income.

In-kind transfers are a different matter. That they further reduce poverty is clear from columns 3 and 4 of Table 9-12, which reveal that 4.3 million families were raised above the poverty level in 1975 as a consequence of receiving food stamps, child nutrition, housing assistance, and Medicare and Medicaid services—benefits which are not included in the listings of income distribution in Tables 9-2 and 9-5. This left about 6.4 million families, roughly 8 percent of the total, below the poverty level in that year, with the incidence of poverty being considerably higher among single-person than multiple-person families. Interestingly, that total rose slightly (to 6.6 million families, or 8.3 percent of the total) when income was calculated on an after-tax, after-transfer-payment basis. Such an adjustment provides a slight clue to the regressive nature of payroll taxes, which are lumped with federal and state income taxes in column 6 of Table 9-12 to determine "net" poverty in the United States.

It should be quickly added that considerable care must be exercised in interpreting the data presented in Table 9-12 or in accepting the conclusion that transfer payments markedly reduce the incidence of poverty. For one thing, the "inclusion of in-kind benefits in any measure of income is controversial and almost certainly overstates the value of such transfers to recipients,"[16] who,

Table 9-11 Government Income Maintenance Programs

Program	Date enacted	Form of aid	Source of funds	Fiscal year 1977	
				Benefit payments (billions of dollars)	Beneficiaries (millions)
Social insurance					
Old age and survivors' insurance	1935	Cash	Federal	71.3	28.5
Medicare	1965	In-kind	Federal	20.8	25.4[1]
Unemployment insurance	1935	Cash	Federal and state	14.3	9.8
Disability insurance	1956	Cash	Federal	11.1	4.7
Workers' compensation	1908	Cash	Federal and state	6.7	2.6
Veterans' compensation	1917	Cash	Federal	5.7	3.5
Railroad retirement	1937	Cash	Federal	3.8	1.0
Black lung	1969	Cash	Federal	1.0	0.5
Public assistance					
Medicaid	1965	In-kind	Federal and state	16.3	21.6
Aid to families with dependent children	1935	Cash	Federal and state	9.8	11.2
Supplemental security income	1972	Cash	Federal and state	6.2	4.3
Food stamp program	1964	In-kind	Federal and state	5.0	17.1
Child nutrition	1946	In-kind	Federal	3.5	28.0
Verterans' pensions	1933	Cash	Federal	3.1	3.4
Housing assistance	1937	In-kind	Federal	3.0	7.1
Basic opportunity grants	1972	Cash	Federal	1.4	2.0
General assistance	[2]	Cash	State	1.3	0.9
Earned income tax credit	1975	Cash	Federal	1.3	6.3

[1] Eligible to receive benefits as of July 1, 1977.

[2] Varies by state.

Source: Adapted from Economic Report of the President, January, 1978, 1978, p. 222.

Table 9-12 Families below the Poverty Level before and after the Effects of Income Maintenance Programs and Taxes, Fiscal 1976[1]

			Families below the poverty level, based on income					
	Before taxes and before transfers (1)	Before taxes and after cash transfers[4] (2)	Before taxes and after cash and in-kind transfers[2]		After taxes and after cash and in-kind transfers[3]			
Kind of family			Excluding medical benefits (3)	Including medical benefits (4)	Excluding medical benefits (5)	Including medical benefits (6)
All families						
Number (millions)	21.4	10.7	9.0	6.4	9.2	6.6
Percent of all families	27.0	13.5	11.3	8.1	11.5	8.3
Single-person families						
Number (millions)	10.3	5.4	5.0	3.5	5.1	3.7
Percent of single-person families	47.8	25.0	23.2	16.4	23.8	17.0
Multiple-person families						
Number (millions)	11.1	5.3	4.0	2.9	4.0	2.9
Percent of multiple-person families	19.2	9.2	6.9	5.0	7.0	5.1

[1] Data based on 1975 Current Population Survey, with adjustments to reflect underreporting of income and changes in the characteristics of the population between the survey year (calendar year 1974) and fiscal year 1976.
[2] In-kind transfers include food stamps, child nutrition assistance, housing assistance, Medicare, and Medicaid.
[3] Taxes include federal personal income and employee payroll taxes and state income taxes.
[4] Cash transfers include payments under government-financed social insurance and public assistance programs.
Source: Adapted from Economic Report of the President, January, 1978, 1978, p. 225.

unsurprisingly, have been found to favor cash over in-kind benefits because of the greater freedom it affords. Medical benefits are an especially troubling item in this regard; they are at best difficult to allocate among the low-income population, and they seemingly imply that the more illness the poor suffer, the better off they are. But the alternative would be to overlook such benefits, and we have noted that this is a major limitation of the data on income distribution derived from the Current Population Survey. Moreover, it is undeniable that those who receive medical services without charge are better off than if they had not received them. Such benefits should not be ignored, even if their magnitude or their impact on the incidence of poverty can be only roughly estimated. Stated in a positive way, then: "The present income maintenance system significantly improves the distribution of income that would otherwise exist."[17]

And some would go considerably further than this. For example, Browning recently observed that in-kind transfer payments of the type referred to above rose from $42 to $657 per poor person between 1964 and 1973, an increase of 1464 percent, while direct cash transfers rose by only 172 percent over the same period.[18] When such in-kind payments are taken into account, Browning contends, "The average poor family in 1973 had an income that was approximately 30 percent *above* the poverty line."[19] This leads him to conclude that there is practically no poverty, statistically speaking, in the United States and that only "our accounting procedures have to be modified to record this achievement."[20] One need not agree with this view to recognize the importance of in-kind payments to the measurement of poverty.

On the question of income distribution among families, Browning is also critical of conventional data of the type reported earlier in Table 9-2. He notes that such data exclude not only in-kind transfers and taxes but also the benefits of public education and differences in average family size among the quintiles. Making such adjustments to official data changes the relative distribution of family income considerably, as shown in Table 9-13a and b. In 1972, for example, the lowest quintile received 5.4 percent of all family income by conventional measures, but it received almost 12 percent when adjusted for in-kind transfers, education, and taxes and when converted to a per capita basis. This is more than a doubling of that quintile's relative income share. The same adjustments reduced the highest quintile's relative income share from more than 41 percent to less than 33 percent in 1972, while raising the second quintile's share from 12 percent to 15 percent. Even more instructive is the trend toward equality of relative income shares over the 20-year period covered in Table 9-13a and b when the data are adjusted in the manner described above. This is most clearly evident in the income share for the lowest quintile of families, which rose from 8.1 percent in 1952 to 11.7 percent in 1972, or "an improvement of 44 percent in the relative position of low-income families."[21]

Still another criticism of data on income distribution concerns their highly aggregative, static nature, which results in their failure to inform us about the extent of income mobility experienced by individuals. As Schiller states,: "It is

**Table 9-13   (a) Relative Income Distribution
(Expressed as Percentage Share of Total Money
Income Received by Families, by Quintile)**

Year	Lowest quintile	Second quintile	Third quintile	Fourth quintile	Highest quintile
1952	4.9	12.2	17.1	23.5	42.2
1962	5.0	12.1	17.6	24.0	41.3
1972	5.4	11.9	17.5	23.9	41.4

**(b) Adjusted Relative Income Distribution (Expressed
as Percentage Share of Income Received, by Quintile)**

Year	Lowest quintile	Second quintile	Third quintile	Fourth quintile	Highest quintile
1952	8.1	14.2	17.8	23.2	36.7
1962	8.8	14.4	18.2	23.1	35.4
1972	11.7	15.0	18.2	22.3	32.8

Source: Adapted from Edgar K. Browning, "How Much More Equality Can We Afford?" *The Public Interest,* **43**:93(1976).

possible . . . that the observed rigidity of the distribution of income is entirely consistent with widespread opportunities for individuals to alter their own status . . . —the essential test of socio-economic opportunity."[22] If this proposition were shown to be true, it would counter the assumption that, for example, the richest or poorest 20 percent of income recipients in any particular year are the same persons who constituted the richest or poorest 20 percent at a prior point in time. Utilizing data on social security rather than conventional census data for a random sample of almost 75,000 male workers who (1) earned at least $1000 in 1957, (2) were between 30 and 34 years old in that year, and (3) were still employed in 1971, Schiller sought to determine whether the "high" earners in the earlier period were still "high" earners later on or whether they had switched relative positions with other workers. Observe that earnings from employment are only one type of income, and so this study is not fully informative about individual mobility within the structure of income distribution in the United States. Nevertheless, Schiller's findings, summarized in Table 9-14, are instructive.

Dividing the sample into twenty categories (dubbed "ventiles") of 5 percent each ranked according to their 1957 distribution of earnings, Schiller discovered that 71 percent of all workers were mobile across at least two ventiles over the period 1957–1971. The *average* move was more than four ventiles (twenty percentiles), "or over one fifth of the way from one end of the [income] distribution to the other."[23] Hence, mobility of *earnings* status was relatively large among this sample, even if few who were at the bottom in 1957 had made it to the top in 1971, and vice versa. And, even though half of the highest earners in 1957 were among that group in 1971, while one-third of the lowest earners in 1957 were in that same category 14 years later, "the fact that half of

Table 9-14   Boundaries of Relative Earnings Positions and Racial Patterns of Mobility among a Sample of Males Aged 30 to 34 in 1957[1]

Ventile[2]	1957	1971	Percent of workers who are mobile		Average move (in ventiles)	
			White	Black	White	Black
1	$9,502 and over	$17,665 and over	52	93	−4.12	−7.21
2	$7,453–$9,501	$14,956–$17,664	58	90	−4.19	−7.97
3	$6,745–$7,452	$13,430–$14,955	69	84	−4,27	−7,68
4	$6,253–$6,744	$12,311–13,429	72	85	−3.73	−6.83
5	$5,851–$6,252	$11,528–$12,310	73	85	−3.30	−6.10
6	$5,522–$5,850	$10,842–$11,527	75	83	−2.82	−5.15
7	$5,220–$5,521	$10,220–$10,841	75	80	−2.32	−4.44
8	$4,933–$5,219	$9,632–$10,219	76	77	−1.48	−2.20
9	$4,654–$4,932	$9,067–$9,631	76	74	−0.87	−2.34
10	$4,371–$4,653	$8,501–$9,066	76	78	0.54	−1.76
11	$4,092–$4,370	$7,945–$8,500	77	77	0.31	−0.55
12	$3,812–$4,091	$7,443–$7,944	76	80	0.64	−0.67
13	$3,497–$3,811	$6,906–$7,442	75	74	1.33	−0.36
14	$3,073–$3,496	$6,193–$6,905	74	71	1.91	0.42
15	$2,623–$3,072	$5,398–$6,192	74	63	2.54	0.58
16	$2,106–$2,622	$4,449–$5,397	70	61	2.56	0.88
17	$1,540–$2,105	$3,373–$4,448	67	56	2.90	1.39
18	$915–$1,539	$2,160–$3,372	65	53	3.57	1.93
19	$343–$914	$854–$2,159				
20	$1–$342	$1–$853	71	70	−0.93	−0.77

[1] Based on 2 percent of all workers covered by social security. The sample consisted of 74,227 males.
[2] Each ventile includes 5 percent of all male workers aged 30 to 34 in 1957.
Source: Adapted from Bradley R. Schiller, "Equality, Opportunity, and the 'Good Job,'" *The Public Interest,* **43:** 114–117 (1976).

those who start at the top end up further down the distribution . . . while nearly two-thirds of those who begin at the bottom later move up, constitutes irrefutable evidence of extensive fluidity in the socio-economic structure."[24]

The one discordant note in this analysis is the relative lack of earnings mobility among black males compared with that among white males (see Table 9-14). Blacks at the bottom of the earnings distribution in 1957 were much less likely than their white counterparts to improve their status by 1971. Blacks at the top of the earnings distribution in 1957 were much more likely than whites to suffer declining economic status in the subsequent 14 years. Among blacks who did improve their relative earnings position, the rate of improvement was, on the average, 1.6 ventiles less than that among whites. Finally, the average position of black workers in this sample remained virtually unchanged at about the 13th ventile during the period under study, a period, as noted earlier, during which various civil rights and equal employment opportunity initiatives were mounted. Consequently, if "the rigid shape of the aggregate income distribution is a misleading index of opportunity stratification because it camouflages a great deal of individual mobility between the separate points of that distribution," as Schiller concludes, then it must be added that, for blacks, "the inequalities observed at any moment tend to be permanent rather than transitory."[25] The longitudinal data of Table 9-14 attest to the continued stratification of economic opportunity across racial lines.

THE DISTRIBUTION OF WEALTH

So far, the focus of the debate about economic inequality has been on earnings and income, but a few words are in order about the distribution of wealth—of owned assets such as stocks and bonds, real estate, and works of art. Succinctly stated, the distribution of wealth seems to be much more skewed—that is, more unequal—than the distribution of income. This is clear from the data in Tables 9-15 and 9-16.[26]

Table 9-15, which is based on a study by the Federal Reserve Board, shows that, in the early 1960s, the poorest 25 percent of the American populace had no net assets, in contrast to the top 19 percent of the population, which had more than three-quarters of all wealth. Well over half of total wealth rested with a mere 7.5 percent of the citizenry, and fully one-quarter of total wealth was owned by only one-half of one percent of the population. Though this study was not replicated in the 1970s, there is little reason to believe that the distribution of family wealth has changed significantly from that shown in Table 9-15.

Somewhat different data on the distribution of wealth are available for a more recent period, however, and these are given in Table 9-16. They are based on estate tax collections, but because such taxes are obtained by the Internal Revenue Service solely from estates exceeding $60,000, only about 7.5 percent of the population provides the basis of this sampling of the distribution of

Table 9-15 Distribution of Family Wealth in the United States in 1962[1]

Percent of total families by wealth	Percent of total family wealth
Lowest 25.4	0.0
Next 31.5	6.6
Next 24.4	17.2
Top 18.7	76.2
(Top 7.5)	(59.1)
(Top 2.4)	(44.4)
(Top 0.5)	(25.8)

[1] Based on Dorothy S. Projector, *Survey of Financial Characteristics of Consumers*, Federal Reserve Bulletin 50, March 1964, p. 285.

Source: Adapted from Lester C. Thurow, *Generating Inequality*, Basic Books, New York, 1975, p. 14.

Table 9-16   Distribution of Wealth in 1969[1]

Net assets (in dollars)	Percent of population with gross assets over $60,000	Percent of total assets of these with gross assets over $60,000
Under 50,000	20.1	6.0
50,000–100,000	38.8	19.1
100,000–150,000	18.2	14.1
150,000–300,000	14.4	18.6
300,000–1,000,000	7.1	21.8
1,000,000–5,000,000	1.2	13.4
5,000,000–10,000,000	0.07	2.8
Over 10,000,000	0.04	4.2

[1] Based on Internal Revenue Service, *Statistics of Income, 1969: Personal Wealth,* Publication 482, 1973.
Source: Lester C. Thurow, *Generating Inequality,* Basic Books, New York, 1975, p. 15.

wealth. Nevertheless, Table 9-16 shows that even among this privileged group, totaling fewer than 10 million persons, most of the wealth is owned by the richest members. Slightly more than 8 percent of this group—which, again, constitutes about one-half of one percent of the entire population of the United States—owns 42 percent of all assets of the top 7.5 percent of the citizenry. Moreover, longitudinal analysis of data on estate taxes shows little change in the concentration of family wealth. From the mid-1950s to the mid-1970s, the top one-half of one percent of the population owned between 20 and 24 percent of total wealth, and the share of the top 1 percent ranged between 25 and 29 percent.[27] These estimates are remarkably similar to those derived in the late 1960s and early 1970s for the United Kingdom, where the top one-half of one percent of the population owned between 22 and 27 percent of total wealth, and the share seems not to have changed much over time.[28]

Finally, it should be recognized that individuals in the same income classes have very different amounts of owned wealth. This is clearly seen from the data in Table 9-17, which is also based on the study of the Federal Reserve Board. Observe that among all families, 8 percent had a negative net worth in the early 1960s, more than half had a net worth of less than $10,000, 7 percent had a net worth of $50,000 or more, and 1 percent had a net worth of at least $200,000. Within an income class such as the $10,000-to-$15,000 group, some families had a negative net worth, some had a net worth of over $100,000, and four out of ten had a net worth of at least $25,000.

Among the lowest-income families there was still one out of four with a net worth of $10,000 or more. At the other end of the scale, 95 percent of families with a minimum of $100,000 of income had a net worth of at least $500,000, and more than one-third exceeded 1 million. Hence we agree with a recent student of this subject who concludes that "no assessment of the distribution of economic prizes is complete if it examines either income or wealth alone."[29] In some countries where such assessments have been made—for example, in

Table 9-17   Net Worth of Consumers within Specified Groups, December 31, 1962[1]

Group characteristic	All families	Percentage distribution of families, by net worth											Mean (dollars)	Median (dollars)
		Negative	0–$999	$1,000–$4,999	$5,000–$9,999	$10,000–$24,999	$25,000–$49,999	$50,000–$99,999	$100,000–$199,999	$200,000–$499,999	$500,000–$999,999	$1,000,000 and over		
All families	100	8	17	17	14	24	11	5	1	1	[2]	[2]	22,588	7,550
1962 income														
0–$2,999	100	12	31	16	15	17	7	1	[2]	[2]	[2]	[2]	8,875	2,760
$3,000–4,999	100	15	22	22	12	17	8	3	[2]	1	[2]	[2]	10,914	3,320
5,000–7,499	100	7	14	21	17	28	8	4	1	[2]	[2]	[2]	15,112	7,450
$7,500–9,999	100	3	5	19	16	37	14	5	2	[2]	[2]	[2]	21,243	13,450
$10,000–14,999	100	1	3	9	13	34	24	11	4	1	[2]	[2]	30,389	20,500
$15,000–24,999	100	[2]	2	2	8	18	30	26	7	7	1	[2]	74,329	42,750
$25,000–49,999	100	1	[2]	[2]	1	2	7	20	31	30	5	3	267,996	160,000
$50,000–99,999	100	[2]	[2]	[2]	[2]	[2]	1	3	13	37	27	20	789,582	470,000
$100,000 and over	100	[2]	[2]	[2]	[2]	[2]	[2]	[2]	[2]	4	61	35	1,554,152	875,000

[1] Data based on Dorothy S. Projector, *Survey of Financial Characteristics of Consumers*, Federal Reserve Bulletin, 50, March 1964, p. 285.
[2] Less than 0.5 percent.

Source: Lester C. Thurow, *Generating Inequality*, Basic Books, New York 1975, pp. 12–13.

France and the United Kingdom—they have led to proposals for enacting taxes on wealth so as to bring about more equal distributions of income.

Inheritance and Economic Success

Even a brief examination of the distribution of personal wealth among the populace leads us to wonder about the extent to which individual economic success —especially success in the labor market—is a function of one's economic origins. More generally, the question may be posed as follows: "Do the material conditions into which one is born essentially determine one's subsequent economic experience?" If the answer to that question is "yes" or "largely yes," this suggests that income inequality has a persistent, intergenerational dimension. If the answer is "no" or "largely no," this implies that individual ability and initiative can overcome inherited disadvantage and that income inequality will diminish over time. Few questions could be as momentous or as deserving of an informed response as this one, which, in reality, has been posed in numerous ways and at various times throughout history.

What does the empirical evidence provide in the way of an answer to the question of economic origins and eventual economic success? The answer seems surprisingly clear: economic inequality, whether measured by income, wealth, or a combination of the two, apparently is transmitted over successive generations and thus persists through time. The key implication of this finding for public policy is also of momentous importance, as reflected in this statement by a leading authority on the subject: "The strong role of inherited advantage and disadvantage bolsters the case for the redistribution of rewards to moderate that component of inequality which is due to circumstances over which the individual has no control."[30] In other words, recent efforts to alter the distribution of personal income in the United States, some of which were reviewed earlier in this chapter, apparently rest on a solid foundation of evidence. Before pursuing this admittedly controversial conclusion further, however, it is necessary for the reader to know something more about recent and, we think, exciting studies of this subject.

A major study of economic inequality across generations is *The Inheritance of Economic Status,* by John Brittain.[31] The main data base for Brittain's analysis consisted of a survey of 659 persons who died in the Cleveland metropolitan area during 1964 and 1965 and a subsequent survey of their survivors. The data subsequently analyzed were restricted "to families for which information was available on two or more brothers."[32] Different combinations of responses to the surveys yielded samples ranging from 115 to 231 brothers who were fairly representative of American men in the labor force in the mid-1960s in terms of age, income, wealth, and educational attainment and somewhat less representative in terms of religious affiliation and size of family from which they had come. It is important to know this because judgments about the role of inheritance in explaining variation in economic success are formed by comparing adult children of the same parents with adults generally. The standard for evaluation is clearly stated by Brittain: "The less the variation [in economic status] among brothers relative to that among all men, the stronger the role of inheritance in determining [economic] outcomes; the greater the variation among brothers, the weaker is inheritance as a determinant of economic status."[33]

The methodological advantages of a sample of brothers in this type of analysis are also important. One is that the effects of family background on the sons' economic status may be judged without reference to actual data on the parents themselves—parents' influences on their sons are held constant. Another is that a wider range of parental influences is held constant in a sample of brothers than in a sample of nonbrothers. Brothers share a wide variety of family influences other than the objective characteristics—education, occupation, income—of their parents, and they tend more than unrelated men to be alike in ability and exposure to environmental conditions. Proceeding from these premises, two empirical estimates of the degree of inheritance were obtained. The first measured the effects of family characteristics, known and unknown, on the economic status of brothers. The second estimated the ratio of standard deviations between and within families; the lower that ratio, the greater the influence of factors affecting brothers in common.

The principal findings of Brittain's study are that between one-third and two-thirds of the brothers' economic status was "explained" by family influences (the first measure referred to above) and that the standard deviation of the brothers' economic status was somewhat larger than half the measure of family influences. The meaning of these summary conclusions is more clearly seen by comparing the predicted family incomes of brothers with advantageous backgrounds with those of brothers who are less well endowed. (Note that we often will use the term "son" or "sons" when referring to members of this sample of brothers.) A son ranking in the top 10 percent in terms of family background had better than a 50 percent chance of earning $25,000 or more in 1976, compared with only a 2 percent chance for a son ranking in the bottom 10 percent. A son ranking in the top 5 percent in terms of family background had almost four chances in ten of earning at least $35,000, while the chances of this were virtually zero for a son ranking in the lowest 5 percent and only about 2 to 3 percent for a son with roughly an average—middle-ranking—family background.

The educational attainment of sons is also a strongly inherited characteristic. If men ranking in the top and bottom 5 percent in terms of family background are once again considered, the former can be expected to complete between 16 and 17 years of schooling, and the latter only about 9 years. The son who is less well-off thus goes to school a bit more than half as long as the well-endowed son. This is a particularly important finding in view of the key role played by educational attainment in occupational status, earnings, and, more generally, personal experience in the labor market. As Brittain himself notes, these predictions—probabilities, really—are subject to many qualifications. Nevertheless, even if individual incomes, or other aspects of economic success are regarded as being determined largely by chance, as in a gigantic lottery, some persons are much more likely to do better than others:

> This [lottery] . . . is fixed in favor of those with advantageous backgrounds. It is as though the lottery gave discounts to participants with privileged socio-economic backgrounds. And if the most privileged were given the largest discounts, the lottery would begin to resemble the one that generates our income distribution of today.[34]

In terms of individual characteristics of family background, those most important to the subsequent economic success of male offspring were found to be high educational level of parents (positively correlated), large family size (negatively correlated), and being white (positively correlated). These findings attest to the strong contrast between the chances of success of sons from upper socioeconomic backgrounds and those of sons from lower socioeconomic backgrounds. However, we may take some solace from the finding, derived from a study of a larger sample of men, that "disadvantaged children overcame their initial handicap more frequently than those with a head start slipped downward."[35] In a study of an even larger sample that included both sons and daughters, it was found that about two-thirds of the offspring rose from the lowest fifth of the index of economic status, compared with one-third who dropped from the top. Despite these results, though, the aggregate findings on mobility across all samples in Brittain's study showed that economic status is a strongly inherited phenomenon in that intergenerational upward mobility is quite low.

How does this process of inheritance work in practice? What are the specific linkages between a person's economic status in life and that of his or her parents? One, alluded to previously, is education or, more accurately, educational opportunity. Separating out the inherited effect of educational attainment from the total effect of socioeconomic background, Brittain estimated that between 25 and 40 percent of the impact of socioeconomic background on a son's economic status is conveyed indirectly through its impact on the son's education. To understand what this means in terms of earnings, consider the comprehensive analysis of brothers, which led to the prediction of a 174 percent income advantage for a son ranking in the top 5 percent in terms of family background over a son ranking in the bottom 5 percent. If it is assumed that 35 percent (rather than, say, 25 or 40 percent) of family influence works indirectly through education, elimination of the inherited educational differential, perhaps by means of public policy, would reduce the expected income gap from 174 to 92 percent.

Of course, educational attainment has an independent effect on a son's economic status apart from that due to its association with parental characteristics and family background. This can be demonstrated by assuming a man who is average in all the respects treated by Brittain's study except education, where he ranks in the top 5 percent. He would have a 30 percent chance of ending up in the top 10 percent in terms of economic status, compared with about 1 chance in 120 for a comparably average man who ranked in the bottom 5 percent in terms of educational attainment. Over the entire sample, a son born in 1925 who obtained a college degree would probably earn a lifetime income 24 percent higher than that earned by a man of the same age who completed only high school.

If the income differential attributable to an additional year of schooling was in excess of 5 percent and if one further assumes two men born in 1925 who are average in all respects, including schooling, they could be predicted to have average incomes over their lifetimes. But if one of them completes some graduate school and the other completes only grade school, the first is fifteen times more likely than the second to earn double the average income. These are very large differentials for men whose backgrounds are in large part held constant, though the independent effects of ability, motivation, and other unknown factors could not be independently controlled for in Brittain's study.

Choice of a Mate

Even these significant findings, however, leave unexplained a majority of the influence of socioeconomic background on the economic status of sons. There seems to be some family influence, perhaps working through values, mannerisms, speech, dress, diet, or other avenues, that rubs off on children and cannot be isolated by analyzing educational inheritance alone. Such reasoning led Brittain to examine a second factor in the intergenerational transmission of economic status: choice of a mate.

To do this, he focused on daughters' choices of husbands in relation to their socioeconomic background and economic status. Because married daughters in this sample were mainly housewives for whom no suitable measures of occupational status and earnings capacity were available, their economic status was pragmatically defined as that of their husbands. Samples of 231 sons and 199 sons-in-law provided the data base for the subsequent analysis. If the daughters' choices of husbands were such as to result in the husbands' being randomly distributed among men ranked according to economic position, the fraction of variation in the daughters' economic status that is explainable by family background would be lower than that of the men who were brothers in Brittain's sample. This would be a factor acting to reduce economic inequality over time.

But the empirical analysis revealed that such choices are far from random. Women in the sample tended to marry men with backgrounds so similar to their own that the consequences for inequality (hardly any reduction) would have been virtually the same if they had married their brothers. The result is that the economic status of men is almost as closely related to the backgrounds of the women they marry as to their own.

Part of the total effect of the background of daughters on the status of sons-in-law worked through the women's education. When the relatively lower education of daughters was controlled for, the net relationship between sons-in-law and parents-in-law was almost the same as that between sons and parents. For specific comparative purposes, forty of the wives of sons-in-law came from the top fifth socioeconomic group, and fifteen of those forty women had married men who themselves ranked in the top fifth. This is almost as high a ratio as that of the sons from the top fifth who subsequently remained in that position. Thus it is that "marital selection, like education, has an intermediate role in transmitting the force of family background as a perpetuator of inequality."[36]

Other Evidence

The results of Brittain's study as they have been summarized here are consistent with, but also modify, previous research on the subject of intergenerational transfer of economic status. For example, writing in 1967, the sociologists Blau and Duncan concluded that the influence of family structure and climate on the occupational achievement of males is transmitted very largely through education. They put it this way: "The family into which a man is born exerts a profound influence on his career, because his occupational life is conditioned by his education and his education depends to a considerable extent on his family."[37] To this we might now add choice of a mate as an important determinant of intergenerational economic status.

Mention should also be made of the recent research of Sewell and Hauser.[38] Unlike Brittain's study and others reported in the literature, Sewell and Hauser's sociological analysis included specific data on parental and family characteristics for a sample of several thousand persons who were surveyed in 1957 about their future plans while in their senior year at one or another high school in Wisconsin. The sample is also distinguishable from others in that it included both men and women. The respondents were interviewed again in 1964 and in 1975, as the investigators sought further data on educational, occupational, and economic attainment; life history; activity in the labor market; and social background.

Sewell and Hauser's findings show that for both men and woman, socioeconomic status is an important determinant of educational attainment at every level of schooling and that this holds true when intelligence is controlled for. Intelligence becomes more important for both men and women than socioeconomic status as one progresses through levels of schooling, but socioeconomic background is always of some importance in determining subsequent educational attainment. The researchers also found that socioeconomic status has no effect on performance independent of academic ability but that it has strong direct and indirect effects on educational and occupational aspirations and, through these, on educational and occupational attainments. Academic ability itself was found to have a strong direct effect on performance in high school independent of socioeconomic status, as well as direct and indirect effects on educational and occupational attainments.

The investigators' quantitative model relating family background to the economic status of offspring was able to explain almost 60 percent of the variance in sons' and daughters' educational attainment after graduating from high school and about 40 percent of the variance in early occupational attainments of males in the sample. A subsequent test of an extended version of their model yielded even better predictive results for educational and occupational accomplishments (though relatively poor results for the variance in earnings) and for the influences of family background on achievement. In controlling for individual ability and intelligence and relating these to economic status, Sewell and Hauser improved upon Brittain's methodology, while providing evidence which tends to support his findings and conclusions.

Finally, in a study published in 1976, Behrman and Taubman analyzed data drawn from a survey by the National Academy of Science and the National Research Council of some 2000 pairs of twin white males born between 1917 and 1927.[39] They sought to estimate the effects of genetic endowment and family environment (called "common environment" by the authors) on earnings and other indices of individual attainment, principally education. The use of a sample made up of twins permitted the investigators to hold constant genetic characteristics and characteristics of the family environment so as to determine the influence of other (noncommon) environmental factors, including luck or chance, on subsequent individual attainment and on intergenerational inequality.

In their highly technical analysis, which we shall summarize only briefly, Behrman and Taubman found that genetics plus common environment accounted for 79 percent of the variance in education, 20 percent of the variance in the socioeconomic status of the twins' initial occupations, 45 percent of the variance in the socioeconomic status of their later occupations (measured in 1967, when the twins were about 45 years old on the average), and 53 percent of the variance in subsequent (1973) earnings. Stated the other way around, the "noncommon environment . . . accounts for 21 per cent of the variation in education, 77 percent of the variance in initial occupation, 50 percent of the variance in mature occupational status, and 43 percent of the variance in subsequent earnings."[40]

The authors concluded from their analysis that the contributions of education to achieving equality of opportunity are significantly overstated in relation to both occupational status and earnings and, more basically, that "an economic-political system that is basically free enterprise will be one in which inequality will be passed on from one generation to another via genetic endowments and family environment."[41] Rarely does one find so clear a statement linking economic inequality among individuals to the nature of the economic system itself.

Taken cumulatively, these studies suggest that a goodly portion of an individual's economic status is inherited and that economic inequality therefore has a persistent, intergenerational quality. If this is so, it provides empirical underpinnings for efforts to redistribute personal incomes in ways that make them less unequal, that is, more just. But exactly how this might be achieved and what amount of redistribution is "just" are controversial matters indeed, ones which require explicit consideration of value preferences. Moreover, a society that relies on competitive capitalism to distribute rewards in the form of economic prizes to individuals may encounter much tension between this goal and that of achieving greater economic equality among individuals. Such tension is clearly evident in the contemporary debate over income inequality in the United States.

INCOME EQUALITY AND REDISTRIBUTION

If one believes that the distribution of income is highly unequal—unfairly so in light of the role of inheritance in perpetuating differential economic status—uncertainty may nevertheless remain about the appropriate instruments of public policy to use in redistributing income among groups or individuals. One such instrument is tax policy, although here, too, there are widely differing views about the components which merit primary emphasis. Some advocate closing the "loopholes" for the rich, which may mean increasing the tax rate on capital gains, raising estate and inheritance taxes, eliminating certain categories of deductions for income tax purposes, and so on.

One problem with this approach is that it would seemingly affect individuals other than simply the rich. More broadly, proposals for tax reform commonly seek to increase the progressivity of the individual income tax structure. One such proposal offered in early 1978 by the Carter administration called for a revised rate structure, reductions in itemized deductions, and alteration of provisions for personal credit. When combined with changes in the social security tax actually adopted by Congress in 1977, these reforms would have raised the income level at which a family of four begins to pay taxes from $7200 to $9256, according to estimates of the Council of Economic Advisers.[42] But such *tax* reforms do not contain any specific provisions for redistributing the revenues raised.

Another potential way of obtaining a redistribution of income, this one oriented to the long run, is for public policy to foster education. Brittain's work, in particular, supports this policy prescription, given that he found sons' economic success to be significantly affected by their own educational attainment. Individual investment in education, which may be in small or large part financed through the public purse, is also supported by the human capital approach, which emphasizes differential productivity resulting from education as a key source of earnings variation in the labor market. But education also tends to be inherited, thereby contributing "to the role of socioeconomic background in perpetuating inequality."[43] Perhaps the way to regard this observation, however, is to judge the equalization of educational attainments as directly promoting economic equality, but also as doing so indirectly by reducing the differentials due to inheritance.

Others are less sanguine about the equalizing properties of education. Most studies which attempt to control for family background, age, and cognitive skills find that an additional year of schooling increases annual earnings by roughly 8 to 10 percent, but, as Taubman points out, these research efforts are not very successful in actually controlling for parental characteristics or differences in ability.[44] In his own research on identical twins, for example, he found that each additional year of schooling added only about 4 percent to annual earnings and accounted for only 5 percent of the variance in earnings among the subjects. Other studies employing human capital analysis provide comparable results for the relationship between education and earnings, leading Taubman to conclude that "a policy to equalize education would result in no more than a six percent reduction in the inequality of lifetime earnings."[45] This impact is quite a bit smaller than that suggested by Brittain in his discussion of public policy concerning education.

If feasible tax, income, and educational policies have very limited ability to affect a redistribution of income, then attention naturally turns toward more direct income transfers, which are also intimately connected to policies of taxation and expenditure. It should be noted that transfer payments increased almost sixfold in the United States between 1964 and 1978, rising to more than $212 billion.[46] We saw previously that in-kind transfer payments in particular have brought about some redistribution of income in the United States. Yet the subjects of income inequality and of the appropriate role of policies for transfer payments continue to be widely debated, with basic positions on this issue resting fundamentally on value judgments.

As an example, consider this statement by Schorr: "The distribution of income should be shifted sufficiently to double the share of the bottom quintile, that is, to increase its share from roughly five to a little over ten percent of personal income."[47] Consequently, the solution to the problem of unequal income distribution that Schorr prefers is to shift the relative shares among family quintiles as shown in the table below:

Income distribution	Lowest fifth	Second fifth	Middle fifth	Fourth fifth	Highest fifth
Actual, 1972	5.4	11.9	17.5	23.9	41.3
Proposed by Schorr	10.4	13.9	17.5	21.9	36.3

Schorr does not tell us why roughly 10.4 percent is the appropriate income share for the lowest fifth of families or why 36+ percent is suitable for the highest fifth, but consider the contrasting view of Nisbet, who claims that "all evidence suggests that a very large number of Americans are indifferent, if not actually hostile, to any idea for national social policy that has substantial equalitarianism behind it."[48] Or recall Browning's conclusion that, in 1972, the lowest quintile of families *had already* increased their relative income share to almost 12 percent.

Equality as a Trade-off

Clearly, these views are so different as to appear irreconcilable. Yet whether one is for or against greater equalization of incomes, the underlying concern— and the real issue—is: What has to be given up to gain additional equality, that is, what is the price to be paid for further reductions of inequality? For insight into this question, we turn to Okun, who recently described the tension between the political principles of democracy and the economic principles of capitalism—between equality and efficiency—as the key issue in American society.[49] Okun links the question of equality directly to the nature of the American economic system, as Behrman and Taubman did previously.

In 1975, Okun proposed a "leaky-bucket" experiment to test one's views about the trade-off of efficiency for equality. The experiment involves the transfer of income from the richest 5 percent of families (whose average income in 1974 was $45,000) to the poorest 20 percent of families (who averaged $5000 of income in the same year). A proposal is made to tax the top group of families by an additional $4000 each, or roughly 9 percent, with the funds thus generated going to aid low-income families. Since the latter group contains four times as many families as the affluent group, this proposal apparently should finance a $1000 grant or transfer to the average low-income family. But there is a fly in the ointment, an unsolvable technical problem: "The money must be carried from the rich to the poor in a leaky bucket."[50]

The leak represents an inefficiency which, in the real world:

> . . . includes the adverse effects on the economic incentives of the rich and the poor, and the administrative costs of tax collection and transfer programs. [Consequently] . . . some of [the money] . . . will simply disappear in transit, so the poor will not receive all the money that is taken from the rich. The average poor family will get less than $1,000, while the average rich family gives up $4,000.[51]

Okun disdains to measure the actual leak in favor of encouraging his readers to decide how much leakage each would accept "and still support the Tax-and-Transfer Equalization Act."[52] He presents hypothetical cases in which the leak ranges from 10 to 99 percent, with poor families receiving $900 and $10, respectively, in the two extreme situations. His principal point is that an answer to the question, "Where would you draw the line?" cannot be right or wrong, just as one's selection of a particular flavor of ice cream cannot be right or wrong.

But if that is so, it has not prevented critics from arguing strenuously against one or another plan for income redistribution, including Okun's. For example, Browning contends that the *marginal* tax rates for low-income families covered by the aforementioned plan would be pushed up close to 100 percent (since any additional earnings over, say, their average $5000 income in 1974 would reduce their receipt of a cash transfer on virtually a one-to-one basis), while the marginal rates for the affluent families who are already in the 40 to 45 percent tax bracket would be in the 65 to 80 percent range.[53] Such disincentives, according to Browning, would produce a significant reduction in earnings by the top-income group of families, a conversion of income into nontaxable forms (made possible by tax loopholes), and fewer families inclined to "acquire the skills, shoulder the responsibilities, and make the effort necessary to move into this [top] income class."[54] And if this occurs, he goes on to say, aggregate taxable incomes might well fall by 10 percent, in which case the tax revenues collected from families would be no different from those obtained under the prevailing tax system and distribution of family income.

This objection is very much like one presently heard in numerous countries around the world—the United Kingdom and Sweden, for example—where efforts to redistribute income outpace those in the United States and have much longer traditions. It can be said that those who offer this objection prefer a small—or smaller—leak from the redistribution bucket and thus favor efficiency over equality.

Alternatively, others clearly vote for equality over efficiency, where equality has an important economic component. This is the position of Rawls, for example, who contends that "to provide genuine equality of opportunity, society must give more attention to those with fewer native assets and to those born into the less favorable social positions."[55] His emphasis on equality, which requires a "just" distribution of income, is grounded in a basic notion of the rights and duties of citizens in a democracy. To ensure and exercise these rights and duties, individual behavior should not depend on class position or relative standing in terms of assets and liabilities. Where behavior is so dependent, redress should be sought which will give precedence to rights over the marketplace and to justice and equality over efficiency. Hence, the intellectual rationale of Rawls's socio-political paradigm leads to the support of economic equality.

For Okun, the solution to the problem he originally posed is more complex; as he puts it, "My answer isn't neat."[56] He takes issue, for example, with Rawls, whose concept of equality is apparently so strong as to require one to prefer a society that guarantees every family $14,000 a year (no more and no less) over one that provides 1 percent of all families with $13,000 and 99 percent of them with $20,000. If the citizenry was indeed in a position to decide its social constitution, as in the starting point of Rawls's analysis, Okun would urge that society "weigh equality heavily" but "not seek to settle forever the precise weighting of inequality."[57] Differing as well with critics like Browning, Okun would favor with enthusiasm equality over efficiency in the leaky-bucket experiment if the leakage were only 10 or 20 percent; he would also favor the trade-off, but without enthusiasm, if the leakage was as much as 60 percent. Whatever Okun's preference in this regard, however, it remains for each person to recognize and to calculate his or her own trade-off of equality for efficiency and for society to make a collective judgment about this as well. Such decisions flow from underlying values rather than from any neat formulas or data bases that automatically generate policy prescriptions.

But if individual values shape one's views about the trade-off between equality and efficiency, it may be helpful to keep in mind one or two facts about income distribution. The first is that the number of families and persons that can be considered rich is quite small. If $50,000 of income separates the rich from the nonrich, less than 3 percent of families and less than one half of one percent of unrelated individuals were among the rich in 1977.[58] If $35,000 of income conveys a "rich" economic status, then one-eighth of all families and roughly 1.5 percent of unrelated individuals were in that position in 1977.

Second, we saw earlier that though the tax system is proportional for most families, it is significantly progressive for the top 5 percent of them. As Pechman and Okner suggest, the very rich, among whom ownership of wealth is concentrated, pay high taxes in large part because much of their income comes from property.[59] In 1972, when federal personal income tax bills averaged 11 percent of the income of all persons, they averaged 27 percent of the income of families earning $50,000 or more. Of this group's total tax bill in that year, some $22 billion, about $13 billion (the difference between 11 percent and 27 percent) was due to the progressive nature of the tax structure. As Okun notes, this was more than the combined federal cost of Medicaid, welfare, food stamps, and public housing in 1972, precisely those transfer payments which have been instrumental in raising the relative income share of low-ranking families and in reducing the incidence of poverty in the United States.

None of this is to say that the rich pay taxes at rates approaching the 70 percent statutory maximum presently in effect for personal incomes or that public policies could not be adjusted to reduce the "tax escape clauses" which the rich and the very rich are able to use to their advantage far more than others. It is to say, however, that to effectuate substantially greater income redistribution in the United States would require increasing the taxes of some (perhaps many) of the nonrich, who may include or be described as the "well-off" or the "middle class" majority. Even more, given the lack of deductions from, and offsets against, income available to the lower-middle-income groups—to the average wage earner, if you like—they too may have to be more heavily taxed in order to raise the relative income standing of the poor, working or not working. These are among the reasons why the distribution of income preferred by Schorr (whether you agree with him on this point or not) would be more difficult to achieve than he seems to realize. Is there any doubt, then, why inequality and income redistribution are such controversial topics or why the trade-off between equality and efficiency is a key issue?

Limiting Producers' and Consumers' Choice

So far in our discussion of inequality, we have focused on mechanisms for transferring funds from those at the upper part of the income distribution to those at the lower end. But a few words are in order about proposals which, while clearly concerned with inequality and income redistribution, are more strongly oriented toward limiting the production of certain consumer goods. In brief, the argument underlying such proposals is as follows.

An affluent society witnesses the production and consumption of certain goods and services—yachts, exotic furs, chauffeur-driven limousines, 12-year-old scotch, cameras that produce a photograph within seconds, beach-front hideaways—which are an excessive indulgence, which have no redeeming social value, and which form part of a vicious cycle whereby consumption is for consumption's sake alone. Such consumption should be limited by putting a cap on incomes—perhaps $35,000 annually per family—or by heavily taxing or prohibiting the production of such consumer goods. The revenues thereby obtained could then be used to satisfy presumably more pressing societal needs. An older but still useful statement of this position is the following: "The solution is a system of taxation which automatically makes a pro rata share of increasing income available to public authority for public purposes. The taxes of public authority, like that of private individuals, will be [used] to distribute this increase in accordance with relative need."[60] Such proposals are somewhat like those which seek to remove tax deductions for such business expenses as conferences in South Sea locations, company airplanes, and three-martini lunches.

Now it is not at all difficult to sympathize with critics of mindless consumption or to prefer to see human and capital resources employed in the production of goods and services which may be deemed necessities rather than luxuries. It is quite another thing, however, to seek to impose this view on others so as to prevent them from producing or consuming particular goods and services. Pragmatically speaking, some items—air conditioning is a prime example—which once were regarded as luxuries come over time to be regarded as necessities, and thus their production satisfies a rather pervasive societal need. On a more principled basis, the restraint of certain kinds of production and consumption imposes the values of some people on others. Apart from its strong elitist connotation, this rank ordering of values, to the extent that it is translated into public policy, restricts the freedom of individuals to make choices in the marketplace. It is precisely that freedom which a capitalist economy was designed to foster, as Adam Smith pointed out in 1776 and as others have done since then.

In a market economy, "instruction" is presumed to pass from the consumer to the producer,[61] not the other way around, or from the public authority to the private citizen. To be sure, a market economy requires regulation through law and a governmental presence. Further, it may happen that, in some sectors and at some points in time, "instruction" is given by producer-monopolists to individual consumers, just as in some labor markets wages are set below competitive levels by producer-monopsonists (labor is exploited). And it is well known that a substantial portion of the economy is highly concentrated, that is, oligopolistic or imperfectly competitive. But that does not gainsay the freedom-reducing propensities of policies that make more costly or prohibit the production and consumption of selected goods and services which a few regard as antithetical to an "enlightened" society. Nevertheless, in the face of limitation of some strategic resources and pressures for equitable distribution of the goods which they make possible, the trade-off between equality and market efficiency may lead in this direction.

Inequality and Meritocracy

Having said this, we come now to a key dimension of the contemporary debate about inequality: meritocracy. The term itself refers to the dominance of society by an elite which attains its position as a result of intelligence and achievement instead of through ascription, that is, assignment or inheritance. This may strike some readers as an odd formulation indeed, since the history of western civilization can be read as a struggle of the populace to overturn the domination of society and economy by a privileged class whose ascribed status and owned wealth gives it the power to rule over the many, sometimes benevolently but more often despotically. The replacement of ascension to elite positions through inherited nobility with ascension based on intelligence, skill, and achievement—in a word, merit—would thus seem to make for a more egalitarian society.

But if merit has become the basis for upward mobility in modern society, the critics contend that the transformation has had an unexpected outcome. "Previously, talent had been distributed throughout the society, and each class or social group had its own natural leaders. Now all men of talent were raised into a common elite, and those below had no excuses for their failures; they bore the stigma of rejection, they were known inferiors."[62] In other words, society has developed a new class structure based not on inheritance but on merit —a meritocracy.

In the late 1950s, the sociologist Michael Young used this scenario as a point of departure to write a predictive fable in which, during the twenty-first century, the citizenry would revolt against meritocracy and replace it with a classless society based upon the principle of equality.[63] For the present period, Bell tells us that "the Populist revolt . . . has already begun, at the very onset of the post-industrial society," and he cites as evidence of this attack the derogation of the intelligence quotient (IQ) and genetic theories of intelligence, the demand for "open admissions" to colleges and universities, the pressure for increased representation of minorities and women on university faculties, the onslaught against credentials, and the criticism of schooling as a determinant of one's position in society.[64] To this list others would add most basically the pursuit of income equalization.

Perhaps the most controversial element of this debate, and the one that has particularly fueled popular discussion of meritocracy and equality, is that of IQ. The publication in late 1969 of an article by Jensen caused many to accuse him of being racist and fanatical and trying to provide a "factual" basis for discrimination against blacks, whom he found to have systematically lower IQs than whites.[65] Few bothered to consider that Jensen himself provided no new data on this subject or that IQ scores are, on the evidence, not very closely related to earnings and other measures of activity in the labor market.[66]

More relevant to our present concern, however, Herrnstein later extended Jensen's analysis to draw out its implications for the consequences of policies to reduce inequality.[67] He reasoned that if difference in mental abilities are inherited, if society requires such abilities, and if the environment is truly equalized, then social standing will be based largely on inherited differences. Consequently, he suggests, if equality of opportunity *is* fully realized (if the social environment is equalized and thus held constant) and if all persons are given an equal start, heredity will be the decisive factor, and meritocracy based on IQ will result. Those with low intellectual capacity will be unable to compete, and a genetically determined caste system will have evolved.

Lest we go too far, however, with such speculation about the unexpected consequences of equality, consider that the notion of a meritocracy is debunked by many, including Okun, who states:

> The spectre that fair races [for prizes] will produce a hereditary caste system of meritocracy . . . [is] farfetched. . . . That argument must rely on the conjecture that gearing market rewards more precisely to abilities will eliminate the lottery aspects of today's income distribution and reveal a truly hereditary elite that earns the top prizes generation after generation: Such speculation is totally [unsupportable]. . . .[68]

Clearly, this complex issue requires further investigation and can in no way be resolved in a few short paragraphs. But consider that researchers on both the British and American scenes tell us that those societies are in fact *not* becoming more meritocratic, even if they are also not necessarily becoming more equal in terms of the personal distribution of income.[69] To this it can be added that the evidence presented at various points in this book attests to elements of mobility and fluidity in the economy and in society, even if we are far short of the goal of perfect mobility or equality of social and economic position.

Equality and Efficiency

By the same token, those who are concerned about the disincentives to productive efficiency that they see emanating from the pursuit of equality, especially through income redistribution, should recognize that the dominant theme of this movement remains one of *equality of opportunity,* not equality of result. Admittedly, employment quotas and specific percentage targets for income redistribution may suggest a push for equality of result, but substantial opposition has arisen to both of these. Just as the negative consequences of policies of open admissions to colleges and universities (where they were adopted) caused many of them to be modified or abandoned, and just as IQ tests continue to be used (rarely alone, incidentally), despite the very legitimate concern about what it is they measure and what factors affect one's scores, so too does society respond to what it considers other excesses in the pursuit of equality. Less could hardly be expected of a society that also seeks to curb the excesses of competitive capitalism. We have seen this in the area of quotas for admission to schools, with the Supreme Court ruling against them in the *Bakke* case (re-

viewed in Chapter 8) *even as it supported affirmative action to increase repre-*
sentation of minorities in the student body. We see it again in the raising of the
question concerning income redistribution: "Have we gone far enough?"

More generally, a society that embraces competitive (or not so competitive) capitalism does indeed expect differences—inequalities—to occur in income, in wealth, and in status among the populace. This is so because if rewards bear any relationship to performance—put differently, if the marginal
productivity theory of wages is *at all* valid—and if abilities, intelligence, and,
to be sure, luck are not evenly distributed among individuals, then differential
outcomes—that is to say, inequalities—inevitably will result. And this does
produce a form of meritocracy. What is critical to this process, however, is that
the chances, the opportunities, for upward mobility in an economic system in
which merit is highly valued not be so unevenly distributed among the citizenry
that some members are foreclosed from improving their economic position,
while others are always and fully protected against a weakening of their status.
If such inequality of opportunity does exist, it may be defined as unjust by the
populace, who will then seek to redress that situation. The data on distribution
of income, ownership of wealth, differentials in earnings and unemployment
between blacks and whites, and the inheritance of economic success certainly
provide a basis for seeking greater equality of opportunity among the nation's
citizens, even if they do not lead to policies which will swiftly and automatically accomplish such an objective.

Also note that the issue of economic inequality among individuals and families is worldwide; it is present in communist and socialist nations as well as
capitalist and mixed capitalist economies. In view of all this, it is perhaps a trib-
ute to the American character and to the economic and political systems of the
United States that the drive for equality of opportunity has made undeniable
progress without so straining those systems that they can no longer function. It
is also perhaps a measure of the success of this effort that it is today the subject
of intense questioning and reappraisal. Wherever one stands on this issue,
though, it is important to recognize that personal values determine one's preferences in the trade-off between efficiency and equality and to keep in mind the
distinction between equality of opportunity and equality of result.

The Labor Market, Once Again

All that has been said here about income distribution and the issue of inequality
may seem to downplay or go against the operation of labor markets in a capitalist, free enterprise economy. After all, if one argues for the redistribution of
income among families or individuals and if the bulk of that income is obtained
in the form of wages and salaries paid for gainful employment, then one is implicitly saying that the market's pattern of income allocation to labor is wrong.
More than that, one is raising a fundamental question about the social contract,
about the consensus in society that economic status is properly determined
principally by one's success in the private labor market rather than by income
allocation through the political system.

To analyze this concern properly, consider that the rise of the labor market in countries of the western world brought freedom to countless millions who otherwise would have been—whose counterparts in earlier times were—forced to toil permanently for one or another employer at legally established maximum rates of pay which workers could not legally seek to alter. Even less freedom, of course, was the lot of those who worked as indentured servants or slaves. In these varying modes of employment and economic systems, society was truly highly stratified, and the notion of mobility, horizontal or vertical, was virtually absent. Payment for work performed often was in kind rather than in money; under those circumstances, employers' control over workers' disposition of income was almost as complete as their control over the amount of income that workers received. Ashton vividly describes the situation facing workers in early-eighteenth-century England and contrasts it with the free labor market that emerged there in the following century:

> Most of the workers were paid by the piece . . . and a delay in transport or the closing of a market might mean that they were deprived of their earnings for many weeks or even months. . . . The domestic workers were often debtors to their employers, not only for material, but also for emergencies of birth, sickness, death, or removal to a new home. The claims of the lender were met by deductions from future earnings, and sometimes children were set to work for the employer without wages, as a means of settlement. . . .
>
> [But] by 1830, Britain had, in one way or another obtained a body of wage-paid workers, acclimatized to factory conditions and able to move from place to place, and from employment to employment, as occasion required. Rates of pay had come to respond more quickly to local changes of demand and supply, and to vary with the upward and downward swings of general activity. Wages in one industry were linked to those in another, and, in particular, the earnings of farm laborers and builders moved up and down with those of factory operatives. Instead of a number of local and imperfect markets in which men offered their services to a few employers on whose goodwill they depended for work, there was coming into being a single, increasingly sensitive, market for labor.[70]

So it is that, from a historical perspective, the freedom to seek work, to change employers, to change employment sectors, and to aspire to mobility in the labor market emerged relatively recently. Compared with the generally downtrodden position of most men, women, and children throughout much of recorded history, this new freedom associated with individual behavior and initiative provided a type of liberty unknown in preindustrial societies. We sometimes lose sight of this in our understandable earnestness to remedy problems of the labor market.

However, although some considered individual freedom and liberty to be fostered by a labor market guided by the laws of supply and demand, others regarded this development as abhorrent because it brought about a rapid disruption in social relations and resulted in the treatment of human beings as commodities. Polanyi, in particular, saw the self-regulating market as a fiction,

as an attempt to foist upon people an unnatural state opposed to their basic in-
stincts of reciprocity, community, and shared interests. He cited numerous examples—trade unionism, legislation concerning factory working conditions,
social insurance, poor laws, combinations of employers—to support his view
that the capitalist economy, with the self-regulating market at its center, was
but a temporary historical aberration, preceded and followed by attempts to
control and to suppress the market within a larger system of social relations. For
Polanyi, *humans seek freedom from the market rather than through the market,*
and it is this guiding principle which, in his view, will cause the transformation of capitalism into an economic system based on society rather than the
individual.[71]

One needn't accept this verdict about the dynamics of social and economic
organization or favor it to appreciate the evils that accompanied the benefits of
industrialization or to recognize the tendency of individuals to combine and
collectively attempt to protect themselves from the unadulterated forces of the
market.[72] This was made abundantly clear in Chapter 3 which outlined the development of unionism in the United States, and earlier in this chapter in the
discussion of efforts to overcome income inequality, efforts which by definition
necessitate public, collective decisions. The fact is that any issue that involves
a trade-off of equality for efficiency almost certainly requires consideration of
collective versus individual decision making.

While at an earlier point in our history we chose a form of economic organization which emphasized individual decision making rather heavily, especially in the labor market, since the mid-1930s we have given relatively greater
weight to collective decisions, which necessarily circumscribe the scope of
issues left solely to the market. But these developments, and, more recently,
the drive for equal opportunity and the attack on poverty have occurred within
a framework of economic and social organization which remains based largely
upon individual (or individual household) decision making. Nowhere is this
more evident than in the American labor market, which encompasses a broader
set of decisions about wages and employment than that of almost any other
country in the western world. The labor market continues to be the primary
arena in which the claims of individual employees and those of workers in general to shares of national income are played out. That is the basis of the social
contract prevailing in the United States between individual citizens and society, even if an important portion of that social contract also stresses some
collectively determined protections from the market and some income transfers
to the working and nonworking poor.

Doubtless, this condition reflects the pragmatic rather than ideological orientation of American society, but it is by no means an unprincipled pragmatism. The United States does not operate under a pure form of capitalism, as
apparently no other county operates under a pure form of socialism or communism. Instead, a balance is sought between those issues decided privately in the
marketplace and those decided collectively in the public, political arena. The
balance to be struck is a delicate one, and it changes from time to time as so-

ciety experiences shifting values. If the discussion of income distribution and
the issue of inequality presented here poses problems for the reader, so be it, for
this is an enduring, pervasive problem not susceptible to solution by an easily
stated preference for ''equality'' or ''efficiency'' or even by the more closely
considered view that ''the market needs a place, and the market needs to be
kept in its place.''[73] Were these preferences or slogans clear guides to action,
we might long ago have resolved the question of income distribution, perhaps
in the same way that we might like to resolve the debate over human capital
versus segmented-labor-market theories.

But that brings us full circle back to the point at which we started in Chapter 7, the first of three chapters devoted to selected aspects of the labor market.
Our preference is to leave readers with still unanswered problems that pertain
to the labor market—leaving them, it is hoped, more informed than before—
and to move on to other issues. Fortunately for us, we reached that decision
individually *and* collectively.

SUMMARY

In this chapter, we reviewed the distribution of national income among factors
of production and among individuals in the United States. Changes in these distributions over time were also explored. We saw that policies concerning taxes
and transfer payments to reduce income inequality and especially poverty have
had some success, particularly when in-kind transfers are taken into account.
Evidence was presented which showed that a considerable amount of economic success is inherited, and this conclusion tends to support policies to redistribute income. In all these efforts, there is an inherent trade-off of efficiency
for equality, with individual and societal values basically determining the trade-
off in a particular nation at any point in time. The trade-off is not something
peculiar to the United States or to capitalist economies, for it is faced by communist and socialist nations as well. On the American scene, however, the
dominant objective concerning equalization seems to be one of equality of opportunity rather than equality of result, though sometimes this distinction is
clouded or overruled by public policy.

In Chapter 10, we move on to consider income supplements and social protections provided to citizens of the United States, but we also draw on selected
examples from other nations, many of which have longer-standing and more
comprehensive policies than our own. Such supplements and protections are
intended partly to prevent excessive reliance on the market for distributing income and thus an exploration of them follows logically upon the subject matter
of this chapter.

NOTES

1   For insightful analyses of this subject, see Stanley Lebergott, ''Factor Shares in the
    Long Term: Some Theoretical and Statistical Aspects,'' in National Bureau of Eco-
    nomic Research, *The Behavior of Income Shares: Selected Theoretical and Empiri-*

cal Issues, Princeton, Princeton, N.J., 1964, p. 83; also Jean Marchal and Bernard Ducros (eds.), *The Distribution of National Income,* Macmillan and St. Martin's, New York, 1968.

2 *Year Book of Labor Statistics, 1976,* International Labour Office, Geneva, 1976, pp. 759–763, table 24.

3 A. B. Atkinson, *The Economics of Inequality,* Oxford University Press, London, 1975, p. 167.

4 Some older but still useful works include Walter S. Measday, "Labor's Share of National Income," *Quarterly Review of Economics and Business,* **2:**25–33 (1962); and Clark Kerr, "Labor's Income Share and the Labor Movement," in George W. Taylor and Frank C. Pierson (eds.), *New Concepts in Wage Determination,* McGraw-Hill, New York, 1957, pp. 260–298.

5 Albert Rees, *The Economics of Trade Unions,* rev. ed., University of Chicago Press, Chicago, 1977, p. 90.

6 Rees, p. 90.

7 See F. Ray Marshall, Allan M. Cartter, and Allan G. King, *Labor Economics: Wages, Employment and Trade Unionism,* 3d ed., Irwin, Homewood, Ill., 1976, p. 371.

8 Marchal and Ducros, *"Distribution of National Income,"* p. 11. The authors are paraphrasing the remarks of Armen A. Alchian.

9 U.S. Bureau of the Census, *Current Population Reports: Money Income and Poverty Status of Families and Persons in the United States: 1977* (Advance Report), ser. P-60, no. 116, 1978, p. 1. This volume and others in the Current Population Survey are the source of the data in this section, unless otherwise noted. They will not be repeatedly cited, though particular tables presented here contain explicit page references to these and other volumes.

10 These findings are discussed in Atkinson, p. 249. For some data on pay differentials in Russia, China, Cuba, and other communist nations, see Henry Phelps Brown, *The Inequality of Pay,* University of California Press, Berkeley, 1977. Brown does not find the occupational pay structures of these countries to be very different from those of western capitalist and socialist countries.

11 For more on this, see U.S. Bureau of the Census, p. 29.

12 Joseph A. Pechman and Benjamin A. Okner, *Who Bears the Tax Burden?* Brookings, Washington, 1974. We rely heavily on this volume for a portion of the discussion in this section.

13 Pechman and Okner, p. 64. By "proportional," the authors mean that the incidence of taxes is in proportion to the income of taxpayers. If taxes were disproportional, there would be a major redistribution of after-tax as compared with before-tax incomes in the United States.

14 Atkinson, p. 52. For additional data on changes over time in before-tax and after-tax income distributions in developed nations, see Malcolm Sawyer, "Income Distribution in OECD Countries," *OECD Economic Outlook, Occasional Studies,* Organization for Economic Co-operation and Development, Paris, July 1976, pp. 26–29.

15 *Economic Report of the President, January, 1978,* 1978, p. 221. The following discussion draws freely from this report.

16 *Economic Report of the President, January, 1978,* p. 224.

17 *Economic Report of the President, January, 1978,* p. 225.

18 Edgar K. Browning, "How Much More Equality Can We Afford?" *The Public Interest,* **43:**90–110 (1976), especially p. 91.

19 Browning, p. 92.

20 Browning, p. 92.

21 Browning, p. 93.

22 Bradley R. Schiller, "Equality, Opportunity, and the 'Good Job,'" *The Public Interest,* **43:**113 (1976).

23 Schiller, p. 115.

24 Schiller, p. 116. Schiller's study, in effect, holds age constant, but the reader should be aware that age and earnings (as well as income) are, in general, positively correlated. However, that relationship is strongest for the middle years—25 to 44—and tends to be reversed at older ages.

25 Schiller, pp. 118–119. On this issue see also U.S. Department of Labor, *Income Inequality and Employment,* Research and Development Monograph 66, Washington, 1978.

26 These data are presented in Lester C. Thurow, *Generating Inequality,* Basic Books, New York, 1975, pp. 11–19.

27 Thurow, pp. 15–16; and U.S. Bureau of the Census, *Statistical Abstract of the United States: 1978,* pp. 475–476.

28 Atkinson, pp. 125–132; and Royal Commission on the Distribution of Income and Wealth, *Second Report on the Standing Conference,* Report 4, H. M. Stationery Office, October 1976, pp. 47–90. The second of these sources shows a secular decline in the concentration of wealth in the United Kingdom, but the data and methods used to analyze them are disputed for earlier periods (and presumably would be for later periods) by Atkinson.

29 Atkinson, p. 14.

30 John A. Brittain, *The Inheritance of Economic Status,* Brookings, Washington, 1977, p. 3.

31 Brittain, p. 3.

32 Brittain, p. 13.

33 Brittain, p. 14.

34 Brittain, p. 17.

35 Brittain, p. 22.

36 Brittain, p. 27. The only caveat here is that, given family background and education, daughters tended to end up having a somewhat lower economic status than sons. If this study of choice of a mate were to be replicated in the 1980s, it probably would be possible to examine directly a sample of married women with experience in the labor market, given recent increases in their rates of participation in the labor force.

37 Peter M. Blau and Otis Dudley Duncan, *The American Occupational Structure,* Wiley, New York, 1967, p. 330, as cited in William H. Sewell and Robert M. Hauser, "On the Effects of Families and Family Structure on Achievement," in Paul Taubman (ed.), *Kinometrics: Determinants of Socioeconomic Success within and between Families,* North-Holland Publishing Company, Amsterdam, 1977, p. 257.

38 Sewell and Hauser, pp. 255–286.

39 Jere Behrman and Paul Taubman, "Intergenerational Transfer of Income and Wealth," *The American Economic Review, Papers and Proceedings,* **66:**436–440 (1976).

40 Behrman and Taubman, p. 438.

41 Behrman and Taubman, p. 440. Much of the popular debate about inequality was sparked by Christopher Jencks et al., *Inequality: A Reassessment of the Effect of Family and Schooling in America,* Basic Books, New York, 1972. See also Mary

Corcoran, Christopher Jencks, and Michael Olneck, "The Effects of Family Background on Earnings," *The American Economic Review, Papers and Proceedings,* **66:**430–435 (1976).

42 See *Economic Report of the President, January, 1978,* pp. 219–221, for an elaboration of these proposals.

43 Brittain, p. 33.

44 Paul Taubman, *Income Distribution and Redistribution,* Addison-Wesley, Reading, Mass., 1978, pp. 102–103.

45 Taubman, *Income Distribution and Redistribution,* p. 103.

46 *Economic Report of the President, January, 1979,* p. 203, table B-18.

47 Alvin L. Schorr, "Fair Shares," in Alvin L. Schorr (ed.), *Jubilee for Our Times: A Practical Program for Income Equality,* Columbia, New York, 1977, p. 19.

48 Robert Nisbet, "The Pursuit of Equality," *The Public Interest,* **35:**105 (1974).

49 Arthur M. Okun, *Equality and Efficiency: The Big Tradeoff,* Brookings, Washington, 1975.

50 Okun, p. 91.

51 Okun, p. 92.

52 Okun, p. 91.

53 Browning, pp. 108–109.

54 Browning, p. 109.

55 John Rawls, *A Theory of Justice,* Harvard, Cambridge, Mass., 1971, p. 100.

56 Okun, p. 92.

57 Okun, p. 93.

58 Derived from U.S. Bureau of the Census, p. 2.

59 Pechman and Okner. The remaining data in this paragraph are from Joseph A. Pechman and Benjamin A. Okner, "Individual Income Tax Erosion by Income Classes," in *The Economics of the Federal Subsidy Programs,* a compendium of papers submitted to the Joint Economic Committee, pt. 1, *General Study Papers,* 92d Cong., 2d Sess., 1972, and cited in Okun, p. 103.

60 John K. Galbraith, *The Affluent Society,* Houghton Mifflin, Boston, 1958, p. 242. Interestingly, since Galbraith sounded this call the public sector has grown faster than any portion of private industry, and transfer payments have increased dramatically.

61 For an analysis of this doctrine as it was first articulated by Adam Smith, see Paul J. McNulty, "The Consumer and the Producer," *The Yale Review,* **58:**537–548 (1969).

62 Daniel Bell, "On Meritocracy and Equality," *The Public Interest,* **29:**29–30 (1972).

63 Michael Young, *The Rise of Meritocracy, 1870–2033,* Thames and Hudson, London, 1958.

64 Bell, p. 31.

65 Arthur C. Jensen, "How Much Can We Boost I.Q. and Achievement?" *Harvard Educational Review,* **39:**1–123 (1969).

66 For evidence on this point, see John C. Hause, "Ability and Schooling as Determinants of Lifetime Earnings, or If You're So Smart, Why Aren't You Rich?" in F. Thomas Juster (ed.), *Education, Income and Human Behavior,* McGraw-Hill, New York, 1975, pp. 123–149.

67 Richard Herrnstein, *I.Q. in the Meritocracy,* Little, Brown, Boston, 1973. The present discussion draws partly from Bell, pp. 31–34.

68 Okun, p. 85.

69 Jencks et al., and Atkinson, especially pp. 86–97.
70 T. S. Ashton, *The Industrial Revolution: 1760–1830*, Oxford University Press, London, 1969, pp. 37, 39, 87.
71 Karl Polanyi, *The Great Transformation*, Beacon Press, Boston, 1944, passim, but especially chaps. 3, 5–6, 18–19, 21.
72 For another view of capitalism's demise and socialism's ascendancy, see Joseph Schumpeter, *Capitalism, Socialism and Democracy*, 3d ed., Torchbooks, Harper & Row, New York, 1942, especially chaps. 7–8, 13–14.
73 Okun, p. 119.

ADDITIONAL READINGS

Atkinson, A. B.: *The Economics of Inequality*, Oxford University Press, London, 1975.
Brittain, John: *The Inheritance of Economic Status*, Brookings, Washington, 1977.
Brown, Henry Phelps: *The Inequality of Pay*, University of California Press, Berkeley, 1977.
Economic Report of the President, January, 1978, 1978; also for 1979.
OECD Economic Outlook, Occasional Studies, Organization for Economic Co-operation and Development, Paris, July, 1976.
Okun, Arthur M.: *Equality and Efficiency: The Big Tradeoff*, Brookings, Washington, 1975.
Pechman, Joseph A., and Benjamin A. Okner: *Who Bears the Tax Burden?* Brookings, Washington, 1974.
Royal Commission on the Distribution of Income and Wealth: *Second Report on the Standing Reference*, Report 4, H. M. Stationery Office, London, October 1976.
Taubman, Paul (ed.): *Kinometrics: Determinants of Socioeconomic Success within and between Families*, North-Holland Publishing Company, Amsterdam, 1977.
Thurow, Lester C.: *Generating Inequality*, Basic Books, New York, 1975.

FOR ANALYSIS AND DISCUSSION

1 If changes in industry mix explain much of the increase in the share of national income going to labor, what explains the relatively larger increase in fringe benefits than in wages and salaries? Compare the fringe benefits component of employee compensation in the United States with the fringe benefits components of compensation in two other developed nations. Is it larger, smaller, or about the same? Why? What is the source of your information?

2 Examine the most recent issue of the Current Population Survey contained in your school's library and locate the volume dealing with consumer income (for 1977, this will be marked Series P-60, No. 116). What kinds of income are included in this report? What kinds of income do you believe are excluded? Of what importance are these exclusions in comparing income shares among subgroups of the population?

3 Figure 9-1 shows a Lorenz curve, which has often been used to depict the degree of inequality in a country's income distribution. The 45-degree line starting at the origin shows what the distribution would look like if each income unit—say, each family—received equal shares of income. The departure of an actual income distribution curve from this 45-degree line represents the extent of inequality; as graphed,

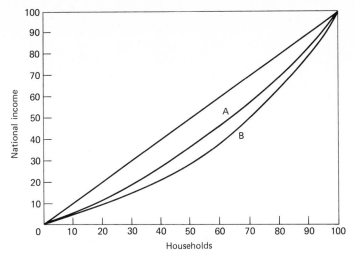

Figure 9-1 Lorenz curves for two hypothetical income distributions.

country A's income distribution is more equal than country B's. If you were to graph the Lorenz curves of the countries listed in Table 9-3, which would be furthest from the 45-degree line? Which would lie closest to it. Why?

4 Two teams of three students each should debate the following proposition: "Resolved: Transfer payments have substantially reduced the amount of poverty in the United States in the last 15 years." The remainder of the class should pose questions to the teams following the conclusion of the debate. The instructor should serve as moderator.

5 Prepare a position paper that argues for an increase in the progressivity of the federal income tax. Support your position with reference to data on income distribution and personal wealth. Be sure to address what you believe to be some of the possible negative consequences of a more progressive income tax structure.

6 Summarize the present evidence concerning the inheritance of economic status. How large is the data base upon which conclusions about inherited economic status rest? If you feel that this data base is inadequate, how do you believe it should be improved? How might a study of the inherited economic status of women be carried out?

7 Compare the occupation of your father with that of a friend's father. Ask your father how he entered his occupation, how his education relates to his occupational standing, and how his occupation and income compare with those of his father. Compare his answers with those of a friend's father who has been queried on these points. If your mother also works, ask her the same questions and compare her answers with those of a friend's mother who is employed.

8 Consider the leaky-bucket experiment proposed by Okun, which was discussed in this chapter. What is your own judgment concerning the point at which a trade-off of efficiency for equality is "too large"? Do you believe that this point has been reached, generally speaking, in the United States? How is your answer affected, if at all, by the data in Tables 9-2, 9-3, and 9-9?

9 Read Milton Friedman's *Capitalism and Freedom* and Karl Polanyi's *Great Transformation*. Compare and contrast the concepts of freedom employed by the two authors. How does each of these authors envision the nature and function of the labor market? Which of these works has "more to say," in your judgment, about contemporary American capitalism? Why?

10 In view of the evidence presented in this chapter, how do you evaluate the human capital approach and segmented-labor-market theories presented in Chapter 7? Which of them seems to you to better explain the distribution of income in the United States? In other nations? Summarize your position in a short essay. Compare your views and analysis with those of a classmate.

Income Supplements and Social Protection

In this chapter, we sketch out the leading income supplements provided to the American labor sector by programs of social insurance established in federal and state laws. Through them, members of the labor sector have established further claims to shares of national income, preferring not to be dependent solely on wage and salary income earned in the marketplace for their economic and social well-being. Treated here are the federal social security system, state workers' compensation programs, and the federal-state unemployment insurance program. Each of these is financed through contributions by employers to one or another level of government and, in the case of social security, by employees' contributions as well. Government, not employers, administers the programs and pays the funds to recipients. However, employers in both the private and the public sectors may establish their own retirement and disability programs, and private programs are now widespread on the American scene. In this connection we shall also briefly examine the federal Occupational Safety and Health Act of 1970 (OSHA) and the Employee Retirement Income Security Act of 1974 (ERISA), which were intended to strengthen income protections for workers who are in ill health or who are retired, respectively.

In this chapter we shall also discuss the Fair Labor Standards Act (FLSA), which limits the working hours of some groups of employees, establishes requirements concerning pay for overtime in private industry, and specifies minimum wage rates for most of the private sector. The chapter concludes with a look at the growth record of aggregate expenditures on social welfare in the United States in the post-World War II era. The experiences of foreign countries with income supplements and social protection are introduced at various points in the analysis. We begin our discussion with an overview of the philosophy underlying programs for income supplements and social protection as they have evolved in the United States.

THE PHILOSOPHY OF AMERICAN SOCIAL INSURANCE

We noted in Chapter 9 that the rise of a market for labor in western industrialized nations was regarded by some as a boon to human freedom and by others as fundamentally debilitating to humanity. Whichever of these views is more accurate, there is little doubt that, in the United States, protections *from* the market in the form of legislative initiatives began to emerge during the Depression of the 1930s and have continued apace for four decades.

It may seem like ancient history to today's readers, but it was less than half a century ago that a typical American worker—well-off by the standards of other nations—could nevertheless be refused a job because of race, religion, or union sympathies; could be disciplined by a supervisor or fired for any reason whatsoever without recourse to grievance procedures or other forms of due process; was solely responsible for determining how to make ends meet if unable to work because of sickness, accident, or old age; could be required to work extremely long hours and with no premium pay whatsoever; and had to rely totally on personal or family resources to locate a job. Although the economic system prevailing at the time worked well by many tests of performance, by present standards of equity it bred misery and degradation for millions of workers.

Today, of course, the typical worker (with some exceptions) can call upon the public employment services for help in locating a job; receives at least the minimum wage established by law and time-and-a-half base pay for hours worked in excess of 40 per week or 8 per day; receives workers' compensation if injured on the job and unemployment insurance if laid off from a job; receives a government-administered pension upon retirement from work; and cannot be legally refused a job, laid off from work, or otherwise discriminated against in employment because of union sympathies, race, religion, age, sex, or national origin.

If this does not add up to complete "womb to tomb" security, it is nevertheless an impressive array of programs for social protection and income supplementation. Indeed, many worry that it is precisely these efforts that have played a leading role in converting the American capitalist system into a welfare state, indistinguishable from collectively organized economic systems found elsewhere in the modern world. Those who hold this view feel that the fundamental American values of enterprise, independence, and especially individualism—in a phrase, the work ethic—have been basically threatened if not supplanted by the panoply of state-run social insurance programs now in existence. They fear that, as a result of the welfare state, capitalism and individual freedom are being undermined and will eventually be supplanted by socialism and collective decision making.

It is important not to dismiss these concerns as the prattlings of simple-minded reactionaries. It is quite appropriate, for example, to worry about the ability of the American economy to finance even larger programs of income supplements and social protection, especially in light of changes in the structure of the economy which have made the growth rates to which we became accustomed in the first half of this century considerably more difficult to achieve today. The level of transfer payments has grown so rapidly in the third quarter of the twentieth century, and is now so large, that even liberals who strongly favor such transfers and the programs from which they stem are increasingly concerned about the nation's ability to fund and maintain them.

Yet, in retrospect, we can see that the thrust of the New Deal social programs was essentially conservative, where that term is used to mean "in keeping with the American character and work ethic," and this is also true of many other programs that have evolved since then. That is so because virtually all the programs to be reviewed in this chapter *are aimed at those who have already demonstrated an attachment to the labor market*—either by being at work or by having previously been employed for a sufficiently long period to qualify for one or another income supplement or protective benefit. This is absolutely fundamental to an understanding of the discussion in this chapter of labor as the subject of social protection in the United States, and it is distinguishable from the rationale underlying some of the income maintenance programs—for example, public assistance and income redistribution—discussed in Chapter 9. The latter are aimed primarily at those who cannot compete in the labor market because of age, disability, or family responsibilities. Although expenditures for welfare programs have risen rapidly, as have those for social insurance programs to pay benefits earned as a "right" by participants in the labor force, that is no reason for failing either to distinguish the one from the other or to analyze them separately.

To conclude this introduction, the philosophy of American programs for income supplements and social protection is to help make the existing economic system work better rather than to supplant it. Until a person has built up at least a minimally acceptable record of steady employment, he or she won't be able to qualify for the benefits of most of the programs to be reviewed in the following sections. In this respect, such claims to benefits of the "welfare state" must first be established as earned rights. That may accord well or poorly with the reader's preferences regarding programs of income supplements and social protection, but it is a basic feature of the American system and is quite in keeping with this nation's form of political economy as it has evolved over the last several decades.

THE AGED AND THEIR ECONOMIC CIRCUMSTANCES

The need for economic assistance to older workers is generally well recognized. Once out of work, some older persons are forced into premature retirement. If laid off, they may draw unemployment compensation for a while, but after the maximum eligibility period has passed and they have spent many months fruitlessly searching for work, the realization sets in that they are not likely to work again. They must then somehow make a living without earning a regular paycheck.

Until recently, older workers were required by company (organizational) policy to retire at a specified age, commonly 65 or, less often, 68. However, in early 1978, Congress changed the law to prohibit private firms from mandating retirement before age 70.[1] This may become the age at which most people retire in the United States. Whatever the age, though, retirement may mean a substantial loss of income to the individual and his or her immediate family. Further, while many workers are quite ready to retire at 62, 65, 68, or 70, others are not. Some would like to continue employment in a familiar work environment and to associate with their colleagues. Mandatory retirement prevents this, and so it may create a loss of purpose as well as a loss of income for some older workers.

Another consequence of retirement may be a deterioration of social status. In earlier times and in more rural environments, the elderly enjoyed a respected and sometimes even governing role in an extended family that included their children and grandchildren. Today, they are likely to live apart and to lead a rather lonely existence, with their views tolerated or humored more than respected. Once retired, they cease to have any real social status in terms of a household with which they are identified or which is their own. Roughly half of all people over 65 years of age live alone as single individuals away from family members. Add to this the likelihood that an older person's physical condition will be impaired—if not at retirement, then a short while afterward—and the difficulties he or she faces in obtaining adequate medical care with a postretirement income. This is not to say that some older persons do not enjoy their retirement years or do not have private pensions and various forms of personal wealth which permit a comfortable—in some cases, opulent—existence. However, upon retiring, the bulk of the elderly face a loss of social status, a deterioration in health, and a decrease in income. So far, public policy and private initiatives have addressed the last two of these concerns but not the first, and they have treated loss of income more comprehensively than loss of health.

Before considering some of these policies, observe in Figure 10-1 the increasing proportion of the population that the aged represent. In 1977, they totaled 10.8 percent of the population, or double the proportion in 1929.[2] Moreover, the group of persons 65 years old and older, which now totals about 23.5 million, is expected to reach about 32 million by the year 2000 and, by one projection (Series I in Figure 10-1), to represent fully 20 percent of the popu-

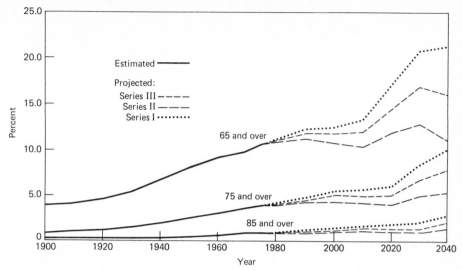

Figure 10-1   Percent of the total population in the older ages, 1900–2040. Notes: (1) Estimates and projections are as of July 1, except for 85 and over, 1900–1930, which relate to April 1. (2) Points are plotted for years ending in zero except for 1975. (3) The three series of population estimates use different assumptions about fertility, thus yielding widely varying projections of the elderly population in 2040. (*Source: U.S. Bureau of the Census, "Demographic Aspects of Aging and the Older Population in the United States,"* Current Population Reports, ser. P-23, no. 59, U.S. Government Printing Office, Washington, D.C., May 1976, p. 4.)

lation by the end of the first quarter of the twenty-first century. Indeed, the American population in general will continue to age over the remainder of this century and to be, on the average, 35 years old at its end. In 1977, the median age of the population was 29.4 years.

These trends reflect the remarkable growth in life expectancy. The average American born in 1900 could expect to live only until age 47, while those born today have a life expectancy of better than 75 years. This development represents progress in many ways, but it also means that everyone's chances have increased of reaching an age at which financial support no longer derives from paid employment. Further, if some of the aged are elderly couples struggling to make ends meet, others (about one-half, actually) are unmarried—the widowed, widowered, divorced, and separated and those who never married. A large majority of the unmarried are women, who tend to outlive their husbands or to remarry less often than widowers. Consequently, any adequate retirement program must include benefits for survivors as well as wage earners, since many women have not been wage earners (a problem that will decline over time, given the great but recent increase in participation by women in the labor force) and have no independent pension claims. We see, then, that an individual's income position after retirement is of importance to others as well as to that person. Let us now consider what some of these sources of retirement income are and how they have changed over time, recognizing that in our mixed capitalistic-welfare society people seek to insure against risk in old age by combining social security, savings, private pension benefits, and accumulated capital goods (a home, furniture, a car, and the like.)

Social Security Benefits

The Social Security Act of 1935 provided old-age benefits to retired workers. The law has been amended and expanded several times since then, and today the social security system includes four separate programs: old-age and survivors insurance, disability insurance, hospital insurance, and supplementary medical insurance. The first two of these are cash-benefit programs that replace earnings lost because of retirement, disability, or death; the last two, known more popularly as "Medicare," provide payments for medical services to the elderly and to disabled workers. Collectively, these provisions are referred to as the national Old-Age, Survivors, Disability and Health Insurance (OASDHI) system.

About 90 percent of all wage and salary workers are covered by the OASDHI system, considerably more than are subject to minimum wage, workers' compensation, and unemployment insurance programs.[3] The major exclusions are government employees, including all who work in the federal sector (which has a separate retirement system), and about 25 percent of those employed at the state and local levels. Also excluded are some employees of nonprofit institutions and workers who do not earn enough to meet minimum legal requirements for coverage. In 1977, roughly 106 million workers paid in $93 billion to the OASDHI system.

Two eligibility tests are applied to determine a person's qualification for OASDHI benefits. First, an individual must show some history of working for a living. This is measured in "quarters of coverage." Since 1978, a person is credited with one-quarter of coverage for each $250 of annual earnings, with the base amount to be increased in future years to take account of increases in average wages. A worker with forty quarters of coverage is fully insured for life, and needs no further employment to qualify for retirement or survivors' benefits. Second, a dollar limit is applied to individual earnings for purposes of determining a person's retirement status under the law. Beginning in 1978, an individual between the ages of 62 and 64 could receive full benefits if he or she averaged less than $3000 of annual earnings after retirement; for each $2 of earnings above that mark, benefits are reduced by $1. For persons between the ages of 65 and 69, the amount of exempt earnings is $4000, and no test of retirement income is necessary for persons 70 years old and older. These limits will rise to $4300 (for 62- to 64-year-olds) and $6000 (for 65- to 69-year-olds), as a result of changes in the Social Security Act made in 1977.

The Benefit Structure A fully insured person who passes the aforementioned eligibility tests draws monthly benefits based on his or her average monthly earnings up to a maximum limit. These benefits and also the worker's actual earnings levels are indexed—that is, updated—to take account of price changes in the economy. The maximum earnings limit is the wage level on which workers and employers pay social security taxes—$22,900 annually in 1979. Consequently, benefits are related to past earnings and contributions, which means that high-wage workers receive larger benefits than low-wage workers. In this sense, the OASDHI program parallels private insurance.

But the wage-benefit relationship under social security is hardly proportional, for the formula has always been weighted in favor of the low-wage worker. For example, the primary benefit for those reaching the retirement age in 1979 is determined according to the following formula: 90 percent of the first $180 of average indexed monthly earnings, plus 32 percent of average indexed monthly earnings over $180 but less than $1085, plus 15 percent of average indexed monthly earnings over $1085 to the maximum earnings limit. A person whose average indexed monthly earnings were $1385 prior to retirement would have received $514 (90 percent of $180 + 32 percent of $1005 + 15 percent of $200) as a monthly social security benefit in 1979. Additionally, however, there is a fixed minimum benefit for social security recipients, estimated at about $121 in 1978, which clearly favors those whose past earnings would otherwise entitle them to less than the minimum.[4] Also, while the provision of additional benefits for a retired worker's dependents can aid both high- and low-wage workers, the criterion of family size further dilutes the relationship between benefits and past earnings or contributions. In these and other ways, the OASDHI system departs from the principles of private insurance and qualifies as "social insurance."

Under certain circumstances, persons can draw benefits early. For example, a worker may retire at age 62 rather than 65 and receive a pension which is permanently reduced to 80 percent of the regular primary benefit. This provision is advantageous for the older worker who becomes unemployed for any reason and, because of age, has difficulty in finding another job. Also, a worker who becomes permanently and totally disabled at any age is eligible for full benefits, provided that he or she is fully insured and has worked in covered employment for 5 out of the 10 years preceding the onset of disability.

In addition to the primary benefit, the pensioner receives supplemental allowances for dependents, typically a spouse and children. The benefit for each dependent usually is 50 percent of the insured's primary benefit up to a maximum family amount fixed by law. In fiscal 1977, this family maximum was $161.90 per month for a worker receiving the minimum primary monthly benefit of $107.90, and it ranged up to $1010.70 for those receiving the highest primary benefit.

Survivors' benefits are also included in the social security program. If the household's breadwinner is fully insured and dies before retirement, his or her survivors are entitled to benefits ranging from 75 percent of the primary benefit for dependent children to 100 percent for a widow aged 65 or over. Benefits are also provided to survivors if the deceased head of the household was "currently insured" at the time of death, but not "fully insured."[5] The law also grants a lump-sum funeral benefit of $255 (in 1977) to the deceased worker's survivors.

Finally, note that a worker who is eligible for social security benefits at age 65 but who delays his or her retirement receives a 3 percent increase in the primary amount for each year of such delay until age 72. Before 1979, the delayed retirement credit was 1 percent per year, and this still applies to those who reached age 62 before that time.

Trends in Benefits We have seen that the benefits an individual actually receives under the social security program depend on a number of variables, such as past earnings, family size, changes in program coverage made by Congress, eligibility tests, benefit formulas, and time of retirement. To see how aged and disabled workers have fared under this program over the years, readers should consult Table 10-1, which presents the average benefits received by different groups between 1940 and 1977 and compares these with trends in hourly earnings and consumer prices over the same period.

Table 10-1 partially belies the common belief that inflation always harms the retired person, who is presumed to be living on a fixed income. To be sure, consumer prices more than quadrupled between 1940 and 1977, but average benefits increased almost elevenfold during this period, surpassing even the rate of earnings growth in the economy. In the highly inflationary 1970s, social security benefits also increased more rapidly than both prices and earnings. Of

Table 10-1 Comparison of OASDHI Benefits, Production Workers' Wages, and Consumer Prices in Selected Years, 1940–1977

	Year				
	1940	**1950**	**1960**	**1970**	**1977**
Average monthly benefit					
Retired worker without dependents	$22.60	$43.86	$ 74.04	$118.10	$242.98
Retired worker and aged wife or husband	$34.73	$67.46	$112.76	$179.89	$366.05
Aged widow or widower	$20.28	$36.54	$ 60.31	$101.71	$221.85
Disabled worker without dependents			$ 89.31	$131.29	$265.19
Average gross weekly earnings of nonagricultural production workers					
	$24.96	$53.13	$ 80.67	$119.83	$203.34
Average gross weekly earnings, manufacturing only					
	$24.96	$58.32	$ 89.72	$133.33	$248.86
Consumer Price Index[1]					
	42.0	72.1	88.7	116.3	181.5

[1] 1967 = 100.

Sources: Adapted from *Social Security Bulletin,* **42**:40 (1979), table M-13, and *Economic Report of the President, January, 1979,* 1979, p. 225, table B-36, and p. 239, table B-49.

course, this is in line (or perhaps not too far out of line) with the intent of Congress in indexing social security benefits to cost of living, a policy which developed in large part out of the erratic pattern of benefit adjustments that historically existed.

But if benefits are protected against inflation, we should not conclude that retired persons are living out lives of comfort under social security. Drawing from a previous example, the worker who earned $1385 per month before retiring receives a benefit upon retirement of less than $515 per month, or a reduction in income of about 63 percent. The personal adjustment to a reduced standard of living that is required of most retirees can be difficult indeed, particularly in light of the adjustments that are necessary in many other dimensions of life. Not all people suffer a reduction in income of the magnitude given in this example, for many receive the additional benefits of private insurance plans, deferred salary payments, and returns to capital. But the vast majority clearly suffer some reduction in their standard of living upon retirement, and if that burden has been lightened in recent years by the indexing of social security benefits, this could be applauded as consistent with the concept of American social insurance and public policy. Recognize, too, that social security in the United States has long been viewed as a supplement to, rather than a replacement for, other sources of income.

Financing the System The scale of the OASDHI system is truly staggering, far surpassing that of any other social insurance or welfare program. In 1977, for example, some 2 million persons were drawing unemployment compensation each month but *34 million* were receiving cash benefits under OASDHI—18 million retirees, 3 million disabled, and 13 million survivors and dependents.[6] In fiscal 1977, the states paid out about $14 billion in unemployment benefits, but cash payments under OASDHI totaled $92 billion.

What is the source of revenue for these tremendous outlays? Although general tax revenues pay a tiny portion of the total cost, on the whole the OASDHI system is self-supporting, with benefits paid out of funds collected from taxes imposed on all covered employees, employers, and self-employed persons. These tax payments go into federally administered trust funds—one for disability insurance and one for old-age and survivors insurance—and the money received can only be used to pay benefits and operating expenses. (The Social Security Administration, incidentally, is one federal agency with an excellent reputation for efficiency, based on its record of keeping down the administrative expenses of this complex operation to about 2 percent of income contributed to it.)

In recent years, the trust funds have developed serious financial problems. As a percentage of annual outlays, assets in the funds declined from a bit over 100 percent in 1970 to 41 percent in late 1977.[7] In 1975, current expenditures began to exceed current receipts, thereby diminishing the actual level of assets. Without remedial action, it was estimated that the assets of disability insurance trust funds would have been exhausted by 1979, and those of old-age and survivors insurance by the early 1980s. This situation was corrected by the 1977 amendments to the Social Security Act, which are discussed further below.

Several factors combined to cause the decline in the trust fund balances of the OASDHI system. One was the indexing of benefits to changes in consumer prices, a practice adopted in 1972, which led to sharply increased expenditures in the highly inflationary mid-1970s. The provision for indexing also caused initial benefits of newly retired workers to rise about 6 percent more rapidly than wages between 1973 and 1977. A second factor was the relatively slow rise in payroll tax receipts during the post-1973 period of high unemployment and slow wage growth. A third was the higher-than-expected number of beneficiaries in the disability insurance program. From a longer-term perspective, the underfinancing of the cash-benefits-programs resulted partly from inflation, the effects of which were magnified—''doubled'' is the precise term—by a technical flaw in the benefit formula. Benefits were first increased on the basis of higher earnings pushed up by higher prices, and then again as the new benefit levels themselves were adjusted for inflation. Double indexing was the result. And, finally, part of the deficit stemmed from sharply expanded projections of the retired relative to the working population after the year 2010. By 2030, for example, it is estimated that there will be 34 persons aged 65 and over for every 100 persons aged 20 to 64, compared with a current ratio of 19:100.[8] This forecast has enormous consequences for the social security system, especially when we consider that more than nine out of ten people who retire in the United States are eligible to draw OASDHI benefits.

It was in recognition of these developments, actual and projected, that Congress amended the Social Security Act in 1977. Among the adopted provisions was one raising the taxable wage base for social security payments as well as the tax rate applied to that base for employers and employees alike. The rates and the base to which they are applied were also raised for the self-employed. The changes occur in a series of periodic steps which are shown in Table 10-2, along with the tax rates and taxable base that would have been in effect under the old, unamended law. Thus, in 1981, for example, the new law requires contributions from employers and employees of 6.65 percent on a maximum of $29,700 of annual wages; a worker earning this amount or more would pay $1975 in social security taxes in 1981, and so would his or her employer. A person earning $15,000 in that year would pay taxes at the same rate, but the total tax would be $997.50 (6.65 percent × $15,000), an amount again matched by the employer. The new provisions contrast markedly, of course, with the 1 percent tax rate and taxable wage base of $3000 adopted at the inception of the social security program in the 1930s. They are intended principally to cover the deficits resulting from demographic changes and patterns of inflation and recession.

Another provision of the 1977 social security legislation changed the procedures for adjusting the benefits of current and future retirees to take account of inflation. Under the previous law, projections of future benefits were heavily dependent upon projections of increases in wages and prices, with the result

Table 10-2 Tax Rates and Taxable Earnings Base for Social Security Trust Funds, Old and New Laws, Calendar Years, 1977–2011, Percent

| | Tax rates | | | | | | | |
| | Prior law | | | | Social security amendments of 1977 | | | |
Calendar year	Total	Old-age and survivors insurance	Disability insurance	Hospital insurance	Total	Old-age and survivors insurance	Disability insurance	Hospital insurance
Employer and employee each								
1977	5.85	4.375	0.575	0.900	5.85	4.375	0.575	0.900
1978	6.05	4.350	0.600	1.100	6.05	4.275	0.775	1.000
1979–1980	6.05	4.350	0.600	1.100	6.13	4.330	0.750	1.050
1981	6.30	4.300	0.650	1.350	6.65	4.525	0.825	1.300
1982–1984	6.30	4.300	0.650	1.350	6.70	4.575	0.825	1.300
1985	6.30	4.300	0.650	1.350	7.05	4.750	0.950	1.350
1986–1989	6.45	4.250	0.700	1.500	7.15	4.750	0.950	1.450
1990–2010	6.45	4.250	0.700	1.500	7.65	5.100	1.100	1.450
2011 and after	7.45	5.100	0.850	1.500	7.65	5.100	1.100	1.450
Self-employed persons								
1977	7.90	6.185	0.815	0.900	7.90	6.185	0.815	0.900
1978	8.10	6.150	0.850	1.100	8.10	6.010	1.090	1.000
1979–1980	8.10	6.150	0.850	1.100	8.10	6.010	1.040	1.050
1981	8.35	6.080	0.920	1.350	9.30	6.7625	1.2375	1.300
1982–1984	8.35	6.080	0.920	1.350	9.35	6.8125	1.2375	1.300
1985	8.35	6.080	0.920	1.350	9.90	7.125	1.425	1.350
1986–1989	8.50	6.010	0.990	1.500	10.00	7.125	1.425	1.450
1990–2010	8.50	6.010	0.990	1.500	10.75	7.650	1.650	1.450
2011 and after	8.50	6.000	1.000	1.500	10.75	7.650	1.650	1.450

(Continued on page 480)

Table 10-2 (Continued)

Taxable earnings base		
Year	Prior law	New law
1977	$16,500	$16,500
1978	17,700	17,700
1979	18,900	22,900
1980	20,400	25,900
1981	21,900	29,700
1982	23,700	32,100
1983	25,800	34,800

Source: Adapted from *Economic Report of the President, January, 1978,* 1978, pp. 235–236.

that replacement rates—benefits as a percentage of preretirement earnings— could increase faster or more slowly than average wages in general. Under prevailing economic projections, replacement rates were predicted to rise faster than average wages in the future. To stabilize these rates, the amended law provided for a new, or "decoupled," basis of future calculation of benefits targeted on a replacement level about 5 percent below that which otherwise would have prevailed.[9] The change, which eliminates the close sensitivity of projected benefit levels to assumptions about inflation and real wage growth, "would stabilize initial benefit levels for a 65-year old retiree who always earned the average wage at about 42 percent of earnings in the year prior to retirement."[10] Most important, this results in roughly a 50 percent reduction in the long-term trust fund deficit.

An alternative treatment of social security would be to fund the system out of general tax revenues instead of relying on the present pay-as-you-go method. This issue has become more important in light of the rising ratio of recipients of benefits to workers contributing funds and the slowdown in economic growth. General tax funding of social security has long been opposed in the United States, but it may become more palatable to policy makers if the aforementioned pressures on the system continue to mount and if voters' resistance to the expanded payroll tax base and tax rates continues to grow. One student of this subject recommends removal of the welfare component from social security—the minimum income guarantee and allowances for dependents—and its funding as a separate program out of general revenues. In that case, social security would revert to the original concept embodied in the 1935 legislation, which was a pensionlike program financed by employers' and employees' contributions collected by a payroll tax.[11]

Social Security in Other Nations How does the system of social security in the United States compare with systems in existence elsewhere in the world? In general, it is less comprehensive and offers lower benefits than most others, though this depends upon the type of benefit being considered. This conclusion is supported by the data in Table 10-3, which shows retirement income allow-

Table 10-3 Retirement Income[1] of a Married Couple, 1975, for Selected Countries, Percent

Country	Gross income comparison			Net income comparison		
	Retirement Income in % of final earnings before deduction of taxes and social security contributions[2]			Retirement income in % of final earnings after deduction of taxes and social security contributions[3]		
	Income category 1 (=100%) (1)	Income category 2 (=150%) (2)	Income category 3 (=250%) (3)	Income category 1 (=100%) (4)	Income category 2 (=150%) (5)	Income category 3 (=250%) (6)
Belgium[4]	46.8	42.9	39.7	60.6	58.1	56.3
West Germany[4]	62.6	60.5	39.3	84.3	84.3	55.7
Finland	78.9	55.7	38.9	95.6	72.5	52.0
United Kingdom	59.1	56.1	63.8	81.6	67.7	64.5
Canada[4]	53.1	35.5	21.3	62.1	44.5	29.2
Netherlands[4]	55.5	37.0	22.2	80.4	53.2	35.2
Austria[4]	79.9	77.2	46.3	90.5	89.6	56.0
Sweden	104.1	81.5	58.2	131.6	103.8	80.2
Switzerland	82.6	76.0	45.6	95.6	91.7	57.6
United States[4]	60.4	47.2	29.1	71.4	59.2	38.6

[1] As a rule, this includes the basic pension of the statutory social-security scheme, complementary retirement benefits from additional social insurance, and/or company-provided pension schemes as well as welfare benefits. The pension computation is based on three different income categories.

[2] Gross pension income as percentage of final gross earnings.

[3] Net pension income as percentage of final net earnings.

[4] Not including retirement benefits of a company-provided pension scheme. Less than one-half of the labor force receives private pension benefits.

Source: Adapted from *Social Security in Ten Industrial Nations*, Union Bank of Switzerland, Economic Research Department, Zurich, April 1977, p. 9.

ances for a married couple in ten industrialized nations in 1975, expressed as a proportion of preretirement earnings before and after taxes at three different levels of income.[12]

Observe that in 1975 a Swedish couple earning the average national income before retirement received 104 percent of their gross earnings after retirement (column 1). No other country approaches Sweden in the generosity of its social security benefits, but several provide payments to recipients that exceed three-quarters of their preretirement income. The United States is in about the middle of this list of nations, permitting a couple with average national earnings to receive about 60 percent of that income level after retirement. Interestingly, the system of social security in the United States is less generous to couples with higher incomes than all but two of the systems of the other countries—Canada and the Netherlands—listed in Table 10-3 (columns 2 and 3). When retirement income is expressed as a proportion of after-tax, preretirement earnings, the United States drops farther down the list in terms of benefits provided to recipients (columns 4, 5, and 6). To some extent, this reflects the higher income tax levels generally prevailing in other nations, which yield lower ratios of disposable personal income to gross income (but higher ratios of retirement income to disposable personal income) than in the United States. Incidentally, the age of qualification for retirement benefits in all these countries is 65 for men and varies between 60 and 65 for women. Early retirement is permitted in only half of these nations, typically at age 60.

Concerning survivors' benefits, the United States turns out to be more generous in terms of percentage payments than most other industrialized nations, though this varies by level of family earnings and is truer when benefits are related to before-tax than to after-tax earnings. As to disability benefits, the United States trails all other nations but Canada and the Netherlands in its percentage payments. Eight of the ten countries listed in Table 10-3 provide disability benefits for accident victims and their families that exceed 100 percent of after-tax earnings, with Austria's percentage benefit levels dwarfing all others. Publicly provided medical benefits are higher in virtually all these nations than in the United States, which is not unexpected since they all have some type of national health insurance. However, this disparity would probably be much smaller if proper account was taken of the medical benefits available to United States citizens under the Medicare and Medicaid programs. Still, the United States remains the only major industrialized nation without such a plan, though several schemes have been proposed in Congress.[13]

The opposition to national health insurance in this country is based in part on a fear of socialized medicine and, more generally, a fear of the advancing welfare state, which, critics charge, is inconsistent with free market capitalism. Other opponents, however, are less concerned with the ideological aspects of national health insurance than with its costs. They worry that a national health insurance plan, if adopted, would add to rapidly rising costs of medical care and to economywide inflation. The result would be a more inefficient allocation of resources and the increased subsidization of some citizens by others. The arguments are similar to those heard in the mid-1960s debate about Medicare, but whether the United States will move to adopt national health insurance in a less stable economic environment than prevailed in the 1960s is uncertain. The debate over this issue is virtually certain to continue, however, even if legislative action on it is not imminent. In this regard, it is important to recognize that medical benefits available under Medicare and Medicaid reduce the gap between the United States and other nations insofar as health care protection is concerned.

If social security benefit levels in the United States (relative to preretirement earnings) are below those existing in most other countries, then so too are the taxes required to finance this nation's social insurance system. Remember that, in most of the countries discussed here, social security is financed by a combination of general tax revenues and payroll contributions. In 1975, income taxes and social security contributions totaled 12.5 percent of gross earnings for a four-person family earning the national average income, which ranked this country with Austria at the bottom of the list of nations.[14] In four countries, such taxes and contributions exceeded 20 percent of gross earnings, falling just short of 30 percent in the Netherlands and Sweden. Indeed, for a high- rather than an average-income family in either of those two nations, the rate rises to almost 50 percent.

But regardless of the differences in their benefit levels, scope of coverage, or method of financing, the industrialized nations of the world face a common problem with their social security systems: actual or potential deficits in funding. As Figure 10-2 illustrates, in 1977 deficits existed in the social security systems of Italy, West Germany, the United States, and France, and they ranged between 0.3 percent and 10 percent of all payments made into the respective systems. Note that these deficits are reported on an annual rather than an actuarial basis; the latter was estimated to be about $2 trillion in the United States prior to the 1977 amendments to the Social Security Act. The deficits have developed despite substantial increases in taxes and in rates of social security contributions by employers and employees, increases which, apart from their other consequences, "can exert a negative impact on employment and economic growth either through raising the rate of inflation . . . or . . . by impairing capital spending activity."[15]

The underlying forces giving rise to such deficits are also the same across the industrialized nations. Working people are retiring earlier, living longer, and receiving larger pensions, while high unemployment in western Europe and North America particularly contributes to the problem of insufficient numbers of worker-contributors to keep social security systems solvent. Moreover, the difficulty will probably be exacerbated by the recent decline in birthrates, as sketched out in Chapter 1.

In Switzerland, for example, the proportion of pensioners to contributors is projected to rise from about 28 percent in 1975 to more than 50 percent in the year 2030, on the basis of assumptions of further declining birthrates and a steady increase in life expectancy.[16] If such assumptions are in fact borne out,

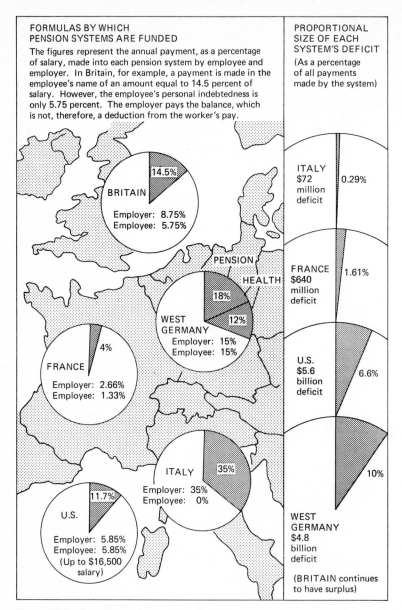

FORMULAS BY WHICH
PENSION SYSTEMS ARE FUNDED

The figures represent the annual payment, as a percentage
of salary, made into each pension system by employee and
employer. In Britain, for example, a payment is made in the
employee's name of an amount equal to 14.5 percent of
salary. However, the employee's personal indebtedness is
only 5.75 percent. The employer pays the balance, which
is not, therefore, a deduction from the worker's pay.

PROPORTIONAL
SIZE OF EACH
SYSTEM'S DEFICIT

(As a percentage
of all payments
made by the system)

14.5%
BRITAIN
Employer: 8.75%
Employee: 5.75%

PENSION
HEALTH
18%
WEST
GERMANY
Employer: 15%
Employee: 15%
12%

4%
FRANCE
Employer: 2.66%
Employee: 1.33%

ITALY 35%
Employer: 35%
Employee: 0%

11.7%
U.S.
Employer: 5.85%
Employee: 5.85%
(Up to $16,500
salary)

ITALY
$72
million
deficit
0.29%

FRANCE
$640
million
deficit
1.61%

U.S.
$5.6
billion
deficit
6.6%

10%

WEST
GERMANY
$4.8
billion
deficit

(BRITAIN continues
to have surplus)

Figure 10-2 Social security systems; funding sources and fund balances. (*Source:* The New
York Times, *May 17, 1977, p. 1.*)

the contribution *rate* (i.e., the payroll tax on employers and employees) to the
social security system in that country, which is presently 8.5 percent, would
have to double by the year 2030. When the problematic nature of future economic growth and the continued rise in the costs of health care are also considered, it is no mere exercise in hyperbole to describe the financing and the

mounting deficits in social security systems around the world as "one of the most critical political and economic issues" of the next several decades.[17] In this respect, the 1977 amendments to the Social Security Act may contain important lessons for other nations, though the many differences between American and foreign systems limit the transfer of social insurance policy across industrialized countries.

Private Pension and Benefit Programs

The social security system is a public effort to provide old-age pensions and financial assistance of various types to retirees. Since 1949, however, there have emerged a very large number of private pensions and other employee-benefits plans instituted by individual companies or employers' associations. Some of these, especially the earliest ones, developed in response to the demands of organized labor, while others were instituted in order to avoid unionization. Today, pension plans are common to both the union and the nonunion sectors, reflecting this nation's mix of private initiatives and social security, rather than one national system of retirement income. Moreover, separate retirement plans are in effect for railroad workers and for many state and local government employees, further illustrating the piecemeal—pluralist—approach to social security in the United States.

One of the most notable collectively bargained pension systems to come into existence before 1949 was in the coal industry, where a 1946 agreement provided for an employer-financed welfare and retirement fund to which contributions were made on the basis of a royalty of so many cents per ton of coal mined. The Supreme Court's 1949 decision in the *Inland Steel* case sustained the view of the NLRB that pensions were a bargainable item; from that point on, employers' resistance to private pension plans fell off, and such plans began to mushroom. So too did other employee-benefit plans, including those covering life insurance and death benefits, hospitalization and major medical expenses, and long-term disabilities.

The data in Table 10-4 show the expansion of these employee-benefit plans over the period 1950–1975. By the mid-1970s, almost three-fourths of all wage and salary workers were covered by life insurance and death-benefit plans, 70 percent by hospitalization plans, and over one-third by "major medical" plans. Among workers in private industry in 1975, roughly 30 million, or 44 percent of the total, were covered by retirement plans, a threefold increase over 1950. Observe that all these employee-benefit plans grew rapidly during the 1950s, but considerably less rapidly in the 1960s and 1970s, with the exception of coverage for major medical expenses. As one authority notes: "Since 1970, this deceleration [in the growth rate of employee-benefit plans] has continued, with coverage barely keeping ahead of the growth in the labor force, except for life insurance and long-term disability."[18]

In the area of health, the trend has been toward providing broadened care for those already having some protection, rather than toward expanding coverage to include larger proportions of workers. In 1950, persons covered by hos-

Table 10-4 Estimated Number of Wage and Salary Workers Covered under Employee-Benefit Plans, by Type of Benefit, 1950–1975, Millions

| | All wage and salary workers | | | | | | | Wage and salary workers in private industry | | | | |
| | | | Hospitalization | | | | | Temporary disability including formal sick leave | | | | |
Year	Life insurance and death	Accidental death and dismemberment	Total	Written in compliance with law	Surgical	Regular medical	Major-medical expenses	Total	Written in compliance with law	Long-term disability	Supplemental unemployment	Retirement
1950	19.4	8.1	24.3	1.2	17.7	8.2		20.1	6.6			9.8
1951	20.8	9.5	27.1	1.4	21.7	10.7		21.7	6.8			10.8
1952	22.3	10.7	28.8	1.5	24.2	12.7	0.2	22.4	7.0			11.3
1953	24.2	11.8	31.0	1.5	26.9	15.8	0.5	23.4	7.0			12.6
1954	25.7	14.0	31.1	1.4	27.8	17.5	0.8	22.9	6.7			13.4
1955	28.1	15.6	32.8	1.4	30.2	20.2	2.2	23.5	6.8		1.0	14.2
1956	29.8	17.3	35.1	1.5	32.4	22.0	3.5	24.7	7.1		2.0	15.5
1957	31.2	18.4	36.4	1.6	34.2	23.9	4.9	24.9	7.2		1.9	16.7
1958	31.7	18.7	36.2	1.4	34.1	24.5	5.9	23.8	6.8		1.7	17.2
1959	33.5	19.7	37.2	1.5	35.4	26.1	7.2	24.4	6.9		1.9	18.2
1960	34.2	20.9	39.3	1.2	37.4	28.2	8.8	24.5	6.8		1.7	18.7
1961	35.5	21.3	39.9	1.1	38.0	29.8	10.3	24.6	6.8		1.9	19.2
1962	36.4	22.6	41.0	0.9	39.0	31.3	11.7	25.3	6.8		1.8	19.7
1963	37.8	24.7	42.6	0.3	40.8	33.3	13.2	23.6	6.2	0.7	1.8	20.3
1964	40.1	26.5	43.9	0.3	41.8	35.4	14.7	23.9	6.2	1.2	2.0	20.9
1965	41.9	28.4	45.7	0.3	43.4	38.2	16.6	24.5	6.4	1.9	2.1	21.8
1966	43.5	28.5	47.2	0.4	45.2	40.2	18.3	25.5	6.6	2.3	2.2	22.7
1967	45.7	30.4	48.7	0.4	47.0	42.5	20.2	26.0	6.7	3.7	2.2	24.3
1968	48.2	33.7	50.1	0.4	48.3	43.6	21.7	27.9	6.7	4.6	2.2	24.8
1969	49.0	36.5	52.1	0.4	50.6	46.1	23.4	29.4	6.9	5.5	2.2	26.0
1970	52.0	38.7	53.1	0.4	51.5	48.0	24.6	29.7	7.1	7.0	2.2	26.1
1971	53.5	39.2	53.2	0.4	51.7	48.3	25.7	30.1	6.9	8.0	2.2	26.4
1972	55.6	40.7	54.2	0.4	52.9	49.4	26.4	31.3	7.1	9.5	2.0	27.5
1973	57.8	42.7	56.8	0.4	55.4	53.7	27.6	32.0	7.2	10.6	2.1	29.2
1974	60.6	44.3	57.6	0.4	56.1	54.9	28.2	31.7	7.0	11.1	1.9	29.8
1975	62.4	46.5	58.2	0.4	56.6	56.1	29.6	31.1	7.0	11.5	1.9	30.3

Source: Adapted from Alfred M. Skolnik, "Twenty-five Years of Employee-Benefit Plans," Social Security Bulletin, 39:5 (1976), and Martha R. Yohalem, "Employee-Benefit Plans, 1975," Social Security Bulletin, 40:20 (1977).

pitalization plans were much less likely to have insurance for surgery and medical expenses. By the mid-1970s, that gap was almost totally closed, and, in addition, almost 30 million workers or 40 percent of the labor sector had major medical insurance. Long-term-disability insurance for privately employed workers began to emerge in the mid-1960s, and over the next decade was extended to 11 percent of the labor force. Supplemental unemployment benefits are still a rarity on the American scene, being available to only 2 percent of wage and salary workers in private industry who work almost exclusively in unionized settings.

In recent years, the most rapid growth of employee-benefit plans has occurred in state and local governments.[19] For example, among full-time state and local government employees, the number with life insurance quadrupled to 4 million between the early 1960s and early 1970s, or almost half of that sector's work force. Over the same period, the number of persons with some form of health insurance increased from under 2 million to almost 6 million, or from one out of three to two out of three employees in state and local governments. This is in keeping with the recent rapid growth of public employment, public payrolls, and public employee unionization in the United States, as described earlier in this book.

Contributions made by workers and employers to employee-benefit plans rose from $3 billion in 1950 to $67.3 billion in 1975.[20] The average annual growth rate of such contributions was 12.3 between 1950 and 1960, slackened off to 10.8 percent during the 1960s, and rose to about 14 percent between 1970 and 1975. The experience of the 1970s reflects the effects of both inflation and expanded coverage. As to benefits paid out under these plans, they increased on the average by 15.6 percent annually during the 1950s, 12.8 percent during the 1960s, and 13 percent during the first half of the 1970s.

Health benefits now account for more than half of all outlays under employee-benefit plans, and retirement payments to privately employed workers for about 30 percent. To a very large extent, health benefits reflect rising hospital costs. Between 1970 and 1975 alone, the proportion of employees covered by cash indemnity policies providing hospital room-and-board benefits of $50 or more per day rose from 13 to 58 percent. Dental plans have been one of the most popular new forms of benefits. In 1975, about one-fifth of all employers had such plans. Coverage for care in a nursing home or extended-care facility is also a rapidly growing benefit, as is insurance for out-of-hospital prescription drugs. These types of health benefits are especially interesting in light of the aforementioned absence of national health insurance in the United States.

Despite the expansion of employee-benefit plans in the post-World War II era, most persons who are presently retired do not have access to retirement income from private pension plans and must rely on their social security benefits alone. This conclusion is supported by a recent longitudinal study of pension coverage and benefits emanating from employment on their longest jobs among a sample of workers who were retired in 1972.[21] Just under one-half of the men and just over one-fifth of the women employed as private wage and salary workers on their longest jobs were covered by pension plans on those jobs. Such coverage tended to be highest (1) for those employed in manufacturing or professional services, (2) for those who were professional operatives or clerical workers, (3) for those employed for 21 years or more on their longest job, (4) for those earning $7500 or above, and (5) for those still employed in the late 1960s. The rates of coverage for men and women were virtually identical.

In contrast to those who had been privately employed, more than 80 percent of all retired government workers had some type of pension coverage in 1972, with the proportion rising to 95 percent for former full-time federal employees.[22] More than half of the retired state and local government personnel had dual pension coverage under one or another civil service retirement system and under the OASDHI system. Interestingly, retired government employees with long service in this sample had substantially higher annual pension benefits than retired workers in the private sector. The figures for 1972 were $4290 and $2230 for men formerly employed in the public and private sectors, respectively, and $3650 versus $1200 for women. No matter what the sector of employment, however, the proportion of retirees receiving a pension increased steadily with years of service.

A major factor in the lack or loss of pension coverage for many retired workers, according to the aforementioned study, was the absence of vesting provisions or the presence of a very stringent vesting requirement.[23] The term "vesting" refers to an employee's nonforfeitable right or entitlement to pension benefits once he or she has worked for a sufficient period of time for a company that has a plan in effect. Another factor in the loss of pension coverage was the withdrawal by employees of their contributions to retirement plans upon termination of employment. Before 1974, the only federal legislation that dealt in any way with private pensions was the Landrum-Griffin Act, reviewed in Chapter 4. Its provisions, however, were limited to union members and attempted to protect from corruption their pension (and other) contributions into trust funds that were administered by labor organizations either alone or jointly with employers. To remedy the more widespread deficiencies in private pension plans and practices, Congress, in 1974, enacted the Employee Retirement Income Security Act (ERISA).

The Pension Reform Law　ERISA—or the pension reform law, as it is popularly known—represented the culmination of a decade-long effort to regulate and provide minimum standards for private retirement plans. A key provision of the law relates to vesting.[24] In adopting this provision, Congress attempted to respond to the complaints of individuals who had worked for many years for a company that had a pension plan, but who still had not qualified for a pension when they quit, were laid off, or retired. The law allows employers to choose from among a variety of vesting provisions, but under any of them the employee's right to pension benefits after a specified period of employment is assured.[25] The law also specifies minimum conditions of eligibility for new employees to participate in a pension plan; they must be at least 25 years of age and have served for 1 year. Additionally, and to help younger workers obtain pension benefits earlier, any employment after age 22 is to be counted in the determination of service to meet the vesting standard.

The pension reform law also sought to address the problem of workers whose pension benefits were jeopardized or eliminated by a plant or business shutdown.[26] It established the Pension Benefit Guarantee Corporation, to which employers with a pension plan must pay an annual premium so as to close any gap between a terminating plan's assets and the amount required to pay all vested benefits. The initial premium levels set by Congress are $1 per covered worker for single-employer plans and 50 cents per covered worker for multiemployer plans. A variety of safeguards in the law are intended to ensure covered workers the receipt of their pension benefits under terminated retirement plans. In this way, an employee's vested benefits continue even if a company's retirement plan folds.

Finally, the pension reform law provides some steps toward the eventual "portability" of retirement benefits—the ability of an individual to take pension credits established at one place of employment to a new job. We say "steps" advisedly because of the many administrative difficulties and the controversy associated with pension portability, factors which were cited in the congressional debate over this issue and which led to a rejection of proposals for comprehensive portability.[27] The present law requires employers to file with the Social Security Administration a record of all departing employees' vested benefits rights, information which the Administration will provide to employees upon their subsequent application for social security benefits. A departing employee is allowed to shift such rights or credits to an individual retirement account or to another plan with the agreement of the employer, and the Pension Benefit Guarantee Corporation will assist individuals and specific employee-benefit plans to achieve greater portability. Hence, this provision of the law provides for strictly voluntary arrangements for pension portability. Observe that social security (OASDHI) is thus superior to private pension plans as regards the problems of vesting, bankruptcy, and portability.

ERISA is too new a piece of legislation for much evidence to have accumulated about its impact on the areas discussed above or on the financial management of private retirement plans with which it also seeks to deal. The law itself is controversial, with many employers, especially those in small businesses, complaining long and loud about the added financial and administrative burdens which the statute imposes on them. Clearly, corporate enterprises have proceeded in the post-ERISA period to reorganize their personnel management staffs to better respond to the federal regulation of private pension plans.[28] Whether the law will prove to be effective or not, few would deny the importance of the problems it attempts to address, the most fundamental of which is the ability of retired workers to live their later years in some financial security, not totally dependent upon the federal system of social insurance. This, too, is a problem in no way confined to the United States.

WORKERS' COMPENSATION

Concern for work-related deaths, injuries, and illnesses in the United States has existed since the industrial revolution. Under common-law doctrine, a worker could sue his or her employer for damages in the civil courts, but had to prove that the injury was due to the employer's negligence in order to obtain a favorable judgment. The many defenses available to employers plus the inability of most workers to underwrite a protracted court battle meant that employees rarely collected money damages for work-related injuries under the common law.[29] Workers were killed or crippled by industrial mishaps for which they were not responsible in any meaningful sense, and yet they or their survivors were often thrown on charity. There was no charge of shiftlessness made against those injured at work, as there was against the unemployed; nevertheless, sudden catastrophes could strike workers and bring economic ruin to them and their families. And not much was changed by subsequent efforts to shift the burden of proof of responsibility from workers to employers, given the increasingly complex operations of industrial organizations, which made it difficult to pinpoint blame for a work-related injury.

In light of these developments, a new approach to the problem of accidents was pioneered in Europe: the "no fault" principle of compensation without respect to responsibility. First in Germany (in 1883) and then in England (in 1897), this principle was incorporated into workers' compensation laws, as they came to be known, which quickly spread to other European countries and eventually to the United States. The first such law in this country was enacted in 1908 for certain federal employees engaged in hazardous work; by 1920 all but six states had adopted similar legislation directed at privately employed workers. These laws were based on the view that injuries sustained on the job were a part of the productive process and that their costs were a proper charge against the expense of production.

Today, workers' compensation laws are found in every state in the Union. Unlike the basic social security program and national labor laws, for which administrative enforcement responsibility rests with the federal sector, workers' compensation systems are dominated by state governments, though some responsibilities for overseeing them are shared with the federal government. However, these arrangements and other aspects of workers' compensation vary considerably across the states. For example, some state laws exempt small employers or specific sectors and particular organizations, such as agriculture, government, and nonprofit employers from coverage, while others limit workers' compensation laws to "hazardous" occupations. Many such laws remain elective in that employers may choose to comply with them or not (though relatively few reject coverage since that leaves them without common-law defenses against suits by employees). Consequently, the proportion of wage and salary workers covered by workers' compensation legislation varies from less than two-thirds in some states to 95 percent or more in others.[30] The proportion of covered employees rose consistently during the early and middle 1970's, reaching 88.5 percent in 1976, or about 69 million workers.[31]

Workers' compensation is financed by employers, as might be expected of a system that presumes injuries sustained at work to be an expense of production. No doubt, some of these costs are passed on to the consumer in the form of higher prices, and perhaps to employees in the form of lower wages. Of course, employers may seek to minimize the costs of workers' compensation by improving safety conditions, engaging in preventive maintenance, and the like. For many employers, such practices and related expenditures became mandatory instead of voluntary with passage in 1970 of the federal Occupational Safety and Health Act (OSHA), about which more will be said later.

Plans devised by states and employers to finance the costs of workers' compensation also vary widely. In most states, employers can insure themselves against accidents with commercial insurance carriers or qualify as self-insurers if they can prove the ability to carry their own risk. In some areas, though, employers must insure with an exclusive state fund, and in still other places such a fund is competitive with private carriers. A federally financed and operated system provides protection to employees in the federal sector. As shown in Table 10-5, the cost of workers' compensation programs to employers generally hovered around 1 percent of total payroll expenditures to the late 1960s, but it has increased in recent years. In 1976, it reached 1.5 percent of all payroll expenditures, reflecting an economywide inflationary spurt but also expanded coverage and benefit provisions under state laws.

Workers' compensation benefits include periodic cash payments, lump-sum payments, medical services to the worker during a period of disability, and

Table 10-5 Statistics on Workers' Compensation Laws in Selected Years, 1940–1977

Year	Benefit payments (in millions)			Benefits as percent of payroll in covered employment	Total cost to employers as percent of payroll in covered employment[1]
	Total	Medical and hospitalization payments	Compensation for wage loss		
1940	$256	$95	$161	0.72	1.19
1946	$434	$140	$294	0.54	0.91
1948	$534	$175	$359	0.51	0.96
1950	$615	$200	$415	0.54	0.89
1955	$916	$325	$591	0.55	0.91
1960	$1295	$435	$860	0.59	0.93
1964	$1705	$565	$1140	0.62	1.00
1967	$2134	$725	$1409	0.63	1.07
1970	$2927	$1050	$1877	0.68	1.13
1973	$5064	$1430	$3634	0.71	1.19
1976	$7463	$2330	$5133	0.88	1.48
1977	$8660	$2770	$5890	N.A.	N.A.

[1] Total cost includes benefit costs plus the overhead costs that employers pay to insure or self-insure the risk of work injury. Included in overhead are such expenses as payroll auditing, claims investigation, legal services, and general administration, plus (in insurance provided by commercial carriers) commissions and brokerage fees, taxes, and profit.
Source: Adapted from *Social Security Bulletin*, various issues to March 1979, passim.

death and funeral benefits to the worker's survivors. Also included are payments to coal miners who suffer from the disease known as black lung. These were authorized by the Federal Coal Mine Health and Safety Act of 1969, with the conditions for benefit payments liberalized thereafter. The benefit structure and standards for qualification were modified again in 1971 with passage of the Black Lung Benefits Reform Act, which was intended to assure miners and their survivors compensation for disability or death resulting from that disease.

Variations in workers' compensation benefits among states are large and are the subject of considerable criticism by students of American social insurance policies. Some states set stringent limits on the amount and duration of workers' compensation payments that may be offered to injured or sick employees, while others have more liberal provisions. States in the south and the midwest have been more restrictive in these respects than states in the western and northeastern regions. Most states liberalized their workers' compensation benefits in the 1970s, and this is reflected in the rapid rise of total benefit payments from \$3.0 billion in 1970 to \$7.5 billion in 1976 (Table 10-5). Of the latter amount, \$2.3 billion was in the form of medical and hospitalization payments, and \$5.1 billion was in the form of compensation for lost wages to disabled workers (\$4.3 billion) and their survivors (\$0.8 billion). Recipients of workers' compensation tend more than other experienced members of the labor force to be older, to be less well educated, to be male heads of households, and to be employed as blue-collar workers in manufacturing organizations. Most of these recipients worked only part of the year, and about one-eighth did no work at all—were totally disabled—during the year, according to a 1973 special Current Population Survey report.[32]

Protection of Workers and Federal Standards

Among the most controversial aspects of state workers' compensation laws is their ability—inability, according to some—to replace a worker's wages that are lost as a result of a disability incurred while at work. The intent of most of the laws is to replace, after a waiting period, from three-fifths to two-thirds of a worker's weekly wage while he or she is temporarily disabled. Most states have raised their statutory maximum benefits, especially during the 1970s. This development was in part a response to the recommendation of the National Commission on State Workmen's Compensation Laws, issued in 1972, which called for a flexible maximum weekly benefit that would automatically adjust to changes in a state's average weekly wage.[33] A maximum equivalent to 100 percent of the statewide average weekly wage was proposed, meaning that a worker whose wage was 50 percent above the average would receive replacement payments at a rate of $66^{2}/_{3}$ percent (100/150).

By 1976, seven states permitted workers' compensation payments of up to 100 percent of the average weekly wage, several others had substantially raised their benefit-wage formulas, and 80 percent were operating with flexible maximum-payment provisions.[34] But because most states remain far short of the rule of "100 percent of average weekly wage," maximum benefits paid by them "are not high enough to allow the statutory percentages to be effective for most workers."[35] Thus, in the mid-1970s, actual workers' compensation payments made to temporarily disabled employees amounted to about 60 percent of the average weekly wage, and about 10 percentage points higher in states that permitted allowances for dependents.

The aggregate percentage is considerably lower, at about the 40 percent level, with respect to the replacement rate of workers' compensation payments made to permanently disabled workers and, in the case of death, to their survivors. Interestingly, the annual average number of workdays for which disabled workers drew workers' compensation benefits increased steadily during the 1970s, rising from 13 days in 1971 to a bit more than 17 days in 1976. Taken together, these factors help us understand the recent pattern of rapidly rising workers' compensation benefits, which amounted to 0.88 percent of total covered payroll in 1976. Total program costs in that year, including benefits paid and administrative expenditures, were about $11 billion.

Note, however, that these aggregate data and trends should not lead us to overlook the remaining shortcomings of the nation's system for workers' compensation. In particular, the absence of federal standards for state systems is a major failing, even if some states were spurred to improve their workers' compensation laws in the 1970s by the aforementioned report of the National Commission on State Workmen's Compensation Laws. The principal author of that report stated in 1972 that "state workmen's compensation laws are in general neither adequate nor equitable"; in 1976, he wrote that "the changes in state law have been, in my view, impressive but insufficient. Thus a national problem still exists."[36]

The problem is reflected in such anomalies as a worker in a small plant or on a farm not being covered by a state workers' compensation law, while comparable workers in larger establishments are covered; a worker in a small plant covered in one state but not in another; and the receipt of, say, $25,000 for the loss of an eye due to a work-related injury in one state but of only $5000 in another state. While these examples may seem compelling in support of federal standards, the competition among states and their officials to attract industry and jobs lends contrary support for state control of workers' compensation programs. These arguments are frequently made under the guise of holding costs down, but Table 10-5 shows that even with recent increases, the costs of workers' compensation are only 1.5 percent of total payroll expenditures. Thus, perhaps it is political factors more than cost or market factors that account for the continued resistance to federal standards for workers' compensation, a resistance which makes "federal involvement for at least the next few years . . . unlikely."[37]

But if federal standards have not yet come to govern workers' compensation programs, they nevertheless have developed elsewhere in relation to work-related accidents and disabilities. Payments to workers suffering from black lung and to the survivors of those who died from it resulted from the 1969 federal legislation and later amendments; such payments totaled about $1 billion in 1976. The federal OASDHI system, reviewed earlier, provides monthly cash benefits to severely disabled workers under the disability insurance component of that program. Similarly, disability benefits are paid to persons who qualify for them under the supplementary security income program. Recipients of supplementary security income must meet a means test, while recipients of disability insurance must show an inability to engage in substantial gainful activity—that is, they must be permanently and totally disabled.

There are still other programs that provide disability payments to workers injured on the job. Indeed, Berkowitz estimates that more than eighty such programs are in existence and that they made total expenditures for income maintenance and support and for medical and other direct services aimed at the disabled of about $83 billion in 1973.[38] Workers' compensation benefits are thus but a small part of total disability expenditures in the United States. Nevertheless, a typical injured worker who received disability benefits in the mid-1970s under workers' compensation laws did better financially than a person enrolled in an alternative program, some of which, such as disability insurance, are purposively skewed in favor of low-wage earners. For this reason, then, several students of the subject conclude that workers' compensation should not be integrated into a general system for coverage of disabilities. As one puts it: "To argue that the victims of work accidents ought to be treated in the same way as those who qualify for the general [disability insurance] provisions is to ignore any special claims that the victims of work accidents have arising from their inability to sue in the event of negligence."[39] From this perspective, federal standards for workers' compensation are not necessarily desirable.

The Occupational Safety and Health Act   In 1970, Congress passed the Occupational Safety and Health Act (OSHA), which established the principle of federal authority over practices in the workplace related to these issues. Three new federal agencies were established under OSHA: the Occupational Safety and Health Administration in the Department of Labor; the National Institute of Occupational Safety and Health (NIOSH) in the Department of Health, Education, and Welfare; and an independent Occupational Safety and Health Review Commission. The first two bodies are empowered to conduct inspections and investigations under the federal law, while the third handles appeals by employers concerning federal actions and decisions in this area. By some interpretations, OSHA preempts the role of state governments in regulating safety and health at the workplace, but the act permits states to establish and enforce their own occupational safety and health plans, provided that these are at least as effective as the federal program. To qualify, state plans must be submitted for approval to the Occupational Safety and Health Administration.

Clearly, OSHA was enacted because of growing worries about industrial practices which, however unintentionally, have a deleterious effect on the short- and long-term health of American workers. Impetus for the legislation developed in part out of the larger, more general concern particularly evident in the later 1960s for environmental preservation and pollution control. That is, control of the working environment and of industrial practices which "pollute the health" of the labor sector is the principal focus of OSHA.

Partly because of the difficulty of relating a worker's health to industrial conditions apart from other contributing factors, no precise estimate is available of deaths, major illnesses, and minor injuries resulting from conditions in the workplace. A widely used estimate of 14,000 work-related deaths in 1972 is itself controversial, and reports of workers' compensation such as that in Table 10-5 remain one of the few systematic sources of data on work-related injuries in the United States.[40] Nevertheless, it is probable that the discovery of a particularly virulent work-related injury, illness, or disease—asbestosis, black lung, or skin cancer, for example—maintains or strengthens support for governmentally regulated practices concerning safety and health at the workplace in a way that large bodies of aggregate data could not. Particularly controversial in all this are concealed work hazards, that is, those which are known to management but not to workers or the public. One way in which such hazards may become better known is for the federal government to conduct surprise inspections of industrial plants and facilities without having first to obtain search warrants from the courts. However, a Supreme Court decision handed down in 1978 prohibited the Occupational Safety and Health Administration from conducting such "warrantless" inspections.[41] The ruling is regarded by some supporters of stronger regulations concerning safety and health at the workplace as imperiling compliance with the 1974 legislation, although that is arguable in view of the Court's support of a speedy procedure to obtain warrants in connection with OSHA investigations.

From the beginning, the enforcement of OSHA by federal agencies has been subject to considerable criticism. Employers decry the burden of meeting federal safety and health regulations, especially when these are claimed to make production unprofitable or to reflect inspectors' lack of knowledge of industrial processes. Organized labor has criticized some OSHA regulations as too stringent when they lead to job reductions and thus reduced employment of union members. At the same time, many organized and unorganized workers criticize the federal government for laxity in enforcing OSHA standards, for ignoring medical evidence about injuries sustained at the workplace, and for too willingly accommodating state officials in the formation of their own occupational safety and health plans. And all parties seem to take the Occupational Safety and Health Administration to task for its alleged preoccupation with minor, nit-picking rules and procedures.[42]

One needn't overlook the strong elements of self-interest in these criticisms to recognize that some of them are justified. Indeed, Secretary of Labor Ray Marshall, in his first year in office, directed the Occupational Safety and Health Administration to eliminate "more than 1,100 provisions of the OSHA safety regulations that have little or no bearing on worker health and safety."[43] Moreover, it is hardly surprising that new federal agencies charged with administering a comprehensive and innovative piece of legislation, but without major powers of enforcement or sizable staffs should encounter resistance from employers and workers or proceed in a tentative, developmental way to form a strategy for enforcement. What is perhaps most instructive about OSHA, however, is the attempt to apply federal standards to the issue of health and safety at the workplace rather than permitting states the latitude to address this concern on their own. In this regard, it contrasts notably with the experience to date under workers' compensation laws, which are themselves concerned with industrial safety and health. This reflects the piecemeal approach generally characteristic of American policies of social insurance and regulation of work practices.

UNEMPLOYMENT INSURANCE

While social security is designed principally to provide income supports during retirement and while workers' compensation is intended to counter loss of wages resulting from work-related disabilities, unemployment insurance seeks to sustain workers economically during periods when they are involuntarily out of work.[44]

In the United States today, almost all workers who are laid off by their employers may qualify for receipt of unemployment insurance benefits. The guiding federal provision was included as Title III of the Social Security Act of 1935 and has been amended several times since then. Fears by Congress that the entire act might be declared unconstitutional led to setting up the unemployment insurance program under the administration of the separate states and the District of Columbia. The federal government limited itself to establishing certain overall standards to which the states had to adhere, but the states were allowed considerable latitude in determining the substantive details of their respective programs.

The federal government ensures compliance with its minimum standards through its taxing powers. It imposes on most employers a tax which, beginning in 1972, amounts to 3.4 percent of the first $6000 of each employee's earnings. Against this, however, the employer is permitted to offset any amount up to 2.7 percent of taxable payroll which is paid to a state unemployment compensation fund meeting federal standards. This portion of the tax is used only to pay benefits, with the remaining 0.7 percent used for federal and state administrative expenses.[45] A state thus has nothing to gain by refusing to join the federal system, since all covered employers would still have to pay the federal tax, and it has much to lose, since all this tax insurance would flow out of the state, whose local workers would be ineligible for any benefits. Given this "choice," every state understandably has elected to establish an unemployment insurance program.

The actual contributions of individual employers to state unemployment insurance funds may vary considerably from the 2.7 percent standard for taxable payroll. This is so because federal law permits each state to establish an "experience rating" in determining the tax liability of employers. Therefore, each employer's tax rate will vary on the basis of the firm's employment experience, the idea clearly being to offer an incentive to an employer to reduce unemployment by stabilizing the size of the work force. Under the most favorable conditions, when unemployment insurance reserve funds are high and unemployment itself is low, actual rates are at or near zero for employers in many states. Under the least favorable conditions, experience ratings rise, and average tax rates for all employers in a state often exceed 4 percent and have gone as high as 6.6 percent. Under normal or moderate economic conditions, tax rates fall between these extremes and are frequently under 2.7 percent in many areas. In mid-1977, the average rate of contribution for employers in all states and the District of Columbia was just under 3.0 percent of taxable payrolls and, because of the ceiling on the taxable wage base, was only about 1.3 percent of total payrolls.[46]

Coverage and Eligibility

Over the years, unemployment insurance has been extended to most of the labor sector. Whereas some 85 percent of the work force was covered in 1975, legislative amendments adopted the next year led the Department of Labor to estimate that, by mid-1978, some 87 million jobs, or 97 percent of all wage and salary employment, were covered by the federal-state unemployment insurance program.[47] In mid-1977, state programs of unemployment insurance covered roughly 71.5 million privately employed workers, while some 2.9 million federal employees were covered by a separate program of unemployment compensation. Other systems are provided for railroad workers and persons leaving the armed services.

Recent amendments to the federal law have extended unemployment insurance coverage to employees who worked in previously excluded sectors. For example, in 1972, employment in small firms, nonprofit organizations, state hospitals, and state institutions of higher education was brought under coverage of the law. In 1978, an amendment to the law became effective which required state insurance programs to cover some—but only some—employment in agriculture and domestic service and nearly all employment in state and local governments. Earlier, a few states had extended coverage to portions of these sectors, but the actions were entirely voluntary and sporadic. The amendment was sought to systematize and extend unemployment insurance to these sectors. Note, however, that, except in four states, most domestic employment in private homes remains excluded from coverage, as does casual labor that is not directly related to an employer's trade or business. Agriculture is an example of an industry in which casual labor is widely used, but each state is permitted to define such labor for itself, and this gives the states some control over the scope of unemployment insurance coverage for this type of worker.

To be eligible for unemployment benefits in most states, a worker must have earned a certain minimum amount—say, $1,200—in the 1-year base period preceding his or her claim. This period may be the preceding 52 weeks, but more often it is the first four of the last five completed calendar quarters. Earnings typically are required to be distributed over two or more of the quarters in the base period. A few states have a flat earnings standard to qualify for unemployment insurance benefits irrespective of the amount or spread of employment. Fourteen states have formulas for qualification based on weeks of employment; this ranges from 14 to 20 weeks, and in each of the weeks a minimum amount of earnings is required of the claimant. Fulfillment of only a minimum earnings or employment requirement usually restricts the duration of benefits.

These requirements, which vary from state to state, have the common purpose of testing a claimant's attachment to the work force so that benefits will be reserved for genuine workers and not made available to those looking for a handout. This is a laudable goal, to be sure, but it requires those who qualify for benefits to have been recently employed, and it does not suitably accommodate part-time workers, temporary and permanent, who have become more numerous in recent years. The consequence is to exclude from unemployment insurance coverage some of the employed and the unemployed.

Other rules concerning eligibility reflect a similar problem: how to make benefits available to the majority of workers who "deserve" them while denying benefits to those who do not, without applying a means test or psychoanalyzing each claimant to determine whether he or she "honestly" wants to work. No total resolution of this problem, in the sense of satisfying both critics and supporters of the unemployment insurance system, is available, but the following describes the general pattern of compromises that has emerged over the years:

> All states require that for a claimant to receive benefits he must be able to work and must be available for work. . . . One evidence of ability to work is the filing of claims and registration for work at a public employment office. Most State agencies also require that the unemployed worker make a job-seeking effort independent of the agency's effort in order to qualify for benefits. . . .
>
> The major causes of disqualification for benefits are voluntary separations from work without good cause; discharges for misconduct connected with the work; refusal, without good cause, to apply for or accept suitable work; and unemployment due to a labor dispute. In all jurisdictions, disqualification serves at least to delay a worker's receipt of benefits. The disqualification may be for a specific period [such as 8 weeks] . . . or for the entire period of unemployment following the disqualifying act. Some states not only postpone the payment of benefits but also reduce the amount due to the claimant.[48]

These requirements and limitations are not peculiar to the United States; they are found in unemployment insurance systems around the world.[49] What they reflect is a picture of a "model" claimant: a good worker who has lost a job through no fault of his or her own (for example, because the employer went out of business, relocated, or experienced a seasonal decline in sales), who is conscientiously looking for another job, and who deserves something more than charity to support a family for the few weeks that it takes to find other work. But what if some cases don't quite fit this model? How should they be handled?

Consider, for example, the issue of "good cause" for quitting. No one wants to reward the person who quits a job in order to draw unemployment insurance rather than work for a living, but what if a wife or husband leaves a job to follow a spouse to another city where he or she has found work? What if a black worker quits a job in disgust because the supervisor uses racial slurs, or what if a female office worker leaves her job rather than tolerate the personal advances of her male boss? What of the pregnant woman who quits her job to bear a child but plans to resume work shortly after the child is born? And, even if these are all good causes for quitting, how are the facts in disputed cases to be uncovered, since we know that some workers bend the truth to win benefits and that some employers do the same to keep their experience rating down?

Similarly, the refusal of "unsuitable work" raises thorny questions. Few would support disqualifying for benefits a laboratory technician on temporary layoff in Chicago who refuses a farm job in Nebraska or even a much lower paying technician's position in the local labor market. In the latter case, if the technician had to accept the job, an employer might purposely beat down the market wage, knowing that the worker who refuses to accept it runs the risk of losing unemployment compensation. But where does one draw the line? Should an unemployed (and perhaps high-priced) actor be free to refuse any job outside the theater or, more broadly, the entertainment industry? Can a union carpenter refuse a nonunion job undercutting the union scale? Is a job unsuitable if it requires 2 hours of commuting time?

To deal with these and other questions, the federal law requires every state to establish an appeals procedure comparable in intent to the grievance procedure used to interpret collective bargaining contracts. Any worker whose claim to unemployment benefits is denied and any employer who believes that benefits should not have been granted to a former employee may appeal through administrative channels—first to an impartial referee and then to a board of review—and these decisions may in turn be appealed to the courts.

Finally, even if a worker passes all these tests of coverage and eligibility, he or she is by no means insured against every day out of work. Virtually all states require a waiting period, typically 1 week, before payment of unemployment benefits can begin, and only a few states (ten, to be precise) pay benefits retroactively for the waiting period. Once payments begin, every state also limits the period over which they can be paid to a fully qualified recipient. In the mid-1970s, this ceiling varied from 20 to 39 weeks, with 26 weeks being most common. Additionally, most states vary the maximum period according to the weeks worked or wages earned by a claimant in the base period before the involuntary unemployment occurred. Thus, in the same state, some recipients may be cut off from benefits after 10 weeks, while others receive benefits for 20 or 30 weeks. In late 1974, when very high levels of unemployment persisted in the United States, a special temporary emergency program was enacted to extend the duration of benefits, their payment being "triggered" when statewide unemployment rates reached specified high levels; with such supplemental benefits, it was possible in 1975 and 1976 for some claimants to draw up to a total of 65 weeks of unemployment compensation.

Evaluating Unemployment Insurance

In spite of these and other regulations governing eligibility, there is, it seems, always a brisk market for editorials, articles, and opinions attacking the "scandalous fraud" attending the unemployment compensation program. But the evidence tells us that most alleged abuses of unemployment insurance are in fact either run-of-the-mill cases, in which a critic disagrees with the law as written by a state legislature, or borderline cases of interpretation, in which a critic disagrees with the verdict reached after extensive argument before administrative tribunals and the courts. Any legislative or judicial decision is, of course, fair game for criticism, but dark hints about fraud or scandal are something quite different.

Furthermore, some behavioral aspects of unemployment insurance are not so much abuses of the system as they are factors embedded in it. Consider, for example, that some employers regularly lay off workers rather than dismiss them because they regard it as inhumane or unjust to deny people benefits that the law permits them to receive—and at very little cost to the employers themselves. In some plants and industries, there is an established pattern of combining earnings with unemployment insurance benefits through regular layoffs. Consider that, for many years, the automobile companies and the United Automobile Workers (UAW) have negotiated supplemental unemployment benefits, which are directly tied to the volume and duration of unemployment insurance payments. The same is true of some other industrial firms and industrial unions. These employers and unionists have been able to take advantage of a publicly sanctioned plan for economic security in protecting their particular interests, and most observers would regard this as innovative rather than fraudulent behavior.

In a different example, some construction workers, who expect the seasonal unemployment characteristic of their industry, willingly seek layoffs during the winter so that they can temporarily move south and west to enjoy a warmer climate. Also, the consequences of unemployment are different for a son or daughter living at home and for a principal wage earner, and this may influence an employer's decision whether to lay off a worker or a wage earner's decision to file for unemployment insurance benefits. All these examples attest to the diversity of experience against which a national policy of economic protection can be evaluated; they should give pause to those who readily charge fraud in the unemployment insurance program.

More sobering, perhaps, is the theoretical and empirical literature concerning the extent to which unemployment insurance acts as a disincentive to work—in particular, the extent to which it acts to increase unemployment. To measure these effects is a very tricky problem indeed, and we do not have space to review in detail the important studies of this subject that have emerged in recent years.[50] To summarize them briefly, these studies tend to find that increases in maximum weekly unemployment benefits (calculated as a ratio of average earned wages) do lead to an increase in measured unemployment. A study of unemployment insurance claimants in Pennsylvania and Arizona, for example, found that an increase in the weekly ratio of benefits to wages in 1968 led to an increase of 0.4 percentage point in overall unemployment rates for those states. A similar study using a five-city sample obtained comparable results, as did another investigation employing a national sample of unemployed workers. The last of these, however, found a more significant relationship between higher benefits and unemployment for older men (45 to 49 years of age) than for other groups in the labor force (women aged 30 to 44 and people of both sexes aged 14 to 24).[51]

Of course, these findings are not conclusive and should not be considered apart from other, related issues. They are based on the low unemployment experiences of the late 1960s and may not be an accurate indicator of benefit-unemployment relationships in periods of less than full employment, such as the 1970s. Also, the relationships uncovered are unlikely to be linear, and thus unemployment may rise by less (or more) than estimated at different benefit levels or with different rates of change in maximum benefits. Additionally, by encouraging unemployed workers to search longer for work, unemployment insurance may lead to improved job matching in the labor market, which in turn may be "socially productive if [it] . . . reduces labor turnover and increases output over the long run."[52] This theory concerning job search is quite difficult to test empirically, but it reminds us that the possible multiple effects of unemployment insurance, including the returns to better job matches, "should be considered in any discussion of whether it is desirable to expand or contract present levels of . . . benefits."[53]

At a more general level of analysis, account must be taken of the implications of the unemployment insurance system for stability in society. The recession of 1974–1975 was the nation's most severe since the Great Depression. The high and rapidly rising levels of unemployment in the mid-1970s might well have produced so profound a level of dissatisfaction among the labor sector as to cast doubt upon, and precipitate major change in, the economic foundations of American capitalism. This is a strong statement, to be sure, but one which draws empirical support from historical developments in other nations and from this country's own experience in the 1930's. However, the direct effects of this recession were to an important extent mitigated by the unemployment insurance system, which paid out almost $18 billion in benefits in 1975 and over $16 billion in 1976, compared with an average $5.5 billion annually between 1970 and 1974.[54]

It is true that about half of the states exhausted their unemployment insurance reserves in the mid-1970s and that the federal government had to adopt emergency measures to supplement benefits and increase their duration. But the ability to do this, the capacity to use an existing component of the social welfare system to satisfy the claims to income of a significant number in the

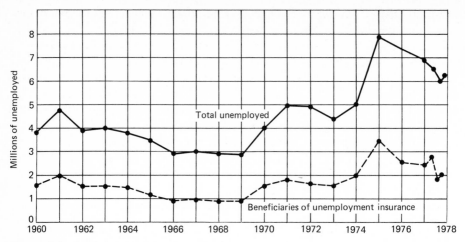

Figure 10-3 Total unemployed versus beneficiaries of unemployment insurance, 1960–1978. (*Sources:* Social Security Bulletin, **42**:71, *February, 1979, table M and* Monthly Labor Review, **102**:75–76, *March, 1979, tables 1 and 2.*

labor sector, and thereby at least partially protect them against economic destitution during a severe recession, should properly be recognized as an important national accomplishment. More than that, it should be assigned some evaluative weight in an attempt to assess fully the federal and state unemployment insurance system. That may challenge current concepts of social programs and methodologies for evaluating them, but the alternative is to settle for much narrower and perhaps erroneous assessments of programs and judgments concerning policy.

Before turning to the adequacy of benefits under unemployment compensation, let us recognize that all the aforementioned exclusions from coverage and restrictions on receipt of payments mean that fewer than one-half of those unemployed at any given time actually receive unemployment compensation. In 1977, for example, total unemployment averaged 6.85 million persons each month, but an average of 2.18 million persons collected unemployment benefits each month—or 32 percent of the total number of jobless persons. The proportion of the jobless receiving unemployment compensation rises during recessions, as many experienced workers are laid off and as the share of entry and voluntary unemployment drops, but even then coverage seldom approaches 50 percent. Figure 10-3 shows the changes in this relationship between 1960 and mid-1978.

Adequacy of Benefits

The major characteristics of unemployment compensation bear a striking resemblance to those of workers' compensation, discussed earlier. First, both types of laws proclaim an ideal standard of benefits. Whereas most workers' compensation statutes aim to replace two-thirds of the income lost by a worker injured on the job, the goal of most state unemployment insurance laws is to replace one-half of the worker's income lost as a result of involuntary unemployment. The different objectives may reflect the suspicion that although relatively few workers would deliberately invite injury in order to collect benefits, many of the able-bodied might welcome or needlessly continue unemployment if benefits were too generous. Though plausible, this reasoning does not explain why standards for income restitution are two-thirds and one-half for the two programs, respectively, instead of, say, 100 percent and 75 percent.

Second, the insured unemployed may not receive even 50 percent of their previous wage, just as injured workers may fail to receive the two-thirds standard under workers' compensation. The reason is the same in both cases: some states have established dollar maximums on weekly benefits and have failed to increase those maximums in step with increases in wages. Thus, in 1977, the average recipient of unemployment compensation was paid about $79 a week, or approximately 42 percent of the average weekly wage among covered workers.[55]

Third, benefits paid out as unemployment compensation vary greatly among the states, just as they do in the case of workers' compensation. In August 1978, for example, when the average weekly unemployment compensation benefit was $81.53 nationally, it ranged from a low of $57.63 in Mississippi to a high of $103.58 in the District of Columbia.[56] The proportion of lost wages made up by unemployment compensation thus may vary roughly between one-third and two-thirds, depending upon where one becomes unemployed. While it may indeed be difficult to specify the "ideal" benefit that a jobless worker should receive, it is equally difficult to rationalize this marked variation in benefits from one state to another by reference to the cost of living or some other standard.

Finally, the inadequacy and variability of benefits under both types of laws spring largely from the same cause—competition among the states to retain or attract industry by minimizing the tax burden on employers. At first glance, the unemployment insurance system would seem to have neutralized this competitive factor by imposing a uniform federal tax on all covered employers in all states. However, the maintenance of a relatively low taxable wage base for unemployment compensation, now $6000 per worker, and the use by states of experience ratings to lower the tax liability of all employers so as to better compete for new industry with other states (instead of using the ratings to encourage individual employers to stabilize their work forces) tend to undermine the effectiveness of the federal standard.

A Comparative Perspective   To gain greater perspective on the adequacy of benefits available under the American system of unemployment insurance, consider the data presented in Table 10-6, which shows estimated weekly benefits for a hypothetical involuntary unemployed worker in nine industrialized nations and nine states of the United States as of 1975.[57]

The benefits ranged between 40 and 80 percent of the average weekly wage

Table 10-6   Estimated Weekly Benefit Amount Payable to Hypothetical Unemployed Worker and Percentage of Wage Loss Compensated in Nine Countries and Nine Selected States of the United States, 1975

Country and currency	Average weekly manufacturing wage, 1974[1]	Weekly benefit amount payable, 1975[2]	Benefit amount as a percent of average wage
Austria (schilling)	1,780	833[3]	46.8
Belgium (franc)	4,586	2,751	60.0
Canada (dollar)	170	113	66.5
France (franc)	360	145[4]	40.3
West Germany (Deutsche mark)	373	187.80	50.3
Japan (yen)	33,825	20,295	60.0
Netherlands (guilder)	363[5]	290.40	80.0
Norway (krone)	735	325[3]	44.2[6]
United Kingdom (pound)	49.10[7]	33.03	67.3
United States (dollar)			
Arkansas	129.36	65	50.2
California	188.25	82	43.6
Illinois	198.37	135[3]	68.1
Massachusetts	165.98	95[3]	57.2
Michigan	232.19	128[3]	55.1
Mississippi	125.29	60	47.9
New York	178.48	90	50.4
Texas	166.06	63	37.9
Wisconsin	197.43	99	50.1

[1] For countries other than the United States, represents 1974 wages as derived from data in *Yearbook of Labor Statistics*, International Labor Office, Geneva, 1975, tables 13B and 19B; for selected states of the United States, represents average weekly earnings in 1974 of production workers in manufacturing taken from *Employment and Earnings*, U.S. Department of Labor, Bureau of Labor Statistics, May 1975, pp. 136–140.

[2] For the nine countries, based on provisions displayed in table 6 of the source listed below; for the United States, based on *Significant Provisions of State Unemployment Insurance Laws*, U.S. Department of Labor, Manpower Administration, July 15, 1975.

[3] Includes dependents' supplements.

[4] Unemployment assistance supplements of 21.60 francs per day also payable—and without an income test during first 3 months of unemployment.

[5] Estimated for October 1974 by applying percentage change in wage-rate index from 1973 to 1974 to October 1973 weekly wage.

[6] Under an altered benefit formula that became effective in late 1975, the weekly benefit amount payable would have compensated 53 percent of the wage.

[7] For male workers.

Note: It is assumed that, when employed, the worker had supported a wife and two children on the 1974 average weekly wage in manufacturing.

Source: Adapted from Saul J. Blaustein and Isabel Craig, *An International Review of Unemployment Insurance Schemes*, Upjohn Institute, Kalamazoo, Mich., 1977, pp. 68–69.

paid in manufacturing in these nations and states, and they exceeded 60 percent in five countries. In the nine American states, benefits as a percentage of wages were as low as 38 percent and as high as 68 percent, with the average benefit being about 50 percent. In absolute terms, Texas had the lowest weekly benefit in 1975—\$63—and Illinois had the highest—\$135. The relatively low benefit level reported for France is somewhat misleading in view of the generous plan for supplementary benefits applicable in some parts of its manufacturing sector and the availability, without a means test, of paid unemployment assistance for the first 3 months of unemployment.

Note that the data in Table 10-6 relate unemployment benefits to gross average earnings and do not take account of taxes and social insurance contributions normally withheld from workers' paychecks. Consequently, net wage losses due to unemployment will be smaller than gross wage losses, especially since unemployment insurance benefits are not taxable in most countries. Unlike most of the nations listed in the table, the United States does not provide allowances for children or other family members (though eleven states pay supplements or higher benefits to claimants with dependents) and does not permit payment for partial unemployment—a temporary reduction of working hours below normal levels. In many other respects, however, the American system of unemployment insurance closely resembles the systems of other developed nations.

To conclude our discussion of unemployment insurance, we should note that it is rather remarkable that the system as operated in the United States continues to be based on the presumption, reflected in experience ratings, that employers cause unemployment and will cure the problem if given a tax break. If the economic record of the last several decades tells us anything on this score, it is that aggregate forces (monetary and fiscal policies of government, most prominently), rather than heartless employers, fundamentally determine the volume of unemployment that exists at a particular point in time. Consequently, a strong case can be made for eliminating experience ratings altogether. This would not magically solve all the problems of unemployment insurance, nor would a major raising of benefit levels or a reduction of variation in benefits among states. Together, though, such initiatives might effectively deal with some of the leading deficiencies of the unemployment insurance system, even if the issue of incentives under that system remains especially troublesome.

MINIMUM WAGE AND MAXIMUM HOURS

The programs of social insurance that have been discussed so far have in common the attempt to provide income supports to workers who are away from the job because of retirement, work-related injuries, or involuntary unemployment. The nation's minimum wage law differs from these programs in that it seeks to establish a wage floor for paid employment. Its objective is to reduce poverty by raising wages to an above-subsistence level. This rationale was clearly expressed by a former Secretary of Labor, who commented as follows concerning the raising of minimum wages and the extension of coverage in the 1960s to previously excluded groups in the labor force:

> [These actions] went a long way toward the development of a philosophy . . . consistent with . . . the attack on poverty. Increases in the minimum wage level . . . brought it roughly in line for the first time with at least the low side

of what is considered a minimal decent subsistence income. . . . The extension of coverage . . . reflected the Congress' recognition that the human needs of the principal contributors to the economy were entitled to at least as much considera-tion as the enterprises involved. There was clear indication that the self-interest pressure groups which have been responsible for the large scale exemptions and exclusions from the coverage of the Act will have an increasingly difficult time in the future in pressing their claims against the broader national interest in seeing to it that a day's work gives whoever does it a day's decent living.[58]

In contrast to this opinion stands the view expressed by Milton Friedman, whose remarks are still to the point, even if the terminology is somewhat dated:

The fact is . . . the minimum wage rate is a major cause of Negro teenage unem-ployment. Of all the laws on the statute books of this country, I believe the mini-mum wage law probably does the Negroes the most harm. It is not intended to be an anti-Negro law but, in fact, it is. . . . The real tragedy of minimum wage laws is that they are supported by well-meaning groups who want to reduce poverty. But the people who are hurt most by higher minimums are the most poverty-stricken.[59]

Which of these sharply differing views is the more accurate? We shall at-tempt to judge this in light of recent empirical evidence obtained from studies of minimum wage legislation, but first let us review the governing statute in this area. The Fair Labor Standards Act (FLSA), adopted by Congress in 1938, spe-cifies the national minimum wage for employment in covered industries. The legal minimum rate was first set at 25 cents per hour, but through a series of amendments it was raised to $2.90, effective January 1, 1979; $3.10, effective January 1, 1980; and $3.35, effective January 1, 1981. The new rates were part of a package amendment passed in 1977, at which time the national minimum wage was $2.30 per hour.[60] Figure 10-4 details the amendments to the minimum wage provisions of FLSA since the inception of the law. Also shown in the fig-

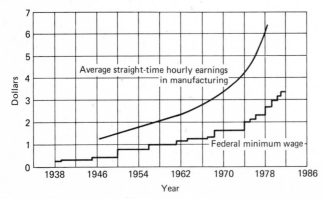

Figure 10-4 Earnings versus the federal minimum wage, 1938–1986. (*Sources:* Economic Report of the President, 1979, *U.S. Government Printing Office, Washington, D.C., 1979, table B-35, p. 224; and periodic reports of changes in the FLSA minimum wage provisions.*)

ure are changes over time in average hourly earnings in manufacturing between 1938 and 1978. For this period, the minimum wage was most commonly about 45 percent of the wage in manufacturing.

Like that of other social legislation, the coverage of the minimum wage law has expanded over time to additional sectors of the labor force. For example, amendments to FLSA in 1961 and 1966 added about 14 million previously uncovered workers to the law's jurisdiction, with most of them employed in the retail trade, hospital, hotel, restaurant, laundry, and construction industries. The 1966 amendments established a minimum wage of $1 per hour for farm workers, who were previously uncovered by the act. This minimum rose to $1.30 per hour in 1969 and will be $3.35 by 1981, or the same as for nonfarm workers. Still other amendments to FLSA in 1974 extended coverage to domestic workers and to other retail and service personnel.[61] In total, approximately 52 million workers, or 65 percent of the labor sector, came under coverage of FLSA in the late 1970s.

Union Views of Minimum Wage Laws

Because minimum wage legislation in the United States has been directed at the lowest-paid workers and because labor unions have generally achieved their organizational successes among semiskilled and skilled employees earning well above the minimum rates, there is reason to question whether the labor movement has any real interest in this component of FLSA. Indeed, early in its history, American labor was hardly enamored with minimum wage legislation, its leaders regarding the law as an alternative to collective bargaining. In 1937, William Green, president of the AFL, commented that collective bargaining should be extended so as to "establish minimum rates in every industry and then, as that is extended, let the Government recede."[62] Since that time, however, labor unions not only abandoned their opposition or indifference to minimum wage legislation but also have become among its strongest supporters. Commenting on the 1977 amendments to FLSA, for example, George Meany, president of the AFL-CIO, said that "the higher minimum wage would give the great mass of people a greater purchasing power."[63] The labor movement led by Meany expended much in the way of personnel and money in pushing for the 1977 amendments to the minimum wage law, just as it had done in the 1960s.

Organized labor's support of FLSA is, of course, not hard to understand. Consider the case of a union whose wage scales begin at, or are slightly above, the legal minimum wage. If the hourly minimum is $2.30, as it was in 1977, and a labor union, perhaps consisting of garment workers, has negotiated a starting hourly wage of $2.65 with firms that employ its members, then the union should be expected to support raising the legal minimum wage to $2.65. Then, when the minimum is achieved, the union will bring pressure on employers to increase collectively bargained wage rates by 35 cents per hour in order to preserve the "historical differential" over other workers (or firms). Or if semiskilled workers have been receiving $2.65 per hour in a given firm and unskilled workers have been receiving $2.30, the amended minimum rate will spur the union to seek an adjustment in wages that will preserve the prevailing occupational wage differential. Such a "ratcheting" effect begins to indicate the potential impact of increases in the minimum wage beyond those workers who receive immediate gains from adjustment of their rates to new minimum levels.

Not to be overlooked in this discussion is the reduction of interregional wage differentials stemming from higher federal wage floors and the related consequences for competition among areas for businesses and jobs. The textile and clothing industries are good examples in this regard; employers in these industrial sectors in the north often have joined with their organized employees to support higher federal minimum wages in order to stem the flow of firms and jobs—that is, of competition—to the south. A reduction of interregional wage differentials induced by the minimum wage would lessen the south's competitive advantage over the north in both labor markets and product markets. This is yet another reason why labor unions ardently support both the raising of the minimum hourly wage and its extension to uncovered portions of the labor sector.

Finally, the labor movement's active support of minimum wage laws may help build alliances among diverse unions and among workers who differ by age, race, sex, education, and other characteristics. There are not many issues that a decentralized, heterogeneous labor movement can uniformly rally around, and thus the minimum wage has important symbolic and coalition-building dimensions for leaders of the AFL-CIO. These should not be overlooked in seeking to understand the American labor movement's prolonged support of minimum wage legislation.

Economic Consequences of Minimum Wage Legislation

Among the intended consequences of minimum wage legislation are to move low-income workers closer to a decent standard of living, to compensate for the weak bargaining power of workers who are relatively immobile, to eliminate competition which is based on depressed wage rates, to act as a protection against the downward spiral of wages and prices in times of recession, and to serve as a stimulus to the economy by augmenting the purchasing power of a low-income group who can be counted on to spend what they earn. There are many, however, who question whether minimum wage legislation will achieve the intended objectives and who criticize the law on one ground or another.

The strongest criticism of a legal wage floor is that it will create unemployment among workers whose value to employers is less than the legal minimum. This view is based on the assumption that employers actually pay workers according to their marginal value product, an assumption which, as we noted in Chapter 7, may be erroneous in individual situations. But where workers do receive pay that is roughly equal to their marginal value, minimum wage legislation may indeed have adverse effects on those very people whom it is designed to help.

Some employees who are paid relatively little because their marginal product is low (and not because their employers exploit them) will be priced too high when their wages are "artificially" raised by a new legal minimum. Such workers will be laid off. Moreover, they cannot find jobs in other covered industries because their contribution to production in them will presumably also be less than their cost. Consequently, these workers are driven into uncovered industries where they compete for jobs with many others, thereby further depressing wage rates in those industries. The logic of the argument remains the same as coverage of the minimum wage law expands to most employment sectors, except that those who are displaced by the new wage floor will be unable to obtain jobs anywhere or may be supplanted by relatively less expensive capital.

An alternative response by employers to increases in the minimum wage is to raise the prices of their products and thus transfer the cost of improving the pay of low-wage workers to the consuming public. The more inelastic the demand for the firm's product and the wider the impact of minimum wage legislation in the industry in which the firm operates, the more likely this is to occur. By some standards, it may seem fair for the public to pay the cost (in the form of higher prices) of improving the lot of low-wage workers, especially if affected workers are retained rather than laid-off, but remember that the public includes some low-income people who may themselves not have benefited from minimum wage legislation.

A third criticism of a minimum wage applied to the entire economy is that it prevents areas with surplus labor from attracting industry because of their low wage rates. The only two cures for labor surpluses and low wages are an increase in the demand for labor, as new industry moves into an area, and an emigration of some portion of the labor supply to other areas which offer inducements sufficient to attract workers. A wage level which is low relative to levels in other areas is thus the incentive *both* for firms to move into, and for workers to move out of, the locale in question. As labor demand and labor supply come to a new balance in the area, wage rates will rise to the levels prevailing elsewhere. But a minimum wage law establishing a wage floor throughout the economy reduces wage differentials and thereby removes some of the inducement for capital to enter and for labor to leave.

As might be expected, supporters of minimum wage legislation have counterarguments to those posed by the critics. Generally, they believe that there are more than just a few cases in which workers are paid less than the value of their marginal product and that an increase in the legal minimum wage therefore brings pay and (marginal) productivity into closer balance. In this scenario, there is little danger that unemployment will result from higher minimum wages. Supporters of the law also contend that the less efficient firms in particular are affected by minimum wage legislation and that this induces them to tighten up operations—to improve quality controls, to reduce scrap, to improve their utilization of labor, to upgrade their products, and so forth. It is argued still further that if price increases are in fact necessary to pay "decent" wages to all workers, this is a result which society should be prepared to accept. Otherwise, consumers rather than producers are, in effect, exploiting those whose bargaining power is weak.

In sum, the arguments over minimum wage laws are essentially the same as those over the effect of unions on wages. If laws (or unions) can really raise wages above market levels without hurting anyone, ask the critics, why don't we make everybody rich simply by legislating a wage floor of $10 or $20 or $30 an hour? When the question is stated so extremely, everyone can readily visualize the disastrous effects on prices and employment that would result; why doubt that the same thing will occur, by a smaller magnitude, when the artificial wage floor is raised from $2.30 to $3.35 an hour (or when unions raise wages by only 10 or 15 percent instead of 50 or 100 percent over market levels)?

And the response from the other side is also the same, whether collective bargaining or minimum wage laws are at issue: forces in the market certainly do impose limits beyond which wages cannot be driven at any given time without generating all the repercussions predicted by orthodox theory, but those restraining limits are not as narrow and predictable as the competitive model implies—as proved by the prevalence of large wage differentials for the same skill even in nonunion markets. In view of such glaring imperfections in "natural" market forces, it is argued, there is both the room and the need for some intervention by government (and unions) in the wage-setting process.

The Evidence Summarized Over the years, a considerable body of empirical work has built up concerning the effects of minimum wages on employment. However, this evidence has not resolved the controversy surrounding minimum wage laws, though it has enlightened us somewhat about the groups in the labor force that are most likely to be affected by increases in the federal minimum wage.

An early example of this empirical controversy is provided by studies conducted by the Department of Labor of the effects of FLSA and by subsequent critiques of these studies. Summarizing the research carried out by the federal government to the late 1960s, a former Secretary of Labor concluded that "employment in the areas affected by the extension of coverage of FLSA has increased, and there is no evidence of any restraining effect of the broader coverage of employment opportunity."[64] Subsequent studies by the Department of Labor and statements by Secretaries of Labor have proceeded largely to these same conclusions and are often cited by union officials as clear evidence of the salutary effects of minimum wage legislation.[65]

But the critics of minimum wage laws are hardly convinced by this evidence. For example, Macesich and Stewart analyzed a special survey of eleven low-wage industries classified by regional location and wage levels before the establishment of new minimum wages in the mid-1950s and found subsequent relationships between wages and employment to be precisely those predicted by competitive-labor-market theory—work force reductions were greatest in the plants in which minimum wage laws had had the most impact (the lowest-wage plants).[66] Later, the same authors found low-wage firms increasing their capital investment by significantly greater amounts after establishment of a new minimum wage. They also detected major increases in violations of the law after new minimum wages went into effect, a finding that matched earlier results obtained by Peterson in an examination of three low-wage industries covered by FLSA and three groups of workers subject to state minimum wage laws.[67] All these actions are, again, consistent with the predictions of competitive theory.

More recent research using newer quantitative techniques has focused heavily on the effects of minimum wage legislation on employment of teenagers.[68] In one study, Adie and Moore found most of the teenage groups they examined—younger workers who differed by age, race, and sex—to have suffered significant additional unemployment in the late 1960s and early 1970s as a result of higher minimum wages. But Kaitz and Lovell, who studied the same groups, found little compelling evidence of such effects. The critical difference between the two studies is the inclusion or omission of controls for growth in the teenage population. When this growth is not controlled for, as in the first study, increases in the minimum wage have a significant effect on unemployment of teenagers; when the variable is accounted for, as in the second study, the effect is insignificant. Thus, "no satisfactory estimates emerge from the two studies, yet such estimates are crucial if employment losses are to be compared to wage gains,"[69] and, one might add more generally, if the outcomes of minimum wage legislation are to be properly evaluated.

A more comprehensive study of the consequences of minimum wage legislation was recently completed by Gramlich.[70] His findings are instructive not only for what they uncovered but also for what they failed to resolve about the effects of minimum wage legislation. First, Gramlich makes the important point that the actual coverage of the federal minimum wage law is considerably narrower than one might think. Over the period 1973–1975, for example, between 22 and 45 percent of the work force in mining and manufacturing, transportation and communications, and construction was still earning below the minimum wages prevailing in those years. In 1975 alone, the exclusions ranged from roughly 37 percent in public administration to 70 percent in private household services.

What this means is that compliance by employers with the minimum wage provision of FLSA, $2.10 per hour in 1975, was well below 100 percent. This may have been due to technical factors (such as part-time workers who work fewer hours than are required to meet the federal standard for coverage), to incomplete coverage in the law as written, to the willingness of employees to take subminimum wages for fear of losing their jobs, or, more likely, simply to willful failure of employers to comply with the law. Whatever the principal reason, "the message is that a very high percentage of low-wage workers make subminimum wages, and . . . industrial variations in the percentage of low-wage workers covered seem to be only modestly influenced by whether or not the industry is covered by the legislation."[71] Consequently, the minimum wage "is simply less of a force for good or evil than people have believed."[72]

Second, Gramlich investigated the effects of higher minimum wages on pay rates above the minimum. He estimated that the 1974 increase in the minimum wage from $1.60 to $2 per hour raised the overall wage bill by about 0.8 percent. This was not a very large boost, but if the increase in the minimum wage had been, say, from $1.60 to $3 per hour (88 percent) instead of from $1.60 to $2 per per hour (25 percent), the direct impact on the wage bill alone would have been 6 percent and the indirect impact would have been considerably higher than that. The reader might want to consider this conclusion in light of the 1977 federal legislation raising the minimum wage under FLSA from $2.30 to $3.35 per hour by 1981.

Third, Gramlich examined the effects on employment of minimum wage increases in the early 1970s. He discovered that a higher minimum wage for teenagers did not cause them to be unemployed so much as to force them (at the margin) out of full-time and into part-time work, where, in general, the wage rates were lower and the jobs were poorer. However, Gramlich also found that adult males benefited somewhat from increases in the minimum wage during the 1970s; of special significance he found that adult females were the main beneficiaries of increases in the minimum wage. The last result is based on the apparent conversion of part-time adult female workers into full-time personnel, although that may further force teenagers into part-time work. In any case, the consequences of minimum wage legislation for other groups in the labor force besides teenagers should be taken into account in evaluating FLSA.

The principal implications of this analysis for public policy are twofold. First, minimum wages set at too high a level will have negative effects on those whom they are intended to help. Gramlich suggests that 40 to 50 percent of the median hourly wage in manufacturing is about the right level for the federal minimum rate. As the minimum increases beyond this range, it will force more and more workers to "confront the grab-bag combination of a higher wage but a reduced probability of having a job."[73] Second, a differential minimum wage should exist based upon the age of the worker. The present minimums seem too low or about right for adults, but too high for teenagers. Gramlich recognizes the possibility, often noted by labor union leaders, that employers might substitute lower-wage teenagers for higher-wage adults if differential minimums were to exist, but for him this does not overturn the case for a youth differential under FLSA or other minimum wage statutes.[74]

By now the reader has no doubt recognized that, as with so many other issues involving the labor sector, analysis of the effects of minimum wage legislation is a tricky empirical task filled with methodological pitfalls. Properly to control for and measure the many variables other than the minimum wage that affect wage levels, employment, unemployment, and shifts in the labor force, and to do this over time, is a herculean task made more difficult, of course, by the absence of systematic cross-sectional and longitudinal data or by the availability of only small amounts of such data. That some of the best minds in labor economics have studied this issue for more than three decades and have yet to resolve the controversy over the effects of minimum wage legislation provides ample testimony to this point.

While it is increasingly clear that, among groups in the labor force, teenagers, especially black teenagers, may on balance suffer from, rather than be helped by, minimum wage legislation—a fact which supports the call for a separate minimum wage for young people—it is not at all clear what the total effects of FLSA and similar legislation at the state level are or what they will be, given recent amendments to the federal law. In a dynamic economy, other, more fundamental forces are at work which can support or override the intended consequences of minimum wage laws. Unquestionably, such forces mask whatever effects do flow from minimum wage legislation. It is perhaps for this reason more than any other that judgments about the efficacy of the minimum wage law still rest heavily on personal values, especially one's belief in competitive labor market theory, even among those who have studied this issue at firsthand. In any case, it may well be that the consequences of the minimum wage provisions of FLSA are quite different from those intended by the framers and supporters of the law. If so, a reappraisal of FLSA may well be in order, as is perhaps also true of other legislation for social protection in the United States.

Further Aspects of FLSA and Related Laws

Although we do not have space to discuss in detail other dimensions of FLSA, the reader should note that this law also contains limitations on the use of child labor and requires that hourly paid workers in covered sectors be paid at the rate of time and a half for hours worked beyond 8 per day or 40 per week. Intended to protect workers from economic exploitation and to encourage the shortening of working hours, especially in light of employment conditions that prevailed earlier in the twentieth century, these provisions have in recent years been subject to some criticisms and modifications. For example, because they make production a more expensive proposition beyond the 40-hour weekly standard, the overtime provisions of FLSA are alleged by some to reduce output, and therefore, consumer choice. Others point out that, at the hourly pay rates prevailing in the modern economy, these overtime requirements should be less rigid and may be altogether unnecessary. In contrast to these views is the criticism that the overtime payments provided for in FLSA are not high enough to encourage the hiring of new workers, for employers choose to pay overtime to presently employed workers. From this perspective and to permit broader sharing of work opportunities among members of the labor force, the law's requirements concerning pay for overtime should be raised, and their enforcement strengthened. In some industries where labor is scarce and production is threatened, strong support has emerged for the use of child labor under special and protected circumstances. Thus, in 1978, the Department of Labor proposed regulations to permit the employment of 10- and 11-year-olds in the hand-harvesting of short-season crops.[75] The regulations require the integration of such work with school hours and also specify a number of other conditions, but they provide another indicator of how a provision of the law is adjusted to fit changing economic and social circumstances.

In all this, we would do well to keep in mind the original purpose of FLSA, which was to protect the worker—adult or child, man or woman, immigrant or native-born—from exploitation at the hands of employers. One may analyze any or all aspects of FLSA and other protective legislation from an economic point of view, and it is important that such evidence be taken into account in evaluating the law and proposing changes in it. But like the laws pertaining to labor-management relations, which were reviewed in Chapter 3, FLSA had and still does have a fundamental social purpose: to guard against misuse of the nation's human resources by outlawing some employment practices and making others more costly to employers. The consequence was to recognize and formally establish certain rights of the labor sector and to limit the extent to which the market alone would determine labor's condition. In any such legislation, a balance must be struck between competing rights and interests: of business owners and managers to produce, of citizens to purchase and consume, and of labor to work under fair terms and conditions of employment. That balance may change over time, but it should not be lost sight of in proposing or evaluating reforms of FLSA and legislation for social protection.

As to the number of working hours put in by members of the American labor force, this declined rather steadily, from well over 60 per week on the average at the beginning of the twentieth century to about 40 per week by mid-century. While FLSA may have contributed to this development after 1938 by raising the cost of hours worked beyond specified limits, the reduction in the number of working hours was due in large part to increasing economic growth and to the desire of employees and employers to reduce industrial fatigue and improve workers' productivity and morale.

Interestingly, as recent analyses have shown, the number of average weekly working hours in the United States has fallen hardly at all in the post-World War II period, when changes in the industrial mix and the composition of the labor force are taken into account.[76] During the recession of 1974–1975 in particular, many proposals for shorter workweeks were voiced, mainly out of a desire to share the available work among more employees and thereby reduce unemployment. There are, moreover, industries and occupations—retail trade and some skilled craft jobs, for example—in which the average workweek is close to 30 or even 25 hours. But so too are there instances in which workweeks average upward of 50 or 60 hours—among some firefighters, for example, and also among some managers and professionals. But in the main, the average workweek in the American economy is between 35 and 40 hours. Whether it will decline noticeably in the near future is problematic, but so far little pressure has emerged for lowering the overtime provisions of FLSA below 8 hours per day and 40 hours per week.

Finally, we have said nothing and can say only little about prevailing wage laws in the American economy which attempt to specify the appropriate wage or basis of wage setting for one or another sector of employment or group of employees. Two of these laws are the Davis-Bacon Act and the Walsh-Healey Act. Under the former, the Secretary of Labor is empowered to determine the prevailing rates paid in the geographic area surrounding each federal construction project for every laboring occupation—from skilled electrician to unskilled helper—and to require that those occupational rates be the minimum paid on the federal site by all private contractors. The Walsh-Healey Act applies the same principle to most federal procurement contracts (for supplies, equipment, and the like), except that it requires that only the prevailing minimum rate in an area be paid for the type of work for which the contract is let.

In the federal government itself, the Federal Salary Reform Act (1962) and the Federal Pay Comparability Act (1970) codified the principle that employees of the national government should be compensated on the basis of wages and salaries prevailing in private industry. Quite similar laws and policies exist in many of the nation's state and local governments. Most of the evidence obtained about the effects of these varied statutes, including the Davis-Bacon Act and the Walsh-Healey Act, indicates that, for most jobs, they raise wages beyond levels that would otherwise prevail and increase costs and prices (that is, taxes) to the public.[77] Again, one can argue that this is a suitable objective which the public should be willing to support (and pay for), though most analysts of the subject tend to conclude otherwise.

More generally, what we see in these laws is much like what we have observed in federal minimum wage laws and other legislation for social protection: efforts to improve economic security and provide social justice or equity for many of the nation's citizens. Virtually all these measures, however, are aimed at those who are or have been more or less regularly attached to the labor force. In this sense, they are quite in keeping with the dominant work ethic of American culture and with the pragmatic nature of most of our policies for social protection. Whether these policies have their intended results is a different question, one which we have shown is not easily answered. Rather than try to provide an overall answer ourselves, we urge the reader to keep an open mind on this question and to consider carefully the evidence that bears upon it.

SOCIAL WELFARE IN THE UNITED STATES

Before concluding this chapter, let us briefly consider the aggregate volume of expenditures on social welfare in the United States. The relevant data are given in Table 10-7.[78] They include expenditures for social programs tied to prior or existing attachment to the labor force as well as those for public assistance (welfare), education, health and medical care, and housing. The dominant conclusion to be drawn from these data is that expenditures on, and activity concerning, social welfare have grown enormously in the post-World War II era. Expenditures rose from $23.5 billion, or about 9 percent of the nation's gross national product (GNP) in 1950, to $331.4 billion, or 20.6 percent of GNP in

Table 10-7 Social Welfare Expenditures under Public Programs, Selected Fiscal Years, 1950–1976, Millions

Program	1950	1960	1965	1970	1971	1972	1973	1974	1975	1976
Total	$23,508.4	$52,293.3	$77,175.3	$145,855.7	$171,907.9	$191,357.0	$213,941.8	$239,313.6	$286,521.9	$331,366.3
Social insurance	4,946.6	19,306.7	28,122.8	54,691.2	66,368.7	74,809.4	86,165.5	98,953.0	122,947.4	146,592.5
Old-age, survivors, disability, and health insurance	784.1	11,032.3	16,997.5	36,835.4	43,122.8	48,229.1	57,766.6	66,286.6	78,429.9	90,440.7
Health insurance (Medicare)				7,149.2	7,875.0	8,819.2	9,478.8	11,347.5	14,781.4	17,777.4
Railroad retirement	306.4	934.7	1,128.1	1,609.9	1,928.9	2,141.2	2,477.5	2,692.6	3,085.1	3,499.6
Public employee retirement	817.9	2,569.9	4,528.5	8,658.7	10,226.0	11,920.4	14,010.8	16,677.5	20,118.6	24,425.0
Unemployment insurance and employment service	2,190.1	2,829.6	3,002.6	3,819.5	6,665.3	7,651.0	6,065.9	6,661.6	13,871.2	19,699.9
Railroad unemployment insurance	119.6	215.2	76.7	38.5	49.6	86.0	45.2	25.6	41.6	148.2
Railroad temporary disability insurance	31.1	68.5	46.5	61.1	53.0	42.1	34.9	31.5	32.9	78.6
State temporary disability insurance	72.1	347.9	483.5	717.7	773.1	783.7	848.2	915.4	989.5	1,049.2
Hospital and medical benefits	2.2	40.2	50.9	62.6	68.4	68.3	69.8	70.7	72.9	73.6
Workers' compensation	625.1	1,308.5	1,859.4	2,950.4	3,550.0	3,955.8	4,916.5	5,662.3	6,378.7	7,251.2
Hospital and medical benefits	193.0	420.0	580.0	985.0	1,090.0	1,185.0	1,355.0	1,600.0	1,860.0	2,125.0
Public aid	2,496.2	4,101.1	6,283.4	16,487.8	21,262.0	26,078.3	28,691.3	31,520.3	40,709.2	48,945.6
Public assistance	2,490.2	4,041.7	5,874.9	14,433.5	18,075.0	21,895.0	24,002.6	23,827.4	26,758.2	31,171.5
Vendor medical payments	51.3	492.7	1,367.1	5,212.8	6,277.5	7,751.6	9,208.6	10,371.9	12,984.2	15,320.0
Social services				712.6	950.4	2,160.5	2,306.2	2,155.0	2,622.4	2,968.6
Supplemental security income							45.7	2,831.4	6,091.6	6,548.1
Food stamps			35.6	577.0	1,576.3	1,866.8	2,212.9	2,838.9	4,693.9	5,691.8
Other	6.0	59.4	373.0	1,477.3	1,610.7	2,316.4	2,430.2	2,022.6	3,165.5	5,534.2
Health and medical programs	2,063.5	4,463.8	6,246.4	9,906.8	11,086.7	12,865.7	13,447.1	14,953.1	17,436.9	19,192.5
Hospital and medical care	1,222.3	2,853.3	3,452.3	5,313.4	5,935.9	6,791.3	7,413.1	8,034.3	9,490.4	10,133.6
Civilian programs	886.1	1,973.2	2,515.5	3,553.8	3,979.3	4,450.3	4,945.1	5,293.2	6,405.4	6,901.6
Defense Department	336.2	880.1	936.8	1,759.6	1,956.6	2,341.0	2,468.0	2,741.0	3,085.0	3,232.0
Maternal and child health programs	29.8	141.3	227.3	431.4	403.3	495.3	455.3	493.4	545.5	592.9
Medical research		.6	4.3							
Medical research	69.2	448.9	1,165.2	1,635.4	1,659.7	1,872.0	2,114.0	2,222.0	2,599.0	2,972.0
School health (education agencies)	30.6	101.0	142.2	246.6	271.9	281.3	300.0	325.2		
Other public health activities	350.8	401.2	671.0	1,348.0	1,578.4	2,002.3	2,065.7	2,531.3	2,953.0	3,255.0
Medical-facilities construction	360.8	518.1	588.3	932.1	1,237.5	1,423.5	1,099.0	1,347.0	1,849.0	2,239.0
Defense Department	1.1	40.0	31.1	52.5	74.1	100.0	76.0	86.0	96.0	171.0
Other	359.8	478.1	557.2	879.6	1,163.4	1,323.5	1,023.0	1,261.0	1,753.0	2,068.0
Veterans' programs	6,865.7	5,479.2	6,031.0	9,078.0	10,456.0	11,522.4	13,026.4	14,112.4	17,018.8	19,005.8
Pensions and compensation	2,092.1	3,402.7	4,141.4	5,393.8	5,877.5	6,209.3	6,605.8	6,777.4	7,578.5	8,269.3
Health and medical programs	748.0	954.0	1,228.7	1,784.0	2,026.9	2,431.4	2,766.1	2,983.6	3,516.7	4,102.2
Hospital and medical care	582.8	879.4	1,114.8	1,651.4	1,873.9	2,255.6	2,587.3	2,786.6	3,287.1	3,793.2

Hospital construction	161.5	59.6	77.0	70.9	85.1	109.8	104.8	118.9	136.7	212.0
Medical and prosthetic research	3.7	15.1	36.9	61.8	67.9	66.0	74.0	78.0	93.0	97.0
Education	2,691.6	409.6	40.9	1,018.5	1,622.4	1,924.6	2,647.9	3,206.9	4,433.8	5,336.2
Life insurance	475.7	494.1	434.3	502.3	526.6	523.7	532.2	538.5	556.1	564.2
Welfare and other	858.3	218.8	185.8	379.4	402.5	433.3	474.4	606.1	933.7	733.9
Education	6,674.1	17,626.2	28,107.9	50,845.5	56,704.7	59,385.1	64,733.7	70,499.3	77,910.5	86,425.5
Elementary and secondary	5,596.2	15,109.0	22,357.7	38,632.3	42,910.8	44,524.0	48,076.9	52,424.6	56,822.1	62,400.9
Construction	1,019.4	2,661.8	3,267.0	4,659.1	4,551.9	4,458.9	5,008.6	4,979.0	5,492.0	5,982.5
Higher	914.7	2,190.7	4,826.4	9,907.1	10,834.9	11,582.5	12,940.0	13,955.8	16,384.1	18,793.8
Construction	310.3	357.9	1,081.4	1,566.9	1,565.5	1,481.9	1,483.2	1,386.4	1,512.7	1,614.9
Vocational and adult	160.8	298.0	853.9	2,144.4	2,718.1	3,021.0	3,453.9	3,880.4	4,441.2	4,956.0
Housing	14.6	176.8	318.1	701.2	1,046.8	1,332.4	2,179.6	2,554.0	2,966.5	3,127.8
Public housing	14.5	143.5	234.5	459.9	608.2	731.1	1,101.9	1,233.1	1,456.4	1,443.7
Other	0.1	33.2	83.6	241.3	438.6	601.3	1,077.7	1,320.9	1,510.1	1,684.1
Other social welfare	447.7	1,139.4	2,065.7	4,145.2	4,983.0	5,363.9	5,698.2	6,721.5	7,532.6	8,076.5
Vocational rehabilitation	30.0	96.3	210.5	703.8	800.8	875.5	911.7	967.5	1,036.4	1,088.3
Medical services	7.4	17.7	34.2	133.8	162.8	179.2	175.0	185.2	217.7	228.9
Medical research		6.6	22.4	29.6	17.0	17.0	15.0			
Institutional care	145.5	420.5	789.5	201.7	224.7	251.1	263.5	284.8	296.1	299.9
Child nutrition	160.2	398.7	617.4	896.0	1,204.5	1,502.3	1,707.0	2,025.8	2,517.6	2,825.7
Child welfare	104.9	211.5	354.3	585.3	596.8	532.0	526.0	510.0	597.0	640.0
Special OEO and ACTION programs			51.7	752.8	784.9	782.7	894.9	766.7	638.3	621.5
Social welfare, not elsewhere classified	7.1	12.4	42.3	1,005.6	1,371.3	1,420.2	1,395.1	2,166.7	2,447.2	2,601.1
GNP (in billions)	264.8	498.3	658.0	960.2	1,019.8	1,111.8	1,238.6	1,361.2	1,452.3	1,611.8
Social welfare expenditures as percent of GNP	8.9	10.5	11.7	15.2	16.9	17.2	17.3	17.6	19.7	20.6

Source: Adapted from Alfred M. Skolnik and Sophie R. Dales, "Social Welfare Expenditures, Fiscal Year 1976," *Social Security Bulletin,* **40**:5, 10 (1977).

1976. Stated differently, over the period 1950–1976, GNP rose by a bit over 600 percent, while expenditures on social welfare advanced by better than fourteenfold. The increases have been particularly sharp since 1965, when many of the Johnson administration's Great Society programs were put into effect. Indeed, since that time, aggregate expenditures on social welfare have risen by 14.2 percent on an average annual basis. In 1975, they were just about 20 percent larger than they had been a year earlier, as expenditures under various social programs—unemployment insurance, public aid, supplementary security income, food stamps, and emergency employment and training—increased rapidly to combat the effects of the recession of 1974–1975. That economic downturn also affected the volume of expenditures on social welfare in 1976, which rose by almost $45 billion, or 16 percent over the 1975 level.

Of all these expenditures, social insurance is the largest single category, accounting for well over 40 percent of the total. Within this grouping, OASDHI is the major component, dwarfing all other items. Public aid (welfare) is the third largest overall category of expenditures on social welfare, but it has been the fastest-growing in recent years, rising by 29 percent in 1975 and by 20 percent in 1976. Also increasing rapidly, though a small portion of the total, are expenditures for all health and medical care, which grew by about 50 percent over the period 1974–1976. Expenditures on education have risen relatively slowly in recent years, in part reflecting the change from a tight to a loose academic labor market from the late 1960s to the mid-1970s. On a per capita basis, expenditures on social welfare in the United States were $1514 in 1976, or about 4¼ times larger than in 1950, *even allowing for the effects of inflation.*

The proportion of expenditures on social welfare emanating from federal funds has also increased notably, especially since 1965. In that year, federal funds accounted for 48.5 percent of all expenditures on social welfare under public programs; by 1976, they accounted for 60 percent of the total. In 1976 as well, 56 percent of all federal and 67 percent of all state and local government expenditures were for social welfare programs, both historic highs. The remaining funds were spent on national defense, environmental control, highways, and the like. Federal expenditures for social welfare programs as a proportion of GNP rose from 4.0 to 12.3 percent between 1950 and 1976, and state and local expenditures rose from 4.9 to 8.3 percent.

All these data attest to the growing importance of the role of the federal government in providing income supplements and social protection to the citizenry, even if many of the programs provide for revenue sharing and other pass-throughs of funds from the federal government to state and local governments. Perhaps this trend helps explain the tensions which have sometimes arisen between federal and nonfederal governments in establishing qualifying requirements for some of the social programs listed in Table 10-7 and in administering them.

The magnitude of expenditures on social welfare in the United States today may seem to provide a substantive basis for the concern expressed by many about the development of a welfare state in what has fundamentally been conceived of as a capitalist nation. But rather than try to resolve what is probably an irreconcilable division between liberals and conservatives on this issue —labels which themselves may not be very enlightening—we would prefer instead to note that economic growth is the key to the ability of any nation to finance continually expanding programs of social welfare. The recent record of the United States is not very good in this regard, productivity having increased less than 2 percent annually since 1970 (compared with roughly 3 percent annually in the earlier part of this century).[79] As rates of economic growth lag, the resources available to finance enlarged social programs and even existing ones dwindle. Unless sustained economic expansion occurs, such programs may have to be cut back; otherwise, the citizenry must be willing to give up larger amounts of personal income in the form of taxes. And that willingness unquestionably has limits in a free society.

As we have seen in our review of systems of social security and other programs, this has become a pressing problem throughout the developed economies of the world. Tensions between the public good and individual freedom are not unexpected in industrialized nations, but for those tensions not to become overt conflicts requiring major restructuring of society seems to require sustained economic growth. Whether such growth will be experienced in the United States and other countries in the remainder of the twentieth century is uncertain. From the perspective of a labor sector that seeks some income supplementation and protection from the market, this is a fundamental challenge facing the western world and its political leaders.

But if economic growth is central to the provision of present and future social welfare benefits, it comes about only at certain costs. In an industrial or postindustrial society, these include pollution of the environment; congestion in central cities, suburbs, and recreational areas; and a sense of aesthetic deterioration reflected in the phrases "neon-sign civilization," "fast-food alley," "plastic society," and the like. What we face here, again, is a dilemma: the fruits of growth must be weighed against the spoilage that growth brings about. Offering "no growth" as a solution does not resolve the dilemma, for the same evaluative process applies to it. If society is to provide economic welfare and social protection to its citizens, and to its labor sector in particular, then growth at least permits an enlarging of the resource pie. The alternative is to attempt to satisfy the claims of interest groups to larger shares of national income by redistributing a stable or declining pie. The conflicts that this latter policy are likely to engender suggest that its costs may outweigh its benefits and render it inferior to a policy that attempts to promote economic growth, albeit controlled to ward off some of its more undesirable consequences.

SUMMARY

In this chapter we reviewed some of the key programs of income supplements and social protection prevailing in the United States. Social security is the largest of these, but important as well are worker's compensation laws, unemployment insurance, and the Fair Labor Standards Act. Brief attention was also given to some legislative initiatives of the 1970s, including the Occupational Safety and Health Act and the so-called "pension reform law" (ERISA). In general, programs for social welfare in the United States are not as comprehensive or of as long standing as those found in other industrialized nations, but they have expanded greatly in recent years. Surprisingly, the tax levies necessary to finance programs for social welfare and income redistribution are in many respects quite similar among the developed countries, including the United States, though there remain some notable differences among them. All these nations share a common problem of achieving the necessary economic growth to generate the resources required to sustain and expand public programs of social welfare and income redistribution.

In Chapter 11, we move on to consider another important area of governmental activity related to the labor sector: the training and development of workers. Comparisons will once again be made with the experiences of other industrialized nations, and some attention will also be given to private efforts at training and development. All these programs are intended in one way or another to improve the match between the demand for, and supply of, labor—and thereby to assist part of the labor sector in the marketplace.

NOTES

1   For an account of this action, see "Carter Signs Retirement Bill: Differences Voiced on Its Impact," *The New York Times,* Apr. 7, 1978, pp. A1, D9. Excluded from the new retirement provision are federal government employees, personnel in higher education, and executives and managers eligible for retirement benefits of $27,000 or more.

2   The data in this paragraph can be found in U.S. Bureau of the Census, *Statistical Abstract of the United States: 1978,* 99th ed., p. 8, and U.S. Bureau of the Census, *Current Population Reports: Demographic Aspects of Aging and the Older Population in the United States,* Special Studies Series, no. 59, May 1976. p. 59.

3   The data in this section and the next are from *Economic Report of the President, January, 1978,* 1978, pp. 232–237; and John Snee and Mary Ross, "Social Security Amendments of 1977: Legislative History and Summary of Provisions," *Social Security Bulletin,* **41:**3–20 (1978).

4   See Snee and Ross, pp. 12–14.

5   The terms distinguish between those who had and had not met the test of quarters of coverage under social security, respectively.

6   "Social Security in Review," *Social Security Bulletin,* **42:**36 (1979).

7   *Economic Report of the President, January, 1978,* p. 233. We rely heavily on this source in the present section.

8   *Economic Report of the President, January, 1978,* p. 234. Observe that this estimate relates the proportion of the elderly in the population to a younger subset and not to the population as a whole. Hence, it is different from the projection discussed earlier and referred to in note 2 above.

9   *Economic Report of the President, January, 1978,* p. 235; and Snee and Ross, pp. 12–13.

10 *Economic Report of the President, January, 1978,* p. 235.

11 See Alicia H. Munnell, *The Future of Social Security,* Brookings, Washington, 1977, as reported in "Which Way for Social Security?" *The Brookings Bulletin,* **14**:7 (1978).

12 The source of these data and the basis for much of the discussion in this section is *Social Security in Ten Industrial Nations,* Union Bank of Switzerland, Economic Research Department, Zurich, April 1977. Note that private pension benefits are included in the computation of retirement income for four of the countries listed in Table 10-3. This may overstate the differences between these countries and others in terms of retirement income as a proportion of pre-retirement income.

13 See *Social Security in Ten Industrial Nations,* especially the tables on pp. 14, 17, and 20, for details concerning survivors, disability and medical benefits. For data on health insurance coverage in the United States, see Marjorie S. Carroll, "Private Health Insurance Plans in 1976: An Evaluation," *Social Security Bulletin,* **41**:3–16 (1978). For a view which suggests that medical insurance has raised the cost of health care in the United States but not the cost of such care to the recipient, see Martin S. Feldstein, "Consequences of Hospital Controls," *The Wall Street Journal,* April 12, 1979, p. 22.

14 *Social Security in Ten Industrial Nations,* pp. 25–27.

15 *Social Security in Ten Industrial Nations,* p. 33.

16 *Social Security in Ten Industrial Nations,* p. 34.

17 See Craig R. Whitney, "Social Security a Major Issue Troubling West," *The New York Times,* May 17, 1977, pp. 1, 14.

18 Alfred M. Skolnik, "Twenty-five Years of Employee-Benefit Plans," *Social Security Bulletin,* **39**:5 (1976). Also Martha R. Yohalem, "Employee-Benefit Plans, 1975," *Social Security Bulletin,* **40**:19–28 (1977). These sources provide basic data for the discussion in the present section.

19 Skolnik, pp. 5–6.

20 Yohalem, p. 22.

21 Gayle B. Thompson, "Pension Coverage and Benefits, 1972: Findings from the Retirement History Study," *Social Security Bulletin,* **41**:3–17 (1978). For another study showing that employees who earned $15,000 per year and who worked for 30 years retired on pensions totaling one-fifth of their final year's earnings, see James H. Schulz et al. "Private Pensions Fall Far Short of Preretirement Income Levels," *Monthly Labor Review,* **102**:28–32 (1979).

22 Thompson, p. 6. Note that, except for temporary personnel, federal workers are not covered by OASDHI.

23 Thompson, p. 15.

24 See, for example, Peter Henle and Raymond Schmitt, "Pension Reform: The Long, Hard Road to Enactment," *Monthly Labor Review,* **97**:3–12 (1974).

25 Presuming, of course, that the worker's employer has a pension plan. The choices available to employers concerning the vesting of pension benefits are as follows: (1) graded vesting, beginning with 25 percent of pension benefits after 5 years of service and increasing by 5 points each year for 5 years and 10 percent annually thereafter until 100 percent is reached after 15 years of service; (2) 100 percent vesting after 10 years of service; or (3) 50 percent vesting for employees who have 10 years of service or who have reached age 50, with the percentage then increasing by 10 points annually.

26 A classic case of a business shutdown was the Studebaker Corporation's closing of its plant in South Bend, Ind., in 1963. Several thousand employees were dismissed, most were still looking for work many months later, a few retired on their social security benefits, and none received private pension benefits from the company, despite having made contributions to the company's pension plan.

27 Henle and Schmitt, p. 9.

28 For evidence supporting this conclusion, see Allen Janger, *The Personnel Function: Changing Objectives and Organization,* Conference Board, New York, 1977, especially pp. 98–109.

29 On this point, see Herman M. Somers and Anne R. Somers, *Workmen's Compensation,* Brookings, Washington, 1961, chap. 1.

30 For background information, see Alfred M. Skolnik, "Twenty-five Years of Workmen's Compensation Statistics," *Social Security Bulletin,* **29**:4 (1966).

31 Daniel N. Price, "Workers' Compensation: Coverage, Benefits, and Costs, 1976," *Social Security Bulletin,* **41**:30 (1978).

32 See Daniel N. Price, "A Look at Workers' Compensation Beneficiaries," *Social Security Bulletin,* **39**:38–48 (1976).

33 *Report of the National Commission on State Workmen's Compensation Laws,* 1972.

34 The data supporting the conclusions offered in this paragraph are contained in Price, "Workers' Compensation: Coverage, Benefits, and Costs, 1976," pp. 30–34.

35 Price, "Workers' Compensation: Coverage, Benefits, and Costs, 1976," p. 32.

36 John F. Burton, Jr., "Federal or State Responsibility for Workers' Compensation?" *Proceedings of the Twenty-ninth Annual Winter Meeting of the Industrial Relations Research Association, 1976,* Madison, Wis., 1977, p. 225. For additional information on recent developments in this area, see Gerri Minor, "Workers' Compensation Laws—Key Amendments of 1978," *Monthly Labor Review,* **102**:43–50 (1979).

37 Burton, p. 226.

38 Monroe Berkowitz, "Workers' Compensation in a General Disability System," *Proceedings of the Twenty-ninth Annual Winter Meeting of the Industrial Relations Research Association, 1976,* Madison, Wis. 1977, p. 212.

39 Berkowitz, p. 218.

40 See U.S. Department of Labor, *News,* May 2, 1974, p. 2. Note, however, that the U.S. Bureau of Labor Statistics now conducts an annual survey of occupational injuries and illnesses. On this point see Norman Root and David McCaffrey, "Providing More Information on Work Injury and Illness," *Monthly Labor Review,* **101**:16–21 (1978).

41 See *Marshall et al. v. Barlow's Inc.,* discussed in Bureau of National Affairs, *Daily Labor Report,* May 23, 1978, pp. 1–2, D1–D9.

42 For these and other perspectives on OSHA, see "An Assessment of Three Years of OSHA," *Proceedings of the Twenty-seventh Annual Winter Meeting of the Industrial Relations Research Association, 1974,* Madison, Wis., 1975, pp. 31–51. This is a collection of three papers offering the views of labor, management, and government, respectively. For a somewhat more analytical approach, see "Health and Safety Programs: Industrial Relations Perspectives," *Proceedings of the 1975 Annual Spring Meeting of the Industrial Relations Research Association,* Madison, Wis., 1975, pp. 486–507. This is a collection of four papers and comments on industrial fatalities and alcoholism on the job.

43 U.S. Department of Labor, *News,* Dec. 5, 1977, p. 1.

44 We save for Chapter 12 a discussion of the major types of unemployment that occur in

the American economy. Note, though, that unemployment insurance is most concerned with cyclical unemployment, the type that results from downturns in the economy. It is also directed at seasonal unemployment, the type resulting from largely expected changes in the demand for a good or service, and hence the demand for labor, during the year.

45 For details of recent changes in the law which raised the taxable wage base and contribution rate for unemployment insurance, see *Employment and Training Report of the President, 1977,* 1977, pp. 64–65. The previous contribution rate of 3.2 percent will be in effect again once loans from the federal unemployment trust fund made in the aftermath of the recession of 1974–1975 have been repaid. For more recent developments, see Diana Runner, "State Unemployment Insurance: Changes During 1978," *Monthly Labor Review,* **102:**13–16 (1979).

46 U.S. Department of Labor, Employment and Training Administration, *Unemployment Insurance Statistics, August–September, 1977,* 1977, pp. 11–13.

47 *Employment and Training Report of the President, 1977,* p. 64. Also *Employment and Training Report of the President, 1978.* The ensuing discussion relies heavily on these sources and on U.S. Department of Labor, Employment and Training Administration.

48 U.S. Department of Health, Education, and Welfare, Social Security Administration, *Social Security Programs in the United States, 1964,* 1968, p. 59.

49 See Saul J. Blaustein and Isabel Craig, *An International Review of Unemployment Insurance Schemes,* Upjohn Institute, Kalamazoo, Mich., 1977.

50 Several of these studies are reported in Arnold Katz (ed.), "The Economics of Unemployment Insurance: A Symposium," *Industrial and Labor Relations Review,* **30:**431–526 (1977).

51 Arnold Katz and Joseph E. Hight, "Overview," *Industrial and Labor Relations Review,* **30:**431–437 (1977).

52 Katz and Hight, p. 432.

53 Katz and Hight, p. 432. For criticism of the assumptions and methodology of the aforementioned studies, see Clare Vickery, "Unemployment Insurance: A Positive Reappraisal," *Industrial Relations,* **18:**1–17 (1979).

54 "Currrent Operating Statistics," *Social Security Bulletin,* **42:**28 (1979), table M-1.

55 "Current Operating Statistics," p. 63, table M-41. In 1977 average weekly earnings in the American economy were $188.64.

56 "Current Operating Statistics," p. 63, table M-41.

57 The source of these data and the basis for the following comparative analysis of unemployment insurance systems is Blaustein and Craig.

58 U.S. Department of Labor, Wage and Hour and Public Contracts Division, *Minimum Wage and Maximum Hours Standards under the Fair Labor Standards Act, 1969,* 1969, pp. 3–4.

59 *The Minimum Wage Rate: Who Really Pays?* an interview with Yale Brozen and Milton Friedman, Free Society Association, Washington, 1966, pp. 11, 26–27.

60 See "Carter Signs Minimum Wage Bill, Giving Raises of 45 Percent by '81," *The New York Times,* Nov. 2, 1977, p. A14.

61 FLSA, which requires time and a half for hours worked over 40 in a week and 8 in a day, was also extended to state and local governments in 1974. However, a Supreme Court Decision 2 years later declared that extension unconstitutional. See *National League of Cities v. Usery,* as discussed in Bureau of National Affairs, *Government Employee Relations Report,* June 28, 1976, pp. AA1–AA6, E1–E14.

For information on the most recent amendments to FLSA, see Peyton Elder, "The 1977 Amendments to the Federal Minimum Wage Law," *Monthly Labor Review,* **101**:9–11 (1978).

62 Fair Labor Standards Act of 1937, *Joint Hearings before the Joint Committee on Education and Labor, United States Senate; and the Committee on Labor, House of Representatives,* 75th Cong., 1st Sess., pt. 1, 1937, p. 217.

63 "Carter Signs Minimum Wage Bill."

64 U.S. Department of Labor, Wage and Hour and Public Contracts Division, p. 1. See also U.S. Department of Labor, Wage and Hour and Public Contracts Division, *Hired Farmworkers: A Study of the Effects of the $1.15 Minimum Wage under the Fair Labor Standards Act,* 1969.

65 As an example, see Rudolph A. Oswald, "Fair Labor Standards," in Joseph P. Goldberg et al. (eds), *Federal Policies and Worker Status since the Thirties,* Industrial Relations Research Association, Madison, Wis., 1976, pp. 107–134, and the studies conducted by the federal government cited therein.

66 George Macesich and Charles T. Stewart, Jr., "Recent Department of Labor Studies of Minimum Wage Effects," *Southern Economic Journal,* **26**:281–290 (1960).

67 John M. Peterson, "Employment Effects of Minimum Wages, 1938–50," *The Journal of Political Economy,* **65**:412–430 (1957); and "Employment Effects of State Minimum Wages for Women: Three Historical Cases Re-examined," *Industrial and Labor Relations Review,* **12**:406–422 (1959). See also, John Peterson and Charles T. Stewart, Jr., *Employment Effects of Minimum Wage Rates,* American Enterprise Institute, Washington, 1969.

68 The studies discussed here are cited and reviewed in Robert S. Goldfarb, "The Policy Content of Quantitative Minimum Wage Research," in *Proceedings of the Twenty-seventh Annual Winter Meeting of the Industrial Relations Research Association, 1974,* Madison, Wis., 1975, pp. 261–268.

69 Goldfarb, p. 264.

70 Edward M. Gramlich, "Impact of Minimum Wages on Other Wages, Employment, and Family Incomes," *Brookings Papers on Economic Activity, 2, 1976,* Brookings, Washington, 1976, pp. 409–451, plus discussion comments to p. 461.

71 Gramlich, p. 426.

72 Gramlich, p. 426.

73 Gramlich, p. 450.

74 For a critical review and questioning of Gramlich's analysis, See Michael L. Wachter, "Comments and Discussion," in Gramlich, pp. 455–461.

75 See U.S. Department of Labor, *News,* Apr. 13, 1978, pp. 1–2.

76 See, for example, Thomas J. Kniesner, "The Full-Time Workweek in the United States, 1900–1970," *Industrial and Labor Relations Review,* **30**:3–15 (1976). However, in the 1970s there have been considerable increases in the proportions of part-time employees at work and in the use of "flexitime" (flexible hours for reporting to, and leaving from, work) in industry. On the latter, see John D. Owen, "Flexitime: Some Problems and Solutions," *Industrial and Labor Relations Review,* **30**:152–160 (1977).

77 See, for example, Armand J. Thieblot, Jr., *The Davis-Bacon Act,* University of Pennsylvania, The Wharton School, Philadelphia Industrial Research Unit, Philadelphia, 1975; and Walter Fogel and David Lewin, "Wage Determination in the Public Sector," *Industrial and Labor Relations Review,* **27**:410–431 (1974).

78 The discussion in this section is based on data in Alfred M. Skolnik and Sophie R. Dales, "Social Welfare Expenditures, Fiscal Year 1976," *Social Security Bulletin*, **40:**3–19 (1977).

79 See *Economic Report of the President, January, 1979*, p. 227, table B-38, and p. 68.

ADDITIONAL READINGS

Ashford, Nicholas A.: *Crisis in the Workplace: Occupational Disease and Injury*, M.I.T., Cambridge, Mass., 1976.

Blaustein, Saul J., and Isabel Craig: *An International Review of Unemployment Insurance Schemes*, Upjohn Institute, Kalamazoo, Mich., 1977.

Boskin, Michael J., George F. Break, et al.: *The Crisis in Social Security: Problems and Prospects*, rev. ed., Institute for Contemporary Studies, San Francisco, August, 1978.

Bowen, William G., Frederick H. Harbison, Richard A. Lester, and Herman M. Somers (eds.): *The Princeton Symposium on the American System of Social Insurance: Its Philosophy, Impact, and Future Development*, McGraw-Hill, New York, 1968.

Davis, Karen, and Cathy Schoen: *Health and the War on Poverty: A Ten-Year Appraisal*, Brookings, Washington, 1978.

Goldberg, Joseph P., et al. (eds.): *Federal Policies and Worker Status since the Thirties*, Industrial Relations Research Association, Madison, Wis., 1976.

Hamermesh, Daniel S.: *Jobless Pay and the Economy*, Johns Hopkins, Baltimore, 1977.

Munnell, Alicia H.: *The Future of Social Security*, Brookings, Washington, 1977.

Report of the National Commission on State Workmen's Compensation Laws, 1972.

United States Social Security Administration, *Social Security Bulletin*, published monthly.

FOR ANALYSIS AND DISCUSSION

1 Select any two western European countries and compare their systems of social welfare with the system of the United States. How do they differ? How are they similar? What are the major philosophical underpinnings of the systems you are comparing? Ask a classmate to undertake a similar analysis, but for nations other than the ones you have chosen. Compare your analyses.

2 It is often said that social security taxes are regressive in that they are highest for low-income persons. As an example, a nominal tax rate of 6.65 percent on earnings up to $29,700 (the rate and taxable base scheduled to go into effect in 1981) works out to an effective rate of 6.65 percent for an employee earning $25,000, but to a rate of only 3.95 percent for one earning $50,000. Evaluate the merits of this criticism and indicate how the financing of social security might be altered to deal with it. In your judgment, should such a change in policy be made?

3 Ask one of your classmates to join you in preparing a report on the Employee Retirement Income Security Act of 1974 (ERISA). Interview a company official, a union leader, and, if possible, an actuary, soliciting their views about ERISA's impact on private pension arrangements. In your report, be sure to address the appropriateness of present provisions for vesting specified in the law and also indicate whether changes should be made in the provisions related to portability of pensions. Ask those whom you interview to give you a critique of your report.

4 Read the report of the National Commission on Workmen's Compensation (issued in 1972). Then gather evidence about the extent to which individual states in the United States have implemented the Commission's recommendations. What do you conclude from your study of this issue about the need for stronger federal standards to regulate workers' compensation in the United States? How do your conclusions compare with those of the authorities on this subject quoted or cited in Chapter 10?

5 Two teams of three students each should debate the following proposition: "Resolved: The federal-state unemployment insurance system should be modified to permit payments to persons who have never been employed but who have searched for full- or part-time work for at least 3 months." In preparing for this debate, examine the requirements for receipt of unemployment insurance payments in other industrialized nations. The instructor should moderate the debate, and the other class members should pose questions to the teams following the conclusion of the debate.

6 Select four states, one each from the western, southern, north central, and northeastern regions. Compare their requirements concerning eligibility to receive unemployment insurance, the levels of benefits paid, the duration of benefits, and rates of employers' contributions. How do these differ? How are they similar? Have the differences moderated or enlarged over time? What are the sources of your data?

7 Should unemployment insurance benefits be indexed to changes in consumer prices in the way that social security payments and some wages under collective bargaining agreements are indexed? Why or why not? Should states decide this issue for themselves, or is a federal policy required in this regard? What should that policy be?

8 Select a recent empirical study of the effects of minimum wages on employment, possibly one of those cited in this chapter. What major independent variables *other than* the minimum wage are "controlled" by the investigator? How are these variables measured? What is the magnitude of their relationship to, or impact on, unemployment, and how does this compare with that of the minimum wage? What implications for public policy concerning minimum wage laws do you draw from your analysis of the study you have selected?

9 Examine the data on expenditures on social welfare presented in Table 10-7. Why did these expenditures increase so much more rapidly in the period after 1965 than before? What significance do you attach to the observation that these expenditures on social welfare represented more than 20 percent of GNP in the mid-1970s? Should that percentage be higher or lower? Why? How does the proportion of the GNP of the United States accounted for by expenditures on social welfare compare with the proportions accounted for by such expenditures in other developed nations?

10 Most social welfare payments made to citizens of the United States require the recipients to be more or less regularly attached to the labor force. Analyze this fact in terms of its implications for the "social contract" that exists in the United States. What is the meaning of this term, as you define it, and how does the social contract that prevails in this country compare with that of another, say, Great Britain, West Germany, Sweden, or Japan? Consider how the labor market and economy of any one of those nations differ from the labor market and economy of the United States.

Chapter 11

Human Resources
Planning and Development

Among the industrialized nations of the world, the United States has a relatively brief history of initiatives set by public policy to assist in planning, developing, and improving the working experiences of members of the labor sector. In this chapter, we shall review these initiatives, some of which—such as the Wagner-Peyser Act of 1933—are of long standing, but most of which have emerged since 1960. The Manpower Development and Training Act of 1962 was a particularly important measure in this regard, and a more recent milestone was the Comprehensive Employment and Training Act of 1973, which sought to codify and integrate existing federal policies governing human resources training and development.

Evidence pertaining to the effectiveness of selected human resources programs will be summarized. Also to be treated is the experimentation in the 1970s with public service employment—government jobs created specifically, if temporarily, for those who have been unsuccessful in finding employment elsewhere. We shall also examine the role of education in economic development, as we return to the theme of education as an investment in human resources. We then move on to consider the limited involvement of the private business sector in public human resources policy, and also the human resources development and planning activities of the firm for itself, which have grown rapidly in recent years. Comparative examples of, and experiences with, human resources policies are presented next. The chapter concludes with a discussion of some key issues that are currently being debated.

At the outset, let us recognize that the term "manpower" which has been widely used in the United States, particularly with regard to public policy, is less accurate in describing both the substance and the approach of present initiatives in this area than "human resources." The prominence of human resources planning in private business and the substantial public and private investment in human resources provide additional support for using the term "human resources" (which also has the advantage of not being sexist).[1]

Despite their rather short history, human resources policies underscore the fact that the claim of the labor sector to a share of national income is made tangible principally through paid employment. When such employment is difficult to come by because of limited experience, training, or information about the labor market—or, more generally, because of a disadvantaged background —federal policy provides that individuals can avail themselves of temporary financial support and improved preparation for the world of work by enrolling in one or another human resources program. Sometimes the labor sector is more broadly aided by governmental human resources policies, such as those funding institutions of higher education and public service jobs. Thus, like the policies concerning antidiscrimination, income maintenance, economic security, and social welfare reviewed in previous chapters, human resources policies reflect the prevailing social contract in the mixed capitalist economy of the United States whereby government provides members of the labor sector with protection from the market while also offering assistance to them in dealing with the market.

THE PUBLIC EMPLOYMENT SERVICE

The beginnings of American human resources policy can be dated from 1933, when Congress passed the Wagner-Peyser Act, creating the Employment Service. The legislation called for "the establishment of a national employment system and for cooperation with the states in promotion of such system."[2] The Wagner-Peyser Act provided federal funds (drawn from general revenues) to the states and an incentive to encourage them to establish their own employment services. Half of the states availed themselves of this option during the first 2 years of the law's existence. The remaining states followed suit after 1935, when Title III of the Social Security Act created the first trust fund for payment of unemployment compensation, but linked receipt of such funds to a claimant's ability and willingness to work. Responsibility for this function was assigned to the Employment Service, and funds to support it were provided out of the unemployment insurance payroll tax. Faced with the choice of creating and administering a fully federally financed employment service or losing tax proceeds to other states, each individual state quickly joined up.

The early activity of the Employment Service in the depression-ridden, high-unemployment era of the 1930s centered on the screening of applicants for welfare and work relief projects. Later, when the United States entered World War II and labor markets became increasingly tight, the Employment Service was placed under the jurisdiction of the federal War Manpower Commission and undertook the allocation of scarce human resources. With the end of the war, the Employment Service assumed its former status, but also became heavily involved in the demobilization effort. Its program providing employment counseling and information about the labor market to ease the adjustment of returning veterans was later applied to the demobilization after the Korean war and became a more general model for its activities during the 1950s.

In that decade, however, the Employment Service grew increasingly moribund. This occurred despite passage in 1946 of the Employment Act, which presumably committed the nation to a full-employment policy and, one might have thought, an active policy regarding the labor market. Recurrent, if mild, recessions generated high unemployment insurance caseloads and turned the attention of the staff of the Employment Service toward the administration of unemployment insurance and away from employment services—which it was not specifically mandated to provide in any case. Most local offices of the Employment Service were content to process unemployment insurance claims, while residually matching a few prospective employees with available jobs offered by employers. By the end of the decade, the agency's budget was smaller than it had been 10 years earlier.

The stagnant role of the Employment Service was described and roundly criticized in 1958 by Secretary of Labor James P. Mitchell, who focused not only on the agency's evolving characteristics, as noted above, but also on its provision of employment services largely to low-skill workers rather than to high-level technical and professional workers. As a Presidential candidate, John F. Kennedy promised in 1960 to improve the Employment Service, and, following plans drafted by personnel of the Department of Labor, he began to do so in the early 1960s after his election to office. Increased funding for the agency and recovery from the recession of 1961 permitted the Employment Service to increase its volume of placements considerably. Moreover, a reorganization in 1962 of the agency mandated it to take on expanded responsibilities as a manpower agency concerned with all aspects of manpower. The reorganization envisaged the agency as becoming the local community human resources center, but linked to a nationwide network of offices operating to meet national purposes and goals. The overall objective was to promote more efficient operations in the labor market and to improve workers' experiences in the labor market, which required the Employment Service to become deeply involved with employers, schools, unions, community development agencies, and the like. Ironically, the new thrust of the agency's activity, aimed in part at white-collar and professional labor markets, engendered opposition from private employment agencies, which grew rapidly in the late 1950s and early

1960s, and also from the College Placement Council, an organization that helped college graduates find jobs.

Whether or not the Employment Service successfully achieved the goals set forth in its new charter is problematic—most informed observers would say it did not—but through the 1960s the scope of its activities widened as it was invested with additional responsibilities. For example, the Manpower Development and Training Act of 1962 (and subsequent amendments) aimed to improve the qualifications of the unemployed and required the Employment Service to identify occupations with "reasonable expectations of employment," recruit the unemployed and underemployed as trainees, work with vocational educators to set up training courses, and place graduate trainees. Programs of relocation assistance and related moving allowances were also offered by the agency. In the mid-1960s, a new director reoriented it principally to serve the disadvantaged located in urban slums and pockets of rural poverty. In the late 1960s, the Employment Service was given yet additional responsibilities in the labor market under the provisions of one or another federal programs—the Comprehensive Employment Program (CEP), the Work Incentive (WIN) program, the Jobs in the Business Sector (JOBS) program, and the Cooperative Area Manpower Planning System, to name but a few. The agency also undertook the development of computerized "job banks" to improve the matching of the supply of labor to the demand for labor, and it became involved in programs and experiments in the areas of vocational rehabilitation, work evaluation, and work adjustment.

In the 1970s, internal reorganization of the Department of Labor eliminated the Bureau of Employment Security, within which the Employment Service had been housed, and led to the agency's being renamed—and recast as—the United States Employment and Training Service (ETS). It operates today as a major arm of the Labor Department's Manpower Administration and serves as the federal government's human resources link, in matters of policy, to regional human resources administrators and state employment services. Many of these changes occurred in the face of what observers had thought were insurmountable obstacles facing the ETS in terms of politics and personnel.[3]

If the ETS has indeed been reoriented and reorganized in recent years toward the goal of making it an active, aggressive human resources development agency, it still is a very long way from achieving that objective. The reasons for this have less to do with weaknesses in structure and personnel than with the limited confines within which any type of public employment service must operate in a strongly competitive, largely decentralized economy of the type found in the United States. Consider, for example, that apart from some federal contractors, employers are not required to register their job vacancies with the ETS, nor are they in any way obligated to hire potential employees referred to them by the agency. This means that every state employment service and the local offices which it operates are dependent on the willingness of employers to make their vacancies known and to hire referred personnel.

Clearly, the ETS must cultivate contacts among employers and truly service employers' needs in a system in which voluntarism rather than fiat is the order of the day. But when they do this, state employment services inevitably are criticized by those who argue that servicing the unemployed—and, more generally, the labor sector—should take precedence over servicing employers. In an environment of such contending interests, it is perhaps not surprising that the ETS has never closely approached becoming a labor exchange of the type found in other nations. It is also in large part for this reason that some students of the ETS contend that it should organize its activities so as to "(1) make easily accessible all possible information about where to search for whatever jobs exist, and (2) teach job seekers how to effectively search for employment."[4]

A second critical dimension of the ETS concerns those groups in the labor sector which should be the primary focus of its activities. We noted earlier that, especially in the mid-1960s, the disadvantaged were the principal target group of the Employment Service, with the placement of disadvantaged and minority-group applicants serving as a key measure of its activity. Some observers believe that this is an appropriate strategy for the ETS irrespective of the state of the labor market: "The direction of change is clearly toward serving those most in need of service at the expense of those who can best get along by themselves . . . [even if] attracting employers to use a service with a reputation for emphasis on the disadvantaged may be difficult."[5] Others contend that the ETS should provide resources to all who need them, irrespective of status, and that only by servicing all types of workers, occupations, and employers can the agency hope to improve its own standing and the experiences of the work force in the labor market.

Whether the disadvantaged should be the primary target group of ETS activity or not, they in fact represent a large proportion of actual placements made. This is evident from Table 11-1, which shows the representation of veterans, women, the poor, minority groups, young and old workers, and the handicapped among the 4.1 million persons who were placed in jobs as a result of referrals by the ETS during fiscal 1977. Note that the aggregate volume of placements has increased in recent years, being fully 1 million larger in 1977 than in 1975.[6] The ETS's heavy load of counseling and testing activities is also discernible from Table 11-1, as is the related representation of target groups. These data confirm that the ETS is by no means an inactive agency, and perhaps also that its operations and success should not be measured solely in terms of job placements.

Finally, the ETS continues to face undeniable problems concerning its image owing to the fact that state employment offices distribute unemployment insurance payments to claimants while simultaneously attempting to provide them with employment services. Given that most of the unemployment insurance claims are entirely legitimate and that the ETS is the agency invested with the responsibility for administering the legally mandated eligibility test to recipients of unemployment insurance, it is still regarded by many as an unemployment office rather than an office for employment services or human resources development. The image persists in spite of increased separation over the years

Table 11-1 Members of ETS Target Groups Who Received Reportable Services, All Sources of Funding, Fiscal Year 1977 (Percent Distribution[1])

Selected services	Total number[2] (thousands)	Veterans	Migrant and seasonal farm workers	Women	Minority-group members	Economically disadvantaged workers	Handicapped workers	Older workers (45 and older)	Young workers (under 22)
Applications taken	15,817	16.5	1.3	44.7	28.6	28.3	5.7	14.2	31.8
Counseled	961	20.2	1.1	49.1	36.0	53.0	15.2	11.2	31.1
Tested	738	11.4	0.4	66.0	28.7	26.7	5.8	6.7	37.2
Enrolled in training	178	11.8	1.0	55.5	44.6	70.8	6.3	4.6	43.2
Received job development[3]	1,310	26.6	1.6	40.8	34.7	33.3	7.9	13.1	26.9
Placed									
In all jobs	4,139	17.4	2.2	41.3	31.6	34.0	5.0	9.4	43.3
In nonagricultural industry	3,960	17.7	0.8	41.9	31.1	33.9	5.1	9.2	43.2

[1] Percentages are based on total new and renewal applications filed in local employment service offices during fiscal 1977. Not included are those applications made earlier than Oct. 1, 1976, that were still active during fiscal 1977. Because the same individual may be a member of more than one target group, the sum of percentages for a selected service will equal more than 100.

[2] Figures are for all new and renewal applicants.

[3] The process of soliciting a public or private employer's order for a specific applicant for whom the local office has no suitable opening currently on file.

Source: Adapted from Employment and Training Report of the President, 1978, 1978, p. 60.

between unemployment insurance functions and employment service functions within the ETS. There are, of course, other policy constraints and operational weaknesses which limit the ETS's ability to serve workers and employers effectively, but those which have been described here are sufficient to illustrate the nature and force of these limitations. The fact of the matter is that the ETS has never been assigned a central role in determining policy for human resources training and development. The American tradition of private job hunting and training and the fear of public controls of market activity underlie the limited utilization of this agency.

THE HUMAN RESOURCES REVOLUTION OF THE 1960s

The 1960s bore witness to an unprecedented volume of human resources programs authorized by federal legislation, and one might naturally conclude that this reflected a new public mandate to attack head on and to reform basic weaknesses in the economy as they were manifested in labor markets. But some informed observers tell us quite the opposite: that "no basic reforms were in demand," that "economic and labor market research had stored up little intellectual capital upon which to draw and never did catch up with the demand for policy decisions until the end of the [1960s] decade," and that the human resources programs of that era were "just ad hoc responses to political demands and trial and error search for solutions to dimly perceived problems."[7] Those problems were generally defined as high unemployment and worsening race relations.

From one perspective, the initial human resources program of the 1960s was the Area Redevelopment Act, passed in 1961, which contained funds for employment assistance and training for residents of depressed areas. But the bill was a limited one, concerned with the provision of aid to isolated pockets within what was judged to be a basically sound economy. It certainly did not apply to the entire economy.

The first significant human resources legislation of the period and the best known was the Manpower Development and Training Act of 1962 (MDTA). The early focus of MDTA was on structural unemployment in the economy, especially the displacement through automation and technological change of employed workers, notably skilled personnel. Unemployment in 1961 exceeded 7 percent of the work force, the highest annual rate in the post-World War II era to that time, and the concern of legislators was with those whose substantial skills had suffered technological obsolescence and who needed retraining. But as unemployment rates began to fall in the 1960s, as the employment of skilled workers and married men picked up, and as unemployment among young people emerged as a major social problem, the focus of MDTA soon became the provision of training to new entrants to the labor force who lacked work experience, rather than retraining for displaced, seasoned workers.

Unlike vocational training in the high school setting, however, the developing thrust of MDTA required the federal government, working with local agencies, to provide (1) remedial education for adults, (2) orientation of the uninitiated to the world of work, and (3) guidance in occupational choice, personal counseling, and other support services, which were to be offered in institutional settings. The available techniques for providing such training were woefully inadequate, however, and the institutions to provide the training were virtually nonexistent. Consequently, a long period of trial and error was necessary before institutional training under MDTA became viable. Even then, it tended to be most effective where jobs were available and in areas where problems of housing, transportation, and discrimination did not combine to thwart the intent of MDTA.

In 1963, Congress passed the Vocational Education Act, which emphasized the provision of education and training to individuals for development of skills. The law recognized, in a way that earlier legislation had not, that in a mature, industrialized nation, education and training are necessary for entry into all but the jobs requiring the fewest skills. In that same year, efforts to establish an act to create jobs for young participants in the labor force were unsuccessful, but they paved the way for subsequent, more fruitful initiatives.

In the aftermath of the assassination of President Kennedy and the succession of Lyndon Johnson to the Presidency in late 1963, Congress proved willing to enact several important pieces of legislation. One of these called for major tax reductions,[8] and another, the Civil Rights Act of 1964, committed the nation to a policy of equal opportunity in employment. Another statute that emerged in this burst of legislation was the Economic Opportunity Act of 1964, which represented the leading edge of the Johnson administration's War on Poverty.

At the base of this legislation was a Community Action Program which sought the development of grass-roots organizations to permit the "maximum feasible participation of the poor" in the program. The act created the Neighborhood Youth Corps (similar in concept to the National Youth Administration of the 1930s) and also the Job Corps, which operated on the premise that some young people were so overburdened by circumstances in their homes and communities that they could not be suitably prepared for work unless they were moved to a controlled situation. Consequently, Job Corps conservation and urban centers were established, and eventually these tended to use vocational education methods, although their administrators had initially disavowed that traditional approach. Originally limited to young men, the Job Corps also began to enroll young women after 1967, when its founding legislation was amended to eliminate the exclusion of females. The Labor Department took over the operation of the Job Corps from the Office of Economic Opportunity in 1969.

The Economic Opportunity Act was amended several times during the 1960s, those actions creating the Neighborhood Youth Corps (NYC), which was intended primarily to provide low-wage summer jobs; Operation Mainstream, a rural work-relief program which was later folded into the Concentrated Employment Program (CEP); and New Careers, a program to develop paraprofessional personnel to take on some of the less critical tasks performed by professionals. Another noteworthy human resources effort of the 1960s was the Jobs in the Business Sector (JOBS) program, promoted by the National Alliance of Businessmen (NAB) and the Johnson administration; this program sought pledges from private employers to hire the disadvantaged. Upon application of the employer, training of the disadvantaged was subsidized by federal funds. The only other significant legislative enactment on the human resources front in the 1960s was the Work Incentive (WIN) program, which came into being as part of the 1967 amendments to the Social Security Act. WIN offered work and training incentives to welfare recipients enrolled in the program, each of whom received a monthly dollar allotment on top of public assistance payments. The WIN program also featured a work requirement as well as a range of services to make recipients more employable.

The aforementioned legislative initiatives and related amendments—the Area Redevelopment Act of 1961, the Manpower Training and Development Act of 1962, the Vocational Education Act of 1963, the Civil Rights Act of 1964, and the Economic Opportunity Act of 1964—constituted the basic tools of American human resources policy in the 1960s. Compared with past efforts, they may have appeared novel, prodigious, and even revolutionary. But as one seasoned student of this subject points out, the human resources programs of the period 1962–1968 "never achieved enrollments exceeding one percent of the labor force and never comprised as much as two percent of the federal budget."[9] The single policy decision of this period aimed at the general level of employment was the tax cut of 1964, which sought to overcome problems of the labor market by raising the demand for labor irrespective of what could be done on the supply side to improve skills, abilities, and work experience. The Civil Rights Act clearly represented intervention by the federal government in the job market, but it required those who suffered discrimination in employment to initiate actions for redress, and the enforcement machinery of the law relied on voluntary compliance by employers.

Thus it is perhaps quite accurate to regard these efforts in the aggregate as "trial-and-error experimentation" intended to bring "the outs in to share whatever was available at the lower margins of the labor market."[10] Like other public policies that have come into being on the American scene, including some of those reviewed in earlier chapters, the plethora of human resources legislation in the 1960s authorized programs which were not carefully planned, researched, integrated, or monitored. Despite this, the programs of the 1960s worked reasonably well in that their costs seemed justified by the benefits they generated for the recipients and for society.

PUBLIC SERVICE EMPLOYMENT

As the economic expansion of the 1960s turned into recession at the end of the decade, pressures emerged for the use of human resources outlays as a countercyclical measure. Thus, in 1971, the Nixon administration proposed that additional funds for human resources development become available—triggered —when the total national unemployment rate averaged or exceeded 4.5 percent for 3 consecutive months. At the funding level prevailing at the time for all human resources programs, about $2 billion, this proposal would have made available about $200 million, or 10 percent more money. The "trigger" concept for expenditures on human resources was exactly the same as the one (described in Chapter 10) that emerged in the recession of 1974–1975 to extend unemployment insurance benefits for additional periods, again as a countercyclical measure.

An even more explicit example of a countercyclical strategy was the proposed expansion of public employment during periods of economic decline. This policy called for the creation of specific public service jobs to combat the effects of recession, with the volume of such jobs linked to the severity of the economic downturn. The proposal was incorporated into the Emergency Employment Act, signed into law in 1971, which provided for a public employment program. It authorized outlays of $1 billion in fiscal 1972 and $1.25 billion in fiscal 1973 to create approximately 130,000 public service jobs. The legislation was implemented with considerable speed, funds being distributed among states, cities, and counties with populations of 75,000 or more.

Significantly, maximum authority and responsibility for the public employment program resided with state and local rather than federal officials. This reflected the more general trend that began to emerge in the late 1960s toward the decentralization of American human resources policies and programs. The result was that local officeholders and political party officials significantly affected the hiring and retention of employees under the Emergency Employment Act, and some public jurisdictions transferred work traditionally performed by regular civil service personnel to federally funded, public service employees. Officially, jobs provided under the Emergency Employment Act were targeted for the unemployed and underemployed and were regarded as transitional in nature. Funding was geared to the aggregate employment rate, the aforementioned 4.5 percent generally serving as a trigger, but with one-fifth of the total slotted for areas with 6.5 percent or more unemployment. Half of the jobholders were expected eventually to move onto permanent payrolls. In all, about 350,000 persons were employed under the temporary program between 1971 and 1973, in addition to 317,000 summer employees.[11]

The Comprehensive Employment and Training Act

If the creation of specific public service jobs to combat recession-induced unemployment was considered a novel measure in the early 1970s, it soon became a basic component of human resources policy. Title II of the Comprehensive Employment and Training Act (CETA), adopted in 1973, institutionalized the role of transitional public service employment on the American scene and specified that 20 percent of the funds available for such jobs were to be allocated to those areas in which there was 6.5 percent or more unemployment in any 3 consecutive months. Remaining funds were to be distributed at the discretion of the Secretary of Labor to areas experiencing even more severe unemployment. Under the program, priority was to be given to veterans returning home after 1964, the long-term unemployed, and graduates of training programs. Some $250 million was appropriated for Title II public service employment in fiscal 1974, with the total rising to well over $1 billion in fiscal 1977.[12]

Further, in 1974, Congress enacted the Emergency Jobs and Unemployment Assistance Act, which added Title VI to CETA authorizing a second public service employment program that provided additional money to areas of high unemployment. Of these Title VI funds, half were designated specifically for areas with 4.5 percent or more unemployment, and another one-quarter for areas with more substantial unemployment. Subsequent legislation extended this countercyclical public service employment program (Title VI) of CETA through the late 1970s and authorized new public service job projects and programs. Titles II and VI of the 1973 law remain the guiding provisions of policy governing public service employment in the United States.

Beyond codifying and extending public service employment programs as a component of human resources policy, CETA had several other important objectives and provisions. Fundamentally, this legislation sought to decentralize and decategorize American human resources programs. Prior to CETA, funds for training, development, and public service employment were distributed by the Department of Labor under a system of some 10,000 direct grants for categorical—that is, specific—human resources programs. The thrust of CETA was to make available to state and local governments and their elected officials funds for human resources training and public service employment which, within limits, could be used as these political leaders saw fit, rather than being expended strictly for one or another federally mandated program. State and local officials would decide what human resources services to provide, whom to serve, and whom to use as deliverers of the services. Title I of CETA provides for the funding and administration of services and programs through a system of "prime sponsors," described as:

> A state [or] a unit of general local government which has a population of 100,000 or more persons . . . any combination of units of general local government . . . any unit of general local government or any combination of such units, without regard to population, which, in exceptional circumstances, is determined by the Secretary of Labor.[13]

It is the task of these prime sponsors to use their own judgment to determine which training and employment programs best fit the needs of their particular areas and labor markets. But they must do so within the structure of a planning council that includes representatives of concerned groups such as labor, business, recipients of services (clients), and community-based institutions. The council's job is to set goals and policies, evaluate existing programs, make appropriate recommendations for change, and analyze the local labor market. However, the council is an advisory body to the prime sponsor—a city mayor, a state governor, or other elected head of the unit of government in question. A State Manpower Council whose members are appointed by the Governor reviews the plans of each prime sponsor in the state and monitors program operations.

To qualify for CETA funds, a prime sponsor must outline its plan to meet the needs of target groups and must work with existing government services and facilities, such as a public employment program. Title I requires funds to be allotted to states and localities on the basis of prior funding levels, the number of unemployed persons, and the number of adults in low-income families. In exercising discretion to allot funds for employment and training, the Secretary of Labor is mandated to "take into account the need for continued funding of programs of demonstrated effectiveness."[14]

It should be kept in mind that considerable decentralization of human resources programs had occurred in the late 1960s, and thus CETA tended to endorse, legitimize, and extend what was in many areas already a fact of life. The repeal of MDTA and most of the Economic Opportunity Act by Title VI of CETA was thus less significant than might have appeared at first glance. But the decategorization of human resources programs was given an emphasis under CETA that, by and large, had not been present before 1973. The twin thrust of CETA, decentralization and decategorization of American human resources programs, was consistent with the concept of "the new federalism" that prevailed in the early 1970s; it placed responsibility on "governors, mayors and county officials who face voter retribution if they do not perform satisfactorily."[15] Interestingly, the decentralization of human resources programs in the 1970s contrasted notably with the efforts to centralize and enlarge the role of the federal government in some of the programs for income supplements and social protection reviewed in Chapter 10.

Besides Titles I, II, and VI, to which we have already referred, CETA contains five other major provisions. Title III in effect continues some preexisting categorical grant programs under the jurisdiction of the Department of Labor. It identifies special target groups and projects—summer jobs for economically disadvantaged young people, migrant farm workers, Indians, older workers, criminal offenders, and persons with limited knowledge of English—for which specific financing is provided. Additionally, the Secretary of Labor is given authority to conduct human resources research and demonstration projects and to develop a computerized job bank based upon information received from national, state, and local labor markets. The Secretary also is empowered to fund special programs to help young people in rural and urban areas acquire employment and training, integrated with their school attendance.

Title IV of the 1973 legislation speaks directly to the Job Corps program, mentioned previously. The legislation authorized the transfer of the Job Corps out of the Economic Opportunity Act to the Secretary of Labor, but that merely confirmed what had occurred operationally 5 years earlier. The Secretary is charged with developing "a program of education, vocational training and counseling, and related activities for low-income youth between the ages of 14 and 22 from culturally deprived or disoriented homes who could complete and secure the full benefits of the program.''[16] Title IV sets out criteria and provisions for both residential and nonresidential training centers, and it pointedly authorizes the increased enrollment of women so that they will make up from 25 to 50 percent of the Job Corps. The Secretary of Labor may establish rules for screening and selecting applicants for enrollment in the Job Corps and is expected to work with local and community action organizations to recruit young persons into the program.

Title V of CETA established the National Commission for Manpower Policy, a seventeen-member body whose task is to advise the Secretary of Labor on national issues concerning human resources. The Commission was charged specifically with studying the impact of the energy crisis of the mid-1970s on human resources needs, with assessing the effectiveness of various programs and services in achieving CETA goals, and with examining the interrelationships among human resources programs, including the Work Incentive (WIN) program. (In late 1978 the Commission was renamed the National Commission for Employment Policy.)

Title VII contains general provisions which apply to all other titles of CETA. They include definitions of terms, conditions of work and training, prohibitions against discrimination and political activities, and procedures for managing programs authorized by the act. Finally, Title VIII, which was added to CETA as a result of legislation passed in 1977, established the Young Adult Conservation Corps to provide employment to youth in conservation work and related projects on public lands and waters.

The Politics of Human Resources Legislation These various titles begin to suggest the political forces at work in American human resources legislation. Those groups which served as the targets of human resources programs in the pre-CETA era by and large continued to do so after passage of the 1973 law. When a particular group is the focal point of a specific public program, it becomes a constituency supporting retention or expansion of that program. This is so whether we are dealing with human resources training and development or some other issue. Consequently, elected officials could not simply overturn the human resources programs authorized by previous legislation and start afresh with an entirely new law, pressed as they were by various target groups who wanted to retain the benefits that earlier laws had given them. Instead, Congress retained most of those programs in CETA, decategorizing them to be sure, and later expanded public service employment because that seemed a suitable political response to the economic problem of recession. In this sense, CETA was evolutionary rather than revolutionary human resources legislation, established, like all public policies, through the political decision-making processes of government.

Similarly, a mere recitation of CETA's main titles provides little in the way of clues to the many conflicts that occurred in the early 1970s between the Nixon administration and Congress and between the House of Representatives and the Senate over the appropriate regulation of American human resources policy.[17] Particularly spirited was the maneuvering of positions over the control of human resources programs and the role of public service employment in the overall effort. The nature of program control as it emerged in CETA reflects a compromise between the position of decentralization (favored by the administration), on the one hand, and the desire of many congressional legislators to retain federal monitoring of, if not responsibility for, state and locally operated CETA programs, on the other. The result was the requirement that state and local governments submit their specific plans to the Secretary of Labor for review and approval prior to the authorization of funds. Further, the Secretary can cut off CETA funds to prime sponsors who do not carry out the intent of the legislation or can refuse to award such funds. At the same time, the law preserves the right of court appeal by prime sponsors who disagree with the Secretary's decision to cut off funds. And finally, the law requires all Labor Department guidelines for implementing CETA to be submitted to Congress 30 days in advance of their being put into effect. Proponents of the law believed that this provision would ensure the carrying out of Congress's legislative mandates.

As to public service employment, it survived numerous efforts by the administration to emasculate it, and, as we noted earlier, Title II deals explicitly with this component of human resources policy. The funding level authorized by the 1973 legislation ($250 million in the first year), which was supposed to generate about 40,000 public service jobs, may not have seemed large in relation to total unemployment in the American economy. However, any statutory support for a permanent public service employment program must be considered an important achievement in light of the forces which opposed such action. After all, the "new federalism" (the term itself signifying the role of partisan politics in decisions on public policy), emphasizing, as it did, local control of human resources programs, also rested in part on the assumption that the private sector was the ultimate repository of the skills of workers who were trained and developed through publicly funded initiatives. Indeed, if training and development was not intended to make the unskilled, inexperienced, and disadvantaged members of society fit for competition in the private labor market, what was its purpose?

If that perspective on human resources policy is extended to its logical conclusion, however, it suggests that a program for public service employment should be only temporary or transitional in nature, rather than permanent. Yet CETA authorized just such a permanent program, and later a temporary (countercylical) one on top of it, and thus the legislative achievements of the early 1970s in this area may be regarded as quite considerable. What is perhaps most remarkable in analyzing human resources policy in this period is the apparent absence of recognition that, since the early 1950s, employment in the United States had grown more rapidly in the public than in the private sector. Hence preparation for employment in the public sector could well have been deemed more suitable than preparation for employment in the private sector for individuals occupying avowedly transitional public service jobs. But that might have conflicted with the preferences of employers to have the public sector pay the costs of training and developing individuals for subsequent employment in the private sector, as in the case of public education, for example. In any event, the reader is encouraged to consider the politics as well as the economics of human resources policy in order to have a balanced perspective on this issue.[18]

Program Performance under CETA[19]   In fiscal 1977 almost $13 billion, or between 0.6 and 0.7 percent of GNP, was expended on the various human resources programs reviewed above. Of this amount, $8.4 billion was for programs (principally public service employment) under Titles II and VI of CETA, the last of which alone absorbed approximately $6.8 billion. About $1.9 billion was spent on employment and training services under Title I, and an additional $1.4 billion was devoted to programs for young people under Title III. Roughly 2.8 million persons were employed in, or serviced by, CETA programs in 1977, and another 570,000 were enrolled in the WIN program. In that year, there were 445 prime sponsors who carried out one or more CETA human resources programs within their local communities.

Recall that Title I of CETA is heavily aimed at the disadvantaged and seeks to improve the employability of individuals by upgrading their education and skills, providing subsidized work experience, and offering counseling and support services. In contrast, Titles II and VI provide short-term public service jobs that are expected eventually to lead to permanent employment. As a result, the characteristics of participants in CETA differ considerably as between Title I and Titles II and VI. This is evident from the data in Table 11-2, which compares enrollees in CETA programs under the three main titles in the period 1975–1977 with unemployed persons generally.

Observe that participants in Title I programs were predominantly young (52 percent were under 22 years of age), economically disadvantaged (78 percent fell in this category), and of relatively low educational attainment (50 percent had less than a high school education). They also included more women and minorities than participants in other CETA programs. The participants in Title I programs in 1977 were not much different from participants in earlier years including the pre-CETA categorical program era. But of course they were quite different from those enrolled in the public service employment program under Titles II and VI, who tended to be more like the unemployed in general. Participants under these two titles were more apt to be men in the prime working years (ages 22 to 44) and to be better educated, and they were less likely to be women or members of a minority group than Title I enrollees. Less than half of Title II participants, but about two-thirds of Title VI participants, were economically disadvantaged in 1977.

Data pertaining to outcomes of programs under CETA over the period 1975–1977 are presented in Table 11-3. Focusing on 1977, about 70 percent of the enrollees in the three major programs were "positively terminated," in the sense of being placed in unsubsidized employment, finding jobs on their own, or engaging in other activities that increased their employability. A small pro-

Table 11-2 Characteristics of Participants in CETA and Other Programs and of the Unemployed Population, Fiscal Years 1975–1977, Percent

Characteristic	CETA									U.S. unemployed population		
	Title I			Title II			Title VI					
	1975	1976	1977[1]	1975	1976	1977[1]	1975	1976	1977[1]	1975	1976	1977[1]
Total	100.0	100.0	100.0	100.0	100.0	100.0	100.0	100.0	100.0	100.0	100.0	100.0
Sex												
Male	54.4	54.1	51.5	65.8	63.8	60.0	70.2	65.1	64.1	54.9	55.5	53.2
Female	45.6	45.9	48.5	34.2	36.2	40.0	29.8	34.9	35.9	45.1	44.5	46.8
Age												
Under 22 years	61.7	56.7	51.7	23.7	21.9	20.3	21.4	22.0	20.3	34.8	33.6	34.2
22–44 years	32.1	36.5	40.8	62.9	64.0	64.2	64.8	64.1	64.9	46.0	46.6	47.2
45 years and over	6.1	6.8	7.4	13.4	14.1	15.5	13.8	13.9	14.8	19.1	19.8	18.6
Education												
8 years and under	13.3	11.9	10.0	9.4	8.0	7.3	8.4	8.1	8.2	15.1	12.9	13.0[2]
9–11 years	47.6	42.9	39.8	18.3	17.9	15.2	18.2	17.7	18.9	38.9	28.7	29.9[2]
12 years and over	39.1	45.2	50.2	72.3	74.1	77.5	73.3	74.2	72.8	46.0	58.4	57.1[2]
Economically disadvantaged	77.3	75.7	78.3	48.3	46.5	48.9	43.6	44.1	66.6[3]	[4]	[4]	[4]

Race												
White[5]	54.6	55.3	56.7	65.1	61.4	70.6	71.1	68.2	66.2	81.1	80.7	79.2
Black	38.5	37.1	34.7	21.8	26.5	22.9	22.9	23.0	25.9	18.9	19.3	20.8
American Indian	1.3[6]	1.4[6]	1.4[6]	1.0	1.3	1.4	1.1	1.8	3.0			
Other[7]	5.6	6.2	7.2	12.1	10.8	5.0	4.9	7.0	4.9			
Hispanic origin	12.5	14.0	13.7	16.1	12.4	13.5[8]	12.9	9.9	12.0[8]	6.5	6.5	6.0
Limited English-speaking ability	4.1[6]	5.1[6]	5.2[6]	8.0	4.3	2.5	4.6	3.5	2.9	[4]	[4]	[4]
Veterans												
Special Vietnam era[9]	5.2	3.6	2.7	11.3	10.1	7.4	12.5	8.7	6.5	7.5	8.0	7.9
Other	4.4	4.5	7.4	12.6	11.4	15.2	14.6	12.0	18.4	9.4	9.7	8.0

[1] Data for the period Oct. 1, 1976, to Sept. 30, 1977, cumulative.

[2] Data are based on the month of March 1977 only.

[3] Not strictly comparable to data for earlier fiscal years because of a change in the definition of "economically disadvantaged." Prior to fiscal 1977, the determination was based, in part, on whether the participant was a member of a family whose annual income in relation to family size and location did not exceed the most recently established poverty levels as determined by the Office of Management and Budget. The current determination is based on either the poverty level or 70 percent of the Bureau of Labor Statistics lower living standard income level—whichever is higher.

[4] Not available.

[5] Includes Hispanic origin Americans (Cubans, Puerto Ricans, Mexican Americans, and Latin Americans) as well as those who do not appear to belong to one of these groups but who have last names of Hispanic origin.

[6] Special programs for Indians and those with limited English-speaking ability operate under Title III of CETA.

[7] A large portion of this group reflects the nonclassification by race.

[8] Estimated.

[9] A veteran who served in Indochina or Korea, including waters adjacent thereto, between Aug. 5, 1964, and May 7, 1975, inclusive, and who received other than a dishonorable discharge.

Note: Detail may not add to totals because of rounding.

Source: Adapted from *Employment and Training Report of the President, 1978,* 1978, p. 42.

Table 11-3 Cumulative Terminations from Programs Conducted under CETA Titles I, II, and VI, Fiscal Years 1975–1977, Percent

Type	Total			Title I			Title II			Title VI		
	1975	1976	1977[1]	1975	1976	1977[1]	1975	1976	1977[1]	1975	1976	1977[1]
All terminations	100.0	100.0	100.0	100.0	100.0	100.0	100.0	100.0	100.0	100.0	100.0	100.0
Positive	60.9	67.5	70.7	62.7	68.0	70.2	54.3	75.8	83.2	45.6	61.4	54.2
Placements	30.7	28.9	34.5	31.8	31.0	38.9	23.4	17.2	17.5	29.0	26.8	33.8
Direct[2]	9.8	6.9	4.7	11.3	9.1	6.5	1.4	.7	.3	1.0	1.3	.5
Indirect[3]	14.9	15.5	21.7	15.3	16.2	24.5	13.7	11.2	11.9	12.3	15.3	19.2
Self and other[4]	6.0	6.5	8.1	5.2	5.7	7.9	8.3	5.3	5.3	15.7	10.2	14.1
Other[5]	30.2	38.6	36.2	30.9	37.0	31.3	30.9	58.6	65.7	16.6	34.6	20.4
Nonpositive[6]	39.1	32.5	29.1	37.3	32.0	29.7	45.7	24.2	16.5	54.4	38.6	45.5

[1] Data for the period, Oct. 1, 1976, to Sept. 30, 1977, cumulative.

[2] Direct placements: individuals placed in unsubsidized employment after receiving only outreach, intake, assessment, and/or job referral services from CETA.

[3] Indirect placements: individuals placed in unsubsidized employment after participating in CETA training, employment, or supportive services.

[4] Self and other placements: individuals who found jobs through their own efforts or means other than placement by the prime sponsor.

[5] Other positive: individuals who left a CETA program to enroll full time in an academic or vocational school, to enter a branch of the armed forces, to enroll in a human resources program not funded under CETA, or to engage in any other activity that increases employability. This category also includes an undetermined but relatively large number of transfers between Titles II and VI.

[6] Nonpositive: individuals who dropped out or left for reasons unrelated to jobs or activities that increase employability.

Note: Detail may not add to totals because of rounding.

Source: Adapted from *Employment and Training Report of the President, 1978,* 1978, p. 43.

portion of this total resulted from transfers between the two public service employment programs under Titles II and VI, which are counted by the federal government as activities enhancing employability. Between 1975 and 1977, the incidence of positive terminations from these CETA programs increased by about 10 percentage points, though it declined somewhat in Title VI programs during the last of these years.

How the thrust of Title I programs differed from that of programs under Titles II and VI is illustrated in Figure 11-1. Work experience and classroom training accounted for most activity by enrollees under Title I programs between 1975 and 1977, with almost 80 percent of the 1.4 million participants active in either of these two components during the last year of this period, but with only 2 percent active in public service employment. By way of contrast, 96 percent of Title II participants and 94 percent of Title VI enrollees were in public service jobs during fiscal 1977. Taking the three titles together, some 922,500 persons, or 40 percent of all CETA enrolless, were in public service employment during the year.[20] Approximately 588,000 persons were in work experience programs under CETA during 1977, with a considerable proportion of the jobs in that category closely paralleling those officially designated as public service positions. These data attest to the significant role that public service employment has come to play in American human resources policy.

Recall that the Job Corps Program, subsumed under Title IV of CETA, is directed specifically at disadvantaged young people aged 16 to 21 years and seeks to provide them with basic education and vocational training at both residential and nonresidential centers. Of the 41,000 new Job Corps enrollees in 1977 roughly 70 percent were male and under 19 years of age, 85 percent had less than a high school education, 54 percent were black, 11 percent were Spanish-speaking, and 70 percent were from families on public assistance or earning less than $5000. In the same year, the Job Corps had a placement rate of about 93 percent. Of 29,600 total placements, roughly 20,000 were in paid employment, with the remainder returning to school or entering military service. These characteristics of the Job Corps closely parallel those of prior years.

Even this brief review of the operations of human resources programs would be incomplete without consideration of the Work Incentive Program (WIN). Intended to help employable welfare recipients find jobs, the WIN program became subject to new regulations in 1976 which were intended to streamline and improve its operations. Under the Intensive Employment Services (IES) component of the program, enrolled welfare recipients are interviewed by a placement specialist and are promptly given information about the labor market.[21]

The factual record of WIN registrants and job entrants for 1977 is shown in Table 11-4. We see that registrants were overwhelmingly female, mostly white, and in their twenties and thirties and that they generally had less than a high school education. In terms of their experiences, in the labor market, "the job-finding difficulties encountered by many women, youth, minorities and older workers are reflected in the job entry experience of WIN registrants."[22] Men,

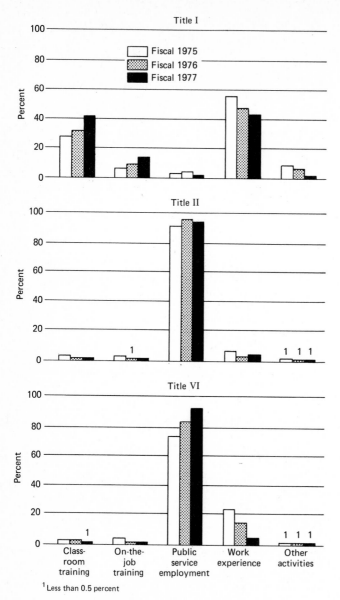

Figure 11-1   Activities of enrollees under CETA programs, fiscal years 1975–1977. (*Source: Employment and Training Report of the President, 1978, U.S. Government Printing Office, Washington, D.C., 1978, p. 41.*)

whites, and the more highly educated were better represented among those who found jobs than among registrants, and older persons (in this case, over 40 years of age) were less well represented.

What were the kinds of jobs and the pay rates obtained by WIN registrants who entered employment in 1977? Figure 11-2 shows that over one-half of the

Table 11-4   WIN Registrants and Job Entrants, by Selected Characteristics, Fiscal Year 1977
(Percent)

Characteristic	Registrants	Job entrants
Total	100.0	100.0
Sex		
Male	27.5	37.7
Female	72.5	62.3
Age		
Under 22 years	15.7	15.3
22–39 years	62.4	69.3
40 years and older	21.9	15.4
Education		
Under 8 years	10.3	6.3
8–11 years	48.7	45.2
12 years	33.2	38.8
Over 12 years	7.8	9.7
Race		
White	55.8	67.5
Black	38.7	28.9
Other	2.8	2.6
Information not		
available	2.7	1.0

Source: Adapted from *Employment and Training Report of the President, 1978*, 1978, p. 55.

women but less than one-fifth of the men became employed as clerical and service workers. Men most often found jobs related to manufacturing and construction. As to pay rates, over 60 percent of the men who found jobs in 1977 received at least $3 an hour, while more than 70 percent of the women earned less than that amount. In fact, 19 percent of the men but only 3 percent of the women earned a minimum of $5 an hour. Note that, in 1977, average hourly earnings throughout the economy were $5.24, in manufacturing they were $5.63, and in retail trade they were $3.83. Among the total group of WIN registrants who found jobs, blacks received lower pay on the average than whites (70 versus 54 percent, respectively, earned less than $3 in 1977), and younger persons earned less than older ones. These data indicate that of those who are able to secure paid employment and leave welfare—keep in mind that most welfare recipients are female heads of households with young children—the vast majority apparently become part of the working poor.

Because the relationship of work to welfare in the United States has been especially subject to both popular debate and public policy, it is instructive to summarize a recent evaluative study of the WIN program.[23] Conducted between 1974 and 1975, the study sought to measure net gains in earnings as well as reductions in welfare payments experienced by active WIN participants. The total sample of 5300 WIN registrants distributed among some seventy-eight program sites was divided into two groups; one consisted of participants who received WIN services, and the other consisted of nonparticipants who

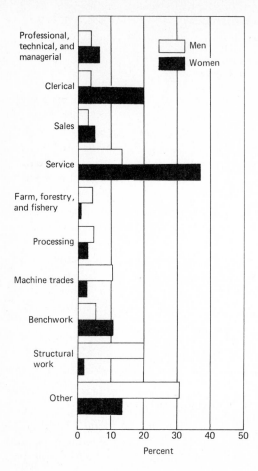

Figure 11-2 Ocupational placements of registrants in WIN programs, fiscal year 1977. (*Source:* Employment and Training Report of the President, 1978, *U.S. Government Printing Office, Washington, D.C., 1978, p. 54.*)

received no services. In scientific parlance, the former was the experimental group, and the latter was the control group—although a sound argument could be made for adding nonregistrants and even poverty-stricken persons not on welfare as additional controls.

The study yielded several conclusions: the first-year earnings of recipients of WIN services were about $400 greater than the earnings of nonrecipients, and their employment lasted about 3 weeks longer; the largest net earnings gains were achieved by those with the least amount of recent work experience; net annual earnings benefits were about $580 more for participating than for nonparticipating white men and $635 more for participating than for nonparticipating white women, but only $255 more for participating than for nonparticipating black women, and there was no difference between the annual earnings benefits of participating and nonparticipating black men; and net earnings gains were substantially greater for participants who received both classroom training and placement services instead of just the latter. As to net reductions in welfare payments, probably the key issue of public concern, these were quite limited

($165 for men and $105 for women in the first year), and WIN participants were no more likely, on the average, to leave welfare than nonparticipating registrants with similar characteristics.[24]

The methodology employed in this assessment of the WIN program is commonly used to evaluate social programs generally. For example, commenting on the Job Corps, three noted experts on human resources observe that ultimately this program, "like any other skill training program, must defend itself on the basis of its trainees' subsequent employment experience."[25] To determine that experience, it is necessary to match a group of training recipients to a comparable group which differs only in that its members do not receive the training in question. Once such comparability has been achieved, the groups must be followed, observed, or surveyed over some period of time following completion by the "experimentals" of their training program. Then the researcher analyzes the data and, it is hoped, is able to attribute any differential experiences in the labor market—earnings, duration of employment, occupational attainments, spells of unemployment—to the investment in human resources training.[26]

Obviously, such differentials may not in fact exist, and the ability to control for the significant factors affecting observed differentials may be quite limited. Is it any wonder, then, that in terms of federal human resources initiatives, no comprehensive or "really rigorous evaluation has been made of the effect of these programs on the employment and income of the people who went through them?"[27] Suffice it to say that soundly conceived evaluations of particular human resources programs, as well as broader, impressionistic judgments reached by experienced researchers and informed observers, seem to support the conclusion that these programs have worked in that "most of the people who went through [them] came out sufficiently better off in employment stability and income to justify the expenditure."[28] Put differently, the overall result of these programs was to move participants closer to escaping poverty status than they otherwise would have been.[29] Thus, the most balanced judgment that apparently can be rendered about the programs carrying out American human resources policies is that they have been modestly successful. This does not take into account, however, the commitment to human resources planning and development which is reflected in the totality of American programs and which merits some weight in forming an evaluative scorecard on this issue.

It is possible to apply still another evaluative criterion to these programs, namely, their impact on unemployment in the American economy. The fact of the matter is, though, that until recently the levels of federal expenditure authorized for human resources programs were simply not large enough to affect the aggregate unemployment rate or the rates for major subgroups of the labor sector. Whether the $12.7 billion spent on human resources in fiscal 1977, for example, had any actual impact on unemployment or not remains to be determined by empirical study, but this will depend greatly on the extent to which those who were hired into public service employment jobs or trained for employment in the private and public sectors had relatively few skills and had been previously unemployed for that reason. With the 725,000 public service employment job slots authorized for fiscal 1978 and a total of about 1.4 million people expected to occupy them over the course of the year, it was theoretically possible for this program to reduce economywide unemployment by about one-half of one percent. That is an extremely unlikely result in the real world, however, given that some participants in public service employment would otherwise have been employed and that some of the projects they worked on would have been funded from regular state and local sources rather than from federal funds. This phenomenon of "fiscal substitution" is difficult to avoid in a decentralized human resources program and when elected officials in some states and localities have had to lay off regular civil service personnel because of fiscal stringency; nevertheless, it limits public service employment and other human resources programs from having much of an impact on aggregate unemployment in the United States.

More generally, in an economy in which the GNP is rapidly approaching $2 trillion and in which the number of unemployed persons in recent years has ranged between roughly 6 and 8 million, expenditures on human resources programs of $12 billion or so cannot have much of an impact on measured employment. Recognize that this should not in any sense be taken as evidence of the ineffectiveness of human resources programs, even though, depending upon one's values, it might be regarded as a failure of policy. It may be that further increases in total expenditures on human resources and major expansion of public service employment jobs to a level of, say 1.4 million, as was proposed by the Carter administration in 1978 as part of an overall welfare reform package, would produce an impact on (that is, reduce) national unemployment.[30] At the very least, congressional approval of such increases in expenditures and expansion of existing programs would offer an opportunity to study and measure the effects of human resources policy on unemployment, in addition to the effects of specific programs on the experiences in the labor market of those for whom they are intended.

EDUCATION AND HUMAN RESOURCES DEVELOPMENT

We noted in Chapter 7 that the human capital approach to labor market analysis emphasizes education and training as important determinants of individual productivity and personal earnings growth over a lifetime. When this approach is applied to the economy as a whole, it similarly "explains" an important part of a nation's development over time—that is, its economic growth record—and, more importantly, differences in economic growth rates among nations.

For example, in the early 1960s, Harbison and Myers studied seventy-five nations, ranging from the most to the least advanced, and uncovered a correlation coefficient of .89 between these countries' indices of levels of human resources development and their gross national products (GNPs).[31] The index for each country was composed of several factors, but education of the labor force played the most prominent role. The researchers also found that the most advanced nations (for example, the United States, New Zealand, Japan, France, Israel, Argentina, and West Germany) were spending proportionately more of their national income on education than the remaining countries, although among the latter the least developed were investing in education more heavily than the partially developed or semiadvanced nations. These findings were interpreted to mean that the "have" nations were widening the gap between themselves and the "have-not" nations in the sphere of investment in human resources, much as they were alleged to be doing in the case of capital investment. A decade or so later, Harbison and his colleagues replicated the earlier study and found the major conclusions largely unchanged.[32]

That education may represent a nation's most important investment in human resources is well recognized today, but it was not always so. Writing in 1961, Theodore W. Schultz, then president of the American Economic Association, admonished his fellow economists for failing to treat rigorously and incorporate into their analytical frameworks expenditures on education— whether at the national level or at individual levels.[33] He reasoned that such expenditures could be examined and explained in the same way as expenditures on land, machinery, equipment, and capital improvements. This was the origin of the modern "education-as-investment" approach, or, more generally, the human capital approach to labor market analysis. In 1960, total expenditures in the United States on education were $25 billion; by 1978, they were $142 billion.[34]

Substantial debate over the connection between education and individual productivity emerged almost simultaneously with the human capital approach to labor market analysis. But such controversy aside for the moment, the rising educational level of American workers is an undeniable fact of life. Over the period 1952–1977, for example, the median number of years of schooling completed by the civilian labor force rose from 10.9 to 12.6; the proportion with some college education more than doubled, from 16.2 to 33.2 percent; and the proportion with less than a high school education dropped by over one-half, from 56 to 27 percent.[35] As noted in Chapter 8, black workers not only shared in this advancement of educational levels but also substantially closed the gap between themselves and white workers. By 1977, black men had only one-half year less schooling, at the median, than white men (12.1 versus 12.6 years, respectively), and the difference was even smaller between black and white women (12.6 versus 12.3 years, respectively).[36]

The growth of higher education in particular has, of course, been a major development of the post-World War II era. Indeed, it recently was described by one group of authorities as "a virtual educational revolution, paralleled only by the extension of universal secondary education nearly 40 years ago"[37] (in 1936). Figure 11-3 shows the growth of the college-age population and college enrollments from the beginning of the twentieth century to the late 1970s; it also projects these totals to the year 2000. By then, it is expected that between 15

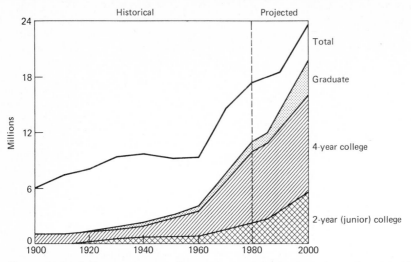

Figure 11-3 College-age group (18 to 21 years) and selected enrollments, 1900–2000. (*Source: F. Ray Marshall, Allan M. Cartter, and Allan G. King,* Labor Economics: Wages, Employment, and Trade Unionism, *3d ed., Irwin, Homewood, Ill., 1976, p. 558.*)

and 20 million persons will be enrolled in institutions of higher education, and this in spite of the declining rate of increase in enrollment expected to occur after the mid-1980s or thereabouts. Increases in enrollments in junior colleges and community colleges (2-year institutions) and professional degree programs have been especially marked and seem likely to continue into the foreseeable future. The production of those holding a doctorate, which increased throughout the twentieth century but most sharply over the last two decades, is more problematic for the 1980s and beyond in view of the downturn in the academic labor market that began in the early 1970s. Still, by the end of the century, "it appears likely that there will be as many persons receiving the doctorate . . . as received the baccalaureate in 1928."[38]

Clearly, the enhanced education of the American labor force is a development of enormous significance. The data presented in earlier chapters indicated that the higher an individual's educational attainment, the more likely he or she is to be in the labor force, to be employed rather than out of work, to be unemployed for only short periods when changing jobs or reentering the work force, and to have a professional or skilled technical position. Many studies testify to the significant positive correlation between investments in education and lifetime earnings. And, of course, there are additional benefits to be derived from the attainment of higher educational levels—psychic, cultural, and intellectual benefits—which may not relate directly or at all to the income-generating effects of such attainment. These benefits reflect the "consumption" component of education, in contrast to the "investment" component.

The significance of these rising educational levels for human resources development is that they have been promoted in part and strongly supported by public policies at all levels of government. So-called "free public education," at least through high school, has been a long-standing practice on the American scene, a practice, incidentally, that was once considered feasible only in a non-capitalist society.[39] Virtually every local public school district in the United States is financed through property taxes or a combination of property taxes and state aid (itself derived from income taxes). It is the expressed policy of these taxes to support the early development of the nation's human resources through the public educational system, even as some segments of the populace avail themselves and their children of primary and secondary education through private schools. In 1978, all expenditures for elementary and secondary education totaled $92 billion, or some 5 times larger than in 1960.[40] At this level, the expenditures may be so large and the tax burden borne by the citizenry may be so great as to threaten the continuance of public education on this scale. Numerous signs of taxpayers' resistance to larger expenditures on education (and, more generally, to larger expenditures by government) were evidenced during the 1970s.

In terms of higher education, in 1862 Congress enacted the Morrill Act which provided for a system of land-grant colleges and out of which emerged the nation's public university systems. More recently, especially since the mid-1960s, the junior college as a component of the country's higher educational system has expanded dramatically. Like the public schools, it is financed almost solely by government expenditures deriving from local or state sources. Students enrolled in such colleges typically pay only a nominal registration fee, as the cost of their education is supported through taxes levied on the citizenry. This is much like the situation prevailing in public 4-year colleges and universities, where tuition charges do not cover the actual expenses of instruction, the bulk of which are paid for from tax receipts. In 1978, total expenditures for institutions of higher education were $50 billion, or double the 1970 figure and 7½ times larger than in 1960. Of the former amount, all but 15 percent came from state and local government sources.[41]

Beyond these measures, the federal government further contributed to the growth of college enrollments in the post-World War II era by subsidizing the education of veterans under the GI Bill of Rights; by making low-interest, long-term loans available to millions of students; and, after 1957, when the Russians launched the first man-made satellite into space, by increasing severalfold its financial contributions to programs of higher education. Federal funds were instrumental to the expansion of various academic curricula during the 1960s, especially in the natural and physical sciences and in engineering. Basic research was generously supported, to the point where about one-half of the annual revenues received by some of the nation's leading colleges and universities flowed from the federal government. And this support generated further demands for trained researchers, skilled assistants, and apprentice graduate students, and ultimately for entry into institutions of higher education.

It is not without good reason that this period was regarded by many—college and university officials, most of all—as the golden age of higher education in the United States, for when the sustained expansion of the 1960s turned into the cyclical and "stagflation-ridden" 1970s, federal expenditures for training high-level human resources were not as easily forthcoming. The academic labor market, which could rightly be characterized as a booming one until the late 1960s, began to turn down thereafter. For the most part, the 1970s witnessed excess supply in the academic labor market and numerous of its subspecialties, in contrast to the excess demand that prevailed throughout much of the 1960s. As a result, public and private institutions of higher education, both of which are recipients of federal funds, began more carefully to scrutinize their programs and to prune some of them.

Still, the federal government remains a major financier of higher education in the United States, reflecting the continuance of a long-standing policy to develop the nation's human resources by means of direct and indirect investments. In 1978, it provided some $8 billion in grants to institutions of higher education, about ten times the level of support that prevailed in 1960.[42] If this policy is sometimes called into question, we would do well to remember the conclusion reached by Schultz, namely, that an important source of economic growth in modern industrialized nations has been the improved quality of their human resources over time. Education has been a fundamental element in this record of improvement.

But can there be too much education or too heavy an emphasis on education? The question may seem heretical, but many informed observers have answered it with a resounding "yes!" Advocates of the human capital approach, for example, regard the decision to invest in education (at any level) on a par with other investment decisions. When rates of return on investments in education are high relative to rates of return on other investments, they will attract new entrants into the market, who will bid up the demand for education. With a stable or less rapidly growing supply of educational programs and the employment opportunities associated with them, rates of return on investments in education will fall. In this fashion, forces in the market provide one answer to the question of too much (or too little) investment in education. Incidentally, this analysis fits well the workings of the college labor market in the United States between 1969 and 1974, as analyzed by Freeman, using the human capital approach.[43]

Recognize, however, that even if market forces suggest too heavy an emphasis on education at a particular point in time or during a specific era, other forces are at work supporting continuance and even expansion of educational activity. These include the managers and administrators of educational institutions, manufacturers of school supplies and facilities, and teachers in schools and colleges who, it should be remembered, have increasingly joined labor organizations in recent years. Some of the interest groups that have supported human resources programs also favor expanded educational programs. And, of course, students are unlikely passively to accept a judgment that the national investment in education may somehow be too large. Since so much of the educational activity in the United States is funded with public money, which goes in part to private as well as public institutions, these interest groups—an educational lobby, we might say—can be expected to play important roles in national, state, and local decisions concerning educational policy. Thus, the question of education has both economic and political dimensions, as is true of any issue that affects the labor sector, and that is a matter of public policy.

Others have also concluded that there has been too heavy an emphasis on educational attainment in the United States, but for very different reasons from those suggested by advocates of the human capital approach. These critics contend that employers prefer better-educated personnel for subjective reasons rather than because of their potential productivity. That is, employers use education as a screening device to "select in" those whom they prefer and who presumably can do at least reasonably well on the job, while "selecting out" those whom they do not prefer but who might be equally capable, if not more capable, of performing on the job. Thus, employers are conspicuous consumers of education, which is valued for its own sake or for the personal attributes associated with it rather than because it enhances productivity.[44]

One needn't wholeheartedly embrace this thesis to recognize its applicability in a variety of settings. A college graduate lacking a teaching credential or a fifth year of higher education may be rejected for a position in a public school in favor of a more "qualified" candidate, even when the two are equally capable of performing the job. Or the holder of a bachelor's degree may be summarily rejected for entry into a management training program in favor of a candidate with a master's degree in business administration. Or a high school dropout may be deemed less preferable than a high school graduate for admission into an apprenticeship program leading to a skilled trade when the two may be equally capable of learning the job. Additionally, surveys of personnel specialists have shown them systematically to overstate the qualifications required for entry into various positions in their firms relative to the characteristics possessed by present occupants of such positions.[45] These examples do not, of course, prove that the more educated candidates could not outperform the less well educated candidates; in fact, we know very little about this, for, as was pointed out in Chapter 8, most employers' selection devices have not been properly validated. But in the absence of compelling evidence, both explanations of the role of education in personnel selection practices—that based on screening and that based on performance—can be argued by their respective advocates and can continue to vie for supremacy.

From a broader perspective, the more pernicious effect of an overly heavy emphasis on education as a qualification for employment is that its impact is likely to be greatest on those at the bottom of the occupational (and income) ladder. If some persons are displaced from high-ranking jobs by more highly educated individuals (either directly or by not being chosen for vacant positions), they are unlikely to go unemployed for long. Instead, they may "bump" (again, directly or indirectly) from other jobs those with still less education. If this process continues, the result is that workers in or near the lowest-ranking jobs are displaced from employment by the marginally more educated. Here we see a "trickle-down" effect of an overemphasis on educational credentials in the labor market, the brunt of which is borne by those with the fewest alternatives in the market—and the fewest opportunities to increase their level of education.

Again, one needn't accept this scenario fully to recognize the important point that it raises concerning formal education as a human resources development policy. To the extent that such a policy has contributed to the inflation of requirements for job entry, to screening, and to credentialism, it has nurtured structural rigidities in labor markets and has denied opportunities to members of the labor sector who may be productive enough to perform on certain jobs but who do not have enough education to obtain those jobs. Certainly "there is strong evidence that in the 1960s education was somewhat overemphasized as a necessary preparation for employment."[46] If this did not generate an excessive amount of national resources going to education, it nevertheless did result in an "unrealistic expectation of what education could do in the short-run for problems of long standing,"[47] and perhaps it also caused an overestimation of the contribution of education to national and personal incomes.

This is not to deny that the economic and technological changes looming on the scene portend relatively rapid growth of occupations with considerable intellectual content for which aspirants will require higher levels of education. It is to say, however, that public policies in support of education for human resources development are not inherently good or proper. Like the policies for training and the related human resources policies previously reviewed, they need to be carefully framed and closely evaluated so that their achievements and shortcomings may be known and so that changes in them may rest on an appropriate analytical base. Certainly that is the least that can be expected of this most fundamental area of public policy concerned with the development of the nation's human resources.

THE ROLE OF THE BUSINESS SECTOR

Historically, the business sector of American society has had little involvement in the development or implementation of governmental human resources policies. This may appear surprising in view of the objective of most human resources policies and programs, which is to equip and train individuals for permanent attachment to the labor force and for jobs in the private sector. But it is less or not at all surprising when one considers that the American business sector, operating in the context of a free society and a capitalist economy, tends to separate its activities from those of government and to regard public incursions into the former as unwarranted intrusions on private decision making. Such a blanket generalization must, of course, have many exceptions, and the JOBS program, described earlier in this chapter, is a good example (and a controversial one to boot) of cooperation between the public and private sectors. But more generally there are "important differences in attitudes and behavior with respect to [business's] interaction with government on manpower [policy and] . . . programs."[48] Businesspeople tend to look askance at deep involvement in advice and consultation on human resources policy in the public sector, "since, in the last analysis, the decisions would be made by legislators and administrators who had to respond to political pressures."[49]

These comments from a 1975 Washington conference on the role of the business sector in human resources policy do not indicate lack of interest on the part of businesspeople so much as they describe a view prevalent among business leaders that government can do little for them or their organizations directly in terms of meeting needs for human resources at the level of the firm. Certainly the business managers and executives who attended this conference, and many of their counterparts who did not, were concerned about the high levels of unemployment, the rapidly escalating expenditures on unemployment insurance, the exhaustion of state unemployment insurance reserve funds, and the mounting welfare costs that were induced by the recession of 1974–1975. Perhaps a conference held during a more buoyant economic period would have produced different views about the role of business in human resources policy. In any case, it is well to remember that the primary concern of businesspeople is with inflation in the economy (prices also rose by record amounts during the recession of the mid-1970s). In reacting to a variety of public policies regulating the use or affecting the costs of human resources—ERISA, OSHA, EEO, FLSA, unemployment insurance, social security, and the Taft-Hartley Act— business owners and managers reflect their general unease about a close involvement with the federal government in the area of human resources policy.

Like the labor sector, however, the business sector is hardly monolithic, and thus one can identify a diversity of opinion on this issue. For example, Jerome R. Rosow, former Assistant Secretary of Labor, proposed in 1975, when he was manager of public affairs planning at Exxon Corporation, that the following human resources policies be adopted by industry:[50]

Work sharing, achieved through a 4-day workweek and reduction of overtime assignments.

Corporation-sponsored retraining programs for new occupations in lieu of layoffs, to be offered in conjunction with community institutions supplying vocational training and with federally financed training and benefit programs.

Early-warning systems to provide substantial advance notice of layoffs, combined with pay in lieu of vacation and the integration of company-provided benefits beyond supplemental unemployment benefits with unemployment insurance.

Extension under a single umbrella of protections provided by employee-benefit plans to laid-off workers, either for specific time limits or until they find new jobs.

Expanded programs of early retirement as an alternative to layoffs and to extend the concept of minimum lifetime income, with management permitted the option of selecting for retirement the least productive among older workers.

As Rosow himself notes, "many of these ideas are already in practice, especially among the larger, more progressive corporations."[51] But where in existence, they emerged voluntarily with the aim of optimizing the use of human resources rather than being mandated by public policy. Indeed, the extent to which the practices proposed above should be totally integrated with national policies or broad economic and social objectives "is another question."[52] And it is a larger question because industry leaders see important differences between decisions that are reached internally and voluntarily for sound business reasons and those imposed upon them by government. This is true even if the focus of a particular governmental human resources policy or program squares closely with a specific company's objectives and practices concerning utilization of human resources.

To illustrate this point further, consider that in times of labor scarcity, when educational and training institutions cannot fully supply needed human resources, private firms will undertake such activity. This was most clearly demonstrated during World War II, when businesses hired and trained the unskilled and those with little education and also upgraded a wide variety of workers into skilled jobs, including women into craft positions. This was done not out of altruism or in accordance with a specific public policy concerning human resources but because labor shortages were widespread during the war years and because the costs of training and upgrading could be incorporated into the prices charged for products sold to the government and other businesses. American business also broadened its educational and training activity in the tight labor markets during the period of the Korean war and in the late 1960s. Again, these actions were undertaken primarily because they served business interests, not because they met objectives of public policy (even if they did). When labor markets are relatively loose, as they have been at most times in the post-World War II era, business is quite content to have its needs for human resources met at minimal cost by relying on existing educational and training institutions for supplies of labor.

Nevertheless, the diversity of opinion about human resources policy that prevails in the private business sector is further reflected in a 1978 statement on national policy by the Committee for Economic Development (CED).[53] This well-known organization, which enrolls the leaders of scores of major American companies, called for a new partnership between the public and private sectors to deal with human resources policy, and it also called for the creation of jobs for the hard-to-employ. Upon closer inspection, though, the policy initiatives proposed by the CED reflect the priorities which, as we noted above, are most commonly shared by businesspeople on the American scene. Chief among these is a strong economy, which can be achieved by "appropriate demand-management policies that aim at steady but vigorous economic growth."[54] Closely related to this recommendation is another for anti-inflation policies which take care to avoid "serious . . . capacity and supply bottlenecks . . . and cost-push pressures."[55] Only after treating these two issues does the CED deal with human resources policies, suggesting that they be used to attack structural unemployment, that is, the mismatch between the skills and abilities required to perform available jobs and those possessed by the unemployed.

If these are the components of an integrated employment strategy, according to the CED, then the implementation of that strategy should feature the following measures: adoption on a much wider scale of private programs, presently in place in some firms, which work effectively to reduce structural unemployment, including special training and efforts to create jobs; stronger mechanisms for active participation by business in devising training and employment opportunities, particularly at the local level and in consortia with community organizations, labor unions, and government units; greater reliance on special "jobs corporations" aimed at developing the employability of the hard-core unemployed and on intermediate nonprofit organizations (such as the Opportunities Industrialization Centers of America) that concentrate on skill development and job placement for minority-group members; federal subsidies to create job-training positions in the private sector, largely for unemployed veterans; and the reduction of disincentives for private firms to invest in training and jobs for the hard-to-employ, including the introduction of a lower minimum wage under FLSA for teenagers, older workers, and the partially disabled, together with exemptions for certain groups from existing minimum wage requirements.

Clearly, some of these proposals—the last, for example—are quite controversial, others are closely akin to recommendations concerning tax reduction and subsidization made by business leaders on different issues, and, as a group, they reflect the view that "if just given the tools," business in the private sector can "do the job" in the areas of employment and human resources development, as it has in other spheres of economic activity. But policy makers have shown themselves to be of a different mind, as reflected in recent and contemplated expansions of public service employment, which, incidentally, the CED opposes. One needn't criticize the objectives or deride the motives of business leaders to recognize that the views they hold differ in some significant respects from those of public officials and policy makers. This is reflected in the contemporary debate over human resources policy in the United States, and it helps us understand why, on the American scene, the private sector hasn't been and still isn't closely involved in the development and implementation of governmental human resources policies and programs.

Human Resources Planning in the Firm

But if this is so, it is also the case that government policies in a variety of areas, including human resources, together with other forces operating in the economy and in work organizations, have resulted in a considerably greater emphasis today than before on human resources planning in the business firm. This is especially true of large companies. More than that, these forces, which will be taken up in more detail below, are spurring the transformation of the traditional personnel department from one which typically operates with a short-term orientation to fill the most urgent vacancy and cope with the latest "people" problem into a more analytical functional unit which adopts a long-term perspective more consistent with the firm's basic objectives and which provides systematic data useful for decision making—hence the ongoing evolution of the terms "human resources planning" and "human resources management." In pursuing our discussion of these developments, however, we shall initially focus on personnel planning in business. Recent surveys show that the vast majority of large companies engage in such planning activity,[56] and, although the specific tasks encompassed within the planning function may vary from firm to firm, they commonly are carried out within a framework that stresses "proposed designs and methods of action or procedure in using manpower resources to attain organizational objectives."[57]

Consider that personnel planning at the level of the firm has been stimulated by government monetary and fiscal policies that filter down to affect the labor market. For example, federal policies concerning taxes and expenditures in the middle and late 1960s were instrumental in the development of tight labor markets, in which unemployment dropped to 3.5 percent (in 1968 and 1969) and was considerably lower for particular subgroups of the labor force and for certain occupational specialties. With many firms experiencing shortages of labor and expecting others to develop, with expenditures on wages and benefits rising rapidly, and with the costs of recruitment, selection, and transfer also mounting as employers searched more widely and intensively for workers, increased attention was paid to personnel planning in business organizations. Personnel audits, including future projections of staffing needs, became more popular in the late 1960s and were conducted for blue-collar and clerical personnel as well as for relatively more scarce professional and managerial employees. In about one out of two large companies, internal and external sources of labor supply were systematically explored and projected, and instruction in such analysis and planning was given in about the same proportion to first-line supervisors. Job analysis also became a more popular activity, and a majority of large companies surveyed developed coordinated staffing practices to transfer personnel among divisions, balancing surpluses against shortages.

Out of this flurry of activity emerged a model of the personnel planning function in the firm, as depicted in Figure 11-4. It begins with the demand for the firm's products or services, which may change over time because of conditions in the market or because of internal decisions concerning efficiency or expansion of production. From this multifaceted demand are derived the firm's personnel planning requirements, which are made specific in terms of the occupational mix required for the jobs to be performed. To meet these requirements, the firm taps two major sources of supply or markets: external and internal. Employees may be recruited, selected, and placed from either type of market, although both typically will be used by a business firm, especially a large firm. Different sources of external supply prevail for various occupational specialties, while, internally, training, development, upgrading, and promotion are among the managerial tools to be used in meeting personnel requirements. The quantitative decision sciences are an important tool to aid in the application of this personnel planning model to the firm.

Despite the apparent thrust toward personnel planning at the level of the firm that developed in the late 1960s, some observers believed it to be a short-

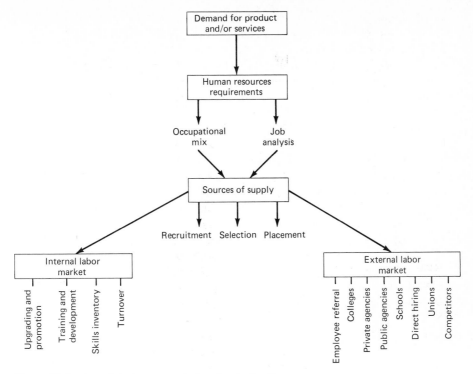

Figure 11-4   A model of personnel planning in the firm.

term phenomenon that would dissipate as soon as labor markets loosened. Such a view was expressed by researchers at the University of Minnesota, for example, who pointed out that, as imbalances in the labor supply eased, the costs of personnel planning and development might well exceed the benefits to the firm.[58] The logic of this position is sound; moreover, it is consistent with the reality that American labor markets have generally been loose in comparison with those in, say, western Europe. And, indeed, the literature of the early 1970s on such planning seemed to reflect disenchantment with it.

However, other complicating factors emerged in all this which were to reenergize the personnel planning function in the firm but also to alter it quite considerably. One of these was the increasingly service-oriented nature of the economy, requiring larger proportions of skilled, high-talent personnel in private firms. Another was the growth of two-earner families as well as smaller families, which resulted in some rethinking of policies for recruitment, selection, placement, promotion, and transfer in business organizations. Still another contributing factor was the increased incidence of mergers, acquisitions and diversification among American business organizations in the 1970s, all of which spurred greater attention to the coordination of personnel utilization across strategic and often highly diverse business units. But the most important development affecting personnel planning in the firm was the heightened incidence of government regulatory activity.

In earlier chapters, we traced the evolution of federal (and some state) policies governing equal employment opportunity, occupational safety and health, private pension arrangements, collective bargaining, minimum wages, unemployment insurance, social security, and retirement practices. The newer of these policy initiatives and changes in some of the older ones may seem to impose only one or another specific requirement on the firm in terms of its treatment and utilization of personnel. Taken together from a broader perspective, though, and in conjunction with the other forces noted above, they have engendered important changes in the way in which managers of modern business firms (again, large firms more than smaller ones) view their personnel and, more broadly, human resources management.

Examples of this altered perspective abound. One is the growing replacement of the term "personnel management" with "human resources management," a change that is at least as substantive as it is cosmetic. A second is the upgrading of human resources managers and of the function itself in an attempt to place it truly on a par (and not merely at the same level on the formal organization chart) with other key functional components of business organizations. Additional evidence of this upgrading is the movement of key executives in human resources management to the uppermost ranks within their organizations and the more general use of this function as an avenue or career path to top-management positions. But the most compelling evidence of an altered perspective on human resources management in the firm is the emerging attempt to link human resources planning to overall strategic business planning.

How widespread such efforts may be is unknown, as are their successes and failures, for no systematic survey of them exists for the business sector as a whole. But examples of such attempted linkages in some of the nation's best-known firms have been reported in the literature,[59] and, if history is any guide on this score, they can be expected to spread to other parts of the business sector. Essentially, the newer focus on human resources planning in the firm ties it to, and attempts to integrate it with, planning for the organization as a whole, rather than treating it as a separate and subordinate activity. Human resources planning thus becomes a component of total system planning within the organization, as depicted, for example, in Figure 11-5. Note the point at which human resources planning enters into this model, as compared with that shown in Figure 11-4. The newer model emphasizes the derivation of the objectives of the human resources system from overall company objectives, in the same way that marketing, production, finance, and other functional objectives are adduced.

Observe further that company objectives must be incorporated into a strategic business plan, which is first formulated and then implemented. Similarly, a strategic plan is formulated for each of the organization's key functional components, including human resources management. This formulation of strategy, whether for the organization as a whole or for the human resources function in

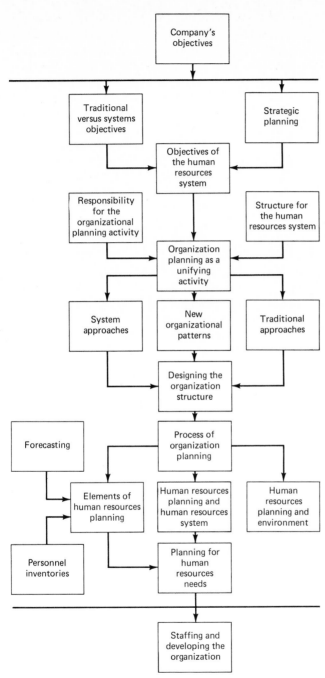

Figure 11-5 A model of organizational and human resources planning. (*Source: Adapted from Lawrence E. Klatt, Robert G. Mendick, and Fred E. Schuster,* Human Resources Management, *Irwin, Homewood, Ill., 1978, pp. 50–51.*)

particular, requires analysis of the environmental forces—economic, political, legal, social, and technological, for example—affecting the business or the specific function in question. For the human resources management function, the legal force of government policy (in equal employment opportunity, occupational safety and health, and other areas previously described) is a major environmental variable to be taken into account in formulating and implementing a strategic plan. And, as we have seen, it is these developments in public policy which have been so instrumental first in raising the consciousness of business leaders and managers about personnel planning and, more recently, in reorienting human resources management within business organizations. Where this reorientation will eventually lead is uncertain in terms of the effective utilization of human resources, but its emergence is observable and undeniable.

Before concluding this section, we must recognize that one of the ways in which public policies to regulate the utilization of human resources in the private sector have affected business organizations is by causing them to obtain more systematic information about this particular management function, information which may then become useful for internal decision making. This was an unexpected but largely positive consequence of federal regulatory policies concerning human resources. For example, in undertaking analyses of the racial composition of the local labor market and of its own work force in order to meet federal equal employment opportunity requirements, a firm also obtains useful data about the state of the market (excess supply, excess demand, or a rough balance) for specific occupations. This permits the firm better to tailor its recruitment, selection, and placement practices to conditions in the real world. Similarly, the gathering of data about its work force permits the firm to build a skills inventory and to assess its internal labor market as a source of supply to higher-ranking jobs, which may not be easily filled from the external market. Relatedly, a firm's training and development policies can be more closely linked than before to the characteristics and deficiencies in skill of its own work force and can be directed toward those employees with potential for greater responsibility and upward mobility. In still another instance, the gathering of information about safety and health conditions in local plants to satisfy federal reporting and regulatory requirements can assist the firm in diagnosing and correcting particularly deleterious conditions; also, and more broadly, such information can help in the design of basic production processes and in training first-line supervisors to enforce safety regulations.

It is especially the generation of information which is useful for decision-making purposes that has recently helped elevate human resources management in business organizations. Such information is important not only in dealing with specific components of the function and in meeting external legal requirements but also in demonstrating to other parts of the business organization that human resources management can help them diagnose and effectively deal with their particular problems. Thus, if American business is not heavily or directly involved in government programs, its own human resources policies and practices nevertheless have been strongly affected by government actions aimed at protecting and regulating the use of the labor sector.[60]

HUMAN RESOURCES POLICY IN COMPARATIVE PERSPECTIVE[61]

It has sometimes been fashionable for observers of human resources policies in foreign nations, especially western European countries, to describe them as successful and to argue for their importation to the American scene. Or at least this was so before the extraordinarily severe recession of 1974–1975, which raised unemployment rates in many of those nations from the 1 to 2 percent range to around 5 percent. In the 1960s and early 1970s, European countries had quite understandably concluded that they knew how to manage their economies so as to achieve full employment—if not also stable prices and free collective bargaining. This record of success served to substantiate the claims that the United States had much to learn from other nations about human resources policy, and that it should adopt some of the better-known initiatives of foreign countries for its own use. However, the recession-induced increases in unemployment abroad weakened these arguments and policy prescriptions considerably, as they threw foreign expertise on human resources into question.

But just as low unemployment rates in some countries do not necessarily mean that these countries' human resources policies are working well or should be closely copied elsewhere, neither do high unemployment rates in other nations mean that these nations' policies should be ignored or that useful lessons may not be learned from them. Instead, it is well to remember that "manpower policies and programs are a characteristic of modern nations and those which would become modern" and also that "those policies reflect the particular countries' economic environment and social value systems, with limited possibilities for effective transfer to contrasting settings."[62]

With respect to the United States, its ethnic and racial diversity has almost no parallel abroad. This is not to deny the significant internal tensions among racial, ethnic, and also religious groups that have occurred in several foreign nations, especially those which have imported labor from other, often less developed countries to perform tasks requiring the least amount of skill. But such conflicts hardly begin to compare with those in the United Sates, which are deep-seated, involve institutionalized discrimination in the case of race, and reflect marked differences between subgroups of the labor sector in terms of preparation for employment. Further, the population and labor force of most European countries are far smaller than those of the United States. For example, the work force of the United States is three times the size of West Germany's and the United Kingdom's, four times the size of Italy's, and twenty times the size of Sweden's. Similarly, job mobility and occupational mobility are greater in the United States than abroad. These are only some of the distinguishing characteristics of the American economy and society which frustrate simple efforts to apply the human resources policies of other countries to the American scene. Having underscored this point, we now move on to examine briefly some of the more important human resources policies that have prevailed abroad in recent years.

The transition from school to work has traditionally been less of a problem (almost nonexistent, in fact) in western Europe than in the United States, given the very different educational systems and their interfaces with employment in these two parts of the world. In Europe, relatively few students continue on to receive higher education. Young people are screened early and competitively, with small proportions typically entering universities. In general, by the age of 14 and certainly by age 16, the great majority of Europeans have left school and embarked on working careers. Moreover, the shortages of workers experienced in many European nations in the 1960s and early 1970s permitted the absorption into paid employment of younger members of the labor force who preferred not to continue their education or were incapable of doing so. Also, the states of technology and economic development in those nations were for the most part not so highly developed as to make the skills of these workers redundant. In other words, younger workers were readily integrated into the labor sectors of European countries, at least through the early 1970s.

More recently, however, this has changed, especially after the recession of 1974–1975, whose international dimensions were so pervasive that it left in its wake significantly higher unemployment rates in those European nations which historically had prided themselves on the achievement of full employment.[63] The impact on unemployment of young people was especially marked, with the result that their transition from school or training institutions to work has rather quickly become a key human resources problem on the European scene. In combination with the higher incidence of unemployment among immigrant workers (both young people and adults) to various European nations, unemployment among young people abroad is a potential form of social dynamite. Recognizing this, political leaders in European nations have begun to search for solutions to the relatively new problem (for them) of such unemployment.

Unemployment among young people has been a significant problem in the United States for many years, its incidence being roughly three times the national average for the labor force as a whole. The post-World War II baby boom, relatively slow economic growth to the mid-1960s, frequent cyclical swings in the 1970s, and rapid advances in technology that generated further shifts toward professional and technical job skills have combined to make difficult the absorption of younger workers directly into the labor force. Moreover, the incidence of unemployment among young people in the United States would very likely be higher, both in absolute terms and relative to other nations, if not for the requirement of compulsory education, typically to age 16. We must recognize that length of schooling is considerably greater, on the average, for American youth than for their counterparts abroad, with about four out of five who enter high school actually graduating from it, half of these going on to college, and half of these receiving their degrees.[64]

Nevertheless, the problem of the high school dropout in the United States (which, it should be noted, is ameliorating) remains a concern in part because of the single-minded funneling of the nation's youth into the educational system. And there is a severe problem as well with those who graduate from high school but who do not possess sufficient verbal, mathematical, or vocational skills to hold down steady jobs. In other developed nations, most young people traditionally were considered to have completed their education at earlier ages, with a few going on to higher education, but with most attaching themselves to an industry or a trade through participation in well-established programs of apprenticeship and training. This too has changed, however, as the demand for professional and white-collar workers in these nations has grown and as their educational institutions have been opened to more than just the top strata of society. Thus, somewhat ironically, European nations may follow the United States in the use of education to develop human resources and to treat, in part, the problem of unemployment among younger workers.

Still, in preparing young people for work, apprenticeship is widely used in European nations. Recently, it has been subsumed under more comprehensive programs of training which are sometimes organized on an industry-by-industry basis. This is the pattern in the United Kingdom, where the Industrial Training Act of 1964 authorized the Minister of Labour (the equivalent of the American Secretary of Labor) to establish industrial training boards. These are composed of employers, employees, educators, and representatives from the Labour Ministry, and they bear the responsibility for training in each industry. Notably, such training programs are financed by tax levies imposed on firms in the industries for which training is provided. Programs for retraining adults and upgrading their skills are included with apprenticeship training for youth under this arrangement, with each board recommending the requisite training modes and specifying completion times for stages of the process.

In West Germany, apprenticeship is also oriented toward specific industries, but apprentices are expected to develop skills that are applicable to diverse firms within an industry rather than limited to any single organization. In France, apprenticeship has been institutionalized in vocational training and education centers, financed, as in the United Kingdom, by a tax on employers. The small size of the typical French enterprise militates against on-the-job training of any substantial sort, and thus institutionalization of apprenticeship training is the preferred, more realistic alternative in that economic and industrial setting.

In the Netherlands, the system of junior technical schools is the vehicle for training in the crafts and trades. Apprentices are obtained from these institutions, and, for each industry, a joint employer-employee board provides direction for apprenticeship programs and standards. In Italy, apprentices are obtained by firms from local employment offices. Under that nation's Apprenticeship Act of 1966, the Ministry of Labor formulates guidelines for apprenticeship programs. These are then carried out by the local offices, with which aspiring apprentices must register. Like Italy, Sweden was rather late in formulating a national policy governing apprenticeship. Central guidance of apprenticeship programs is provided by the National Board of Vocational Education, which includes representatives from industry, labor, education, and government. A separate body, the Royal Vocational Training Board, supervises and subsidizes some of the apprenticeship programs for artisan trades, although much of this training is carried out independently.

The retraining of adult workers has been pursued far more aggressively in Europe than in the United States. This is consistent with the shortages of labor experienced by many European nations in the post-World War II period (though these have partially disappeared in the wake of the recession of the mid-1970s), in contrast to the relative surpluses of labor in the United States. European efforts at retraining have sought to overcome shortages of skills in critical occupations and industries, thereby attempting to promote economic growth and ameliorate conditions in the labor market contributing to inflation. These efforts have also had a social dimension, which is the intended resettlement of veterans, the disabled, and the unemployed in rural areas. As European labor markets tightened in the 1960s and early 1970s, efforts to retrain adults increasingly focused on groups of the hard-to-employ, such as the mentally and physically handicapped and older workers. As labor markets loosened thereafter, efforts at retraining swung back in the direction of less marginal groups requiring upgrading of skills. This experience parallels somewhat that of the earlier MDTA program and, more recently, programs under Title I of CETA in the United States.

In its emphasis on redressing some of the consequences of economic distress, the western European community of nations has also experimented with "sheltered employment"—jobs whose occupants are in some way protected from traditional pressures at the workplace—for groups in the labor force who are difficult to place and for the handicapped, that is, the physically and mentally disabled and workers suffering from alcoholism or other diseases. These efforts include special public works and outdoor projects, homework, and sheltered workshops, the last of which are also found in the United States. Whether in Europe or the United States, these programs are specialized efforts aimed at particular groups rather than basic actions to assist in achieving full employment.

Also notable in the European countries are various measures for relocation, which are almost totally absent from the American scene. These include travel expenses for workers who search for jobs in new locations, moving allowances for wage earners and their families, and assistance with housing. Despite such efforts, the limited supply of good housing is an important factor in the high incidence of "reverse relocation" among European workers, who often find their new surroundings to be physically as well as culturally unsuitable. Note, too, that the rapid economic growth and severe shortages of labor in European nations during the third quarter of the twentieth century resulted in vigorous encouragement of immigrant labor. Workers from southern Italy, Turkey, north Africa, Yugoslavia, Spain, Portugal, and elsewhere were recruited into jobs located in western Europe. Though such policies were helpful in filling the demand for labor and promoting economic growth, they nevertheless exacerbated ethnic and social conflicts, increasingly so in recent years when labor markets in these nations loosened considerably.

The postrecession era in western Europe has witnessed substantial increases in unemployment insurance and other social welfare benefits, payment for hours not worked as a form of work sharing, accelerated retirement of persons in their late fifties and early sixties, and public subsidies to private employers to help them remain in business. Interestingly, such measures have been widely supported, while, at the same time, public service employment and expanded public works projects, so heavily emphasized in the United States in recent years, have been strongly opposed in Europe. These developments are perhaps quite the opposite of what one might have predicted in more collectively oriented societies than the United States, but they may well reflect the "strong anti-government bias in countries with large public sectors and predictably rising expenditures for social services."[65]

European experts on human resources have become increasingly concerned about structural rigidities in the labor market that may be induced by the policies governing work sharing, early retirement, and social welfare payments noted above. They also worry about the apparent increasing segmentation of European labor markets into sectors of "good" and "bad" jobs, that is, into primary and secondary labor markets of the type discussed in Chapters 7 and 8. This development is in some ways similar to the weakening of Japan's system of "permanent employment."[66] Together they may indicate that other developed nations are moving closer to, rather than farther away from, the types of practices found in the American labor market. If this is so, then those nations may come to adopt some of the United States' human resources policies rather than providing pace-setting models to be replicated here and elsewhere.

Again, these observations underscore the caveat that, in the area of human resources policy, caution should be exercised in applying the "solutions" developed in one nation to another nation or to a group of nations. Cultural differences between civilized peoples of the world are substantial enough to frustrate facile attempts to transport one nation's policy prescriptions across international boundaries. That is true in the area of human resources, just as it is in other dimensions of economy, society, and the labor sector.

SOME UNRESOLVED ISSUES

We conclude this chapter with a short discussion of some issues which are the subject of intense debate. The first of these is the transition from school to work and the extent to which this process might be improved so as to ameliorate the problem of unemployment among young people, which, as we noted above, has been quite severe in the United States (we shall discuss this further in Chapter 12). A recent collection of papers prepared for the National Commission for Employment Policy and discussed at a national conference addresses this issue.[67]

To summarize briefly, in the United States the student labor force continued to grow in the 1970s even as the youth and student populations expanded, with much of the former group's work experience obtained in "secondary" jobs; the distinction between in- and out-of-school youth in terms of their activity in the labor market continued to be stronger than in other nations; younger workers were particularly short of information about occupations, aptitudes, careers, job openings, and institutional linkages to employment; the largest disadvantages in the labor market experienced by young people were associated with sex (being female) and race (being black or belonging to another minority group); high unemployment rates among young people were related to (and not totally distinctive from) job changes and movement in and out of the labor force among all workers; and the advantages of a high school diploma were considerable, while those of specialized training were not so great.[68]

As to policy recommendations for improving the transition from school to work, the Commission conferees strongly supported better coordination at all levels of government of human resources policies aimed at youth, but also (following the European lead) a much stronger emphasis on local action.[69] From this perspective, the role of federal policy is to stimulate "local projects that have the merit of bringing together several of the critical participants in a school-to-work transition."[70]

Such efforts might include local councils composed of educators, employers, union members, parents, representatives of community organizations, and students. These councils would devise specialized projects and pilot programs to assist in the transition to adulthood and to full participation in the labor force; community employment counseling services for high school students to help them learn about occupations and their related points of entry; and model employment placement services, perhaps offered through high school consortia, the United States Employment and Training Service (ETS), volunteer organizations, or combinations thereof to provide part-time work opportunities for young people still in school, career opportunities for others, feedback to the guidance organizations about barriers to success in employment, and follow-up of dropouts, graduates, and young workers placed in jobs. These efforts could also consist of community internship programs to supplement jobs in the private sector, permitting experiential learning to be combined with more formal education; model delivery systems to match student applicants with available or sponsor-developed part- and full-time jobs; various demonstration projects funded in part by the federal sector to identify, expand, improve, and publicize employment opportunities for youth; development of local occupational inventories of entry-level jobs for high school seniors; and selected comparisons of the job performance of 18-year-olds with that of other workers, with the hope of overcoming employers' resistance to hiring persons under 21 years of age. This ambitious agenda was accompanied by recommendations to expand and improve career education, linking hands-on experience to classroom training, and to focus more heavily on the process of counseling and guidance.[71]

The last of these is most sorely neglected in the bulk of local school systems, perhaps suggesting that federal standards and funding might be needed for the process to be improved. Additionally, Barton strongly recommended changes in the system of measuring the labor force that would make it possible to begin tracking the work and life experiences of young people at about the age of 14, when they begin to be independent from their families, rather than at age 16, 18, or 21.[72] He also proposed that the experiences of young people who are institutionalized in health, penal, or military institutions be measured as well. At present, institutionalized persons—young, middle-aged, and old alike—are excluded from statistics on the labor force. Finally, the National Commission for Employment Policy itself offered the following recommendation:

> That provision be made through Title III of CETA for the Secretary of Labor, in cooperation with the other agencies concerned with youth employment problems, to experiment with a limited number of pilot models (five or so) of a Youth Employment Corporation, with the aim of determining whether a unified management structure, in cooperation with employers, unions, and other groups concerned with creating meaningful job opportunities, can assure a more effective transition of disadvantaged youth into a regular labor market.[73]

In supporting this proposal, the Commission observed that with annual expenditures in excess of $2 billion on human resources services for youth, most of which in reality provide income maintenance, an improved system to deliver those services holds promise of potentially high returns. A modified version of this proposal was adopted by Congress in 1977, when it passed the Youth Employment and Demonstration Projects Act authorizing employment and training programs similar to those under Title I of CETA, a conservation corps made up of young adults, incentive projects, and community conservation and improvement projects. Under the research provisions of this legislation, the initial question to be studied is whether staying in school increases the future employability of potential dropouts and the disadvantaged.[74]

This measure, together with other proposed initiatives, attests to widespread concern about the transition from school to work of American youth. If that process is improved by adoption of services to aid in this transition found in other nations; by enactment of a special, lower minimum wage for teenagers; by a broader commitment to full-employment policies in the United States; or simply by the aging of the population, which is presently under way, so much the better—though the importance of these factors to unemployment among young people is open to question. But such developments would hardly be reason to avoid further attempts to make American human resources policies better able to serve a key segment of the labor sector, namely, the nation's youth.

A second important issue of human resources policy, only briefly touched on in the discussion above, is the more general delivery of services under CETA. Students of this subject are of a similar mind in advocating improved program coordination at all levels to overcome differences between prime sponsors in planning cycles, terminology, and reports in order to give them an improved base of information about the labor market and to elicit greater cooperation between them and non-CETA program managers.[75] Also recently proposed were a reordering of priorities under Title I to emphasize skill training in a period of economic recovery; improving linkages between CETA and the Trade Adjustment Assistance program, which provides income support for workers adversely affected by foreign trade; and (related to the discussion earlier in this section) making decisions on funding for the summer youth program early rather than late in the budgeting cycle to permit orderly planning for use of the funds by prime sponsors.[76]

At the same time, however, concern was expressed that, as a relatively new program, "the present CETA structure be given a fair chance to prove itself"[77] before being subjected to a major overhaul aimed at reversing the principles of decategorization and decentralization upon which it is based. Within this framework of delivery of services, one authority on the subject proposes to:

> Strengthen CETA consortia incentives, disperse the balance-of-state responsibility among local prime sponsors except in states of small population where one statewide prime sponsorship should prevail, train and strengthen prime sponsor planning councils, discourage program operation and service delivery by prime sponsors, and seek to defend the local labor market planning concept. . . .[78]

It should be recognized that proposals to strengthen local control of, and involvement in, human resources programs for youth and for others are controversial because partisan politics often enter into decisions about who should receive federally funded jobs and training.[79] Some better-connected youths—relatives and friends of local officials, for example—may be favored over others for these opportunities, and patronage employees may be preferred over regular civil service personnel when federal funds are awarded or withdrawn. Also, it may be difficult for mostly white local officials and school administrators to overcome racial tensions in attempting to improve the transition from school to work of black and other minority students, who are in the majority in some inner-city schools—especially if those same local officials and administrators engage in or are perceived as engaging in partisan politics over the allocation of moneys for human resources development. In a political democracy, this may be an inherent price that must be paid for the decentralization of human resources programs, and clearly it complicates the improved coordination of these programs within an overall policy framework.

A third area of concern is income maintenance, especially the unemployment insurance system. If not formally designated a human resources policy, unemployment insurance nevertheless has important implications for participation in the labor force (as was noted in Chapter 10), and it shares with policies more conventionally regarded as oriented toward human resources a concern with the economic well-being of the nation's workers. Some believe that unemployment insurance should be linked to training, with stipended training offered as an alternative following, say, 5 weeks of unemployment benefits. Also proposed has been the termination of unemployment insurance after 26 weeks and enrollment of recipients in public service employment programs.[80] More fundamentally, the National Commission for Employment Policy has called for improved unemployment insurance benefits, inclusion in the system of those presently uninsured, revamping of the system's financing, and the permanent adoption of benefit extensions to the long-term unemployed, which were temporarily authorized during the recession of the mid-1970s.[81]

Most policy recommendations in the area of income maintenance and the welfare system call for imposition of a mandatory requirement on all states (some now do this voluntarily) to accept into the Aid to Families with Dependent Children program those families in which both parents are present but which are in need because of unemployment of the father. Only about half the states permit the payment of welfare benefits to such families, and only when certain eligibility standards are met. Other proposals are directed at improving the effectiveness and equitability of procedures for testing willingness and ability to work contained in the unemployment insurance, food stamp, and WIN programs. Still others call for the federal government to assess the magnitude of foreclosures of home mortgages and expiration of health insurance coverage resulting from unemployment. For welfare recipients who are female heads of families with dependent children, Mangum proposes that public service employment and training be discretionary and that only they and the disabled receive cash and in-kind payments. All other heads of families with dependent children would be provided "last resort" public service employment under this scheme.[82]

As to public service employment more generally, experts on human resources policy are not all of the same mind. Some believe that public service employment should be strengthened, expanded, and made the centerpiece feature of human resources policy in the United States. On the basis of the evidence presented earlier in this chapter, it could be argued that this has already occurred. Others view public service employment as only a temporary, last-ditch effort which should be aimed most heavily at disadvantaged workers and workers in depressed areas. The National Commission for Employment Policy, which, keep in mind, advises federal officials in this regard, generally is of the first view. It recently proposed an expanded federal program for creating jobs in the public sector, but conceived and operated more as a developmental tool than as a countercyclical measure. More specifically, the Commission recommended that public service employment be restructured to better focus on specific groups in the labor force, including the hard-to-employ; that a household income ceiling for eligibility under the program be established; and that more systematic information about jobholders in public service employment be obtained so that the results of the program in terms of reaching targeted groups can be better evaluated.[83]

At the same time, however, this advisory commission does not regard public service employment as a program to be used as a final repository for those otherwise unsuccessful in the job market. Indeed, as between Titles II and VI of CETA, under which the nation's public service employment programs are authorized, the Commission favors the former: ''With its emphasis on transitional opportunities for the hard-to-employ . . . the Title II approach [should] continue to be emphasized to the maximum possible extent.''[84] The Commission also has called for the Secretary of Labor to review the steps which might be taken to strengthen the transitional process of public service employment, whereby persons are expected to move into regular jobs in either the private or the public sector. Cognizant of the economic downturn and related layoffs experienced by some state and local governments in the middle to late 1970s, the Commission also proposed increased use of private nonprofit and other community-based organizations in managing and operating public service employment programs.[85] Clearly, these proposals do not reflect a view of public service employment as an alternative to private employment for the nation's unemployed.

If there are in general few advocates of large-scale or permanent (as opposed to transitional) public service employment programs, then economic circumstances can produce some pragmatic supporters of them. We have seen how the cyclical economy of the 1970s, with first a mild and then a severe recession, generated political forces that strengthened and broadened what initially was a small, temporary, and transitional public employment program. If full employment could be achieved or closely approached, then public service employment and selected other human resources policies would be less pressing matters (although, as in Europe, other policies might then come into vogue). It is hardly a coincidence that those who advise and offer recommendations about human resources policy are of a single mind in proposing full employment as an overriding national goal.[86] Attainment of that goal would do more to improve the experiences in the labor market of American workers, especially the disadvantaged—minority-group members, the young and the old, women, the mentally and physically handicapped, and veterans—than any initiative in the sphere of human resources policy.

If human resources policies in the United States must operate within the context of loose labor markets, as they have had to do for the bulk of two decades, then few should be surprised that they focus on special groups in the labor force rather than on the improvement of labor markets or, more basically, the economy.[87] For a long period, European human resources policies were directed at improving the operation of labor markets, but the changed economies (and labor markets) of those countries during the 1970s seem to presage a different orientation in the future. In the remaining decades of the twentieth century, it may be the United States which experiences economic conditions which will lead to the development of human resources policies that will be regarded as forerunners of things to come elsewhere. Until then, however, human resources policies in this country apparently will continue to be directed toward those whose position renders them the most disadvantaged in—periph-eral to—the labor market.

SUMMARY

This chapter reviewed the development and selected aspects of human re-sources policy in the United States. These range from the early Employment Service (now the United States Employment and Training Service), authorized by the Wagner-Peyser Act of 1937, to very recent programs of public service employment. For the most part, American human resource policies and the programs they spawned have been piecemeal and were formed ad hoc in re-sponse to a series of particular problems in the labor market. The Comprehen-sive Employment and Training Act of 1973 to some extent codified these poli-cies, but its principal accomplishment was to decategorize and decentralize human resources programs. Since then, public service employment has evolved into the nation's leading human resources program. Policies in other developed nations generally are more comprehensive and of longer standing than those in the United States. At the same time, a large amount of human resources training and development activity has emerged in the private busi-ness sector, with the most recent emphasis placed on the integration of human resources management and planning with total organizational planning.

In Chapter 12, our attention turns to the fundamental issues of full employ-ment and the relationship between unemployment and inflation in the modern economy.

NOTES

1 Note further that the word "manpower" is no longer used in federal agencies and publications, partly because of its sexist connotation, but also because it does not adequately represent public policy in this area. Thus, in the mid-1970s the Depart-ment of Labor's Manpower Administration was renamed the Employment and Training Administration, and *Manpower Report of the President* was changed to *Employment and Training Report of the President*.
2 For detailed histories of the Employment Service, see William Haber and Daniel H. Kruger, *The Role of the United States Employment Service in a Changing Econ-omy,* Upjohn Institute, Kalamazoo, Mich., 1964; and Arnold Nemore and Garth L. Mangum, *Reorienting the Federal-State Employment Service,* University of Michi-gan and Wayne State University, Detroit, 1968.
3 For more on recent developments in the ETS, see Frank H. Cassell, *The Public Em-ployment Service: Organization in Change,* Academic Publications, Ann Arbor, Mich., 1968; Stanley H. Ruttenberg and Jocelyn Gutchess, *The Federal-State Em-ployment Service: A Critique,* Johns Hopkins, Baltimore, 1970; Miriam Johnson, *Counterpoint: The Changing Employment Service,* Olympus, Salt Lake City, 1973; and U.S. Department of Labor, *The Employment Service: An Institutional Analy-sis,* Research and Development Monograph 51, 1977.

4 Garth L. Mangum, "Afterword," in Johnson, p. 185.

5 Sar A. Levitan, Garth L. Mangum, and F. Ray Marshall, *Human Resources and Labor Markets*, Harper & Row, New York, 1972, p. 374.

6 *Employment and Training Report of the President, 1978*, 1978, p. 59, table 6. A total of 3.1 million persons were placed by the ETS in fiscal 1975, and 3.4 million in fiscal 1976.

7 Garth L. Mangum, *Employability, Employment, and Income*, Olympus, Salt Lake City, 1976, p. 41.

8 It could well be claimed that the tax cut of 1964 was the most significant "human resources" policy of the period, for together with subsequent expenditures (and federal deficits), it spurred a sustained economic expansion that eventually reduced unemployment to 3.5 percent (in 1968 and 1969). This underscores the fact that human resources policies per se are unlikely to have anything approaching the effects on the labor market of fiscal and monetary policies.

9 Mangum, *Employability, Employment, and Income*, p. 54

10 Mangum, *Employability, Employment, and Income*, pp. 54–55.

11 Sar A. Levitan, "Creation of Jobs for the Unemployed," in *Proceedings of a Conference on Public Service Employment: A Special Report of the National Commission for Manpower Policy*, May 1975, p. 155. For a good short account of these early efforts at job creation, see Sar A. Levitan, "Manpower Programs for a Healthier Economy," in Lloyd Ulman (ed.), *Manpower Programs in the Policy Mix*, Johns Hopkins, Baltimore, 1973, pp. 111–113.

12 For an early account of this legislation, see Charles Howe, "The Comprehensive Employment and Training Act," *New Generation*, **56**:1–11 (1974). Data for fiscal 1977 are from *Employment and Training Report of the President, 1978*, p. 40.

13 Howe, p. 3.

14 Howe, p. 4.

15 Mangum, *Employability, Employment, and Income*, p. 69.

16 Howe, p. 5.

17 In this section, we rely on the lively account of CETA's emergence contained in Howe, pp. 6–11.

18 Recognize, though, that the legislation clearly mentions the private *and* the public sectors as suitable places of employment for workers in transitional public service employment jobs. The preference for the private sector was most strongly expressed in the (partly rhetorical) statements of elected officials, including the President.

19 Unless otherwise indicated, the data presented in this section are from *Employment and Training Report of the President, 1978*, pp. 37–56.

20 At the end of the fiscal year, Sept. 30, 1977, about 600,000 persons were in public service employment jobs under Titles I, II, and VI of CETA. That was a large majority of all enrollees in CETA programs. See *Employment and Training Report of the President, 1978*, pp. 40, 307, table F-2.

21 For further information about the IES, see *Employment and Training Report of the President, 1977*, 1977, pp. 57–58.

22 *Employment and Training Report of the President, 1977*, p. 58.

23 The study is reported in *Employment and Training Report of the President, 1977*, pp. 60–62.

24 Further details of these findings and related studies are given in *Employment and Training Report of the President, 1977*, pp. 62–63; and U.S. Department of Labor,

Employment and Training Administration, *The Work Incentive (WIN) Program and Related Experiences: A Review of Research with Policy Implications*, R & D Monograph 49, 1977.

25 Levitan, Mangum, and Marshall, p. 336. Actually, the quoted passage should more appropriately end with "labor market experiences," for these include employment, unemployment, wage rates, hours of work, and other factors. Also see U.S. Department of Labor, *The Noneconomic Impacts of the Job Corps*, Research and Development Monograph 64, 1978.

26 An application of this design and methodology is found in Earl D. Main, *A Nationwide Evaluation of MDTA Institutional Job Training Programs*, National Opinion Research Center, Report 118, University of Chicago Press, Chicago, October 1966.

27 F. Ray Marshall, Allan M. Cartter, and Allan G. King, *Labor Economics: Wages, Employment and Trade Unionism*, 3d ed., Irwin, Homewood, Ill., 1976, p. 578.

28 Garth L. Mangum, "Manpower Policies and Worker Status since the 1930's," in Joseph P. Goldberg et al. (eds.), *Federal Policies and Worker Status since the Thirties*, Industrial Relations Research Association, Madison, Wis., 1976, p. 150.

29 Mangum, "Manpower Policies and Worker Status since the 1930's," p. 150. For a different view, see Michael E. Borus, "Indicators of CETA Performance," *Industrial and Labor Relations Review*, **32:**3–4 (1979).

30 For further details of this proposal for welfare reform, see *Economic Report of the President, January, 1978*, 1978, pp. 174–176, 221–237; and *Employment and Training Report of the President, 1978*, pp. 123–136. Note that because funding for public service jobs is tied to the amount of unemployment in the economy, the number of such jobs began to decline as the unemployment rate dipped in 1978 and 1979. Thus, whereas 725,000 public service jobs were funded for fiscal 1977 and 1978, about 625,000 were funded for fiscal 1979 and 1980, with the total of year-end slots projected at 467,000 for fiscal 1980. See "Labor Department Budget—Fiscal Year 1980," in U.S. Department of Labor *News*, Jan. 22, 1979, pp. 2, 12–13.

31 Frederick Harbison and Charles A. Myers, *Education, Manpower and Economic Growth*, McGraw-Hill, New York, 1964.

32 See Frederick Harbison, Joan Maruknick, and Jane R. Resnick, *Quantitative Analysis of Modernization and Development*, Research Report Series 115, Princeton, Princeton, N.J. 1970.

33 Theodore W. Schultz, "Investment in Human Capital," *American Economic Review*, **51:**1–17 (1961). See also Theodore W. Schultz, "Capital Formation by Education," *Journal of Political Economy*, **68:**571–583 (1960).

34 U.S. Bureau of the Census, *Statistical Abstract of the United States, 1978* (1978), p. 136, table 212.

35 *Employment and Training Report of the President, 1978*, p. 247, table B-9.

36 *Employment and Training Report of the President, 1978*, pp. 248–249, table B-9.

37 Marshall, Cartter, and King, p. 556.

38 Marshall, Cartter, and King, p. 557.

39 See, for example, Samuel H. Beer (ed.), *Marx and Engels: The Communist Manifesto*, Appleton-Century-Crofts, New York, 1955, p. 32, where "free education for all children in public schools" is listed as one of the leading goals of the communist society, which presumably would supplant capitalism.

40 U.S. Bureau of the Census, p. 136, table 212.

41 U.S. Bureau of the Census, p. 136, table 212.

42 U.S. Bureau of the Census, p. 136, table 212.

43 See Richard B. Freeman, "Overinvestment in College Training?" *Journal of Human Resources,* **10:**287–311 (1975).

44 This view is forcefully argued in Ivan E. Berg, *Education and Jobs: The Great Training Robbery,* Praeger, New York, 1970.

45 See M. A. Blaug, M. H. Peston, and A. Ziderman, *The Utilization of Educated Manpower in Industry,* University of Toronto Press, Toronto, 1967. This is a study set in the British engineering sector.

46 Levitan, Mangum, and Marshall, p. 111.

47 Levitan, Mangum, and Marshall, p. 111.

48 National Commission for Manpower Policy, *Proceedings of a Conference on the Role of the Business Sector in Manpower Policy,* November 1975, p. 3.

49 National Commission for Manpower Policy, p. 3.

50 Jerome R. Rosow, "Corporate Personnel Policies during High Unemployment," in National Commission for Manpower Policy, pp. 12–21. In 1979, Rosow served as president of the Industrial Relations Research Association, the same post that Secretary of Labor Ray Marshall held in 1977.

51 Rosow, p. 31.

52 Rosow, p. 31.

53 See *Jobs for the Hard-to-Employ: New Directions for a Public-Private Partnership,* Committee for Economic Development, New York, January 1978.

54 *Jobs for the Hard-to-Employ,* p. 34.

55 *Jobs for the Hard-to-Employ,* p. 35.

56 See Bureau of National Affairs, *Effective Utilization of Manpower,* Personnel Policies Forum Survey 83, August 1968; and *The Personnel Function: Changing Scope and Objectives,* The Conference Board, New York, 1977.

57 U.S. Department of Labor, *Employer Manpower Planning and Forecasting,* Manpower Research Monograph 19, 1970, p. 3. Note that in the text "personnel" is used in place of "manpower," and "human resources planning" is considered much broader than "personnel—manpower—planning."

58 *Manpower Planning and Forecasting in the Firm: An Exploratory Probe,* University of Minnesota, Industrial Relations Center, Minneapolis, March 1968.

59 For a popular account, see Herbert E. Meyer, "Personnel Directors Are the New Corporate Heroes," *Fortune,* **93:**84–88, 140 (1976); and "Personnel Chiefs Gain in Significance and Stature at Many Companies," *The Wall Street Journal,* Dec. 13, 1977, p. 1. For a more sober perspective, see Edgar H. Schein, "Increasing Organizational Effectiveness through Better Human Resource Planning and Development," *Sloan Management Review,* 1–20 (1977).

60 Recognition of this development is further reflected in the formation in 1975 of the Human Resources Planning Society, which seeks to "exchange experience, pool knowledge, advance the state of the art and foster professional development" in this relatively new and rapidly evolving field of management (quoted from a brochure of the society's 1978 conference in Atlanta).

61 Some useful sources of information on this subject are National Commission for Manpower Policy, *Reexamining European Manpower Policies,* Special Report 10, August 1976; and Rudolf Meidner and Rolf Andersson, "The Overall Impact of an Active Labor Market Policy," in Ulman, pp. 117–158.

62 Levitan, Mangum, and Marshall, p. 549.

63 Some data on changing unemployment rates abroad are shown in Table 1-5 (page 15).

Note the significant increases during the mid-1970s in the unemployment rates of the countries listed in the table.

64 On this point, see Levitan, Mangum, and Marshall, p. 553.

65 National Commission for Manpower Policy, *Reexamining European Manpower Policies*, p. 5.

66 The phrase refers to the arrangement whereby "an employee enters a large firm after school graduation—whether it be middle school, high school or university— and receives in-company training and remains an employee in the same company until the retirement age of 55." See Robert E. Cole, "Permanent Employment in Japan: Facts and Fantasies," *Industrial and Labor Relations Review*, **26:**615 (1972). Cole notes that this arrangement, historically confined to males, has recently become less common.

67 National Commission for Manpower Policy, *From School to Work: Improving the Transition*, 1976.

68 National Commission for Manpower Policy, *From School to Work*, pp. 297–303.

69 See especially Paul E. Barton, "Youth Transition to Work: The Problem and Federal Policy Setting," in National Commission for Manpower Policy, *From School to Work*, pp. 1—19. Also see U.S. Department of Labor, *From Learning to Earning: a Transnational Comparison of Transition Services*, Research and Development Monograph 63, 1979.

70 Barton, p. 6.

71 Barton, pp. 9–13.

72 Barton, pp. 13–16.

73 National Commission for Manpower Policy, *An Employment Strategy for the United States: Next Steps*, December 1976, p. 78.

74 For more on this, See *Employment and Training Report of the President, 1978*, pp. 69–81.

75 See National Commission for Manpower Policy, *An Employment Strategy for the United States*, pp. 72–78; and Mangum, *Employability, Employment, and Income*, pp. 304–305.

76 National Commission for Manpower Policy, *An Employment Strategy for the United States*, pp. 77–78.

77 National Commission for Manpower Policy, *An Employment Strategy for the United States*, p. 77.

78 Mangum, *Employability, Employment, and Income*, pp. 304–305.

79 Some examples are offered in John Herbers, "Federal Job Program Aids Cities, but Fraud Reports Mar Success," *The New York Times*, May 14, 1978, pp. 1, 18.

80 Mangum, *Employability, Employment, and Income*, p. 304.

81 National Commission for Manpower Policy, *An Employment Strategy for the United States*, pp. 69–71.

82 Mangum, *Employment, Employability, and Income*, p. 304.

83 National Commission for Manpower Policy, *An Employment Strategy for the United States*, pp. 65–68.

84 National Commission for Manpower Policy, *An Employment Strategy for the United States*, p. 67.

85 National Commission for Manpower Policy, *An Employment Strategy for the United States*, p. 68.

86 See National Commission for Manpower Policy, *An Employment Strategy for the*

United States, pp. 27–30; and Mangum, *Employment, Employability, and Income,* pp. 299–302.

87 That American human resources policy should be comprehensive and not limited to special groups in the labor force is forcefully argued by E. Wight Bakke, *The Mission of Manpower Policy,* Upjohn Institute, Kalamazoo, Mich., 1969.

ADDITIONAL READINGS

Ashenfelter, Orley, and James Blum (eds.): *Evaluating the Labor Market Effects of Social Programs,* Research Report Series 120, Princeton University, Industrial Relations Section, Princeton, N.J., 1976.

Freeman, Richard B.: *The Overeducated American,* Academic, New York, 1976.

Jobs for the Hard-to-Employ: New Directions for a Public-Private Partnership, Committee for Economic Development, New York, January 1978.

Lewin, David, Raymond D. Horton, Robert Schick, and Charles Brecher: *The Urban Labor Market: Institutions, Information, Linkages,* Praeger, New York, 1974.

Mangum, Garth L.: *Employability, Employment, and Income,* Olympus, Salt Lake City, 1976.

National Commission for Manpower Policy: *From School to Work: Improving the Transition,* 1976.

National Commission for Manpower Policy: *Reexamining European Manpower Policies,* Special Report 10, 1976.

Patten, Thomas H., Jr.: *Manpower Planning and the Development of Human Resources,* Wiley-Interscience, New York, 1971.

U.S. Congressional Budget Office: *Report of Congressional Budget Office Conference on the Teenage Unemployment Problem,* 1976.

Watts, Harold W., and Albert Rees: *The New Jersey Income Maintenance Experiment,* vol. I–III, Academic, New York, 1976, 1977.

FOR ANALYSIS AND DISCUSSION

1 Two teams of three students each should debate the following proposition: "Resolved: American human resources programs are cost-effective and should be expanded in terms of both funds and target groups." The instructor should moderate the debate, and the remainder of the class should pose questions to team members at the conclusion of the debate.

2 Select any single federal human resources program (for example, the Job Corps, the WIN program, or public service employment) and summarize the available evidence concerning its effectiveness. What are the sources of your data? How recent is the information provided in them? How "scientific" are the procedures and methods used to make these assessments? Ask a classmate to review the same evidence and compare your judgments about the effectiveness of the program.

3 Contact your community's local office of the United States Employment and Training Service (ETS). Inquire about the office's volume of activity, its placement record, the services it provides to job applicants, and its follow-up of applicants referred to employers. Then ask about the office's ability to serve employers as well as job applicants and about its ability to provide employment services while also

Table 11-5 Rates of Unemployment among Teenagers in Nine Countries, 1960–1975

Country	Age	Teenage unemployment rates (annual average)					
		1960	1965	1968	1970	1974	1975
United States	16–19	14.7	14.8	12.7	15.3	16.0	20.2
Out of school	16–19	15.6	13.3	12.5	17.2	14.6	
In school	16–19	10.0	10.9	10.9	15.7	19.4	
Australia	15–19			4.2	3.9	6.9	
Canada	15–19	13.1	8.8	11.3	14.3	12.2	
France	16–19	6.6	5.1	7.6	7.0		
West Germany	15–19			3.8	2.0	1.8	
Italy	14–19	9.3	10.3	13.6	12.9	18.4	
Japan	15–19	1.5	1.5	2.3	2.0	2.6	
Sweden	16–19		2.9	5.6	4.5	6.8	5.7
United Kingdom	15–19	0.8	1.5	3.0	4.4	4.2	

Note: Data for the nine countries are not necessarily for the same months. Data for 1968–1974 adjusted to international concepts, except for British unemployment rates.

Sources: National data for 1960, 1965, 1975. For 1968–1974 (except British unemployment rates), U.S. Department of Labor, Bureau of Labor Statistics, Office of Productivity and Technology, Division of Foreign Labor Statistics and Trade. Adapted from Beatrice G. Reubens, "Foreign and American Experience with the Youth Transition," in National Commission for Manpower Policy, *From School to Work: Improving the Transition*, 1976, p. 277.

disbursing unemployment insurance funds. Using these data, prepare a short position paper on the scope of activity and the effectiveness of the local ETS office.

4 Examine the unemployment rates among teenagers shown in Table 11-5. Why should these rates be so much higher in the United States than in other countries? What is the importance of the distinction between in-school and out-of-school status for unemployment among teenagers? What is the significance of changes in these rates over the period 1960–1975? Discuss the data and their implications with your classmates and then attempt to locate more recent comparative data on unemployment among young people.

5 Appraise the objectives of decategorization and decentralization of the Comprehensive Employment and Training Act (CETA). Do you agree or disagree with these objectives? Why? Is the decentralization of human resources programs consistent with the policies governing other social welfare programs, for example, unemployment insurance and workers' compensation?

6 Select one western European and one Asian country and compare their leading human resources development policies. How are they similar? Are they fundamentally different from those prevailing in the United States? Have they changed over time? Be sure to identify the sources of your data for this exercise.

7 Contact two large business firms in your local community and inquire into the role and operations of their human resources management function. What components of the function are most heavily emphasized? To what extent do the firms engage in human resources planning? Write a brief report of your findings for a class presentation.

8 How would you go about improving the transition from school to work? Do the recommendations offered by the National Commission for Employment Policy in this regard seem sensible or likely to work if put into practice? What is the basis of your

judgment? Have you used the services of your school's guidance counselor or placement office? Are they useful sources of information about the labor market? What could be done to improve them?

9 Prepare a short position paper on the role of public service employment in human resources policy. Assume that the paper will be used to support or oppose (you decide which) an expansion of public service employment to provide 1.5 million jobs. Be sure to address the relationship between various levels of public service employment and the aggregate unemployment rate. Also consider the extent to which public service employment should be apportioned between Titles II and VI of CETA, which provide for transitional and countercyclical programs, respectively.

10 Review some of the literature (such as the sources cited in this chapter and listed under Additional Readings) on the "human resources revolution of the 1960s" in the United States. What seems to be the leading interpretation of the experience with human resources policy during that era? What is your appraisal of that experience? Compare your views with those of a classmate who has undertaken a similar analysis of human resources policy in the 1970s. Using the two analyses, prepare a short summary of human resources policy in the United States from 1960 to 1980.

Full Employment and Inflation

INTRODUCTION

In this final chapter we will explore two issues that are central in every modern economy and society: full employment and price stability. These, along with free markets—meaning a minimum of government controls over such matters as wages, prices, and collective bargaining—are the three goals which politically democratic and economically advanced countries, the United States among them, persistently seek but rarely attain.

The chapter begins with some data about unemployment in the United States and definitions of the various types of unemployment that commonly occur in an industrialized society. Particular attention is paid to the concept of full employment and to the level of unemployment (above zero) which may be consistent with it. Possible changes over time in the "full employment level of unemployment" are closely considered. We then move on to examine the record of price changes in the United States in the post-World War II era, with recent inflation drawing the bulk of attention.

The intense and long-standing debate over the relationship between the unemployment rate and the rate of inflation is reviewed, together with the recent evidence on this issue. We then examine the use of wage and price guidelines and controls in the United States to combat inflation, assessing the record of their effectiveness. Foreign nations have experimented with these and other "incomes policies," and we briefly review that record as well.

As will be evident, there are no instant or easy solutions to the problems of unemployment, inflation, and maintenance of free markets, for they are interrelated; to attempt to resolve any one of them may severely exacerbate one or both of the others. As an example, a public policy to reduce inflation significantly might involve the imposition of wage and price controls and might bring about a major increase in unemployment. Alternatively, a policy to reduce unemployment substantially through the stimulation of aggregate demand might overheat the economy to the point of drastically increasing inflation. And in still another instance, a government policy to refrain from instituting wage and price controls might preserve free markets but be unable to combat those concentrations of power in the economy which contribute to worsening inflation.

Rather than being achievable in pure form, then, a balance must be struck between the three goals of full employment, price stability, and free markets, *and this balance is determined politically*. The issues of unemployment, inflation, and free markets have major economic implications, of course, and may be discussed in economic terms, but they are fundamentally political because decisions about how to treat them are arrived at through the political process. Interest groups in society bring different values to this process, and out of the clash of contesting wills in the public arena are determined the policies which a nation employs to deal with the central problems of political economy.

As far as the labor sector is concerned, its claims to a role in the production of national wealth and to a share of national income manifest a strong preference among its members for full employment in the economy. Indeed, although the prevailing social contract in the United States, about which we have spoken in earlier chapters, incorporates a variety of protections from the market, it embodies an even more basic commitment to paid employment as the principal generator of labor's share of income. When unemployment is high and the social contract is therefore being violated for more than just a few of the nation's citizens, there are political pressures on government to adopt policies that, it is hoped, will ameliorate the problem. If unemployment is especially widespread and prolonged, it can lead to mass social protest and political upheaval.

But the labor sector also consists of consumers who are concerned about prices and who, when inflation is particularly virulent, seek protection against it. For those who are organized into unions, such protection may come about through escalator clauses in collective bargaining agreements. More generally, though, members of the labor sector will advocate that government undertake stronger anti-inflation policies. If political leaders fail to initiate such measures or if their policies are unsuccessful in curbing inflation, especially a rapid inflation, they may be turned out of office by the voters, who include members of the labor sector desirous of protecting their interests as consumers.

Finally, a government that attempts to deal with inflation through wage and price controls may earn the enmity of a substantial portion of the labor sector, namely, organized workers who feel that they are made to bear the costs of government policy in this area. Believing that their freedom to negotiate and their share of income are being unfairly restricted, even as business owners and managers snipe at the fundamentals of collective bargaining, organized workers (perhaps joined by a significant portion of the business sector) may try to bring strong political pressure on elected officials to alter their policies. Whether elected officials will actually do so depends upon how they weigh the opposition to controls in relation to the support for them, but, again, this is fundamentally a political judgment.

Thus, we observe within the labor sector those conflicting values and multiple desires which testify to the elusiveness of the goals of full employment, price stability, and free markets. In plunging more deeply into these issues, we encourage the reader to consider whether these goals are attainable and how that bears upon continuation of the mixed capitalist system which has evolved in the United States.

THE EXTENT AND MEASUREMENT OF UNEMPLOYMENT

The extent of unemployment in the United States for the period 1929–1978 is shown in both absolute and percentage terms in Table 12-1. The deleterious effect of the Great Depression is simply but starkly revealed in the rate of joblessness that prevailed in the 1930s—one out of four persons in the work force was unemployed. During World War II, the armed services drained off 10 million men and women from the supply of civilian labor, and the early postwar years saw less joblessness than had been anticipated, but between 1949 and 1974 the unemployment rate ranged between 3 and 6 percent, and on two occasions it approached 7 percent. The recession of 1974–1975 acted to increase unemployment sharply, the aggregate rate rising to 8.5 percent in 1975. It began to decline thereafter, averaging 7.0 percent in 1977 and 6.0 percent in 1978.

The fact that unemployment receded *to* 6 percent of the American work force in the late 1970s, when the measured rate only rarely surpassed that level for more than three decades (1942–1974), suggests why there has been concern over the causes of fluctuations in unemployment, the best ways of helping the jobless, and, most fundamentally, the definition of full employment and means of achieving it. It also indicates why unemployment is a fundamental issue of political economy rather than simply an economic phenomenon. The extent of unemployment will strongly influence the political actions taken to deal with it, and the policies that emerge out of the political process will, in turn, influence the workings of the economy. Thus, even without many of the measures for income supplements and social protection described in previous chapters, the role of politics in the economic process, particularly with respect to unemployment, substantiates the view that mixed capitalism rather than pure free market capitalism characterizes the United States.

Table 12-1 Unemployment in the United States, 1929–1978[1]

Year	Number of persons (in thousands)	Percent of civilian labor force	Year	Number of persons (in thousands)	Percent of civilian labor force
1929	1,550	3.2	1954	3,532	5.5
1930	4,340	8.7	1955	2,852	4.4
1931	8,020	15.9	1956	2,750	4.1
1932	12,060	23.6	1957	2,859	4.3
1933	12,830	24.9	1958	4,602	6.8
1934	11,340	21.7	1959	3,740	5.5
1935	10,610	20.1	1960	3,852	5.5
1936	9,030	16.9	1961	4,714	6.7
1937	7,700	14.3	1962	3,911	5.5
1938	10,390	19.0	1963	4,070	5.7
1939	9,480	17.2	1964	3,786	5.2
1940	8,120	14.6	1965	3,366	4.5
1941	5,560	9.9	1966	2,875	3.8
1942	2,660	4.7	1967	2,975	3.8
1943	1,070	1.9	1968	2,817	3.6
1944	670	1.2	1969	2,831	3.5
1945	1,040	1.9	1970	4,008	4.9
1946	2,270	3.9	1971	4,993	5.9
1947	2,311	3.9	1972	4,840	5.6
1948	2,276	3.8	1973	4,304	4.9
1949	3,637	5.9	1974	5,076	5.6
1950	3,288	5.3	1975	7,830	8.5
1951	2,055	3.3	1976	7,288	7.7
1952	1,883	3.0	1977	6,855	7.0
1953	1,834	2.9	1978	6,155	6.0

[1] Data for years prior to 1947 are for all persons 14 years of age and over in the civilian labor force; from 1947 on, data are for all persons 16 years of age and over. This difference is insignificant for most purposes; the two measures yield nearly identical unemployment rates.

Sources: Adapted from *Economic Report of the President, 1979*, 1979, p. 214, table B-27, and prior issues.

But how is it that we come to know the level and rate of unemployment that exists in the economy at any point in time? Again, this reflects a political judgment that unemployment is an important problem meriting treatment by means of policy and a related decision that government should bear the responsibility for gathering information about unemployment. The basic source of data is the set of responses to a survey questionnaire administered as part of the monthly Current Population Survey by the Bureau of the Census, whose interviewers visit a sample of about 56,000 households.[1] That sample is selected to represent (within a statistically acceptable margin of error) the population as a whole, and it is rotated regularly. The Census interviewers obtain information about the employment status of each household member 16 years of age and above during the week of the month containing the twelfth day, the so-called "survey week." The survey data are then "blown up" into estimates for the labor force as a whole, using the following distinctions between the employed and the unemployed:

> Employed persons are those who, during the survey week, worked at least one hour as *paid* employees, or in their own business, profession, or farm, or who worked 15 hours or more as *unpaid* workers in a family business, or those who were not working but had jobs or businesses from which they were temporarily absent because of illness, bad weather, vacation, or labor dispute.
>
> Unemployed persons include those who did not work at all during the survey week but made specific efforts to find a job within the previous four weeks and were currently available for work, plus those who did not work at all but were available for work and were waiting to be called back to a job from which they had been laid off or were waiting to report to a new wage or salary job within 30 days.[2]

The sum of these two groups is the civilian labor force of the United States, with all other persons 16 years and over classified as "not in the labor force." Few observers question the statistical soundness of the household sample, but many question whether the above measures present a true picture of unemployment. Among the critics are those who favor narrowing the concept of unemployment, but also, as noted briefly in Chapter 1, those who support its expansion. The first group generally proposes (1) limiting the unemployment count to full-time primary earners who lose their jobs through no fault of their own, that is, "breadwinners" who support themselves and others, and (2) counting only those who are actively attached to the labor force during the survey week rather than engaged in some other major activity such as keeping house or going to school. Constraining measured unemployment in this way would exclude from its ranks "most part-time jobseekers, married women, youth, job leavers, new and reentrants to the labor force, and persons fired for cause."[3]

In contrast, proponents of an expanded concept of unemployment recommend several changes which would permit it to be used as a measure of personal hardship or inadequate labor supply. For example, Levitan and Taggart propose an index of employment *and* earnings inadequacy which would reflect the proportion of people working, looking for work, or discouraged from job seeking who cannot secure a minimum income by themselves or through other employed family members.[4] This is a variation on the subemployment index offered by Spring, Harrison, and Vietorisz, as described in Chapter 1. Short of such a major change, others advocate a broadening of the concept of unemployment to include discouraged workers who do not actively search for work because they feel that none is available and persons who are on part-time work schedules even though they would prefer to be fully employed. Still others favor taking account of "the desires or rights of individuals to a job,"[5] that is, making measured unemployment reflect the potential labor supply. This approach would require identifying the number of people who want jobs and finding out for what wages and under what other terms of employment they would be willing to offer their services.

These various (and in some cases, strongly contrasting) proposals illustrate the role of value judgments in the measurement of unemployment. Following through on any one or any group of them would affect reported unemployment rates, in some (but not all) cases significantly. This is observable from Figure 1-1, showing Shiskin's compilation of seven measures of unemployment, ranging from the most restrictive (U_1) to the most comprehensive (U_7). The latter yields a considerably higher unemployment rate than the former; if adopted by the government as an official statistical indicator, it might thrust public policy more strongly toward combating unemployment and away from the other goals of society to which we referred at the beginning of this chapter.

We must recognize that debate about the propriety of national unemployment statistics has been going on for many years and has sometimes led to formal reappraisals of the conceptual and measurement bases upon which the data rest. The most recent of these efforts was authorized by Congress in late 1976, when the Emergency Jobs Program Extension Act created a nine-member Commission on Employment and Unemployment Statistics. That body, under the chairmanship of Sar Levitan of Georgetown University, is completing its analysis and report at the time of this writing.[6]

More generally, the controversy over concepts of, and data on, unemployment provides a basis for examining the types of unemployment that occur in the American economy and for taking up the critical issue of full employment. While there are many types of unemployment, four will be specifically considered here: frictional, seasonal, structural, and cyclical.

Frictional unemployment is joblessness, usually of a short-term variety, that results from the voluntary and involuntary movement of people between jobs; this is an unavoidable aspect of any labor market. Indeed, from the perspective of labor as a factor of production to which some mobility attaches, worker mobility is desirable. After all, no worker is unalterably tied to a job or to an employer any more than he or she is guaranteed a paid position. In the labor market, there normally is a churning of people looking for jobs and of employers searching for workers, especially in prosperous times.

In earlier chapters, we reviewed the incidence of job mobility and also occupational mobility in the American economy, noting their widespread incidence and increased frequency during expansionary periods. But because changes in employment rarely proceed with timing so precise that a worker leaves one job at 5 P.M. on Friday to take another starting at 9 A.M. on Monday, there is often a period of unemployment between jobs. Further, because of miscalculation or misfortune, some firms are forced to lay off workers, and the same can occur in expanding companies that close some plants or move others elsewhere. This transitional unemployment—transitional because laid-off workers are expected to find jobs with other firms soon—also falls into the frictional category. So, too, does that of new entrants to the labor force who are looking for their first jobs and also that of reentrants who are searching for employment. At the other end of the spectrum are older employees, who, once laid off, may incur brief spells of unemployment and then leave the labor force to begin retirement. Here is another instance of frictional unemployment.

Seasonal unemployment is quite a different phenomenon. It stems from weather (affecting employment in agriculture and construction, for example, and also dependent industries such as food processing), from annual style and model changes which lower production levels during changeovers (as in garment and automobile manufacturing), and from customary purchasing patterns such as those associated with major holidays (Christmas and Easter, most notably).[7] All these factors create shifts in the demand for labor over the calendar. Additionally, a major supply factor affecting the seasonality of unemployment is the large number of students who temporarily leave school during the summer, not all of whom are able to find jobs. Thus for workers under age 25, unemployment typically reaches its peak in June, when it may be half again or more above the annual average for that age group. For the same workers, unemployment is at its seasonal low in early fall, with the resumption of school, when it drops back to about three-quarters of the annual average rate. For men over 25 in the labor force, the seasonal low point of employment is in February, reflecting layoffs in outdoor jobs, while for women it occurs in January, when clerical and sales forces are reduced after the holiday period.

In order to take account of these events, the federal government (specifically, the Bureau of Labor Statistics) makes seasonal adjustments to the raw data on unemployment. To appreciate the effects of these adjustments, consider the data presented in Table 12-2. Over an entire year, the adjusted and unadjusted data are identical. During the year, however, seasonal adjustments sometimes yield substantially different unemployment rates from those originally reported. Note particularly the differences between unadjusted and adjusted rates early and late in the year, and also at midyear. The data in the lower part of Table 12-2 show how seasonal adjustments of a specific monthly unemployment rate affect its magnitude and also the magnitudes of unemployment rates of specific groups in the labor force and workers in specific areas. Comparable adjustments to data on unemployment reported late in the year serve to raise rather than lower the published rates.[8]

Structural unemployment arises from major imbalances in the demand for, and supply of, particular kinds of labor. As noted in Chapter 11, the term is often applied to the hard-to-employ who are not just temporarily out of work as

Table 12-2   Unemployment Rates with and without Seasonal Adjustments, 1978 and January 1979

	Not seasonally adjusted	Seasonally adjusted
1978		
Total	6.0	6.0
January	7.0	6.3
February	6.9	6.1
March	6.6	6.2
April	5.8	6.1
May	5.5	6.1
June	6.2	5.8
July	6.3	6.1
August	5.8	5.9
September	5.7	5.9
October	5.4	5.8
November	5.5	5.8
December	5.6	5.9
January 1979		
Total civilian labor force	6.4	5.8
Men 20 years and older	4.8	4.0
Women 20 years and older	6.1	5.7
Both sexes, 16–19	17.1	15.7
Whites	5.7	5.1
Black and other	11.7	11.2
California: total civilian labor force	7.2	6.3
New York: total civilian labor force	7.7	7.0

Source: Adapted from Council of Economic Advisers, *Economic Indicators, January, 1979,* 1979, p. 11.

they change jobs or unemployed as the result of seasonal lags in particular industries or a major slump in the economy as a whole. Instead, even if jobs go unfilled, these people cannot fill them because they have insufficient or unwanted skills or because they live in deteriorating regions. In other words, the structure rather than the level of demand does not match supply in many labor markets, and the impact of this imbalance falls heavily on particular groups in the labor force.

Where skin color, religion, race, or sex is used to "select out" individuals and groups of workers, public programs attempt to provide remedies: for example, Title VII of the Civil Rights Act of 1964, federal contracting procedures to ensure equal employment opportunity, and related measures which were reviewed in Chapter 8. But where skill, experience, and verbal, mathematical, and reasoning abilities fall short of the mark, public programs sometimes attempt to overcome these deficiencies through classroom or subsidized on-the-job training. Improvement in the quality and availability of information about the labor market (presently supported by the federal government) and relocation allowances (supplied by some European governments) are also intended to combat structural unemployment. Though its magnitude is sharply debated and though it is not without controversy, the concept of structural employment nevertheless has gained wide acceptance on both the American and the European scenes, especially with the growing influx into the labor force of young workers, who often are not well prepared for employment.[9]

Cyclical unemployment is perhaps the most familiar form and is reflected in the periodic rise and fall of the rates presented in Table 12-1. As a recession or depression spreads, its effects are felt by most firms, most industries, and most groups of workers. The resulting unemployment is not due to seasonal factors which may shortly play themselves out, to the frictions of voluntary and some involuntary job changes, or to structural imbalances in the labor market. Rather, it results from a generalized condition of economic decline, the recession of 1974–1975 standing as the most recent case in point. As the contraction reaches its trough and begins to reverse direction, however, people's spirits revive, firms commence rebuilding depleted inventories and adding new or repairing old equipment, government expenditures swing toward stimulation of the economy, employment rolls start to rise, and unemployment begins to decline. The prosperity phase eventually supplants the recovery period, and the cycle begins once again.

A business cycle may be of long or short duration, and sometimes short cycles are superimposed on long ones with disastrous results. It is quite unlikely, however, that the nation will again suffer a massive depression like that of the 1930s, for the "Keynesian revolution" in economic thought apparently convinced all but a few that government should attempt to avert any major economic collapse—even if far more than a few question government's effectiveness in this regard. But the persistence of the recession-recovery-prosperity (or quasi-prosperity) pattern of economic events indicates that cyclical unemployment remains an ever-present threat.

UNEMPLOYMENT AS AN ISSUE OF PUBLIC POLICY

Having identified four major types of unemployment and, in other chapters, having reviewed the differential incidence of unemployment among subgroups of the labor sector, let us now take up the treatment of unemployment as a major issue of public policy. We have already dealt with some measures that are intended to offset the debilitating effects of unemployment, for example, unemployment insurance and others such as human resources policies that attempt to upgrade workers' skills and improve the matching process in labor markets. At this point, though, our focus is on the broader policy sweep as it reflects society's concern about unemployment or, more properly, full employment, but in relation to other goals such as stable prices and free markets.

A useful starting point in this regard is the Employment Act of 1946. It served irrevocably to indicate that labor and product markets would not be allowed to operate unchecked and that public policy would play a primary role in shaping economic activity. Observe that this measure emerged only after public sentiment had been mobilized behind programs of governmental economic planning for full employment. Crystallization of that sentiment was, in turn, due to three influences: the Great Depression of the 1930s, Keynesian economics, and wartime planning for production. The first of these, which at its height engendered not only a 25 percent unemployment rate but also great insecurity among jobholders concerning their future livelihood, aroused strong interest in government actions to ensure employment opportunities for all who wished to work. Certainly the New Deal policies initiated by President Franklin D. Roosevelt had this objective, even if they did not precisely spell out the goal.

The second major influence came in 1936, when John Maynard Keynes published his *General Theory of Employment, Interest, and Money,* which provided a theoretical framework for full employment policy. Challenging conventional doctrine, which viewed price dislocations as the principal cause of unemployment, Keynes argued that unemployment could emerge and persist whenever the amounts individuals were willing to invest balanced the sums which individuals were willing to save at some aggregate level of expenditure below that necessary to employ the entire labor force. His work traced through the dynamics of this suboptimal savings-investment scenario and then dwelt on the actions necessary to overcome substantial and persistent unemployment. These were government initiatives, such as directly undertaking an investment program or indirectly encouraging private expenditures by reducing taxes, insuring loans, or lowering interest rates. Keynesian theory thus seemed to offer an acceptable rationale for governmental full employment policies and a framework within which governments might initiate comprehensive planning to prevent the emergence of unemployment.

Finally, the sharp contrast provided by "overfull" employment during World War II (see Table 12-1 again) and the dismal unemployment of the preceding decade led many to question why, if an economy could be mobilized for maximum production for the destructive purposes of war, it could not also be mobilized for the constructive purposes of peace.

As powerful as these forces may have been, and despite the concerted attacks on unemployment mounted in many developed nations of the world, the new American legislation fell considerably short of full-blown planning to promote full employment policy. In the debate that preceded the 1946 statute, conservative economists claimed that economic planning could not proceed without a centralization of authority that spelled a loss of people's liberties. By undertaking large-scale public works and investment projects, it was charged, government officials would drive business people out of the field because they would fear being steamrollered by the new, large, public competitor. And, as government assumed more and more responsibility for investment, it might well be drawn into regulating wages and prices and then into taking partial or direct control of industry, thereby leading to "creeping socialism."

In reply to these arguments, liberal proponents of a full employment policy contended that political freedom is an empty abstraction to a person without a job and that no society which fails to provide jobs for its citizens can long retain its democratic base. Furthermore, they noted, a free society seldom must choose between total controls and no controls, for it places some limits on every political freedom—of speech, the press, assembly, and religion—without fully constraining them. The same could be done, it was argued, in partially regulating economic activities.[10]

We have dwelt on the debate during the 1940s over the appropriate role of government in a democratic society and capitalist economy because it is one that continues up to the present. The most recent version of this debate will be considered later in this chapter when we discuss legislation enacted in late 1978 to require balanced growth and economic planning in the United States. For now, it suffices to say that, as so often happens, the sharp contention between opposing views led to something of a compromise position, as reflected in the Employment Act of 1946. Originally presented as a bill entitled the "Full Employment Act," the adopted version pledged the government only "to promote maximum employment, production and purchasing power . . . in a manner calculated to foster and promote free competitive enterprise." Nevertheless, the policy seed had been planted, and every subsequent administration has pledged itself *to attempt* to achieve full employment.

But what is full employment, how does it relate to other national goals, and what is the cost of achieving it? These questions have persisted, and the answers to them are as elusive now as they were before. Consider that the ink was hardly dry on the Employment Act of 1946 when inflation displaced unemployment as the nation's chief domestic problem. Consumer prices rose by more than 14 percent in 1947, and producer prices rose by about 23 percent (see Table 12-3), while unemployment remained slightly under 4 percent of the work force. With the removal of controls on wages and strikes, strife in the labor market mounted in the immediate postwar period, leading to record levels of both lost working time and increases in negotiated pay and benefits. Many observers attributed the inflationary spiral of that period to collective bargaining, but in retrospect it seems to have been a classic case of "too many dollars chasing too few goods."

Ironically, this resulted largely from the effectiveness of wartime rationing and wage and price controls, which permitted consumers to save a considerable portion of their relatively high wartime earnings, which they then used to bid up the demand for goods and services. Labor unions may have intensified or prolonged the resulting inflation, but not by much, and they were hardly its basic source. Similarly, they contributed only marginally to inflation during the early 1950s, rising prices in that period being attributable mainly to the stresses of the Korean war.[11]

Examining the data presented in Table 12-3, we may think it surprising, maybe even foolish, for anyone to have been concerned about inflation from the mid-1950s to the mid-1960s. After all, in those years, consumer prices never increased by as much as 4 percent annually and only twice experienced more than a 2 percent rise. But this analysis from hindsight overlooks the view then prevailing that prices needn't rise at all and might even drop a little in a stable,

Table 12-3   Changes in Consumer and Producer Price Indexes, United States, 1947–1978[1]

Year	CPI[2] All items		PPI[3] All commodities	
	Index	Percent change	Index	Percent change
1947	66.9	14.4	76.5	22.8
1948	72.1	7.8	82.8	8.2
1949	71.4	−1.0	78.7	−5.0
1950	72.1	1.0	81.8	3.9
1951	77.8	7.9	91.1	11.4
1952	79.5	2.2	88.6	−2.7
1953	80.1	0.8	87.4	−1.4
1954	80.5	0.5	87.6	0.2
1955	80.2	−0.4	87.8	0.2
1956	81.4	1.5	90.7	3.3
1957	84.3	3.6	93.3	2.9
1958	86.6	2.7	94.6	1.4
1959	87.3	0.8	94.8	0.2
1960	88.7	1.6	94.9	0.1
1961	89.6	1.0	94.5	−0.4
1962	90.6	1.1	94.8	0.3
1963	91.7	1.2	94.5	−0.3
1964	92.9	1.3	94.7	0.2
1965	94.5	1.7	96.6	2.0
1966	97.2	2.9	99.8	3.3
1967	100.0	2.9	100.0	0.2
1968	104.2	4.2	102.5	2.5
1969	109.8	5.4	106.5	3.9
1970	116.3	5.9	110.4	3.7
1971	121.3	4.3	114.0	3.3
1972	125.3	3.3	119.1	4.5
1973	133.1	6.2	134.7	13.1
1974	147.7	11.0	160.1	18.9
1975	161.2	9.1	174.9	9.2
1976	170.5	5.8	188.0	4.6
1977	181.5	6.5	194.3	7.7
1978	195.3	7.6	NA[3]	NA[3]

[1] 1967 = 100.

[2] Through 1977 data are for urban wage earners and clerical workers. For 1978 data are for all urban consumers.

[3] Formerly the Wholesale Price Index (WPI). Through 1977 the data are for all commodities including farm products. For 1978 data are published separately for farm products and industrial commodities, without an aggregate index. Farm products increased in price by 9.5 percent in 1978, industrial commodities by 7.3 percent.

Sources: Adapted from Employment and Training Report of the President, 1978, 1978, p. 333, table G-6; Monthly Labor Review, **102**:93, table 22 (1979); and Economic Report of the President 1979, 1979, p. 248, table B-57.

smoothly functioning economy. Moreover, if prices were increasing only slowly, perhaps creeping along at between 1 and 2 percent a year, who was to say that inflation could not suddenly expand at higher rates? Notice, too (in Table 12-1), that unemployment, which had averaged about 3 percent of the work force in the early 1950s, moved upward to 5.5 percent in 1954 and averaged almost exactly that rate over the next decade. Clearly, at those rates unemployment represented more than mere frictional joblessness, but if public policy attempted to achieve some full-employment level—say, 3 percent—wouldn't inflation gallop rather than creep ahead? Thus, far from being insignificant, the data seemed to reveal a classic and painfully clear dilemma, one that required policy makers to choose between combating inflation and combating unemployment.

Of course, the combinations of inflation and unemployment rates that prevailed in the mid-1950s and mid-1960s appear benign, indeed favorable, compared with those which characterized the mid-1970s. Over the period 1974–1978, for example, inflation as measured by changes in the Consumer Price Index averaged about 8 percent a year, reaching 11 percent in 1974, while unemployment was about 7 percent annually. It is true that more salutary combinations of rates existed in the late 1960s and that both inflation and unemployment began to recede after the recession of the mid-1970s, but doesn't this all suggest that even more undesirable rates might prevail simultaneously at some future point?

Perhaps it does, and it is possible that the development of a heavily service-oriented economy, together with growing economic internationalization, prevents any single nation from attaining historically favorable combinations of inflation and unemployment rates, let alone price stability and full employment. But even if that is so, the question posed earlier—"What is full employment?" —remains to be addressed. It is theoretically possible for it to mean no unemployment, as is claimed to be the case in Russia, China, and some eastern European nations. But those are communist societies in which private ownership of the means of production is not permitted, economic activity is fully planned and controlled by the state, and free labor markets of the type found in western nations do not exist. The communism of the workers presumably ensures that all "returns" to economic activity flow to labor (for there is no capitalist, property-owning class), that labor is fully employed, and that market incentives are not required to manage the production of goods and services. There is, of course, good reason to doubt that the practice of communism fully accords with the ideal of it; it is known, for example, that incentive schemes resembling those used in the west have been employed in the management of large-scale productive enterprises in communist nations and that the occupational wage structures in those nations are quite hierarchical.[12] Consequently, it would not be too surprising to find some unemployment in communist nations, even though it is supposedly absent from them by definition.

Nevertheless, in some capitalist societies unemployment can be close to, if not at, zero. This has been true of Japan and West Germany, where unemployment rates were slightly above and slightly below 1 percent, respectively, in the early 1970s. Since then, unemployment has risen to about 2 percent in Japan and 4.5 percent in West Germany, rates which are considered to represent departures from full employment in these nations. In Chapter 1 we observed that in socialist countries unemployment rates of between 1 and 2 percent have generally been considered to represent full employment. These also worsened considerably in the 1970s (see Table 1-5), however, and thus by their own standards socialist countries are perhaps further away from achieving full employment than the United States is.

In this country during the 1960s, full employment was commonly (which is not to say unanimously) considered to be in the 3 to 4 percent range. Both the Kennedy and the Johnson administrations accepted these as the boundaries of unemployment consistent with full employment and adopted fiscal, monetary, and human resources policies designed to achieve the goal. The intellectual basis of those initiatives set by policy, especially fiscal policy, was the so-called "GNP gap," the difference between the actual output of goods and services in the national economy and the potential output at full employment. Walter Heller, chairman of the Council of Economic Advisers in the Kennedy administration, provides an illustrative example of this approach:

> For 1962, when the unemployment rate averaged 5.6 percent—1.6 percentage points above 4 percent [defined as full employment]—the gap between potential and actual GNP was estimated at around $30 to $35 billion, or a little over 5 percent of a potential $585 to $590 billion. . . . The trend line projection . . . yields a potential GNP rate of $629 billion in the fourth quarter of 1963. This is over $65 billion, or nearly 12 percent, above the level of $563.5 billion actually achieved in the last quarter of 1962. Thus it appears that an increase of some $65 billion in aggregate monetary demand would be needed to create the 3.1 million jobs that would reduce unemployment from the 5.5 percent rate that prevailed in the fourth quarter of 1962 to the interim goal of 4.0 percent by the fourth quarter of 1963.[13]

This analysis was instrumental to the Kennedy administration's proposal, submitted to Congress in 1963, for a major tax reduction. Tragically, Kennedy did not live to see the enactment in 1964 of this fiscal measure, which sought to stimulate economywide demand, reduce unemployment, and bring about enhanced economic growth. And, in fact, those consequences did materialize, although the additional growth of federal expenditures over the period 1965–1969 to finance the Vietnamese war was instrumental in raising the rate of inflation from less than 3 percent to beyond 5 percent by the end of the decade.

We must recognize that Kennedy and Johnson's policies sought principally to overcome the type of unemployment that, within our fourfold definition, most closely fits the cyclical category. Not only did the recessions of 1954 and 1958 bring about increased unemployment, but also the rather sluggish recoveries from them, especially the second, did not induce substantial declines in joblessness. Indeed, Kennedy's 1960 Presidential campaign, built on the theme of "getting the country moving again," was focused heavily on the problem of unemployment, which, it was charged, had been largely ignored during the two-term Eisenhower administration of the 1950s. Consequently, in the 1960s strong emphasis was placed on remedying the deficiency of aggregate demand in the economy. True, human resources policies were adopted in those years to combat structural unemployment, but even more fundamental was the belief that the state of economic affairs could be actively and positively affected by government action, in particular that management of aggregate demand was an appropriate subject of public policies. This was basic to Kennedy and Johnson's initiatives of the 1960s. And the intellectual rudder for moving in this direction was provided by Keynes and his disciples, who, as noted earlier, revolutionized macroeconomic thought and the role of public policy.[14]

But if Keynesian economic policies seemed finally to have produced a mechanism for achieving sustained growth and control of the economy, with only "fine tuning" required every now and then, subsequent events were rudely to shatter that idyllic expectation. The destabilizing effects of the buildup in Vietnam in the late 1960s have already been noted. As the weight of national concern once more shifted to the control of inflation, economic policies were adopted by the Nixon administration, which took office in 1969, to cool down the overheated economy. Fiscal policy was directed at reducing government expenditures, with some social welfare and human resources programs pared down or eliminated, and monetary policy was also tightened. Unemployment rather predictably moved upward, but inflation proved more intractable, and in the period 1969–1970 the nation experienced its first economic recession in over a decade, as real GNP declined by 0.3 percent.

The combination of persistent inflation and economic recession raised basic questions about management of the economy through public policy and about the staying power of the "new economics" of the 1960s. Despite the recovery from the recession that was under way in 1971, the administration looked for still more effective anti-inflation measures. Seeking and receiving legislative authority from Congress, the Nixon administration imposed a wage and price freeze on the economy in the summer of 1971 and, 3 months later, a program of wage and price controls which lasted until early 1973.[15]

All these measures, but the last especially, may seem in retrospect to have worked inasmuch as inflation declined to little more than 3 percent in 1972, unemployment fell below 5 percent in the following year, and the economy in general experienced a boom over the period 1972–1973. But inflationary forces already were at work in the period following controls. The progressive breakdown of the international monetary system, the large deficits in this country's balance-of-payments accounts which preceded and followed it, and the onset of the Arab oil embargo in late 1973 combined to plunge the United Sates (indeed, the world) into a major recession which lasted well into 1975. Moreover, in the crisis of Watergate, which brought Gerald Ford to the Presidency, relatively scant attention was paid to the federal government's management and coordination of economic policy.

Given these developments, real GNP declined, inflation moved to double-digit levels, and unemployment shot past 9 percent in mid-1975, averaging 8.5

percent over the entire year. Although mild versions of "stagflation"—the combination of inflation and recession—had appeared on the scene in the late 1950s and again in the period 1969–1970, it developed with a vengeance during 1974 and 1975. One was tempted to ask, "If full employment had been difficult to achieve in an era when it was assumed that public policies could bring about effective management of the economy, could attainment of that goal be seriously considered in an economy apparently out of control?"

Patterns of Unemployment—and Employment

Well, one could consider it, to be sure, but some students of the labor sector cautioned that, in doing so, we should look afresh at employment and unemployment, lest we be saddled with outmoded notions about the level of joblessness consistent with full employment.[16] As noted in Chapter 1, the composition of the labor force underwent changes in the 1960s and 1970s, with the proportions of women and young people increasing and with the proportion of males decreasing. The first two groups historically have had higher unemployment rates than the third, as shown in Table 12-4, but more important are the reasons accounting for these different rates.

Like all other workers, teenage members of the labor force are affected by cyclical unemployment, but they differ from other workers in the fluidity of their attachment to the labor force. A considerable amount of unemployment among teenagers, especially among white teenagers, results from decisions to leave and reenter the work force. For the bulk of younger teenagers in the labor force, those 16 and 17 years old, employment is a second- or third-order activity, while for older teenagers, the trial-and-error process of locating suitable employment and career paths also leads to relatively high rates of turnover.[17]

To appreciate better the relatively high rates of turnover among the teen-

Table 12-4 Unemployment Rates by Race, Sex, and Age, Selected Periods, 1956–1978

(Percent[1])

Group	1956	1965	1968	1973	1975	1978
Total	4.1	4.5	3.6	4.9	8.5	6.0
Whites						
Males 20 years and over	2.0	2.9	2.0	2.9	6.2	3.7
Females 20 years and over	3.7	4.0	3.4	4.3	7.5	5.2
Teenagers	10.2	13.4	11.0	12.6	17.9	13.9
Blacks and others[2]						
Males 20 years and over	7.4	6.0	3.9	5.7	11.7	8.6
Females 20 years and over	7.8	7.5	6.3	8.2	11.5	10.6
Teenagers	18.2	26.2	25.0	30.2	36.9	36.3

[1] Percent of civilian labor force in group specified.
[2] Blacks make up about 89 percent of total blacks and others in the labor force.
Sources: Adapted from *Economic Report of the President, January, 1979*, 1979, p. 218; *Employment and Training Report of the President, 1978*, 1978, p. 190; and U.S. Bureau of Labor Statistics, *Employment and Earnings*, January 1979, p. 161.

Table 12-5   Unemployment Rates by Reasons for Unemployment, 1978
(Percent)

Group	Total[1]	Males 20 years and over[2]	Females 20 years and over[2]	Teenagers[2]
Total labor force	6.0	4.2	6.0	16.3
Job losers	2.5	2.6	2.3	3.1
Job leavers	0.8	0.6	1.0	1.7
New entrants to the labor force	1.8	0.9	2.4	4.7
Reentrants	0.9	0.2	0.4	6.8

[1] Percent of civilian labor force.
[2] Percent of civilian labor force in sex and age group specified.
Source: Adapted from U.S. Bureau of Labor Statistics, *Employment and Earnings,* January 1979, p. 166.

age work force, study the data for 1978 presented in Table 12-5, which shows that teenagers have an incidence of involuntary job loss a little higher than other workers but that they leave their jobs voluntarily about twice as often. Note, further, the much larger disparities between teenagers and adults in the incidence of new entrants and returnees to the work force. This is not to suggest that unemployment among teenagers should not be taken seriously or to overlook the fact that some reentrants among them may have dropped out of the work force because they became discouraged about the prospects of finding a job. But the data do indicate that a large portion of the difference in rates of joblessness among teenagers and adults "clearly reflects the former's high rate of voluntary job mobility prior to settling on a stable career."[18]

Less easily explained by turnover, however, are the vastly different unemployment rates of black and white teenagers—36.3 and 13.9 percent, respectively, during the calendar year 1978 (see Table 12-4). The proportion of black teenagers who quit work only slightly exceeded that of white teenagers, and the evidence tells us that black teenagers (like black adults) have much more difficulty than white teenagers in locating employment. Additionally, the disparate rates of participation in the labor force of black and white teenagers—45 and 65 percent, respectively, in 1978—suggest a higher incidence of discouragement about job prospects among the former. If these dropouts from the labor force had been counted as unemployed, the unemployment rate among black teenagers in 1978 might have been as much as 20 percent higher than the reported 36 percent.[19]

Still, because white teenagers outnumber their black counterparts by about 9 to 1, the extent of unemployment among all teenagers, some 16.3 percent in 1978, must be recognized as stemming in large part from their relatively high incidence of voluntary turnover and their low incidence of attachment to the labor force. In turn, because the proportion of teenagers in the civilian labor force increased from about 7 percent in 1960 to 10 percent by 1978, their high rate of unemployment, voluntary and otherwise, has raised the average rate of unemployment in the economy.

Similarly, adult women have a higher incidence of voluntary turnover than prevails among the work force as a whole (see Table 12-5). However, adult women are much less likely than all teenagers, but more likely than adult men, to reenter the work force following a period of absence. Much of that absence is accounted for by married women who drop out of the labor force to bear children and then return to work later. Some of the reentry of adult women no doubt reflects prior discouragement about finding a job, but the lack of sufficient opportunities for part-time work is a more important factor in women's leaving (and subsequently reentering) the work force. All this is to say that women still are somewhat less attached to the work force than men, despite the enormous increases over time in their rates of participation in the labor force. Because women represent almost 42 percent of the civilian labor force (in 1978), their unemployment rate—which is higher than that of men, even if well below that of teenagers—also tends to raise the unemployment rate for the economy as a whole.

It is these changes in the composition of the work force (that is, the increased participation in the labor force of teenagers and women, among whom voluntary turnover is greater than among adult men) that some students of the labor sector instruct us to consider in approaching the subject of full employment in the modern economy.[20] To recognize this, we repeat, is not to gainsay the importance of unemployment among teenagers and women or to argue that, because of them, full employment is unattainable. Rather, it is to sort out the differential causes of that unemployment in order to learn how they bear upon the question of full employment.

Additional insights into this issue are provided by a brief review of changes over time in the level of employment as distinct from the level of unemployment in the economy. In 1961, total civilian employment in the United States stood at roughly 65,775,000 persons, or not quite 9 million more than in 1947, when systematic data on the labor force began to be assembled.[21] By 1968, employment had risen to just under 76 million. The next year some 2 million persons were added to the employment rolls, and the volume of jobholders continued to mount through the recession of 1969–1970 and beyond, *averaging* more than 1.8 million new additions over the period 1971–1974. The severe recession of the mid-1970s caused a momentary decline in employment of over 1 million, but in the recovery period of 1975–1977, employment grew by almost 7 million, or 3.4 million annually. That pace was maintained in 1978 as total employment approached 96 million.[22]

By any historical or contemporary standard, these are extraordinary levels of job creation. They demonstrate the economy's ability to absorb increasingly large proportions of new entrants into the labor force, many of them teenagers and adult women. This fact can be further appreciated by examining Figure 12-1, which shows the employment-population ratio as well as the unemployment–labor force ratio in the United States from 1960 to 1978. These two measures are not parallel, as Figure 12-1 suggests. At the beginning of the period, the employment-population ratio was under 55 percent. It grew to 56 percent in

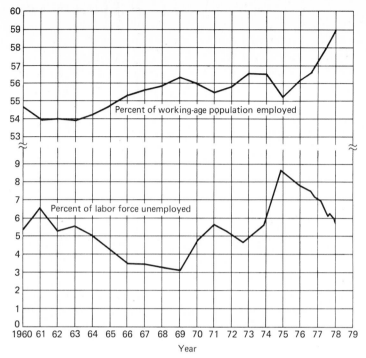

Figure 12-1 Employment-to-population ratios and unemployment rates, 1960–1978. (*Sources:* Economic Report of the President, 1979, *U.S. Government Printing Office, Washington, D.C., 1979, table B-27, pp. 214–215; and Philip L. Rones and Carol Leon, "Employment and Unemployment During 1978: An Analysis,"* Monthly Labor Review, *102:3–12 (1979).*

1968, a year of low unemployment, and rose and then fell back to that level in 1972 and again in 1976, but it moved upward to near 58 percent by the end of 1977 and was at a record 59 percent at the end of 1978. The employment-population ratios for teenagers and adult women also reached new highs by the end of this period. Thus recent decades, the 1970s especially, have witnessed a major expansion of employment, even as unemployment also increased.

Adding together these observations about the changing composition of the labor force, employment, and unemployment, we begin to see that "full employment" in today's economy may not necessarily mean the same thing that it did in the mid-1960s or even the early 1970s. If 3 to 4 percent unemployment was once consistent with full employment in the United States, a somewhat higher rate may well be consistent with it as the decade of the 1980s begins to unfold. What is the new rate of unemployment, or range of rates, that signifies full employment? No one can say with authority, but 5 to 5½ percent is often cited by experts on this subject.[23] By that standard, the United States may have been relatively close to full employment in late 1978 and early 1979, when unemployment was below 6.0 percent.[24]

According to one observer:

> Today's six percent unemployment may actually mean as tight a job market as the four percent rate of the booming sixties. . . . Women and young, single workers constitute the fastest growing groups within the work force, and both traditionally exhibit higher unemployment rates than older men and heads of households. Since more of the newcomers are now classified in the labor market, they automatically push up unemployment. . . . So let us dethrone the unemployment rate. No single statistic tells how close the economy is to what used to be called "full employment." . . . Changing the rules of the game gives us no right, of course, to rationalize away unemployment. . . . But the blind worship of outmoded unemployment targets isn't helping anyone.[25]

Unquestionably, there is a danger in revising our estimates of the full-employment level of unemployment. Specifically, we run the risk of defining away the problem of unemployment by merely raising the "acceptable" rate of it. And this danger should not be taken lightly, for several authorities have suggested that the incidence of unemployment in the United States is considerably understated. Recognizing this danger, however, anyone who is seriously interested in the labor sector must keep abreast of new developments and be willing to reexamine the relevant data for their empirical content and implications for public policy.

The cost to the nation of unemployment beyond that consistent with full employment is amply demonstrated by the data in Table 12-6 which was compiled by the President's Council of Economic Advisers. A full-employment level of unemployment (referred to in Table 12-6 as the "benchmark unemployment rate") was assumed for each year over the period 1952–1978.[26] On this basis, the lost production of goods and services in the economy owing to excess unemployment has approached $375 billion just since 1970 and was $256 billion for the period 1975–1978 alone. That is a very high price indeed to pay for the failure to employ the nation's human resources fully, and it suggests to us why liberals and conservatives—Democrats, Republicans, and independents alike—all agree on the need for full employment, even as they differ over the level of unemployment that is consistent with it.

Inflation and Unemployment: Is There a Trade-off?

Earlier we observed that policy makers seem to face a dilemma in that by choosing to combat unemployment, they may trigger increasing rates of inflation, and vice versa. The intellectual basis of this apparent trade-off stemmed largely from the empirical studies of the late A. W. Phillips.[27] Plotting changes in wages against unemployment in the United Kingdom over the 96-year span from 1861 to 1957, Phillips uncovered a rather strong and consistent relationship between them. From this analysis, he concluded that when the rate of unemployment was about 2½ percent of the work force, increases in wages would be no greater than the general increase in productivity, and prices would re-

**Table 12-6   Potential Gross National Product and
Benchmark Unemployment Rate, 1952–1978**
(Billions of 1972 Dollars, Except as Noted)

Year	Potential GNP	Actual GNP	GNP gap (potential less actual)	Benchmark unemployment rate (percent)
1952	584.9	598.5	−13.6	4.0
1953	603.2	621.8	−13.6	4.0
1954	629.7	613.7	16.0	4.0
1955	651.4	654.8	−3.4	4.0
1956	673.9	668.8	5.1	4.0
1957	697.2	680.9	16.3	4.0
1958	721.3	679.5	41.3	4.0
1959	746.2	720.4	25.3	4.1
1960	771.9	736.8	35.1	4.1
1961	798.6	755.3	43.3	4.1
1962	826.4	799.1	27.3	4.1
1963	857.1	830.7	26.4	4.2
1964	890.3	874.4	15.9	4.3
1965	925.0	925.9	−0.9	4.4
1966	960.3	981.0	−20.2	4.5
1967	996.3	1007.7	−11.4	4.4[1]
1968	1031.7	1051.8	−20.1	4.4
1969	1068.3	1078.8	−10.5	4.4
1970	1106.2	1975.3	30.9	4.5
1971	1145.5	1107.5	33.0	4.6
1972	1186.1	1171.1	15.0	4.7
1973	1227.0	1235.0	−8.0	4.9
1974	1264.2	1217.8	46.4	5.0
1975	1302.1	1202.3	99.8	5.1
1976	1341.1	1271.0	70.1	5.1
1977	1381.4	1332.7	48.7	5.1
1978	1422.9	1385.1[2]	37.8[2]	5.1[3]

[1] Shift in benchmark unemployment rate from 1956 to 1967 because of 1967 change in sampling procedure in the Current Population Survey.

[2] Preliminary.

[3] Shift in benchmark unemployment rate from 1973 to 1978 based on revised estimates of potential output and unemployment-output relation.

Source: Adapted from *Economic Report of the President, January, 1978,* 1978, p. 84, and *Economic Report of the President, 1979,* 1979, p. 75.

main stable. Unemployment rates below this level led to an upward movement in wages and, presumably, prices. If wages were held steady and productivity increases were distributed throughout the economy in the form of reductions in prices, unemployment, according to Phillips, had to rise to about 5½ percent. The implication for public policy seemingly inherent in these findings was a trade-off between unemployment and changes in wages and prices.

Phillips's analysis was for the United Kingdom, but other economists replicated his study using data for the United States. Samuelson and Solow, for example, examined data on wages, prices, and unemployment for the United States between the turn of the century and the late 1950s (excluding wartime periods) and found the bulk of their observations to accord rather closely with those of Phillips.[28] Around 1946, however, the pattern seemed to change. Before that time, when the level of unemployment was about 3 percent, annual increases in wages could be kept at about 2 to 3 percent or roughly equal to the rate of increase in economywide productivity, but in the post-World War II era it took an unemployment rate almost double the earlier one to hold wage increases to the same level. And to keep money wages absolutely stable would require an unemployment rate of perhaps 8 percent. On the basis of these findings, Samuelson and Solow concluded that, in the future 4 to 5 percent unemployment would be required to keep wage increases at a 3 percent annual rate, while to achieve 2½ percent unemployment would require price increases of 5 to 6 percent annually.[29]

All this is shown in Figure 12-2, with rates of price change scaled on the vertical axis, and unemployment rates scaled on the horizontal axis. Point A corresponds to price stability, but at a 5½ percent level of unemployment. Point B combines a lower unemployment rate, 3 percent, with a 4½ percent rate of price increase. Different combinations of inflation and unemployment prevail all along this "Phillips curve," and policy makers presumably could de-

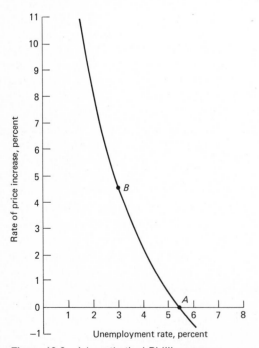

Figure 12-2 A hypothetical Phillips curve.

termine which mix of rates best fit the preferences of society, though it was considered unlikely that any nation would select one or another polar extreme.

Phillips-type analyses boomed in the 1960s and 1970s, as a veritable industry of scholars sought to measure trade-offs between inflation and unemployment in various countries and over time. From the perspective of public policy, the Phillips curve seemed an insightful guide to action. For example, if 7 percent unemployment existed at a point in time, as was the case in the United States in 1961, fiscal and monetary policies apparently could be made more expansionary to reduce the rate to around 5½ percent. With a curve of the type sketched in Figure 12-2, such a reduction of unemployment would be entirely a net gain, for it would have come at no cost in terms of inflation. As public policy stimulated even higher levels of demand, unemployment could be reduced still further, but only at a cost of rising prices. And the trade-off would worsen as unemployment was pushed even lower—going from 5½ to 4 percent unemployment would involve a 2 percent rate of annual price increase, while movement from 4 to 3 percent unemployment would be associated with a 4½ percent rate of inflation.

Preferred combinations of unemployment and inflation would differ from nation to nation, according to the values of the society. In Chapter 1, we reviewed data which show that the United States prefers higher unemployment and lower inflation than most other developed countries. The additional insight offered by the Phillips-type analysis, though, was that the curve itself could be pushed to the left over time, permitting a total range of more favorable trade-offs between inflation and unemployment than originally prevailed. The device for accomplishing this shift was human resources policy, which, by providing training, employment services, and information about the job market, would diminish structural unemployment in the economy.[30] If such unemployment were totally eradicated, then point B on the curve of Figure 12-2 would represent only frictional joblessness. Here seemed to exist the analytical apparatus for achieving a close to ideal state of tolerable inflation and full employment.

As is invariably the case, though, and especially with the labor sector, things turned out not to be so simple. In focusing heavily on the Phillips relation and its attendant implications for public policy, attention was diverted from the question of the stability of any such relationship. Yet as early as 1960, Samuelson and Solow suggested that the relationship between inflation and unemployment would change over time, and this prediction was borne out, perhaps even more strongly than they expected. Economists began rapidly to accumulate evidence which showed that the Phillips curve was anything but stable. The principal variable at work in this regard was expectations about inflation, particularly as they were manifested in labor's estimates of future price changes.[31]

At any point in time, workers will anticipate a certain price level, very likely that which presently exists or that which prevailed in the recent past. Suppose, however, they anticipate that prices may rise by 5 percent and, in addition, they expect their rate of wage increase to be 7 percent. To depict this expected rate of inflation in conjunction with the state of the labor market, as represented by the unemployment rate, we can draw the short-run Phillips curve (SRP_1) in Figure 12-3. If workers expected a higher rate of inflation and, correspondingly, larger wage increases for the same state of the labor market, we would have a curve such as SRP_2. In fact, depending upon different expected rates of inflation, there can be a whole series of short-run Phillips curves, and it is the adjustment of these expectations of workers to the incidence of inflation over time that is at the center of the analysis.

To illustrate, assume a starting point A (in Figure 12-3), showing the economy experiencing 7 percent unemployment and 5 percent inflation. Next, an expansion sets in, and unemployment declines to 5 percent, with the result that we move to point B on curve SRP_1. But now an unexpected development occurs in this expanding economy; instead of rising by 5 percent, as workers had anticipated, prices increase more rapidly, say, by 8 percent. Observing this higher inflation, workers will demand higher wages to offset the erosion of their earnings.

At an inflation rate of 8 percent, workers will pursue wage increases of 10 percent, whereas formerly, with 5 percent inflation, they would have been satisfied with a 7 percent wage boost. By seeking the new rate of wage increase, workers demonstrate their adjustment to the new inflation rate and their changed expectations about the rate that will prevail in the future; they are on a new short-run Phillips curve (SRP_3) at point C combining 5 percent unemployment and 8 percent inflation. By connecting points A and C, we derive a long-run Phillips curve (LRP), which yields a less preferable combination of unemployment and inflation—a higher inflation rate for any given unemploy-

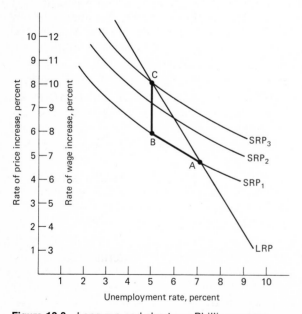

Figure 12-3 Long-run and short-run Phillips curves.

ment rate—than any of the short-run curves. Thus it is that there is no stable Phillips relationship, principally because workers' expectations about inflation are always adjusting to the changing realities of inflation.[32]

Note that the entire Phillips analysis seems to assume the centrality of collective barganing to this price-wage feedback and adjustment process. Workers' wage demands, formulated and reformulated in light of inflation, are made known and become the basis for wage bargains struck in negotiations with employers. This is the mechanism by which workers' changing expectations about inflation presumably are translated into higher wages and prices. Yet not all unions have the power to translate their members' preferences concerning wages into reality—organized textile workers and printers generally are in a less powerful bargaining position than organized airline pilots and construction workers, for example—and only about one-quarter of the American work force is organized. Unless union-negotiated wage increases spread throughout much of the unorganized sector, something which we noted in Chapter 7 appears doubtful, it is hard to see how collective bargaining can be the principal vehicle for bringing about wage and price adjustments to anticipated inflation. It is more likely that employers in unorganized labor markets, by adjusting wages, prices, and their expectations about inflation, play a significant part in the instability of the Phillips curve.

Even the long-run Phillips curve in Figure 12-3 is challenged by those who, in essence, contend that the trade-off of inflation for unemployment is based on a money illusion in which workers and others never consistently get their expectations about changes in wages and prices into line.[33] The critics contend that people will indeed come to learn the true rates of wage and price inflation, factor them into future outlooks, and seek complete protection against them, as, for example, when unionized workers negotiate full cost-of-living provisions into their agreements with employers. In such circumstances of fully adjusted expectations, the long-run Phillips relation would be nothing other than a straight line standing at some "natural rate of unemployment," as shown in Figure 12-4. The level of this natural rate, so the argument goes, depends on frictional and structural characteristics of the labor market and cannot be reduced by public policies to raise aggregate demand because the consequences of those actions in terms of wages and prices eventually are fully anticipated.

It should not surprise the reader that the concept of a natural rate of unemployment has come under considerable attack.[34] It is, after all, an argument that posits long-run equilibrium, that is, an eventual steady-state condition. But a dynamic economy constantly experiences disequilibrium, and that condition may continue long into the future to prevent attainment of the steady state. Moreover, the long run can be very, very long; in the interim, "society may well have been torn apart by voter revolt, urban riots, and unemployment-induced hardships and dissatisfactions."[35] Further the argument for a natural unemployment rate posits a total labor supply, a single wage rate, and an *aggregate* level of unemployment, whereas we have frequently observed that there

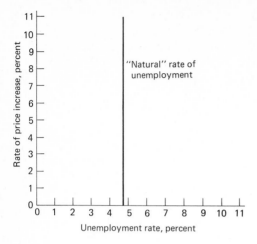

Figure 12-4 Natural rate of unemployment.

are many labor markets—some characterized by excess supply, others characterized by excess demand, and still others in rough equilibrium. As one authority observes, "The fact that excess demand raises wages while excess supply fails to reduce them helps to explain the inflationary bias of the economy and also the characteristic tilt of the Phillips curve."[36]

All in all, if recent research casts doubt on macroeconomic efforts to combat unemployment, it clearly tends to undermine the Phillips curve. Not only are there short-run curves and long-run curves, but also none is stable except, perhaps, in the very short run. Hence, they cannot provide workers, consumers, business people, or policy makers with firm predictions about rates of changes in wages and prices in relation to rates of unemployment. One need only examine the data in Tables 12-1 and 12-3 and observe the Phillips curves shown in Figure 12-5 to appreciate this fact.

Nevertheless, if there is no predictable or precise or unchanging trade-off of inflation for unemployment, there is still some trade-off. Otherwise, policy makers could attack unemployment without concern for inflation, and vice versa. That they cannot do so—that inflation will not be the same when unemployment is low as when it is high, and vice versa—testifies to the painful trade-offs which confront an advanced, industrialized society and which make so difficult the achievement of the three goals of full employment, stable prices, and free markets.

Before turning to a more intensive examination of recent inflation, we must recognize that the different relationships between inflation and unemployment shown in Figures 12-2, 12-3, and 12-4 nevertheless lead to some common policies for remedying unemployment. This is so because in all of them unemployment is made up partly of the structural type, which we described previously. Policies and programs to educate, train, and upgrade the work force; offer counseling and employment services to workers and potential workers; and improve information about the labor market can diminish structural unemployment and thereby push any Phillips curve to the left, as in Figure 12-5, which represents an improved trade-off between unemployment and inflation. So, too, would such measures as instituting computerized systems for providing information about the labor market, strengthening the guidance and counseling function to ease the transition from school to work, and providing training for workers with middle-level skills in order to open up jobs for the less skilled and less experienced unemployed.[37]

There has perhaps been insufficient recognition of the fact that while the debate over the Phillips curve calls into question the use of macroeconomic policy to combat unemployment, it seems to support human resources policy in pursuing this objective. Indeed, to the extent that there is any trade-off of inflation for unemployment, anything other than a vertical Phillips "curve," human resources policies can also contribute to a reduction of inflation (by moving the curve to the left).[38] If human resources policies have these potential benefits, then perhaps we shall see an expansion of expenditures for them beyond the $10 billion or so annual level of the late 1970s and of specific programs within the policy mix.[39] Additional support for such initiatives is provided by the aforementioned increased participation in the labor force of teenagers and women, who are more prone to structural unemployment than the work force as a whole. Thus, by illuminating the difficulties involved in trying to resolve the dilemma of unemployment and inflation at the macroeconomic policy level, the Phillips analysis underscores the usefulness of structural and human resources (i.e., microeconomic) approaches to these problems.

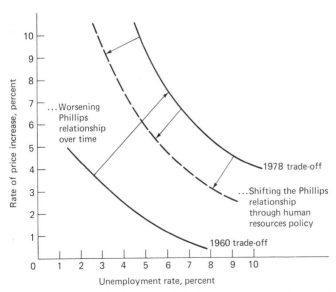

Figure 12-5 Shifts in the trade-off between inflation and unemployment.

More on Inflation

Just as there are many different labor markets which cannot adequately be represented when subsumed under an aggregate unemployment rate, as in the Phillips analysis, so too are there varying markets for goods and services which cannot be appreciated when combined in a single measure of price change. Therefore, in addition to changes in the (retail) prices of all items that make up the Consumer Price Index (CPI), Table 12-7 lists changes in the prices of several specific components of that index over the period from 1970 through 1978. If price changes for any of these components were scaled against unemployment rates in a Phillips-type analysis, the resulting curves would be even more unstable than that based on all items combined (that is, the CPI).

While the prices of many consumer items have fluctuated considerably in recent years, food prices have been subject to particularly wide swings. This conclusion is borne out by the data in Table 12-7, which shows that retail food prices rose more rapidly than the CPI as a whole in 5 of the 9 years between 1970 and 1978. Over that period, the average annual change in food prices was close to 8 percent, compared with 6.8 percent for the index as a whole. In the period 1973–1978, the CPI rose at an average annual rate of 8.1 percent, but food prices shot up an average of almost 10 percent. Further, food was second only to housing in relative importance among the components of the consumer market basket of goods and services, accounting for almost 18 percent of all expenditures made annually by all urban consumers.[40]

The diversity of price experience in product markets is further illustrated by the data for other components of the CPI listed in Table 12-7. For the entire period 1970–1978, energy prices rose more rapidly than any other category, averaging about 9.1 percent annually. Of course, the rate of increase was far greater following the onset of the energy crisis in 1973 than before it. Among the items listed in Table 12-7, mortgage interest payments grew least rapidly

Table 12-7 Percentage Change in Consumer Prices, All Items and Selected Components, 1970–1978

	Percentage change[1]								
Component	1970	1971	1972	1973	1974	1975	1976	1977	1978
All items	5.5	3.4	3.4	8.8	12.2	7.0	4.8	6.8	9.0
Food	2.2	4.3	4.7	20.1	12.2	6.5	.6	8.0	11.8
Other commodities	4.8	2.3	2.5	5.0	13.2	6.2	5.1	4.9	7.7
Energy[2]	4.5	3.1	2.8	16.8	21.6	11.6	6.9	7.2	8.0
Services	8.2	4.1	3.6	6.2	11.3	8.1	7.3	7.9	9.3
Medical care	7.3	4.8	3.3	5.2	12.4	9.9	10.1	8.8	8.8
Mortgage interest	6.9	−11.0	−.9	14.7	10.5	−3.1	−4.8	1.9	9.7

[1] Change from December to December, not seasonally adjusted.

[2] Gas and electricity, fuel oil and coal, and gasoline and motor oil.

Sources: Adapted from *Economic Report of the President, January, 1978,* 1978, pp. 140–318, and U.S. Bureau of Labor Statistics, *CPI Detailed Report, December 1978,* 1979, pp. 7–9 and 19.

during the period 1970–1978, averaging about 2.7 percent annually over the entire span and some 3 percent in the last 5 years. However, mortgage interest was the most volatile of the items, the difference between its lowest (negative) and highest (positive) annual rate totaling more than 25 percentage points. These fluctuations derive from changes in the money market for housing, which in turn is susceptible to the sharp expansions and contractions of federal monetary policy which have occurred in recent years.

Observe that services have undergone more rapid price changes since 1975 than food or other commodities. Indeed, between 1976 and 1978, the price of services rose faster than the price of energy. Among the services which have undergone the most pronounced price increases is medical care (which is first included in services and then shown separately in Table 12-7). Since 1974, consumers have paid an average 10 percent more each year for medical care, and the item was the fastest-rising component of the CPI over the period 1976–1978. Within the category of medical care, price increases for hospitalization have been especially pronounced, surpassing even increases in professional fees. Recall that the economy is becoming continuously more service-oriented, and thus the prices of services (and the wages of service employees) may be expected to rise more rapidly than other prices in the near future.

Continued rapid increases in the cost of medical care, however, may help bring about the enactment of national health insurance in the United States. The irony of that eventuality, should it materialize, is that other federal policies, Medicare and Medicaid in particular, have been instrumental in raising the demand for, and the price of, medical services. If the costs of services in general or of medical care specifically were scaled against unemployment in a Phillips-type analysis, the derived curve would be even more unstable than earlier ones. And, we might ask in this case, "What would be the long-run period required for expectations about prices to adjust to the reality of them?"

Further, some product markets are far from the ideal of competitive-labor-market theory; in such markets, prices may be unresponsive to shifts in demand and supply or responsive to factors other than such shifts. In the area of medical care, for example, increases in the supply of doctors to some geographic areas have not resulted in greater price competition, and medical fees apparently are highest where the supply of doctors is greatest.[41] In another instance, the raising of the prices of American-made small cars seems to have been in response to actions of foreign producers rather than to factors of supply or demand. These and other situations aggravate inflation and bring about a major problem of political economy in that government officials may be strongly urged by the public to adopt one or another policy to spur competition or, alternatively, to provide consumers with protection in the form of insurance against rapidly rising prices that result from the lack of competition. Thus, the goal of full employment aside, there may also be some incompatibility between the goals of price stability and free markets.

As we have often done in regard to other issues, we may employ comparative analysis to broaden our perspective on inflation. Table 12-8 lists changes in

Table 12-8 Changes in Consumer Price Index in Nine Countries, 1970–1977

Year	United States	Canada	Australia	Japan	France	West Germany	United Kingdom	Italy	Sweden
				Consumer Price Index[1]					
1971	104.3	102.9	106.1	106.0	105.5	105.3	109.4	104.8	107.4
1972	107.7	107.8	112.3	110.9	112.0	111.1	117.2	110.8	113.8
1973	114.4	115.9	122.9	124.0	120.2	118.8	128.0	122.8	121.5
1974	127.0	128.6	141.5	154.1	136.7	127.1	148.4	146.3	133.5
1975	138.6	142.5	162.8	172.4	152.8	134.7	184.4	171.1	146.6
1976	146.6	153.2	184.9	188.4	166.9	140.8	214.9	199.8	161.7
1977	156.1	165.4	207.6	203.6	182.7	146.3	249.6	NA	180.1

[1] 1970 = 100.

Source: Adapted from United Nations, Department of Economic and Social Affairs, *Monthly Bulletin of Statistics,* **32**(4):178–187 (1978), table 61.

the Consumer Price Indexes of nine developed nations over the period 1970–1977, with 1970 being the base year for calculating subsequent price changes. Among the nations, the United States experienced the second smallest increase in consumer prices between 1970 and 1977 (56 percent), and West Germany had the best record in this regard (a 46 percent increase). In contrast, consumer prices rose by almost 150 percent in the United Kingdom during these years, by over 100 percent in Australia and Japan, and by around 80 percent in France and Sweden. In all the countries, inflation advanced at a much more rapid pace in the mid-1970s than in the early portion of the decade.

These data tell us that the United States has fared comparatively well in the fight against inflation. This is not to overlook the more rapid rate of price increases that have prevailed since the energy crisis and major recession of the mid-1970s; in fact, it is to recognize that, even with such developments, price instability has been less pronounced in the United States than almost anywhere else. In terms of the Phillips analysis, it might at one time have been said that other nations simply preferred higher inflation rates as the cost of keeping unemployment down to levels unknown in the United States, under 1 percent in some cases. But if the Phillips relation has been unstable in this country, it has been almost mercurial abroad. All the countries listed in Table 12-8 except Sweden have witnessed substantially increased unemployment since 1973 (see Table 1-5). They are no longer able to keep the ranks of the unemployed low by suffering relatively high rates of price increase. Indeed, they are not able to maintain stable (predictable) inflation rates. For them, as for the United States, the trade-off not only has worsened but also has changed shape in such a way as to call into question existing analytical frameworks and policy prescriptions for dealing with inflation and unemployment.

It is, in general, true that falling unemployment will be accompanied (with a lag) by more rapidly rising prices and that declining rates of inflation will be accompanied by rising unemployment. As we have said, this is a real problem of trade-offs and thus of political economy. If, for example, the government runs up a very large federal deficit in stimulating the economy and cutting unemployment, inflation will be aggravated. And if the government severely pares the federal budget or greatly increases taxes in order to control inflation, unemployment will worsen. Thus it is that unemployment and inflation in modern society are negatively, if imperfectly, correlated.

To recognize this, however, is not to expect the correlation to persist or to believe that policies based upon it will lead to precisely predictable results. Many social phenomena can be negatively or positively associated in a statistical sense, but to jump from association to causation can be a snare and a delusion.[42] Many variables are at work affecting something as complex as rates of inflation or unemployment. Unless some conception of these variables is formulated and an analytical framework is developed to relate them systematically to one another, public policies undertaken to deal with either (or both) of them can have only limited success—barring that enduring imponderable, luck. Even if this is the only lesson to be learned from the rise and decline of the

Phillips curve, then that intellectually fascinating construct may have indeed contributed a lasting benefit.

INCOMES POLICIES

Apart from fiscal and monetary policy, many of the world's developed nations have attempted to deal with the problems of inflation and unemployment through one or another "incomes policy." The term covers a wide range of initiatives which have in common their intention directly to influence wages, prices, and incomes in the economy. If these rise by some "appropriate" standard (generally set by government), then presumably inflation can be kept within reasonable bounds, thereby contributing to real economic growth and the attainment of full employment. In a Phillips-type analysis, one can conceive of an incomes policy as an attempt to shift the curve downward or to the left.

In the United States, the term "incomes policy" generally means wage and price controls.[43] Prior to the 1970s, these had been legally mandated only during wartime. However, a full wage and price control program emerged with suddenness in 1971 during the Nixon administration. It was regarded as the first peacetime controls program in the United States, even though at its inception the Vietnamese war was still winding down. Before discussing the Nixon controls program, however, let us go back to the period of Kennedy and Johnson to explore the incomes policy then prevailing. That effort represented this nation's first major policy thrust toward developing standards of wage and price behavior in the post-World War II economy.

In 1962, the Council of Economic Advisers to President Kennedy formulated the concept of wage and price guidelines. These were undertaken to provide labor and management in the private sector with specific standards by which to judge the appropriateness of wage and price increases. In the Council's words:

> The general guide for noninflationary wage behavior is that the rate of increase in wage rates (including fringe benefits) in each industry be equal to the trend rate of overall productivity increase. . . . The general guide for noninflationary price behavior calls for price reduction if the industry's rate of productivity increase exceeds the overall rate, for this would mean declining unit labor costs; it calls for an appropriate increase in price if the opposite relationship prevails; and it calls for stable prices if the two rates of productivity increase are equal.[44]

However, to recognize varying conditions across labor markets, the Council spelled out additional components of the guidelines:

> Wage rate increases should exceed the general guide rate in an industry which would otherwise be unable to attract sufficient labor or where wage rates have been exceptionally low. . . . Wage rate increases should be less than the general guide rate in an industry which could not provide jobs for its entire labor force even in times of generally full employment, or where wage rates have been exceptionally high.[45]

Price guidelines were similarly modified to take account of different conditions in product markets and the movement of capital in and out of industries. Together, these guidelines formed the basis of the administration's official policy, that is, incomes policy. The Council's estimate of annual increases in productivity in the economy during the early 1960s was 3.2 percent, and this became the specific guideline for noninflationary increases in employee compensation. Wages and benefits could rise by that percentage without being inflationary, for they would be fully offset by gains in productivity and would not add to unit labor costs.

The guideline approach to incomes policy of the 1960s has several important implications. First, regardless of its actual impact on wages and prices, a subject to be discussed shortly, it helped cement the notion of productivity as the basis of real earnings gains and real economic growth in the economy. Adjustments in wages and benefits, especially under collective bargaining, could be rationalized on several grounds—cost of living, comparability, ability to pay —but only increases in compensation based on productivity made all workers, all employers, and society as a whole better off. Recall from Chapter 6 that this realization has only recently begun to emerge in the public sector, where collective bargaining has become the order of the day.

From a macroeconomic perspective, productivity is the output per hour of all persons in the economy. However, it is measured only for the private business sector inasmuch as no system has yet been devised for evaluating output in the public sector. The latter is entered into the national income and product accounts of the United States as the sum of all wages, salaries, and benefits paid to public employees; in other words, the output—productivity—of the public sector is defined as the value of the labor input to it. Within the private economy, moreover, actual measurement of productivity is far more easily accomplished in goods-producing than in service-producing industries. Despite these limitations, changes over time in output per hour can be gauged for the private sector; for major components of it, such as manufacturing, agriculture, and nonfinancial corporations; and for specific industries. In conjunction with changes in hourly compensation, this permits one to determine trends in unit labor costs and, relatedly, pressures on inflation.

Second, Kennedy and Johnson's guidelines were a voluntary effort at wage and price controls. Business and labor were not compelled to abide by them or penalized for failing to follow them (except by Presidential opprobrium and, it was hoped, by adverse public opinion). Put differently, employers and workers incurred no cost other than the potential wrath of the President and the citizenry if they agreed to increases in wages and benefits beyond those set by the guidelines. Similarly, individual firms could raise prices beyond the levels "justified" by the behavior of labor costs and not be subject to formal government sanctions.

Third, the experience of the 1960s showed that voluntary guidelines will be more or less adhered to as long as they make rough sense to those who must reach decisions on wages and prices, that is, as long as they are reasonably in tune with wage and price developments in the economy. When they get out of tune, private parties disregard them in favor of decisions guided by more pressing economic realities. Thus, Kennedy and Johnson's guideline of 3.2 percent for noninflationary increases in compensation worked reasonably well (in the sense that few major wage adjustments exceeded it) in the period 1962–1965, when unemployment was relatively high and rates of price increase were rather low (see Tables 12-1 and 12-3 again). Major labor agreements reached during that period called for increases in pay and benefits at or around the recommended guideline percentage. In 1966, however, as labor markets tightened and inflation accelerated, the pressures on wages and prices grew and led to sharply expanded rates of increase. The guidelines were freely violated, and even though President Johnson's Council of Economic Advisers adjusted the allowable increase in compensation upward to 3.6 percent, the guidelines concept soon was abandoned as official administration policy. By 1968, increases in pay and benefits of 6 and 7 percent were common, and prices were rising in excess of 4 percent on an annual basis.[46]

Fourth, the guidelines were undertaken virtually without prior discussions with representatives of the business and labor communities. Lack of such advance consultation might be expected to foretell doom for any policy that depends upon the voluntary compliance of important parties, and that seems especially true of the United States, where economic decision making is individualistic and decentralized and where consensus among government, business, and labor on any key issue of policy is rare. This lack of consultation may also have been due to the administration's view that "big business" and "big labor" were the main economic actors and that controlling their actions would do the trick insofar as the aims of public policy were concerned. But by the mid-1960s, the growth of the service, trade, and public sectors, together with the continued decline of union membership as a proportion of the work force, meant that decisions on wages and prices in the economy were becoming less rather than more centralized. Hence, even successful control of a few big collective bargaining settlements was not likely to extend conformity with the guidelines to the remainder of the economy.

Finally, strict adherence to the guidelines would have resulted in maintenance of the proportionate shares of national income going to workers and employers. That is, if prior to the guidelines two-thirds of national income had been distributed to workers in the form of wages and salaries and one-third had been distributed in the form of returns to owners and investors of capital, subsequent wage boosts that were fully offset by gains in productivity would have preserved this 2-to-1 allocation. Taking a specific example, assume that employee compensation averages $6 per hour in the economy and (the value of) output per hour averages $9. Assume further that, over time, average output per hour rises to $12. If compensation is then to rise at the same rate as output, average hourly pay and benefits will be $8, or one-third larger than before. The return to capital also rises by one-third to $4, and thus the new proportionate income distribution between the two factors of production (land has been lumped with capital) remains the same. Since the guidelines called for noninflationary increases in pay and benefits, compensation would rise only as much as productivity advanced, as shown in this example, thereby preserving relative income shares. Some critics of the guidelines were especially vociferous about this issue, contending that public policy was defining the existing distribution of income as somehow correct when that judgment should have been left to the workings of a decentralized economy based on individual decision making.[47]

Wage and Price Controls in the Early 1970s

The guidelines of the 1960s emerged against a backdrop of mild recovery from recession, rising prices, increases in the level of labor settlements, and relatively high unemployment, and so too did the wage and price controls program of the early 1970s. But in contrast to the voluntary approach to incomes policy, the Nixon controls program was a legislatively authorized, legally enforceable set of directives to be followed by business and labor in their decisions on prices and wages. Ironically, the legal basis of these controls was provided by congressional extension of the Economic Stabilization Act of 1970, which had been passed in spite of strong opposition by the administration. That statute gave the President wide authority "to stabilize wages, prices and rents without recourse to the Congress and left him unfettered by any procedural niceties."[48] Furthermore, the President and his principal advisers had long been adamantly opposed to any system of wage and price controls, and so the adoption of them represented a complete reversal of the administration's policy on this issue. Thus just a few months after stating that "I do not intend to impose wage and price controls," and "neither do I intend to rely upon an elaborate facade that seems to be wage and price control but is not,"[49] President Nixon set in place a full-blown program of wage and price controls.

It began on August 15, 1971, with the sudden announcement of a freeze on wages, prices, and rents that took virtually everyone but a few close Presidential advisers by surprise. Enforced by a new Cost of Living Council (COLC), the freeze was intended to demonstrate in a dramatic way the administration's concern about inflation, a concern that had sharpened in the wake of a collective bargaining settlement in the can industry which spread to others and called for an estimated 16 percent increase in first-year compensation. Rising unemployment seemed not to lessen unionized workers' bargaining demands during this period, and so even though consumer prices in mid-1971 were rising less rapidly than they had in the preceding 4 years—specifically, under 4 percent on an annual basis—the public and the administration nervously anticipated more rapid increases in the future. This specter of heightened inflation was strong enough to counter the administration's prevailing opinion and bring about a freezing of incomes of all sorts.

The freeze lasted for 90 days, at the end of which a continuing format for wage and price controls went into effect. Known as "Phase II," the program created a seven-member Price Commission and a fifteen-member Pay Board which bore responsibility for the enforcement of price controls and wage controls, respectively. The former body was made up entirely of representatives of the public, while the latter was tripartite in nature, consisting of five representatives each of business, labor, and the public. The activities of the two new bodies were coordinated by the COLC, which had been created at the inception of the freeze.[50]

The administration's objective was to reduce inflation to about 2½ percent by the end of 1972. With that percentage serving as the allowable base of price increases and with an assumed annual growth rate in productivity of 3.0 percent, wages under the controls program were permitted to rise by 5.5 percent per year. Recognizing the variation in conditions across labor markets and the special difficulties that this standard might pose in some instances, the Pay Board did authorize some pay increases of up to 7.0 percent.

Additionally, wage adjustments beyond the 5.5 percent level were allowed if offset by accompanying gains in productivity. Labor and management were required to submit to the Pay Board for review and approval any negotiated agreement calling for productivity-based wage increases above the mandated limit. Another Board policy established a maximum limit for fringe benefits plans. Contributions to such plans could rise by 0.7 percent of total compensation. Thus, when added to the 5.5 percent pay limit, the Board's standard for permissible total increases in compensation under Phase II was 6.2 percent. Workers earning less than $2.75 per hour were exempted from wage controls.

The enforcement of these pay (and price) controls under Phase II varied across three major categories of businesses. The first encompassed firms which employed 5000 or more workers or which had $100 million or more of annual sales; they were required to apply—to the Pay Board or the Price Commission —for *advance approval* of wage and price increases. The second category included firms with 1000 to 5000 employees or with $50 million to $100 million in annual sales; they were required to report wage and price increases *after* making them. The third grouping, which covered the vast majority of American businesses, included medium-sized and small firms that fell below the aforementioned minimums in terms of employment and annual sales; they were not required to report or request approval of their wage and price actions, but they were expected to conform to the standards for acceptable increases and, like larger businesses, were subject to penalties for failing to follow the standards. Thus, the Nixon administration's controls program, like the wage and price guidelines which preceded it, focused on large institutions in the belief that restraint in terms of wages and prices exercised by big labor and big business would set an example for others and thus have consequences throughout the economy.

Phase II of the program lasted to January 1973, when President Nixon, in essence converted the program from a mandatory to a voluntary one. The wage and price limitations of Phase II were in general carried forward, but with some relaxation of restrictions on profits and limits on wages. The proportion of workers excluded from the program rose markedly, as the original low-wage exemption was increased from $2.75 to $3.50 an hour. Most important, the enforcement structure was altered to eliminate the mandatory advance approval of some wage and price increases and the required reporting of others. The Pay Board and the Price Commission went out of existence, and the largely voluntary controls program of Phase III was administered by the Cost of Living Council. The administration's new policy was intended to eliminate red tape, delays, inequities, and interference with the private economy and to encourage efficiency and investment in an expansionary period.

Although some of those objectives were laudable and a few may have been achieved, the pace of inflation quickened markedly during the first half of 1973, to the point where a new wage and price freeze was announced in mid-June of that year. Known as Phase III½, the freeze lasted for only 60 days, during which time the administration ostensibly was designing a Phase IV controls program. However, after only about a month, the freeze was lifted from all food prices except beef to counteract the shortages which had rapidly developed at the retail level; later, controls on beef prices were dropped as well. In August 1973, Phase IV controls went into effect for the remainder of the economy.

From its inception, the program permitted cost increases to be passed through in the form of price increases on a dollar-for-dollar basis, though prenotification to the COLC of such actions was required of larger firms. Wage requirements operative in earlier phases were carried through to Phase IV, but as time passed, more and more exemptions from them were authorized. At the termination of Phase IV in April 1974, when Congress failed to renew the original enabling legislation for economic stabilization, relatively few industries remained subject to wage and price controls—and, it should be added, inflation was well into double digits.

The wage and price controls program of the Nixon administration provides even stronger evidence than Kennedy and Johnson's guidelines of the politics of inflation. When the economic system fails to perform in a manner acceptable to the public, elected officials take action. And, while their actions are undertaken in the hope that they will deal with the particular problem at hand—in this case, inflation—the more basic motive behind them, given that they flow from the political process, is to curry the political favor of voters. The actions demonstrate that government leadership is responsive to the public's will, and certainly there were strong public pressures for the Democratic administrations of the early 1960s and the Republican administration of the early 1970s to "do something" about inflation. The subsequent responses to those pressures demonstrate that elected officials do not simply interfere with what is otherwise objective, professional management of the economy. Rather, they are attempting to apply political solutions to political problems—which is not to say that the solutions work well or that the problems are not also economic in nature.

This was shown once again in late 1978, when President Carter announced a new anti-inflation policy, which included wage and price standards.[51] Under the program, wages and fringe benefits in 1979 were to rise by no more than 7 percent annually, and individual firms were to limit their cumulative price increases to one-half of a percentage point below the firm's average annual rate of price increase during 1976–77. By obtaining adherence to these standards and assuming annual productivity growth of 1.75 percent, the Carter administration aimed to reduce inflation to 5.75 percent.

Low-wage workers, meaning those earning less than $4 an hour, were exempted from the standard, as were pay agreements reached in collective bargaining prior to announcement of the program. Further, the Carter program permitted wage increases beyond the standards if they stemmed from changes in work rules that demonstrably improved productivity or if they were required to preserve historical pay relationships between employee groups where one of them had negotiated an increase before the program began. These exemptions and special provisions are comparable to those contained in the guidelines and controls programs of previous administrations, and they reflect the need for political leaders to consider strongly the equity aspects of incomes policies. In this respect, a novelty of the Carter program was the proposal for ''real wage insurance'' to workers, whereby employees who adhered to the 7 percent wage standard were eligible for a tax refund to the extent that the CPI advanced by more than 7 percent annually, but subject to a ''reasonable limit'' clause.[52] (This wage-insurance program was, however, rejected by Congress.)

The Carter program was voluntary, and the responsibility for monitoring it was assigned to the Council on Wage and Price Stability. In the period 1974–1978, or between the end of the Nixon controls program and the beginning of the Carter wage and price standards, the Council's function was to provide information about sectors of the economy and analyze them in terms of their actual and potential inflationary effects.[53] Its reports permitted the President to express concern over especially inflationary sectors and forces and bring these to the public's attention. They also could have provided the President a basis for ''jawboning'' employers and organized workers to moderate their price and wage behavior, although relatively little of that occurred during the first 2 years of the Carter administration.

Under the voluntary wage and price standards program, the Council's function remained largely that of a monitor of inflation, but its activities and staff were considerably expanded, and it had specific bench marks by which to judge the inflationary potential of particular decisions on wages and prices. In instructing the Council to monitor the wage and price actions of some 400 large firms (defined as those with $500 million or more of annual sales) and the terms of major collective bargaining agreements, the Carter administration showed that its program, like others that preceded it, was focusing on ''big business'' and ''big labor,'' though other sectors and institutions received selected attention. While the future of this voluntary program of wage and price standards is problematic, the AFL-CIO, in a major change of position, has expressed doubt over its effectiveness and a preference for compulsory controls on wages, prices, profits, rents, mortgage payments, and interest rates.[54] Such are the pressures on government leaders to recognize inflation as a political issue and to develop political responses to it; recent Presidents have shown no reluctance to do so.

Their actions provide ample testimony, if more is needed, to the difficulty of maintaining stable prices while also trying to achieve full employment and preserve free markets.

The Impact of Incomes Policies

But what of the actual effectiveness of incomes policies? Have wage and price controls or voluntary guidelines and standards had an impact on inflation? Have they moderated rates of increases in wages and prices compared with what would otherwise have occurred? The Carter program is too new to evaluate, but, unsurprisingly, the available evidence on this issue provides mixed results. On the one hand, several studies of the experience with guidelines in the 1960s have concluded that both wages and prices rose less rapidly in the early 1960s than they would have in the absence of guidelines. For example, Perry found that wages rose about 1 percent more slowly each year from 1961 to 1965 than they would have if the guidelines had not been operative.[55] This slowdown effect was considerably larger in highly concentrated, "visible" industries such as steel, aluminum, and automobiles than elsewhere, as might have been expected under an anti-inflation policy that focused on major collective bargaining settlements. As to prices, several students of this subject concluded that they too rose more slowly in the early 1960s because of the presence of the wage and price guidelines. Thus, Solow estimated that prices rose about 0.7 of a percentage point more slowly between 1962 and 1965 than they would have without the guidelines.[56]

On the other hand, some observers have come to quite different conclusions about the effects of the guidelines. For example, Black and Kelejian point to the stable composition of aggregate demand as the key variable explaining the moderate behavior of wages and prices in the economy during the period 1962–1966.[57] Gordon tested several econometric models over the same span and, unlike Perry, found no evidence of an independent effect of the wage and price guidelines.[58] Concerning the impact of the guidelines on collective bargaining between labor and management in the early 1960s, John Dunlop, who was to serve as director of the Cost of Living Council and later as Secretary of Labor, commented as follows:

> The guideposts probably have had no independent restraining influences on wage changes in private industry. . . . I know of no person actually involved in wage setting on the side of industry, labor organizations, or as a government or private mediator or arbitrator who thinks that the guideposts have had on balance a constrictive [result].[59]

Concerning the effectiveness of the formal controls program of the early 1970s, the evidence is similarly in dispute. Most of this evidence pertains to Phase II of that program, which, the reader will recall, was in effect from late 1971 to early 1973.[60] Ashkin and Kraft used three different models of the private nonfarm economy to assess the impact of Phase II on average hourly earnings and on the implicit price deflator for the economy. They concluded that the direct effect of controls during that period was to reduce the annual rate of price increase by between 1 and 2 percentage points, while the impact on annual wage changes was between -0.5 and $+1.0$ percentage points. A more inclusive set of total annual impacts on prices and wages ranged between -1.2 and -2.6 and between -1.5 and $+0.1$ percentage points, respectively. Lanzelotti and Roberts judged Phase II to have lowered inflation by about 2 percent annually, while having no impact on wages. Further, de Menil, who limited his study to prices, estimated Phase II to have reduced the average annual rate of price increase by 1 percent.

Feige and Pearce reached different conclusions. They uncovered no impact of Phase II on rates of price change in the economy, contending that the slowing of inflation in 1972 relative to prior periods would have occurred even in the absence of controls. However, they attributed to the controls program a reduction in the rate of wage increase in 1972 of almost 1 percent. In a comprehensive analysis of Phase II wage controls, Mitchell concluded that there was a significant impact on major collective bargaining agreements during 1972, the average first-year adjustment under such agreements declining to little more than 7 percent from more than 11 percent in the previous year.[61] Mitchell's findings are instructive, for he coupled them with the conclusion that "Phase II was too brief, and its impacts too concentrated on new union adjustments, for aggregate equations [of the type employed in the other studies reviewed here] to pick up much of anything."[62]

This conflicting evidence on the effectiveness of American incomes policies and the inability to more precisely measure that effectiveness leaves much room for strong opinion and debate about this issue. Thus, George Shultz and Kenneth Dam, both former officials in the Nixon administration, contend that the experience of the controls program of 1971–1974 showed once again that controls create distortions in both product and labor markets and that those charged with enforcing a controls program cannot cope with a dynamic economy and a rapidly changing business environment.[63] They also assert that the Nixon program was adopted primarily for political rather than economic reasons, and they point out the need to "grasp the political dimension of that important economic policy decision."[64]

In response to these charges, Arnold Weber and Daniel Mitchell, both of whom served with the Cost of Living Council, argue that the distortions occurring under the controls program of 1971–1974 were "extremely mild, and probably minimal."[65] More specifically, Weber and Mitchell find no evidence that the Pay Board's compensation guidelines acted as a floor in collective bargaining, that escalator clauses tended to spread during Phase II, or that the incidence of strikes increased during the period. Nor did the administrative apparatus for enforcing the controls develop into a self-perpetuating bureaucracy, as had been charged. Interestingly, Weber and Mitchell do not quarrel with Shultz and Dam's judgment about the politics of the controls program; in this they support the view that the politics dominate the economics of anti-inflation policies.[66]

Thus the debate over incomes policies in the United States seems to differ little from period to period. Even the newest, most sophisticated measurement techniques do not yield exact, quantitative impacts of incomes policies on wages, prices, and, ultimately, inflation. Lacking precise evidence, intellectuals, opinion makers, public officials, and the citizenry are all able to state their firm—and conflicting—judgments about incomes policies. But despite the empirical complexity of this issue and the absence of consensus on it, we believe that some conclusions are in order about recent incomes policies in the United States.

Consider first that virtually all estimates of the impact of incomes policies, whether informal guidelines or enforceable wage and price controls, yield small results, typically 1 percent or so on annual rates of wage and price increases in the economy. Such effects can be important to particular economic sectors or groups of workers, but their aggregate impact is modest indeed. And incomes policies are concerned primarily with aggregate economic behavior, with the performance of the economy as a whole.

Second, no informed observer recommends incomes policies as the prime tool for managing the economy or as a panacea for major economic problems. Fiscal and monetary policies are the fundamental macroeconomic instruments. An incomes policy that is inconsistent with them will have its effects "swamped" by those emanating from the government's policies concerning taxes, expenditures, interest rates, and the money supply—and an incomes policy consistent with them is likely also to have minimal effects. As Weber and Mitchell note, "Few practitioners or serious students of industrial relations would argue that wage controls should be initiated except under grave circumstances."[67]

Third, an incomes policy that is put in place without close consultation with, and the active support of, the labor and management communities is unlikely to endure or to have much success. In the United States, both the wage and price guidelines of the 1960s *and* the wage and price controls program of the early 1970s were undertaken by political leaders who, while attempting to respond to public concern about inflation, did not see fit to develop close working relationships with the labor and business communities. The same appears true of the Carter administration's wage and price standards program of the late 1970s. Even the staffing of the Pay Board in 1971 with five representatives of labor and five representatives of management was more of a generalized appeal for cooperation than an example of their being closely integrated into the processes of policy formulation and implementation. Such integration is almost certainly a more difficult task in the United States than abroad, given this nation's free enterprise ideology (and business unionism) and its basically capitalist economy. Moreover, it is no guarantee of successful incomes policies, as is attested to by the experience of foreign nations.[68] But it is undeniably a necessary condition for an incomes policy to have any chance of success.

Fourth, to operate incomes polices on an ad hoc or interim basis, as has been the case in the United States, generates expectations that wage and price behavior will be allowed to return to "normal," whatever state of affairs that label may describe. Rates of wage and price increase may be temporarily moderated during a controls program, as the parties simply delay the actions they would like to take until the controls are lifted. From this perspective, ad hoc rather than sustained incomes policies enable employers, workers, and consumers to adjust behavior in anticipation of the removal of controls. Stated harshly, private economic actors may suspect that public officials who advocate ad hoc incomes policies do so for short-term political purposes rather than as part of a long-term integrated strategy for managing the economy. In this light, people adjust their expectations about incomes policies in precisely the same way that they adjust their expectations with regard to inflation generally, and so in the end incomes policies may be totally ineffective. Again, there is no guarantee that sustained incomes policies will work any better than piecemeal ones, but the former do suggest a stronger seriousness of purpose than the latter.

Fifth, the focus and enforcement of incomes policies seem inevitably to be most heavily directed at collective bargaining—at the control of "cost-push" inflation. This is clear from a reading of this country's experience with wage and price guidelines, standards, and controls. Labor settlements which involve large numbers of workers and which occur with regularity are well known, and so they understandably become a prime focal point for jawboners and controllers. Wage changes in unorganized labor markets (including those for managers and executives) and price changes in the firm are less visible actions that are more difficult to monitor or control than collective bargaining agreements. Additionally, the logic of controls means that a single figure or percentage can be popularized for wages (3.2 and 5.5 and 7.0 percent are recent examples), but this is much harder to do for prices or profits, since these vary greatly by productivity and other factors about which information is unknown—unknown to those in charge of the controls, that is. As a result, organized labor may quickly conclude that an incomes policy in effect means the tight control of union members' wages and benefits and looser control of other incomes. Such perceived (and often factual) inequity can precipitate a posture on organized labor's part of noncooperation with incomes policies.

This leads to our final and most basic conclusion about incomes policies: whatever their form, they have a major political component and can have major political consequences. This tends to be better recognized in Europe than in the United States, for in European nations controls are often regarded as a mechanism for explicitly planning the distribution of income. Indeed, in some instances, an incomes policy is the primary instrument for forging the social contract between labor, business, government, and other interest groups in society. Where this occurs, the political aspects of an incomes policy can strongly overshadow the economic aspects and, especially if the policy is judged to be ineffective or inequitable, can exacerbate social tensions.[69]

This point merits further consideration with respect to the American scene, where an incomes policy can affect the distribution of income, even if that is not its express or primary purpose. Recent experiences with incomes policies in the United States have deepened normal resentment against wage and price guidelines, standards, and (particularly) controls, notably among organized labor, whose leaders have taken such actions as resigning official roles in the government's apparatus for wage control[70] and forcefully opposing other controls to demonstrate their belief that such anti-inflation efforts are inimical to the interests of workers. More broadly, these incomes policies have engendered wide debate about government-planned versus market-determined income shares and also controversy (here and abroad) over the equity or justice of such policies. Whether those who are worst off economically should suffer the least from an incomes policy is an especially critical issue in this regard.

In sum, when government invokes an incomes policy in pursuit of price stability, the freedom of individuals and groups to make their own decisions must to some degree be sacrificed. And in carrying out an incomes policy, public officials must be alert to perceptions of inequity or injustice among those whose actions the government is attempting to affect. These are the political dynamics of incomes policies wherever and whenever they are used. They must be considered together with the economic evidence in any comprehensive assessment of incomes policies.

Experiences of Other Countries

We can conclude this section by asking and very briefly answering the question, "What can be learned from the record of other developed nations with respect to incomes policies?" The apparent answer is, "probably not a great deal," because even though some other nations have experimented with incomes policies considerably more than the United States, their efforts have not been very successful. For example, in analyzing the experience with incomes policies of western European nations to the late 1960s, Ulman and Flanagan report that no one of them had solved the problem of simultaneously achieving stable prices and full employment, to say nothing of their success in preserving free collective bargaining.[71] Most of these countries were willing to accept high rates of inflation, by American standards, in the belief that this was the price of attaining relatively low unemployment. Some observers suggested that the United States should do the same, that is, alter its preferred (Phillips curve) combination of inflation and unemployment to more closely approximate combinations prevailing in Europe and adopt one or another of the incomes policies practiced there. But in the 1970s, the trade-offs between inflation and unemployment worsened considerably abroad, and incomes policies therefore appeared even less useful than before to the countries that employed them and to others that sought lessons from them. Thus Ulman and Flanagan's judgment about incomes policy in Europe is even more instructive in light of events of the 1970s: "There is growing appreciation that its potential usefulness is limited, that it was originally oversold, and that it cannot be expected to bridge an inflationary gap, however wide."[72]

Still, some characteristics of the experiences of other countries with incomes policies merit further discussion. Consider that income distribution is of paramount importance in western European experiments with income policies. Abroad, labor unions, which generally represent much larger proportions of workers than in the United States, are adamant about increasing labor's share, not simply maintaining it. This continues to be true today, and thus any policy initiative in western Europe designed to preserve the division of national income between capital and labor is strongly opposed. And this applies to both the public and the private sectors, suggesting that a policy of wage restraint focused on government employees, some working in essential services, is no more likely to be successful than a controls program oriented toward the private sector.

Furthermore, European incomes policies do not come and go with changes of political administration. They are modified, to be sure, but as a case in point, the United Kingdom has continued to employ incomes policies under Labour and Conservative governments alike. Indeed, in the early 1970s, the experience there closely paralleled that in the United States, as Prime Minister Edward Heath, like President Nixon, adopted wage and price controls in spite of his professed opposition to them. Even the Scandinavian countries, which have enjoyed relative economic stability together with widespread collective bargaining, have in recent years adopted some form of incomes policy. They too, however, are undergoing worsening trade-offs between unemployment and inflation, and thus their controls programs are not doing much better than those of other countries. In fact, one observer proposes that "Socialist governments, because of their reliance on trade union political and financial support, may be less able than nonsocialists to make the tough decisions required to implement economic controls."[73]

Moreover, in some western European nations, workers are paid wages above official rates set in collective bargaining, a phenomenon known as "wage drift"; other workers receive their pay in cash in a more surreptitious form of drift from collectively bargained rates or from those formally sanctioned by an incomes policy; and some workers take on night and weekend jobs to augment their individual earnings and, as a group, increase their income share above allowable levels. When such practices prove insufficient, workers sometimes take direct political action to secure higher wages and modify the wage limits mandated by an incomes policy. Barkin graphically describes these developments on the European scene to the mid-1970s:

> Older systems of wage settlement [have] disintegrated in many countries. The Netherlands' long-standing formal plan of wage restraint gave way to newer arrangements. Wage controls elsewhere did not long survive. . . . Workers often took the initiative in securing adjustments through direct appeal and stoppages. . . . Political action appeared more neccessary than before; workers realized most poignantly that the government was setting many policies and making decisions that controlled their very lives as well as the conditions and terms of employment.[74]

So it is that the developed nations of the world are suffering increased economic strain and experiencing greater militancy among workers, neither of which seems controllable by governmental macroeconomic policies, let alone by incomes policies. Again, from a comparative perspective, as Barkin suggests, the United States is less troubled than most other nations. Nevertheless, here as well as abroad, higher levels of inflation *and* unemployment have brought about a fundamental rethinking of the structure of the economy and of the relationship between the public and the private sectors. It is to this subject that we turn our attention next, as we conclude our study of the labor sector.

NATIONAL ECONOMIC PLANNING

At the height of the recession of 1974–1975 in the United States, Senators Javits and Humphrey introduced into Congress a bill calling for national economic planning. Entitled the "Balanced Growth and Economic Planning Act of 1976," the bill was drafted by the Initiative Committee for National Economic Planning, a group composed of prominent academics, labor leaders, and business executives.[75] It called for the creation of an Office of National Economic Planning in the executive branch of the federal government which would "be in a position to perceive our country's economic and social needs . . . and to provide the public, Congress and the executive branch with alternative plans of action . . . to guide the economy in a direction consistent with our national values and goals."[76]

In pursuit of this broad objective, the proposed office would (1) provide a central repository of information on the economy, (2) examine long-term economic trends in order to work out national economic programs for periods of up to 25 years, (3) devise intermediate-length plans as steps toward long-range objectives, and (4) specify the resources, labor, and financing required to achieve agreed-upon programs and plans. While the office would not set specific goals for individual companies, "it would indicate the number of cars, the number of generators, and the quantity of frozen foods we are likely to require in, say, five years, and it would try to induce the relevant industries to plan accordingly."[77]

The bill quickly generated major debate between supporters of economic planning and advocates of a free market system. For example, Arthur Schlesinger, Jr., writing in *The Wall Street Journal*, defended the planning bill as necessary to cope with problems that are essentially political rather than economic in nature, and he also argued that it would be regarded as innocuous in any other highly industrialized country.[78] Henry Hazlitt took quite a different view, commenting editorially in *Barron's* that the bill was a blueprint for disaster that would elevate the decisions of less knowledgeable government bureaucrats over those of individual citizens, who, following the profit motive of the free market system, constantly strive to maximize their income.[79] Thus, the argument was joined.

Interestingly, however, the original proposal was soon supplanted by the

Humphrey-Hawkins bill, which dropped the phrase "economic planning" entirely.[80] Known as the "Full Employment and Balanced Growth Act," a modified version of the Humphrey-Hawkins bill was approved by the Ninety-fifth Congress just prior to its adjournment in October 1978 and was signed into law shortly thereafter by President Carter, who had described the bill as "must" legislation.[81] Its principal provisions call for the reduction of unemployment to 4 percent in 1983 and of inflation to 3 percent by the same year and to zero by 1988. It is the President's responsibility to present each year a detailed plan for the attainment of full employment and price stability, including numerical goals, specific policies and programs, and 5-year budget projections. Beginning in 1980, the President is permitted to reset the unemployment goal to a later year, but he cannot alter the 4 percent standard. Moreover, the law states that the "inflation goals are not to be designed so as to 'impede' achievement of the unemployment target by 1983."

While the private sector is assumed to be the chief generator of employment, the Humphrey-Hawkins legislation mandates the federal government to use its economic policy instruments—taxes, expenditures, public service employment—to promote jobs in the effort to achieve full employment. Additionally, the Federal Reserve Board is required explicitly to take into account national goals concerning unemployment and inflation in its conduct of monetary policy. All these initiatives are to be consistent with the overall presidential plan for full employment and price stability, and that plan is to be presented annually to Congress for review. Consequently, though the law itself authorizes no new programs or expenditures to create jobs or fight inflation and though it hardly provides for national economic planning, it does seek to establish a framework for integrating decisions on economic policy reached by political leaders and institutions through processes of government.

With this legislation, the nation in a sense turned full circle back to the events that preceded and followed passage of the Employment Act of 1946. Recall that earlier versions of the immediate postwar legislation called for an explicit national commitment to full employment. Congress, however, worried about the country's ability to achieve that goal and, of course, about the possible costs of doing so. In the end, the federal government went on record to define unemployment as an important national problem that was properly the subject of public policy, but it stopped short of specifying a full employment target and of a pledge to aim policy at that objective above all others. Very quickly thereafter, the citizenry's and the government's primary concern shifted to the control of inflation.

And that concern remains uppermost in the minds of many Americans, despite the high rates of unemployment that have prevailed in the United States during the 1970s, the growing internationalization of the economy, and the enlarged role of government as a regulator and as a business. So strong is this concern that the Humphrey-Hawkins bill, which began as an attempt to legislate economic planning to achieve full employment, was enacted only after very specific and, by recent standards, very stringent goals concerning inflation were added to it. Because of this, many supporters of the bill contend that it "evolved into nothing more than a set of symbols, and . . . was not the kind of message that had been originally intended when the measure was introduced" (in 1976).[82] But if it differs from the Employment Act of 1946 in mentioning and defining price stability, the Humphrey-Hawkins legislation also differs from the earlier law in defining full employment. The larger question is, of course, "Are the goals which the law sets out attainable?"

There will be, as there have been before, a plethora of doctrinaire arguments to support a "yes" or a "no" answer to this question. We do not wish to add to these but, rather, to help the reader sort out his or her own thinking about this matter. To begin with, consider the meaning of full employment in the modern American economy. Previously, we reviewed the evidence concerning the changing composition of the labor force and expanded programs of social protection, developments which appear to have elevated the level of unemployment consistent with full employment beyond that of earlier periods. Among the types of unemployment that occur in a developed economy, frictional and structural unemployment seem to be especially important on the American scene and to have increased in recent years. The cure for the second of these is not the same as that for unemployment due to deficient demand. Thus, when supporters of the Humphrey-Hawkins law claim that it "would put an end to the cyclical process of redefining full employment upwards to five, six or even seven percent in order to explain the failure of economic policies,"[83] it behooves the student of the labor sector to ask whether 4 percent unemployment remains consistent with full employment in today's economy. And that must be done with reference to the costs of achieving full employment, that is, in terms of price stability, which the Humphrey-Hawkins law also identifies as a national goal.[84]

Similarly, those who strongly endorse the reduction of inflation, especially to the levels specified in the Humphrey-Hawkins Act, must ask what it would cost in terms of unemployment. Recall (from Table 12-1) that as recently as the mid-1960s, 3 percent inflation was generally considered to be quite high, whereas today it seems an optimistically low standard. And that is just the point. Given the worsening (and unstable) Phillips relationship, a policy to slow down the economy to the point of reducing inflation to 3 percent (or, later, to zero) would be very likely to engender a deep recession and to result in a major increase in unemployment. That would be a very costly policy indeed, not just economically in terms of lost GNP and personal income, increased unemployment insurance and welfare payments, and the like, but socially and politically as well. True, economic and social protections are available to workers today that did not exist in the Great Depression of the 1930s, but most of them were present in the recession of 1974–1975, when unemployment went beyond 9 percent, and they did not serve to quell national concern over unemployment and subsequent political actions to reduce it. Such protections ameliorate somewhat the personal hardships that unemployment brings about—that is their intent, after all—but they do not overcome the basic fact of unemployment, the consequent reduction of part of the labor sector's claim to a share of national income, and, in the case of large-scale unemployment, violation of the prevailing social contract. Supporters of the inflation targets set forth in the Humphrey-Hawkins Act must bear these facts in mind.[85]

In the final analysis, decisions about unemployment and inflation are made politically, not in a pejorative sense, but in terms of their being public actions reached through democratic processes. Because unemployment and inflation are political issues, we believe it unlikely that elected officials of whatever party or personal persuasion will push down unemployment *or* inflation to the levels specified in the Humphrey-Hawkins law if the attainment of one of those objectives is perceived to severely worsen the other. To ignore either full employment or price stability is to proceed at one's peril, politically speaking.

All this may seem to suggest that the Humphrey-Hawkins Act is to some degree contradictory, as indeed we believe it is. More generally, however, we seek to encourage those who are seriously interested in the labor sector and in public policy to undertake the difficult analytical task of subjecting to close scrutiny every policy and every proposal for improving the nation's welfare. In a world of scarcity, attainment of one's preferred objective comes at a cost. It is only by knowing or attempting carefully to estimate the economic and noneconomic costs and benefits of a particular initiative set by public policy that one can make intelligent, realistic choices. This holds true in the areas of unemployment and inflation, just as it does in the areas of union wage policy, social security, and countless other dimensions of modern economic and political life.

Beyond this, we also ask the reader to ponder why serious debate continues over national economic planning, recognizing that the Humphrey-Hawkins Act authorizes only an integrated framework for national economic policy making, rather than full-scale planning. In approaching this issue, consider that recurring recessions and expansions during the 1970s have cast major doubts on the nation's ability to manage a complex, increasingly service-oriented economy. Keynesian macroeconomic tools no longer seem capable of doing the trick. For some, this means that we should undertake a wholesale reappraisal of public policies concerning a private market economy, with a view toward diminishing the governmental presence. Proponents of this position call into question the wisdom of governmental actions undertaken since the New Deal days of the 1930s. They regard the many public policies that have emerged since that time as of a piece in unduly constraining a free market economy that would, if left largely to its own devices, truly maximize the welfare of society.

For others, including some supporters of the Humphrey-Hawkins Act, there exist failures of policy which imply that new governmental initiatives must be charted to manage the economy. From this perspective, the most pressing issue is the coordination of disparate, sometimes contradictory economic policies that harm the general welfare and portions of the labor sector in particular. To achieve such coordination requires long-range planning and the specification of interim targets and programs instead of ad hoc responses to first one problem and then another. What is advocated by proponents of this view is sounder and broadened governmental policy making, that is, an expansion of the public presence in economy and society rather than greater reliance on the private marketplace.

Nor is the United States alone in debating the proper relationship between the public and private sectors, between markets and government. Virtually every developed nation of the world, whether capitalist, socialist, or communist, is wrestling with the issue. Much has been heard in recent years about the experiments with market-type incentives in professedly egalitarian communist countries and about the rethinking of governmental operation of large enterprises in socialist nations. In the sphere of labor relations, attention abroad is turning to bargaining and grievance procedures of the type found in the United States, even as this country has begun to experiment with European-type plans for broadened participation by workers in decision-making.

Regarding inflation and unemployment, a recent report sponsored by the Organization for Economic Cooperation and Development (OECD) advocates the following common objectives for member nations of that organization: rapid economic growth, a progressive return to full employment and price stability through steadier monetary and fiscal policies, improved reconciliation of the claims of competing interest groups, firmer guidelines for public expenditures and close review of the efficiency and effectiveness of public programs, better functioning of labor and product markets, and more vigorous energy policies.[86] There are few who would quibble with this menu of objectives; the larger question is whether such goals are attainable, especially in light of recent international economic developments, the slowing of growth in many advanced economies, and the apparent inability of traditional policies—and perhaps traditional politics—to accomplish them.

Consider, further, that while objectives of the OECD are widely approved, not everyone may agree to them or share their underlying values. In the United States, for example, labor leaders have expressed alarm about what they perceive as a new onslaught by management against unions and collective bargaining. They cite as examples the strategy used by some companies (dubbed the "southern strategy") by which operations are shifted to the south, where unionism is less of a factor than in other parts of the country; the well-financed campaign of the National Right-to-Work Committee to eliminate the legal protection of union security provisions; and initiatives toward work redesign and job enrichment, which, as we noted in previous chapters, are viewed by some union leaders as thin disguises for broadening management's authority over labor. In light of these perceptions, the continuing decline of union membership as a proportion of the work force, and the view of organized labor that it has been unjustly treated by past incomes policies, one may understandably wonder whether the labor movement can be counted on to cooperate in subsequent initiatives toward incomes policies or in furthering the integration of national economic policy making, let alone economic planning. Consequently, the "improved reconciliation of the claims of competing interest groups," of which labor and management are only two examples, may be especially difficult to achieve—and may be necessary to attainment of the other objectives which the OECD recommends to us.

We have no special insights to offer the reader in considering these most fundamental of issues, no compilation of "new thought" that can suddenly illuminate a clear path or guide policy through the thicket of political economy. Industrialized societies of the west have long struggled simultaneously to obtain full employment, price stability, and free markets, especially free collective bargaining. These three goals involve a balancing act in which the balance to be struck is determined through the interplay of political forces. Out of that balance emerges the social contract which binds together a nation's interest groups, which legitimizes their claims to shares of national income, and which represents rough agreement about the allocation of national income and mechanisms for allocating it.

If, in the United States, the public sector has somehow grown "too large," then the corrective political forces of interest-group pluralism may emerge to right the balance, as has occurred in the narrower area of labor-management relations. Indeed, there is some evidence to suggest that this has already begun to happen.[87] If the trade-off between inflation and unemployment has in fact worsened over time, then reassessments of desirable positions and the means of attaining them are in order. The labor sector, however, will continue to press its claims for a role in the production of the nation's wealth and a fair share of national income. The trick in all this is somehow to preserve the (mostly implicit) social contract which prevails in any nation and which links its leading interest groups in common acceptance of the underlying system. That appears to be the fundamental challenge facing the industrialized and postindustrial nations of the world in the last decades of the twentieth century, a challenge which is most heavily focused on the labor sector and which will play itself out largely in the treatment accorded this sector.

NOTES

1 The Census Bureau conducts the Current Population Survey for the Bureau of Labor Statistics, which analyzes the data on the labor force and publishes them in various forms. The Current Population Survey is also the source of data for the *Current Population Reports,* which are published by the Census Bureau. The Appendix to this book further describes these publications.

2 Julius Shiskin and Robert L. Stein, "Problems in Measuring Unemployment," *Monthly Labor Review,* **98:**4 (1975). For more on survey methodology and historical comparability of unemployment data, see U.S. Bureau of Labor Statistics, *Employment and Earnings,* January 1979, pp. 203–213.

3 John E. Bregger, "Establishment of a New Employment Statistics Review Commission," *Monthly Labor Review,* **100:**16 (1977).

4 Sar A. Levitan and Robert Taggart, *Employment and Earnings Inadequacy: A New Social Indicator,* Johns Hopkins, Baltimore, 1974.

5 Bregger, p. 16.

6 Prior reviews of concepts and measures of the labor force were carried out by the

federal government in 1948, 1954–1955, and 1961–1962. The last was conducted by the President's Committee to Appraise Employment and Unemployment Statistics, chaired by Robert A. Gordon of the University of California at Berkeley. The Committee published a distillation of its work, *Measuring Employment and Unemployment*, 1962. For more on these appraisals, see Bregger, pp. 14–17. Note that the present head of the Commission, Sar A. Levitan, together with Robert Taggart, proposed the aforementioned employment and earnings inadequacy index, cited in Levitan and Taggart.

7 Another form of seasonal unemployment, somewhat different from the types already mentioned, occurs when labor and management purposely arrange annual working hours to incorporate periods of unemployment. Cases in point are the maritime industry and the Internal Revenue Service (IRS), the latter relying on regular part-time employees who collect unemployment benefits for about 6 months each year.

8 For example, in December 1978, the unadjusted unemployment rate for the civilian labor force was 5.6 percent, and the adjusted rate was 5.9 percent. The December rates for the seven subgroups of the labor force listed in Table 12-2 were increased from 0.0 to 0.7 of a percentage point by the seasonal adjustment.

9 See, for example, Charles R. Killingsworth, "The Fall and Rise of the Idea of Structural Unemployment," paper presented to the Thirty-first Annual Winter Meeting of the Industrial Relations Research Association, Chicago, Aug. 30, 1978. Interestingly, the widely feared (if only minor actual incidence of) technological displacement of skilled workers in the early 1960s was a major factor in expanding public recognition of structural imbalances in the labor market.

10 The vigor of this debate over government planning is suggested by the titles of the major books on this issue that appeared between 1944 and 1948: William Beveridge, *Full Employment in a Free Society*, Norton, New York, 1945; Henry A. Wallace, *Sixty Million Jobs*, Simon and Schuster, New York, 1945; Friedrich A. Hayek, *Road to Serfdom*, University of Chicago Press, Chicago, 1944; Herman Finer, *Road to Reaction*, Little, Brown, Boston, 1945; John Maurice Clark, *Alternative to Serfdom*, Knopf, New York, 1948; Barbara Wootton, *Freedom under Planning*, University of North Carolina Press, Chapel Hill, 1945; and John Jewkes, *Ordeal by Planning*, Macmillan, New York, 1948.

11 For the definitive expression of this analysis of inflation in the 1940s, see Walter A. Morton, "Trade Unionism, Full Employment, and Inflation," *American Economic Review*, **40:**13–19 (1950). On inflation during the period of the Korean war, see Walter Galenson, *A Primer on Employment and Wages*, Vintage Books, New York, 1966, pp. 93–94.

12 See, for example, Barry M. Richman and Melvyn R. Copen, *International Management and Economic Development*, McGraw-Hill, New York, 1972; and E. H. Phelps-Brown. *The Inequality of Pay*, Oxford University Press, 1977, especially chap. 2.

13 Walter W. Heller, "The Administration's Fiscal Policy," in Arthur M. Ross (ed.), *Unemployment and the American Economy*, Wiley, New York, 1964, p. 106. The concept of the "GNP gap" seems to have originated with Arthur M. Okun. See his "Potential GNP: Its Measurement and Significance," in *Proceedings of the Business and Economic Statistics Section of the American Statistical Association*, 1962, pp. 98–104.

14 Heller, pp. 93–115. For a defense of those policies some dozen years later, see

Walter W. Heller, "What's Right with Economics," *The American Economic Review, Papers and Proceedings of the Eighty-sixth Annual Meeting of the American Economic Association,* **64:**1–14 (1974). Note that in this paragraph we have followed the interpretations of key economic spokesmen for the Kennedy and Johnson administrations, for example, Heller, "The Administration's Fiscal Policy." It can be argued that the Keynesian approach to economic policy was to a degree accepted in the Truman and Eisenhower administrations, and also that there was close harmony between the macroeconomic and structural policies concerning the labor market during the Kennedy and Johnson years.

15   The political forces which led to these actions are detailed in Arnold R. Weber, *In Pursuit of Price Stability: The Wage-Price Freeze of 1971,* Brookings, Washington, 1973.

16   For example, Geoffrey H. Moore, "A Measuring Stick for Unemployment," *The Wall Street Journal,* May 6, 1975, p. 20; and Geoffrey H. Moore, "Some Secular Changes in Business Cycles," *American Economic Review, Papers and Proceedings of the Eighty-sixth Annual Meeting of the American Economic Association,* **64:**133–137 (1974).

17   For further evidence on this point, see *Economic Report of the President, January, 1978,* 1978, p. 163.

18   *Economic Report of the President, January, 1978,* p. 164

19   *Economic Report of the President, January, 1978,* p. 164. This source refers to 1977, when inclusion of potentially discouraged black teenagers would have raised the official unemployment rate for this group from 38 to 57 percent. The same result would seem as applicable to 1978. Consider that the substantial unemployment rate for black youth may account in large part for their high representation among enlisted military personnel (28 percent in 1978).

20   Note that some offset to these changes in the labor force should have been provided by the increasing education of the labor sector, which presumably ameliorates one structural component of unemployment. If that did indeed occur, then the full significance of unemployment among women and young people may not be evident from statistics on the labor force.

21   The data in this section can be found in *Economic Report of the President, January 1979,* 1979, pp. 214–215, table B-27.

22   In December 1978 total employment was 95.9 million. Over the year 1978 it averaged 94.4 million. See U.S. Bureau of Labor Statistics, *Employment and Earnings,* January 1979, p. 21.

23   See, for example, Moore, "A Measuring Stick for Unemployment," p. 20.

24   Unemployment was 5.9 percent during the fourth quarter of 1978 and 5.8 percent during the first quarter of 1979.

25   Peter Passell, "The Illusory Arithmetic of Unemployment," *The New York Times,* May 29, 1978, p. 12.

26   The benchmark rates were adjusted for changes in the composition of the work force in terms of age and sex. See *Economic Report of the President, January, 1978,* p. 83, and *January, 1979,* p. 75.

27   See A. W. Phillips, "The Relation between Unemployment and the Rate of Change of Money Wage Rates in the United Kingdom, 1861–1957," *Economica,* **25:**283–299 (1958). A most useful companion piece is Richard G. Lipsey, "The Relation between Unemployment and the Rate of Change of Money Wages in the United Kingdom, 1862–1957: A Further Analysis," *Economica,* **27:**1–31 (1960).

28 Paul A. Samuelson and Robert A. Solow, "Analytical Aspects of Anti-Inflation Policy," *American Economic Review, Papers and Proceedings of the Seventy-second Annual Meeting of the American Economic Association,* **50:**177–194, 1960.

29 Samuelson and Solow, pp. 192–193.

30 For more on this view, see the papers in Lloyd Ulman (ed.), *Manpower Programs in the Policy Mix,* Johns Hopkins, Baltimore, 1973.

31 See Edmund S. Phelps, "Money Wage Dynamics and Labor Market Equilibrium," *Journal of Political Economy,* **76:**687–711, pt. 2 (1968); Edmund S. Phelps (ed.), *Microeconomic Foundations of Employment and Inflation Theory,* Norton, New York, 1970; Milton Friedman, "The Role of Monetary Policy," *American Economic Review,* **58:**1–17 (1968); and Robert E. Lucas, Jr., and Leonard R. Rapping, "Price Expectations and the Phillips Curve," *American Economic Review,* **59:**109–120 (1969).

32 This process is also at work when a slowing of the economy or a recession brings about an increase in unemployment and a decline in inflation. This could be shown as a movement to the right of curve SRP$_3$ in Figure 12-3. Because the new rate of price increase is lower than expected, however, workers will adjust downward their expectations of future inflation. If the new rates of unemployment and price increase are, say, 7 and 5 percent, respectively, this adjustment process would result in a return to point A in Figure 12-3, that is, the trade-off of inflation for unemployment as revealed in the long-run Phillips curve (LRP).

33 Friedman; Lucas and Rapping; and Phelps, "Money Wage Dynamics and Labor Market Equilibrium."

34 See James Tobin, "Inflation and Unemployment," *American Economic Review,* **62:**1–18 (1972); and Albert Rees, "The Phillips Curve as a Menu for Policy Choice," *Economica,* **37:**227–238 (1970).

35 Paul A. Samuelson, *Economics,* 10th ed., McGraw-Hill, New York, 1976, p. 835.

36 Lloyd G. Reynolds, *Labor Economics and Labor Relations,* 7th ed., Prentice-Hall, Englewood Cliffs, N.J., 1978, p. 214.

37 Keep in mind that shifting the Phillips curve to the left does not require agreement about the shape of the curve. The curves shown in Figure 12-5 are based on rates of price increase and unemployment prevailing in 1960 and 1978, as reported in Tables 12-1 and 12-3, but the curves shown in Figures 12-2 to 12-4 would serve equally well for this purpose. On recent experience of the Employment and Training Service (ETS) computerized job bank system, see Joseph C. Ullman and George P. Huber, *The Local Bank Program: Performance, Structure, Direction,* D.C. Heath, Lexington, Mass., 1973.

38 See Charles C. Holt, C. Duncan McRae, Stuart O. Schweitzer, and Ralph E. Smith, "Manpower Policies to Reduce Inflation and Unemployment," in Ulman, pp. 51–82.

39 *Employment and Training Report of the President, 1978,* 1978, p. 40. More specifically, the estimated federal outlays for employment and training programs in fiscal 1978 were $12.7 billion; about $8.4 billion was for public service employment, and the remainder was for training.

40 *Economic Report of the President, 1978,* p. 140; and U.S. Bureau of Labor Statistics, *CPI Detailed Report, December 1978,* pp. 7–8. Readers should be advised that the Consumer Price Index has undergone major changes in terms of concept and measurement, the most recent of which, effective January 1978, expands the coverage to all urban consumers rather than limiting it to urban wage earners and clerical workers. See U.S. Bureau of Labor Statistics, *The Consumer Price Index Revision —1978*, 1978; and U.S. Bureau of Labor Statistics, *The Consumer Price Index: Concepts and Content over the Years,* Report 517, 1977. Note that there are several different measures of inflation for the American economy: the Consumer Price Index, the Producer Price Indexes, and the "GNP deflator."

41 For supporting evidence, see Boyce Rensenberger, "Health Analysts Ask If the Nation Can Afford More Physicians," *The New York Times,* May 7, 1978, p. 1; and Council on Wage and Price Stability, *13th Quarterly Report,* April 1978.

42 For example, Gregory R. Kunkle, *How to Use (and Misuse) Statistics,* Prentice-Hall, Englewood Cliffs, N.J., 1978, especially pp. 182–183.

43 For a review of the American experience with wage and price controls, see Milton Derber, "The Wage Stabilization Program in Historical Perspective," *Proceedings of the Annual Spring Meeting of the Industrial Relations Research Association, 1972,* Madison, Wis., 1972, pp. 453–462.

44 *Economic Report of the President, 1962,* 1962, p. 189. The rate referred to here is the annual average percentage change in output per worker hour in the economy during the latest 5 years.

45 *Economic Report of the President, 1962,* p. 189.

46 See successive issues of the *Economic Report of the President* between 1962 and 1968 for changing policy on wage and price controls during that era.

47 See, for example, the papers and discussion in George P. Schultz and Robert Z. Aliber, *Guidelines: Informal Controls and the Market Place,* University of Chicago Press, Chicago, 1966, pp. 17–78, pt. 1.

48 Arnold R. Weber, *In Pursuit of Price Stability: The Wage-Price Freeze of 1971,* p. 5.

49 *Economic Report of the President, January, 1971,* 1971, p. 7.

50 For background and highlights of this experience with an incomes policy, see the various papers in John Kraft and Blaine Roberts (eds.), *Wage and Price Controls: The U.S. Experiment,* Praeger, New York, 1975; and Daniel Q. Mills, *Government, Labor and Inflation,* University of Chicago Press, Chicago, 1975. For more on the initial freeze, see Weber, p. 5.

51 See *White Paper: The President's Anti-Inflation Program,* Oct. 24, 1978, and U.S. Council on Wage and Price Stability, *Fact Book: Wage and Price Standards,* Oct. 31, 1978.

52 *White Paper,* pp. 11–12. This provision would have required Congress to amend the Internal Revenue Code.

53 See, for example, U.S. Council on Wage and Price Stability, *Collective Bargaining: Review of 1976, Outlook for 1977,* February 1977; U.S. Council on Wage and Price Stability, *Differences among Hospitals in the Rates of Increase of Costs and Related Characteristics,* December 1976; and U.S. Council on Wage and Price Stability, *Increased Freight Rates and Charges, 1977,* 1977.

54 See "Meany Prefers Mandatory Controls over Voluntary Guidelines," *John Herling's Labor Letter,* **28:**1–2 (1978). Meany's expression of the official position of the AFL-CIO on this issue by no means reflects the unanimous view of labor leaders, even among the heads of unions affiliated with the AFL-CIO.

55 George L. Perry, "Wages and the Guideposts," *American Economic Review,* **57:**897–904 (1967). For a comprehensive review of the evidence, see John Sheahan, *The Wage-Price Guideposts,* Brookings, Washington, 1967.

56 Robert M. Solow, "The Wage-Price Issue and the Guideposts," in Frederick H. Harbison and Joseph D. Mooney (eds.), *Critical Issues in Employment Policy,*

Princeton University, Industrial Relations Section, Princeton, N.J., 1966, pp. 57–73.

57 S. W. Black and H. H. Kelejian, "A Macro Model of the U.S. Labor Market," *The Review of Economics and Statistics,* **38:**712–741 (1970).

58 Robert J. Gordon, "The Recent Acceleration of Inflation and Its Lessons for the Future," *Brookings Papers on Economic Activity, I,* Brookings, Washington, 1970, pp. 8–41.

59 John T. Dunlop, "Guideposts, Wages and Collective Bargaining," in Shultz and Aliber, p. 84.

60 In this section, we rely on John Kraft and Blaine Roberts, "Wage and Price Controls: Success or Failure," in Kraft and Roberts, pp. 143–149, in which the research reported here is summarized.

61 Daniel J. B. Mitchell, "Phase II Wage Controls," *Industrial and Labor Relations Review,* **27:**351–375 (1974).

62 Mitchell, p. 372.

63 George P. Shultz and Kenneth W. Dam, "Reflections on Wage and Price Controls," *Industrial and Labor Relations Review,* **30:**139–151 (1977).

64 Shultz and Dam, p. 141.

65 Arnold R. Weber and Daniel J. B. Mitchell, "Further Reflections on Wage Controls: Comment," *Industrial and Labor Relations Review,* **31:**151 (1978).

66 For more on this, see George P. Shultz and Kenneth W. Dam, "Reply," *Industrial and Labor Relations Review,* **30:**159–160 (1978).

67 Weber and Mitchell, p. 158.

68 For an account of that experience, see Lloyd Ulman and Robert J. Flanagan, *Wage Restraint: A Study of Incomes Policy in Western Europe,* University of California Press, Berkeley, 1971.

69 See, for example, Daniel J. B. Mitchell, "Incomes Policy and the Labor Market in France," *Industrial and Labor Relations Review,* **25:**315–335 (1972).

70 As occurred in 1972. Only Frank Fitzsimmons, president of the International Brotherhood of Teamsters, remained on the Pay Board. The resignees included George Meany, president of the AFL-CIO.

71 Ulman and Flanagan.

72 Ulman and Flanagan, p. 69.

73 See Walter Galenson's review of Ulman and Flanagan's book in *Industrial and Labor Relations Review,* **25:**599 (1972).

74 Solomon Barkin (ed.), *Worker Militancy and Its Consequences, 1965–75,* Praeger, New York, 1975, p. 370.

75 See Initiative Committee for National Economic Planning, "For a National Economic Planning System" *Challenge,* March–April 1975, pp. 51–53.

76 Initiative Committee for National Economic Planning, p. 51.

77 Initiative Committee for National Economic Planning, pp. 52–53.

78 Arthur M. Schlesinger, Jr., "Laissez Faire, Planning and Reality," *The Wall Street Journal,* July 30, 1975, p. 22.

79 Henry Hazlitt, "Planning Disaster: Government Blueprint for the Economy Would Cost U.S. Dear," *Barron's,* Mar. 24, 1975, p. 7.

80 See Full Employment Action Council, *A Summary of the Full Employment and Balanced Growth Act,* 1978. For a discussion and contrasting views of the modified bill, see Peter H. Schuck, "National Economic Planning: A Slogan without Substance," *The Public Interest,* **45:**63–78 (1976); and George Meany, "Jobs," *The American Federationist,* **84:**1–6 (1977).

81 As reported in Bureau of National Affairs, *Labor Relations Reporter,* **99**:141–142 (1978). The bill retained the name of its original cosponsor, Senator Hubert H. Humphrey, who died in early 1978. His widow and successor, Senator Muriel Humphrey, offered an amendment to the bill calling for the achievement of 3 percent unemployment at the earliest possible date, but it was rejected by the Senate just before passage of the legislation.

82 Bureau of National Affairs, p. 142.

83 Shuck, p. 65.

84 One critic claimed in 1977 that the start-up costs of attaining 4 percent unemployment would be $48 billion and that continuing annual costs would be about half that amount. See Raymond J. Saulnier, "A Critique of the Humphrey-Hawkins Bill," *Business Horizons,* **20**:21 (1977). Another observer pointed out in 1978 that the economy would then have to expand in real terms at an average annual rate of more than 5 percent over a 5-year period in order to reduce aggregate unemployment to 4 percent. He argued that this would push output to the limits of productive capacity and help touch off a new inflationary round; for that reason, he was dubious that the unemployment goal of the Humphrey-Hawkins bill will be pursued "as vigorously as its advocates anticipate." See Andrew Brimmer, "Economic Perspectives: The Humphrey-Hawkins Bill," *Black Enterprise,* March 1978, p. 55. Finally, Secretary of Labor Ray Marshall estimated in 1977 that two tax reductions of about $20 billion each plus 2 million public service jobs would be required to reduce unemployment to 4 percent by 1983.

85 For an estimate of the GNP gap to 1981 resulting from the failure to attain full employment, see *Economic Report of the President, 1978,* p. 85. That estimate is far below what would be predicted for 1983 and 1988 (the dates mentioned in the Humphrey-Hawkins bill) on the basis of the goals of 3 percent and zero inflation, respectively. On this see *Economic Report of the President, 1979,* pp. 106–124, especially p. 109, table 22. Note, further, that full employment might be defined as a series of unemployment rates for particular groups in the labor force, rather than as a single aggregate rate. On this point, see Robert A. Gordon, "Another Look at the Goals of Full Employment and Price Stability," in National Commission for Manpower Policy, *Demographic Trends and Full Employment,* Special Report 12, December 1976, pp. 5–26, especially pp. 17–26.

86 See *Towards Full Employment and Price Stability,* Summary of a Report to the OECD by a group of independent experts, Organization for Economic Cooperation and Development, Paris, 1977. See also *Socially Responsible Wage Policies and Inflation: A Review of Four Countries' Experience,* Organization for Economic Cooperation and Development, Paris, 1975.

87 For example, in the cutting of state and local government services and payrolls during the financial crises of the mid-1970s that afflicted many public jurisdictions and in the approval by California voters (June 1978) of Proposition 13, which slashed property taxes by some $7 billion, or more than 50 percent.

ADDITIONAL READINGS

Brunner, Karl, and Allan H. Meltzer (eds): *The Phillips Curve and Labor Markets,* American Elsevier, New York, 1976.

Kraft, John, and Blaine Roberts (eds.): *Wage and Price Controls: The U.S. Experiment,* Praeger, New York, 1975.

Levitan, Sar A., and Robert Taggart: *Employment and Earnings Inadequacy: A New Social Indicator,* Johns Hopkins, Baltimore, 1974.

Malinvaud, Edmond: *The Theory of Unemployment Reconsidered,* Wiley, New York, 1977.

Mills, Daniel Q.: *Government, Labor and Inflation,* University of Chicago Press, Chicago, 1975.

Morley, Samuel: *The Economics of Inflation,* The Dryden Press, Hinsdale, Ill., 1971.

Phelps, Edmund S. (ed.): *Microeconomic Foundations of Employment and Inflation Theory,* Norton, New York, 1970.

U.S. Bureau of Labor Statistics: *The Consumer Price Index: Concepts and Content over the Years,* Report 517, 1977.

Weber, Arnold R.: *In Pursuit of Price Stability: The Wage-Price Freeze of 1971,* Brookings, Washington, 1973.

Weber, Arnold R., and Daniel J. B. Mitchell, *The Pay Board's Progress: Wage Controls in Phase II,* Brookings, Washington, 1978.

FOR ANALYSIS AND DISCUSSION

1 Prepare a short position paper on the adequacy of unemployment measures in the United States. What are their principal benefits and shortcomings? How might the statistics be altered to take "discouraged workers" into account? Should something other than the aggregate unemployment rate be the main indicator of the state of the labor market? Explain your answers to these questions.

2 Briefly discuss with your classmates the major types of unemployment that prevail in the labor market. In your judgment, which of these presents the most severe problem for public policy? Which is most amenable to remedy through public policy? How is measured unemployment affected by seasonal adjustment of the data?

3 Examine the differences in unemployment rates among the groups in the labor force listed in Table 12-4. Why is the unemployment rate among teenagers so much higher than that among adults? Why has the disparity increased over time? Why is the incidence of unemployment among black and other minority-group teenagers so much greater than that among white teenagers? Ask your local or regional office of the Bureau of Labor Statistics about unemployment among teenagers in your community.

4 Some authorities believe that the Consumer Price Index (CPI) is a misleading indicator of inflation because it does not fully reflect changes in the quality of goods and services that make up the index's "market basket." Evaluate this argument and go on to suggest how the CPI might be modified to incorporate such changes.

5 Compare the changes that took place after World War II in the CPI, the Producer Price Index (PPI), and the GNP deflator. Do the indexes "tell the same story"? What are the basic differences between them in terms of concept and measurement? Is there reason to believe that the PPI or the GNP deflator provides a better index of inflation than the CPI? What appear to be the leading consequences of the 1978 revisions in the CPI?

6 Using the data in Tables 12-1 and 12-3, plot a series of Phillips curves for the United States since 1950. Is there a pattern to the shifts of these curves? In light of the changing Phillips curve for the United States, how do you evaluate the more general argument advanced by some that the long-run curve is in fact a straight line, yielding a natural rate of unemployment?

7 Outline the possible uses of human resources planning and development policy as an anti-inflation device. Is a Phillips-type analysis helpful in carrying out this task? What level of expenditures for human resources policy would be required to have an impact on unemployment of, say, 1 percent? Does the distribution of funds between (1) public service employment and (2) training have any bearing on the effectiveness of human resources policy in reducing either inflation or unemployment?

8 You and your classmates should conduct a round-table discussion of an incomes policy for the United States. In doing so, consider the political support that exists in American society for an incomes policy, the type of policy that might best fit the American economy, and the general as well as specific goals that should be established for such a policy. Do you personally favor an incomes policy for the United States? Why or why not?

9 Two teams of two students each should debate the following proposition: "Resolved: The United States should begin immediately to undertake a full-scale program of economic planning," Be sure to make your positions specific, indicating what planning would consist of, how it would be enforced, and how its effectiveness would be evaluated. The instructor should moderate the debate, and the remainder of the class should pose questions to the teams upon conclusion of the debate.

10 Now that you have finished reading *The Labor Sector,* prepare a brief summary of the major issues that you believe will be the critical subjects of public policy debate in the United States during the 1980s. How do these differ from the major issues of the 1960s? The 1970s? Compare your views with those of a classmate. Then compare your analysis with that of a classmate who has performed this exercise for another developed nation.

Data Sources

In this appendix, we provide a selected, annotated list of data sources that students may find helpful in studying the labor sector. We have drawn on these sources for much of the data presented in this book and believe it important for students to be familiar with them. Note that most of these sources tell the reader how the basic data they contain were gathered, how often the data are collected, and what adjustments are made to the data by the agencies responsible for obtaining and publishing them. Each of the items listed here is regularly or periodically updated, and thus a student who is familiar with the basic sources will be able to obtain the most recent data available concerning the labor sector. Some comparative data are contained in these publications, but the student who is especially interested in comparative dimensions of the labor sector should examine publications of the United Nations, the International Labor Organization (ILO), the World Bank, and, of course, individual nations.

Current Population Reports   Many reports throughout the year, U.S. Bureau of the Census, Department of Commerce, with series identification code and number. Detailed reports and statistics on population, family and individual income, poverty, aging, educational attainment, fertility, mobility, ethnic and racial minorities, and other socioeconomic characteristics of the population and labor force. The publications in Series P-20, *Population Characteristics*, and P-60, *Consumer Income*, are especially useful for studying the labor sector.

Handbook of Labor Statistics Periodically, U.S. Bureau of Labor Statistics, Department of Labor. Historical data (1909 to date) on the labor force; employment; unemployment by age, race, sex, marital status, occupation, industry, and education; and reasons for nonparticipation in the labor force. Also contains data on earnings, unionization, consumer prices, and occupational injuries, as well as statistics on labor markets in other countries.

Employment and Earnings Monthly, U.S. Bureau of Labor Statistics, Department of Labor. Detailed household data on the labor force, total employment, and unemployment; establishment data on employment, hours, earnings, labor turnover, output per hour, hourly compensation, unit labor costs, and insured unemployment nationally and by state and area; special articles presenting data on various aspects of the labor force; charts; and technical notes on concepts and methods.

Monthly Labor Review Monthly, U.S. Bureau of Labor Statistics, Department of Labor. Articles on a wide range of subjects in the field of labor: employment, the labor force, wages, prices, productivity, collective bargaining, and developments abroad. Departments appearing regularly: Anatomy of Price Change, Book Reviews, Communications, Conference Papers, Conventions, Current Labor Statistics, Developments in Industrial Relations, Foreign Labor Developments, Labor Month in Review, Major Agreements Expiring Next Month, Productivity Reports, Research Summaries, Significant Decisions in Labor Cases, and Special Labor Force Reports. Includes statistical tables.

Economic Report of the President Annually, together with the annual report of the Council of Economic Advisers. Reports economic trends, the economic outlook, and major issues of economic policy. Contains detailed statistical tables relating to income, employment, and production.

Employment and Training Report of the President (**formerly** *Manpower Report of the President*) Annually, Employment and Training Administration, Department of Labor. Reviews the employment and unemployment situation, special developments in the labor force, and the progress of related government programs. Presents detailed statistics on the labor force, training programs, unemployment insurance, etc., and contains projections concerning population and the labor force.

Current Wage Developments Monthly, U.S. Bureau of Labor Statistics, Department of Labor. A monthly report on employee compensation. Covers changes in wages and benefits resulting from collective bargaining settlements and unilateral decisions by management; statistical summaries; and special reports on wage trends. Also includes strikes and lockouts and major agreements expiring during the month.

Wage Chronologies Periodically, U.S. Bureau of Labor Statistics, Department of Labor, with bulletin number. Traces changes in wages, benefits, and selected working conditions negotiated between employers and unions. Provides discussion and analysis of key bargaining issues, developments, and provisions. Individual chronologies are updated and occasionally supplemented with a special publication. For example, *Wage Chronology: Martin Marietta Aerospace and the Auto Workers, March, 1944–November, 1975*, Bulletin 1884, with supplement, 1975–1978. See U.S. Bureau of Labor Statistics, *Directory of Wage Chronologies 1948–June, 1977*, Report 503, for a complete listing.

Directory of National Unions and Employee Associations Biennially, U.S. Bureau of Labor Statistics, Department of Labor. A fact book on many aspects of union structure and membership. Provides names of major officers and officials, number of members, locals or affiliates of each organization, and location of union headquarters. Summarizes significant developments in organized labor and discusses union functions, activities, and structure. Contains detailed statistics on union organization and membership and discusses the methods by which these were obtained.

Analysis of Work Stoppages Annually, U.S. Bureau of Labor Statistics, Department of Labor, with bulletin number. Provides detailed information on strikes by size, duration, industry group, occupation, location, and issue. Covers the private and public sectors and reports on procedures used to settle disputed issues. Contains some historical data and gives the scope, definitions, and methods used to collect data on strikes.

Characteristics of Major Collective Bargaining Agreements Periodically, U.S. Bureau of Labor Statistics, Department of Labor, with bulletin number. Reports on agreements covering 1000 or more workers in the private sector. Provides information on the following categories of contractual provisions: union security and management's rights, wages, hours and overtime pay, seniority, paid leave and vacations, job security, grievance procedures, and strikes and lockouts.

Characteristics of Agreements in State and Local Governments Periodically, U.S. Bureau of Labor Statistics, Department of Labor, with bulletin number. A companion volume to the one listed above. Reports the same types of contractual provisions as in agreements in the private sector, but it is not limited to those covering 1000 or more workers.

Social Security Bulletin Monthly, U.S. Social Security Administration, Department of Health, Education, and Welfare. Provides reports, statistical tables, and special articles on social security, workers' compensation, unemployment insurance, health care, the elderly, public welfare, and many other aspects of income maintenance. Program statistics are reported monthly, quarterly, and annually.

The Federal Civil Rights Enforcement Effort Periodically, U.S. Commission on Civil Rights. A multivolume report that covers the efforts aimed at antidiscrimination and equal employment opportunity of the U.S. Office of Personnel Management, the Department of Labor's Office of Federal Contract Compliance Programs (OFCCP) and Wage and Hour Division, the Equal Employment Opportunity Commission, the Department of Justice, and the Equal Employment Opportunity Coordinating Council. Contains selected statistical data concerning compliance review and resources, litigation, and related activities.

News Free press releases of the Bureau of Labor Statistics, Department of Labor, covering many subjects, including the following:

Consumer Price Index, monthly
The employment situation, monthly
Employment and wages, quarterly
Labor force developments, quarterly
Labor turnover in manufacturing, monthly
Major collective bargaining settlements, quarterly
Real earnings, monthly
Work stoppages, monthly
Comprehensive Employment and Training Act, occasionally
Trade adjustment assistance, occasionally
Equal employment opportunity, occasionally
Occupational safety and health, occasionally

Special Labor Force Reports (Free mailing.) Occasionally, U.S. Bureau of Labor Statistics, Department of Labor. Reprints from the *Monthly Labor Review* with supplementary tables and technical notes.

Publications of the Bureau of Labor Statistics Semiannually. Subject index of publications issued during the period covered.

Unpublished Data U.S. Bureau of Labor Statistics, Department of Labor. The computer data bank and retrieval system known as "LABSTAT" contains unpublished data on the labor force. The Bureau can also generate special data on the labor force through use of the Current Population Survey's individual record (micro) tapes. These tape files contain responses to the monthly household survey. Tapes are available for all months since January 1976 and for some prior months. Inquiries should be sent to the Office of Systems and Standards, Bureau of Labor Statistics, Washington, D.C. 20212.

Index

Aaron, Benjamin, 262*n.*, 313*n.*, 412*n.*
Abel, I. W., 192, 209*n.*, 250
Adams, Arvil V., 407, 414*n.*
Adams, J. F., 362*n.*
Affirmative action programs, 244 – 245
  Bakke case and, 403 – 405
  construction industry and, 395 – 396
  EEOC and, 389
  Executive Order No. 11246 and, 390, 391
  HEW and, 392
  human resources management and, 401
  OFCCP and, 390, 391
  seniority versus, 401 – 403
Age discrimination, 379 – 381
Age Discrimination in Employment Act, 242, 393
Aged, social insurance for, 472 – 489
  population trends and, 472 – 473
  private pension programs, 485 – 489
  retirement, 472 – 473
  social security and (*see* Social security system)
Agency shop, 122, 281

Agricultural Relations Act (California), 121
Agriculture industry, unionization of, 121
Aid to Families with Dependent Children program, 573
Alexander v. Gardner-Denver, 242
Aliber, Robert Z., 636*n.*
Alioto, Joseph, 287 – 288
Allen Bradley case, 108 – 109
Amalgamated Clothing and Textile Workers Union (ACTWU), 184
Amalgamated Meat Cutters and Butcher Workmen of North America (AMCB), 255
American Anti-Boycott Association, 103
American Civil Liberties Union, 173
American Federation of Government Employees (AFGE), 181, 184, 203, 302, 304
American Federation of Labor (AFL), 101 – 102, 164
  corruption in, 116
  craft versus industrial unionism and, 113 – 115

American Federation of Labor (AFL):
  discrimination and, 117
  opposition to, 103 – 104
  political activities of, 194 – 196, 201
American Federation of Labor-Congress of
      Industrial Organizations (AFL-CIO),
      80, 147, 150, 192, 301
  civil rights legislation and, 198, 388,
      395 – 396
  Ethical Practice Code on Union Democratic
      Processes, 175, 180
  Ethical Practices Committee, 117
  expulsion from, 117, 162, 163, 187
  financing of, 167 – 170
  illegal aliens and, 387
  Landrum-Griffin Act and, 173, 175
  limited power of, 160, 162
  Meany and, 116, 184, 190, 193, 507
  merger, 116 – 117, 163, 164, 196
  political activities of, 196 – 206
  political philosophy of, 195
  structure of, 160 – 164, 193
      autonomy and, 162 – 163
      exclusive jurisdiction and, 116, 163 – 164
  Taft-Hartley Act extension and, 305
  UAW and, 189, 190
  wage and price controls and, 620
American Federation of State, County and
      Municipal Employees (AFSCME), 162,
      170, 197, 202
  collective bargaining and, 280, 281, 286, 296,
      299, 305
  membership of, 147 – 151, 181
  New York fiscal crisis and, 290 – 291
American Federation of Teachers (AFT), 119,
      150, 170, 184, 290 – 291, 305
American Management Association (AMA),
      145 – 146
American Nurses Association (ANA), 150
American plan, 107
American Postal Workers Union (APWU),
      181, 301
American Telephone and Telegraph Company
      consent decree, 400 – 401, 409
Anderson, John C., 208n.
Andersson, Rolf, 578n.
Apex v. Leader, 108
Applebaum, Leon, 208n.
Apprenticeship programs:
  construction industry and, 395 – 396
  European, 567 – 568
Arbitration, 223
  binding, 278, 302, 303
  compulsory, 278, 279
  expedited, 240

Arbitration:
  final-offer, 278 – 279
  grievance, 238 – 243
    cost of, 239 – 240
    legal standing of, 240 – 242
    permanent umpire for, 240
    time and, 240
  interest, 238
  opposition to compulsory, 232
Area Redevelopment Act, 533, 535
Ashenfelter, Orley, 208n., 360n., 361n., 408,
      412n. – 415n., 580n.
Ashford, Nicholas A., 525n.
Ashton, T. S., 460, 466n.
Associated Industries of Seattle, 107
Atkinson, A. B., 463n., 464n., 466n.
Attitudes toward work (*see* Job attitudes)
Attitudinal structuring, 216, 249
  in public sector, 297
Automobile industry, 247, 251 – 255
Automobile Workers, United (*see* United
      Automobile Workers)

Baer, George, 226
Bakaly, Charles G., 414n.
Bakery and Confectionery Workers'
      International Union of America, 117
Bakke, E. Wight, 580n.
Bakke case, 403 – 405
Bancroft, Gertrude, 85n., 86n.
Barbash, Jack, 156n.
Bargaining (*see* Collective bargaining)
Bargaining power, 214 – 215, 249
  costs of agreement or disagreement and,
      214 – 215, 228 – 234
    in public sector, 279, 283
  defined, 214
  management function and, 228 – 230
Bargaining unit, 218 – 222
  characteristics of, 219 – 222
  criteria for, 112
  legal determinant of, 219
  NLRB and, 111 – 112, 218 – 219, 299
  in public sector, 299
Barkin, Solomon, 154n., 156n., 209n., 626,
      627, 637n.
Bartel, Ann, 361n.
Barton, Paul E., 571, 579n.
Beal, Edwin F., 312n., 313n.
Beame, Abraham D., 290, 291
Beck, Dave, 187
Becker, Gary, 358n., 362n., 371 – 373, 410n.,
      415n.
Becker, Howard S., 25, 47n.

Beer, Samuel H., 577*n.*
Begin, James P., 312*n.*
Behrman, Jere, 450, 453, 464*n.*
Bell, Daniel, 47*n.*, 457, 465*n.*
Beller, Andrea, 408, 414*n.*
Bendix, Reinhard, 35, 48*n.*, 87*n.*, 88*n.*
Benefit seniority, 243
Bennett, William J., 413*n.*
Berg, Ivar E., 261*n.*, 359*n.*, 413*n.*, 578*n.*
Berkowitz, Monroe, 494, 522*n.*
Bernstein, Irving, 156*n.*
Beveridge, William, 633*n.*
Bill of rights under Landrum-Griffin Act,
      174 – 176, 183
Black, S. W., 621, 637*n.*
Black Lung Benefits Reform Act, 492
Blackmun, Harry A., 404 – 405
Blacks:
   distribution of family income and, 428 – 432
   human resources programs and, 527 – 575
   income mobility of, 441 – 442
   job mobility of, 55, 56
   minimum wage laws and, 506
   occupational choice and, 26 – 27
   occupational mobility and, 29, 34
   participation rates, 8 – 10, 366, 378 – 379
   poverty and, 40, 431, 432
   unemployment rates, 11 – 12, 379, 598 – 601
   unions and, 117, 139 – 144
   (*See also* Discrimination)
Blaine, Harry R., 208*n.*
Blau, Peter M., 29, 35, 48*n.*, 49*n.*, 449,
      464*n.*
Blaug, M. A., 578*n.*
Blauner, Robert, 89*n.*, 359*n.*
Blaustein, Saul J., 523*n.*, 525*n.*
Blue-collar workers, 13, 22 – 23
   choosing similar work and, 72 – 73
   income, 37 – 39, 65 – 66, 327 – 331, 349
   job mobility, 55, 59 – 63, 65 – 66
   occupational mobility of, 28 – 29, 35
   unemployment rates, 11, 12
   in unions, 134
      discrimination and, 140 – 144
   work characteristics and, 70 – 74
Blum, James, 415*n.*, 580*n.*
"Bogus" typesetting, 246 – 247
Bok, Derek C., 153*n.*, 156*n.*, 193, 204, 209*n.*,
      210*n.*
Bornstein, Leon, 209*n.*
Borus, Michael E., 577*n.*
Boskin, Michael J., 525*n.*
Bottomore, T. B., 87*n.*
Boulware, Lemuel, 248
"Boulwarism," 248 – 249

Bowen, William G., 525*n.*
Bowles, Samuel, 359*n.*
Boycotts, 233
   secondary, 115
   Sherman Antitrust Act and, 105
Boyle, W. A. "Tony," 188 – 189
Brecher, Charles, 580*n.*
Bregger, John E., 632*n.*
Brennan, Peter, 206
Briggs, Vernon M., 362*n.*
Brimmer, Andrew, 638*n.*
Brittain, John, 33, 48*n.*, 49*n.*, 207*n.*, 445 – 452,
      464*n.*, 465*n.*, 466*n.*
Brotherhood of Railway, Airline and
      Steamship Clerks, Freight Handler,
      Express and Station Employees
      (BRASC), 197
Brown, Charles, 263*n.*
Brown, David G., 87*n.*
Brown, Gary D., 410*n.*
Brown, Henry Phelps, 463*n.*, 466*n.*
Brown, Scott C., 48*n.*, 411*n.*
Brown v. Board of Education, 403
Browning, Edgar K., 439, 452 – 454, 463*n.*,
      464*n.*, 465*n.*
Brozen, Yale, 523*n.*
Brunner, Karl, 638*n.*
Bryan, E. James, 88*n.*
BSN-Gervais Danone, 259
Buchholz, Rogene A., 88*n.*
Burke, Donald R., 208*n.*
Burton, John F., Jr., 87*n.*, 270, 283 – 284,
      310*n.*, 311*n.*, 312*n.*, 522*n.*
Business cycles:
   human resources outlays and, 535 – 536
   job mobility and, 59
   national income and, 419
   unemployment and, 379, 591
   unemployment insurance and, 499 – 500
   unions and, 95
Business sector and human resources planning
      and development, 556 – 565
Business unionism, 99, 122, 146, 225
   development of, 102 – 104
   thrust of, 138
Butler, Richard, 406, 407, 411*n.*, 414*n.*
Byrne, James J., 48*n.*, 86*n.*

Cain, Glen G., 49*n.*, 359*n.*, 362*n.*
Campbell, Angus, 210*n.*
Campbell, John P., 88*n.*
Canada, public sector labor relations in,
      306 – 307
Carey, James, 248

Carpenters and Joiners of America, United
    Brotherhood of (UBCJA), 147 – 151,
    184, 219
Carroll, Marjorie S., 521*n.*
Carroll, Norman E., 311*n.*
Carter, Jimmy, 121, 190, 199, 200, 202, 206,
    235, 300, 628
  incomes policy of, 619 – 621, 623
Cartter, Allen M., 358*n.,* 463*n., * 577*n.*
Cassell, Frank H., 575*n.*
Centers, Richard, 200, 209*n.*
Chamberlain, Neil W., 86*n.,* 260*n.,* 262*n.,*
    358*n.*
Chavez, Cesar, 121
Chemical and General Workers' Union,
    International Federation of (ICF),
    – 258 – 259
Chernish, William, 263*n.*
Cherns, Albert G., 88*n.*
Chickering, A. Lawrence, 310*n., * 313*n.*
Child labor, 513 – 514
Chrysler Corporation, 230, 252 – 253
Cigar Makers International Union, 101, 102
Civil Rights Act, 183, 198, 242, 388 – 391, 395,
    402, 534, 535
  apprenticeship programs and, 395 – 397
  effectiveness of, 406 – 409
  passage of, 388
  Title VII of, 388 – 391, 395, 396, 590
    Supreme Court's interpretation of, 398
  voluntary actions and, 401
Civil service (*see* Public sector)
Civil Service Commission, 300 – 302, 391, 394
Civil Service Employees Association, Inc.
    (CSEA), 147, 151, 294
Civil Service Reform Act, 300, 302, 304
Clark, John Maurice, 633*n.*
Clarkson, Kenneth W., 47*n.*
Classified federal employees, 301
Clayton Act, 106, 195
Closed shop, 97, 113, 281
  prohibition of, 115
Clothing and Textile Workers Union,
    Amalgamated (ACTWU), 184
Coercive comparisons, 345 – 346
Cole, Robert E., 89*n., * 579*n.*
Coleman, James S., 209*n., * 210*n.*
Collective bargaining, 94 – 95, 213 – 309
  abroad, 222
  administering agreements, 235 – 247
    grievance procedure, 235 – 243
    seniority, 243 – 245, 401 – 403
    work rules, 245 – 247
  bargaining power and (*see* Bargaining power)

Collective bargaining:
  behavioral bases of negotiations, 215 – 218
    attitudinal structuring, 216, 249
    distributive bargaining, 215, 249, 254
    integrative bargaining, 215 – 216, 254
    intraorganizational bargaining, 216 – 217,
      249
  continuous, 251
  cooperative initiatives, 254 – 257
  coordinator of, 229 – 230
  costs of agreement or disagreement,
    214 – 215, 228 – 234
  dynamics of, 248 – 253
    in automobile industry, 251 – 253
    in electrical equipment industry, 248 – 249
    in steel industry, 249 – 251
  as government policy, 109
  incomes policy and, 614 – 627
  inflation and, 607
  internal bargains, 216 – 217
  internal union management and, 194
  job enrichment and, 81 – 82
  multinational, 257 – 259
  negotiating tactics and strategy, 230 – 235
    bluffing, 231, 232
    concessions and, 234
    costs and, 230 – 234
    strikes and, 230 – 234
  new dimensions of, 254 – 257
  NLRB and, 111 – 113, 218 – 219, 222, 225
  nonunion employees and, 45, 111, 125 – 126,
    219
  origins of, 96 – 97, 102
  pensions and, 485
  primary labor market and, 42
  productivity and, 81, 254
  provisions of, illustrative, 223 – 225
  in public sector, 267 – 309
    abroad, 306 – 309
    Civil Service Reform Act and, 300
    costs of agreement or disagreement, 279,
      283
    currents of change, 282 – 292
    diversity, 291 – 292
    Executive Order No. 11491 and, 118,
      299 – 300, 302
    extension of Taft-Hartley Act to,
      305 – 306
    federal, 118 – 120, 203, 299 – 304
    final-offer arbitration, 278 – 279
    fiscal crises of mid-1970s and, 282 – 284
    governmental sovereignty, 268, 281, 302
    grievance procedure, 295, 302 – 303
    how different is?, 268 – 272, 286

Collective bargaining:
  in public sector: legal regulation, 272–282
    management policy, 296–297
    management prerogatives, 225–226
    monopolistic governmental services and,
      268–269, 286
    multiemployer, 297–299
    multilateral bargaining, 270–272
    in New York, 286–287, 289–291
    personnel administration, 269–270,
      295–296
    public ratification of agreements, 306
    resolving impasses, 276–279, 303
    in San Francisco, 286–289
    scope of, 302
    second generation of, 283–286
    strikes, 118–120, 269, 273–276,
      283–286, 302, 303
    structure of, 297–299
    summary, 309
    supervisory and management personnel,
      280–281, 284, 286
    tax revolt, 282
    union representation and, 300–301
    unionization of military, 121, 304–305
    unresolved issues of, 304–306
    wage determination, 271–272
  ratification of agreements (*see* Contracts)
  scientific management and, 104
  scope of, 222–230
    bargaining power and, 228–230
    management function and, 228–229
    management's prerogatives and, 225–228
    NLRB and, 112–113, 222
  on single-employer basis, 222
  statistics on, 219–222
  structure of union and, 162–170
  summary, 259–260
  unfair labor practices and, 110
  wages and (*see* Wages)
  Wagner Act and, 109–110, 113
College Placement Council, 530
Colosi, Thomas R., 313*n.*
Committee for Economic Development (CED),
  558–559
Committee on Political Education (COPE)
  (AFL-CIO), 196, 197
Commons, John R., 359*n.*
Commonwealth v. Hunt, 97–98
Communications Workers of America (CWA),
  184, 219
Communism, 82–83, 116, 249, 338–341
  full employment and, 595
Community Action Program, 534

Company unions, 106–107
Competitive-labor-market theory, 53–54, 60,
  83, 317–336
  assumptions of, 318–319
  conditions in labor market and, 318
  demand for labor: aggregate, 321–323
    individual firm's, 319–321
  equilibrium in labor market and, 326–327
  job information and, 54, 318
  supply of labor: aggregate, 323–325
    to firm, 325–326
    human capital approach to, 331–336
  wages and, 53–54, 317–336
    empirical patterns of, 327–331
Competitive-status seniority, 243
Comprehensive Employment Program (CEP),
  530
Comprehensive Employment and Training Act
  (CETA), 536–539
  decentralization of human resources
    programs and, 537–538
  expenditures for, 536–537, 541
  objectives of, 536–537
  politics and, 539–541
  program performance under, 541–550
    characteristics of participants,
      541–543
    Job Corps, 545
    outcomes of programs, 541, 544–545
    summary, 549–550
    WIN, 545–549
  proposed improvements in, 571–572
  Title I, 537, 541–546, 572
  Title II, 536–537, 540–546, 574
  Title III, 538, 541, 571
  Title IV, 538–539, 545
  Title V, 539
  Title VI, 537, 538, 541–546, 574
  Title VII, 539
  Title VIII, 539
Compulsory arbitration, 278, 279
Concentrated Employment Program (CEP),
  534
Conciliation, 276, 278
Congress of Industrial Organizations (CIO),
  189
  break with AFL, 114–115, 164
  described, 114–116
  leadership of, 114, 116, 117, 188, 192
  political activities of, 195, 196
  (*See also* American Federation of
    Labor-Congress of Industrial
    Organizations)
Conspiracy doctrine, 97–98, 108

Construction industry and apprenticeship
  programs, 395 – 396
Consumer Price Index (CPI), 593 – 595,
  610 – 613
Consumption, limiting, 455 – 456
"Contracting out" political contributions,
  196 – 197
Contracts:
  administering, 235 – 247
    grievance procedure, 235 – 243
    seniority, 243 – 245, 401 – 403
    work rules, 245 – 247
  expiration of, and strikes, 232
  ratification of, 185 – 186, 233
  public, 306
Converse, Phillip E., 210n.
Cook, Alice H., 207n.
Cooper, Carole L., 312n.
Cooperative Area Manpower Planning System,
  530
Copen, Melvyn R., 633n.
Corcoran, Mary, 464n. – 465n.
*Coronado Coal Company v. United Mine
  Workers,* 105, 108
Corporate profits, 419 – 421, 427
Correge, Joy, 262n.
Cost of Living Council (COLC), 617 – 619
Costs of agreement or disagreement, 214 – 215,
  228 – 234
  in public sector, 279, 283
Council of Economic Advisers, 596, 614 – 616
Council of unions, 170
Council on Wage and Price Stability, 620
Cox, Archibald, 155n.
Craft doctrine, 114
Craft severence, 111 – 112
Craft unionism, 95 – 100, 104
  construction industry discrimination and, 395
  industrial unionism versus, 113 – 115
Craig, Isabel, 523n.
Craypo, Charles, 257, 258, 264n.
Cross, John G., 261n., 362n.
Cullen, Donald E., 263n.
Cyclical unemployment, 591

Dales, Sophie R., 525n.
Dalton, Gene W., 359n.
Dalton, James A., 360n.
Dam, Kenneth, 622, 637n.
Danbury Hatters' case, 105
David, Henry, 154n.
Davis, Karen, 525n.
Davis, Louis, 88n.

Davis-Bacon Act, 515
De Maria, Alfred T., 156n.
Democracy in unions, 159 – 194
Democratic party and unions, 199 – 202
Dennis, Barbara D., 262n.
Department of Health, Education, and Welfare
  (HEW), U.S., 68, 69
  regulating discrimination and, 391 – 392
Department of Justice, U.S., 391, 395, 400
Department of Labor, U.S.: CETA and,
  536 – 540, 574
  child labor and, 513 – 514
  Davis-Bacon Act and, 515
  fiscal responsibility violations and, 189
  minimum wages and, 505 – 506, 510
  Occupational Safety and Health Act and,
    494, 495
  regulating discrimination and, 390 – 393,
    395, 400
    Bureau of Apprenticeship Training, 395,
      396
    Wage-Hour and Public Contracts
      Division, 392, 393
  union elections and, 176, 178, 180, 188
Derber, Milton, 313n., 636n.
Disability benefits, 474, 475, 482, 490 – 496
Discrimination, 9, 365 – 410
  bargaining and, 229, 242
  changes in, over time, 376 – 386
    age, 379 – 381
    education, 379 – 386
    occupational distribution, 374 – 386
    participation rates, 378 – 379
    ratios of income, 376 – 386
    summary of, 384, 386
    unemployment, 379, 380
  cost of, 371 – 372
  defined, 371, 372
  dual-market theory and, 42, 339, 341
  economic perspectives on, 371 – 373
  equal employment opportunity laws and,
    44 – 45
  experiences in labor market, 366 – 371
  illegal aliens, 386 – 387
  income and, 367 – 387, 406 – 408
  informal labor market contracts and, 64
  measuring, 373 – 375
  regulating, 388 – 409
    affirmative action aggreements and,
      389 – 392, 401 – 403
    Age Discrimination in Employment Act,
      393
    apprenticeship programs and construction
      industry, 395 – 396

Discrimination:
  regulating: AT&T consent decree, 400 – 401,
    409
    Bakke case, 403 – 405
    Civil Rights Act, 388 – 391, 397
    Department of Health, Education, and
      Welfare and, 391 – 392
    Equal Employment Opportunity Act, 394
    Equal Employment Opportunity
      Commission, 388 – 391
    Equal Employment Opportunity
      Coordinating Council, 394 – 395
    Equal Pay Act, 392 – 393
    evaluating, 406 – 409
    Executive Order No. 11246, 390, 391, 397
    Executive Order No. 11478, 394
    Griggs v. Duke Power Company case and,
      397 – 400, 409
    monitoring equal employment progress,
      401
    Office of Federal Contract Compliance
      Programs, 390 – 391
    Office of Personnel Management,
      394 – 395
    review of, 388 – 389
    seniority and, 401 – 403
    summary, 396 – 397, 409 – 410
    Taft-Hartley Act, 393 – 394
    valid selection of employees and,
      398 – 400, 405
    voluntary actions and, 401
  reverse, 403 – 405
  sex-role stereotyping, 375 – 376
  as social issue, 366
  summary, 409 – 410
  by unions, 117, 139 – 144, 388, 395 – 396,
    407
Distributive bargaining, 215, 249, 254
District organization of unions, 170
Division of labor, 67 – 68
Doeringer, Peter B., 49*n.*, 359*n.*, 362*n.*
Douglas, Paul H., 117
Dual labor markets, 41 – 43, 336 – 338
  key aspect of, 337
Ducros, Bernard, 463*n.*
Dues checkoff, 122, 281
Duncan, Otis Dudley, 29, 35, 48*n.*, 49*n.*, 449,
  464*n.*
Dunlop, John T., 153n., 156*n.*, 193, 204, 209*n.*,
  210*n.*, 360*n.*, 361*n.*, 621, 637*n.*
Dunnette, Marvin D., 88*n.*
Dyer, Lee, 264*n.*

Eastland, Terry, 413*n.*

Eck, Allan, 48*n.*
"Economic man," 63, 69
Economic Opportunity Act, 534, 535, 538
Economic Stabilization Act, 617
Edelstein, J., 210*n.*
Education:
  costs and benefits of, 332 – 336
  discrimination and, 367 – 371, 379 – 386
    Bakke case and, 403 – 405
    Griggs case and, 398 – 400
    HEW and, 391 – 392
  income and, 367 – 371, 379 – 386
  inheritance and, 446 – 449
    socioeconomic status and, 449 – 450
  occupational achievement and, 29, 32, 33
  occupational choice and, 25 – 27
  on-the-job training, 334 – 335, 340
  redistribution of income and, 451 – 452
  social welfare expeditures on, 517, 518
  transition from school to work, 566,
    569 – 571
  (*See also* Human resources planning and
    development, education and)
Education Association, National (NEA), 119,
  150, 151, 164, 305
Edwards, Richard C., 359*n.*
Efficiency versus equality, 452 – 455, 458 – 459
Ehrenberg, Ronald G., 359*n.*, 361*n.*, 362*n.*
Eight-hour workday, 100, 106, 513, 514
Eisenhower, Dwight D., 597
Elder, Peyton, 524*n.*
Electrical equipment industry, 248 – 249
Electrical, Radio, and Machine Workers of
  America, United (UE), 249
Electrical, Radio, and Machine Workers,
  International Union of (IUE), 163, 248,
  249
Electrical Workers, International Brotherhood
  of (*see* International Brotherhood of
  Electrical Workers)
Emergency Employment Act, 536
Emergency Jobs Program Extension Act, 588
Emergency Jobs and Unemployment
  Assistance Act, 537
Employee associations, 123 – 129
  autonomy of, 162
  financing of, 167 – 170
  membership in, 147 – 151, 158
  public sector and, 120, 126 – 129
  white-collar workers and, 131, 134, 135
  women and, 134, 136 – 138
Employees' Retirement and Income Security
  Act (ERISA), 198, 488 – 489
Employers' associations, 217

Employment:
  full (*see* Full employment)
  level of, versus unemployment, 600–602
    (*See also* Unemployment)
  status, 6–7
Employment Act, 539, 591–599
  issues behind passage of, 592
  purpose of, 593, 628, 629
Employment agencies:
  blue-collar workers and, 60
  Employment Service and, 529
  white-collar workers and, 61–62
Employment Service, 528–530
  (*See also* United States Employment and
    Training Service)
Entrepreneurial income, 419–421
Epstein, Edwin M., 197, 209n.
Equal Employment Opportunity Act, 394, 400
Equal Employment Opportunity Commission
    (EEOC), 388–391
  affirmative action versus seniority and, 402
  AT&T consent decree and, 400
  effectiveness of, 406–408
  OFCCP and, 391
  role and function of, 389, 395
  state and local commissions and, 390, 407
Equal Employment Opportunity Coordinating
    Council, 394–395
Equal Pay Act, 242, 392–393
Equality versus efficiency, 452–455, 458–459
Estey, Martin S., 210n.
Executive Order No. 10988, 118, 299, 303
Executive Order No. 11246, 390, 391, 395,
    397, 408
Executive Order No. 11478, 394
Executive Order No. 11491, 118, 302
  provisions of, 299–300
Expedited arbitration, 240
Experimental Negotiating Agreement (ENA)
    and, 192, 251

Factfinding, 278
Fair employment practice laws, state (FEP),
    390, 407
Fair Labor Standards Act, 306
  child labor and, 513–514
  Equal Pay Act amendment, 392–393
  maximum hours and, 513
  minimum wage and, 506–514
  purpose of, 514
Family income, 39–40
  (*See also* Income distribution, personal
    income)

Farber, Henry S., 310n.
Farm workers:
  income, 37–39
    distribution of, 418
    reduced numbers of, 22
Farm Workers of America, United (UFWA),
    121
Farrah Manufacturing boycott, 233
Federal Coal Mine Health and Safety Act, 492
Federal Election Campaign Act (FECA), 197
Federal Elections Commission, 197
Federal Labor Relations Authority (FLRA),
    300, 302, 303
Federal Labor Relations Council, 299
Federal Mediation and Conciliation Service
    (FMCS), 255, 256, 276
Federal Pay Comparability Act, 119, 304, 352,
    515
Federal Pay Council, 301
Federal Reserve Board, 628
Federal Salary Reform Act, 119, 304, 352, 515
Federal Service Impasses Panel, 299
Fein, Mitchell, 70, 87n.
Feldstein, Martin S., 521n.
Feller, David E., 262n.
Ference, Thomas P., 156n.
Feuille, Peter, 279, 297, 310n., 311n., 312n.,
    314n.
Final-offer arbitration, 278–279
Finer, Herman, 633n.
Fire Fighters, International Association of
    (IAFF), 165, 170, 280
Fischer, Ben, 262n.
Fitzsimmons, Frank, 187, 188, 206
Flanagan, Robert J., 264n., 360n., 406, 414n.,
    625, 637n.
Fleisher, Belton M., 85n.
Fletcher, Arthur, 395
Fogel, Walter, 310n., 361n., 387, 411n., 412n.,
    524n.
Food industry, 255–256
Ford, E. J., 360n.
Ford, Gerald R., 199, 200
Ford Motor Company, 251–253
Fottler, Myron D., 361n.
Fox, Alan, 260n.
France, public sector labor relations in, 307
Frankfurter, Felix, 153n.
Franklin, Ben A., 209n.
Fraser, Douglas, 184, 190
Freeman, John, 207n.
Freeman, Richard B., 25, 47n., 156n., 362n.,
    406, 407, 411n., 414n., 554, 578n.,
    580n.

Frictional unemployment, 588 – 589
Friedlander, Stanley, 26 – 27, 47n., 359n.
Friedman, Marcia, 49n.
Friedman, Milton, 468n., 506, 523n., 635n.
Friend, Edward H., 260n., 361n.
Fringe benefits, 419 – 423
Fuchs, Victor F., 17, 47n., 49n.
Full employment:
    composition of work force and, 598 – 602
    defined, 12 – 13, 595 – 596
    Employment Act and, 591 – 593
    "GNP gap" and, 596
    inflation and, 593 – 595, 597 – 598
    management of aggregate demand and,
        596 – 597
    national economic planning and, 627 – 632
    opposing views on, 592 – 593
    public sentiment for, 591 – 592
Full Employment and Balanced Growth Act,
    628

Gain sharing, 81
Galbraith, John Kenneth, 19, 47n., 465n.
Galenson, Walter, 154n., 207n., 358n., 633n.,
    637n.
Garfinkel, Stuart, 85n., 86n.
Garraty, John A., 154n
General American Transportation Corporation
    case, 241 – 242
General Electric Company, 248 – 249
General Motors, 251 – 253, 255
*General Theory of Employment, Interest, and
    Money* (Keynes), 592
Gerhart, Paul F., 204, 210n.
Getman, Julius G., 154n., 157n.
GI Bill of Rights, 553
Ginzberg, Eli, 21, 47n.
Glazer, Nathan, 411n., 413n.
Glover, Robert, 414n.
"GNP gap," 596
Gold, Charlotte, 89n.
Goldberg, Arthur, 118
Goldberg, Joseph P., 263n., 265n., 524n.,
    525n., 577n.
Goldberg, Stephen B., 154n., 157n.
Goldfarb, Robert S., 524n.
Goldfeld, Stephen, 414n.
Goldstein, Gerald S., 361n.
Goldstein, Morris, 415n.
Gomberg, William, 263n., 313n.
Gompers, Samuel, 102, 194 – 195
Gordon, David M., 359n.
Gordon, Margaret S., 47n., 86n.

Gordon, Robert A., 47n., 621, 633n., 637n.,
    638n.
Gotbaum, Victor, 202 – 203, 210n.
Gould, Jay, 100
Government Employees, American Federation
    of (AFGE), 181, 184, 203, 302, 304
Government employment, 20 – 22
    (*See also* Public sector)
Gramlich, Edward M., 511 – 512, 524n.
Great Britain, 307, 435
Great Depression, 45
    full employment policies and, 592
    rental income and, 419 – 422
    unionism and, 107 – 109
Great Society, 518, 534
Green, William, 507
Greenberg, David H, 360n.
Greene, Nathan, 153n.
Greenstone, David J., 210n.
Gregory, Charles O., 154n.
Grievance procedure:
    administering, 235 – 238
        contract disputes and, 235 – 236
        discipline and, 236
        trouble spots and, 236
    appraising, 238 – 243
    arbitration under, 238 – 243
    collective bargaining and, 223
    example of, 236 – 238
    management's use of, 236
    in public sector, 295, 302 – 303
Griggs v. Duke Power Company, 397 – 400,
    409
Grodin, Joseph R., 313n.
Gross, James A., 263n.
Gunderson, Morley, 313n.
Gurman, Richard, 156n.
Gutchess, Jocelyn, 575n.

Haber, William, 575n.
Hackman, J. Richard, 88n.
Hall, W. Clayton, 311n.
Hamermesh, Daniel, 313n., 361n., 525n.
Hammarstrom, Olle, 88n.
Hampton, Robert E., 412n.
Hanslowe, Kurt L., 263n.
Harbison, Frederick H., 525n., 550, 551,
    576n., 577n.
Hardman, J. B. S., 207n.
Harmon International Company, 255
Harrington, Michael, 209n.
Harrison, Bennett, 47n., 359n., 588
Hart, Wilson R., 155n., 313n.

Harvard University admissions program, 403–405

Hatch Act, 195, 204

Hause, John C., 465n.

Hauser, Robert M., 449–450, 464n.

Hausman, Leonard J., 410n., 411n., 415n.

Hayek, Friedrich A., 633n.

Hayford, Stephen, 311n.

Hayghe, Howard, 86n.

Haymarket riot, 100–101

Hazlitt, Henry, 627, 637n.

Health care industry, unionization of, 120–121

Health care insurance, 472, 474, 482, 611
  employee-benefit-plans, 487
  national, 482–483

Healy, James J., 262n., 263n.

Heath, Edward, 626

Heckman, James J., 406–408, 411n., 414n.

Heller, Walter, 596, 633n.–634n.

Henle, Peter, 521n., 522n.

Herbers, John, 579n.

Herman, Jeanne, 154n., 157n.

Herrnstein, Richard, 457–458, 465n.

Herzberg, Frederick, 88n.

Hickman, Charles W., 207n.

Hicks, John, 261n.

Hiestand, Dale L., 21, 47n.

Hight, Joseph E., 523n.

Hill, Herbert, 157n.

Hoffa, James R., 179, 187, 346

Holmes, Justice Oliver Wendell, 97

Holt, Charles C., 635n.

Hoover, Herbert, 108

Horton, Raymond D., 309n., 311n., 312n., 314n., 361n., 580n.

Hot cargo, 116

Hotel and Restaurant Employees and Bartenders International Union (HREU), 184

Household life-cycle, 9–10

Howe, Charles, 576n.

Hoxie, Robert, 102, 154n.

Huber, George P., 86n., 635n.

Hughes Tool case, 393

Human capital approach to labor supply, 331–336
  cost and benefit analysis and, 332–333
  defined, 331–332
  discrimination and, 371, 372, 374
  education and, 550–551, 554
  empirical support for, 335–336
  on-the-job training and, 334–335
  present value of money and, 333–334

Human resources planning and development, 527–575
  CETA (*see* Comprehensive Employment and Training Act)
  comparative perspective on, 565–569
    apprenticeship, 567–568
    education, 566–568
    ethnic conflicts, 565, 568–569
    public service employment, 569
    relocation, 568
    retraining, 568
    sheltered employment, 568
    unemployment, 566
  education and, 550–556, 566–568
    college, 551–554
    economic growth rates and, 550–551
    educational lobby and, 554–555
    expenditures for, 553
    overemphasis on, 554–556
    rates of return on investment in, 554
    rising level of, 551–553
    as screening device, 555
  introduction, 527–528
  public employment service (*see* United States Employment and Training Service)
  public service employment, 535–550, 569, 573–574
  reducing inflation and, 608–609
  revolution of 1960s, 533–535
  role of business sector in, 556–565
    CED on, 558–559
    diversity of opinion about, 556–559
    in firm, 559–565
    personnel planning and, 559–565
    Rosow plan for, 557
    voluntarism and, 558
  summary, 575
  unresolved issues in, 569–575
    CETA, 571–572
    public service employment, 573–574
    transition from school to work, 569–571
    unemployment insurance, 572–573
    welfare, 573

Humphrey, Hubert, 202, 627

Humphrey-Hawkins Act, 628–630

Hutchinson, John E., 208n., 210n.

Illegal aliens, 386–387

Illegal Purpose doctrine, 97–98, 109

Incentives, 254

Income:
  discrimination and, 367–387, 406–408

Income:
  family, 39–40
  mobility and, 58–59, 64–66
  personal, 37–39
  poverty and, 40–41
  rental, 419–422
  (*See also* Wages)
Income distribution, 417–462
  incomes policy and, 624–625
    in Europe, 626
  introduction, 417–418
  national income, 418–424
    categories, 418–421
    corporate profits and, 419–421, 427
    entrepreneur's share, 419–421
    foreign comparisons, 422
    labor's share, 418–424
    public sector and, 419–421
    rental income and, 419–422
    unions and, 422–424
  personal income, 424–442
    equality of, 439, 440, 452–455
    foreign comparisons, 425–427, 435
    income mobility and, 439–442
    inequality of, 424–431, 452
    poverty and, 429–432, 436–439
    race and, 428–432
    stability of, 427–428
    taxes and, 431–435
    transfer payments, 435–442
  summary, 462
  (*See also* Redistribution of income; Wealth,
    distribution of)
Income equality and redistribution (*see*
    Redistribution of income)
Income mobility, 439–442
Income supplements (*see* Social insurance;
    Transfer payments)
Income tax, 425, 426, 431–435
Incomes policy, 614–627
  abroad, 625–627
  under Carter, 619–620
  conclusions, 623–625
  impact of, 621–625
  intention of, 614
  under Kennedy and Johnson, 614–617
  under Nixon, 597, 617–619, 622
  politics and, 619–622, 624–625
  productivity and, 614–615, 618
  wage and price controls, 617–621
Industrial democracy, 227–228
Industrial unionism, 113–115
Industrial Workers of America, International
    Union of Allied (AIW), 258

Industrial Workers of the World (IWW)
    ("Wobblies"), 101–102
Inflation, 610–614
  abroad, 612–613
  Consumer Price Index, 593–595
    610–613
  human resources policy and, 609
  incomes policy and (*see* Incomes policy)
  national economic planning and, 627–632
  OASDHI benefits and, 476–480
  politics and, 619–622, 624–625
  post-World War II, 593
  unemployment and (*see* Unemployment,
    inflation and)
Inheritance and economic success, 445–448
  choice of mate, 448–449
  education and, 446–449
Inheritance of Economic Status, The (Brittain),
    445–450
Initiative Committee for National Economic
    Planning, 627
In-kind transfer payments, 436–439
Inland Steel case, 485
Integrative bargaining, 215–216, 254
Interest arbitration, 238
Interest rates, 422
Internal bargains, 216–217
Internal mobility, 53
International Association of Fire Fighters
    (IAFF), 165, 170, 280
International Association of Machinists and
    Aerospace Workers (IAM), 80,
    147–151, 197
International Brotherhood of Electrical
    Workers (IBEW), 114, 163, 219
  fiscal responsibility violations of, 181
  membership in, 147–151
  women, 138
  Sherman Antitrust act and, 108–109
International Brotherhood of Teamsters (*see*
    Teamsters, International Brotherhood of)
International Federation of Chemical and
    General Workers' Unions (ICF),
    258–259
International Ladies' Garment Workers Union
    (ILGWU), 138, 184
  pricing policy and, 222–223
  work rules and, 247
International Longshoremen's Association
    (ILA), 116, 246
International Typographical Union (ITU), 162,
    184
  "bogus" typesetting and, 246–247
  described, 190–191

International Union of Allied Industrial
    Workers of America (AIU), 258
International Union of Electrical Radio and
    Machine Workers (IUE), 163, 248, 249
International Union of Operating Engineers
    (IUOE), 181, 184, 297
International unions (*see* National unions, *and
    specific international unions*)
International Woodworkers of America (IWA),
    184
Intraorganizational bargaining, 216 – 217, 249
    in public sector, 271
IQ (intelligence quotient), 457 – 458
Ives, Irving M., 117

J. P. Stevens boycott, 233
Jacobs, Carl D., 88*n*.
James, Estelle D., 207*n*., 210*n*.
James, Ralph C., 207*n*., 210*n*.
Janger, Allen, 522*n*.
Janus, Charles J., 207*n*.
Japan, public sector labor relations in, 308
Javits, Jacob, 627
Jedel, Michael Jay, 312*n*.
Jencks, Christopher, 464*n*., 465*n*., 466*n*.
Jennings, Ken, 313*n*.
Jensen, Arthur C., 457 – 458, 465*n*.
Jersey Central Power and Light Company case,
    402
Jewkes, John, 633*n*.
Job attitudes, 67 – 74
    choosing similar work, 72 – 73
    dissatisfaction, 67 – 74
        (*See also* Job enrichment)
    division of labor and, 67 – 69
    hierarchy of needs and, 74
    ratings of characteristics, 69 – 74
    "Taylorism" and, 68 – 69
Job bank program, 63 – 64, 530
Job clusters, 356
Job Corps, 534, 549
    CETA and, 538 – 539, 545
Job design, 74 – 83
Job Diagnostic Survey, 78
Job enlargement, 74, 75
Job enrichment, 74 – 84
    business-team concept, 76 – 77
    at Cummins, 76
    limitations of, 77 – 83
        decision-making participation and, 79 – 83
        Job Diagnostic Survey and, 78
        lack of evaluation, 77
        lack of performance data, 77 – 78

Job enrichment:
    limitations of: older setting, 80
        performance-satisfaction relationship and,
            78 – 79
        unions, 80 – 82
    at Saab, 74 – 75
    summary, 84 – 85
    UAW and, 75 – 76
    at Volvo, 74, 75
    at Xerox, 76
Job evaluation, 354 – 356
Job mobility, 52 – 67
    age and, 55 – 57
    anatomy of, 54 – 57
    competitive-labor-market theory and, 53 – 54
    defined, 53
    determinants of, 57 – 66
        how workers find jobs, 60 – 64
        income, 64 – 66
        why workers change jobs, 59 – 60
        workers' opinions, 58 – 59
    historical perspective on, 460
    interim appraisal, 66 – 67
    introduction, 52 – 53
    labor force subgroups and, 55 – 57
    types of, 57
    (*See also* Occupational mobility)
Job rotation, 74, 75
Job satisfaction, 67 – 74
    performance as determinant of, 79
Jobs in the Business Sector (JOB) program,
    530, 535
Johnson, Beverly L., 46*n*.
Johnson, George E., 208*n*., 360*n*.
Johnson, Lyndon B., 198, 366, 388, 518, 534,
    535, 596, 597
    incomes policy of, 614 – 617, 619
Johnson, Miriam, 575*n*.
Joint board of unions, 170
Jones, Ralph, 312*n*.
Jong Oh Ra, 209*n*.
Juris, Hervey, 312*n*., 314*n*.
Jurisdictional dispute, 116
    AFL-CIO and, 163 – 164

Kahn, Mark L., 263*n*., 265*n*.
Kahn, Robert L., 69, 87*n*.
Karsh, Bernard, 153*n*.
Katz, Arnold, 523*n*.
Katz, Harry C., 310*n*., 311*n*.
Katzell, Raymond, 89*n*.
Kauterman, Frances E., 208*n*
Kelejian, H. H., 621, 637*n*.

Kendrick, John, 24
Kennedy, John F., 117, 118, 299, 388, 529, 596 – 597
  incomes policy of, 614 – 617, 619
Kerr, Clark, 463*n*.
Keynes, John Maynard, 591, 592, 597
Kidder, Alice, 408, 414*n*.
Kienast, Philip K., 312*n*., 313*n*.
Kiker, B. F., 358*n*
Killingsworth, Charles R., 633*n*.
King, Allan G., 358*n*., 463*n*., 577*n*.
King, Martin Luther, Jr., 388
Kingsley, Robert, 361*n*.
Kleingartner, Archie, 312*n*.
Kloch, Joseph J., 208*n*.
Knapp, Charles, 414*n*.
Kniesner, Thomas J., 524*n*.
Knights of Labor, 99 – 102
Koch, Edward I., 291
Kochan, Thomas A., 264*n*., 271, 310*n*., 311*n*., 314*n*.
Kohler Company strike, 233
Kornhauser, Arthur, 209*n*.
Kornhauser, Ruth, 201, 210*n*.
Kraft, John, 621, 636*n*., 637*n*., 638*n*.
Krendel, Ezra, 155*n*., 313*n*.
Krider, Charles E., 283 – 284, 311*n*.
Krischer, Gorden E., 414*n*.
Kruger, Daniel H., 575*n*.
Kuhn, James W., 89*n*., 260*n*. – 264*n*., 309*n*., 312*n*., 314*n*., 361*n*.
Kühne, Robert J., 89*n*.
Kunkle, Gregory R., 636*n*.
Kwitny, Jonathan, 208*n*.

Labor force, 1
  composition of, 598 – 602
  occupational choice and, 24 – 27
  occupational mobility and, 27 – 37
  participation rates, 3, 6 – 10, 324, 366 – 367, 378
    sex-role stereotyping and, 375
  search for security, 43 – 46
  service sector, 16 – 22
  summary, 46
  white-collar jobs, 22 – 23
Labor injunction, 98, 108, 109
Labor laws:
  public sector: collective bargaining, 272 – 282
    organizing, 118 – 120
    political activity of, 203 – 204
  unions and, 105 – 122

Labor laws:
  unions and: internal affairs of, 172 – 183
    political activity of, 194 – 199
  (*See also specific laws and cases*)
Labor-Management Relations Act (*see* Taft-Hartley Act)
Labor-Management Reporting and Disclosure Act (*see* Landrum-Griffin Act)
Labor-Management Services Administration, 176 – 178
Labor market:
  class and, 339 – 340
  competitive (*see* Competitive-labor-market theory)
  defined, 317
  described, 317 – 319
  discrimination in (*see* Discrimination)
  dual, 41 – 43, 336 – 338
  external, 337 – 338
  internal, 337, 338, 356, 357
  neoclassical, 41, 43, 44, 318, 334, 357
  primary, 42, 336 – 337
    tiers within, 338 – 339
  public, 351 – 354
    (*See also* Public sector)
  radical theories of, 339 – 341
  redistribution of income and, 459 – 462
  scope of, 317 – 318
  segmented (*see* Segmented-labor-market theories)
  summary, 357 – 358
Labor movement:
  history of, 95 – 122
  idealism and reform, 98 – 102
  origins of, 95 – 97
  structure of, 160 – 194
  (*See also* Unions)
Labor Party (Great Britain), 204 – 206
Labor supply:
  aggregate, 323 – 325
  business cycles and, 95
  to firm, 325 – 326
  human capital approach to, 331 – 336
  illegal aliens and, 386 – 387
  unionization and, 95
    labor's share of national income and, 423
Labor unions (*see* Unions)
Laborers' International Union of North America (LIUNA), 149 – 151, 184
Labor's share of national income, 418 – 422
  impact of unions on, 422 – 424
Ladies' Garment Workers Union, International (ILGWU), 138, 184, 222 – 223, 247
LaFollette, Robert, 195

Landes, William M., 407, 414n.
Landrum-Griffin Act, 110, 198
  evaluation of, 183–186
  objective of, 172, 186
  provisions of, 173–174
    bill of rights, 174–176, 183
    election procedures, 167, 176–179
    fiscal responsibility, 180–182
    trusteeships, 179–180
  union corruption and, 117, 173, 187
Lansing, John B., 60, 64, 86n., 89n.
Law of diminishing returns, 320
Lawler, Edward E., III, 88n.
Lawrence, Paul R., 359n.
Lebergott, Stanley, 462n.
LeGrande, Linda H., 156n.
Lester, Richard A., 412n., 525n.
Letter Carriers of the United States of
    America, National Association of
    (NALC), 301
Levine, Richard J., 47n.
Levinson, Harold M., 263n., 265n.
Levitan, Sar A., 413n., 576n.–579n.,
    587–588, 632n., 633n., 639n.
Lewin, David, 86n., 261n., 291–292,
    309n.–312n., 360n., 361n., 524n., 580n.
Lewis, Anthony, 413n.
Lewis, H. Gregg, 347–349, 360n.
Lewis, John L., 114, 188, 346
Liebow, Eliot, 26, 48n.
Ligget, Malcolm, 414n.
Lindsay, John, 289–290
Lipset, Seymour M., 35, 48n., 209n., 210n.,
    358n., 360n.
Lipsey, Richard G., 634n.
Lipsky, David B., 264n.
Litton Industries, 257–259
Livernash, E. Robert, 262n., 263n.
Local government employment, 20–21
  unionization and, 120
  (See also Public sector)
Local unions:
  autonomy of, 162
  business agent of, 166
  council of, 170
  described, 165–166
  dispersed, 165–166, 171
  district organization of, 170
  financing of, 167, 170
  joint boards of, 170
  national unions and, 160, 166, 167
  trusteeships and, 179–180
  turnover of officers of, 184–185
Lockout, 232–233

London, Jack, 153n.
Longshoremen's Association, International
    (ILA), 116, 246
Loomba, R. P., 87n.
Lorenz curve, 466n.–467n.
Lorsch, Jay W., 359n.
Lucas, Robert E., Jr., 635n.
Luxuries, limiting production of, 455–456

McAdams, Alan K., 209n., 210n.
McAndrew, Ian, 313n.
McBride, Lloyd, 192, 251
McCaffrey, David, 522n.
McClellan, John L., committee hearing of, 117,
    173, 179
McCullough, George E., 88n.
McDonald, David J., 192, 250
Maceskich, George, 510–511, 524n.
McGillivray, Patrick J., 310n., 361n.
McGovern, George, 162, 200, 202, 203
Machinists and Aerospace Workers,
    International Association of (IAM), 80,
    147–151, 197
McKersie, Robert B., 215–218, 260n., 265n.,
    294, 312n.
Maclachlan, Gretchen, 49n.
McLaughlin, Doris B., 210n.
McLennan, Kenneth, 310n.
McMurray, Donald L., 153n.
McNulty, Paul J., 465n.
McRae, C. Duncan, 635n.
Madden, Janice Fanning, 415n.
Main, Earl D., 577n.
Malinvaud, Edmond, 639n.
Malkeil, Burton G., 411n.
Malkeil, Judith A., 411n.
Malm, F. T., 86n.
Management:
  as coordinator of bargaining, 229–230
  function of, 226–227
    nature of, 228–230
  legal basis of, 227
  policy of, in public sector, 296–297
Management's prerogatives, 225–228
  property rights and, 227
  threats to, 225–226
  workers' perspective on, 227–228
Managerial unionism, 115, 144–146
Mangum, Garth L., 413n., 575n.–580n.
Manpower (see Human resources planning and
    development)
Manpower Development and Training Act
    (MDTA), 530, 533–535, 538

Marchal, Jean, 463n.
Marginal value product (MVP), 319–336
  minimum wage and, 508–509
  in public sector, 352
Marshall, F. Ray, 157n., 358n., 413n., 463n.,
  576n.,-579n.
Marshall, Ray, 264n., 407n., 414n., 415n., 495
Martin, James E., 312n., 313n.
Maruknick, Joan, 577n.
Marx, Karl, 67, 68, 338–341
Maslow, Abraham H., 74, 87n.
Maximum hours of work, 100, 106, 513, 514
Mayer, Albert J., 209n.
Mayo, Elton, 227–228
Meany, George, 116, 184, 190, 193, 202–203,
  206, 507, 637n.
Measday, Walter S., 463n.
Meat Cutters and Butcher Workmen of North
  America, Amalgamated (AMCB), 255
Mediation, 276, 278
Medicaid, 482, 483, 611
Medicare, 474, 482, 483, 611
Medoff, James L., 156n., 263n.
Meidner, Rudolf, 578n.
Meiners, Roger E., 47n.
Meltzer, Allan H., 638n.
Membership agreements, 122
Merit Systems Protection Board (MSPB), 300
Meritocracy, 457–458
Mexico, illegal aliens from, 386–387
Meyer, Herbert, 578n.
Meyers, Frederic, 262n.
Meyers-Milias-Brown Act (California), 287
Miles, Raymond E., 88n., 89n.
Military, unionization of, 121, 304–305
Miller, Arnold, 189
Miller, S. M., 35, 37, 48n.
Miller, Warren E., 210n.
Mills, Daniel O., 265n., 636n., 639n.
Mincer, Jacob, 358n., 359n.
Mine Workers of America, United (see United
  Mine Workers of America)
Minimum wage, 199, 505–515, 559
  contrasting views on, 505–513
  economic consequences of, 508–513
    summarized, 512–513
  increases in, 506–507
  "ratcheting" effect of, 507–508
  union views on, 507–508
Minor, Gerri, 522n.
Mitchell, Daniel J. B., 360n., 622, 623, 637n.
Mitchell, James P., 529
Monopsony, 342–344
Moore, Geoffrey H., 634n.

Moore, William J., 156n.
Morgan, James N., 415n.
Morley, Ian, 265n.
Morley, Samuel, 639n.
Morrill Act, 553
Morse, Dean W., 86n.
Morton, Walter A., 633n.
Moscone, George, 288
Moskow, Michael H., 310n.
Moynihan, Daniel P., 49n.
Mueller, Eva, 60, 64, 86n., 89n.
Multilateral bargaining, 270–272
Multinational bargaining, 257–259
Munnell, Alicia H., 521n., 525n.
Murray, Philip, 192
Muste, A.J., 172
Myers, Charles A., 550, 576n., 577n.

National Advisory Commission on Civil
  Disorders, 366, 376, 378, 386
National Alliance of Businessmen, 535
National Association of Letter Carriers of the
  United States of America (NALC), 301
National Association of Manufacturers
  (NAM), 103, 106
National Civic Federation, 103
National Commission for Employment Policy,
  539, 569, 571, 573
National Commission for Manpower Policy,
  539
National Commission on State Workmen's
  Compensation Laws, 492, 493
National economic planning, 627–632
National Education Association (NEA), 119,
  150, 151, 164, 305
National GM-UAW Committee to Improve the
  Quality of Work Life, 255
National health insurance, 482–483
National income, distribution of (see Income
  distribution, national income)
National Industrial Conference, 106
National Industrial Recovery Act, 109
National Institute of Occupational Safety and
  Health (NIOSH), 494
National Labor Relations Act (see Wagner
  Act)
National Labor Relations Board (NLRB),
  109–110
  appointments to, 206
  arbitration and, 241–242
  bargaining subject matter, 112–113, 222
  bargaining unit and, 111, 218–219, 299
  "Boulwarism" case, 248, 249

National Labor Relations Board (NLRB):
defeated proposals for, 121 – 122
discrimination and, 393 – 394
jurisdiction, 112, 163, 164, 173
new areas under, 199
pensions and, 485
public sector and, 301
recent decisions of, 110, 225
strikes by interns and residents and, 121
unfair labor practices and, 110 – 113
union election procedures and, 111 – 112, 218 – 219
National Labor Union, 99
National Metal Trades Association (NMTA), 103
National Right to Work Committee, 226, 631
National unions:
autonomy of, 162 – 163
conventions of, 166, 167
described, 166 – 167
elections of, 167
financing of, 167 – 170
government of, 170 – 172
local unions and, 160, 166, 167
membership in, 147 – 151
power of, 160
trusteeships and, 179 – 180
turnover of officers of, 184
(*See also specific unions*)
National Wage Policy Committee, 301
Negative income tax, 431, 433
Neighborhood Youth Corps, 534
Nemore, Arnold, 575*n*.
Neoclassical labor market theory, 41, 43, 44, 318, 334, 357
Nesbitt, Frederick H., 210*n*.
Net worth, distribution of, 442 – 451
New Careers program, 534 – 535
New Deal social programs, 470, 471, 592
Newman, Robert J., 156*n*., 412*n*.
Nisberg, Jay N., 88*n*.
Nisbet, Robert, 452, 465*n*.
Nixon, Richard, 118, 162, 186, 198 – 206, 299, 535 – 536, 539
incomes policy of, 597, 614, 617 – 622
No-raiding pacts, 116, 163
Norris-La Guardia Act, 98, 108, 109
Northrup, Herbert R., 258, 259, 263*n*., 264*n*., 265*n*., 415*n*.
Norton, Eleanor Holmes, 390
Nurses Association, American (ANA), 150

Oaxaca, Ronald, 373 – 374, 410*n*., 411*n*.

Oberer, Walter E., 209*n*.
Occupation, defined, 24 – 25, 28
Occupational achievement, 29, 32 – 33
Occupational choice, 24 – 27
defined, 24 – 25
process of, 25 – 27
(*See also* Occupational mobility)
Occupational distribution, discrimination and, 374 – 386
Occupational inheritance, 29, 32 – 37
Occupational mobility:
appraisals of, 33 – 37
education versus family and, 29, 32 – 33
into elite occupations, 35 – 37
income and, 38 – 39
nature of, 27 – 29
perfect, 34
prediction for, 24
volume of, 28, 30 – 31
(*See also* Job mobility)
Occupational Safety and Health Act (OSHA), 198, 242, 256, 491, 494 – 496
enforcement of, 495 – 496
principal focus of, 494 – 495
Occupational Safety and Health Administration, 494, 495
Occupational Safety and Health Review Commission, 494
Office of Federal Contract Compliance Programs (OFCCP), 390 – 391
impact of, 408
Office of National Economic Planning (proposed), 627
Office of Personnel Management (OPM), 300, 302
regulating discrimination and, 394 – 395
Oi, Walter, 358*n*.
Okner, Benjamin A., 433 – 434, 455, 463*n*., 465*n*., 466*n*.
Okun, Arthur M., 453 – 455, 458, 465*n*., 466*n*., 633*n*.
Old-Age, Survivors, Disability and Health Insurance (OASDHI) system:
benefits: disability, 494
structure of, 474 – 476
trends in, 476 – 477
eligibility for, 474
expenditures for, 516, 518
financing of, 477 – 480, 483 – 485
inflation and, 476 – 480
portability of, 489
public employees and, 488
Oldham, Greg R., 88*n*.
Olneck, Michael, 465*n*.

On-the-job training, 334 – 335, 340
Operating Engineers, International Union of
(IUOE), 181, 184, 297
Operation Mainstream, 534
Opportunities Industrialization Centers of
America, 559
Organization for Economic Cooperation and
Development (OECD), 631 – 632
Orodovic, Josip, 89*n*.
Osterman, Melvin, 294, 339
Osterman, Paul, 49*n*., 311*n*., 359*n*.
Oswald, Rudolph A., 524*n*.
Overtime, 513, 514
Owen, John D., 524*n*.

Palzer, Doris, 208*n*.
Parker, John E., 87*n*.
Parnes, Herbert S., 64, 86*n*., 87*n*.
Parsons, Donald O., 358*n*.
Part-time employment, 11, 13, 14
Passell, Peter, 359*n*., 634*n*.
Patten, Thomas H., Jr., 580*n*.
Pechman, Joseph A., 433 – 434, 455, 463*n*.,
465*n*., 466*n*.
Pencavel, John H., 358*n*., 360*n*.
Pension Benefit Guarantee Corporation, 489
Pension programs:
private, 485 – 489
health benefits, 487
loss of coverage of, 487 – 488
pension reform law and, 488 – 489
public sector and, 487, 488
trends in, 485 – 487
public (*see* Old-Age, Survivors, Disability
and Health Insurance system)
Pension reform law (ERISA), 198, 488 – 489
Perfect mobility, 34
Perlman, Selig, 95, 102, 153*n*., 154*n*., 157*n*.
Perry, George L., 621, 636*n*.
Personal income, 37 – 39
(*See also* Income distribution, personal
income)
Personnel administration, 152
human resources planning and, 559 – 565
altered perspective of, 561 – 564
government regulation and, 562, 564 – 565
model of, 560, 561
private sector, 269
public sector, 269 – 270, 295 – 296
Peston, M. H., 578*n*.
Peters, Edward, 261*n*.
Peterson, John M., 511, 524*n*.
Phelps, Edmund S., 635*n*., 639*n*.

Phelps-Brown, E. H., 633*n*.
Philadelphia Cordwainers case, 97
Phillips, A. W., 602 – 604, 634*n*.
Phillips curve, 604 – 609, 613 – 614
expectations of inflation and, 605 – 608
natural rate of unemployment and, 607 – 608
stability and, 605, 608, 613
Picketing:
as form of free speech, 108, 109
prohibition of, 115
Taft-Hartley Act and, 115 – 116
Pierson, Frank C., 361*n*., 463*n*.
Pilkington Brothers, Ltd., 258, 259
Piore, Michael J., 49*n*., 358*n*., 359*n*., 362*n*.
Pluralistic Economy, The (Ginzberg et al.), 21
Polanyi, Karl, 68, 87*n*., 460 – 461, 466*n*.,
468*n*.
Population changes:
birthrates and, 2
components of, 4 – 5
geographic, 2 – 3
urban areas and, 3
Porter, Lyman W., 88*n*.
Postal employees, 301 – 303
Postal Reorganization Act, 301
Postal Workers Union, American (APWU),
181, 301
Poverty, 40 – 41
dual labor markets and, 41 – 43
incidence of, 429 – 432
threshold level, calculation of, 431
transfer payments and alleviation of,
436 – 439
War on Poverty, 534
Powderly, Terence V., 99, 100
Prasow, Paul, 261*n*.
Prevailing-wage rule, 352
Price, Daniel, 522*n*.
Printing industry, 246 – 247
Producer Price Index (PPI), 594, 610
Production, limiting, 455 – 456
Productivity:
collective bargaining and, 81, 254
labor-management ventures and, 254 – 257
wage and price controls and, 618
wage and price guidelines and, 614 – 615
Productivity bargaining, 81, 254
in public sector, 293 – 295
Professional Drivers Council on Safety and
Health (PROD), 187 – 188
Professional organizations, 119, 120
Property rights, 103
management's prerogatives and, 226, 227
Proposition 13, 282

Public employment service (*see* United States Employment and Training Service)
Public sector:
collective bargaining in (*see* Collective bargaining, in public sector)
employment in, 20—22
Executive Order No. 10988 and, 118, 299, 303
Executive Order No. 11491 and, 118, 302
provisions of, 299—300
fiscal responsibility in, 181—182
labor organizations in, 120, 126—129, 147—151
internal governments of, 181, 193
managerial unionism in, 145
national income and, 419—421
organizing, 118—120
growing pains and legal treatment, 119—120, 126
pension programs and, 487, 488
political activity and, 203—204
wages in, 271—272
impact of unions on, 349—354, 422—424
prevailing-wage rule and, 352—354
Public service employment, 535—550, 569
proposals for, 573—574
Purcell, Theodore V., 413*n*.

Quandt, Richard, 414*n*.
Quinn, Robert P., 87*n*.

Raffaele, J. A., 262*n*.
Railroad industry, 247, 255
Railway, Airline and Steamship Clerks, Freight Handlers, Express and Station Employees, Brotherhood of (BRASC), 197
Railway Labor Act, 109, 195, 196
Raimon, Robert L., 64, 86*n*., 87*n*., 360*n*.
Rapping, Leonard R., 635*n*.
Rawls, John, 454, 465*n*.
Redistribution of income, 451—462
efficiency versus equality, 452—455, 458—459
equality as trade-off, 452—455
investment in education and, 451—452
labor market and, 459—462
limiting choices, 455—456
meritocracy and, 457—458
tax reform and, 451, 453—455
(*See also* Transfer payments)
Rees, Albert, 86*n*., 89*n*., 348—349*n*., 360*n*., 362*n*., 412*n*., 413*n*., 415*n*., 463*n*., 580*n*.

Rehmus, Charles M., 210*n*., 263*n*., 265*n*., 313*n*., 314*n*.
Reich, Michael, 359*n*.
Rensenberger, Boyce, 361*n*.—362*n*., 636*n*.
Rental income, 419—422
Repas, Robert F., 312*n*.
Representation plans, 106—107
Republican party and unions, 199—202
Resnick, Jane R., 577*n*.
Retail Clerks International Association (RCIA), 138, 147, 149, 151, 255
Retail, Wholesale and Department Store Union (RWDSU), 184
Retirement, 472—473
(*See also* Aged, social insurance for)
Reubens, Beatrice G., 21, 47*n*.
Reuther, Walter, 116, 189—190, 205
Reverse discrimination, 403—405
Reynolds, Lloyd G., 265*n*., 635*n*.
Rezler, Julius, 207*n*.
Richman, Barry M., 633*n*.
Right to work, 122
Rival unionism, 163, 164
Roberts, Blaine, 636*n*., 637*n*., 638*n*.
Rock, Eli, 311*n*.
Rockwell International, 255
Ronner, Sam, 207*n*.
Roosevelt, Franklin D., 107, 273, 390, 592
Root, Norman, 522*n*.
Rosen, Hjalmar, 260*n*.
Rosen, Sherwin, 359*n*.
Rosow, Jerome R., 557, 578*n*.
Ross, Arthur M., 360*n*.
Ross, Mary, 520*n*.
Rottenberg, Simon, 86*n*., 358*n*.
Rowan, Richard L., 258, 259, 264*n*., 265*n*.
Roy Robinson, Inc. case, 242
Royal Typewriter, 257—258
Rubin, Lester, 208*n*.
Rungeling, Brian, 362*n*.
Runner, Diana, 523*n*.
Rus, Veljko, 89*n*.
Rustin, Bayard, 415
Ruttenberg, Stanley, H., 575*n*.
Rynecki, Stephen B., 313*n*.

Sabrosky, Alan, 155*n*., 313*n*.
Sadlowski, Edward, 192, 251
Saint-Gobain-Pont-a-Mousson, 258
Samoff, Bernard, 155*n*., 313*n*.
Samuelson, Paul A., 604, 605, 635*n*.
Sandstrom, Thore, 88*n*.
Saulnier, Raymond J., 638*n*.
Sawyer, Malcolm, 463*n*.

Scandinavia, public sector labor relations in, 308
Scanlon plan, 81, 254
Schein, Edgar, H., 578*n.*
Schick, Robert, 580*n.*
Schiller, Bradley R., 439–442, 464*n.*
Schlesinger, Arthur M., Jr., 627, 637*n.*
Schmidt, Peter, 360*n.*
Schmitt, Raymond, 521*n.*, 522*n.*
Schoen, Cathy, 525*n.*
Schorr, Alvin L., 452, 455, 465*n.*
Schubert, Richard F., 415*n.*
Schuck, Peter H., 637*n.*, 638*n.*
Schultz, George P., 622, 636*n.*, 637*n.*
Schultz, Theodore W., 551, 554, 577*n.*
Schulz, James H., 521*n.*
Schumpeter, Joseph, 466*n.*
Schwab, Charles, 107, 154*n.*
Schwartz, Louis B., 414*n.*
Schweitzer, Stuart O., 635*n.*
Scientific management, 68–69, 104
Seasonal unemployment, 589
Secondary boycotts, 115
Security, search for, 43–46
Segmented-labor-market theories, 41–43, 336–341
  discrimination and, 371
  dual labor market, 41–43, 336–338
  radical, 339–341
  three-tiered, 338–339
Seidman, Joel, 153*n.*
Selznick, Phillip, 262*n.*
Senate Committee on Improper Activities in the Labor or Management Field, 117, 173, 179
Seniority, 243–245
  affirmative action versus, 401–403
  wages and, 356–357
Service Employee's International Union (SEIU), 149–151, 280, 281, 286, 288, 299, 305
Service sector, 13, 16–22
  defined, 17–19
  government employment, 20–22
  unemployment rates in, 11
Service workers, 13
  income, 37–39
  unemployment rates, 11
Service-workers occupation, 19
Services industry, 18–19
Severn, Alan K., 87*n.*
Sewell, William H., 449–450, 464*n.*
Sex-role stereotyping, 375–376
Shapiro, David, 361*n.*
Shaw, Justice Lemuel, 97

Sheahan, John, 636*n.*
Sheppard, Harold L., 209*n.*
Sherman Antitrust Act, 105–106, 195
  reversal of early applications of, 108–109, 195
Shiskin, Julius, 47*n.*, 588, 633*n.*
Shultz, George P., 86*n.*, 87*n.*, 89*n.*
Simkin, William, 208*n.*
Sinicropi, Anthony, 311*n.*
Skolnik, Alfred M., 521*n.*, 522*n.*, 525*n.*
Slaiman, Donald, 415*n.*
Slichter, Summer H., 262*n.*, 263*n.*
Slovenko, Ralph, 207*n.*
Smith, Adam, 67, 87*n.*, 328, 358*n.*
Smith, Barton, 412*n.*
Smith, James P., 411*n.*
Smith, Lewis H., 362*n.*
Smith, Ralph E., 635*n.*
Smith, Robert S., 415*n.*
Smith, Sharon P., 310*n.*, 362*n.*
Smith-Connolly Act, 195–196
Snee, John, 520*n.*
Snow, Charles C., 88*n.*, 89*n.*
Social insurance, 469–520
  aged and, 472–489
    private pension and benefit programs, 485–489
    Social Security benefits, 474–485
  concern over, 470–471
  history of, 470–471
  minimum wage, 505–515
    economic consequences of, 508–513
    further aspects of FLSA, 513–515
    union views of, 507–508
  philosophy of American, 470–471
  social welfare expenditures, 515–519
  summary, 519–520
  unemployment insurance, 496–505
    adequacy of benefits, 502–505
    coverage and eligibility, 497–500
    evaluating, 500–502
  workers' compensation, 490–496
    federal standards and, 492–496
Social Security Act, 195, 474, 535
  Employment Service and, 528
  1977 amendment of, 478–480, 483, 485
  unemployment provision of, 496
Social Security Administration, 477
  pension reform law and, 489
Social security system, 474–485
  OASDHI, 474–480
  in other nations, 480–485
  programs of, 474
Social welfare expenditures, 515–519

Socialism, 101
  "creeping," 592
  full employment and, 596
Solomon, Lewis C., 362*n*.
Solow, Robert A., 604, 605, 621, 635*n*., 636*n*.
Somers, Anne R., 522*n*.
Somers, Gerold G., 262*n*.
Somers, Herman M., 522*n*., 525*n*.
Sommers, Dixie, 48*n*.
Spence, Michael A., 358*n*.
Spring, William, 47*n*., 588
"Stagflation," 597–598
Stagner, Ross, 260*n*.
Staines, Graham L., 87*n*.
Stanley, David T., 312*n*.
State, County and Municipal Employees,
  American Federation of (*see* American
  Federation of State, County and
  Municipal Employees)
State government employment, 20–21
  unionization and, 119–120
  (*See also* Public sector)
Steel industry, 249–251, 254, 346
Steelworkers of America, United (*see* United
  Steelworkers of America)
Stein, Robert L., 632*n*.
Stephenson, Geoffrey M., 265*n*.
Stern, James L., 313*n*.
Stevens, Carl, 310*n*.
Stevens, Uriah, 99
Stewart, Charles T., Jr., 510–511, 524*n*.
Stieber, Jack, 209*n*.
Stigler, George J., 86*n*.
Stoikov, Vladimir, 87*n*., 360*n*.
Stokes, Donald E., 210*n*.
Stoner, J. A. F., 156*n*.
Strauss, George, 88*n*., 89*n*., 208*n*.
Strauss, Robert, 360*n*.
Strikes, 232–234
  in automobile industry, 252, 253
  contract expiration and, 232
  in electrical equipment industry, 249
  employer's counter to, 232–233
  ENA and, 192, 251
  impact of, in 1970s, 233
  by interns and residents, 121
  IWW and, 101–102
  jurisdictional, 116
  Knights of Labor and, 100
  labor injunction and, 98
  negotiating tactics and, 230–234
  by public employees, 118–120, 269, 302,
    303
    legal regulation of, 273–276, 283–286

Strikes:
  by public employees: in New York, 289
    in San Francisco, 287–289
  Sherman Antitrust Act and, 105, 108
    in steel industry, 250, 251
  Taft-Hartley Act as response to, 115
  Wagner Act and, 109
Structural unemployment, 589–591, 597,
  608–609
Subcontracting, 113
Survey of Working Conditions (University of
  Michigan), 69–72
Survivors benefits, 474–476, 482
Sylvis, William H., 99

Taft, Philip, 154*n*., 211*n*.
Taft-Hartley Act, 110, 122, 164, 173, 183, 186,
  198, 248, 250
  arbitration and, 241, 242
  areas not covered by, 115, 121, 144, 181, 305
  discrimination and, 393–396
  health care industry and, 100, 120
  political contributions and, 196, 197
  public sector and, 118, 280, 301, 305–306
    strikes by, 273
  unfair labor practices and, 110, 113, 115
  union power and, 115–116
  union security and, 122, 199, 281
Taggert, Robert, 587–588, 632*n*., 633*n*., 639*n*.
Tannenbaum, Arnold S., 88*n*., 89*n*.
Tarnowieski, Dale, 156
Taubman, Paul J., 362*n*., 450–453, 464*n*.,
  465*n*., 466*n*.
Tax-and-Transfer Equalization Act, 453
Taxes:
  distribution of family income and, 425, 426,
    431–435
  education financing and, 553
  OASDHI system and, 477–480
  redistribution of income and, 451, 453–455
  transfer payment financing and, 435–436
  unemployment insurance and, 496–497
Taylor, Frederick W., 68–69, 104
Taylor, George W., 119, 361*n*., 463*n*.
Taylor law (New York), 119, 286
Teachers, American Federation of (AFT), 119,
  150, 151, 170, 184, 290–291, 305
Teamsters for a Democratic Union, 188
Teamsters, International Brotherhood of, 121,
  170, 187–188, 206, 219, 255
  described, 187
  dissident groups within, 187–188
  expulsion from AFL-CIO, 117, 162, 187

Teamsters, International Brotherhood of:
  fiscal responsibility violations of, 181,
    187 – 188
  government of, 171
  membership in, 147 – 151, 187
  political orientation of, 201, 344
  trusteeships and, 179
Technological change and work rules,
    245 – 247
Teen-age workers:
  minimum wages and, 511 – 513
  unemployment rates, 11, 12, 581, 598 – 601
Textile Workers of America, United (UTWA),
    184
Thal-Larsen, Margaret, 86n.
Thieblot, Armand J., Jr., 524n.
Thompson, Gayle B., 521n.
Thornhill v. Alabama, 108
Thurow, Lester, 371 – 373, 411n., 415n.,
    464n., 466n.
Tichy, Noel M., 88n.
Tobin, James, 635n.
Trade Adjustment Assistance program, 572
Trade agreement, 102
Transfer payments, 435 – 442
  effectiveness of, 436 – 439
  income mobility and, 439 – 442
  increases in, 452
  in-kind, 436 – 439
  listing of, 437
  social insurance programs, 435 – 439
  welfare, 435 – 439
  (*See also* Social insurance)
Transition from school to work, 566, 569 – 571
Transitional unemployment, 589
Transport Workers Union of America
    (TWUA), 150, 151
Treas, Judith, 48n.
Trow, Martin, 209n., 210n., 360n.
Trusteeships under Landrum-Griffin Act,
    179 – 180, 183
Typographical Union, International (*see*
    International Typographical Union)
Tyree, Andrea, 48n

Ullman, Joseph C., 86n., 312n., 635n.
Ulman, Lloyd, 154n., 157n., 576n., 625, 635n.,
    637n.
Underemployment, 13 – 14
Unemployment:
  abroad, 14 – 16, 595 – 596
  concept of, 587 – 588
  cost of, 602, 603

Unemployment:
  cyclical, 379, 591
  defined, 12 – 13, 587
  duration of, 13
  employment levels and, 600 – 602
  frictional, 588 – 589
  incomes policy and (*see* Incomes policy)
  inflation and, 593 – 595, 597 – 598
    Consumer Price Index, 593 – 595,
      610 – 613
    negative correlation of, 613
    Phillips curve and, 604 – 609, 613 – 614
    "stagflation" and, 597 – 598
    tradeoff between, 602 – 614
  as issue of public policy, 591 – 614
    acceptable levels of, 596
    Employment Act and, 591 – 592
    "GNP gap" and, 596
    Great Depression and, 592
    inflation and, 593 – 595, 597 – 598,
      602 – 614
    Keynesian theory and, 592, 597
    opposing views on, 592 – 593
    patterns of unemployment, 598 – 602
    World War II employment and, 592
  labor-market theories and, 319
  MDTA and, 533 – 534
  measurement of, 13, 14, 585 – 591
    Current Population Survey, 587
    proposals for, 587 – 588
    seasonal adjustments, 589, 590
    value judgments and, 588
  national economic planning and, 627 – 632
  politics and, 585, 587
  public assistance for, 45 – 46
  rates, 1, 6 – 7, 10 – 12, 585 – 591
    natural, 607 – 608
    by reason for unemployment, 599
    of subgroups, 11 – 12, 366, 379, 380,
      598 – 602
  seasonal, 589
  structural, 589 – 591, 597, 608 – 609
  transitional, 589
  types of, 588 – 591
  (*See also* Human resources planning and
    development)
Unemployment insurance, 496 – 505
  adequacy of benefits, 502 – 505
    comparative perspective, 503 – 505
  compared to workers' compensation,
    502 – 503
  coverage and eligibility, 497 – 500
    appeals procedure for, 499
    ceiling on, 499 – 500

Unemployment:
  coverage and eligibility: disqualification, 498
  as disincentive to work, 500–501
  ETS and, 531, 533
  evaluating, 500–502
  implications of, for stability, 501–502
  proposals for, 572–573
  recipients of, 502
  taxes and, 496–497
Unfair labor practices, 110–113, 115, 118
Union security, 122, 199, 226
  in public sector, 281–282, 284, 286, 302
Union shop, 94, 118, 122, 199, 281–282
Unions, 42, 45, 69, 92–212
  abroad, 94–95
  administration of, 192–194
  as agents, 93, 102, 123
  agricultural, 121
  autonomy of, 162–163
  business agent, 166
  business unionism, 99, 102–104, 122, 138, 225
  collective bargaining and (*see* Collective bargaining)
  company, 106–107
  complacency, 116–117
  conspiracies, 97–98, 108
  contemporary patterns of, 123–153
  corruption, 116, 117, 162, 173, 181, 187–189, 193
  democracy in, 159–194
    ITU and, 190–191
    summary, 192–194
    two kinds of government and, 170–172
    UAW and, 189–190
  development of, 95–122
  discrimination, 117, 139–144, 388, 395–396, 407
  financing of, 93, 167–170
  functions of organizations, 165–170
  government of, 170–173
  government support of, 106, 109, 113, 118–119
  great Depression and, 107–108
  health care industry and, 120–121
  hiring halls and, 94
  how they represent workers, 94–95
  idealism and reform, 98–102
    AFL, 101–102
    Knights of Labor, 99–102
  intermediate bodies and, 170
  internal regulation of, 172–194
    bill of rights, 174–176, 183
    election procedures, 111–112, 176–179

Unions:
  internal regulation of: evaluating, 183–186
    fiscal responsibility, 180–182
    trusteeships, 179–180, 183
    variations in, 186–192
  international (*see* National unions)
  job enrichment and, 80–82
  jurisdictional disputes, 116, 163–164
  labor's share of national income and, 422–424
  laws regulating, 105–122, 178–183, 194–199
    (*See also specific laws and cases*)
  local (*see* Local unions)
  managerial, 115, 144–146
  membership, 100, 101, 106, 115, 117, 123
    abroad, 123, 125
    apathy among, 185–186
    black, 139–144
    federal, 301–302
    in individual, 147–151
    by industry, 126–133
    by occupation, 131, 134
    trends in, 123–126, 138–139, 158
    women, 134, 136–139
  military, 121
  minimum wage laws and, 507–508
  national (*see* National unions)
  objectives of, 93, 342
  officers of, 165–167, 193
    turnover of, 184–185, 193
    (*See also specific individuals*)
  opposition to, 103–107, 115–117, 152
  origins of, 95–97
    dual orientation of, 96
  political activities of, 94–100, 114–115, 194–207
    civil rights legislation and, 198, 388
    dues for, 196–197
    effectiveness, 198–199
    history of, 194–198
    increased involvement in, 197–198
    labor leaders in government, 206
    Labor Party, 204–206
    party alignments and, 199–203
    public employees and, 203–204
  power of, 115–117
  in public sector (*see* Public sector)
  purpose of, 93
  recognition of need for, 106, 107
  scientific management and, 104
  structure of, 160–194
  summary, 153
  trade agreements and, 102

Unions:
  wages and: impact on relative, 347 – 349,
    422 – 424
    public sector and, 349 – 354
    (*See also* Wages)
  why workers join, 93 – 94
  World War I and, 106
  World War II and, 115
United Automobile Workers (UAW),
    111 – 112, 162, 189 – 190, 197, 206, 219
  AFL-CIO and, 189, 190
  collective bargaining and, 251 – 253, 255
  commitment to democracy of, 189 – 190
  described, 189
  financing of, 167
  job dissatisfaction and, 75 – 76
  membership in, 147 – 151
  unemployment benefits and, 500
  work rules and, 247
United Brotherhood of Carpenters and Joiners
    of America (UBCJA), 147 – 151, 184,
    219
United Electrical, Radio, and Machine
    Workers of America (UE), 249
United Farm Workers of America (UFWA),
    121
United Mine Workers of America (UMW),
    114, 184, 188 – 189
  Coronado case, 105
  described, 188
  Miller and, 189
  trusteeships and, 180
  Yablonski murders and, 188 – 189
*United Packinghouse, Food and Allied
    Workers v. NLRB* case, 394
United States Employment and Training
    Service (ETS), 63 – 64
  constraints on, 530 – 531
  disadvantaged and, 530, 531
  Employment Service and, 528 – 530
    early activities of, 529
    establishment of, 528
    opposition to, 529 – 530
    reorganization of, 529 – 530
    stagnation of, 529
  job placements of, 531, 532
  unemployment insurance and, 531, 533
United States Steel, 250, 346
United Steelworkers of America (USA), 118,
    191 – 192, 219, 344
  collective bargaining and, 249 – 251
  Experimental Negotiating Agreement (ENA)
    and, 192
  history of, 192

United Steelworkers of America (USA):
  membership in, 147 – 151
  union election laws and, 178
  wage agreements of, 346
United Textile Workers of America (UTWA),
    184
Unorganized workers:
  collective bargaining benefits, 45, 111,
    125 – 126, 219
  explaining, 150, 152 – 153
Uphoff, Walter H., 261*n.*

Valdes, William C., 312*n.*
Valid selection of employees, 398 – 400
  racial quotas and, 405
Verdier, Jean-Maurice, 313*n.*
Vickery, Clair, 523*n.*
Vietnamese war, 596, 597, 614
Vietorisz, Thomas, 47*n.*, 588
Vocational Education Act, 534, 535
Vollmer, Howard M., 310*n.*, 361*n.*

Wachter, Michael L., 411*n.*, 524*n.*
Wage-board federal employees, 301
Wage contours, 356
Wage patterning, 346
Wage and price controls:
  Carter and, 619 – 620, 623
  conclusions, 623 – 625
  as incomes policy, 614
  Nixon and, 597, 617 – 619, 622
    legal bases of, 617
    Phase II of, 617 – 619, 621 – 622
    Phase III of, 619
    Phase IV of, 619
    politics and, 619
    productivity and, 618
Wage and price guidelines, 614 – 617
Wage and price standards, 619 – 620
Wage rigidity, 348
Wage system, 98 – 99
  acceptance of, 101, 102
Wages:
  coercive comparisons and, 345 – 346
  competitive-labor-market theory and,
    53 – 54, 317 – 336
    empirical wage patterns and, 327 – 331
  controls on, 199
  determination of, 341 – 358
    economic influences on, 341 – 344, 351
    political influences on, 344 – 346, 351
    summary, 357 – 358

Wages:
  illegal aliens and, 386–387
  impact of unions on relative, 347–349
    countercyclical, 348, 351
  job clusters and, 356
  job evaluation and, 354–356
  minimum (*see* Minimum wage)
  monopsonist and, 342–344
  negotiating tactics and, 230–231
  OASDHI benefits and, 475–477
  pay relationships, 354–357
  in public sector, 271–272
    impact of unions on, 349–354, 422–424
    prevailing-wage rule and, 352–354
  reference groups and, 345
  seniority and, 356–357
  supplements to, 419–423
    (*See also* Social insurance)
  tradeoffs in, 342–344
  (*See also* Income)
Wagner, Martin, 313*n*.
Wagner, Robert, 289, 290
Wagner Act (National Labor Relations Act),
    195, 393
  described, 109–110
  public employees and, 118, 280
  secondary boycotts and, 115
  significance of, 109, 183
  union elections and, 111
Wagner-Peyser Act, 528
Wallace, George, 200
Wallace, Henry A., 633*n*.
Wallace, Phyllis A., 412*n*.
Walsh-Healey Act, 515
Walton, Richard E., 208*n*., 215–218, 260*n*.,
    265*n*.
War Labor Board, 106
War Manpower Commission, 529
War on Poverty, 534
Warner, David, 210*n*.
Warner, Malcolm, 208*n*., 210*n*.
Warren, E. Kirby, 156*n*.
Watts, Harold W., 580*n*.
Wealth, distribution of, 442–451
  inequality of, 442–445, 450–451
  inheritance and, 445–448
    choice of mate and, 448–449
    education and, 446–450
    socioeconomic background and, 449–450
Weaver, Warren, Jr., 413*n*., 414*n*.
Weber, Arnold R., 264*n*., 359*n*., 622, 623,
    634*n*., 636*n*., 639*n*.
Weinberg, Edgar, 89*n*., 90*n*., 264*n*.
Weiss, Leonard, 360*n*.

Weisskopf, Thomas E., 359*n*.
Welch, Finis, 411*n*.
Welfare programs, 471
  expenditures for, 516, 518
  proposals for, 573
  WIN program and, 547–549
Welfare state, 44–45, 470–471, 518–519
Wellington, Harry H., 268–269, 309*n*., 314*n*.
West Germany, public sector labor relations in,
    307–308
White, Bernard J., 70, 72, 73, 87*n*.
White-collar workers, 22–23
  attitude toward union membership, 138
  choosing similar work and, 72–73
  described, 138
  income, 37–39, 65–66, 327–331, 349
  job mobility, 55, 59–63, 65–66
  in labor organizations, 131, 134, 135
    discrimination and, 140–144
  professional organizations of, 119, 120
  unemployment rates, 11, 12
  work characteristics and, 70–74
Whitney, Craig R., 521*n*.
Wickersham, Edward D., 312*n*., 313*n*.
Wilson, Woodrow, 106
Winchester, David, 313*n*.
Winpisinger, William, 80, 88*n*., 89*n*.
Winter, Ralph K., Jr., 268–269, 309*n*.,
    314*n*.
Wirtz, Willard, 395
"Wobblies," 101–102
Wolkinson, Benjamin W., 407, 414*n*.
Women:
  choice of mate, 448–449
  competitive-labor-market theory and, 324
  discrimination against: Civil Rights Act and,
      388–389
    income and, 367–386
    sex-role stereotyping, 375–376
    (*See also* Discrimination)
  income of, 37, 38, 367–386
  Job Corps and, 534, 539
  job mobility, 55, 56
  labor organization among, 134, 136–139,
      141
  occupational shifts of, 28, 31
  participation rates, 3, 8–10, 324, 366, 375,
      378–379
  population changes and, 2
  poverty and, 431, 432
  unemployment rates, 11, 12, 598–601
  WIN program and, 545–548
Woodcock, Leonard, 184, 190, 206
Woodward, Joan, 359*n*.

Woodworkers of America, International (IWA), 184
Wool, Harold, 87*n.*
Wootton, Barbara, 633*n.*
Work in America (HEW), 68–73
Work Incentive (WIN) program, 530, 535, 539, 541
  program performance, 545–549
Work rules, 245–247
Workers, decision-making participation by, 79–83
Workers' compensation, 490–496
  benefits, 491–492
  coal miners and, 492–494
  compared to unemployment insurance, 502–503
  federal standards and, 492–496
    OSHA and, 494–496
  financing of, 491
  "no fault" principle and, 490
  variations in, 490–493

Works councils, 106
World War I and unions, 106
World War II:
  full employment policies and, 592
  union and, 115
Wurf, Jerry, 202

Yablonski, Joseph, 188–189
Yankleovich, Daniel, 89*n.*
Yavitz, Boris, 86*n.*
Yellow dog contracts, 107, 109
Yohalem, Martha R., 521*n.*
Young, Michael, 457, 465*n.*
Youth Employment and Demonstration Projects Act, 571

Zalusky, John, 262*n.*
Ziderman, A., 578*n.*
Ziskind, David, 273, 310*n.*